AF888861

Zhanqi Village Over Fifty Years

Xiaodan Dong

Zhanqi Village Over Fifty Years

The Micro-foundation of Chinese De-dependency

北京大学出版社
PEKING UNIVERSITY PRESS

palgrave
macmillan

Xiaodan Dong
Renmin University of China
Beijing, China

ISBN 978-981-97-5425-0 ISBN 978-981-97-5426-7 (eBook)
https://doi.org/10.1007/978-981-97-5426-7

Jointly published with Peking University Press
The print edition is not for sale in China Mainland. Customers from China Mainland please order the print book from: Peking University Press
ISBN of the Co-Publisher's edition: 9787301320440

© Peking University Press 2024

This work is subject to copyright. All rights are solely and exclusively licensed by the Publisher, whether the whole or part of the material is concerned, specifically the rights of translation, reprinting, reuse of illustrations, recitation, broadcasting, reproduction on microfilms or in any other physical way, and transmission or information storage and retrieval, electronic adaptation, computer software, or by similar or dissimilar methodology now known or hereafter developed.
The use of general descriptive names, registered names, trademarks, service marks, etc. in this publication does not imply, even in the absence of a specific statement, that such names are exempt from the relevant protective laws and regulations and therefore free for general use.
The publishers, the authors, and the editors are safe to assume that the advice and information in this book are believed to be true and accurate at the date of publication. Neither the publishers nor the authors or the editors give a warranty, express or implied, with respect to the material contained herein or for any errors or omissions that may have been made. The publishers remain neutral with regard to jurisdictional claims in published maps and institutional affiliations.

Cover illustration: Maram_shutterstock.com

This Palgrave Macmillan imprint is published by the registered company Springer Nature Singapore Pte Ltd.
The registered company address is: 152 Beach Road, #21-01/04 Gateway East, Singapore 189721, Singapore

If disposing of this product, please recycle the paper.

About This Book

Drawing upon extensive archival research, documentary sources, and field investigations, this book chronicles the transformative journey of Zhanqi (battle flag) Village in Sichuan Province over 55 years, commencing from the inception of the exemplary rural reform (the "Learn from Dazhai in agriculture" campaign, 农业学大寨). It delves into the intricate interplay between macro policy adjustments and internal mechanisms that shaped the village's evolution.

The essence can be encapsulated as "four threads": One nucleus—rural areas as China's microfoundation for emancipation; Two perspectives—harmonizing macro and micro, intertwining temporal and spatial dimensions; Three phases—the "scarlet zhanqi" during politicized rivalry, the "gilded zhanqi" during industrialized competition, and the "verdant zhanqi" during ecological contention; Four illuminations—internalizing costs, rationalizing communal life, safeguarding resource sovereignty, and championing spatial justice.

Anchored in the synergistic prowess of "Three Lives, Three Governance"[1] and the sagacity of village communities, the rural fabric adeptly absorbs macro risks, thus fortifying China's sovereignty, security, and independence amidst global uncertainties.

[1] Translator's note: "三生" (three lives; three 生) is a collective term referring to production (生产), existence (生活), and ecology (生态). It stems from the report of the 18th National Congress of the Communist Party of China, which put forward the requirement of "promoting intensive and efficient production spaces, comfortable and moderate living spaces, and pristine and beautiful ecological spaces."

"三治" (three governance, three 治) refers to self-governance (自治), governance by law (法治), and governance through virtue (德治). In 2019, the Central Committee of the Communist Party of China and the State Council issued the "Guiding Opinions on Strengthening and Improving Rural Governance," which outlined 17 key tasks aimed at building well-governed rural areas—it emphasized the need to establish a rural governance system that combines self-governance, governance by law, and governance through virtue.

Contents

List of Figures

Chapter 2

Chapter 3

Chapter 4

Chapter 6

Chapter 7

Chapter 8

Chapter 9

Chapter 12

Chapter 13

Chapter 14

Chapter 15

Chapter 17

List of Tables

Chapter 9

Chapter 10

Chapter 11

Chapter 12

Chapter 13

Chapter 14

Chapter 17

Chapter 18

Chapter 19

CHAPTER 1

Preface: The Great Struggle of Rural Collectives- China's Micro-foundation for De-dependence

In this preface, we delve into the realm of "rural collectives." Their greatness lies in the intertwined existence of village ecosystems, where communal boundaries shape their rights. This intrinsic fabric becomes the bedrock for localized rural growth, aligned with the imperatives of global challenges and comprehensive security. Thus, the immense struggle of rural collectives emerges as the rightful "political direction" for rural revitalization. By objectively analyzing the Zhanqi Village experience, we capture the grand battle of Chinese farmers fighting for autonomous development.

With a stroke of the pen, a fleeting pause, "Looking back, the figure lingers in dimmed lights"…

For over 15 years, our team has tirelessly compared regional development experiences, aiming to distill their essence and create a compelling series. A decade ago, "Interpret Southern Jiangsu (解读苏南)" and "Interpret the Pearl River Delta (解读珠三角)" took shape. Then, "Interpret Chongqing (解读重庆)" and "Review Southern Jiangsu (再读苏南)" followed suit. Three years ago, the groundwork was laid for "The Struggle of a Village: 1965–2020," documenting the arduous journey of Zhanqi Village. "Southern Jiangsu" graced the shelves five years ago, and now, "Interpret Zhanqi Village (解读战旗村)" triumphs ahead of "Interpret Chongqing," while our exploration of other "interpretive" studies continues.

© Peking University Press 2024
X. Dong, *Zhanqi Village Over Fifty Years*,
https://doi.org/10.1007/978-981-97-5426-7_1

1 "Thanks to Our Wing Under Huang Gonglue."[1]

In the year 2017, whether you observed or turned a blind eye, two paramount policies swept across the vast tapestry of China's developmental trajectory—an unyielding force impossible to overlook. The initial surge arrived with the "Agricultural Supply-Side Structural Reform," an audacious endeavor to combat surplus within the agricultural framework, steering the nation toward an unequivocal transformation: embracing the verdant embrace of eco-friendly production methods. And then, on the eve of the year's curtain call, the Communist Party of China, during the momentous Nineteenth Congress, etched into history the "Rural Revitalization Strategy." Its resolute vision and meticulous orchestration unfolded at the year-end Central Rural Work Conference, laying the groundwork for an epic struggle, empowering China's farmers to unite collectively, ascend to self-determined prosperity, and claim their sovereign right to independent growth.

These grand orchestras shaped the year's symphony—manifesting in the "Agricultural Supply-Side Structural Reform" at its inception and the "Rural Revitalization Strategy" at its twilight hour. The "No. 1 Central Document" of 2017 heralded an unprecedented paradigm, urging a paradigmatic shift toward emerald production techniques to ameliorate the excesses of an agrarian tapestry. Then, on that fateful October 18th, the Communist Party of China elevated the Rural Revitalization Strategy during the venerable Nineteenth Congress. As the year drew to a close, a unified blueprint was meticulously woven during the Central Conference on Rural Work, beckoning Chinese farmers to unite in their collective quest for self-empowerment, casting an indomitable vision upon the canvas of their struggle for autonomous development.

[1] From Mao Zedong's poem "March From Tingzhou to Changsha—to the tune of Die Lian Hua (蝶恋花·从汀州向长沙)":

In June Heaven's armies chastise the corrupt and evil,
Seeking to bind roc and whale with a league-long cord.
Red glows the far side of the Gan,
Thanks to our wing under Huang Gonglue.
六月天兵征腐恶，
万丈长缨要把鲲鹏缚。
赣水那边红一角，
偏师借重黄公略。

Undoubtedly, the agricultural supply-side reform aims to address "structural excess," mirroring the industrial supply-side reform's call to "reduce excess capacity, inventory, leverage, and costs" in 2015. However, this poses a challenge for vested interests and departments accustomed to a paradigm of "expansive quantitative growth," hindering the rural revitalization agenda. Consequently, a significant political arrangement emerged: General Secretary Xi Jinping, along with all members of the Communist Party of China Central Committee Political Bureau elected at the 19th Party Congress, attended the rural work conference in late 2017 to fortify the unified determination to implement the rural revitalization strategy, with Xi delivering a crucial address.

In alignment with this, on February 12, 2018, Xi Jinping inspected the development of rural revitalization and the collective economy in Zhanqi Village, Sichuan Province. Notably, Zhanqi Village became the first village visited by Xi after the Party Central Committee designated rural revitalization as a national strategy, emphasizing the "reconstruction of a novel collective economy" as its hallmark. Xi commendably acknowledged the accomplishments in Zhanqi Village's collective economic development, affirming the village's reputation as a symbol of success.

Subsequently, the Pidu District, where situated in the Zhanqi Village, took a groundbreaking step by establishing the "The Zhanqi Training Institute for Rural Revitalization (四川战旗乡村振兴培训学院)." This institute invited our experienced team, committed to "rural reconstruction action," which the fifth plenary session of the 19th Central Committee specifically highlighted. It is worth emphasizing that "rural reconstruction" extends beyond conventional infrastructure projects, embodying a broad-based and pragmatic movement for rural improvement, void of radicalism.[2] Originating over a century ago, this movement

[2] The document from the 5th Plenary Session of the 19th Central Committee of the Communist Party of China specifically emphasizes the "Rural Reconstruction" action. It's important to note that "Rural Reconstruction" is not just about physical infrastructure development. It is a broad-based, "de-radicalization" movement for rural improvement that involves wide participation from various sectors of society. This movement, rooted in the principle of "integrating theory with practice," was initiated by predecessors more than a century ago and has continued for over two decades in the twenty-first century.

During this time, not only have there been thousands of pilot projects and initiatives across the country bearing the name of "Rural Reconstruction," but also a plethora of scholarly papers, reports from various regions, and various publications from rural development teams have been produced. Furthermore, this movement has also had a positive impact internationally.

integrates theory and practice, garnering widespread participation across society. Over the past two decades, numerous pilot projects and initiatives bearing the name of rural reconstruction have proliferated nationwide. Our involvement extends beyond research and training; we have also established the "Wen Tiejun Workshop" for localized endeavors, as well as the "Gao Demin Workshop (高德敏工作室)," named after Zhanqi Village's Party Secretary. Consequently, our research team collaborates with Zhanqi Village's officials and residents to meticulously analyze and synthesize the village's experiences, elevating them from the specific to the general.

Amidst a momentous shift, as Chinese individuals conscientiously adjust their ecological civilization strategy to align with human development, a symphony of events unfolds elsewhere. Upon assuming office, President Trump swiftly declared China as a new ideological adversary, sparking a "trade war" in 2018, followed by a "technology war" and an "education war" to stifle China's progress. Unilateral sanctions, branded as a "financial war," were imposed to curb China's overseas investment. These disruptions defied the established international order and prompted China to confront unprecedented challenges by proposing rural revitalization in 2019 and embracing a strategy of dual circulation in 2020, emphasizing domestic focus.

Amidst the recurring globalization crises, the Zhanqi village of farmers emerges as a development force with assets and negotiation power. They lead the way by implementing the "three transformations"[3] reform,

[3] Translator's note: The "three transformations" reform (三变改革) in rural areas refers to the transformation of resources into assets, government funding into shares, and farmers into shareholders.

1. Resources into Assets: This means that rural collectives transform collective natural resources such as land, forests, and water areas into assets through methods like equity participation to make them more productive.

2. Government Funding into Shares: Without changing the nature and purpose of the funding, various financial inputs from higher levels of government, such as funds for agricultural production development (excluding subsidies, relief, and emergency funds), agricultural resources and ecological protection subsidies (excluding those directly given to farmers), poverty alleviation funds, rural infrastructure construction funds, and funds supporting collective village development, are quantified as collective shares and invested in various operating entities. Village collectives and farmers, especially those in poverty, participate in profit-sharing.

3. Farmers into Shareholders: This means that farmers invest their personal resources, assets, funds, technology, skills, etc., into operating entities and become shareholders, participating in profit-sharing.

restructuring a new collective economy, and embracing "green production methods." This exemplifies the "confidence in the path" of socialism with Chinese characteristics in the new era, as championed by Xi Jinping. The profound connection between the inherent rural essence and national development makes the experiences of this village profoundly significant. They provide guidance on implementing the rural revitalization strategy in the era of "domestic circulation as the mainstay" and fostering the synergy between domestic and international realms. Moreover, they shed light on realizing the value of rural ecological resources and promoting holistic development encompassing ecology, politics, economy, society, and culture through deep-rooted reforms.

2 Unearthing China in Rural Realms and Reconstruction

Zhanqi Village, since its inception in the 1950s, carries a profound backdrop of era-defining shifts at every major juncture in its history. This process encapsulates the essence of China's magnificent resurgence over the past 70 years.

While some visitors perceive Zhanqi Village as exceptional, our research unveils its replicable developmental insights. Modern or traditional, other villages share the underlying mechanisms that propelled Zhanqi's growth. This book distills the experience of autonomous rural development, addressing the elemental questions of capital accumulation, village restructuring, and collective economic revival. Our investigation delves into the capacity of collective economy to "internally address externalities," searching for universality.

By adhering to customary research methods, we initially encounter a village on the Western Sichuan Plain. Scrutinizing its current state and history becomes our foundation. Subsequently, we discern the imprints of national progress, originating from this village's evolutionary course. Yet, prevailing research predominantly emphasizes the microcosm, neglecting the macroscopic. Rare are the village studies that incorporate both local cultural insights and broad perspectives, depicting China's five-millennium-old civilization.

Guided by an ardent desire to fathom Chinese civilization, our study unites micro and macro lenses, historical context, and practical actions within a comprehensive framework. This endeavor unearths China in rural landscapes and unveils China's essence in rural development. We seek to discover distinctive qualities that set China apart from other nations or civilizations, drawn from an exploration of rural realms.

Driven by a profound sense of duty to scrutinize the depths of Chinese civilization, this research undertaking embarked upon its journey by encompassing the microcosm, macrocosm, historical heritage, and practical endeavors of the Zhanqi Village within a grand framework. Herein lies the dual purpose: unearthing China amidst its rustic landscapes and unveiling China through the very act of rural rejuvenation. Discovering China within rural realms denotes the quest for distinctive qualities setting China apart from other nations and civilizations.

Since the modern era's dawn, China has witnessed a convergence of cultures with various nations, compelling scores of intellectuals to dissect this phenomenon. Prof. Fei Xiaotong's seminal work, "From the Soil (乡土中国)," so aptly titled, underscores his belief that China, owing to its rural fabric, bears unique traits divergent from other civilizations. This classic opus stems from a comparative perspective, a scholarly triumph born of observing rural landscapes. Today, numerous scholars champion the cause of studying rural China in comparative contexts, exemplified by luminaries like Professor Zhang Xiaode of the National Academy of Governance, Professor Liu Zhiwei of Sun Yat-sen University, Researcher Sun Ge of the Chinese Academy of Social Sciences, and Professor Zhao Yuezhi of the Communication University of China. Their clarion call resonates: rural landscapes serve as a "methodology," a touchstone for humanistic and social sciences, challenging the Western-centric paradigms. Indeed, rural domains possess methodological significance.

Our pursuit encompasses not only discovering China within the bucolic idyll but also constructing China within its verdant embrace. As sage words from Mr. Liang Shuming echo, "To engage in rural endeavors without considering the overarching tapestry of China is to falter in our understanding of the rural conundrum and render our efforts inconsequential.[4] Hence, rural development transcends its nominal confines, harboring aspirations to edify the entire Chinese society—an endeavor akin to birthing a nation." Zhang Jian, the vanguard of modern Chinese social enterprises, ardently championed the cause of "village-orientedism," for he perceived the village as the bedrock upon which China's ascension within the realm of modernization is predicated.

[4] Liang Shuming. The Complete Works of Liang Shuming, Volume II, Shandong People's Publishing House, 2005.

Thus, "unveiling China amidst rustic frontiers and fashioning China within pastoral realms" evokes a profound lineage of theoretical sagacity and historical praxis. It epitomizes the tenets upheld by discerning intellectuals in modern times, fervently committed to indigenous knowledge production and ardently involved in "grounded" community development—a thematic vista that illuminates the pages of this tome.

If there is divergence, it lies primarily in our team's enduring commitment to "action research," where theory and practice intertwine. Unlike the writer's discovery of China in the countryside and its subsequent depiction of rural China's transformation, we embody the roles of both researchers and participants in the rural development process, delving deeper into comprehending the essence of China. This stems from our team's origin, forged within the crucible of diverse grassroots initiatives, tightly bound with local volunteers and grassroots leaders. Furthermore, our mentors, including luminaries such as Huang Ping, Wang Hui, Liu Jianzhi, Zhang Xiaoshan, Zhang Xiaode, Dai Jinhua, Xu Baoqiang, Zhou Li, Tong Zhihui, and others, imparted invaluable perspectives

Through a multidimensional lens encompassing political economy, institutional history, cultural evolution, social flux, and global comparisons, they astutely elevated our grassroots experiences to a profound theoretical plane, broadening our vista to apprehend the essence of rural China. Amidst our on-the-ground research, we have experienced a sense of profound clarity akin to reaching for the heavens while maintaining a foothold on Earth, affording us the unique opportunity to survey the course of human history across millennia and, concurrently, paint a vivid portrait from the microscopic perspective of this book, intimately bridging the gap with our readers. This harmonious convergence, reminiscent of the yin-yang symbol, interweaves macroscopic and microscopic insights, thereby endowing our conclusions and the very research process with replicability. From a single drop, we discern the radiant sun, just as behind every village, the specter of China's accumulated civilizational history emerges. Each pivotal juncture in our nation's narrative finds a parallel thread within rural praxis.

Naturally, China's tumultuous development, the toil and travail endured over the years, inexorably accumulated in myriad manners within rural environs. It may burgeon with exuberance or become stilted and distorted, resembling the winds aloft that propel clouds to soar and, simultaneously, stir up the earth, creating a cascade of swirling soil. The stratified layers of dust, painstakingly amassed by the relentless passage of time, imbue the collective soul of rural China with humility, yet remain veiled, not readily discernible. In essence, the researcher's task mirrors that of an archeologist, meticulously reconstructing the ephemeral "soil and dust dancing in the breeze" of bygone eras. By shattering the rigid confines of ideologically manipulated collective memories, we illuminate the panorama of objective rationality, where the grand and minute intricately converge. This pursuit is undoubtedly arduous. Shall we then surrender to the tempestuous nature of our quest and meekly submit to the whims of public opinion, attributing the convoluted tapestry of history to mere subjective predilections, or even worse, assigning the enigmatic underpinnings to the realm of irrational folkloric phenomena?

This book carries forward our team's steadfast tradition of embedding the research subject within the vast tapestry of China's historical saga. Our writing team, with an unwavering purpose, aims to evoke the essence of "China within the battle flag, and the battle flag within China." While we acknowledge the gap that separates us from the ideal, the youthful cohort undertaking this writing endeavor strives to unravel, with commendable zeal, the profound metamorphosis of a village spanning three distinct epochs across a span of 55 years. Their endeavor commends admiration, as they deftly unravel the intricate economic bedrock that underpins this remarkable narrative.

3 The Dao That Can Be Spoken of Is Not the Eternal Dao[5]: A Village Case Study Merging Macro and Micro Perspectives

In the words of Karl Marx, humans forge their own historical paths, yet not in a capricious manner, nor within self-imposed confines. Rather, they shape their destinies amid predefined, ancestral circumstances they directly encounter.[6]

Simplicity in speech, complexity in action. In modern China, be it urban sprawl or rural hamlets, the grand tapestry of the macro environment weighs heavily on the cost and reward calculus of individual actors. Thus, this macro backdrop assumes its pivotal role as the prime

[5] Translator's note: 道可道，非常道, the first sentence of "道德经.".

[6] Karl Marx. The Eighteenth Brumaire of Louis Bonaparte[M]. Nanjing: Jiangsu People's Publishing House, 2011.

catalyst of historical creation. However, apprehending the historical flux of this expansive milieu proves a daunting obstacle on the path to genuine comprehension. It is here that our team diverges from convention, embracing the extraordinary. Leveraging our interpretive opus on China's macroeconomic undulations, christened "Eight Crises," as our foundation, we enshrine the notion of rural terrain as the bedrock for China's emancipatory endeavors.[7] We then resituate Zhanqi Village's saga, spanning five and a half decades, within the ebb and flow of the macrocosm. Only thus can we seamlessly intertwine pivotal events and transformative measures undertaken by Zhanqi Village with its geographical bearings, alongside the intricate dance of political and economic forces that shaped its moments of consequence. The culmination of this approach yields a resounding symphony of research, persuasive in its harmonious conviction.

To facilitate comprehension, let me elucidate with examples.

Firstly, the whereabouts of Zhanqi Village.

The standard response places Zhanqi Village snugly at the base of Hengshan Mountain, along the tranquil banks of the Baitiao River in Tangchang Town, Pidu District, Chengdu City, Sichuan Province. However, such a plain explanation hardly delves into the profound essence of Zhanqi Village. On a two-dimensional plane, it rests in the southwestern reaches of China. Yet, if we venture beyond the realms of latitude and longitude, elevating our perspective to encompass the majestic heights, an ethereal panorama of a "snow-crowned mountain's foothills" emerges, unveiling a tapestry of geographic and anthropological significance.

The disparity of human civilization hinges upon the superficial geological endowments they owe their existence. The ceaseless tapestry of Chinese civilization, spanning five millennia, is no exception. In the 1980s, Chinese geologists conceived the notion of a "Third Pole." The poles of the Earth, the Arctic and the Antarctic, are known as the icy frontiers that invigorate global atmospheric and hydrological circulation, fueled by the temperature variance betwixt temperate realms and the tropics. Yet, in proximity to the Tropic of Cancer, the Asian landmass boasts another bastion—the Qinghai–Tibet Plateau, the planet's "Third Pole." This colossal altitudinal plateau heeds a clarion call, its uplift

[7] Wen Tiejun, et al. Eight crises: China's real experience 1949–2009[M]. Beijing: Oriental Publishing House, 2013.

instating a realm of profound influence on the climate throughout the vast Asian expanse.

The ascent of the Qinghai–Tibet Plateau bequeaths an aerie of low-pressure ambiance, drawing forth neighboring winds to supplement its aura. Behold the birth of this "superlative windmill," where climatic dispositions undergo a metamorphosis, begetting the audacious dichotomy of "rain-kissed Jiangnan, versus the autumnal gales of the northern frontiers." The pursuit of geographical scholarship unveils an intimate correlation among the contemporary natural geography of Asia, the rhythmic monsoons, and the uplifting of the Qinghai–Tibet Plateau. Through the metamorphic stages of the Qinghai–Tibetan tectonic movements, the Kunlun–Yellow River tectonic movement, and the Gonghe tectonic movement, the zenith of the Asian monsoon climate system was reached, eclipsing planetary air currents and fostering the edenic foundations of Asia—a resplendent sanctuary teeming with natural abundance, cultural grandeur, and flourishing prosperity.[8] Thus, Zhanqi Village finds itself ensconced within the plains, gracefully descending from the lofty periphery of the Qinghai–Tibet Plateau to the Chengdu Plain, where it embraces the bountiful blessings of the plateau's aqueous snowmelt, yet remains at the mercy of seasonal deluges, thereby beckoning the discourse on water management.

If we observe the humanistic features and incorporate a temporal perspective alongside the spatial one, the whereabouts of Zhanqi Village, approximately 20 kilometers from Dujiangyan, become discernible. The murmuring waters of the ancient two-thousand-year-old irrigation system flow through the village, inducing a lingering chill even as one strolls along its banks during the summertime. It is widely recognized that Dujiangyan, a hydraulic endeavor overseen by Li Bing and his progeny at the behest of King Zhao of Qin during the twilight of the Warring States era, holds tremendous historical significance for the nation's political landscape. The Chengdu Plain, once a capricious domain of floods and droughts, witnessed a transformative metamorphosis with the advent of the Dujiangyan project. This ingenious hydraulic feat bifurcated the Min River into the Inner River and the Outer River, allowing the former to meander through the Chengdu Plain via an intricate network of irrigation channels. Employing astute design, a self-regulating water allocation

[8] Li Jijun. Uplift of the Tibetan Plateau and Environmental Evolution in Asia—Selected Papers of Academician Li Jijun [M]. Beijing: Science Press, 2006.

mechanism was attained: during times of scarcity, 60% of the water coursed into the Inner River, ensuring the irrigation needs of hundreds of thousands of arable acres; conversely, during times of abundance, 40% proved sufficient to sustain the plain's agriculture, while the remaining 60% was discharged into the Outer River, preventing inundation and sparing the populace from the perils of floods. Henceforth, the Chengdu Plain became a realm where "floods and droughts come from people, as people never know about famine anymore."[9] Thus, an age-old adage echoes through time: "First conquer Long (陇), then seize Shu (蜀), and finally triumph over the world," underscoring the pivotal role this region played in shaping the entire Chinese realm.

A deeper contemplation reveals the profound tapestry of human endeavor woven into the fabric of Dujiangyan. The construction of Dujiangyan stands as an archetypal manifestation of statehood. It interweaves the prosperity of the nation with the welfare of its people, fostering an inextricable nexus between governmental authority and hydraulic infrastructure. Common sense readily elucidates that the enterprise demanded not only the mobilization of labor during the construction phase but also the perennial maintenance of the entire water system. Consequently, a symbiotic relationship between the nation and the rural grassroots was necessitated, epitomizing a perennial interaction. Questions abounded: how to apportion irrigation water annually, levy water fees, and orchestrate manpower to periodically cleanse the irrigation channels of sediment and silt to ensure unimpeded flow? Thus, the interaction between the state and the local grassroots regarding water management metamorphosed into a well-oiled governance machinery. The inscription "Dig deep into the bottom of the beach to make a weir (深掏滩底作堰)" preceding the Erwang Temple, venerated as a shrine to Li Bing and his progeny, encapsulates the profound wisdom accumulated over the course of two millennia in Dujiangyan's vigilant guardianship. This terse phrase embodies the quintessence of the region's agrarian and national governance. While Zhanqi Village only attained the status of an autonomous production brigade in 1965, it, as a fundamental organizational unit steeped in historical lineage and cultural continuum, had already forged an enduring operational paradigm in its institutional ties with the nation, a template meticulously honed over two thousand years.

[9] Translators' note: 水旱从人, 不知饥馑, from Records of the Huayang Kingdom (《华阳国志记》).

Secondly, what is the "Zhanqi" (battle flag; 战旗)?

Zhanqi Village, situated within the domain of Chongning County's Lingsheng Township during the Republic of China era, found its place among the "sanjia" (三甲) classification. But mind you, "sanjia" does not imply a podium finish for the imperial examination, rather it signifies its inclusion within the "baojia" (保甲) system prevalent during that time. This exemplifies the adjustment of the nation's grassroots governance structure, in tandem with the demands of modernization.

In retrospect, this marked an endeavor of exorbitant costs. Primarily, the feeble economic foundation of the agrarian society, shackled by paltry surplus, proved inadequate to bear the burden of constructing a modernized edifice. The upper echelons of the Republic of China's governance were tasked with incessantly communicating the nation's intent through the baojia framework to the rural expanse. However, any government intending to administer in accordance with modernized architectural paradigms would inevitably incur exorbitant systemic costs. Alas, the vulnerable economic foundation of the countryside proved incapable of shouldering the weight of such grandiose structures, consequently engendering grave predicaments in societal governance.

Moreover, the bedrock of mutual benefits and shared natural and market risks between the peasantry and landlords, prevalent in the agricultural sphere of yore, was shattered by the advent of a modernized economy. In bygone days, farmers would dutifully render their harvest shares to the landlords once the autumn yielded its bounty. The division of spoils, be it an even fifty–fifty split or a lopsided forty–sixty or thirty–seventy, always bore witness to the ebb and flow of production. In essence, it symbolized the traditional coalescence of risk-sharing between the tenant and the landlord. However, as the Republic of China surged forth with its industrialization and urbanization during the golden decade, the narrative took a somber turn. Scores of landlords flocked to urban centers, embarking upon commercial and industrial pursuits, prompting a paradigm shift in the rural landscape. A dire transformation unfolded. Farmers were now coerced into tendering cash rents, forepaying their dues ahead of the land lease, effectively transmuting the divisible rent into an unyielding fee. The dynamic of downward rent shifted upward, leaving the farmer alone to bear the capricious whims of nature, while simultaneously shouldering the volatile burden of market fluctuations. Irrespective of market conditions, farmers found themselves entrapped within the confines of predetermined output prices, thus perpetuating an unending cycle of burdensome fixed rents. Consequently, the small-scale farmers faltered under the weight of dual risks, resulting in a deluge of bankruptcies. Alas, the baojia system of the Republic of China succumbed to failure, plunging countless rural enclaves into decay, sowing the seeds of peasant revolutions, and beyond.[10]

After the birth of the New China, the nation remained steadfast in its pursuit of modernization. The indissoluble bond between the village and the fate of the country finds its most conspicuous manifestation in the perpetual metamorphosis of Zhanqi Village, formerly known as JiJifeng Village (集凤村).

In the year 1952, Jifeng Village came into existence as the first production mutual aid group in the enchanting enclave of Lingsheng Township, nestled within the embrace of Chongning County. From this humble genesis sprouted a primary agricultural production cooperative, solidifying its roots. By 1954, the audacious experiment of the Jinxing Agricultural Production Cooperative (金星农业生产合作社) in the realm of Lingsheng Township unfolded, casting ripples of change. The year 1956 witnessed the ascension of an advanced agricultural production cooperative, ultimately giving rise to the institution of the people's commune. In the annals of 1965, Jifeng Village emancipated itself from the once-familiar embrace of the Jinxing Brigade (金星大队), asserting its unique identity as the "Jinxing Third Brigade" (金星三大队)...

The intricate tapestry of these incessant recalibrations beckons thorough analysis, for it is clear that Jifeng Village, situated at the very heart of grassroots accounting organizations, experienced an ebb and flow that stemmed from China's momentous acceptance of Soviet assistance in the post-1952 era, entwined with the cascading consequences resulting from the near-cessation of aid after the year 1957 Necessitated by these mounting pressures, Jifeng Village adroitly navigated the tempestuous currents by deftly adjusting the tapestry of rural management systems, defying the imminent crisis. Those who have perused the pages of our team's work (the "Eight Crises") will assuredly recognize this pivotal juncture.

With the dawn of the industrialization epoch of the People's Republic of China, an existential predicament reared its head—the perilous specter of a famine. In 1952, the country wholeheartedly embraced Soviet

[10] Wen Tiejun. Research on China's rural basic economic system[M]. Beijing: China Economic Press, 2000.

aid, beckoning forth a surge of individuals to the urban milieu, their purpose, to bolster the foundations of industrial prowess. In the relentless pursuit of progress, the concomitant escalation in urban demand for sustenance strained the conventional mechanisms of rural procurement, thus ushering in a momentous metamorphosis—the advent of a unified system of procurement and distribution in 1953.[11] To pave the way for this transformative endeavor, the intricate labyrinth of transactional costs between the countryside and the humble agrarian was vanquished. Thus, emerged the chrysalis of primary agricultural cooperatives, instilling a renewed sense of organization among the rustic denizens and internalizing the erstwhile transactional tribulations. The year 1956 heralded the mass production of tractors, entailing an imperative for the industrious realm to disperse its bounty to the rural outposts. This called for the formation of the venerated advanced cooperatives, serving as the conduit to further heighten organization and consolidate vast expanses of arable land with resolute audacity.

China then faced its first economic crisis due to the external onslaught of industrialization, labeled as an "imported" crisis, primarily triggered by the abrupt withdrawal of Soviet investments. For developing nations, the sudden halt of colossal international aid, comprising 156 projects worth $5.4 billion, proved disastrous. In China, the present-day narrative remains composed: the "First Five-Year Plan" surpassed expectations, but the subsequent investment in projects lagged behind, thus impeding the formulation of the anticipated "Second Five-Year Plan" in 1957. Yet, with numerous ongoing projects slated for production in 1958 or even 1960, neglecting further investments meant squandering prior efforts. Consequently, the First Zhengzhou Conference[12] proposed a grassroots approach, endeavoring to supplant central industrialization with localized efforts.

[11] Because urban industrialization has driven a large number of people to move into cities, urban food needs cannot be met under the original grain purchase, sale, and stockpile system. Therefore, both rural and urban areas can only be "unified (统)"—unified purchasing (统购) in rural areas and unified distributing (统销) in cities. Together, it's called "unified system of procurement and distribution.".

[12] Translator's note: The Central Committee of the Communist Party of China held a working conference in Zhengzhou from November 2 to 10, 1958, which was attended by some central leaders, regional leaders, and some first secretaries of provincial and municipal party committees, namely the First Zhengzhou Conference. This meeting was held on the initiative of Mao Zedong.

It is worth noting that a contextual understanding of the period is crucial for readers. In the nascent stages of New China, the majority of leaders had been honed through guerrilla warfare, lacking substantial experience in industrial development. Consequently, local industrialization initiatives hinged on mimicking the established blueprint of central industrialization, a structure primarily guided by Soviet experts. The top-down administrative approach adopted by the central government mirrored the Soviet bureaucratic model, while the influx of Soviet foreign investment bolstered the directive nature of the planned economy. As local governments endeavored to replicate this framework for industrialization, they faced a formidable predicament. The transition from a cadre base primarily comprising impoverished farmers and intellectuals to proficient managers of industrialization came with exorbitant learning costs, inadvertently birthing numerous challenges.

Just as the formation of primary cooperatives in 1952 predominantly catered to urban demands, rather than being an organic aspiration of the farming populace, the inception of the People's Communes in 1958 did not stem from agrarian requisites. Instead, it served as a response to the grave crisis of "absolute capital scarcity" (资本绝对稀缺) that plagued national industrialization due to the cessation and withdrawal of Soviet aid between 1958 and 1960. China, forced into self-preservation, resorted to "factor substitution." The pivotal approach involved organizing labor on a communal scale, employing extensive manpower to compensate for the dearth of capital, with the emphasis placed on small-scale industries like steel production. The rural sector's manufacturing of industrial goods sought to alleviate the shortfall of urban-produced commodities, thereby circumventing the predicament.

In our archives, we unearthed records of the nascent Advanced Communes of 1956, meticulously detailing the considerable funds expended and the quantity of "double-disc plows" procured (Soviet-designed agricultural wares) by urban enterprises. To disseminate industrial goods to the hinterlands, amalgamating the small, independently accounted production brigades into larger, consolidated entities became imperative. This approach ensured ample financial means for industrial acquisitions but, alas, expanded the purview of agricultural management, a blueprint conceived over six decades ago to infuse city-born industry into agrarian landscapes. Alas, it has proven ill-suited to the idiosyncrasies of small-scale farmers, impeding agricultural productivity. Yet, a conundrum emerges: the simplistic revival of the "peasant economy" would invariably foster dispersed farmers confronting the scourge of "market failure." Nonetheless, our present predicament affords us an opportunity to architect a compound system, escaping the binary entrapment of decentralization versus centralization.

Following the cessation of strategic aid from the Soviet Union, China found solace solely in its domestic economy, fueling an arduous phase of high-intensity industrialization while endeavoring to discharge mounting debts. Straddling the precipice of economic tension, the government sought respite through systemic adjustments. In 1958, an extensive transfer of enterprises to local authorities occurred, accompanied by the advent of the People's Commune framework across rural landscapes. However, by 1961, the decentralized enterprises were repossessed by the central authority, returning the rural expanse to the rudiments of "three-level ownership, with the brigade as its foundation (三级所有，队为基础)." Consequently, the recalibration of the nation's economic compass reemphasized an agrarian-centric trajectory, birthing the resurgence of rural economies.

Originally, the phrase "the brigade as its foundation" alluded to the premise of the "production teams (生产小队)," natural village entities blessed with a localized radius of influence. Yet, these tenets materialized with disparate manifestations across various regions. While Huaxi Village in Jiangsu, in 1961, commenced its journey toward a "brigade-centric" model, the more conservative hinterlands of Sichuan, epitomized by Jifeng Village, remained subservient to the all-encompassing Jinxing Brigade until 1965. Gradually, the realization of unwieldy managerial reach impeding productivity and efficacy compelled the division of the colossal brigade (生产大队) into smaller production units, with the humble production team as the bedrock of their accounting. Simultaneously, the grassroots administrative framework underwent harmonization, anchoring itself to the brigade echelon. Since then, this administrative architecture has largely endured.

In summation, sans the shackles of ideological scrutiny, the trajectory experienced by Jifeng Village—spanning from the birth of primitive agricultural cooperatives in 1952 to the zenith of collectivization in 1955, culminating in the socio-brigade adjustments during the Socialist Education Movement of 1965—represents an objective portrayal of China's rural economy adapting to the juggernaut of urban industrialization.

Thirdly, why the name "Zhanqi"?

The choice of "Zhanqi" begs the question: What's the underlying macro backdrop?

In 1964, urban industry regained momentum, ushering in the distribution of manufactured goods to rural areas. Simultaneously, agricultural and irrigation projects burgeoned, fostering a tangible exchange of resources between the urban and rural domains. On the one hand, city-produced commodities could reach the countryside, while, on the other hand, the industrial sector received compensation from rural areas in the form of agricultural products. Henceforth, slogans like "Emulate Dazhai in Agriculture (农业学大寨)," "Follow Daqing in Industry (工业学大庆)," and "Adopt Lei Feng's Spirit in the People's Liberation Army (解放军学雷锋)" emerged nationwide.

When Zhanqi emerged as a distinct entity in 1965, it was christened "Jinxing Third Brigade." However, in 1966, Jiang Daxing (蒋大兴), the brigade's party secretary, proclaimed, "We must serve as the vanguard banner of 'Learning from Dazhai in Agriculture' Campaign." Consequently, the village's name underwent a metamorphosis, assuming the profoundly revolutionary mantle of "Zhanqi (战旗)," the battle flag.

This deep-seated bond between peasants and the nation-state in a non-militaristic setting is a rarity throughout China's extensive history. Historically, it was only during periods of dynastic transition that farmers were galvanized for uprisings, thereby propelling rural areas into a proactive role. Revolutions necessitated land redistribution, the mobilization of farmers for warfare, and the establishment and defense of new regimes. However, once the transition concluded, the farmer militias would lay down their arms, reverting to subsistence farming, and the countryside would resume its conservative state. Such was the historical norm. The 1960s, strictly speaking, did not constitute a period of tranquility. Rather, it was an era where "war dictated war," ultimately culminating in the peace that future generations would behold. China, grappling with formidable pressures, embraced the enterprising strategy of "Learning from Dazhai in Agriculture" as a means to reshape the foundations of agriculture and the rural landscape within the confines of limited natural resources. It sought to harness the subjective agency of individuals, infusing rural labor with an intensity that bordered on the extraordinary.

The valiant struggle of the Zhanqi villagers remains an undeniably stirring saga. A united front emerged as the entire village engaged in rigorous militia training, adopting a militaristic approach with resolute dedication. They embarked on the transformative endeavor of "changing fields and learning from Dazhai (条田改土学大寨)," an arduous task that demanded perseverance. Nestled in the low-lying expanse of Zhanqi, their fertile lands were persistently inundated, compelling them to raise the earth's contours and fortify its composition with lime. Diligently excavating peripheral trenches ensured timely drainage, effectively converting saturated fields into bountiful havens. This paved the way for mechanized farming, empowering the surplus labor to flourish in secondary enterprises, and augmenting the collective's overall productivity.

The fourteen syllables, "changing fields and learning from Dazhai, straightening ditches, and planting trees in rows at the end of the ditches (条田改土学大寨，沟端路直树成行)," might effortlessly trip off the tongue, yet for the indomitable Zhanqi residents, it encapsulated a grueling labor that spanned well over a decade. Their relentless toil was so exacting that the village's young bachelors found themselves in the throes of matrimony's quandary, for prospective brides feared the burdens they would inherit.

From a panoramic perspective, it was the concerted effort of over eight hundred thousand villages (brigade), akin to Zhanqi, that enabled China to surmount the tempestuous 1960s. By lavishing untold labor upon rural infrastructure, these vibrant hamlets not only achieved unprecedented milestones in agricultural water management but also propelled the "Third Front" movement (三线建设). This, in turn, engendered a self-sustaining "domestic circulation," chronicling China's awe-inspiring journey of autonomy and self-reliance during the harshest period of the 1960s. A resplendent testament that continues to inspire the embattled nations of our world.

4 Insights on Comprehensive Rural Revitalization by This Book

This book illuminates the profound journey of comprehensive rural revitalization. Our team, amidst a decade-long exploration of regional landscapes, has garnered commendation for its audacious ingenuity. Building upon our previous research, this literary opus unveils a plethora of invaluable discoveries, not only of great scholarly significance but also of pivotal relevance to the holistic advancement of rural renaissance.

In the author's discerning gaze, this tome endures the course of tradition, encapsulating its essence "from one to four." Allow me to expound briefly on these facets:

One nucleus: The bucolic heartland, China's paradigm of emancipation from reliance.

Two perspectives: Marrying the grandiose and the minute, melding temporality with spatiality.

Three phases: The "scarlet zhanqi (红色战旗)" during politicized rivalry, the "gilded zhanqi (金色战旗)" during industrialized competition, and the "verdant zhanqi (绿色战旗)" during ecological contention.

Four illuminations: Internalizing costs, rationalizing rural society, safeguarding resource sovereignty, and championing spatial justice.

Here is a brief explanation of the four illuminations this book draws from the experience of Zhanqi Village to draw readers' attention.

The initial illumination lies in the internalization of costs.

China, once entangled with the two dominant global powers, found itself abruptly severed from their economic grasp after the cessation of Soviet foreign investments and technological aid in 1960. How did the nation, striving for over seven decades, bear the burden of internalizing the costs incurred by this foreign capital rupture? It is worth noting that past dependencies had reaped "dividends." China, fueled by its geopolitical ambitions, had enjoyed the Soviet Union's strategic transfers of equipment, reaping vast financial and technological savings, propelling it swiftly toward industrialization. But when the unexpected "de-dependence" occurred, China faced a dual challenge. On one hand, it had to repay debts; on the other, it had to recalibrate the vested interests embedded within its domestic landscape while continuing to funnel investments into industrialization. The cost of this "de-dependence" nearly doubled, yet these institutional expenses couldn't be shifted elsewhere. Thus, the pressing question emerges: How could the nation ensure its industrialization trajectory wouldn't falter midway? Under the prevailing circumstances, internalizing costs became the sole recourse. A vital foundation for such assimilation was the existence of collective villages. These settlements thrived by substituting a surplus of labor for the dire scarcity of capital, forging an exchange of material goods and essential resources with urban industries. Within this vast, malleable countryside, accommodating the strategic aspirations of the nation, China succeeded in constructing its intricate domestic circulation network. Hence, the birth of Zhanqi Village, emblematic of the nation's drive to internalize external costs, marked a transformative juncture.

The second illumination: the rationality of rural society.

As previously expounded, disparate cultures and microcosmic behavioral rationality emerged in the East and the West owing to geographical resource differentials. In the East, the collective rationality born from the communal existence in village settlements diverged from individual rationality. Zhanqi Village proffers an occasion to witness the mechanics of rationality within the quintessential administrative unit shaping social structures—the village itself.

To this day, Chinese rural life embraces the concept of "Three Lives in One (三生合一)." This convergence encapsulates the fusion of seemingly distinct realms—ecology, production, and existence—into a harmonious amalgam within the rural domain. China's geographic framework, characterized by "seven mountains, two rivers, and one plot of farmland (七山二水一分田)," is further complicated by severe disparities in seasonal and spatial water resource allocation. Natural calamities, recurrent and rampant (marking China as one of the world's most beleaguered nations), exacerbate the challenge of survival amidst resource constraints. Yet, remarkably, China manages to sustain around 20% of the global population in the face of such strained human-land dynamics. Traditional agricultural practices, replete with meticulous cultivation, cyclical utilization, and resource frugality, unite with the denizens sharing the same geographical endowments, fostering a profound and interrelated fabric of the village community. Together, they safeguard the ecological balance, fortify collective resilience against adversity, and nurture various artisanal crafts within their confines, endeavoring to minimize external risks. A localized tapestry of culture and governance—a "trinity of livelihoods" and "trinity of governance"—springs forth from this groundwork.[13]

From the agricultural zenith of Dazhai to the establishment of the Zhanqi Brick Factory, and now in this new epoch, Zhanqi forges ahead with reform, undertaking the "Three Transformations" reforms. This transformative process entails the construction of a novel collective economy, the renaissance of ancestral traditions, and the resurgence of rural craftsmanship. In every milestone, the village community, an intrinsic entity, assumes a paramount role, harmonizing resources and essential elements. Academia, in the 1980s, astutely encapsulated this Eastern paradigm—an intricate interplay between dual layers of households and villages, bound by kinship and geographical proximity,

[13] Wen Tiejun, Yang Shuai. "Three Rural Issues" and "Three Governances" [M]. Beijing: Renmin University of China Press, 2016.

ingeniously internalizing transaction costs—as the "rationality of rural communities."

The third illumination: resource sovereignty.

Our research reveals that a nation can only forge economic sovereignty and safeguard its political autonomy by acquiring and preserving unadulterated "resource sovereignty." For microcosmic entities like villages, possessing a coherent "resource rights and interests" delimited by geographical boundaries becomes imperative to sustain their localized "three lives" and "three governance," thus fashioning an institutional sphere where internalizing external factors thrive. This metamorphosis empowers villages to serve as the microscopic foundation upholding comprehensive national stability and security.

As China endeavors to metamorphose into an ecological civilization in the twenty-first century, the predicament of rural resource rights becomes an inescapable quandary in the throes of profound reform. Alas, urban hegemony has entrenched itself, leaving deep-rooted path dependency saturating all facets of institutional frameworks and narrative discourses. How can China unravel this tangled skein, banishing the chains of dependency, and transition toward a novel amalgamation of urban–rural dynamics?

In this epoch dominated by the ecological civilization ethos, the valuation of rural resources and the equitable distribution of accrued benefits epitomize the essence of village self-determination.

Behold Zhanqi Village, where resources are not transacted in the ephemeral guise of contractual obligations aimed at appeasing investor expectations. Instead, a perpetual state of "win–win" is embraced, adroitly recalibrating the worth of manifest resources and expanding the village's grasp on resource rights and interests. The resulting gains burgeon into a veritable lifeblood for the nascent collective economy. The overarching insight lies in the unequivocal need for other villages to replicate Zhanqi's triumph: an indomitable aspiration hinging on the prerequisite of securing an institutional sphere facilitating comprehensive resource rights and interests. This quandary, by and large, extends beyond the rustic realms. Ergo, our optimism rests with reforms emanating from the supply side of institutional structures, sanguinely yearning for proactive responsiveness from relevant authorities aligning with the nation's cardinal strategic trajectory, and placing primacy on rural realities and the aspirations of its denizens, thereby bequeathing farmers their rightful dominion over autonomous development.

The fourth illumination: spatial justice.

When a village's entire prosperity stems from the autonomous development rights it holds over its internal resources, that prosperity must be shared among all villagers as a socialized allocation of membership entitlements. This "profit-sharing" is what ensures the integration of village resources becomes an enduring and deepening process.

Given that all resources are collectively owned by the village's members, it follows that the benefits should be distributed solely among them. This realization epitomizes the essence of "spatial justice" in the Marxist sense—a manifestation of identity and belonging that resonates with the principles of resource internalization. It is through this framework that continuous mobilization of the villagers occurs during the subsequent capitalization of resources, further strengthening the collective economic organization's capacity to unite individuals.

Moreover, in China, "spatial justice" assumes an additional, profoundly significant macro meaning. Reflecting upon the nation's journey toward independence and development in modern times, the vast geographical depth it possesses emerges as an indomitable foundation. It is perhaps an extension of China's historical wisdom in skillfully navigating its "continental geopolitics" (distinct from the Western countries' reliance on "maritime dominance" in geopolitics). If we consider that China's unique advantage, as a vast continental nation, has always been its ability to leverage space to overcome external crises, it becomes apparent that each custodian of spatial resources deserves equitable distribution—a strategic embodiment of macro "spatial justice."

In essence, the tale of Zhanqi unveils the lingering echoes of China's ever-shifting epochs within a quaint village, offering a profound embodiment of China's intrinsic wisdom. When we delve into the realms of "Chinese experience" and "Confidence in the Chinese path," these notions transcend mere illusions and mirages, for our confidence dwells authentically within the vibrant tapestry of every village's existence. Village studies, akin to this literary work, represent a scholarly endeavor to eloquently narrate the resounding "Chinese story," endowing other fields with a plethora of invaluable narratives. Now, it is within our reach to embark upon an enlightening journey, commencing with a survey of the rural enclaves in our own proximity, embracing a profound understanding of China, and artfully articulating its tale, bolstering the Chinese discourse with a mosaic of captivating chronicles. It is through such endeavors that cultural and institutional fortitude take root.

"A 55-Year Odyssey of Zhanqi Village: 1965–2020" shall soon grace the literary stage, and as the esteemed academic consultant for this opus, my heart brims with contentment. May we aspire not solely to uncover China within Zhanqi Village, but also to unravel the multitude of Chinese narratives concealed within other hamlets.

A preface, thus composed.

Wen Tiejun,

Principal Expert at the Zhanqi Training Institute for Rural Revitalization.

Winter, at the crossroads of the Gengzi and Xinchou years.

CHAPTER 2

Overview: China in the Zhanqi, and the Zhanqi in China

Nestled at the foot of Hengshan Mountain, by the tranquil banks of Baijiao River, lies a village hailed by General Secretary Xi Jinping as an embodiment of its name: a battle flag unfurled with unwavering pride. Amidst its enchanting vistas, a spirit of relentless pursuit and distant horizons thrives.

Zhanqi Village finds its abode beneath the lofty Qinghai–Tibet Plateau and the formidable Hengduan Mountains. Here, the timeless waters of the Minjiang River course through the venerable Dujiangyan Irrigation System, meandering through ordered channels, whispering their way through this humble hamlet. While neighboring villages scramble to catch the speeding train of modernity, Zhanqi Village, fueled by centuries of agrarian toil, metamorphoses into a shining "battle flag" (, Zhanqi) amidst the rural renaissance.

A promenade through Zhanqi Village reveals the graceful silhouette of Mount Siguniang, adorned with its ethereal allure, and the gleaming crown of Xiling Snow Mountain in the distance. On one side, traditional dwellings of Western Sichuan beckon, while on the other, the vista transforms into a tapestry of contemporary agricultural landscapes. Underfoot, a crystalline stream meanders—a living testament to the battle flag's chronicle—a conduit bearing the historical yearning of "Cuckoos told of Emperor Wang's wish in Spring ( )," flowing toward a harmonious coexistence between humanity, nature, and all creation.

© Peking University Press 2024

X. Dong, *Zhanqi Village Over Fifty Years*,
https://doi.org/10.1007/978-981-97-5426-7_2

Amidst lavender-scented meadows, it is inconceivable that this village, too, has not weathered its share of adversities—a tale mirrored by countless others.

Zhanqi Village resides within the embrace of Tangchang Town, Pixian District, Chengdu City, in the bosom of Sichuan Province. Situated where Pixian District, Pengzhou City, and Dujiangyan City intersect, this village once constituted a meager expanse of 2.06 square kilometers, with cultivated lands spanning 1930 mu (around 129 hectares) and a population of roughly 1700.[1] For long epochs, this village languished amidst the vast sea of over 600,000 administrative villages, an embodiment of ordinary rural existence. In its nascent years of 1965, Zhanqi Village, situated within an unclaimed administrative territory, bore the burden of a 700.

yuan debt, its collective assets reduced to a dilapidated shack and a trifling trio of rickety stools. How did this battle flag ascend, defiantly aloft? Beyond trite "one-size-fits-all" descriptions, the crux of curiosity lies in the tale's ebbs and flows, and the transcendent wisdom derived from lucid analysis and synthesis, disentangled from the individual or the particular.

Perhaps someone would argue that not all villages possess the remarkable geographical advantages and centuries of cultural enrichment that Zhanqi Village enjoys by virtue of its place within the Dujiangyan irrigation system. Consequently, skeptics question the representativeness and reproducibility of Zhanqi Village's experience. Such doubts are not uncommon. However, while Zhanqi Village's developmental journey holds distinctiveness, its intrinsic mechanisms are universal and open to replication, imitation, and even substitution. The transformation from "peculiar" to "general" stands as the pivotal test for the success or failure of case studies.

As the celestial bodies dance, from the year 1983 when the revolutionary Zhanqi Brigade initiated the rural household contract responsibility system reform,[2] to the present publication, a span of thirty-eight

[1] However, following the merger with Jinxing Village ( ) in early 2020, Zhanqi Village expanded its reach to encompass 5.36 square kilometers, with cultivated lands spanning 5441.5 mu, and accommodating a total of 1445 households and 4493 individuals. This narrative primarily chronicles the village's pre-2020 history.

[2] In the 1950s, Zhanqi Village was originally named Jifeng Brigade ( ). In 1966, it was renamed Zhanqi Brigade ( ). In 1984, the team was withdrawn to build a village, and it was renamed Zhanqi Village.

years has passed. Within the expanse of the vast cosmos, history has turned to a fresh page—a page characterized by the construction of a novel collective economic structure and the pursuit of communal prosperity. Simultaneously, it marks the juncture where China, amidst the tempestuous global landscape, confronts the challenge of liberation from external dependencies. More than six decades ago, in the shackles of a dual blockade imposed by the United States and the Soviet Union, this very locale, hoisting the banner of Zhanqi Village, rose in resolute defiance. Sacrificing the village's manpower to reclaim marshy fields and untidy plots, they significantly augmented grain production. The relentless struggles of countless Zhanqi Villages epitomized the microcosmic foundation that enabled China to sever its reliance on the Soviet Union in the 1960s. Now, more than sixty years later, guided by the Communist Party, Zhanqi Village propels its collective economy toward rapid growth, elevating the lives of its villagers to unprecedented heights. A scenic haven blessed with an idyllic ecological environment and distinguished regional cultural traits, it served as the inaugural destination for General Secretary Xi Jinping's inspection after the 19th National Congress, a place where he conveyed the resplendent symbol of "auspiciousness"( ) to the nation. It encapsulates the fervent aspirations of General Secretary Xi Jinping, urging the nation to stride at the forefront and set forth a compelling example.

Amidst the torrent of China's accelerated modernization, rural revitalization assumes paramount significance as a critical national strategy with Xi Jinping's Thoughts on Socialism with Chinese Characteristics for a New era. It not only serves as the ballast to counter internal and external risks but also establishes a bedrock foundation for fostering domestic circulation and fortifying sustainable socioeconomic development. This transformative strategy necessitates the emergence of a reinvigorated rural landscape, wherein the pervasive predicament of atomization is transcended, hollowed-out collective economies rejuvenated, and the massive outflow of young rural labor stemmed. No longer can the rustic heartlands be left at the mercy of the market economy, while the urban epicenters remain inundated with a plethora of capital fixated on speculative gains. Against this backdrop, the tales and wisdom of Zhanqi Village attain profound significance, casting a radiant beacon to navigate the path toward surmounting the prevailing challenges.

"Regardless of the trajectory of urbanization, it is an undeniable fact that a substantial rural population will persist. It is untenable for us to witness the prosperity of cities juxtaposed against the backwardness or even decline of our rural hinterlands. The development of rural areas transcends mere industrial progress or materialistic advancement; it necessitates an unwavering commitment to fostering spiritual enlightenment and nurturing a vibrant cultural life."[3] Within China's domestic and international crucibles, rural regions stand as the quintessential fulcrum—steadfastly bolstering the nation's resilience against multifarious risks and challenges. Zhanqi Village, an emblematic standard-bearer, embarks on a profound odyssey, resolutely positioned to navigate the realm of monumental opportunities and adversities confronting the Chinese nation.

1 The Zhanqi Village in a Three-Dimensional Realm

In the realm of three-dimensional space, where the winds of change dance, a battle flag unfurls. Bruce G. Trigger once mused, "Culture, the harmonious marriage of nature's embrace and man's technological prowess, is a tapestry woven by their intricate dance. The diversity that adorns this cultural mosaic reflects the unique demands imposed by each distinctive environment, where the latent potential of ecosystems intertwines with the cadence of economic development, forever entwined with the tapestry crafted by the diverse forms of social structure."[4] The evolution of any society or civilization cannot be disentangled from the inexorable pull of natural resources. China, birthed by the waters it tamed, finds even its fundamental building blocks—the villages—intimately linked with the aqueous realm. Thus, to fathom the enigmatic tale of Zhanqi Village's growth, we must embark on a voyage through the aquatic domain, navigating its currents and eddies.

Across the vast expanse of the Chinese mainland, a tapestry of diversity is woven, its threads spun by the harmonious convergence of longitude, latitude, and altitude—an intricate symphony in the fabric of a three-dimensional space. When the titanic clash of the Indian Ocean Plate and the Eurasian Plate reverberated through the land, the Qinghai–Tibet

[3] Xinhuanet. Xi Jinping emphasized in Zhanqi Village, Sichuan: Cities and villages must develop simultaneously [EB/OL].(2018-02-12)[2021-01-21].xinhuanet.com/2018-02/12/c_1122410506.htm.

[4] Bruce Graham Trigger, Time and Traditions: Essays in Archaeological Interpretation. Edinburgh: Edinburgh University Press, 1978.

Plateau emerged as the terrestrial embodiment of the "third pole," an indomitable force of nature, transcending the realms of the Arctic and Antarctic. As these polar bastions of ice and snow emerged at opposite ends of the Earth, their mercurial dance with the temperate zones spawned a cornucopia of climates, while the "third pole" emerged near the Tropic of Cancer, its influence profound. In the vicinity of the 30° north latitude, the subtropical domain was once an arid expanse, thirsting for sustenance. Yet, the very upheaval of the Qinghai–Tibet Plateau altered the ballet of atmospheric currents, as sun-soaked plateaus, perched high above, absorbed the radiance of the heavens, casting a celestial glow. Such a transformation fashioned a realm of low pressures upon the plateau, defying the arid predilections that once held sway. Furthermore, the geological embrace of tectonic forces etched a grand tapestry, a north–south chasm that bridged the Yunnan–Guizhou Plateau and the Qinghai–Tibet Plateau. Within this ancient gorge, the ebullient monsoons of East Asia and South Asia, carrying a wealth of aqueous tales, converged, their moist whispers echoing amidst the three-tiered geological staircase and the great fissures that bisect the land. In the lofty heights of the plateau, moisture met with a frigid descent, birthing crystalline lakes and frozen rivers—an ethereal symphony of aqueous majesty. Thus, the Qinghai–Tibet Plateau stands as nature's sacred reservoir, nourishing not only the cradle of Chinese civilization—the Yangtze River and the Yellow River—but also the life-giving veins of South Asia and Southeast Asia, such as the Indus River and the Ganges River. Similarly, the plateau's embrace, sculpted by its ascendancy, thwarted the passage of warm and humid currents from the Indian Ocean, rendering the northwest region a desert wasteland, parched and devoid of life's elixir.

The fusion of China's tiered geographical terraces and the five major climate zones creates a mosaic of terrain, weather, and superficial geographic resources, abundantly diverse. Consequently, East Asian agricultural civilization and its ideological framework inherently embody diversity and inclusiveness, finding vivacity in the fabric of its villages. These settlements, birthed by specific mountain and water conditions, nurture a bountiful tapestry of crops and livestock, showcasing a multifaceted array of trades. By minimizing external dependencies, they establish the foundational bedrock to internalize the handling of adverse externalities.

Likewise, the Chengdu Plain, molded by tectonic forces, bears witness to the symphony of plate movements. The northward thrust of the Indian

Ocean plate compresses the Eurasian plate, yielding the majestic rise of the Qinghai–Tibet Plateau. Simultaneously, an eastward motion ensues, exerting pressure upon the serene Sichuan Basin, birthing stress accumulation in the hallowed realm of Longmen Mountain. Thus, the Longmen Mountain fault, ceaselessly ascending and rupturing, begets a landscape adorned with lofty slopes and undulating contours. It is within this frame that the Minjiang River, emanating from the Qinghai–Tibet Plateau, becomes a mineral-laden vessel, serenading the fault zone. Downstream, the river embraces fertile plains and valleys, etching an intricate web of waterways, nurturing the Chengdu Plain's ancient civilization.[5]

In the dawn of human civilization, the Chengdu Plain was christened the "realm of marshes" and the "red basin," its fate entwined with the capricious dance of floods and droughts. The pioneers of Shu ( ), huddled in the upland valleys of the Minjiang River, found solace in the art of foraging and the thrill of the hunt. Far from the polished agrarian civilization of the Central Plains, Bashu ( ) lingered in the shadows of obscurity. Yet, over seven millennia past, the world embraced the embrace of the Holocene climatic zenith, awakening the rapid crescendo of human progress. Thus, the forebears of the Chengdu Plain, seeking greener pastures, embarked on a migratory pilgrimage from the river's upstream sanctum to the fertile embrace of the Chengdu Plain. Two thousand years hence, global temperatures began their slow descent, the climate transitioning from warm indulgence to cold austerity. Humanity's watery liaison shifted from draining canals in the tapestry of irrigation to the nurturing embrace of diversionary waters. Anchored upon the second-tier geological terrace, the Chengdu Plain stood tall, its reservoir of favor overflowing, courtesy of practical hydraulic marvels. None resonates more profoundly than the Dujiangyan Irrigation System, helmed by the stewardship of Li Bing, the sagacious magistrate of Shu County, and his prodigious scion. Carving a passage for the roaring Minjiang River, they conjured an inner fluvial course, harmoniously irrigating the Chengdu Plain through the rhythmic dance of water division. Henceforth, the realm breathed in unison with its waters, undaunted by hunger's specter, emerging as an undisputed haven, truly the land of abundance. Even today, Dujiangyan's legacy continues, orchestrating the symphony of water partition and control.

[5] Yao Lei. Chengdu Plain's Natural Environment and its Relationship with Ancient Civilization. Doctoral Dissertation. Guangxi Normal University, 2013.

Furthermore, the residents of Pidu take great pride in their rich history. This pride stems from the fact that Dujiangyan serves as the birthplace of "enlightenment," attributed to Emperor Wang ( ) of the ancient Shu Kingdom, who encouraged the transition from nomadic herding to stable farming. He advocated for the cultivation of mulberry trees for silk production as a means of adapting to climate fluctuations. Following Emperor Wang's reign, Emperor Cong ( ) assumed leadership and embarked on an extraordinary endeavor: the development of water management systems. He famously declared, "Where the dragon of Wu Mountain contends, obstructing the river's flow, and the people of Shu face adversity, I shall carve through Wu Mountain and unveil the Three Gorges (, , ,)." Emperor Cong, played a pivotal role in the initial stages of constructing the Dujiangyan irrigation system, predating Li Bing's work by a remarkable three centuries. To this day, the Wang-Cong Temple in Pidu District stands as a testament to the reverence held for Emperor Wang and Emperor Cong, housing their honored tombs.

Zhanqi Village, a mere stone's throw away, a scant twenty kilometers distant from Dujiangyan, finds its essence deeply intertwined with the lifeblood of Baijiao River, the foremost tributary meandering forth from the very veins of Dujiangyan. The entirety of Pidu District, encompassing Zhanqi Village, belongs to the domain of Dujiangyan's gravitational irrigation system. Bygone annals recount the zenith of opulence in the Western reaches of Sichuan—the combined dominion of Wen ( ), Pi ( ), Chong ( ), Xin ( ), and Guan (, present-day Guan County, presently christened Dujiangyan City)—revered as the "quintessential five counties." Zhanqi Village, harmoniously nestled amidst the confluence of Chong and Guan (the lion's share of Chongning County subsumed by Pidu County, presently christened Pidu District), takes its rightful place.

In contrast to the Mediterranean region, where favorable harvests often hinge on natural rainfall, Chinese agriculture relies heavily on hydraulic infrastructure. The foundation of China's agricultural prowess lies in its embrace of water management, encompassing two crucial tiers: "national water governance" and "community-based water stewardship," giving rise to two distinct organizational structures—the "water-managing nation" and the "water-managing community." If we were to consider the Dujiangyan irrigation system from over two millennia ago as emblematic of national water management, then the land known as Zhanqi, christened as such in 1966, offers compelling evidence of the enduring logic of "building villages through the harnessing of water" during the latter half of the twentieth century.

This narrative posits that Zhanqi Village's journey unfolds as a pivotal milestone, laden with significance.

For not only does it mark the inception of material capital accumulation in Zhanqi Village but also signals the genesis of social capital consolidation, a force that continues to exert its influence on the village today. It was within the crucible of transforming the dynamic between arable land and water that Zhanqi Village unearthed its most precious asset—human potential. This convergence gave rise to a collective spirit, characterized by unity and competence, with a commitment to justice at its core. At this moment, Zhanqi Village accomplished its "socialist reformation," successfully accumulating the foundation of social capital. Zhanqi Village, thus, unfurls a banner distinct from the conventional narrative of capitalist accumulation—an emblem of "Chinese characteristics" in their unique approach to progress.

2 Zhanqi in the China

2.1 *The Era of Agrarian Transformation*

When one delves into the annals of Zhanqi Village, a storied tapestry of its developmental history unfurls. Administrative boundaries and nomenclature, like the shifting tides of circumstance, underwent constant adjustment. From the bygone days of Lingsheng Township's Sanjia/Sanbao (/) during the War of Liberation, to the agrarian metamorphosis that birthed Jifeng Village, and thence the emergence of the Zhanqi Brigade after the tempestuous Socialist Education Movement—each epoch witnessed its share of harrowing tales.

In 1915, Yuan Shikai restored the imperial system. Yang Jingzhong, a member of Tongmenghui of China, sent a telegram nationwide, declaring the independence of Chongning and establishing the Western Sichuan Expeditionary Army Command ( ). "The revolutionaries in Sichuan are completely concentrated in Chongning, and all actions are issued by Chongning… The Lüzu Shrine is also the secret party organization of Sichuan."[6] The Lingsheng Nunnery and Zitong Palace, located within the area of today's Zhanqi Village, became one of the activity areas of the Western Sichuan Expeditionary Army.

In May 1933, Chongning erupted in an internal conflict within the Sichuan Army, and the villagers suffered the hardships of war. In 1950, on the eve of the first Spring Festival after the founding of the People's Republic of China, as the whole country was immersed in a festive atmosphere, the remnants of the Nationalist Party (Kuomintang), police, and special forces hidden inside and outside Chongning County, along with local feudal landlords and habitual bandits, conspired to launch a counterrevolutionary political upheaval with the intention of overthrowing the Communist Party and the people's government.[7]

Subsequently, armed work teams were stationed in various townships. On one hand, they propagated the policies of the Communist Party, mobilized and organized the masses, and relied on the masses to combat bandits. On the other hand, they provided reassurance to those who were forced to participate in the uprising. Due to the implementation of the Party's policy of "combining repression with leniency" and the principle of "punishing the ringleaders, not asking about the coerced, and rewarding those who make contributions," with a combination of military and political measures, the action had a good effect, and the uprising in the entire county was quickly quelled. As the predecessor of the Zhanqi Brigade Militia Company ( ), the Lingsheng Township Armed Team made significant contributions to defending the newly established Red political power and the revolutionary victories of the people, laying the foundation for the militia construction of the Zhanqi Brigade in the future.

In January 1952, a long-cherished plan for land reform commenced its inexorable march across the verdant precincts of Lingsheng Township. The process began with the meticulous delineation of rural class divisions, adhering to the tenets enshrined in the "Land Reform Law of the People's Republic of China" and the "Supplementary Provisions for Class Division by the Western Sichuan Region Party Committee (《

[6] Zhao Renchun. The Leading Figure of the Alliance Society in the Western Sichuan Region, Yang Jingzhong, and His Self-narrative [J]. Journal of Literature and History, 2011 (6): 10–11.

[7] Sichuan Province Pi County Chronicle Compilation Committee. Pi County Chronicle [M]. Chengdu: Sichuan People's Publishing House, 1989.

》)." Subsequently, exhaustive land surveys, household assessments, and production verifications followed, culminating in the equitable redistribution of the land. Through this profound transformation, the very fabric of land relations underwent a profound metamorphosis. Heretofore, the landlords of Lingsheng reigned supreme over 9099.523 mu of fertile acreage. Yet, post-reform, their dominion diminished to a mere 907.885 mu. While poor peasants formerly claimed ownership of 1272.499 mu, comprising a modest 8.11% of the total arable expanse, their fortunes altered dramatically after the reform, granting them possession of 6316.288 mu—a formidable 40.8% of the entire arable terrain—equating to an average allocation of 2.131 mu per person. The land reform's impact likewise extended to tenant farmers, whose collective share of 2.386 mu prior to the reform represented a paltry 0.01% of the total arable land, amounting to a meager 0.009 mu per person. However, following the reform, the landless tillers were endowed with 532.667 mu, corresponding to 3.47% of the total arable expanse—a marked increase—providing each laborer with an average allotment of 2.156 mu.[8]

History is a tale spun for onlookers, while for those who have lived it, it is a tapestry woven with profound elation and melancholy. "It was the act of wresting land from the oppressive elite that bestowed upon me the chance to pursue education," reminisced villager Luo Huifu ( ), his voice tinged with nostalgia. Little did Luo Huifu know that his humble participation in that movement would catapult him into a pivotal role in the industrialization process of Zhanqi Village, and countless other peasants like him, propelled by the pulse of their era, would silently witness the subtle alteration of their fates. Unbeknownst to them, it was precisely this very movement that thrust them into the limelight during the successive economic crises that would beset the nascent People's Republic.

The 1960s unfolded against a backdrop of international tension, heralding the grand inauguration of a fervent socialist education movement on home soil. In the hallowed halls of a central working conference, Chairman Mao Zedong imparted words laden with significance. "The majority of our cadre, including those who remain anchored to the toils of production and those who have strayed, remain woefully ignorant of the true essence of socialism. To whom does the onus of this

[8] Source: Zhao Renchun. Chronicles of Zhanqi Village (unpublished manuscript).

ignorance fall? Upon ourselves," he intoned with gravitas.[9] Thus, in response to the rampant gluttony, opaque bookkeeping, and pervasive corruption that had taken root among the rural cadres, the Socialist Education movement (also called "Four Cleansing" movement,) was thrust to the forefront of the party's agenda. This clarion call entailed "rectifying accounts, purging warehouses, scrutinizing work allocations, and cleansing financial dealings (、 、 、)," eventually evolving into an all-encompassing crusade to "cleanse the political realm, cleanse the economic sphere, cleanse the organizational structure, and cleanse the realm of ideology."

March of 1965 witnessed the emergence of an autonomous Zhanqi Village, standing apart from its progenitor, the Jinxing Brigade, under the watchful guidance of the "Four Cleansing" work team. It swiftly unfurled as a beacon, serving as a veritable standard-bearer for the entire county during the transformative land reform.

In recollecting the genesis of the name "Zhanqi," Gao Demin ( ), the current Party Secretary of Zhanqi Village, elucidated, "Each member of Zhanqi is an emblem in their own right, akin to a fluttering flag amidst the chaos of battle. Hence, the moniker 'Zhanqi'." Back then, the Zhanqi Brigade remained but a destitute hamlet, characterized by a meager trio of pigsties, a solitary wooden filing cabinet, a trifling assemblage of chairs, and the weight of a 700 yuan debt. Galvanized by the clarion call of the nation's "Agrarian Great Leap Forward," its hardworking denizens emboldened by the creed of self-sufficiency and unwavering perseverance, wholeheartedly embraced the arduous task of cultivating the land. Little could they fathom that decades later, this erstwhile inconspicuous and impoverished village would unexpectedly emerge as a radiant archetype, a resplendent pearl glistening amidst the rugged terrain of Western Sichuan.

In 1965, Jiang Daxing ( ) assumed the position of the village's inaugural secretary. At that juncture, a recent groom named Luo Huifu, heeding the brigade's call, returned to the village to partake in construction. Led by Secretary Jiang Daxing, a cohort of skilled craftsmen, with Luo Huifu as their torchbearer, erected water turbines, the brigade office, a medical station, and a consignment store. Consequently, the Zhanqi Brigade was graced with a semblance of respectable infrastructure. Yet,

[9] Central Compilation and Translation Bureau of the Central Committee of the Communist Party of China, 2013.

as the trajectory of struggle often meanders, impediments failed to stifle the Zhanqi denizens' yearning for a brighter existence; instead, it ignited an even fiercer determination within their souls. Amidst the resounding chorus of "Fear not the inferno's blaze, for Zhanqi's soil shall witness the birth of new horizons (,)," the Zhanqi folk embarked upon the arduous task of rebuilding their abode (as depicted in Fig. 1). Such tales, replete with vicissitudes, recurred incessantly throughout the annals of Zhanqi Village's strife—a testament to the indomitable spirit that courses through the veins of Chinese agrarian warriors. This intrepid ethos, time and again, has woven its tapestry into the fabric of China's historic narrative. As eras ebb and flow, the mountains and rivers persist, and each successive generation grasps the baton from their forebears, resolutely inscribing their own magnificent opus.

In the year 1969, China found itself in a precarious state of tension with both the United States and the Soviet Union. Amidst this backdrop of strained relations, the issue of national defense and security took center stage. It was during these intense times that the concept of military-civilian integration gained momentum throughout the nation, and even the illustrious Zhanqi Brigade was not exempt.

Fig. 1 Renewal of the Zhanqi Village

Under the leadership of Luo Huijin ( ), the Party Secretary of the brigade, a team led by the Deputy Commander of the Wenjiang Military District embarked on a journey to inspect the implementation of militia work in various locations. The Zhanqi Brigade's remarkable achievements in militia construction caught the attention of the Armed Forces Department in Pixian County. They swiftly decided to hold up the Zhanqi Brigade as an exemplar of military-civilian integration, dispatching a dedicated workgroup to reside in Zhanqi. This group would provide guidance and direction for the village's militia work.

Li Shili ( ), the 7th Party Secretary of Zhanqi Village, recollected, "In the past, the primary responsibility for militia work rested upon the Armed Forces Department. Our team and the village committee often labored side by side, engaging in collective toil and shared learning. They assisted us in organizing militia work and conducting military training. Zhanqi Village's military training prowess was renowned throughout the province. When the militia was called to labor, they could assemble within a mere five minutes."

Thus, the disciplined and resolute ethos of the armed forces found its way into the realm of militia training, and in turn, the militia embraced this spirit within their production endeavors. Astonishingly, militia training did not hinder productivity; on the contrary, it heightened efficiency and bolstered crop yields. The Zhanqi Brigade was bestowed with the prestigious title of the "advanced brigade in the 'Learning from Dazhai in Agricultural' Campaign" and was lauded by the former Chengdu Military Region as an exemplary militia unit in the Wenjiang area. The Zhanqi flag soared gallantly over the plains of Chengdu.

In the aftermath, the formidable organizational strength forged through militia construction began to reshape the very fabric of Zhanqi's village landscape and the spirit of its inhabitants. A cadre of youthful leaders emerged from this transformation, and the collective consciousness of Zhanqi's people became deeply ingrained. Inspired by Zhanqi's success, numerous regions sought to emulate its model. In the pursuit of such aspirations, this literary work posits that the crux lies in the ability to foster a resolute spirit akin to Zhanqi—a spirit that fervently espouses the ideals of socialist construction and the zealous transformation of one's homeland. It is only by embarking upon a journey rooted in the essence of the Zhanqi spirit that an indomitable internal drive can truly be awakened.

If the construction of agricultural water conservancy greatly elevated the Zhanqi Brigade's agricultural prowess, satiating the basic needs of the masses, then the post-1975 construction of new village quietly alluded to the Zhanqi people's ascent to a loftier realm in their pursuit of a blissful existence. For an extensive duration, the pursuit of a gratifying life became the Zhanqi people's paramount ambition, crystallizing as the village's very dream. This profound aspiration coursed through the veins of the Zhanqi folk, steadfastly guiding generations at pivotal crossroads. The elderly inhabitants now dwelling within the villas, adorned with resolute Chengdu charm, constructed collectively by the village, certainly reminisce about the toil and sacrifice endured during the 1970s, all for the construction of their new abodes. Following Third Secretary Li Shibing ( )'s return from a visit to Dazhai, and with the support of the county, the Provincial May 7th Cadre School, and the Provincial Construction Commission, along with the active cooperation of the masses, the inaugural concentrated dwelling area for farmers in Pixian County[10]—a community comprising 17 households and 87 persons—was brought to fruition. Amid this process, Zhanqi Village's industrial prowess took root within the curved kilns, where machine bricks were crafted for the nascent settlement. Subsequently, it burgeoned and thrived, effectively shifting Zhanqi's developmental axis from agriculture to industry.

Figure 2 immortalizes a scene of the Zhanqi Brigade's party convening in the 1970s—a testament to their unwavering dedication.

2.2 The Era of Industrialization

In the annals of China's modern history, the year 1978 stands as a pivotal milestone. An article titled "Practice is the Sole Criterion for Testing the Truth ( )" resonated profoundly amidst the somber depths of Chinese society at the time. It heralded a cascading torrent of transformative waves, unfurling like buds after a spring rain, as the Chinese locomotive bellowed its resolute call for change.

During this epoch, as urban economies burgeoned to become the nation's principal financial wellspring, the historical mission of rural collectivization, to furnish the primal accumulations of the state, reached

[10] Pixian County, present-day Pidu District. In December 2016, the State Council approved the abolition of Pixian County and the establishment of Pidu District in Chengdu City, with the administrative region and government residence remaining unchanged.

Fig. 2 Party Branch Meeting

its culmination. Subsequently, the collective rural economy waned, giving way to the implementation of the "household responsibility system" rooted in familial realms.

This movement, in essence, unshackled the productive prowess of rural domains, emancipating farmers from the clutches of their agrarian fetters. The farmers, imbued with an innate impetus, gravitated naturally toward the industrial sphere, ceaselessly seeking avenues for sustenance. It was this inexorable pull that propelled the ascendancy of township enterprises. Amidst this era, Huaxi Village, once a quintessential embodiment of the "Learning from Dazhai in Agriculture" Campaign, contemplated its own metamorphosis. Even in the nascent throes of this transition, the indefatigable Wu Renbao (   ), the Party branch secretary of Huaxi Village, clandestinely established a diminutive hardware factory within the village's confines. "Amidst the crimson flags fluttering in the fields, and the echoing trumpets, when the inquisitive comrades departed, we, too, turned our gaze toward the factory. Why risk venturing into industry? Simply because farming yielded meager profits. While agriculture's total output stood at 240,000 yuan, our modest hardware factory, manned by a mere twenty individuals, achieved an output worth the same amount."[11]

[11] Wu Xiaobo. "The Stirring Three Decades (Vol. 1): Chinese Enterprises 1978–2008." Beijing: CITIC Press, 2017.

If Huaxi Village's transformation appeared stifled and veiled, owing to its early divergence from the prevailing policy currents, the Zhanqi Brigade's banner, in contrast, unfurled with exuberance and audacity, propelled by the propitious winds of the zeitgeist. Distinct from the multitude of grassroots enterprises borne of humble beginnings, the Zhanqi Brigade, from its inception, adroitly forged ties with the Armed Forces Department, leveraging its exceptional militia construction to secure enviable resources. During the construction of the sinuous kiln, the county's Armed Forces Department facilitated the procurement of funds for the Zhanqi Brigade's brick-making apparatus. Concurrently, the Sichuan Provincial Building Materials Industrial Scientific Research Institute initiated a pioneering project within the Zhanqi Brigade's dominion, charged with training villagers and erecting the curved kiln. Bolstered by the influx of external capital and technological succor, the Zhanqi Brigade encountered diminished resistance as it veered from an agricultural economy to an industrial one. In 1976, the curved kiln commenced its official production, channeling its bricks partially toward the edifice of a new village and partially as the foundation for primitive accumulation.

After assuming the mantle of the fourth secretary, Yang Zhengzhong ( ) set forth a visionary plan to erect a rotary kiln upon the foundation of the intermittent kiln at hand. If the intermittent kiln served as the overture to the industrialization symphony of the Zhanqi Brigade, the realization of the rotary kiln, fraught with technical complexities and demanding substantial financial investment, unequivocally heralded the brigade's resolute stride toward modernity. The latter half of 1978 witnessed the commencement of the rotary kiln's construction. Upon hearing murmurs of the Zhanqi Brigade's ambitious endeavor, county party secretary Hu Zhongxiang ( ) sounded the clarion call, prompting the then director of the Planning Commission, Luo Zhengchang ( ), to rally diverse departments in wholehearted support of the brigade's kiln construction. County authorities consented, permitting the Zhanqi Brigade to barter its output of bricks for the cement and steel indispensably required for the kiln's erection. Following ten months of tireless labor, Pixian County proudly unveiled its inaugural rotary kiln in 1979, christened the "Pioneer First Machine Brick Factory ( )," as faithfully depicted in Fig. 3.

Given the prevailing dearth of resources during those times, the brick factory reaped enviable returns, igniting the village collective's zeal to found yet another enterprise—the Broad Bean Paste (Douban) Factory.

Fig. 3 Pioneer First Machine Brick Factory

Consequently, an avalanche of enterprises burgeoned forth, swelling the ranks of Zhanqi Village's collective endeavors to a staggering twelve. With the exception of the joint venture steel foundry, all other enterprises thrived upon the solid foundation of the village-level collective economy. In essence, the village-run enterprises of that era embraced a boundless market, brimming with myriad suppressed desires, poised to burst forth at the cusp of an opportune moment—an era where progress thunderously reverberated in the background, beckoning all to forge ahead with unwavering determination.

In the 1980s, a cascade of policies encouraging the growth of township enterprises swept across the nation, ushering in a remarkable era for these small-scale ventures. Townships bloomed with newfound vigor as policy benefits intertwined harmoniously with burgeoning market demands. By 1987, Zhanqi Village's village-run enterprises proudly generated a staggering output value of 1.5 million yuan, constituting an impressive 46% of Tangchang Township's entire village-run enterprise output. But, just as the collective economic engine of Zhanqi Village surged forth, the winds of policy swiftly shifted.

The tumultuous dual-track price reform of the 1980s exacted a substantial toll on the system, igniting China's fifth economic crisis. In 1993, a trifecta of fiscal, financial, and foreign exchange deficits materialized simultaneously. Necessitated by this crisis, the government disengaged from heavily indebted township enterprises, initiating the advent of shareholding reforms.

In 1995, Zhanqi Village emerged as one of the pioneering villages embracing the transformative mixed ownership reform nationwide. Selecting five village-run enterprises boasting commendable economic efficacy—namely, a brick factory, Huifu Broad Bean Paste Factory, Pioneer Brewing Factory (for Broad Bean Paste), compound fertilizer factory, and flour mill—Zhanqi Village orchestrated their restructuring, birthing the "Jifeng Industrial Corporation ( )." Amidst the mid-1990s, a confluence of factors, including the market economy's sway and internal managerial dynamics, compelled the unfortunate closure of five collective enterprises. Zhanqi Village, ever resilient, embarked upon an arduous quest for novel avenues of growth. It was in this striving that Darwin's "On the Origin of Species" found poignant resonance: the fittest species to endure are not necessarily the strongest or the most intellectually endowed but rather those most adept at responding to the winds of change.

2.3 *The Era of Ecological Transformation*

The mission entrusted to Zhanqi Village in the twenty-first century is to strengthen the village and enrich its people through collective economic development, while continuing to safeguard the dreams and homes of generations. In 2002, during the village committee's transition, Secretary Li Shili and Director Gao Demin took the stage in Zhanqi Village. To address the challenges of a weakening local economy, the prevalence of privatization in surrounding businesses, and the outflow of young laborers, Zhanqi Village embarked on a new era "Long March."

If the memory of 2003 for us was the spread of the "SARS" pandemic and the nationwide fight against it, what happened in Zhanqi Village was a return to their original aspirations. Three significant pressures, including inadequate consumer demand, significant increases in raw material prices, and internal conflicts within collective industries, were hindering economic development. The newly appointed village committee members began their transformation journey with Vanguard's first brick factory, acquiring equity, auditing assets, conducting open tenders, and leasing operations. Subsequently, the other four major enterprises under the Jifeng Industrial Corporation underwent transformation one by one, experiencing institutional changes. The key aspect of the restructuring was the transfer of the enterprise's fixed assets to new operators through leasing and the conversion of liquid assets at market value for sale to the new operators, with unpaid amounts being converted into loans, subject to a 10% interest rate. Through this restructuring, Zhanqi Village not only preserved the accumulated wealth built by generations but also earned the "first pot of gold" for further economic development. The collective enterprises, carrying the memories of the industrialization phase, took new steps in the new era, making the story of restructuring a precious memory for the village.

While the enterprises showed promise after their transformation, the agricultural sector remained barren. At that time, like many other villages across the country, Zhanqi Village faced abandoned farmland and heavy tax burdens on farmers. To address these issues, village officials focused on land and, initially, collected over 100 acres of land by offering to pay agricultural taxes on behalf of villagers. They used this land to grow vegetables after road and field improvements. After the national agricultural tax exemption was announced, Zhanqi Village planned to establish a professional cooperative for mushroom cultivation. With competitive land transfer fees, they centralized 600 acres of land within the village, leasing it externally through the cooperative. They cleverly used a distribution method of "guaranteed rent plus 50% profit-sharing" to stabilize the land and generate income "from the land, back to the land." After several years of land consolidation practices, large-scale farming had become the norm, and Zhanqi Village had emerged from its isolated corner to actively participate in the urban–rural integration development process of Pidu.

In April 2006, Sichuan News Network reported on Zhanqi Village's "cultural experiment of urban–rural interaction." The small village hosted folk artists and groups of university students, allowing villagers to spend five days with city residents. During the five days of interaction and experiences, the concept of urban–rural exchange slowly seeped into the villagers' minds through the personalized expressions of the students. At the same time, the rural traditions of the villagers influenced the city residents. As a pilot village for the experiment established by the Propaganda Department of the Municipal Party Committee, Zhanqi Village not only served as a demonstration but also built bridges for interaction between businesses, urban residents, and rural grassroots. At that time, Zhanqi Village probably did not anticipate that such pairing activities would become a marathon, with outstanding students from major universities leaving their mark there every year. The "university + party branch + household" model brought together a new force that broke through the barriers between urban and rural areas, witnessing Zhanqi Village's progress in the new era's currents. In July of the same year, the construction of the "Cultural Grand Courtyard" in the village began, and subsequently, the village built a rural library, a rural gallery, and a sports plaza. It developed into the largest village-level cultural facility in the Western region, meeting the spiritual and cultural needs of the villagers.

In 2007, the sound of the foundation stone laying for the Zhanqi Community broke the silence of the village, and the project was called "demolish and rebuild." After consolidating the villagers' original residential land and courtyards, a total of 440.8 acres of land were added. Among them, 215 acres were used for the village's own construction, and 208 acres were obtained through the combination of demolition and land consolidation, with more than 90 million yuan in funding from the "land comprehensive improvement increase–decrease linkage project ( )."[12]

In 2009, the construction of the new community was basically completed. The new homes were both simple and elegant, featuring a rustic charm with blue bricks and flying eaves, as well as a modern appearance created by courtyard buildings and dazzling lights. The infrastructure, including a kindergarten, supermarket, and health station, allowed villagers to enjoy the convenience of urban life without leaving the village. Zhanqi Village also became an advanced community, featured in a prestigious national TV program.

Concentrated habitation propelled the consolidation of agricultural land within the village, now under the unified operation of the Vegetable Professional Cooperative (formerly known as the Needle Mushroom Professional Cooperative) nestled in the village's embrace.

Harnessing the spatial resources ingrained in the locale, the village's ecological resurgence was realized through calculated additions and subtractions. On one hand, situated within Chengdu's self-irrigation zone, Zhanqi Village shuttered brick factories, fertilizer plants, prefabricated component facilities, foundries, and quartz sand works, unburdening the terrain and bestowing it with precious construction land. On the other hand, the cooperative fervently enticed diverse industries,

[12] Source: Zhanqi Village Development Summary. 2011 (internal report).

augmenting agricultural earnings. By means of agricultural land transfers and the leasing of collective construction land usage rights, Zhanqi Village forged an alliance with Chengdu Fifth Season Investment Co., Ltd ( ), birthing Pidu District's inaugural 4A-grade creative agricultural sightseeing haven—Mama Farm ( ). Its expansive lavender cultivation grounds bewitch innumerable urban dwellers, heightening Zhanqi Village's prominence: On June 3, 2012, Sichuan TV, Chengdu's primary television network, and Chengdu's fifth television network lauded Mama Farm as the embodiment of purple-hued romance akin to "Chengdu's Provence." Subsequently, on November 14 of the same year, revered regional artist Li Boqing, leading the culinary show "A Taste of Sichuan," descended upon Zhanqi Village's Mama Farm to capture its essence. In 2013, Sichuan Blue Rainbow Ecological Agriculture Co., Ltd ( ) was welcomed, followed by the introduction of Chengdu Yuxiang Agricultural Technology Co., Ltd ( ). In 2014, enhancing the allure of blueberry and strawberry picking amidst joyous revelry. The former fertilizer plant site found renewed purpose as it embraced the arrival of Pixian County Manjianghong Seasoning Food Co., Ltd ( ).[13] Together, they embarked on the processing and commercialization of bean paste, while welcoming visitors to partake in the delights of sightseeing. Figure 4 visually encapsulates the idyllic essence of Mama Farm in Zhanqi Village.

The Zhanqi industry's growth is underpinned by effective grassroots governance and impeccable ancillary services. Secretary Gao Demin fully comprehends that the crux of grassroots work lies in rallying the populace. He once remarked, "The party organization serves as the lifeblood. Initially, you 'speak,' then gradually 'act,' and soon you discern that it is the collective impetus propelling you forward, compelling you to forge ahead." Following his election as the village party branch's secretary, Secretary Gao orchestrated a "Three Questions, Three Reveals" campaign for party members. The three queries—"For what purpose did

[13] The company's investors collaborated in establishing two firms within Zhanqi Village, with Pixian County Manjianghong Seasoning Food Co., Ltd. spearheading Broad Bean Paste Production, while Sichuan Shufu Pidu Bean Paste Co., Ltd. ( ), established in 2015, primarily focused on the tourism project for the Pixian County Broad Bean Paste Museum, hereafter collectively referred to as "Manjianghong" ( ).

Fig. 4 Mama Farm in Zhanqi Village

I join the party?" "What have I accomplished as a party member?" "In what way have I exemplified and spurred others on as a commendable party member?"—were posted within the party members' activity room, demanding profound introspection from each cadre. In actuality, party members ought to proactively "reveal their identities, commitments, and tangible achievements," assuming the role of a formidable bastion. Only through the establishment of such a formidable and combative unit can the village surmount internal conflicts, oversee agricultural and industrial production, and coalesce forces in pursuit of progress. Secretary Gao, reminiscing about his specific undertakings, aptly summarized, "Absence of innovation would preclude the very existence of the present-day Zhanqi Village."

Arising from the village-level elections emerged an innovative entity—the Democratic Supervisory Board—tasked with safeguarding the villagers' exercise of democratic oversight rights. As one of Pixian County's pioneering innovation for rural governance structures, Zhanqi Village erected decision-making and supervisory mechanisms, further enforcing a "triple-convention" system: village meetings, representative assemblies, and villagers' councils. Simultaneously, a six-step operational modus operandi encompassing "propaganda and mobilization, solicitation of opinions, formulation of proposals, public announcement of decisions, organizational implementation, and societal evaluation (、 、 、 、 、)" was embraced, thereby fostering the fortification of public service organizations and the fulfillment of management responsibilities. During a momentous village gathering that witnessed deliberations on the "Zhanqi Village Villagers' Autonomy Charter" and the "Chengdu Jifeng Industrial Corporation Charter," members of the supervisory board attended as observers, meticulously overseeing the electoral process of the task force assigned to reform the village's collective economic organizational structure. Notably, they proffered multiple amendments and recommendations concerning said charters and governing regulations. Promptly, the village committee incorporated alterations in accordance with the village representatives' perspectives. Unquestionably, the comprehensive supervision founded upon democratic principles plays a pivotal role in bolstering the authoritative stature of village-level decision-making and earning the approbation of the masses.

On April 20, 2011, the entire village set the boundaries for 529 households comprising 1704 members of collective economic organizations, officially granting them land rights. Following this, a thorough evaluation and quantification of the collective assets took place, resulting in a total valuation of over 40 million yuan. On August 17, 2015, the registration of Tangchang Town Zhanqi Asset Management Co., Ltd. ( ) in Pixian County, with a registered capital of 17.04 million yuan, marked a significant milestone. Each member held one share valued at 10,000 yuan, pioneering the transformation from "funds into capital" and turning farmers into shareholders. Capitalizing on Pixian County's designation as one of the 33 pilot counties for rural land system reform in China, Zhanqi Village seized the opportunity by listing 13.45 mu of unused construction land on the land resource trading center. After several rounds of bidding, Sichuan Maigao Tourism Resource Development Co., Ltd. (, hereinafter referred as "Maigao Tourism") secured the 40-year land use rights for the construction land at a price of 525,000 yuan per mu. This achievement resounded as the "inaugural gavel" for collective-operated construction land entering the market in the entire province.

Dormant resources within the village were reawakened, and the land unveiled its reform dividends. Seizing the policy opportunities presented by rural land system reforms, Zhanqi Village embarked on a solid stride toward integrated development encompassing agriculture, commerce, culture, and tourism. Jointly establishing Sichuan Huayang Zhanqi Tourism Scenic Area Management Co., Ltd. ( ) in partnership with strategic ally Maigao Tourism, the collective undertook the responsibility of managing idle resources within the village. By discounting the land resources and collaborating on the development of the Fifth Season Fragrance Resort ( ), Zhanqi Village introduced restaurants, hotels, shops, and conference rooms, providing comprehensive hospitality services. Both parties shared the benefits and risks, exemplifying a model of synergistic cooperation between the village and the enterprise. Through these endeavors, Zhanqi Village emerged as a pioneering village at the forefront of implementing the "three transformations," heralding the new era of socialism with Chinese characteristics.

On October 18, 2017, General Secretary Xi Jinping, in the report of the 19th National Congress of the Communist Party of China, articulated the strategy of rural revitalization, outlining the overarching requirements and phased planning for rural development. Zhanqi Village stood as the first exemplar inspected after General Secretary Xi Jinping laid the foundation for the strategy of rural revitalization. On the morning of February 12, 2018, General Secretary Xi Jinping graced Zhanqi Village with his presence, lauding the village's work with utmost praise. In August of the same year, Zhanqi Village independently orchestrated the unveiling of the "Eighteen Rural Alleys ( )," a captivating array of storefronts such as "Uncle Lang," "Honey Fermentation Workshop," and "Shu Embroidery Workshop." These establishments, in the style of a front store leading to a rear lane, guided visitors through a retrospective journey of traditional craftsmanship, including fermented bean curd processing, honey brewing, and Shu embroidery, imparting a profound appreciation for the timeless artisanal spirit. Subsequently, in September, the Pixian County Douban Museum, sprawling across an expanse exceeding 30 mu, ceremoniously opened its doors. The museum ingeniously incorporated historical tools, cultural relics, and finished products, intricately capturing the essence of "Sichuan cuisine's soul" through the meticulous craftsmanship on display. The yeast-making hall, sauce-fermenting platform, and traditional sun-drying fields permeated the air with an aromatic aura. Similarly, the Shu Mansion Pavilion, Ancient Sauce Garden, and Flavors Corridor evoked a lasting sensation, with flavors that lingered on the palate. As the eons passed, the vibrant hues of Douban culture became increasingly apparent, with the memories embraced by Douban resembling the enduring and fragrant essence of finely aged Douban sauce.

The characteristic broad bean paste fermentation jars of Zhanqi Village are elegantly portrayed in Fig. 5: "Open-air Broad Bean Paste Fermentation Jars of Manjianghong."

As Zhanqi Village forges ahead in rural economic development and the propagation of local heritage, it remains committed to societal benevolence. The Vegetable Professional Cooperative, having showcased its merits at the China Public Welfare Charity Project Exchange Exhibition, now proudly bears the certification of "Excellent Chinese Social Enterprise." In 2019, the completion and inauguration of the Zhanqi Training Institute for Rural Revitalization marked an amalgamation of exposition, pedagogy, research, and deliberation, playing host to numerous provincial and municipal forums and conferences. Dignitaries, experts, scholars, and grassroots officials from both domestic and international realms found respite within its premises, as Zhanqi embraced an inclusive disposition.

Fig. 5 Open-air Broad Bean Paste Fermentation Jars of Manjianghong

steadfast in its pursuit to disseminate its enlightening practices nationwide. Undoubtedly, this distinguished institute aspires to become the premier talent cultivation hub harmonizing academia, industry, and research in the southwestern domain.

Zooming in on the present, the village pulsates with vibrant occasions like the "World Bicycle Day" and the exhilarating Tianfu Greenway Cycling Event, as well as the festive Farmers' Harvest celebration and the grand New Year's "Dam Banquet" attended by a multitude. Eclipsing these festivities, the Tianfu Agricultural Culture Museum progressively unfurls an epochal saga of farming spanning a millennium, amidst the resplendent backdrop of the Bashan Mountains and the meandering Shu waters. This ongoing narrative of Zhanqi finds its torchbearers in the contemporary era, fervently inscribing its chapters...

Zhanqi epitomizes a place where candid conversations flourish in the early morn, where neighbors convene in harmonious camaraderie, akin to the formation of a majestic dragon. And as twilight descends, the village reverberates with the lively rhythm of the Dam Banquet, exuding an atmosphere of conviviality... Zhanqi's story is, in essence, a narrative shared by every village as they navigate their own unique journeys. The realization of Zhanqi's dreams materializes as a splendid panorama, illuminating the tapestry of this enchanting settlement. Perhaps, with the passage of time, the tales embedded in the soil shall be enshrined in the annals of history, yet we approach this task with reverence, engaging in a heartfelt dialogue with the village, endeavoring to chronicle the story of Zhanqi. In doing so, we shall etch a captivating tableau within the ceaseless river of time.

3 Observing China Through the Rural Area: 70-Year Evolution of Tournament-Style Political Competition

3.1 *The History of Tournament-Style Political Competition: Three Phases in Seven Decades*

Ever since China's industrialization took flight under the active guidance of local governments in the 1980s, the academic sphere has teemed with discussions on the competition between these governing bodies. Within this discourse, our research team delved into the concept of "corporatization competition by the local governments while risk taken by the central government ( )," positing that the intricate conflicts of interest between the central and local authorities have evolved over the years. These conflicts often leave the central government ensnared in a discomfiting "paralysis" as its macroeconomic oversight collides with the resistance of local administrations.

This convoluted state of affairs can be traced back to two fundamental factors. Firstly, during the mid-twentieth century up until the 1990s, each time China weathered a cyclical macroeconomic crisis, the central government bestowed local governments with more autonomy to stimulate regional economic growth. Consequently, a distinct pattern of corporatization competition emerged, characterizing local governments' actions. While limited in their responsibilities, these authorities conveniently shifted the associated risks to the central government. Even though the tax-sharing reform of 1994 somewhat curbed the chaotic nature of corporatization of local governments, it failed to fundamentally alter the long-standing independent status of local governments as significant stakeholders. In essence, it merely reshaped the distribution of benefits between the central and local governments within the established framework of relative decentralization.

Secondly, the central government predominantly assumed unlimited liability by employing measures such as issuing the currency and national bonds. In stark contrast to the Western system of limited liability, where debts can be left unpaid, China's institutional advantage lies in its unique approach to securing lasting stability and sustainable development for the nation. However, this system faces its most formidable challenge due to its reliance on the somewhat tenuous foundation of the collectively owned economy. As a result, it inadvertently amplifies the symbiotic reinforcement between local industrial competition and central financial monopolies. Over time, this dynamic contributes to the solidification of an economic hierarchy between the central and local governments, making it increasingly arduous for the central government to execute effective regulation amidst normal economic operations. Consequently, a protracted state of imbalanced interests between the central and local authorities becomes the norm. Only when risks accumulate to the point of crisis, and the interests of various factions are jeopardized, does the central government's macroeconomic regulation gain begrudging acceptance from local administrations.

In this scenario, the conception of ecological harmony and the agricultural diversification approach present a viable path for harnessing local resources, easing the competitive risks faced by regional governments, and mitigating the inherent conflicts between central and local interests. The intense rivalry among these authorities can largely be attributed to their control over entities within a uniform and low-tiered realm of the tangible economy. Yet, the truth remains that across vast China, the natural landscapes, cultural heritage, and traditional customs exhibit remarkable diversity, thereby embracing the notion of nurturing varied regional economies that align with the essence of ecological harmony. Thus, under the guidance of this paradigm, even if local governments continue their relentless pursuit of corporate competition, at the very least, it will adopt a distinctive form. Moreover, given the current rise of a green, eco-conscious, and discerning middle class, channeling creative means toward the utilization of local resources for tertiary industry development can serve as a panacea to the issue of surplus productivity, a malady borne from the prolonged emphasis on secondary industry development in disparate locales.[14]

Expanding upon this foundation, our study ventures to extend the institutional framework governing local competition, propounding a three-stage theory of regional government rivalry. This very theory shall serve as the macroscopic scaffold through which we fathom the developmental triumphs of Zhanqi Village nestled amidst the plains. By scrutinizing the behavioral patterns of micro-level actors within this broader panorama, we aspire to trace the unifying thread that unravels the intricate tapestry of the Zhanqi experience.

Enter the hypothesis of "stratified epochs" delineating the evolution of local government competition over the past seven decades: Since 1949, China has traversed three distinct historical phases, each characterized by a distinctive essence of regional competition—politicized rivalry, corporate strife, and ecological contention. Unique to each phase, dissimilar institutional frameworks have woven the fabric of opportunity, influencing the avenues by which participants accrue benefits from established systems, while shouldering the burdens imposed by institutional costs.

[14] Wen Tiejun, Ji Han, Zhang Junna. Central Risks and Local Competition. Journal of the National School of Administration, 2015(4): 23–31.

At a glance, the evolution of local competition unveils a compelling narrative: The prelude to 1978 resonates with a fervor of political mobilization, where competition hinged upon the simplistic deployment of productive resources. A new era emerged in the 1980s, one marked by corporate duels for the acquisition of rent differentials (pertaining to land and labor), leading to the crystallization of industrial capital. As the twenty-first century heralded the dawn of ecological transformation, a fresh realm of competition surfaced, one that celebrates the multifaceted and three-dimensional development of spatial resources.

In the initial phase, from the birth of the People's Republic of China to the advent of reform and opening-up, political competition took center stage. Its essence was an extension of the mobilization mechanisms witnessed during the tumultuous era of land revolution warfare. Between urban and rural areas, as well as in the domains of labor and agriculture, political mobilization became the driving force, urging an unrestrained and intensive input of labor, surmounting the crisis of capital scarcity. Only through the organization of labor on a substantial scale could the dearth of capital be replaced. Thus, it becomes apparent that local governance during this period hinged on the simple mobilization of political forces for horizontal competition. In that epoch of "collective devotion," those ranking among the elite in the competitive arena reaped extra rewards, while the surplus value exacted from the masses assumed a systematic nature.

China, being a nation steeped in a profound tradition of mobilization, witnessed the ascension of social mobilization as a paramount approach to societal governance. During the era of revolutionary warfare, the Chinese Communist Party galvanized the masses on an unprecedented scale, enticing the participation of the middle and lower strata in the revolution, thereby propelling it toward ultimate victory. Following the establishment of the New China, owing to the momentum generated by the revolutionary struggle, societal endeavors continued to rely on social mobilization. From land reform to the propagation to fight US aggression and aid Korea, and even the Three-anti Campaign (1951) and Five-anti Campaign (1952) ( ),[15] the mobilization capabilities of the Party

[15] Translator's note: The Three-anti Campaign (1951) and Five-anti Campaign (1952) ( ) were reform movements originally issued by Mao Zedong a few years after the founding of the People's Republic of China in an effort to rid Chinese cities of corruption and enemies of the state. The result turned into a series of campaigns that

and the government steadily improved. The quintessential character of the mass line approach remained intertwined with class struggle or its extension, ensnaring the societal modes and behaviors of mobilization within the inertia dictated by the crucible of revolutionary experience. Although the 1960s and 1970s marked a relatively placid period of national economic development since the establishment of the New China, they paradoxically bore witness to the apex of social mobilization intensity. Subsequent to the advent of reform and opening-up, the traditional paradigm of extensive mass mobilization gradually morphed into an administrative mobilization spearheaded by the government itself.[16]

The common critique of the politicized phase of competition is that it was dominated by the notion of class struggle. The shift in the Party's fundamental direction to "one central task, two basic points" (、)[17] was underscored after 1984. Yet, in truth, the period of political strife was not solely centered on class struggle. China's economic development has steadfastly revolved around industrialization, never straying from this core. Its objective during this stage was to extract and divert economic surplus. During the early stages of industrialization, when primitive capital accumulation was underway, capital was exceedingly scarce. Conventional market mechanisms alone proved inadequate in surmounting this predicament. Since the inception of the New

consolidated Mao's power base by targeting political opponents and capitalists, especially wealthy capitalists.

The Three-anti Campaign was launched in Northeast China at the end of 1951. It was aimed at members within the Communist Party of China, former Kuomintang members and bureaucratic officials who were not party members. The 3 antis imposed were: anti-corruption ( ), anti-waste ( ), and anti-bureaucratism ( ).

The Five-anti Campaign occurred in the midst of the Korean War and was a key campaign in the Communist Party's effort to eliminate private property. It both extracted funds from the private sector to support China's involvement in the war and further restrained the power of Chinese capitalists. The 5 antis were: anti-bribery ( ), oppositional toward theft of state property ( ), oppositional toward tax evasion ( ), oppositional toward cheating on government contracts ( ), and oppositional toward stealing state economic intelligence ( ).

[16] Liu Yini, A Historical Reflection on the Forms of Social Mobilization, Strategy and Management, 1999 (4): 82–89.

[17] Translator's note: The "one central task and two basic points" proposition—taking economic development as the central task and the Four Cardinal Principles and reform and opening-up as the two basic points—is the core of the Party's basic line for building socialism with Chinese characteristics in the primary stage of socialism. It was established at the 13th CPC National Congress.

China, our experience has taught us to first express economic needs politically, permeating them from top to bottom, and to politically manipulate the demand for capital mobilization. Subsequently, all methods of motivation, oversight, and reward-punishment were administered through political channels. Employing these political means, society's surplus was maximally focused on the path of industrial construction.

By examining the relationship of dependence, one can observe that prior to the rupture between China and the Soviet Union, the latter provided extensive strategic assistance, leading to an effective Sovietization of China. Once the dependency bond was established, it bestowed dividends upon nearly all sectors, affording them short-term stability in returns. This harmonious state fostered a cooperative alliance between urban and rural areas, as farmers eagerly flocked to the cities to bolster the nation's industrialization endeavors. The socialist landscape during this era was truly auspicious, owing to the objective impact of dependency dividends, which stimulated a greater sense of voluntary organization among the populace. Farmers, as an autonomous class, were mobilized by these dividends, giving rise to various collectives, such as the inception of Primary Cooperatives in 1953, followed by the Advanced Cooperatives in 1956, and culminating in the establishment of People's Communes in 1958. Comparatively, the cost of organization during this period remained low, thanks to the dividends covering such expenses, and the prominent role of large-scale organizations as a substitute for capital was not yet apparent. However, the high dependency dividends also implied that the cost of severing this attachment would prove disproportionately burdensome. "De-dependence" entailed not only settling the unpaid costs of the dependency dividend phase but also signified that all future capital inflows into the new dependency system would incur costs exceeding the norm.

In the second phase, spanning from the 1980s to the turn of the twenty-first century, the prevailing policy direction aimed at establishing a socialist market economy system. This involved embracing market-oriented reforms as the primary means of resource allocation. The arena of local competition revolved around the strategic formation of industrial capital, acting as the baton orchestrating industrialized competition mechanisms. The coastal regions, endowed with an array of advantages including capital, technology, and market access, alongside the pivotal hubs of economic development in the inland, were granted an extra tilt in terms of scarce resource allocation, providing them with a motivational edge.

During this evolution, the conduct of local governments underwent a significant metamorphosis. In the vibrant 1980s, they fervently fostered township enterprises, which served as a critical source for their low-cost capital accumulation. This was achieved through the astute capitalization of local land resources, almost free of cost. The land utilization mechanism during this era could be distilled down to "land-driven enterprise growth." However, commencing in the late 1980s, the central authority embarked on a quest to reclaim a portion of rural land revenue rights. These rights were then entrusted to market-savvy, corporatized local governments, allowing them to extensively employ the authoritative power vested in them by the state to influence the metamorphosis of the land tenure system. Consequently, the very foundations of the land resource capitalization mechanism for township enterprises underwent a profound shift. Local governments found themselves liberated from the obligation to "operate" enterprises and, instead, wholeheartedly embraced the pursuit of "land-driven wealth growth" to satisfy their voracious appetite for governmental consumption. It was in the early 1990s that the quest for rapid progress kindled a wave of fervent enthusiasm across various regions, inspiring the establishment of development zones and the feverish pursuit of real estate ventures. This, however, sparked concerns such as excessive investment, inflationary pressures, and the erosion of precious land resources. The advent of the 1994 tax-sharing system reform further cemented land as the primary, most liquid source of immediate revenue for local governments.[18]

As time unfolded, the role of land in the economic landscape experienced a striking transformation. In the 1980s, the land stood as a vital cog, interwoven with tangible assets within enterprises, embodying an invaluable "asset." Its cultivation within the realm of industrial and commercial endeavors yielded remarkable returns. By the early 1990s, however, the land itself assumed center stage, becoming the very subject of operation. The sheer act of land development or its transfer birthed returns that far surpassed the realm of the previous "land-driven enterprise

[18] Yang Shuai, Wen Tiejun. Economic fluctuations, changes in the fiscal and taxation systems and capitalization of land resources—an empirical analysis of issues related to China's "three enclosures" since the reform and opening-up [J]. Management World, 2010 (4): 32–41,187.

growth" era. This shifting paradigm signified a momentous shift within the intrinsic interest structure of corporatized governments. Gradually, they distanced themselves from the shared appreciation of local industrial capital, growing ever fonder of foreign investment untethered by community obligations. Yet, as fate would have it, the mainland regions, bereft of the favorable conditions enjoyed by their counterparts, found themselves ensnared in the clutches of pernicious debt in the aftermath of the 1990s' macroeconomic crisis and the subsequent coping policies. Local governments, too, assumed new guises, adopting altered developmental models. On the one hand, they withdrew from direct engagement in enterprise management through the restructuring of township enterprises. On the other hand, they fervently courted domestic investment, shifting the focus from courting foreign capital. Henceforth, the incentivized outward-oriented economies evolved into the very mechanisms propelling China's overarching globalization…

In the third phase, which commenced in the twenty-first century, the inexorable pull of an export-driven economy led to the withering of domestic resources and the deterioration of the environment. Alongside these perils emerged consequential losses in public welfare, prompting the central government to prioritize sustainable development and the metamorphosis toward an ecological civilization.

In the annals of modernity, a burgeoning scientific and technological wave in the West birthed a period of industrial civilization. Its hallmark was the advent of societal-scale production and the ensuing wave of consumerism, as human existence detached itself from the embrace of nature. While this era engendered vast wealth and fostered economic and social transformations, it also sowed the seeds of grave resource depletion and an ecological crisis. Under the weight of this predicament, society had no choice but to reevaluate the symbiotic bond between humanity and the natural world, embarking on a series of proactive endeavors aimed at fostering sustainable development and effecting a holistic shift toward an ecological paradigm.

At the dawn of the twenty-first century, China consciously undertook a strategic transformation. In the crucible of the 2007 American subprime mortgage crisis, China resolutely embraced the tenets of ecological civilization. Subsequently, during the economic slump precipitated by the global debt crisis in 2012, China formally espoused an all-encompassing national development strategy, charting a course toward a comprehensive transition to an ecological civilization. Moreover, in 2017, China unveiled the "Rural Revitalization Strategy" and initiated the "Agricultural Supply-Side Structural Reform," steadfastly affirming the imperative of green production in the agricultural sector. These historic transformations embody the ardor for China's resurgent destiny and the trajectory of human civilization, constituting vital chapters within the annals of China's noble pursuit of sustainable development.

The ideology of General Secretary Xi coined as the "Three Rural Issues," stands as an integral facet of Xi Jinping's Thought on Socialism with Chinese Characteristics for a New Era. It serves not only as a compass for the rural revitalization strategy but also provides concrete directives for the sustainable development of agriculture. For instance, Xi astutely notes that China's agricultural and rural progress has ascended to unprecedented heights, forging a new historical epoch. Shifting from an overarching scarcity, the primary contradiction within agriculture has morphed into a structural dilemma, predominantly residing on the supply side. In grappling with the multifaceted challenges and contradictions inherent in agricultural and rural development, the quintessential key lies in the depths of comprehensive reform.

Amidst these novel circumstances, deepening rural reform remains intertwined with skillfully navigating the intricate dynamics between farmers and their cherished land. Regardless of the measures undertaken, the delicate equilibrium of collective land ownership mustn't be undermined, nor the reduction of arable land tolerated, nor the enfeeblement of grain production capabilities accepted. Above all, the sanctity of farmers' interests mustn't be compromised. Embarking on the arduous path of agricultural green development engenders a profound revolutionary metamorphosis in the perspective toward agricultural growth. Lucid waters and lush mountains are invaluable assets ( ); in truth, an immaculate ecological milieu constitutes the rural realm's most sublime and invaluable treasure, providing the firm bedrock for the resurgence of the countryside.

The trajectory of agricultural advancement must not only absolve itself from accruing further ecological liabilities but also embark on the gradual atonement of existing ones. Establishing a robust framework of institutional mechanisms and policies for the harmonious integration of urban and rural development assumes paramount significance. The construction of a novel rural milieu necessitates the primacy of authenticity, conforming to the authentic nature of rural life, faithfully adhering to the intrinsic laws of rural growth, amply showcasing its distinctive features, preserving the essence of rustic charm, safeguarding the verdant landscapes and crystal-clear waters, while remaining ever mindful of the poignant nostalgia that permeates the rustic fabric. These groundbreaking ideals chart a compass for the transformation of China's ecological civilization and herald a direction for sustainable agricultural progress in this new epoch.

Following this transformation, the framework of local competition has blossomed into a credo encompassing both "mountains of gold and silver" alongside the flourishing "green mountains and clear waters." The varied means by which diverse interest groups engage in the contest now teem with an effervescent diversity and differentiation. On one hand, regions along the coasts, such as the bountiful and high-quality South China and East China, continue to bask in the limelight of recognition. Simultaneously, the provinces of Zhejiang, Fujian, and Guizhou, embodying the essence of the notion that "Lucid waters and lush mountains are invaluable assets," progressively accrue invaluable practical experience, serving as the bedrock and wellspring of central edicts and policy guidelines. Even prior to the research group's introduction of the "three-tier market" ( )[19] design for the valorization of rural ecological resources, a tapestry of diversified practices had already unfolded nationwide in the exploration and utilization of these resources. Noteworthy endeavors include the pioneering explorations in Zhejiang's Lishui, realizing the materialization of ecological product value; Ningxia's Longde, zealously advancing the reform of stock and rights, augmenting distinctive cultivation and husbandry industries, and propelling collective economic prosperity; Chongqing's Chengkou County, leveraging

[19] The "Three-tier market" framework was proposed by this research team:

In terms of the "First-tier market," the state makes portfolio investments in rural areas and uses this as a lever to form the "three changes" reform conditions (resources into assets, funds into shares, and villagers into shareholders), leveraging "global resources" according to the The principles of the primary stock market are internalized for stock making.

In terms of the "Second-tier market," township coordination and village autonomy improve the negotiating position of village collective asset management companies and unify external investment attractions—various cooperatives serve as secondary market carriers, and village collectives do not participate in direct operations and only collect share income. Villagers make secondary distribution.

The "Third-tier market" uses local equity exchanges to build a "Third market," and promotes off-board transactions through collective asset trust and collective stock pledges. First, local enterprises join the on-board trading of resource-based capital products, and then absorb social capital investment to get funding.

rural ecological resources to steer the "Three Transformations" Reform; Guizhou's Luodian, issuing real estate certificates for individual Hainan yellow pear trees, daringly embarking on the frontiers of property rights exchange; and Shanxi's Daning, probing innovative institutional arrangements to alleviate ecological poverty. While diverging in their specific focal points, methods, and outcomes, these undertakings collectively echo the clarion call of the central authority's vision for ecological transformation.

The foregoing elucidates the rough trajectory of the evolution of local competition rules, which, when viewed through a political lens, reveals a parallel logic. Chinese local officials prioritize incentive models and performance rankings relative to the developmental pace in their respective regions, thereby exerting significant influence on the rise of governing officers in those locales. During historical epochs dominated by political movements, the contest focused primarily on political loyalty. However, in contemporary times, economic performance has gradually supplanted political loyalty. This governance paradigm, which harmonizes concentrated administrative power with vigorous incentives, has, on occasion, yielded a series of distortions, rendering the arduous transition of the Chinese economy from quantitative expansion to qualitative progress all the more formidable. Moreover, this model of governance has engendered myopic tendencies, as evinced by insufficient investment in education, science, technology, and healthcare, while impetuous expansion has begotten concomitant predicaments of environmental pollution and excessive energy consumption. Consequently, since the dawn of the twenty-first century, while highlighting economic growth, the central authority has mandated that greater administrative resources be allocated to non-economic realms, such as ecological preservation and cultural development, with the aim of galvanizing local governments at all levels to enhance their administrative achievements in these domains.

Within the strategic backdrop of precise poverty alleviation and rural revitalization, the ensuing competition for spatial resources will assume increasingly diverse forms, permeating even the humblest villages. Burdened with the onerous responsibilities of rural construction and governance, village-level organizations, as the principal executors of grassroots tasks, will exhibit a propensity toward administrative formalism in their interactions with township governments, gradually evincing a "quasi-hierarchical" structural motif. Envisaging the institutional arrangement of "one group people with names (,),[20]" it is foreseeable that the rural system shall metamorphose into an amalgamation of "ecological civilization" and "village corporatism." Thus, the current flag-bearers' experiences can offer invaluable insights to other rural communities. Furthermore, the central government ought to persevere in actively facilitating rural development, seizing this opportunity to catalyze internal dynamism within the villages by deploying a panoply of methodologies.

3.2 The Origins and Mechanisms of Institutional Benefits in Zhanqi Village's Three Ascensions

By deciphering the experiences of Zhanqi Village, one unearths the grandeur of its present-day accomplishments, stemming in part from the macro institutional dividends procured amidst local rivalries. These gains transcend the conventional confines of market-driven profits (though markets, in their broader sense, do embody a form of institution) or the narrow scope of institutional rewards, as some ideological onlookers claim the village's triumphs arose solely from the might of its collective economy. Nestled in the hinterlands as a rustic gem, Zhanqi Village's primary institutional advantages converge at the initial stage of non-corporate competition, further accentuated by a mitigated corporate rivalry during the third phase. Its developmental trajectory, akin to the tiered majesty of China's geographic landscapes, has been a gradual ascension, scaling the rungs with each institutional metamorphosis. While the pace may have slackened at the second step, Zhanqi Village, when juxtaposed against the majority of its rural counterparts, nevertheless continues to flourish, diligently upholding the reservoir of its communal economy—a feat not to be taken lightly.

In the era preceding 1978, when elemental productive forces competed unabated, the venerable Zhanqi Brigade amassed a formidable stockpile of institutional resources (nurtured by institutional rewards) by dutifully adhering to the central policies. Aligned with the exigencies of constructing the Third Front and safeguarding military preparedness,

[20] Translator's note: at the village level, three names include "Village committee, village party committee, and village collective economic organization."

their compliance proved instrumental, rendering the village's developmental trajectory far loftier than that of contemporaneous hamlets. This simultaneous juncture ushered forth a propitious macro institutional climate, where the leviathan of national funds condescended upon the Western domains during the Third Front endeavor. Consequently, an unprecedented opportunity materialized, wherein urban industrial capital pervaded the rural tapestry—an occurrence, in part, sparked by the fortuitous proximity of the May Seventh Cadre School, endowing the brigade with a chance to undertake road construction projects. Such concentrations of populace ushered in the bountiful yields of diversified agrarian and livestock pursuits, acting as precursors to nascent urbanization within these rustic confines. To wit, Zhanqi Brigade emerged as an early adopter of agricultural standardization, mechanization, rural industrialization, and, to a certain degree, rural urbanization. As the central government unveils its recent plan for rural rejuvenation, one must not forget that Zhanqi Village had already epitomized this vision as early as the bygone 1970s.

After the 1980s, a fierce corporate competition engulfed the local government, propelling rural industrialization to the forefront. However, the coastal regions' inclination toward openness and urban-centric development policies burdened the township enterprises of Zhanqi Village with the weight of regional disparities and urban–rural divides. The collective economy, once an object of envy due to its rapid growth, gradually succumbed to a perilous path of indebtedness. In the late 1990s, under the duress of macroeconomic crisis, the township enterprises underwent a restructuring process primarily guided by privatization. The 1980s witnessed the rise of many collective enterprises, their growth fueled by the trust extended between banks and businesses. However, the subsequent financial reforms in the 1990s profoundly impacted the financing landscape for small and medium-sized enterprises, aggravating the deteriorating business environment for township enterprises.

Post-2003, the industrial capital's differentiated competition spurred a diversification drive, akin to an ecological contest where "each showcases its own beauty," embodying the essence of ecological civilization. Shedding the shackles of fiscal constraints, the government wholeheartedly embraced a new paradigm characterized by people-centered policies, scientific development principles, sustainability, and the transformation toward ecological civilization. While continuing the legacy of corporate competition, greater investments were directed toward the fundamental and social infrastructure in rural areas. At this juncture, a momentous shift occurred, as the substantial sunk costs incurred by the central government, especially through the implementation of new rural construction and rural revitalization strategies, infused rural areas with abundant assets capable of generating tangible returns. Consequently, the once dormant ecological and spatial resources within the countryside awakened, offering novel institutional opportunities distinct from the realms of industrial competition. Zhanqi Village, ever steadfast in its allegiance to the central government, reaped substantial rewards by embracing this momentous occasion.

In summary, if we liken the development of Zhanqi Village to a three-act play, the first act symbolizes the political assimilation of the economy, followed by the second act characterized by the economy's assimilation of politics. During this phase, economic objectives were unduly emphasized, serving as the primary rules of engagement for interregional governmental competition, inevitably accentuating the disparities between various locales. As the story reaches its climactic third act, we witness the transformation of economic competition into a diverse, ecological-driven contest, aimed at rectifying past policy fallacies. Consequently, a dual narrative emerges: one narrative faithfully echoes the previous economic competition, with economically robust provinces in the eastern region also wielding political clout. Simultaneously, there exists a parallel storyline showcasing a select group of regions in Jiangsu and Zhejiang, embodying the new developmental vision championed by the central government, and thereby attaining opportunities infused with political institutional benefits.

In essence, these three acts paint a picture of Zhanqi Village's development, a tale that oscillates from fast to slow growth, and then back to rapid progress, mirroring the delicate dance between tension and reprieve, reminiscent of the artistry displayed in both war and literature.

4 The Illuminations

4.1 Cost Internalization: National "De-dependence"

The theory of "De-dependence," an offshoot of the renowned economist and Marxist thinker Samir Amin's "dependency" theory, finds its microcosmic foundation in the experience of a China that reconstructed its political and economic sovereignty through nationalist revolution.

Professor Wen Tiejun's research team, unearthing the nascent stages of China's "de-dependence" during the early years of the People's Republic, has distilled the process of "dependence-de-dependence-redepence" that unfolded as China became enmeshed in the economic systems first led by the Soviet Union and later by the United States.

Born amidst the pangs of China's "de-dependence" in the 1960s, the War Banner bears enlightening insights that resonate with China's seven-decade developmental voyage.

In the nascent days of New China's establishment in 1949, strategic aid from the Soviet Union fostered a national industrialization system dominated by heavy industry. This system, with its "capital intensification, labor exclusion" mechanisms, emerged to navigate the treacherous political landscape. Limited to collective forms, the government siphoned surplus value from the countryside, thereby nurturing an inward-oriented "primitive capital accumulation" essential for national industrialization.

By the late 1950s, as Sino-Soviet relations soured, China confronted the urgent need to bolster industrialization. Independent efforts to bridge critical industrial gaps and repay debts owed to the Soviet Union became imperatives. Bereft of the ability to externalize costs, the sole recourse was cost internalization. History reveals a pivotal juncture when China's resilience hinged on the vast expanse of countryside that had undergone the forging of the Land Reform Movement. Within the tales of War Banner Village and its environs, the microcosmic constituents of China's "de-dependence" macrocosm, we glimpse the contributions of rural communities as active agents. For instance, in their pursuit of the directive to "raise more pigs in rural areas," collective members meticulously allocated land and agricultural seasons, ingeniously carving out pig-forage fields amidst the bountiful harvests of grains and vegetables. Likewise, confronted with land quality and topography unsuited for cultivation, the Zhanqi Brigade undertook agrarian water conservation projects in the early 1970s. Transforming wetlands and constructing irrigation channels to enhance irrigation, they revolutionized cropping patterns from single-season to dual-season cultivation, resulting in a substantial surge in agricultural yields. Through these written testimonies, we bear witness to the proactive agency of Chinese farmers, as they, armed with their extensive agricultural know-how, innovative organizational acumen, and unwavering spirit of self-sacrifice, not only bore the institutional costs of national "de-dependence" but also gradually elevated the resources and social cohesion within village communities. This formidable foundation paved the path for numerous rural areas in the 1970s, facilitating the internalization of industrial primitive accumulation and embarking on the trajectory of agrarian-village industrialization.

In essence, it is the interplay of two pivotal mechanisms that allows Zhanqi Village to navigate the transformative currents of rural industrialization: the substitution of abundant labor for scarce capital and the dissolution of the negative externalities spawned by capital's primitive accumulation through a self-denying method. The convergence of these forces paves the way for a seamless and swift transition from agrarian roots to an industrial horizon.

As an "external factor," the politicization and mobilization of the broader macro context leave an indelible imprint on Zhanqi Village, gradually molding its own spiritual core and a corresponding modus operandi. These intangible constituents progressively intertwine with the village's developmental fabric, fostering an unwavering resolve in the face of adversity and a resolute march forward. Ultimately, they breathe life into the grand tapestry of Zhanqi Village's triumphs past, its present achievements, and the boundless possibilities that lie ahead.

Within this ethereal realm reside the tenets that fuel Zhanqi Village's collective spirit: guidance by the Party and governmental compass, a tenacious embrace of responsibility; a primacy of the collective, fostering unity and solidarity; the pursuit of audacious toil and a daring foray into innovation; an unwavering adaptability, adroitly navigating policies and embracing the noble spirit of struggle with public welfare as its polestar.

4.2 Rationality of Village Society: "Three Lives" and "Three Governance" in Rural China

In the realm of cultural diversity, East and West, shaped by disparate geographical resources, bear witness to distinctive legacies. The humble Zhanqi Village, as the elemental administrative nucleus shaping the societal fabric, beckons a glimpse into the intricate tapestry of Eastern civilization.

China's rustic hinterlands remain resolute in their "Three Lives in One ( )." This profound concept, wherein the spheres of ecology, productivity, and existence harmoniously converge, finds its embodiment within the spatial confines of rural settlements. Anchored in a land defined by the mantra of "seven mountains, two rivers, and one plot of farmland," these territories confront the gravitas of imbalanced water resources, impeding agricultural pursuits amidst the vexing conundrum of resource scarcity. Remarkably, China surmounts such challenges, defying human-environmental tensions, and nourishing nearly a fifth of the world's populace. This accomplishment owes its gratitude not solely to age-old agricultural practices of meticulous cultivation, resource circuity, and frugality but also to the profound communal interconnections fostering solidarity within village societies. Together, they safeguard the ecological equilibrium, fortify communal resilience against calamities, and mitigate external risks to their artisanal trades, shaping the very bedrock of indigenous cultural mores and governance principles within rural landscapes.

In the realm of entity-based foundations, the concept of "Three Lives in One" finds its counterpart in the elevated structures of rural society, known as the "Three Governance in One." It can be succinctly categorized into governing people, governing water, and governing the village, or more broadly encompassed as political governance, economic governance, and social governance, while also embracing the means of governance through morality, self-governance, and the rule of law.

Within the annals of Zhanqi Village's struggle, the trajectory of governing people, governing water, and governing the village unveils a compelling ascent, akin to a spiraling spiral. At the village's nascency, the scarcity of sustenance loomed large, with food emerging as the tangible conduit to nurture the anticipated harvest and galvanize the collective ardor for production. Thus, the metamorphosis of waterlogged and decrepit fields became the linchpin of water governance. The transformation necessitated an intensive infusion of labor, for in the dearth of capital, it was imperative to marshal the political domain's ideological mobilization and the economic realm's collective accounting to effectively marshal and organize the workforce, constituting the essence of governing people. Moreover, surpassing conventional governance methodologies, Zhanqi Village seized the opportunity to embark on agricultural endeavors through a quasi-military framework. Consequently, the integration of labor resources within the village transcended conventional boundaries, culminating in not only formidable grain and livestock production capabilities but also propitious advancement in rural ancillary industries. Moreover, this fortunate turn of events paved the way for industrialization, imparting a profound expansion to the village's production and governance, thereby earning Zhanqi Village the distinguished moniker of a renowned "battle flag" in the Western hinterlands, epitomizing the essence of governing the village.

This historical chronicle bears immense significance as Zhanqi Village ventures anew into the collective economic trajectory of the post-twenty-first-century era, unfurling itself as a resolute "battle flag" in alignment with the nation's resolute pursuit of rural revitalization. The team characterizes this profound phenomenon as "rationality of village society," a manifestation of collective reason grounded in the interplay of village communities and rural households, where bonds of kinship and geographical proximity intertwine to uphold societal order, harmonize productive pursuits, and efficaciously internalize transactional costs.

4.3 Resource Sovereignty: Achieving and Safeguarding the Complete Benefits of Rural Resources

Development, simply put, entails capitalizing on and reaping the rewards of the natural resources crafted over countless eons—a process known as "resource capitalization." In the modern world, nations or states serve as the primal arena for competition. Within this realm, it is widely understood that a country's territorial boundaries encompass its ownership of resources. Through the capitalization and exploitation of resources, a nation establishes its economic foundation. However, the stark reality remains that numerous developing countries lack the necessary conditions to derive ample sustenance for their citizens' survival and economic progress from their own resources. Either their rights to exploit these resources have been hastily relinquished to multinational corporations or they find themselves restrained by the tumultuous whims of the international market due to their lack of pricing power within the global cycle of exporting domestic resources and importing vital commodities. In essence, the income derived from a nation's resources languishes in a state of uncertainty, incompleteness, and inadequacy, thereby hampering its ability to maintain a coherent domestic and foreign political structure. Faced with this predicament, it is our conviction that a country can only form true economic sovereignty—effectively upholding its political sovereignty—through the attainment of comprehensive "resource sovereignty."[21]

For microcosmic entities such as villages, the possession of relatively comprehensive "resource sovereignty" is paramount, as it serves to uphold the localized tenets of "Three Lives" and "Three Governance" to a considerable degree. This establishes an institutional space wherein villages can become the bedrock for the nation's macro-level quest for emancipation from dependency. In the 1990s, as villages embraced the tenets of the market economy, with urban capital and industrial forces predominantly influencing the allocation of numerous resources, and with nascent forms of urban–rural amalgamation in their infancy, the experiential insights gleaned from Zhanqi Village assumed utmost significance.

Throughout the entire twentieth century, rural China, as a collective entity, functioned predominantly as a reservoir of surplus, nurturing the forces of industrialization and urbanization, all the while grappling with incomplete resource rights and interests. As China enters the twenty-first century, heralding a transition toward ecological harmony, with an emphasis on addressing the prevailing contradiction of imbalanced development as the primary focal point of Xi Jinping's socialism thought with Chinese characteristics, the issue of resource rights and interests in rural regions emerges as an unavoidable quandary demanding "profound transformations." The crux of the matter lies in the long-standing urban dominance over rural surplus, resulting in an entrenched path dependency permeating every facet of institutional dynamics and discourse. How can China liberate itself from the shackles of this path dependency and effectuate a transformative shift toward a novel paradigm of urban–rural integration?

Therefore, the pricing and distribution quandaries concerning rural resources and their increased benefits have emerged as pivotal manifestations of a village's inherent right to self-development.

It is evident that Zhanqi Village persistently expands its internal resource gains through the astute practice to "feed two birds with one scone." Fundamentally, this approach involves reevaluating the value of

[21] Dong Xiaodan, Wen Tiejun. "Breaking Free from Dependence: China's Authentic Experiences in Resolving Its Inaugural Economic Crisis" [M]. Beijing: Oriental Publishing House, 2019.

previously undervalued resources that were allowed to slip away, with the resulting profits serving as a vital catalyst for nurturing a novel collective economy. The initial instance encompasses augmenting collective asset revenues by dissecting fixed and liquid assets of collective enterprises, meticulously accounting for leasing costs and transfer expenditures. Thus, this innovative tactic becomes the auspicious "first pot of gold" propelling the collective economy's renaissance in the twenty-first century. Within Zhanqi Village, the auctioning of liquid assets such as raw materials assumes a momentous role, invigorating collective assets with the replenished cash flow. Portions of these funds are allocated to alleviate financial constraints impeding contractors, fostering a harmonious symbiosis between the village and enterprises. Additionally, a fraction of these proceeds is allocated to internal village affairs, encompassing expenses related to public services, societal and cultural advancements, and the enrichment of the spiritual and cultural lives of the populace. These endeavors further propel organizational and societal cohesion, serving as the bedrock for the village's spatial restructuring.

The second case pertains to cooperative land development endeavors within the concentrated village, engaging external stakeholders. This collaborative process not only thoroughly considers the divergent values inherent in agricultural and construction land but also intricately calculates the realization of the resource value encapsulated within the latter. As the village secures income from leasing rights, it astutely safeguards the ultimate "land bottom rights" associated with construction land, poised to promptly monetize them on equal footing, reaping identical rewards as urban land.

4.4 *Spatial Justice: The Socialized Allocation of Rural Socioeconomic Resources*

The villagers of Zhanqi penned a response, a quintessentially Chinese answer to Marx's call for "spatial justice." In this realm, the village's resources and assets find common ownership among its members, with the resulting benefits socially distributed to all. It is an embodiment of Marx's core principles on property and equitable distribution. Long before Zhanqi's land share cooperative earned the esteemed title of a "Good Social Enterprise in China," the Zhanqi Collective Asset Management Company had already embraced the ethos of a social enterprise.

Beyond the realm of classical political economy, "spatial justice" in China harbors an additional and momentous meaning. Tracing back along the threads of history, one must first acknowledge that as an expansive nation, China has time and again triumphed in its struggle for national independence, leveraging its vast inland expanse. While capitalist nations sought to augment their colonial gains through war, China's substantive experience in defeating colonialism lay in its ability to "buy time through space."

Moreover, during the nascent stages of New China, beset by grave inflation, the fledgling regime confronted the formidable challenge of battling against over half the nation's material resources, financial clout, and speculative capital. Only through this unwavering resolve did they achieve a complete emancipation from financial subjugation. Where speculative capital hinged on financial maneuverings, a realm marked by temporal exploitation of future returns, the new regime, in the absence of sufficient financial credit, resorted to pooling the nation's material and financial resources to curb inflation—an embodiment of spatial concentration. It was this very strategy, akin to the victorious mechanisms witnessed in the "Huaihai campaign" waged in the currency realm, that once again embraced the power of space to gain the precious commodity of time.

In the realm of industrialization for the People's Republic of China, a crisis befell urban capital during the tumultuous 1960s and 1970s. To quell this urban unrest, a curious solution emerged: directing the unemployed denizens toward the rustic countryside. This approach, in essence, tapped into the rural spatial and organizational reservoirs. Even in the wake of reform and the era of openness, space remained an invaluable player in crisis resolution. China's national strategies such as Western Development ( ), the Northeast Area Revitalization Plan ( ), the Rise of the Central China ( ), and the Building New Socialist Villages ( ) effectively absorbed societal employment and redundant capacities, effectively pushing the crisis horizon further back. Essentially, this was a utilization of space to buy time.

Given China's knack for leveraging space to gain temporal advantages, it stands to reason that every individual within the nation's territorial boundaries, every entity intertwined with spatial resources, inherently possesses the right to claim a just share of the accompanying benefits. This, my dear reader, encapsulates the profound concept of macro "spatial justice" bearing China's unmistakable characteristics.

Now, let us cast our gaze upon the micro-foundation. During the era of collectivization, the banner-waving social organizations that dotted the landscape transformed into localized embodiments of societal enterprises, albeit without formal acknowledgment. Bereft of external resource influx, these enterprises found themselves navigating treacherous waters: seeking to satisfy the insatiable hunger of a nation marching toward industrialization while ensuring the very survival of their village constituents. As a result, a discernible pattern emerged, wherein the distribution of spoils adhered to the mantra of "70% population, 30% labor." This egalitarian safeguard of individual survival constituted the bedrock of their "social pedigree." Alas, some voices today label this practice as the vile "communal feast of egalitarianism." However, they fail to perceive the fundamental truth that rural landscapes offered the primordial foundations for national industrialization, only to witness their abundant surplus confiscated by external forces, thereby impeding the conditions necessary for labor-driven distribution within the confines of the village and its communal fabric.

From the late 1970s until the zenith of the 1990s, the village and its communal identity relied upon internal accumulations to nurture a cornucopia of enterprises, including brick factories, soybean paste mills, flour mills, distilleries, and foundries. It proved a delicate dance, a tightrope act of symbiosis. On one hand, these collective enterprises provided sustenance for the village, ensuring employment opportunities and bestowing welfare upon their members. On the other hand, the village collective stood shoulder to shoulder, shouldering the harrowing risks of enterprise operation. As fate would have it, the Production Brigade's collective economy thrived, securing its place at the pinnacle of the county's economic hierarchy, fostering not only the unity of the village collective but also laying the bedrock for the transformative adjustments that lay ahead in the twenty-first century.

As the new millennium emerged from its slumber, witnessing the village's resources once more consolidate, the logic of social enterprise in resource allocation resurfaced with renewed vigor. The entire village embarked upon a four-year odyssey, quantifying and transforming its wealth into shares, thereby anointing its villagers as stakeholders in the realm of collective assets. Through such structural alliances, the village collective economy assumed an unwavering "orchestration" role, fortifying the bond between the village collective and its farming constituents.

Moreover, it fortified the efficacy of government policies, while simultaneously slashing the expenses required for the village to harmonize with external market forces. Undeniably, this reiterates that the rural collective economy stands as a vital component within Xi Jinping's thought of socialism with Chinese characteristics for a new epoch. Indeed, it is only through the cultivation of rural collective economy that comprehensive rural revitalization can be realized, unveiling a resplendent panorama of renewal. And thus, dear reader, we uncover the microcosmic essence of "spatial justice."

PART I

1949–1973: The Scarlet Zhanqi: Catching Up on Socialism Education and the Spark of Rural Vitality

In the era between the 1950s and 1970s, preceding China's venture into reform and opening-up, it was widely regarded as the nascent stage of national industrialization. By adhering to classical theories, this phase embodied the inward-bound accumulation of capital, distinct in its development trajectory from any advanced nation. While the Western world acknowledges capital accumulation as an outward, colonial endeavor steeped in bloodshed, China's pursuit remained inward, indigenous, and burdened with hardship. Consequently, China's initial three decades toward industrialization could be characterized as a saga of unyielding perseverance, stirring and tearful yet grandly resplendent, marred by recurring crises that unfurled an array of movements.

During this transformative era, China confronted not only the taxing ordeal of a new political regime grappling with fiscal deficits and the perils of rampant inflation, which imperiled its very existence, but also the predicament of fragmented agrarian economies and the excessive extraction of agricultural surplus to propel industrialization, resulting in exorbitant transaction costs for small-scale farmers. Additionally, there arose a crisis precipitated by the Soviet Union's withdrawal of investments during the nascent stages of the Second Five-Year Plan, causing a disruption in China's industrialization efforts, plunging it into the pitfall of a "development trap." Furthermore, compelled by three urban economic crises, a vast "Down to the Countryside Movement (上山下乡)" had to be launched to alleviate the surplus labor conundrum in urban centers.

Most significantly, amid these three decades, China confronted a daunting international milieu defined by comprehensive external blockades and heightened geopolitical tensions within its periphery, encompassing the War to resist US aggressors and aid Korea and Soviet investment withdrawal, and unceasing intrusions by American aircraft into Chinese territorial waters. De facto, China found itself teetering on the precipice of a "hot war," amid the Cold War era's frosty standoff between China, the Soviet Union, and Western powers.

In light of these adversities, China was compelled to continually adjust its domestic macroeconomic policies, gradually adopting an economic doctrine of "self-reliance and diligent work," intertwined with the amalgamation of the masses. Drawing upon the political mobilization mechanisms inherited from the era of land revolution, local governments propelled labor force engagement predominantly through political motivations and competitive incentives. This galvanized the workforce to exert themselves relentlessly, often heedless of the incurred costs. With the entire nation embracing frugality and austerity, they overcame a spectrum of crises, including the dearth of capital, embodying the undying spirit of resilience.

China, once a destitute agrarian nation, defied its impoverished state and swiftly embraced industrialization through self-reliance. The conduit for such transformation lay in its organizational prowess. The Chinese Communist Party rallied the fragmented masses of farmers, uniting them like scattered grains of sand, propelling the people to become the driving force behind historical progress. During the era of collectivization, village communities became the bedrock of organization, internalizing the fundamental elements of labor, capital, and land, as postulated by classical economics. The resources subject to the village community's control were judiciously allocated based on varying demands, such as the initial focus on agricultural and hydraulic development, the mid-stage emphasis on integrating cultivation and animal husbandry, and the subsequent promotion of secondary industries. These productive factors, which were readily shaped within the collective, required little in terms of organizational costs, culminating in the accumulation of collective economic strength. Consequently, China achieved the imperative capital original accumulation for industrialization at a notably diminished cost.

Simultaneously, the rural organization process paralleled the profound penetration of the nation's political structure into grassroots society. Since the waning days of the Qing Dynasty, despite the relentless efforts to establish state authority at the grassroots level, it encountered resistance in various degrees. In that era, the ordinary people lacked a concrete understanding of the state, rendering it bereft of the necessary impetus for a momentous industrial transformation However, with the advent of the People's Republic of China, state power permeated the grassroots sphere with greater verticality, delving deep into production teams while expanding its influence horizontally. Besides procuring agricultural produce, facilitating industrial distribution, and levying taxes, the state assumed control over agricultural production management and income distribution. Naturally, the operation of state power within grassroots society faced persistent opposition from traditional customs, particularly from grassroots cadres and members harboring self-interests. The evolution of the relationship between state power, landlords, gentry, and farmers into the interplay between the state, collectives, and farmers ushered China's rural regions through a labyrinthine progression amid the perpetual clash between state rationality, collective rationality, and the opportunist inclinations prevalent among small-scale peasant farmers.

Compared to prevailing academic opinions, which lamented the excessive costs of labor supervision or emphasized economic growth devoid of genuine development during the collective era, our perspective lies in embedding the historical process of collectivization within the confinements imposed by the internal and external circumstances arising from the nascent phases of industrialization. By scrutinizing the specific trajectory of development, concrete instances reveal a spiraling upsurge in the mobilization of farmers during that epoch, with the focus centered on maximizing per unit output rather than labor productivity. Galvanized by an unwavering spirit, the vast multitude of grassroots cadres and impassioned masses actively engaged in the nation's construction, endowing China with an awe-inspiring force capable of reshaping landscapes and transforming the world within this venerable and extraordinary realm. Presenting an authentic account of rural social development, we endeavor to facilitate a fresh understanding of the bewildering assortment of national and individual behaviors characteristic of this distinct phase.

Hence, perhaps it is incumbent upon us to reevaluate China's agrarian collectivization period from the first three decades. Only through an immersive analysis of the internal and external milieu prevalent during that era, and a meticulous disentangling of its institutional mechanisms, can we begin to glimpse the complete tapestry of events. The remarkable experiences and odyssey of the "minuscule" Zhanqi Brigade in Western

Sichuan proffer an exquisite microcosm, shedding light on the panorama of China's evolution during this extraordinary epoch.

In the midst of the 1970s, any rural production brigade embarking on the initial stages of industrialization faced a dearth of capital, technological know-how, and skilled managers. **Survival and growth in the cutthroat market required the discovery of distinctive competitive advantages.** During the collectivization era from 1965 to 1978, the Zhanqi Brigade resolutely upheld the tenet of "political supremacy." It was during this period that they hoisted the flag of revolution, propelled by the mighty force of the people, and etched an epic tale of struggle across the rugged landscapes of the Western territories. This struggle paved the path toward primitive capital accumulation within the village, propelling them gradually onto the road of rural industrialization. This is the microcosmic vantage point from which China, nestled within the folds of the Zhanqi Brigade, crafted its magnificent feats within the span of three decades.

Prior to the splintering of the Zhanqi Brigade, the region, as a fledgling liberated zone, weathered a series of sociopolitical and economic movements. The tumultuous era witnessed grain requisition, campaigns against banditry and feudal overlords, rent reduction and the return of confiscated lands, the transformative land reform, the tide of collectivization, and the establishment of people's communes. These orchestrated movements laid the groundwork for institutional arrangements aimed at extracting the maximum surplus resources from the countryside, propelling the nascent gears of national industrialization. Consequently, a relentless wave of socialist education movements targeted grassroots cadres and members, embarking on an incessant journey of ideological edification, fostering collective consciousness through the lens of "public versus private" and "collective versus individual."

Amidst the dire scarcities of capital, circa 1965 to 1973, the Zhanqi Brigade harnessed the powers of women's mobilization and militia construction to rally a formidable internal labor force, fervently immersing themselves in the realms of agricultural and ancillary industries. Swiftly, agricultural output skyrocketed and swine populations flourished. Guided by the synergy of "tilling and rearing" and adept labor force allocation, the Brigade astutely navigated a realm where the harvest of comprehensive yields was paramount, enabling the completion of the brigade's primordial capital accumulation. Such prowess and the blueprint of the militia training system were, in due course, disseminated by the county committee as a propagandistic example, inspiring a myriad of brigades throughout the county. Within this unfolding narrative, the Zhanqi Brigade emerged as a paragon of excellence.

Between 1974 and 1979, the Zhanqi Brigade, poised at the precipice of agricultural hamlets, boldly embarked on the transformative transition toward a comprehensive domain of agricultural and industrial development. The bounty of social capital amassed during the period around 1973 bestowing them with a modicum of fortuitous advantage and institutional gains, enabled the Brigade to expedite their procurement of equipment, capital, and sundry resources. Bolstered by the collective's unwavering tenacity to harness their collective strength in the pursuit of greatness, the Zhanqi Brigade expediently launched the establishment of a curvaceous kiln, deftly seizing the initiative in the nascent stages of industrialization's awakening, thereby laying an unyielding foundation for future industrial progress.

Zhanqi Brigade's extraordinary experience is no mere coincidence. A discerning examination reveals a striking resemblance in the developmental journeys of collectively prosperous villages. Places like Liuzhuang Village in North China, Huaxi Village in Jiangsu, and Honglin Village in Hubei share a kinship with Zhanqi Village's trajectory. Their collective economic growth, fueled by abundant labor investments, has earned them well-deserved recognition.

Perusing the annals of Zhanqi Village, one witnesses the remarkable organizational prowess of the Communist Party of China at the grassroots level. In a mere handful of years, this party, buoyed by a select few CPC cadres who migrated from the south, established its unassailable authority in the newly liberated territories, seamlessly transferring the reins of power. Moreover, Zhanqi Brigade, deftly adapting its institutional fabric to navigate external political forces, swiftly emerged as a paragon of prowess in vital domains such as grain cultivation, pig husbandry, and civic defense. **Such is China's Battle Flag (Zhanqi), an inseparable fragment of her tenacious struggle and resolute progress.**

This part is divided into two chapters, delineating the development of Zhanqi Brigade during this stage. The initial chapter unveils the political, economic, and social tapestry of Sichuan prior to the birth of the People's Republic of China. It further examines the successive rural reforms and socialist educational endeavors, the bedrock upon which Zhanqi Brigade was forged and its evolution perpetuated. The ensuing chapter narrates the post-establishment exploits of Zhanqi Brigade, as successive branch secretaries masterfully orchestrated an accelerated upsurge in agriculture and ancillary pursuits during the "Learning from Dazhai in Agriculture" campaign. Additionally, this chapter adroitly dissects the mechanisms underlying the internalization of primitive capital accumulation. Moreover, it expounds upon the advantages garnered through astute practices of high accumulation and low consumption, the "bonus rewards" garnered during this phase through surplus agricultural production, and the intricate journey from an agrarian hamlet toward industrialization as it pertains to the crucible of industrial competition.

CHAPTER 3

Catching Up on Socialist Education (Before 1964)

1 Introduction

To delve into the historical development and mechanisms of the Zhanqi Brigade, one must first grasp its backstory and the grand-scale setting it inhabited, establishing the foundation for analytical exploration. Although officially established in 1965, the Zhanqi Brigade had already taken form in various manifestations prior to that, such as Jifeng Village, a segment of the Jinxing Brigade, and the enigmatic Jinxing Third Brigade. This chapter scrutinizes the political, economic, and societal environment in which Zhanqi Village found itself before the dawn of New China. It also examines the subsequent local consolidation of the new regime, the impetus behind collectivization, and the emergence of the socialist education movement.

2 Before the Birth of New China: Political, Economic, and Social Landscape

Zhanqi Village resides within the Chengdu Plain of Sichuan Province, China. The "Shu Jing Lu (蜀警录)," penned by the local official Ouyang Zhi in the waning days of the Ming Dynasty, astutely observed, "When chaos engulfs the realm, Shu treads that path first; when order reigns over the realm, Shu basks in that warmth last." Hence, the significance of the Bashu region becomes evident, possessing four gateways and being acclaimed as the Celestial Land, even tempting ambitions of imperial

© Peking University Press 2024
X. Dong, *Zhanqi Village Over Fifty Years*,
https://doi.org/10.1007/978-981-97-5426-7_3

dominion, casting longing gazes upon the Central Plains. Amid the Xinhai Revolution, the road to political transformation in Sichuan witnessed the demise of the provincial authority held by the Qing Dynasty, crumbling under the pressures of the Railway Protection Movement (保路运动).[1] With the birth of the "Republic of China," Sichuan's provincial institutions experienced mercurial rearrangements. Ostensibly demarcated between military and political domains, the actuality blurred the distinction, with military brass seizing the reins of governance. The year 1919 marked the gradual establishment of the "Defense Zone System" in Sichuan, precipitating the fragmentation of power as warlords of divergent factions claimed dominion over their demarcated territories. These enclaves exhibited an aura of autonomy, with unchecked taxation, donations collected at will, and the appointment of administrative and fiscal officials. Each stronghold resembled an independent fiefdom, rendering Sichuan devoid of unified military and political directives.[2]

The warlords, embroiled in perpetual conflicts, vied for territorial supremacy in Sichuan, ultimately birthing two factions during the era of defense zones. One contingent, led by Liu Xiang (刘湘), was hailed as the Sucheng Faction (速成系), while the other, helmed by Deng Xihou (邓锡侯), Liu Wenhui (刘文辉), and Tian Songyao (田颂尧), was famously known as the Baoding Faction (保定系). From 1926 to 1933, Liu Wenhui's bastion reaped opulence, particularly in the vital southwest regions of Sichuan, encompassing a substantial sway over 70 counties. Liu Xiang, predominantly stationed in the eastern reaches, commanded a narrower defense zone, yet his strategic hub in Chongqing burgeoned as a pivotal commercial entrepôt. Both factions harbored ambitions of unifying Sichuan, precipitating the eruption of the "Two-Liu War" between Liu Xiang and Liu Wenhui in the frigid winter of 1932. This

[1] Translator's note: The Railway Protection Movement, also known as the "Railway Rights Protection Movement," was a political protest movement that erupted in 1911 in late Qing China against the Qing government's plan to nationalize local railway development projects and transfer control to foreign banks. The movement, centered in Sichuan province, expressed mass discontent with Qing rule, galvanized anti-Qing groups and contributed to the outbreak of the 1911 Revolution.

[2] Sichuan Provincial Compilation Committee. Sichuan Province Annals: Chronicles of Political Affairs (Volume 1) [M]. Beijing: Fangzhi Publishing House, 2000.

seismic clash laid the bedrock for Liu Xiang's ultimate consolidation of Sichuan.[3]

After the National Government of the Republic of China (Nationalist Government) made Nanjing its capital, Chiang Kai-shek didn't give much weight to Sichuan, considering it a "remote frontier" for quite some time. The Nationalist Government's perception of Sichuan's political and strategic importance underwent a transformation in 1932–1933, triggered by two critical events: the entrance of the Fourth Red Army into Sichuan and the eruption of the "Two-Liu War" in the same period. These events compelled Chiang Kai-shek to redirect his attention and involvement toward Sichuan's political landscape, igniting a nationwide discourse on the need to reshape its governance.[4]

Amidst internal concerns and external perils, Sichuan gradually assumed the role of a "national revitalization base" in Chiang Kai-shek's eyes, a sentiment echoed by intellectuals throughout the nation, who saw Sichuan as a province capable of serving as the nation's "rear area."

In November 1934, driven by the pursuit of the Red Army, Chiang Kai-shek extended a personal invitation to Liu Xiang, summoning him to Nanjing for discussions—an inaugural venture beyond Sichuan's borders for Liu Xiang. During this encounter, Chiang Kai-shek proposed the formation of a staff unit to assist Liu Xiang in Sichuan, an offer difficult for Liu Xiang to decline. By January 1935, the Generalissimo's Headquarters Staff Group had arrived in Chongqing, paving the way for the establishment of the new government of Sichuan Province in February of the same year.[5] **Consequently, a protracted struggle unfolded between Liu Xiang, and the subsequent Pragmatists of Sichuan, and Chiang Kai-shek, spanning over a decade within the boundaries of Sichuan.**

As the Nationalist Government's political dominion expanded across Sichuan, coupled with the extensive occupation of the mainland during

[3] Sichuan Provincial Committee of the Chinese People's Political Consultative Conference. Sichuan Cultural and Historical Materials: Volume 1 [M]. Chengdu: Sichuan People's Publishing House, 1996.

[4] Huang Tianhua. "From 'Remote Frontier' to 'National Revitalization Base': Chiang Kai-shek's Metamorphosis of the Sichuan Situation on the Brink of the War against Japan." Research on the War of Resistance against Japan, 2012(4): 14–23.

[5] Sichuan Provincial People's Government Office of Advisors, Sichuan Provincial Research Institute of Literature and History. "The Pragmatists of Sichuan and Chiang Kai-shek." Chengdu: Sichuan University Press, 1993.

the all-encompassing war, Sichuan's position as a vital fiscal stronghold assumed ever-greater significance. Chief among its revenue streams was the land tax. In 1939, the land tax accounted for a staggering 45.6% of Sichuan's total annual tax income. Starting from 1941, owing to inflationary pressures and other factors, Sichuan implemented a policy of collecting land tax in kind, directly acquiring physical commodities. The Nationalist Government persistently augmented Sichuan's land tax quotas, surging from 12 million tam (1 tam = 50 kilograms) in 1941 to 20 million tam by 1945. In turn, Sichuan's actual land tax collection as a percentage of the national aggregate escalated from 30% in 1941 to 43.5% in 1945, nearing half of the nation's total land tax revenue. Subsequently, business tax emerged as the second-largest revenue source, trailing only the land tax. Introduced to China from the West during the Nationalist Government era, it was slated for implementation following Sichuan's political consolidation. In order to bolster the Sichuan Army's incursions beyond its borders, the province relentlessly overhauled the business tax system, expanding its ambit and intensifying the collection efforts. Consequently, from 1937 to 1941, Sichuan experienced a marked annual upswing in business tax revenue. In 1941, Sichuan's tax contribution amounted to approximately 55.58% of the national business tax revenue, totaling 166.49 million yuan.[6]

The considerable surge in land taxes and business levies has birthed an upsurge of conflicts between the grassroots of Sichuan and their landlords. Various forms of resistance by merchants and business associations have, at times, compelled the Nationalist Government to yield ground. The tenant-landlord dynamics in the Chengdu Plain, located in Western Sichuan, were inherently intricate, with prevalent practices of rent withholding and land occupation, rendering the actual land ownership a tangled web, with a substantial amount of unaccounted-for lands. To boost land tax revenues, the remeasurement of lands became an urgent task. However, the augmentation of land taxes and the land surveying process inflicted a reduction in landlords' income, prompting them to further shift the tax burden onto tenant farmers. As a consequence, conflicts between landlords and tenants in the Chengdu Plain arose with alarming frequency. In order to pursue comprehensive land

[6] Ke Weiming. "On the Reform of Sichuan's Business Tax System during the War." Research on the War of Resistance against Japan, 2013(3): 116–124.

measurement, the administrative expenses of county governments escalated, thereby transferring the financial burdens to the farmers. Between 1937 and 1938, land measurement stood as a pivotal element of the Xin Du Experimental County. Although over 60,000 mu of unregistered land were unearthed, the discovery kindled intense resistance among the local populace, leading to the infamous siege of the city and consequently shattering the very existence of the experimental county. In a similar vein, the unyielding resistance from business associations ultimately coerced the Sichuan provincial government into making concessions concerning the business tax rates.

Despite the surge in Sichuan's tax capacity, propelled by the exigencies of the Nationalist Government's intervention in the region and the fight for national salvation, their authority never penetrated the grassroots of Sichuan. The implementation of the new county system in July 1940, an endeavor ostensibly aimed at fortifying grassroots administrative capabilities, faltered due to the dearth of wartime funds. Chiang Kai-shek, cognizant of the need for counties to attain an autonomous fiscal position, detached from their subservience to provincial finance, and secure a dependable source of revenue, delineated the tax revenues that counties and townships were entitled to collect. The objective was to propel the development of county and city education, health, transportation, public security, economy, culture, and other sectors. The inclusion of slaughter taxes in the domain of county and city revenues, alongside the previously collected rents from public schools and miscellaneous donations, prompted Chiang Kai-shek to assert the substantial nature of these inflows for counties and cities. Urgent priorities lay in reforming the antiquated tax collection methods, with an unequivocal need for a comprehensive financial overhaul to prevent the few from monopolizing the tax proceeds to the detriment of the masses, failing to serve their interests. **The notion of "autonomous finance (自治财政)" championed by the Nationalist Government necessitated that each county's financial independence and self-sufficiency be upheld under the new county system, effectively shedding burdensome ties.** Although the reorganization of autonomous finance, to some extent, bolstered state control over grassroots affairs, the resultant impact proved meager. For instance, the linchpin of autonomous finance, the slaughter tax and franchise tax, burdened the townships and suffered from long-standing abuses due to the prevalence of contractors. Despite initial attempts at self-collection following the implementation of the new county system, the lack of a comprehensive understanding of grassroots realities rendered the cost of information retrieval exorbitant, compelling a return to the old practice of entrusting tax collection to contractors. Feng Qingyun, a notable figure among contractors, gradually amassed power in Bishan County (now Bishan District of Chongqing City) in eastern Sichuan after 1940, ultimately assuming the position of township head. In 1950, his resistance to grain requisition resulted in his downfall, epitomizing the inherent flaws of autonomous finance.

In the realm of "25% rent reduction" and the easing of agricultural land rent, let us take a glance at the year 1945 when the Nationalist Party's Executive Yuan issued the mandate for "25% rent reduction," urging tenant farmers to pay a quarter less in land rent for the ongoing year. Come 1946, the Sichuan provincial government, citing the burden on landlords exacerbated by escalating land taxes since the anti-Japanese resistance, beseeched for a delay in the implementation of the "25% rent reduction." Alas, the Executive Yuan denied their plea, thus compelling Sichuan Province to persist in its pursuit. Regrettably, compliance with the directive was far from widespread, leading the "25% rent reduction" to its demise. As 1949 rolled in, the plight of the Kuomintang grew increasingly dire, shedding light once more on Sichuan's significance. It was then that Chiang Kai-shek anointed Zhang Qun as the head of the Chongqing Pacification Office, instigating a revival of land reform, notably through the avenue of "rent reduction of agricultural land." The involvement of Y. C. James Yen, an esteemed Chinese organizer for rural reconstruction, in eastern Sichuan's ten-county agricultural land rent reduction effort further embellished this endeavor. With an abundance of archival material at our disposal, one may discern the staunch opposition and earnest pleas from landlords and various administrative bodies at the county and township levels, quickly ensnaring the agricultural land rent reduction in a quagmire, ultimately yielding the predicament of apparent reduction but no substantive respite across most regions.

All in all, this glimpse into the depths of the Nationalist Government's foray into grassroots politics in Sichuan unveils the profound quandaries faced on political, economic, and social fronts. Politically, the tension between the aim to fortify grassroots administrative construction and the paucity of funds loomed large. Economically, the contradictory aspirations of bolstering tax revenues from land taxes, business levies, and slaughter duties clashed with the incapacity to grasp tax collection intelligence. Socially, the dichotomy between dismantling the prevailing power structures of landlords and contractors and reliance on them as revenue sources further compounded the conundrum. These intertwined dilemmas shackled the government, rendering genuine implementation of policies at the grassroots level a Sisyphean task.

While the Nationalist Government's strides in establishing grassroots political authority in the region proved limited, **policies such as the "25% rent reduction" and the alleviation of agricultural land rent gradually kindled the embers of resistance among tenant farmers.** The surge in disputes between primary tenants and their landlords unsettled the previously placid countryside of the Western Sichuan plain, laying a historical foundation for the forthcoming regime to galvanize the populace.

On the auspicious day of December 27, 1949, the Chengdu region embraced liberation. However, the majority of farmers in the newly emancipated territories, unlike their brethren from the erstwhile liberated domains, remained unacquainted with the transformative land reform movement spearheaded by the Communist Party of China and Chairman Mao Zedong. The villagers, blissfully unaware of the Communist Party of China and the socialist order, found themselves thrust into the vortex of the new regime's requisition of grain, land surveys and evaluations, crackdown on banditry and feudalism, rent reduction and deposit restitution, and the seminal land reform movement. Within this cauldron, grassroots cadres and farmers grappled with the colossal social tensions inherited from the era of the Republic of China or born anew. The challenge lay in acquainting these rural denizens with the new regime, enabling their harmonious assimilation and active engagement in the nascent stage of industrialization—an onerous trial that tested the Communist Party of China's prowess in constructing grassroots political authority, reforming farmers' livelihoods, and mobilizing society at large.

3 Blocked Grain Collection and the Cooperative Movement

Today's Zhanqi Village was part of the Jifeng Village, located in Chongning County's Lingsheng Township, freshly liberated from oppression. In December 1949, as Chongning County broke free, military control blanketed the entire region. By January 1950, County Magistrate

Duan Zhensheng assumed his post, spearheading the county-wide effort to collect grains.[7]

Grain collection at that time carried immense significance for the newly liberated regions. The ability to amass sufficient grain would determine whether the fledgling government could establish a foothold in the Western reaches of Sichuan and beyond. Firstly, the new regime grappled with formidable fiscal burdens in Western Sichuan and the broader province. Bereft of adequate manpower due to the southern migration of cadre, the new government primarily took charge of urban centers in the region, while rural areas relied on the remnants of the old Nationalist Government's local personnel. A policy of "inheriting" the existing government and civil service was implemented, leaving township and lower levels under their purview. Moreover, the fledgling government's own armed forces urgently required ample supplies and sustenance. **Secondly, the nation as a whole found itself mired in an economic crisis**, as the departing Kuomintang absconded with the entirety of the national treasury's gold reserves and foreign currencies. To ensure fiscal solvency, the new government resorted to currency issuance, inadvertently giving rise to pernicious inflation. Plagued by this malignant affliction, legitimate enterprises languished without profits, and the economy teetered on the precipice of being detached from reality. Unscrupulous profiteers hoarded goods while the stock market witnessed frenzied speculation. Major urban centers like Shanghai, Tianjin, Wuhan, and Chongqing desperately sought copious quantities of staple commodities such as rice, flour, and cloth to curb rampant price hikes.[8]

Although the grain collection effort strove to impose a reasonable burden, in Western Sichuan, the mounting time constraints compelled local reactionary forces to escalate their resistance, ultimately culminating in large-scale brigandage.

Take, for instance, Pixian County and Chongning County. On February 11, 1950, the residual forces of the Kuomintang—military,

[7] At the close of 1949, the majority of the southern territories were liberated. In the nascent stage of the new regime, with the urgent need to address the food crisis of two million people in the southwestern region, national finances were stretched thin. Thus, grain collection emerged as a pivotal avenue to bolster the state coffers.

[8] Dong Xiaodan, Wen Tiejun. Breaking from Dependency: China's Real Experience in Resolving the First Economic Crisis. Beijing: Dongfang Publishing House, 2019.

police, and secret agents—colluded with local feudal despots and habitual marauders, sparking a grand insurrection that aimed to topple the Communist Party of China and the People's Government. Coinciding with the twenty-fifth day of the lunar twelfth month, this rebellion came to be known as the "25 Uprising." These reactionaries laid siege to the valiant revolutionary troops, pillaging their arms cache and ruthlessly slaying those involved in grain collection as well as Liberation Army soldiers. "On the very day the rebellion erupted, grain collection personnel toiled in various townships. Among the victims were County Magistrate Duan Zhensheng, several local cadres, and over twenty soldiers from the Independent Third Army who had participated in the collection effort, all mercilessly cut down by the marauding bandits."[9]

In the pursuit of retribution and enlightenment, a conference was convened in Chongning County from September 25–27, 1950. Its solemn purpose: to unleash a campaign against bandits and quell the oppressive reign of local tyrants, while also addressing the issues of rent reduction and deposit refunds. As the year drew to a close, the county assembled for its inaugural public trial, swiftly suppressing over ten dissidents—ringleaders of counterrevolutionary upheaval—spies, despots, and landlords alike. Simultaneously, a vigilant pursuit ensued, apprehending a significant cohort of concealed bandits and traitors from the Self-Improvement Personnel Training Class and the Home Guard Training Class. Throughout the townships, People's Courts were erected, where public trials unfolded, sealing the fate of the primary perpetrators of organized revolt and consigning them to the harshest of penalties.

Following suit, on that fateful day of October 25, the Lingsheng Township embraced its own maiden public trial, heralding a public reckoning for those implicated in the upheavals. Amidst the twelve village branches, a remarkable turnout emerged—1617 souls, comprising 6968 individuals from 1568 households—amounting to a formidable 23% of the township's populace. Within this gathering, a chorus of twelve brave souls stepped forth, their anguished voices tearing through the air, unleashing a torrent of accusations aimed at the landlords and despots. As the wheels of justice turned, eighteen denizens of Lingsheng Township

[9] Compilation Committee of Pixian County Chronicle, Pixian County Chronicle. Chengdu: Sichuan People's Publishing House, 1989.

would find themselves silenced, their fates sealed by the grip of suppression. Likewise, those involved in the rebellion within the village faced the grim hand of the law, their sentences proclaimed with finality.[10]

With the tempest of bandits and tyrants quelled, **the Communist Party employed a myriad of stratagems—mass assemblies, the ardent struggle against grain-hoarding landlords—the Party unfurled its grand tapestry of governance.** By September of 1950, the arduous task of procuring public grain in the Western realms of Sichuan was nigh on 85% complete—**a feat that solidified the nascent regime's foothold in the region.** The vigorous endeavor of "field investigation and crop evaluation" unveiled the truths of Western Sichuan's terrain, its topography, the bounty it yielded, and the teeming agricultural populace. **This invaluable trove of knowledge laid the bedrock for the forthcoming land reform, an endeavor that would commence in the year 1951.**[11]

The transformative wave of land reform swept through the verdant expanses of Pidu and Chongning, heralding its arrival in late June of 1951, its departure marked in the waning days of April 1952. A vast expanse—363,545.68 mu—of land was claimed, wrested from the grasp of those who clung to power, usurping a staggering 69.84% of the counties' total domain. Illuminating Table 1, Pi County bestowed parcels of land upon a tapestry of 33,231 households, an overwhelming 85.14% of all rural abodes. Those fortunate recipients swelled to a multitude of 146,191 souls, comprising a formidable 83.76% of Pixian County's inhabitants. Across the fertile expanse, 264,408.61 mu of land were disbursed, a generous endowment averaging 1.81 mu per person. In neighboring Chongning County, 16,687 households basked in the spoils of the reform, a bountiful 73.43% of the county's collective homesteads. The land's bestowal graced the lives of 72,674 individuals, embodying 73% of Chongning County's entire populace. A grand total of 128,194.943 mu of land was apportioned, each person laying claim to an elegant 1.76 mu.

The land reform wrought profound changes in the average extent of land ownership among farmers in two counties. The Lorenz curves, portraying the state of land ownership pre- and post-reform, are vividly depicted in Fig. 1.

[10] Source: Zhao Renchun. Zhanqi Village Annals (Unpublished Manuscript).

[11] Zhang Yang. "The Old Land Tax and the New Tax System: The Collection of Public Grain in the Western Sichuan Administrative Office in 1949." Journal of the Communist Party History Research, 2019 (10): 86–96.

Table 1 The dispensation of land in the land reform of Pidu and Chongning Counties, Unit: mu[12]

Class / *Items*		*Farm laborers*	*Poor peasants*	*Middle peasants*	*Tenant-middle peasants*	*Tenant-rich peasants*	*Rural poor*	*Others*	*landlords*
Pixian County	The number of households gain lands	4186	13,713	891	6166	488	3179	2854	1754
	Accounts for the total number of households in the county (%)	99.86	96.66	42.07	97.63	94.03	83.57	68.89	93.6
	The number of households gain lands	12,034	58,722	5228	37,841	3529	9577	9723	9537
	Accounts for the total number of households in the county (%)	99.39	96.02	44.57	96	97.14	79.46	68.54	89.72
	Total field area	23,727.64	99,620.68	6373.44	78,541.03	5465.23	16,860.74	15,981.91	17,837.94

(continued)

12 Compilation Committee of Pi County Chronicle, Sichuan Province. Pi County Chronicle. Chengdu: Sichuan People's Publishing House, 1989.

Table 1 (continued)

Class / *Items*		*Farm laborers*	*Poor peasants*	*Middle peasants*	*Tenant-middle peasants*	*Tenant-rich peasants*	*Rural poor*	*Others*	*landlords*
	Per capita field area	1.97	1.7	1.22	2.08	1.55	1.76	1.64	1.87
Chongning County	The number of households gain lands	1447	8604	1022	2767	57	808	1238	744
	Accounts for the total number of households in the county (%)	97.64	90.05	45.95	93.64	95	56.74	38.32	82.48
	The number of households gain lands	3815	35,637	5654	16,589	383	2239	4324	4033
	Accounts for the total number of households in the county (%)	97.82	89.44	41.38	94.02	83.08	56.77	38.41	83.65
	Total field area	7859.018	61,689.698	9201.065	30,843.282	697.785	4087.114	6389.526	7427.455
	Per capita field area	2.06	1.73	1.63	1.86	1.82	1.83	1.48	1.84

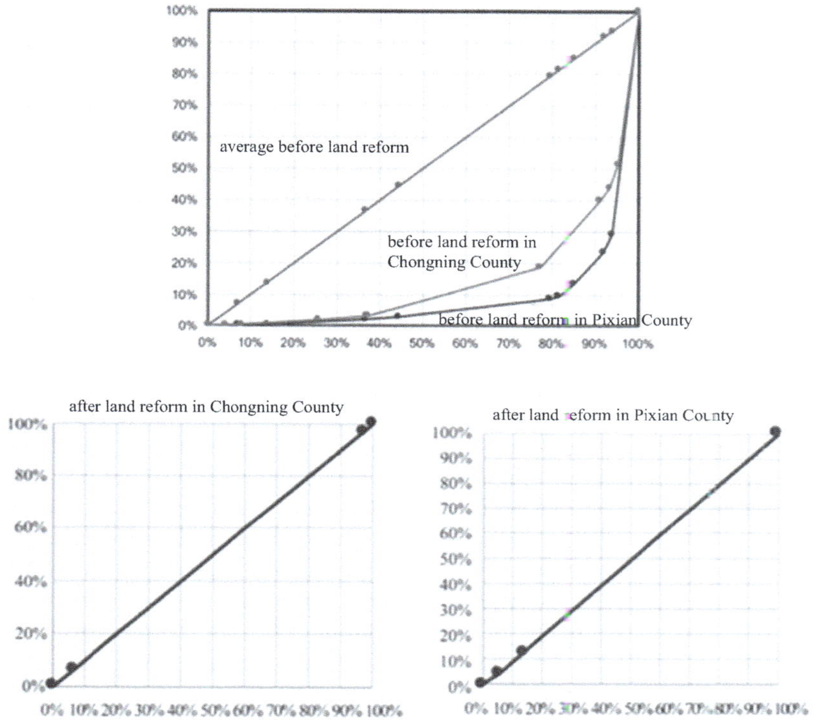

Fig. 1 Lorenz Curves of Land Ownership Before and After Land Reform in Pixian County and Chongning County. *Source*: Compilation Committee of Pixian County Chronicle, Pixian County Chronicle [M]. Chengdu: Sichuan People's Publishing House, 1989

土改前平均 average before land reform.
土改前崇宁 before land reform in Chongning County.
土改前郫县 before land reform in Pixian County.
崇宁土改后 after land reform in Chongning County.
郫县土改后 after land reform in Pixian County.

Calculations reveal that prior to the reform, the Gini coefficient of land ownership in Pixian County reached a staggering 0.82, while Chongning County registered 0.71. By international standards, a Gini coefficient exceeding 0.5 signifies a glaring disparity in land possession. Astonishingly, after the reform, both counties witnessed a Gini coefficient of zero, thus indicating a state of absolute parity. It is, therefore, safe to assert that the land reform not only accentuated equity within the realm of the agrarian society but also bolstered the new regime's ability to rally the masses. In the East Asian context, homogeneity among the populace serves as a distinct attribute of small-scale agrarian societies. According to Hiroshi Miyajima's research, this particular form of small-scale agrarian society emerged during the Ming Dynasty in China and may have surfaced somewhat belatedly in Sichuan. Although a disparity in affluence existed among farmers, the divide between landowners and tenant farmers was remarkably fluid.[13] As each dynasty neared its twilight, this homogeneity inevitably eroded as landlords and powerful magnates amalgamated lands, giving rise to conflicts that, in some instances, spurred dynastic transformations. The land reform subsequent to the birth of the People's Republic of China enabled farmers to secure plots of land, greatly fostering individual productivity. Granted, the reform also exacted a measure of sacrifice in terms of economies of scale. Nevertheless, it bestowed upon the new regime an unprecedented capacity to mobilize politically over more than half of the rural population—an aspect seldom broached within the realm of microeconomics.[14] The land reform, as implemented in Pixian County and Chongning County, compelled the wholesale seizure and requisition of land previously owned by landlords and affluent farmers, thereby irrevocably altering the social fabric and power structures at the grassroots level. Subsequently, the countryside witnessed an evolving trajectory, diverging from the past.

By apportioning land evenly, the land reform galvanized the individual farming populace, instilling a newfound zeal for production. Yet, those farmers who had recently experienced the requisitioning of grains and rampant inflation grew inclined to hoard, rather than sell, their precious harvests. Consequently, rural areas faced the predicament of insufficient commodity circulation. For the burgeoning People's Republic of China, this predicament impeded the dissemination of industrial goods into the countryside, thereby hampering the accumulation of capital required

[13] Hiroshi Miyajima, Zhu Mei. The Formation of East Asian Small Peasant Society [J]. Open Era, 2018(4): 74–91.

[14] Dong Xiaodan, Wen Tiejun. Breaking from Dependence: China's Real Experience in Resolving the First Economic Crisis [M]. Beijing: Dongfang Publishing House, 2019.

for industrial development. "Irrespective of the late-developing nation's chosen path to industrialization, and regardless of the ideological underpinnings it embraces, the conundrum of transaction costs arises in the context of capital's primitive accumulation and the dispersed nature of small-scale agrarian farmers." Moreover, the eruption of the Korean War engendered a substantial inflow of strategic aid from the Soviet Union, precipitating a clash between private and state capital within urban and rural domains.

In tackling the conundrum of land issues and effecting a transformative overhaul of the economic bedrock, the nascent regime, in its wisdom, saw fit to recalibrate the very fabric of grassroots governance, thereby unshackling the antiquated rural power structure of yore. The landmark inaugural People's Representative Congress convened in 1953 by the Wanshou Township's hallowed People's Government stood resolute, embarking upon a resolute mission to dismantle the excessive organizations prevalent in agrarian hinterlands, and to galvanize prodigious strides in productive pursuits. The grand purging entailed the dissolution of over 20 township and village-level entities, coupled with the severance of their numerous administrative acolytes. The roll call of defunct entities and personnel is an extensive one, encompassing the Security and Defense Committee and its coterie of seven, the august Construction Committee and its retinue of seven, the learned Education, Culture, and Health Committee and its entourage of nine, the Veterans and Dependents Committee and its quintet of scribes, the custodians of Public Property Management and their quintet of overseers, the agrarian custodians of the Village Management Committee, whose rank swelled to seven, and lastly, but not least, the solitaires of the Rural Finance Committee, the Civil Affairs Committee, and sundry other vocations, totalling a significant cadre of 23. Likewise, the protagonists of the Patriotic Health Movement Committee, numbering one, the shepherds of the Literacy Campaign Committee, encompassing a baker's dozen, the mediators of the Mediation Committee, comprising five, the helmsman of the Marriage Mediation Committee, the preceptor of the Health Committee, the sentinel of the Rural Finance Committee, and sundry others, were all relinquished from their hitherto held duties. Furthermore, the erstwhile overseers of the Winter Study Committee and its illustrious spearhead, the erstwhile custodians of the Village Loan Committee, and those unfinished tasks were consigned to the watchful aegis of the Production and Construction Committee. Thus, the transient mandates of the erstwhile elected or invited farmer representatives, people's representatives, grain collection representatives, and the earnest exhorters of grain collection have been fulfilled, rendering them obsolete, save for the exigencies of future work that may necessitate provisional arrangements. The sundry responsibilities previously vested in the village directors and their coterie will henceforth be divinely apportioned among the preeminent representatives, the people's representatives, and the motley crew of committee members. The sprawling residencies, previously allocated to subdivisions within each village, will now be entrusted to the stewardship of residential groups, each comprised of 25–30 households, presided over by a newly anointed group leader, charged with the manifold governance of all affairs pertinent thereto. Ergo, the matrimonial arbitration groups and the healthcare brigades within each village shall be disbanded forthwith.[15]

With the demise of the erstwhile establishments, both permanent and transient, and the dethronement of the administrative apparatchiks, the nascent regime undertook a thorough restructuring of grassroots organizations, thereby obliterating the specters of overblown grassroots political clout and exorbitant administrative expenditure. Drawing inspiration from the unfolding metamorphosis in Wanshou Township, we encounter a revamped landscape characterized by a refined organizational edifice and a recalibrated workforce. The political mantle is now worn by a solitary township mayor and a deputy, accompanied by a People's Government Committee comprising nine members, excluding the mayor and deputy. This overarching authority begets the establishment of seven committees, including the Production and Construction Committee, the Education, Culture, and Health Committee, the Veterans Affairs Committee, the Armed Forces Committee, the Finance and Grain Committee, the Public Security and Defense Committee, and the Mediation Committee. Each committee finds guidance in the watchful stewardship of a director, invariably drawn from the ranks of the People's Government Committee, while the remaining committee members are culled from the fourteen villages that dot the township. Furthermore, each village boasts a venerable chief

[15] Source: "Resolution of the First People's Representative Congress of Wanshou Township," archived at the Pixian District Archives, Sichuan Province, Archive No. 152-001-0001-001, Pages 1–6.

and a deputy chief of the People's Representative Congress, with the additional caveat that the chief of each village assumes the mantle of a group leader to guide their constituents. This parsimonious distribution of authority serves to manifest the palpable transformation that has swept through Wanshou Township's grassroots governance, as administrative functionaries shoulder a medley of roles, culminating in a lean contingent of 11 township-level personnel and 28 village-level personnel.

In the intricate dance of intertwining changes between economic foundations and the lofty structures above, 1953 marked the commencement of our nation's pursuit of socialist transformation. A resolute push toward agricultural cooperativization took center stage in the agrarian realm. It was within this crucible that the Central Committee of the Communist Party of China unveiled an audacious vision: to swiftly uplift impoverished farmers and guide them onto the path of abundance, where sustenance and clothing would be plentiful. This ambitious endeavor, aimed at procuring a surplus of essential commodities, including grain and industrial raw materials, was equally focused on bolstering the purchasing power of the agrarian masses, thus providing a fertile market for our nation's industrial prowess. The key, they proclaimed, was organization—mobilizing the collective strength of the people.[16]

Thus, the wheels of progress were set in motion, propelling the growth of agricultural mutual aid cooperation throughout the vast expanse of our land. Semi-socialist in nature, primary agricultural production cooperatives sprouted like seeds in every nook and cranny, heralding a new era. Yet, it is worth noting that synchronized with the organization of farmers, a system of unified procurement and distribution of grain emerged, laying bare its origins in the solemn deliberations of the National Emergency Grain Conference in October 1953. A striking metaphor, Chen Yun (陈云) likened himself to a bearer of explosive burdens: "Before me, a trove of 'black explosives,' and behind, 'yellow explosives.' Devoid of grain, the market would tremor; however, requisitioning carried its own perils, for it might provoke the very farmers we sought to empower. A precarious crossroads, indeed."[17]

[16] Institute of Contemporary China. Chronicle of the People's Republic of China: Volume 1953 [M]. Beijing: Contemporary China Press, 2009.

[17] Chen Yun. Selected Works of Chen Yun[M]. Beijing: People's Publishing House, 1995.

In the fledgling liberated regions, where the mutual aid movement still clung to frailty, the party recognized the need for an initial form of cooperation that would find resonance among the agrarian masses—a temporary, seasonal, and unassuming alliance of labor. Thus, in the sleepy embrace of Chongning County's Wanshou Township, Tang Sixue, an esteemed model of agricultural labor, a torchbearer for the people, rallied seven farmers to establish an unwavering bond of mutual support. Answering the clarion call of the party, they forged an enduring partnership, laying the foundation for Chongning County's inaugural agricultural production cooperative in the winter of 1953. Thirty-two households strong, it would serve as an emblem of progress and a beacon of hope.

In the annals of time, Jifeng Village of Chongning County stood tall as a vanguard, spearheading the charge toward collective prosperity. In 1952, it bore witness to the birth of Chongning County's first production mutual aid group, an offspring that would ultimately mature into the primary and advanced agricultural production cooperatives. As the gentle whispers of spring caressed the land in 1954, the stalwart Chongning County Committee of the CPC breathed life into the Xianfeng Agricultural Production Cooperative of Wanshou Township, the **Jinxing Agricultural Production Cooperative of Lingsheng Township(**灵圣乡金星农业生产合作社**)**—its reach extending to Zhanqi Village—and the resplendent Huohua Agricultural Production Cooperative. Like tender shoots, these three cooperatives emerged, united by the common thread of progress. With 73 households strong and 664 mu of fertile land, they stood in humble infancy, eager to blossom.

And so, with the arrival of spring in 1956, Chongning County, fortified by the nurturing soil of progress, witnessed the dawn of three advanced agricultural production cooperatives, signaling a promising new chapter in the chronicles of collective endeavor.

Although the advanced cooperatives were successfully established, the plans implemented during that period bore evident marks of top-down state determination, leaving grassroots cadres and farmers uncertain about the concept of collectivization. Consequently, work and production encountered various predicaments. Take the Lingsheng Township Party branch, for instance, which exhibited an oscillating stance regarding leadership in collectivization. Party member Yu Yuewei, affiliated with the second Party branch, remarked, "Initially, they feared excessive membership intake; however, later on, they sought to eradicate landlords, wealthy peasants, and counterrevolutionaries at once. Thus, they blindly admitted a portion of members into the cooperative and incorporated a primary cooperative into the advanced one, only to persuade them to depart a few days later." As some Party branch secretaries transitioned to advanced cooperatives, complacency and unwarranted optimism took hold, breeding numerous complications and resulting in losses in both production and labor.[18] According to statistical data on rice production in Chongning County for the year 1956, a decline was noticeable when comparing rice yield per unit and overall output to those of 1955. Table 2 displays the scenario in Lingsheng Township and Wanshou Township, the pioneers in establishing advanced cooperatives.

The vacillating thoughts among cadres and members represent a customary occurrence during the process of socialist collectivization exploration, especially in newly liberated regions devoid of organizational experience. Analysis of Table 2 reveals a decrease in rice production across all townships in Chongning County subsequent to the establishment of advanced cooperatives in 1956. In the Xianfeng Advanced Cooperative of Wanshou Township, the rice planting area encompassed 4394.8 mu, approximately 24.8% of the township's total rice planting area. The yield per unit stood at 464 catties, trailing behind the township's average by 51 catties. Not only did the Xianfeng Advanced Cooperative face challenges

Table 2 Statistical overview of rice production in Lingsheng Township and Wanshou Township, Chongning County, 1955–1956, Measurement: mu, catties (1 catty = 0.5 kilograms)

Township	*Area in 1955*	*Per Mu production in 1955*	*Total production in 1955*	*Area in 1956*	*Per Mu production in 1956*	*Total production in 1956*	*Change in average production in 1956*
Lingsheng	13,508	508.62	6870.439	13,480	500	6,740,000	− 8.62
Wanshou	17,581	526.67	9259.385	17,705	515	9,118,075	− 11.67

Source: "Statistical Table of Rice Production in Chongning County, 1956" (January 21, 1957). Archives of Pixian District, Chengdu, Sichuan Province, File No. 152-001-0005-026, Page 142
Note: The original figure for total production in 1955 appears to be erroneous, as it does not result from multiplying the area by the yield per unit. Therefore, the numbers presented in this table have been rectified

18 "Work Summary of the Lingsheng Party General Branch Member Congress" (May 19, 1956), Archives of Pixian District, Chengdu, Sichuan Province, File No. 152-001-0004-001, Page 3.

in agricultural production, but it also incurred a deficit of 908.85 yuan in pig farming. A substantial sum of 5957.9 yuan was expended solely on piglet acquisition, surpassing the income generated from selling fat pigs, which amounted to 4,102.22 yuan.[19] The loss in the sideline business, to some extent, serves as an indicator of issues within the unified management of advanced cooperatives. The integration of pig farming and other auxiliary enterprises, which were originally the purview of individual households, not only led to escalated costs for piglets and feed but also witnessed a heightened mortality rate among pigs. Naturally, this setback stands in stark contrast to the pig farming experience of the Zhanqi Brigade in the late 1960s and early 1970s, where mother pigs were predominantly collectively cared for, while pigs were privately entrusted to the members. Retaining the control of piglets within the collective proved instrumental in achieving success in pig farming.

During that time, crop yields fell short of expectations, and secondary industries suffered substantial losses. It is evident that the organization and development of collective economy require a protracted summation of diverse experiences and lessons. The Chengdu Plain region still faces an arduous journey ahead.

In 1956, despite the completion of socialism's "Three Major Transformations (三大改造, Socialist transformation of the ownership of the means of production)," farmers remained somewhat resistant to the cooperative movement. The first half of 1957 witnessed farmer unrest and pleas for redress, fueled by grain shortages in certain regions. Leaders grasped the pressing need for farmer education. In August 1957, the Central Committee of the Communist Party of China issued the "Directive on a Widespread Socialist Education Campaign Among Rural Populations (《关于向全体农村人口进行一次较大规模社会主义教育的指示》)," extolling the virtues of cooperatives and the imperativeness of centralized grain procurement and distribution. The Central Committee urged education to unfold through "exploiting gaps in production and leisure time, engaging the entire rural population in spirited debates, raising inquiries, presenting opinions, marshaling evidence, reasoning, reflecting,

[19] "Archives of Pixian District, Chengdu: Pioneer Township File," File No. 152-001-0005-012, Pages 85–90.

and contrasting the changes in farmers' lives before and after liberation and the advent of cooperatives."[20]

In adherence to the Pixian County Committee's plan for socialist propaganda and educational undertakings in rural areas, the Xianfeng Advanced Production Cooperative, ensconced in Wanshou Township, orchestrated a resounding "speak out and let go" campaign in 1957, enlisting the participation of party members and the masses. Almost all of the township's 129 party members wholeheartedly threw themselves into this endeavor. Following an intense 38-day propaganda period, the majority of party members in Wanshou Township underwent profound ideological and class education, cementing their unwavering faith in cooperatives and socialism. In this very event, cooperative members and the general populace received their own share of enlightenment.

As comprehension deepened among cadres and the populace regarding cooperatives and socialism, the Xianfeng Advanced Production Cooperative achieved a more favorable income in 1957 than in 1956, experiencing an overall income surge of 11.4%. The total grain production for the year reached a staggering 3,007,878 catties, with an average household income of 370.7 yuan. Each individual, as depicted in Table 3, received an average allocation of 531 catties of grain.

Through socialist propaganda and education, the cooperative cadre and members saw a certain improvement in their labor enthusiasm. The grain production also gradually bounced back. However, the mismanagement in the senior cooperative posed a problem, leading to an increase in agricultural production costs. Looking at Tables 1, 2, 3, it's evident that the agricultural expenses of the Xianfeng Advanced Cooperative witnessed a yearly surge. Taking 1957 as an example, agricultural expenses reached 72,322.02 yuan, roughly 25.9% of the total income. The primary factors behind this surge were excessive use of commercial fertilizers and increased investment in pig manure by the members. Commercial fertilizer expenses amounted to approximately 38,729.12 yuan, whereas the members' investment in pig manure stood at 29,468.49 yuan. In 1958, agricultural expenses continued to rise, with a total fertilizer input of 69,254.26 yuan, and the members' investment in pig manure soaring to 39,940.46 yuan.

[20] Contemporary China Research Institute. Chronology of the People's Republic of China: Volume for 1957. Beijing: Contemporary China Publishing House, 2011.

Table 3 Xianfeng advanced production cooperative's summary of agricultural and subsidiary industry production from 1956 to 1958

Year	*Rice area (mu)*	*Rice yield (jin)*	*Wheat area (mu)*	*Wheat yield (jin*	*Total grain output (jin)*	*Total grain output value (yuan)*	*Total output value of sideline business (yuan)*	*Agricultural expenditure (yuan)*
1956	4394.81	464	470.03	357	Non calculated	247,523.47	1389.61	58,686.91
1957	4349.32	527	681.48	386	3,007,878	279,315.46	Loss, non calculated	72,322.02
1958	3933.63	1002	551.26	423	4,588,527	340,894.01	– 3173.36	91,067.87

Data sources: "1956 Annual Summary Report of the Xianfeng Advanced Production Cooperative" (December 1, 1956), File No. 152-001-0005-012, pages 85–90; "1957 Annual Summary Report of the Xianfeng Agricultural Cooperative" (December 25, 1957), File No. 152-001-0007-015, pages 80–90; "1958 Annual Summary Report of the Xianfeng Cooperative" (May 1, 1959), File No. 152-001-0008-001, pages 1–6.
Note: The absence of unified conversion standards resulted in the exclusion of total production figures for 1956, owing to the need for calculations involving crops like sweet potatoes. Additionally, due to factors such as the "Great Leap Forward," statistical data for 1958 lacks meaningful reference and shall not be further expounded upon.

From the preceding discourse, it becomes clear that, until 1958, the agricultural cooperative movement in the region was in its embryonic stage. While it did address some issues such as scattered labor, inadequate tools, and low productivity to a certain extent, the management of agricultural and sideline industries remained at a rudimentary level, resulting in losses in the latter and exorbitant agricultural production costs. Moreover, cooperative cadre and farmers exhibited a strong inclination toward petty opportunism, with a greater focus on personal enrichment. During the land reform period, many cadres hailing from impoverished farming backgrounds became the so-called "new middle peasants," rendering them less reliable for the subsequent reforms. As Fei Zhengqing aptly described, "During the land reform, work teams sought out young men (and perhaps a few women) who were rash and audacious and came from humble peasant backgrounds, positioning them at the forefront of the struggle against the old ruling class. These individuals were later absorbed into the Chinese Communist Party, forming the leading force that supported local peasant associations." However, as the Party's objectives changed, and policies shifted toward emphasizing mutual assistance and cooperativization, the heterogeneous amalgamation of local leaders, who had ascended to power during the initial stages of the movement, proved to be a hindrance in implementing these novel policies.[21]

In the Chengdu Plain region, the cooperative movement continued its ebb and flow, marked by cycles of acceptance, resistance, and educational efforts among the cadre and the masses. However, from 1958 to 1960, as the Soviet Union withdrew its investments from China, the nation experienced the initial throes of cyclic economic crises during the industrialization process outlined in the "Great Leap Forward" plan. To sustain industrialization, the Party Central Committee put forth the call for "mobilizing two positives" in early 1958, aiming to rally local finances and ensure the continuance of a national economy predominantly centered around heavy industry. Consequently, local authorities were urged to embark on large-scale development of "five small industries."

[21] R. MacFarquhar, Roderick & Fairbank, John King. The Cambridge History of China, Volume 14: The People's Republic, Part 1: The Emergence of Revolutionary China, 1949–1965. Beijing: China Social Sciences Publishing House, 1990.

Yet, due to mechanical and expedited efforts to drive local industrialization, these initiatives gradually devolved into what modern eyes perceive as the borderline absurdity of the "Great Leap Forward" campaigns.[22]

With foreign capital abruptly severed, the ongoing projects required swift acceleration in construction, and some even demanded premature initiation. The pursuit of industrialization now relied solely on internal resources—mobilizing labor to substitute for capital and extracting surplus grain from rural areas. It was under the dire circumstances of this economic crisis and the scarcely credible backdrop of the "Great Leap Forward" that the People's Communes emerged, as both a response to the crisis and a means to persist with the industrialization process.

4 Collective Economy and the Movement of Socialist Education

In the wake of the People's Commune Movement, Pixian County found itself enmeshed in a fervent atmosphere of competition—a climate seemingly influenced by Chairman Mao Zedong's visit to the Hongguang Agricultural Production Cooperative. On the afternoon of March 16, 1958, Chairman Mao stepped into the realm of the cooperative, delving deep into the homes of its members. He probed into their livelihoods, their pig-rearing ventures, and engaged them in familiar banter. The arrival of the nation's paramount leader to this humble agrarian hamlet in the Western reaches of our land left an indelible impression on the local peasantry, hitherto unacquainted with such lofty dignitaries. It ignited an incandescent zeal among the cadre and the masses, fueling their fervor for socialist advancement.

In September of the same year, both Lingsheng and Wanshou townships within Chongning County birthed their own People's Communes. But come November 11, 1958, Chongning County was expunged and merged into Pixian County, precipitating the consolidation of Wanshou and Lingsheng. From this fusion, the Xianfeng Commune of Pixian County emerged. Henceforth, the territory where the battle flag resided remained an integral part of the illustrious Jinxing Brigade, an arm of the Xianfeng People's Commune, until their subsequent divergence in 1965.

[22] Wen, Tiejun et al. Eight Crises: China's Real Experiences, 1949–2009. Beijing: Dongfang Publishing House, 2013.

The reconfigured Xianfeng People's Commune boasted a total of 3524 households and a population of 14,517, tilling 27,865.79 mu of fertile soil with an additional 1738 mu of land. It stood as an amalgamation of eight formidable brigades—Xianfeng (Vanguard), Lianhe (Union), Xianjin (Advanced), Shuguang (Dawn), Huohua (Spark), Jinxing (Gold Star), Liming (Dawn), and Mingfeng (Phoenix). Notably, the Xianfeng Brigade and the Jinxing Brigade were born directly from the illustrious Xianfeng Advanced Commune and the Jinxing Advanced Commune, respectively. However, the dawn of the Xianfeng People's Commune witnessed a meager collective-owned machinery fleet consisting of a mere eleven tractors and three seeders. Machines such as transplanters, harvesters, and land-leveling bulldozers were conspicuous by their absence, necessitating a torrent of manual labor to compensate for the dearth of capital. In a bid to level the ground and enhance productivity, the Xianfeng People's Commune established a Land Leveling Committee, envisioning a transformation of "lofty land made even, shallow fields raised high," while diligently pursuing the goal of agricultural homogeneity.[23] To further galvanize agricultural yield and bolster industrial construction, it was imperative for the Central Committee of the Communist Party to persist with the pursuit of the People's Commune system.

The Central Committee of the Communist Party of China (CPC) issued the "Resolution on Establishing People's Communes in Rural Areas" simultaneously with the "Directive on Launching a Comprehensive Education Movement on Socialism and Communism in Rural Areas during this Winter and Next Spring (《关于今冬明春在农村中普遍展开社会主义和共产主义教育运动的指示》)." The directive acknowledged the growing political awareness among farmers, forged through nationwide rectification efforts, the struggle against Rightist elements, socialist education movements in rural areas, and propaganda campaigns promoting the general party line. It noted a significant decline in individualistic inclinations focused solely on personal gains or parochial concerns at the team, commune, village, or county level. Nonetheless, to timely assess lessons learned and foster the spirit of communism, debates arose concerning the allocation of income within agricultural cooperatives and

[23] "Planning for Comprehensive Mechanization in the Xianfeng Commune in 1960" (November 26, 1959), Chengdu Pixian District Archives, "Pixian Vanguard Township Files," File No. 152-001-0012-004, pp. 34–36.

the establishment of people's communes, with the consensus deeming a **"widespread education movement on socialism and communism in rural areas during this winter and next spring as necessary." The directive further called for showcasing numerous instances of remarkable production growth, effectively underscoring the superiority of the socialist system, and fortifying the determination and confidence of the majority of farmers to tread the socialist path, while critically dissecting the lingering capitalist tendencies of a few affluent farmers.**[24]

Doubts regarding the system of people's communes swayed certain cadres and collective economy members, revealing the dual nature ingrained within farmers amidst the collective economy's evolution. The aftermath of setbacks, including a decline in grain production amid the grand strides of the Great Leap Forward, only served to further destabilize the wavering faith in socialism, particularly among well-to-do peasants.

In November 1959, Xianfeng Commune launched a socialist education movement to counter the hesitation and skepticism permeating some individuals, particularly those who cast blame upon the commune's missteps and advocated the partitioning of land. Likewise, a handful of party members and cadres, lacking zeal, suffering from waning resolve, and plagued by a sense of lost prospects, demanded special attention.

Beyond the tepid enthusiasm exhibited by cadres and members concerning the collective economy's advancement, the prevalence of localism within Xianfeng Commune cast a heavy shadow. Localist tendencies, inevitably, tarnished the broader national industrialization endeavor. Its symptoms manifested in three primary domains: firstly, hierarchical management dilemmas arose, as select production brigades shunned the jurisdiction of management areas, thereby impeding effective economic governance. Conversely, a few management areas refused to recognize the authority of the commune, effectively hampering industrial grain allocation—an ailment that encompassed the Jingxing Management Area. "The original Lingsheng management areas were supposed to provide 913,000 jin of grain, but in actuality, only 422,500 jin were delivered. When the cadres from the Jingxing Management Area collected grain on behalf of the commune, they unabashedly declared, 'None remains.'" Secondly,

[24] Central Archives, CPC Central Committee Literature Research Office. Selected Works of CPC Central Committee Documents: June 1949–May 1966 [M]. Beijing: People's Publishing House, 2013.

corruption and embezzlement charges emerged, with the concealing of cultivated land and production, and clandestine distribution of grain funds becoming all too commonplace. Statistically, production brigades and individuals clandestinely withheld and divided 320,000 jin of grain. Thirdly, covert alliances materialized between select production brigades and management areas, fostering an atmosphere of mutual support.[25]

After debating and criticizing the aforementioned issues, most cadres and masses have gained a heightened understanding of collectivism. This movement sparked an unprecedented surge of productivity throughout the entire society during that winter. Community cadres rallied the members, particularly focusing on the movement centered around managing small spring fields and manufacturing fertilizers Over a hundred members united to mend every inch of the 1,733 mu of wheat. Regardless of gender, they would venture before dawn to distant places, hauling manure water. Initially aimed at fostering collective and socialist ideology, superseding the personal interests of small farmers, the socialist education movements also unveiled certain quandaries among the cadres, especially those grassroots officials who emerged from grain requisition and land reform since liberation. Following more than a decade of progress, a few cadres with wavering convictions and blemishes gradually emerged, hindering the growth of the collective economy. Song Wenbin, Secretary of the Wenjiang District Committee, asserted during the 1961 County Secretaries Conference that opportunistic activities pervaded the actions of rural grassroots officials, with some regions witnessing severe repercussions. To address this predicament and preempt rural upheaval, Song Wenbin advocated for every county to select a commune for scrutiny and study, identifying a quintessential case for criticism within the rectification movement.

Evidently, in the early 1960s, issues with local cadres were ubiquitous, necessitating a cautious approach by the central government, provinces, and district committees, mindful of their methods and influence. As Fei Zhengqing astutely acknowledged, "Regardless of the circumstances, after 1962, the moral quandary surrounding local cadres became the crux for the Communist Party of China... The efficacy of exemplary indigenous

[25] Report on the Summary of the Socialist Education Movement by the Xianfeng Commune Committee of the Communist Party of China (January 1960), Archives of Pixian District, Sichuan Province, "Xianfeng Township File," Archive No. 152-001-0011-001, pp. 1–9.

leadership remains indispensable for the triumph of collective agriculture."[26] Undoubtedly, the significance of adept local leadership permeates the forthcoming case studies, elucidating how an unwavering cadre deftly guided the brigade toward the triumphant development of the collective economy.

Subsequently, the Socialist Education Movement ("四清"运动, also called the "Four Cleanups" campaign) emerged, chiefly aimed at rectifying the erroneous practices of rural cadres in the realms of economy, politics, ideology, and management. In May 1963, Mao Zedong summoned a select assembly of Political Bureau members and regional secretaries in Hangzhou to deliberate on socialist education in rural areas. Following the discussions, they formulated the "Decision of the Central Committee of the Communist Party of China on Several Issues in Current Rural Work (Draft)" (《中共中央关于目前农村工作中若干问题的决定(草案)》, commonly known as the "First Ten Articles 前十条"), emphasizing the necessity for widespread socialist education in rural regions and mandating all communities to partake in the "Four Cleanups" campaign—comprising an audit of accounts, clearing of storehouses, financial rectification, and equitable redistribution of work points. Consequently, the focus of the socialist education movement gradually shifted toward the "Four Cleanups" endeavor.

As the socialist education movement swept through, cleansing the minds of both cadres and members, the people's commune system underwent constant adjustments and developments amidst its share of setbacks. It all began in 1961 when the Central Guangzhou Work Conference, in a decisive move, adopted the "Regulations on People's Commune Work in Rural Areas (Draft) (《农村人民公社工作条例(草案)》)"—commonly known as the "Sixty Articles on Agriculture." This marked the gradual reform of the system of large communes into a more streamlined and grassroots-oriented model known as the small commune system, where "three-level ownership, with the production team as its foundation," took precedence.

Fast forward to September 1962, at the 10th Plenary Session of the 8th Central Committee of the Communist Party of China, the third iteration of the "Sixty Articles on Agriculture" was passed. The major reform came in the form of designating the production team as the

[26] Roderick MacFarquhar, Michael Schoenhals. Mao's Last Revolution. Cambridge: Harvard University Press, 2006.

fundamental accounting unit for agricultural production—an important decision accompanied by a solemn proclamation of "no change for at least thirty years." These measures effectively bolstered stability within rural society and facilitated the recovery and growth of agricultural production.

Prior to the commencement of the "Four Cleanup" campaign, the Xianfeng Commune boasted a classification of brigades that encompassed the entire county, the entire commune, and even the sprawling Wenjiang Regional Committee. These were brigades known for their formidable mobilization capabilities and commendable strides in development. On the flip side, the Jinxing Brigade, where the Zhanqi Brigade found its footing, seemed to progress at a more ordinary pace. During that period, the Jinxing Brigade (initially referred to as the "Jinxing Management Area") failed to capture the spotlight and to add to their misfortune, they had to borrow a sum of 2000 yuan from the Xianfeng Brigade in 1963.

Following the tumultuous years of the "Great Leap Forward," the Wenjiang Regional Committee found itself grappling with a critical question: should they advocate for the system of responsibility for overall output or persist with the brigade accounting approach? Local leaders found themselves bereft of certainty regarding the future trajectory of the rural collective economy, leaving the Secretary of the Regional Committee with no choice but to glean insights from practical case studies. Consequently, the Xianfeng Brigade emerged as a prime example, acting as a starting point to delve into the collective economic development journey it had embarked upon and the intricate repercussions inflicted upon it by the "Four Cleanup" campaign. Notably, the Xianfeng Brigade had been under the astute guidance of Tang Sixue (唐思学), a cadre hailing from humble peasant origins, since the dawn of liberation.

* * *

Tang Sixue's Personal Journey

Tang Sixue, born on December 12, 1924, was a man of the Xianfeng Brigade in Pixian County. Even at the tender age of seven or eight, he toiled beside his father, hauling carts and bearing the burdens of labor. By thirteen, he had become a hired hand for the landlords, a role he fulfilled until the dawn of liberation. In 1950, he embarked on his professional path, assuming various roles, including Village Armed Committee Member, Armed Squad Leader, Township

Production Committee Member, Deputy Township Chief, Deputy Secretary of the Township Party Branch, Mutual Aid Group Leader, Junior Cooperative Society Leader, and Senior Cooperative Society Director. The year 1952 marked his induction into the Communist Party. From January 1953 to February 1955, he served as Deputy Township Chief of Wanshou Township (later known as Xianfeng Township). From February 1956 to February 1983, he dedicated himself to the post of Secretary of the Party Branch for Xianfeng Village (Brigade) in Xianfeng Township (Commune).

Following the Spring Farming Production Mobilization Conference in 1952, Tang Sixue rallied eight households comprising thirty-nine individuals. Guided by the principles of voluntary participation, mutual benefit, and equitable exchange, he forged the earliest mutual aid group in Pixian County—a testament to his foresight and tenacity. The Tang Sixue Mutual Aid Group breathed life into the dormant spirits of its members, sowing fifty-five mu of rice fields with unwavering zeal. Astonishingly, the average yield per mu soared to six hundred and ten jin, representing a remarkable twenty-seven percent increase compared to the pre-mutual aid era. Notably, one particular plot spanning 1.04 mu yielded an impressive one thousand and forty jin of moist millet, defying expectations.

As the mutual aid group flourished, the Xianfeng Brigade, in turn, spearheaded the establishment of the Junior Cooperative Society and the Senior Cooperative Society—laying the foundation for the Xianfeng Society. On the first day of the year in 1954, the Tang Sixue Mutual Aid Group joined forces with thirty-two households from neighboring groups to create the pioneering semi-socialist entity in the former Chongning County—the Tang Sixue Junior Agricultural Production Cooperative (later rechristened as the Xianfeng Junior Agricultural Cooperative Society). By the end of that same year, the cooperative had expanded its membership to include seventy-two households. By the spring of 1956, seven junior cooperatives and a staggering five hundred and fifty-five households merged to form the all-encompassing socialist venture—the Xianfeng Senior Agricultural Production Cooperative. As the sagacious Secretary of the Party Branch for Xianfeng Brigade, Tang Sixue attended the esteemed Beijing Advanced Producers' Work Conference—an epochal gathering hailed as the "Gathering of Outstanding Talents" during that transformative era.

In the annals of 1963, within the confines of "Exemplary Materials of Comrade Tang Sixue, Secretary of the Xianfeng Brigade of Puxian Commune (《郫县先锋公社先锋大队书记唐思学同志的模范材料》)," a chronicle unfolds with poignant narratives.

Comrade Tang Sixue, a steadfast adherent of the Party's tenets, governed his deeds with unwavering fidelity to its policies. Uttering sagely, he professed that the Party's policies, a bastion of the people's welfare, held steadfast truth. Obeying the Party's counsel would never falter; aligning actions with its policies guaranteed triumph. Such was his modus operandi in the realm of daily production.

In the chill of the winter of 1962, when charting the course for early spring's endeavors, the commune bestowed upon the brigade a directive of 605 mu, a stretch of land measuring 40.3 hectares, for cultivating rapeseed—a notable augmentation of 117 mu from the preceding year. Dissonance in ruminations plagued certain cadres and commune members, suggesting that sowing rapeseed would usurp fertile green expanses, exacerbating the dearth of sustenance for porcine denizens. The grain enthusiasts asserted that grains reigned supreme, relegating rapeseed to future cultivation. Immersed in these conversations, Comrade Tang Sixue and a coterie of committee members embarked on introspective deliberations. An inquiry surfaced: Did the expansion of rapeseed cultivation signify veracity, or did it instead reflect the lingering bias toward "grains over oil" among the masses? Scrutinizing the expanse allocated to various crops, the latter seemed more pervasive than the former.

Ergo, Comrade Tang Sixue, his oratory prowess astir, elucidated to comrades and constituents the benefits of faithfully executing the rapeseed planting mandate, a tenet intertwined with the nation's prosperity and the populace's well-being. Furthermore, he shepherded the production team toward a plan of action, one hinged upon the spirit of harmonious equilibrium and comprehensive arrangements. Dialogues with seasoned agriculturists and cadre members followed suit. In the patch earmarked for tobacco, over 70 mu, an expanse approximating 4.7 hectares, burgeoned with the sprightly saplings of soybeans—a resolute resolution to the predicament of scarce pig feed. By adhering resolutely to the Party's policy prescriptions, Comrade Tang Sixue not only achieved the onerous task of cultivating 605 mu of rapeseed but also transcended the exigencies of local sentiments, deftly unraveling the conundrums that confounded both ideologues and practitioners. Satisfaction, an ardent companion, graced the cadres and the populace alike.

In the labyrinthine web of policy implementation, Comrade Tang Sixue bestowed upon the masses an incomparable gift—patience in unraveling the intricate tapestry of Party policies. In the vernal bloom of 1962, when the commune disseminated the reverberations of the Central Committee of the Communist Party of China, decreeing the transformation of the fundamental accounting unit of the rural people's commune, most cadres, steeped in satisfaction with the Xianfeng Brigade's years of industriousness and its commendable economic foundations, questioned the imperative to reconfigure the bedrock of accounting—preferring to eschew the production team's ascent to primacy. To dispel these reservations, Tang Sixue, true to form, imparted a verbatim elucidation of the Party's precepts to the cadre corps and commoners, fostering an environment of profound deliberation concerning the bounties of the production team as the nucleus of accounting. As the discourse deepened, the policy infiltrated the recesses of hearts, affirming the sagacity of those fixated on the brigade's accounting as a paragon of success, yet oblivious to the schism between production and allocation—an impediment that blunted the ardor of the production team. This newfound cognizance, catalyzed by the delegation of accounting units, surged through the masses, resuscitating their entrepreneurial zeal.

Comrade Tang Sixue, a man of action, eschewed verbosity in favor of unwritten volumes of sagacity.

Two years ago, in 1961, there unfolded a tale. On a certain occasion, a member of the collective approached Tang Sixue, addressing him as "Secretary Tang," with a profound suggestion. Tang Sixue responded with a smile, "Well, go ahead and spill it out." The member expressed his concern, "You know, during the day, your family contributes little in terms of manure. Your father, most of the time, focuses on his own plot, and the folks aren't too pleased about it." That evening, Tang Sixue summoned his family for a meeting, where he addressed his father, "As a family of cadres, our every word and action carries immense weight upon the masses. If we fail to lead by example in executing policies, how can we expect to educate the people?" It was during this family gathering that they established plans for labor and manure contribution, and Tang's father enthusiastically partook in collective labor.

During that same time, a destitute member of the community named Zhou Chuandao succumbed to a grave illness. Neglected and without anyone to attend to his medication or thirst, Comrade Tang Sixue, upon discovering the severity of Zhou Chuandao's condition, promptly arranged for a fellow member to transport him to the city for hospitalization. Eventually, Zhou Chuandao's affliction yielded to the curative powers of medicine. Grateful for his recovery, Zhou Chuandao frequently remarked to others, "In that critical moment, I teetered on the precipice of demise. I owe my life to Comrade Tang; otherwise, my bones would have surrendered long before." This incident sparked an unwavering fervor within Zhou Chuandao, propelling him toward an active role in all endeavors.

As the calendar turned to early 1962, misfortune befell the households of the third and seventh teams, their abodes and furnishings consumed by the flames of fire. In a demonstration of compassion, Tang Sixue not only personally extended his condolences but also engaged in consultations with cadres and the masses. He rallied more than ten skilled carpenters and craftsmen, mobilizing their talents to aid in the reconstruction of houses, restoration of stoves, and the prioritized supply of essential farming implements. The timely assistance offered respite to those burdened by adversity. Even Zhang Yuru, a once-indifferent affluent farmer whose dwelling succumbed to the inferno, found himself moved by the ordeal, declaring, "The Party, the collective, they are indeed a bastion of virtue. For who else would attend to my needs? We must, henceforth, strive to cultivate an environment of collective productivity, a testament to our gratitude for the Party's and the cadres' unwavering care." Under Tang Sixue's influential guidance, his fellow cadres, too, manifested an ardent concern for the well-being of the masses.

Approximations suggest that, in 1962, the entire brigade extended assistance to 186 struggling households. Aided by an allocation of 8560 kilograms of grain and a sum of 3497 yuan in cash, these compassionate efforts resulted in the construction of 1543 dwellings, 32 pigsties, the provision of 326 small agricultural implements, and 227 essential household items. As a result, the masses burgeoned with an intensified affection toward the Party and its devoted cadres. The symbiotic relationship between the Party and the masses, as well as that between the cadres and the masses, thrived harmoniously. On a singular occasion, when Tang Sixue succumbed to illness, the people willingly assumed the mantle of responsibility, promptly seeking medical expertise and acquiring the necessary medications on his behalf.

During the early days of the primary cooperative, Tang Sixue, displaying an unwavering commitment, unfailingly carried provisions on his person when venturing beyond their locale to procure supplies for the collective. Hunger was staved off with these carefully packed rations, and thirst was quelled with a few sips of fortified tea, diligently imbibed during work hours. Never lingering in a hotel, even when dusk descended, he tirelessly pressed onward, ensuring a swift return, thus economizing expenses for the collective's benefit. In 1959, while attending the "Gathering of Heroes" in Beijing, the brigade's travel funds, save for essential transportation costs, were judiciously allocated toward procuring agricultural pesticides and literature on advanced farming techniques, vital resources essential for the communal pursuit of agricultural productivity.

In '63, the tide of socialist education swept across the land, known as the "Four Cleanup" campaign. It entailed an exhaustive process of "clearing accounts, clearing warehouses, clearing finances, and clearing work points." However, just as the echoes of the "Four Cleanup" lingered in the air, a new movement emerged in July '64—the "Four Clearup." This time, its focus shifted toward "clearing politics, clearing the economy, clearing organizations, and clearing thoughts." The "Four Clearup" task force swiftly descended upon the Xianfeng Commune, intertwining with the minority masses, orchestrating covert unveilings that struck hard against countless grassroots cadres. As winter of '64 arrived, the "Four Clears" task force relegated Tang Sixue to the sidelines.

On May 27, '65, an appraisal of Tang Sixue, the Party Branch Secretary of the Xianfeng Brigade, materialized, showcasing his undeniable merits. The document hailed the following virtues within Tang's realm:

(1). Unyielding devotion to the socialist path, perpetually locked in battle against the perversions of the era.
(2). An exemplary steward of productivity.
(3). A guiding light amidst toil.
(4). Enduring austerity, selflessly committed.
(5). An empathetic soul, nurturing the welfare of the masses.

Tang Sixue once confided, "I shun teahouses, I shun taverns, I shun all gourmand retreats. A legend echoes within our commune, a moniker earned by my steadfastness—'Three Unentered,' they call me. A rustic soul, I embody the 'Two Unwanted': shunning travel allowances and abstaining from the scarce luxuries bestowed upon our brigade's cadres."

Come late January '65, the Central Committee disseminated a missive titled "Some Pertinent Queries Amidst the Rural Socialist

Education Movement (《农村社会主义教育运动中目前提出的一些问题》)," rectifying the zealous excesses witnessed within the "Four Clearup" campaign. Thus, the comrades who had borne the brunt of the crack-down were duly reinstated to their erstwhile positions within the Xianfeng Brigade.

June 3, '65 marked the birth of the Council for the Impoverished and Lower-Middle Peasantry in Pixian County. Simultaneously, the brigade established the "Committee for the Impoverished and Lower-Middle Peasantry," an assembly composed of 7–9 members, entrusted with one chairman and one vice-chairman.

Then, in the waning days of '65, a fervor for agricultural revolution swept across Pixian County. Embracing the "three ones" doctrine—merely a clock, a whistle, and an attendance ledger—this endeavor forged the bedrock of agrarian advancement.

On May 16, '66, the Political Bureau of the Central Committee, assembled in a moment of grandeur, sanctioned the proclamation that would forever be etched in history—the "Notice of the Central Committee of the Communist Party of China (《中国共产党中央委员会通知》)" (affectionately dubbed the 516 Notice). Within the Xianfeng Commune, a vanguard of the "Cultural Revolution" took shape, categorizing unit cadres, and galvanizing employees to employ the arsenal of "resounding declarations, resplendent posters, and vigorous debates" to unearth the insidious "counterrevolutionary revisionists" and "anti-Party, anti-socialist elements" that festered within their midst.

In 1966, the Xianfeng Brigade underwent a transformation. Eleven production teams were reshaped into twenty. The original composition shifted: the 1st, 3rd, and 4th teams merged to form the new 1st team, while the 2nd and 19th teams merged to become the new 2nd team. The 5th team inherited the mantle of the original 3rd team, while the 6th team assumed the identity of the former 4th team. The 7th and 20th teams amalgamated into the new 5th team, and the 8th, 9th, and 10th teams merged to form the new 6th team. Likewise, the 11th team became the new 7th team, the 12th team became the new 8th team, the 13th and 14th teams unified to create the new 9th team, and the 15th and 16th teams fused into the new 10th team. Finally, the 17th and 18th teams united to forge the new 11th team.

In the ensuing year of 1967, the clarion call of the "Cultural Revolution" reverberated, thrusting the machinery of party organizations into paralysis. Party members found themselves compelled to halt their activities, and the agricultural domain, in a slow descent, sank into a state of anarchy.

One fine day in January 1967, Tang Sixue ventured forth to Tangchang Town, intent on procuring an official attestation. He had initially planned to embark on a coal-hauling expedition to Pengxian County. Yet, as he traversed the grand arches of Dayun Bridge, his gaze chanced upon a poster scheduled to castigate him the following day. And so, he deftly altered his course, forsaking the coal venture. As the early rays of dawn graced the second day, Tang Sixue stood resolute at the brigade, ready to embrace the forthcoming chastisement. With the denouncement's denouement, Tang Sixue promptly emerged unscathed and unabated, summoning the cadre of each team to remain behind. There, he orchestrated a collective endeavor of enlightenment, emboldening all to seize their roles in the production landscape while reinforcing the paramountcy of rich fertilizer reserves and attentive stewardship of tender spring crops. Whispers emerged in the aftermath, proclaiming, "Tang Sixue, unyielding, dances amidst the blows."

Then, from April 26 through 30 1971, the third Party Congress of Pixian County materialized. Within this solemn occasion, the county committee underwent a reconstitution, heralding the official restoration of the Communist Party of China's (CPC) Pixian County Committee. Consequently, the Xianfeng Brigade witnessed the resurrection of its branch committee, with Tang Sixue bestowed the honor of branch secretary.

Years rolled by, and Tang Sixue remained tethered to the position of village party secretary, steadfast in his duties until the year 1983 when he gracefully embraced a well-earned retreat from the frontline.

Source: Zhao Renchun, edited by Gao Guangjun. "Xianfeng Village Chronicle" (unpublished manuscript).

Rural grassroots cadres are of utmost importance in fostering the development of collective economy. Tang Sixue, hailing from humble peasant origins, matured under the yoke of the old regime and came into his own during the grain requisitioning, land reform, and cooperativization movements that followed the birth of the New China. A staunch advocate of the Communist Party of China, he remained resolute in his commitment to the socialist path, embodying simplicity, selflessness, and unwavering public service. Such virtues propelled the Xianfeng Brigade to the forefront of collective economic advancement even before the inception of the People's Commune. Emerging from the ranks of the Xianfeng Junior Cooperative and subsequently the Xianfeng Senior Cooperative, this brigade evolved to become a symbol of resilience during the rural socialist transformation in Pixian County. In the winter of 1958, as emissaries of their cause, the Secretary and Deputy Secretary of the Xianfeng Brigade attended the pioneering production conference in Beijing and the provincial-level cadre meeting in Chongqing. **It is pertinent to note that Tang Sixue, despite a modest educational background, found himself at the helm of a substantial community comprising over 500 households. Such a position necessitated leaders endowed with formidable administrative prowess, possibly placing the Xianfeng Brigade at a disadvantage compared to its rival, the Zhanqi Brigade, in subsequent battles for supremacy. As the People's Commune advanced into its later stages, the rural landscape witnessed substantial institutional adjustments, accompanied by heightened expectations concerning the managerial acumen of brigade cadres.**

With the advent of the People's Commune system, the Xianfeng Brigade weathered only modest disruptions to its agricultural yield, a testament to the wealth of experience amassed during its tenure as a senior cooperative. By virtue of the "convergence of politics and production" of the People's Commune, the Xianfeng Brigade melded production leadership with administrative oversight, engendering a favorable environment for the coordinated allocation of resources and the unfurling of production. This symbiotic relationship proved pivotal, particularly in the realm of agricultural output, where the transformation of farmland irrigation systems and the fortification of soil fertility reigned supreme. Embracing these imperatives wholeheartedly, the Xianfeng Brigade embarked on ambitious endeavors to bolster its farmland irrigation infrastructure. It mobilized scores of laborers, laboriously repairing and constructing a staggering 250-plus small and large ditches, along with over 130 field ridges—essential conduits for effective water management. By ensuring the ample hydration of their farmland, they paved the way for flourishing agricultural endeavors. Concurrently, diligent hands excavated a drainage channel, breathing new life into more than 400 mu (roughly 26.7 hectares) of underperforming terrain. The Xianfeng Brigade's unyielding commitment to enhancing soil fertility manifested through the extensive mobilization of its members, as they amassed copious amounts of natural fertilizers. Organized efforts diligently traversed the lands of Peng

Table 4 Flourishes of wheat and rice production in the Xianfeng Brigade (1949–1962), Unit: jin

Crop	*1949*	*1956*	*1962*
Wheat	223	357	39,838
Rice	412	464	513

Source: "An Abridged Chronicle of the Xianfeng Brigade's Odyssey within the Xianfeng Commune of Pixian County" (August 1963), Archive Number 152-001-0029-012, pages 109–128

County, Chengdu, and twelve additional towns, gathering an abundance of fertilizer. In 1962 alone, the brigade triumphantly transported back 350,000 jin (175 metric tons) of chicken manure and over 12,000 loads of human excrement, effectively addressing the dearth of chemical fertilizers and galvanizing agricultural productivity—a testament to their unwavering resolve, as beautifully illustrated in Table 4.

In the arduous toil and relentless dedication, the Xianfeng Brigade achieved bountiful harvests in 1962, surpassing the levels of 1956 for major crops like rice and wheat. **The Brigade, resourceful in its rural domain, ventured into diverse subsidiary enterprises. Utilizing the abundance of space, they reared fish and bees, amassing over 30,000 fish and 80 beehives, thus augmenting the collective's supplementary income.** Moreover, the industrious brigade mobilized artisans—the masons, carpenters, tilers, and blacksmiths—to construct new warehouses, diligently renovating more than 170 dwellings for the members. The establishment of a self-sufficient brick and tile factory further fortified the Brigade, providing essential materials for storage and new edifices.

In the realm of pig husbandry, perseverance through trial and error yielded a definitive path: **upholding both collective and private rearing, with sow nurturing remaining a collective endeavor. This strategic approach bolstered the pig population, rendering staunch support to impoverished teams and households, and fostering the expansion of pig farming.** From a modest count of 1506 in 1960, the swine population thrived, reaching a noteworthy 2001 by 1963.

By 1962, the Xianfeng Brigade surpassed the national grain requisition target by a considerable margin—2000 catties. This string of accomplishments propelled the Xianfeng Brigade to be lauded as a crimson standard-bearer, embodying the pinnacle of excellence in Pixian County. The Brigade nurtured 23 national, provincial, and county-level labor exemplars, their commendable feats garnering accolades from the State

Council and regional authorities. A steady stream of over 14,000 officials and brethren from neighboring communes sought inspiration from the Brigade's achievements.

The rice and wheat yields in the Xianfeng Commune revealed a resilient ascent throughout various periods, with exceptions during the advent of advanced cooperatives and the early stages of people's communes. In 1965, the average rice yield reached an impressive 564 catties, while wheat achieved a commendable average of 396 catties per unit. These figures stood unparalleled in the annals of New China's agrarian history, far surpassing national averages, as corroborated by Table 5.

After more than a decade of socialist education and ardent exploration of methods to rally farmers, the Xianfeng Commune's collective economy began to take shape, casting a nascent mold. The indomitable spirits of cadres and members, instilled by protracted periods of spiritual inspiration, propelled them toward new and uplifting horizons, laying a bedrock of unwavering fortitude for future progress.

These movements breathed life into a fresh breed of local luminaries, forging a cohort of ardently altruistic, morally awakened socialist individuals amidst rural expanses. Against this evocative backdrop, a new standard was poised to emerge, poised to pierce the earth's surface with unwavering resolve.

Table 5 Rice and wheat yield per unit in Pixian County Xianfeng Commune and Nationwide from 1949 to 1965, Unit: Catties

Year	Xianfeng rice yield	National rice yield	Xianfeng wheat yield	National wheat yield

Note: □ indicates indiscernible data due to archival limitations

Source: "Basic Information on Pixian County Xianfeng Commune" (August 1964), held at the Pixian District Archives in Sichuan Province, "Files of Pixian County Xianfeng Township," file number 152-001-0033-006, page 26; data from 1964 to 1965 are from "Summary of Agricultural and Secondary Industry Production Increase in Pixian County Xianfeng Commune in 1965," file number 152-001-0038-014, pages 55–61; national data is from the book "Statistical Data of China's Agriculture in 60 Years of New China," published by China Agriculture Press in 2009

CHAPTER 4

Promoting Dazhai's Agricultural Success from the East, Unfurling the Zhanqi in the Western Front (1965–1973)

As the grip of state power extended to rural communities, the ascent and progression of rural cadres underwent rigorous scrutiny from their superiors.

Within this realm, amidst trials and tribulations, the nation nurtured a cohort of youthful, zealous individuals hailing from humble backgrounds, infusing fresh vitality into the Party. In June 1964, Mao Zedong articulated the requisites for a successful socialist education movement: mobilizing the impoverished peasantry, rectifying the quandaries surrounding cadre transparency, fostering labor participation among officials, forging a robust leadership nucleus, and bolstering agricultural productivity.[1]

The pivotal impetus behind the Zhanqi Brigade's secession from the Jinxing Brigade lay in this poignant backdrop. In 1965, the Xianfeng Commune Party Committee astutely determined two factors: firstly, the sprawling expanse and voluminous households of the communes posed difficulties in effective governance, inhibiting timely detection and resolution of prevailing predicaments, thus necessitating a wait for opportune moments to fortify and consolidate the collective economy; secondly, the party's socialist education movement had subjected cadres to appraisal, instilling the ability for autonomous work among these individuals. They could deftly implement the Party's policies, closely engaging with the

[1] Contemporary China Research Institute. "Chronology of the People's Republic of China: 1964 Volume." Beijing: Contemporary China Publishing House, 2019.

© Peking University Press 2024

X. Dong, *Zhanqi Village Over Fifty Years*,
https://doi.org/10.1007/978-981-97-5426-7_4

members and masses. Against this backdrop, the separation of select brigades would catalyze comprehensive production advancement.[2]

Thus, the Xianfeng Commune extracted production teams 11–17 from the Jinxing Brigade, birthing an autonomous entity christened the Zhanqi Brigade (originally dubbed the "Jinxing Third Brigade" upon its inception in 1965, later rebranded as the Zhanqi Brigade in 1966). In its nascent stages, the brigade found its inaugural secretary in Jiang Daxing (蒋大兴), with Luo Huijin (罗会金) commanding the ranks as the brigade leader, while Li Shibing (李世炳) held the mantle of brigade accountant.[3]

The Zhanqi Brigade, stationed in the heart of Jinxing, was once perceived by the commune as a mediocre or lagging unit before 1965. In '63, they sought a cash loan of 2000 yuan from the Xianfeng Brigade, and their agricultural and sideline endeavors were enshrouded in passivity. Even with some assets at their disposal, like water mills and sows, the Jinxing Third Brigade merely scraped together a meager income of just over 200 yuan every six months. The commune placed the blame on the muddled minds of their cadre, who naively heeded the murmurs of the members claiming that feeding pigs was an unprofitable endeavor. Rather than nourishing swine, they suggested selling the bran from the mills to their fellow members, which seemed to offer more favorable returns. Such

[2] Report from the Xianfeng Commune Party Committee on brigade division and production team amalgamation (July 1965), archived at the Pidu District Archives, Chengdu, Sichuan Province, "Archives of Pixian County, Xianfeng Township," Archive No. 152-001-0037-005, pp. 25–28.

[3] Jiang Daxing, then aged 49, emerged from a tenant-peasant background. He assumed the role of Agricultural Association Leader within the Jinxing Brigade in 1952, progressing to Village Committee Director in 1956. During the "Four Cleanups" movement, he faced scrutiny, yet was subsequently chosen as the brigade secretary of the Zhanqi Brigade, assuming responsibility for overseeing the Oil Refinery Factory during the early 1970s. Luo Huijin, born into impoverished farming circumstances, had previously served as a production team leader prior to the establishment of the Zhanqi Brigade. Following in Jiang Daxing's footsteps, he assumed the mantle of the second brigade secretary in 1969, before transitioning to the role of Party Committee Secretary within the commune in 1975. Li Shibing, at the tender age of 26, possessed a secondary education and had imparted knowledge as an educator. His party affiliation commenced in 1966, wherein he shouldered the duties of the Zhanqi Brigade's accountant until his ascension to deputy secretary of the branch in 1971. In 1975, he triumphantly secured the position of the brigade's third secretary, subsequently being reassigned as Party Committee Secretary in Xinminchang Town in 1980.

words shook the foundation of the cadre's resolve.[4] Hence, during the division, as recollected by the cadre at the time, the Zhanqi Brigade was left with a mere pittance—three pigsty rooms, a wooden filing cabinet, three circle chairs, and a debt of 700 yuan. It would not be an exaggeration to label them a "backward brigade, both destitute in the economic realm and bewildered in their thoughts, adrift without a clear direction."[5]

However, come 1973, the Jinxing Third Brigade, rechristened the Zhanqi Brigade, astonishingly found itself reigning supreme in the county and the commune. Their rice and wheat yields per unit area and the number of pigs per capita surpassed all others. The collective grain reserves soared to 240,000 catties, while their public accumulation swelled to a staggering 170,000 yuan. They procured 61 agricultural machinery units, including trusty tractors. Even after fulfilling their national procurement obligations, they managed to exceed expectations by trading an additional 30,000 catties of commercial grain. Their contributions to the country grew steadily, bolstering the collective economy and elevating the living standards of their members.[6] This accomplishment outshone the Xianfeng Brigade mentioned earlier, which had basked in their advanced status from 1958 to 1965 (by 1960, the Xianfeng Brigade had already hoisted the banner high in Pixian County). How, then, did the Zhanqi Brigade in the Western front manage to surge to such great heights? What were the factors that propelled them toward success?

1. "Learning from Dazhai in Agriculture" and Zhanqi's Agricultural Prosperity.

[4] Source: "Briefing on the Development of Collective Secondary Industries by the Xianfeng Commune Party Committee" (January 21, 1964), archived in the Pidu District Archives of Sichuan Province, "Archives of Pixian County Xianfeng Township," file number 152-001-0032-011, pages 48–50.

[5] Other archival records mention the division of a debt nearing 10,000 yuan during the separation, yet this claim remains unverified at present. For more information, refer to the Pixian County Revolutionary Committee: "Investigation on the Situation of Route Education of the Xianfeng Commune Zhanqi Brigade" (September 30, 1971), archived in the Pidu District Archives, "Archives of Pixian County Xianfeng Township," file number 152-001-0098-013, page 50.

[6] Reference: "Continue the Great Struggle for Innovation and Revolutionary Progress" from the "Agricultural Learning from Dazhai" Conference in Pixian County (March 5, 1973), archived in the Pidu District Archives, "Archives of Pixian County Xianfeng Township," file number 152-001-0113-016, pages 142–155.

Following the "Four Cleanups" campaign, the new socialist education became intertwined with initiatives like the implementation of the "Dazhai Work Point System." The progress of agricultural production in the Zhanqi Brigade was closely tied to the nationwide movement known as "Learning from Dazhai in Agriculture." Comrade Li Shibing from the Zhanqi Brigade (then part of the Jinxing Brigade) embarked on a visit to Dazhai in pursuit of knowledge, soon after the Party Central Committee issued the rallying cry for "Learning from Dazhai in agriculture." Starting in 1965, numerous brigades and production teams in Pixian County embarked on their own learning journey inspired by Dazhai. It was in April of that same year when Brigade Leader Luo Huijin proudly declared the motto, "Leaders should emulate Chen Yonggui, while members should learn from the hardworking people of Dazhai," fostering the indomitable spirit of Dazhai.[7] This, perchance, marked the soaring beginnings of Zhanqi, epitomizing the tangible embodiment of "poverty begets transformation."

As the nation fervently pursued Learning from Dazhai in agriculture, the Party Central Committee made a significant economic strategic decision to shift the focus of the third Five-Year Plan, originally centered around "food and clothing," to prioritize "Third Front Construction (三线建设)" in preparation for potential conflicts. In 1964, during a meeting of the CPC Central Committee's Political Bureau Standing Committee, Mao Zedong voiced concerns about insufficient attention given to the construction efforts in the southwestern region.[8] As the international landscape grew increasingly hostile, Mao Zedong repeatedly emphasized the importance of Third Front Construction. It was not until early August 1964, when the United States Huohuaed the flames of aggression with the fabricated Gulf of Tonkin incident, that the fires of war encroached upon China's borders. Consequently, the implementation of the Third Front Construction was urgently demanded, with Sichuan province serving as a pivotal region for this endeavor. Given the colossal investments required for Third Front Construction, the surplus extracted

[7] Source: "Investigation of the ideological education of the Zhanqi Brigade Party Branch of Xianfeng Commune" (September 30, 1971), Pidu District Archives, "Xianfeng Township Volume," File No. 152-001-0098-013, page 55.

[8] Source: Institute of Contemporary China Studies. "Chronological History of the People's Republic of China: Volume for 1964" [M]. Beijing: Contemporary China Publishing House, 2019.

from agriculture became the only viable source, thereby setting the stage for the nationwide surge in Learning from Dazhai in agriculture.

In early 1964, Zhou Enlai recognized the need for a comprehensive study of Dazhai's experience, urging regions to adapt and learn according to their specific circumstances, without neglecting the material aspect while emphasizing the spiritual dimension. Responding to Zhou Enlai's directives, Minister of Agriculture Liao Luyan embarked on a 21-day investigation at the Dazhai Brigade in May 1964 and subsequently submitted the "Investigation Report of Dazhai Brigade" to the central government. This report lauded Dazhai as an exemplar of self-reliance, a bastion of stable and abundant agricultural yields in the face of droughts and floods—an iconic symbol on the national agricultural front.

In April 1968, the Ministry of Agriculture of the People's Republic of China disseminated the "Summary of the National Learning from Dazhai in agriculture Labor Management Experience Field Conference (《全国学大寨劳动管理经验现场会议纪要》)." This publication marked a significant milestone, following two national conferences held at Dazhai, Shanxi in September 1967 and January 1968, which deepened the understanding and propelled the mass movement of "Learning from Dazhai in agriculture" to new heights. In response, the County Committee of Pixian County issued the third Five-Year Plan for "Learning from Dazhai in agriculture' (Draft)" in 1969.

Subsequently, the Xianfeng Commune, gauging its own reality, issued the "Preliminary Draft of the Three-Year Plan for Learning from Dazhai in Agriculture." They rallied under the battle cry of "One flag held high, one line never forgotten, toil relentlessly for three to five years, inducing a triple transformation of mind, land, technique, and yield." Simultaneously, they emphasized the significance of "leveraging exemplary models and setting up a model of excellence at the brigade level, ensuring each production team emulates the achievements of Dazhai." Additionally, they sought to "respond to the populace's requests and voluntarily implement the unified accounting system pioneered by Deyang's Hongguang Brigade, starting with Zhanqi Brigade as a testing ground and gradually expanding upon its success." This historical document reflects the birth of Zhanqi's institutional capacity for concentrated efforts, serving as the fountainhead from which the village's collective economy continues to flourish.

Against this backdrop, Zhanqi Brigade, through the reformation of both cadre and popular mindsets, improvements in agricultural water

Table 1 Zhanqi Brigade's demography and Grain production, 1966–1967, 1972–1973

Year	*Number of households*	*Population*	*Area of rice (mu)*	*Yield of rice (catties/mu)*	*Area of wheat (mu)*	*Yield of wheat (catties/mu)*
1966	248	999	1813	613	427	415
1967	251	1013	174	631	416	366
1972	300	1274	1510	676	485	463
1973	305	1298	1645	762	506	520

Year/Number of Households/Population/Area of Rice (mu)/Yield of Rice (catties/mu)/Area of Wheat(mu)/Yield of Wheat (catties/mu).

Source: "Settlement and Distribution Table for Zhanqi Brigade in 1966, Pixian County," Archive Number 152-001-0086-002, pages 20–38; "Settlement and Distribution Table for Zhanqi Brigade in 1967, Pixian County," Archive Number 152-001-0089-011, pages 165–180; "Settlement and Distribution Table for Zhanqi Brigade in 1972, Xianfeng Commune, Pixian County," Archive Number 152-001-0107-002, pages 16–30; "Settlement and Distribution Table for Zhanqi Brigade in 1973, Xianfeng Commune, Pixian County," Archive Number 152-001-0112-003, pages 36–52.

management, the establishment of militia units, and the mobilization of female labor, witnessed a remarkable surge in agricultural productivity, particularly in rice and wheat. By 1973, Zhanqi Brigade achieved a rice yield of 762 catties per mu and a wheat yield of 520 catties per mu. In stark contrast, the national average for rice yield in 1975 stood at a mere 468.57 catties per mu, with wheat at a modest 218.41 catties per mu. These figures showcased Zhanqi Brigade's impressive grain production, as indicated in Table 1.

1 The Molding of Cadres and the Masses' Thoughts

Once the structure and path are set, the fate of an organization lies in the abilities and qualities of its cadres.

Zhanqi Brigade's cadres possess an exceptional aptitude for learning. Whether it be the inaugural secretary, Jiang Daxing, or his successor, Luo Huijin, they relentlessly rally the cadres and members to delve into the latest decrees of the Party and the nation, fostering profound discussions that align with the brigade's reality. A prime example is Luo Huijin, the second secretary, hailing from the humble ranks of impoverished farmers.

He painstakingly orchestrated the study of Mao Zedong's remarks on "Running a Socialist Society through Diligence and Frugality (《勤俭办社》)" in his work "The Socialist Upsurge in China's Countryside (《中国农村的社会主义高潮》)." Together, they dissected the means to establish and embark on ventures. Through this communal pursuit of knowledge, consensus was reached: it was the indomitable spirit of the "impoverished" and the tenacity of diligent hands that would pave the path of self-reliance and arduous struggle. Once their course was set, the leadership of the brigade's party branch and its members spearheaded the way in every aspect.

Encountering obstacles, the cadres of Zhanqi Brigade are habitually introspective, searching within themselves and dutifully rectifying their leadership. During a particular period, the fields of the 5th production team swelled, sowing crops of disparate quality—a grievous blow to the collective interests and an encroachment on communal lands. Recognizing the transgression, the party branch plunged into exhaustive investigations, unmasking a member of the branch committee implicated in this misconduct. Thus, the party branch convened an extended committee meeting, fostering an atmosphere of constructive criticism and self-reflection that kindled a positive wave of ideological enlightenment. The errant member, now cognizant of the perils of land encroachment, zealously obliterated the widened ridges, galvanizing the masses to curb this deviant trend. Under the cadres' guiding influence, with the members and masses mobilized along the people's path, Zhanqi Brigade sustained its Xianfeng spirit.[9]

Moreover, Zhanqi Brigade's cadres possess an astute ability to discern and address issues within the minutiae. Take, for instance, the year 1973, when the party branch synthesized the experiences of Teams 5 and 8, scrutinizing their merits and flaws. Team 8's leadership, persevering through hardship and pioneering the way, witnessed a triumphant surge in productivity. Conversely, Team 5's leadership clung to archaic traditions, mired in conservative ideologies, resulting in steady albeit lackluster output. The party branch of Zhanqi Brigade perceived that acquiring the audacious fervor of Dazhai necessitated an unwavering leadership team.

[9] Pixian County "Learning from Dazhai in Agriculture" Conference Reference Material 2: "Hard Work and Innovative Industry Continue the Revolution and Move Forward" (March 5, 1973), Archives Collection of Pidu District, Sichuan Province. "Xianfeng Township Archives of Pixian County", Archives No. 152-001-0113-016, pages 143–144.

Thus, the brigade embarked on four comprehensive reform campaigns, mobilizing the masses to unearth contradictions, identify disparities, and propel progress. Resorting to approaches such as "seeing" (organizing external visits to broaden horizons and liberate minds), "comparing" (launching mobile red flag competitions to foster mutual learning), "helping" (assigning specific aid responsibilities to Team 6 cadres), and "debating" (facilitating on-site visits and engaging in comparative deliberations), their efforts resolutely fortified the ideological framework of the production team's leadership.

Through intricate struggles and relentless practice, the 47 cadres of the Zhanqi Brigade honed their martial prowess, embodying the "six tough" arts.[10] Not a solitary cadre dared pilfer a penny or annex a blade of grass from the brigade. Gao Yuhong (高玉洪), a militia platoon leader (and the father of the current Party secretary, Gao Demin 高德敏), embraced moral rectitude by dutifully returning 110 yuan and assorted garments to their rightful owner. Zhou Jiyou (周继尧), the brigade's cashier, exemplified immaculate integrity and unwavering commitment, even harboring thoughts of duty amidst his ailment, hence earning the people's reverence as the "socialist steward." The Zhanqi Brigade, steadfast in organizational fortification, bestowed particular emphasis on nurturing nascent cadres, perpetually selecting and nurturing youthful leaders from among the destitute and lowly farmers. Each of the brigade's nine production teams housed one to two young cadres beneath the age of twenty-five. These youthful Xianfengs infused the leadership echelons with a fresh vitality, fusing the ages together and igniting an effervescent atmosphere, leading the masses valiantly forward.[11]

The Party branch's leading role wielded profound influence over fellow cadres and cooperative members alike. The Zhanqi Brigade's work ethos garnered acclaim from the Xianfeng Commune's Party Committee, inciting the commune's call for assimilating Zhanqi's indomitable spirit. This, in essence, epitomized Zhanqi's acquisition of political resources.

Thus, the Zhanqi Brigade's cadres and the masses willingly embraced labor, diminishing managerial and production costs, curtailing collective

[10] Tough in political ideology, tough in class struggle, tough in work ethics, tough in collective labor, tough in economic resources, tough in leading by example.

[11] Source: "Experience of the Zhanqi Brigade in Rice Production Increase: Be Full of Enthusiasm and Strive for Advancement" (September 20, 1973), Archives of Pidu District, Sichuan Province, File No. 061-001-0025-007, pages 18–20.

and personal expenditures, and elevating the proportion of communal allocations. It was through labor's displacement of capital that they expeditiously achieved primordial capital accumulation.

Foremost, the cadre's meager origins ingrained thrift and parsimony, yielding heightened labor participation and diminished consumption, hence curbing the Zhanqi Brigade's management and production costs. Shifting ideological alignments, the Zhanqi Brigade's Party branch engendered an exemplary leadership cadre. The brigade's entirety bore no indolent beneficiary; for instance, the treasurer Zhou Jiyou who embarked on a 60-mile trek to Guanghan, repairing a noodle contraption, bedded down at the station instead of an inn. Occasionally, business obligations caused him to tarry until five in the afternoon, yet he never squandered on victuals. Such unimpeachable conduct, a beacon of integrity and diligence, radiated as an exemplar to the multitudes. In swine husbandry, they amassed generous natural fertilization, supplementing it with gathered verdant fodder from external sources, which abated their reliance on industrial fertilizers and the acquisition thereof, ergo attenuating production costs.

Secondly, the Zhanqi Brigade, through the power of ideological education, strives to curtail non-essential expenditures and indulgences. Embracing their ancestral ethos, the brigade adheres to a principle: refraining from purchasing any dispensable item. They possess an unwavering resolve to shun ostentatious squandering and dubious shortcuts. When it comes to meetings of the production team or illuminating the water pump station at the breeding farm, they ingeniously employ surplus diesel from the tractor fleet, thus saving a remarkable two-thirds of their annual kerosene consumption. Even the requisites for a dedicated column in the production team are addressed with resourcefulness; instead of purchasing writing materials, they fashion their own rudimentary blackboards from the soil, sparing only a few modest sums for white chalk throughout the year.

Remarkably, the Zhanqi Brigade does not allocate any funds for hospitality during their business trips. On one occasion, when the water pump station generously hosted visiting craftsmen from afar, a suggestion emerged to procure wine and meat from the city for the occasion. Yet, the brigade's officials astutely opted for an alternative path—organizing a study session to scrutinize the "four freedoms," conducting a comprehensive analysis of their course, ultimately elevating the awareness of the members and obviating the need for such an expense.

Another illuminating example transpired amidst the Zhanqi Brigade's burgeoning crop yields and improved living conditions. Some individuals advocated demolishing antiquated structures and erecting new abodes, contending that "a prominent brigade with grand aspirations should not bear the blemish of dilapidated huts." This matter, meriting the earnest attention of the Zhanqi Party branch, led to the mobilization of all officials and masses, who diligently revisited Chairman Mao's resonant address from the Second Plenary Session of the Seventh Central Committee of the Communist Party of China. Reverently, they imbibed the essence of his exhortation to uphold humility, prudence, modesty, and unwavering perseverance, while also retrospectively examining the brigade's laborious entrepreneurial history. Condemning the notion of casual waste under the guise of "large family, large business," they ignited a communal introspection, delving deep into the impact of their chosen path. The impoverished and lower-middle peasants expressed profound sentiments, for they recognized that "the demolition of a few decrepit huts is a triviality when weighed against forsaking the resilient spirit of the downtrodden peasants' relentless struggle. It becomes a profound issue dictating the route we follow and the path we tread." Following ardent deliberation, they unanimously resolved to preserve these aged structures as auxiliary processing quarters, perpetually reminding the officials of the virtues of tenacity and diligence.[12]

Moreover, the Zhanqi Brigade implemented a strategy of reducing individual allocations while concurrently augmenting collective distributions, thereby fostering heightened accumulation. Within the realm of distribution, the state's allotment maintained relative stability (aside from a decrease during the calamitous year of 1972), while the collective retention experienced a gradual ascent. Conversely, individual provisions progressed at a leisurely pace. As evidenced in Table 2, the year 1973 witnessed collective retention accounting for approximately 15.34% of the overall grain allocation, reflecting an increase of roughly 6.16% compared to the figures of 1966. It was this elevated sense of accumulation that bestowed upon the Zhanqi Brigade a formidable sum of 200,000 yuan in public funds and a stockpile exceeding 200,000 catties of grain in 1973.

[12] "The Tradition of Unyielding Struggle Must Persevere: An Inquiry into the Frugal Operations of Zhanqi Brigade in Xianfeng Commune" (February 11, 1972), Archives of Pidu District, Sichuan Province, "Archives of Xianfeng Township in Pixian County," File No. 152-001-0105-007, pp. 30–35.

Table 2 Grain distribution in Zhanqi Brigade, 1966–1967, 1971–1973, Unit: Catties

Year	*Total amount of grains to be distributed*	*National part*	*Collective withdrawal*	*Individual allocation*
1966	1,311,896	675,555	120,378	515,963
1967	1,309,496	694,181	81,036.5	534,278.5
1971	1,537,630	–	–	–
1972	1,379,405	604,388.5	114,297	660,719.5
1973	1,637,364	685,609.5	251,176	700,578.5

Year/Total amount of grains to be distributed/National part/Collective withdrawal/Individual allocation.

Notably, in 1972, Pixian County encountered a harrowing disaster that affected various communes and brigades. Although the Zhanqi Brigade experienced a relatively lesser impact, a decline in production was nevertheless witnessed.

In addition, the Party branch of Zhanqi Brigade deftly employed the method of labor replacing capital. The unified deployment of "Five Artisans" personnel and the utilization of local production materials and tools within the village community exemplified this approach. Following the "Learning from Dazhai in Agriculture" campaign, Pixian County imposed restrictions on the "Five Artisans," mandating that rural craftsmen (including commune construction workers) prioritize agricultural work, local endeavors, and maintenance tasks. Rural artisans engaging in urban or out-of-town artistic pursuits were compelled to return and participate in agricultural labor within their own teams. Consequently, the entire contingent of Zhanqi Brigade's "Five Artisans" united their skills to craft farming implements for the collective.

Furthermore, Zhanqi Brigade mobilized its members to cultivate bamboo, resourcefully sourcing materials without incurring any expense. They achieved complete self-sufficiency in sun mats, brooms, bamboo strips, and cow ropes, all meticulously crafted from the bountiful local bamboo. The brigade's storage room underwent an innovative rejuvenation, embracing a policy of replacing old small agricultural tools with new ones, all while adhering to a quota system. Moreover, they adopted the practice of soaking the hemp strips used for bundling, discarding only those that were truly unusable. Though implementing these regulations proved somewhat cumbersome, they yielded an annual saving of over a thousand kilograms of precious bamboo.

Prior to 1971, the production teams within Zhanqi Brigade were accustomed to procuring bamboo agricultural tools such as ropes, bamboo strips, and brooms through monetary means. However, their resourceful spirit spurred a transformation, as they took matters into their own hands and commenced local production, effectively eliminating this expenditure. In the realm of construction, the year 1971 witnessed the industrious efforts of Zhanqi Brigade's nine production teams, erecting a total of 107 structures comprising storage facilities, cowsheds, pigsties, and buildings for auxiliary activities. Remarkably, the calculated expenses for these endeavors stood at a mere 1900 yuan, a stark contrast to the exorbitant figure exceeding 20,000 yuan that would have been incurred had they purchased all the required materials.[13]

The shaping of ideology within Zhanqi Brigade's cadre and civilian circles was an intricately intertwined process, wherein cause and effect coalesced seamlessly. During the course of collective production and labor, the capabilities and moral rectitude of the brigade's cadre stood resolute in the face of the masses, their prominence reliant solely upon the approbation they received. This served as the mechanism for sieving out and appointing the brigade's leadership. The selected cadre demonstrated exceptional intellectual and ethical acumen, allowing them to effectively educate and galvanize the masses. Thus, a virtuous symbiosis ensued between the cadre and the masses, propelling the enduring advancement of the collective economy.

2 Women's Labor Mobilization and the Work Points System

Having resolved the quandaries of both cadre and populace, the pivotal element for augmenting agricultural output under the prevailing technological and capital constraints was an influx of labor. Among the key factors, hitherto overlooked, lay the mobilization of women's labor force and their substantial participation in agricultural production, effectively bolstering labor input and crop yield.

[13] "Briefing on Distribution Inspection" (January 19, 1972), Archives Collection of Pidu District, Sichuan Province, "Pixian County Pioneer Township Files", File No. 152-001-0104-005, p. 40.

In the Chengdu Plain, where the Zhanqi Brigade was stationed, women once thrived, thanks to a flourishing grassroots market system, finding avenues to showcase their inherent worth through domestic sidelines such as textile crafts. Naturally, opportunities for market engagement varied, contingent upon social strata, age, and chosen occupation. According to G. William Skinner (施坚雅), while Chengdu Plain's women may not have endured the same toils as their counterparts in Fei Xiaotong's research Lulu Village in Yunnan, they were always ready to toil in the fields when necessity beckoned.[14] Rearing children and tending to household duties remained the primary tasks for the majority of ordinary women. Consequently, emancipating them from domestic obligations and effectively organizing their collective strength played an instrumental role in heightening agricultural and ancillary production. Though physically weaker than their male counterparts, women were by no means inferior when it came to laborious tasks that didn't necessitate brute force.

The advent of the work points system, compensating labor under the collective framework, significantly elevated the status of rural women. Subsequently, developments such as the Marriage Law, literacy campaigns, and women's representative assemblies continued to propel the womenfolk's ascendancy. However, the crux determining their standing rested upon the economic bedrock. During the era of household-based agricultural labor, whether engaged in domestic chores, assisting with farming, or partaking in family handicrafts, women found it arduous to have their toil acknowledged or comprehend the true value of their labor. Only when the collective work points system emerged, ushering women entirely into agricultural production and rewarding them commensurate with their output, did each household start acknowledging the existence of female labor, even if recompense often funneled to the male household head. This awareness spawned palpable social effects, for work points vanished in the absence of exertion. As aptly observed by Philip C. C. Huang (黄宗智) although pay parity eluded women in comparison to men, the transformation engendered a twofold surge in agricultural

[14] Li Deying. Rural Women in the Rural Market Structure and Family Handicrafts: An Investigation Centered on the Chengdu Plain (1940-1950s) [J]. Journal of Sichuan University (Philosophy and Social Sciences Edition), 2019 (1): 26–39.

labor within the North China and Yangtze River Delta regions, further stimulating the highly intensive nature of agricultural production.[15]

In addition to the work point system, the Women's Committee (nicknamed "Women's Brigade") played a crucial role in awakening the female population through ideological education. Back in 1963, the Xianfeng Commune's Women's Brigade took a proactive approach by providing concentrated training to female cadres holding the rank of team leader and above. This initiative aimed to empower the majority of women, enabling them to seamlessly integrate agricultural production with domestic responsibilities, thereby elevating their consciousness. Notably, the commune kindled inspiration among women by showcasing exemplary figures like Chen Xiuying, the fearless leader of Huohua Team 7. Known for her remarkable dedication to both fieldwork and household chores, Chen epitomized the ideal female worker. She deftly managed her team's production, handled domestic affairs, tended to her children, and tirelessly led by example. In her spare moments, she even shouldered the responsibility of carrying fertilizer, demonstrating her unwavering commitment to the collective and fostering camaraderie. Her remarkable efforts earned her the esteemed moniker of the "Exceptional One."[16]

To liberate more women from their domestic confines, the Zhanqi Brigade took a commendable stride by establishing kindergartens. Simultaneously, they focused on bolstering the ranks of female cadres and female militia members, instigating a mass influx of women into the realm of large-scale production.

Within the Zhanqi Brigade, however, certain individuals adhered to the notion that rural and urban contexts differed significantly. Consequently, they believed that women need only concern themselves with domestic duties, such as tending to livestock, preparing meals, and caring for children.[17] Moreover, comrades within the brigade failed to

[15] Philip C. Huang. Small Agricultural Family and Rural Development in the Yangtze River Delta [M]. Beijing: Zhonghua Book Company, 2000.

[16] Source: "Summary Report on Women's Work in the Xianfeng Commune of Pixian County" (January 29, 1964), Archives of Pidu District, Chengdu, Sichuan Province, "Archival File of Pioneer Township in Pixian County," File No. 152-001-0017-011, pages 43–47.

[17] Source: "Establishing Kindergartens for the Revolution—Zhanqi Kindergarten in the Xianfeng Commune" (January 1974), Archives of Pidu District, Chengdu, Sichuan Province, "Archival File of Pioneer Township in Pixian County," No File Number, page 118.

fully comprehend the importance of cultivating female leaders. Their narrow perspective dictated that women engrossed in familial obligations would struggle to perform effectively as cadre members. Similarly, they harbored reservations about investing in unmarried female comrades, as they believed that any effort spent on their development would ultimately benefit another party. Furthermore, during militia recruitment, a surplus of additional conditions impeded the acceptance of women into the ranks. Even if women possessed the necessary qualifications as grassroots militia members, those burdened with multiple children were still overlooked.[18]

These notions of women swiftly transformed alongside the resurging wave of "Learning from Dazhai in Agriculture." The Party branch of the Zhanqi Brigade rallied the impoverished and lower-middle-class peasants, urging women to fully embrace their pivotal role. The brigade's women representatives readily responded, proposing the establishment of a brigade-operated kindergarten to address the issue of unattended children, actively spearheading its realization. To inspire hesitant women to enroll their children, brigade officials organized the entire village's womenfolk to study Chairman Mao's discourse on women's work and the cultivation of successors to the proletarian revolutionary cause. Through poignant contrasts and bittersweet reflections, the women at large began to fathom the profound truth that Chinese women embody a formidable human resource, an indomitable force that shapes the destiny of the revolution. Ultimately, the Zhanqi Brigade kindergarten welcomed 164 children, proving instrumental in unleashing women's labor force and bolstering agricultural support. Notably, the entire brigade witnessed an astonishing 90% attendance rate of women in labor. In 1973, the women accomplished the harvest of 520 mu of wheat within a mere day and a half. Moreover, they diligently completed the entire rice-transplanting task in a mere two nights, a staggering seven days ahead of previous years. Thus, the male comrades of the brigade paid homage, acknowledging the unwavering resilience of their female counterparts who "uphold half the sky (妇女能顶半边天)."

The significant role played by women during childbirth can also be confirmed through the oral account of Jiang Zhizhen (蒋志珍), who was the Women's Director at the time. Jiang Zhizhen mentioned several

[18] Source: "Report on the Situation of the Zhanqi Brigade Militia Platoon" (December 14, 1972), Archives of Pidu District, Chengdu, Sichuan Province, "Archival File of Pioneer Township in Pixian County," File No. 152-001-0105-018, pages 123–124.

times in interviews, "At that time, we were really enthusiastic… They gave me the nickname 'Li Shuangshuang[19] of Zhanqi,' which means very spirited." At that time, Director Jiang Zhizhen led the female militia to participate in cultural competitions in Pixian County, and they sang the song "Love Arms, Not Makeup," which further boosted the determination and enthusiasm of the women in the Zhanqi Brigade. Jiang Zhizhen, as a representative of women's work, received numerous commendations and served as a leader and role model.[20]

Jiang Zhizhen, the Women's Director at Zhanqi Brigade, stands as a formidable representative of Women's Brigade. Entrusted with the responsibility of overseeing all female militiamen within the brigade, Jiang Zhizhen garnered numerous accolades for her commendable efforts. Hailing as the fifth offspring in her family, preceded solely by four older sisters, her arrival was met with skepticism by her grandmother, who callously suggested her untimely demise, dismissing her as yet another girl child. Fortuitously, she escaped this grim fate, rescued from the clutches of mortality, a sentiment her mother consistently impressed upon her. Consequently, Jiang Zhizhen harbored an indelible reverence for the Communist Party, convinced that her survival would have remained untenable within the confines of the erstwhile society. Upon completing her junior high education in 1965, she faced financial constraints that thwarted her aspirations of pursuing higher learning. Persuaded by Jiang Daxing, she acquiesced, returning to the village to contribute her labor. Still in her teens, Jiang Zhizhen infused her endeavors in the village's women's work with unyielding zeal. Reminiscing on that era, she fondly recollected, "In those days, our minds were unblemished, united as one brigade. Wherever duty called, without a moment's hesitation, we responded, devoid of grievances or objections to the assigned tasks." The dawn of a new epoch heralded the reconstruction of women's intrinsic value system, reinvigorating their spirit through the judicious allocation of work points.

[19] Translator's note: The story of Li Shuangshuang (李双双) first appeared in The People's Literature in 1960. After becoming a huge success among China's citizens it was made into a movie. Li Shuangshuang is a model member of society who condemns the laziness and corruption of other members of the commune. Shuangshuang, sick of staying at home and working on domestic labor, leads the commune to take part in the progress of The Great Leap Forward.

[20] Source: Interview transcript with Jiang Zhizhen, January 30, 2020.

Under Jiang Zhizhen's guidance, the Zhanqi Brigade delved deeper into their understanding of the female cadre and female militia predicaments, effectively stoking the feminine fervor and yielding remarkable outcomes in agricultural and rural water management. Unfortunately, due to a lack of emphasis on nurturing female cadres, the Zhanqi Militia Company counted only two women in their ranks prior to the unit's overhaul. Addressing this quandary, the Party branch orchestrated a study session on Chairman Mao's enlightened mantra: "Times have changed, men and women are equals; what men can achieve, women are equally capable of." Such tutelage successfully instilled the significance of cultivating female cadres within the militia's endeavors. Consequently, ten valiant women militia members were carefully selected to serve as deputy cadres, empowering the female militia force.

Moreover, the Party branch took proactive measures to rectify the issue of meager female militia numbers. They illustrated the remarkable exploits of a female soldier named Meng Biqun (孟笔群) as an exemplar. Despite her familial obligations—three children to tend to and a husband laboring afar—Meng Biqun consistently exhibited unwavering zeal for militia activities. This poignant exemplar vividly conveyed the notion that a woman's participation in militia activities hinges not on the quantity of her offspring, but rather on her level of education. During the subsequent reorganization, the militia unit graciously absorbed all 48 qualified and burdened women comrades, with 43 of them serving as grassroots militia members.

By 1976, the Zhanqi Brigade boasted a commendable proportion of female militia members. During the militia's experimental phase that year, the restructuring process ushered in 31 new recruits, including 10 women. Among them, five grassroots members advanced to regular status, while one regular member transitioned to grassroots. Furthermore, 23 members departed from the unit. Following the reorganization, the company stood united with 503 spirited militia members, encompassing 36.2% of the total population. Among these ranks, 178 were grassroots militia members, including 80 courageous women; 128 armed grassroots militiamen, with 32 brave women in their midst; and 197 ordinary militiamen, accompanied by 94 resolute women. The staggering figures underscored the near-parity between male and female militia members, validating Jiang Zhizhen's assertion that the two genders stood shoulder to shoulder in their dedication to the cause.

Due to the exponential growth of female militia cadres and their ranks, women's standing and involvement surged. Unleashing their untapped potential, these laborers embraced their roles with unwavering fervor. While women's labor output amounted to a mere eighty percent of their male counterparts, their enthusiasm remained unyielding. For instance, in 1973, amidst the conclusion of the "early spring harvest," the arduous battle of sowing the seeds of the bountiful spring commenced. Male militiamen toiled the fields, tending to the irrigation and fertilization, while all other tasks were shouldered by the capable female militiamen. Unfazed by hardship or fatigue, they tirelessly toiled by day, and under the glow of lanterns and torches, transplanted seedlings well into the late hours of the night. The collective efforts of our militia and commune members bore fruit, leading to an abundant harvest surpassing all historical records...

In the winter of 1971, a select unit of one hundred militiamen was mobilized to form a rapid-response team tasked with the daunting challenge of excavating the treacherous Hengshan lateral canal across the commune. Unyielding in their resolve, these militiamen, regardless of discomfort, exhaustion, or filth, embraced their tools, caked in the earth, with bare hands. On slippery rainy days, they resorted to human chains, triumphing over adversity and completing the assignment half a month ahead of schedule. Fueled by the indomitable spirit of the canal construction militia, their tenacity inspired both the homebound militiamen and commune members to rally together, embarking on ambitious endeavors of fundamental agricultural development. More than 10,000 cubic meters of soil were excavated, and a network of sixteen ditches and canals was opened, spanning an impressive 7500 meters in total.[21]

Furthermore, the Zhanqi Brigade bore witness to the emergence of numerous remarkable women across various endeavors. Take, for instance, the resolute Li Shifang (李仕芳), a female militiawoman and adept tractor operator. During the 1975 "double grab" campaign, when machinery faltered and her right index finger fell victim to an unfortunate fracture,

[21] Source: "Speech Materials of the Advanced Production (Work) Representatives' Congress of Pixian County in 1973: The Basic Line Commands the Three Major Revolutions—The Party Branch of Pixian Xianfeng Commune Zhanqi Brigade" (January 14, 1974), Archives of Pidu District, Chengdu, Sichuan Province, File No. 152-001-0113-013, pages 113–116.

she stoically endured excruciating pain, unwavering in her determination to mend the equipment and ensure the seamless progress of the operation.[22]

In an interview, Jiang Zhizhen proclaimed, "The Zhanqi Brigade has no place for second or third. We must surpass the Xianfeng Brigade in all endeavors. If they claim completion tomorrow, we achieve it today. It is through such tenacious competition that our reputation precedes us, ever at the forefront of innovation." This statement provides a fitting response to the question raised at the outset of this chapter: why did the Zhanqi Brigade transcend the Xianfeng Brigade, an exemplary Xianfeng Commune? It is this comprehensive competitive spirit that propelled the Zhanqi Brigade to stand unrivaled.

While the notion of "equal pay for equal work" advocated during the People's Commune era failed to materialize universally, the work point system substantially elevated the economic status of women as independent contributors within the household. Women were further emancipated, actively participating in agricultural and sideline production, as well as initiatives for agricultural and water conservation transformation. The latent value of these labor forces was maximized. Undoubtedly, during this period, the Zhanqi Brigade embodied the essence of "women upholding half the sky," playing an indispensable role in bolstering agricultural and sideline yields within the brigade.

3 Renovation of Agricultural Water Infrastructure

A surplus of labor merely represents one aspect of agricultural production, for the pivotal key to enhancing agricultural yields lies in the transformation of agricultural water infrastructure. Stirred by the indomitable spirit of self-reliance and tenacious struggle fostered in the Dazhai commune, the Party branch of Zhanqi Brigade roused a substantial workforce to embark on endeavors such as trenching for drainage and deep soil cultivation.

In that era, Zhanqi Brigade possessed over 1800 mu of farmland, nearly half of which suffered from decay and waterlogging. Merely about

22 Source: "Criticizing the Promotion of 'Intelligence Over Ignorance' to Promote Double Grab" (May 21, 1974), Archives of Pidu District, Chengdu, Sichuan Province, File No. 152-001-0120-007, page 205.

400 mu of land, belonging to Teams 2, 4, and 8, could be classified as fertile oil-sand fields. The waterlogged and decaying fields, nestled within low-lying basins, concealed shallow groundwater, with many fields even presenting a crimson-hued rusty water film upon their surfaces. Some of these excessively waterlogged plots transformed into barren soil, rendering any yield unattainable. Owing to the elevated water table and prolonged drainage issues, toiling the land in these fields became an exceptionally laborious task. Numerous waterlogged tracts, once plowed, retained their compactness, necessitating sun-drying until December prior to sowing wheat and rapeseed. Discordance between water, fertilization, air, and heat plagued the crops in the decaying fields, resulting in universally stunted growth and meager output. Numerous fields could only accommodate a single season of barley cultivation, yielding merely a few hundred catties per mu. Following rice maturation each year, the waterlogged fields remained incapable of drainage, condemning farmers to labor within the muddy waters. Moving the threshing machine employed during the harvest required a layer of straw for buoyancy. Despite the farmers' persistent toil, crop yields remained stagnant, ensnaring their livelihoods in impoverishment. A local folk rhyme lamented, "Without planting in the Jiangjiawai (an area in Zhanqi Brigade), perpetual inundation prevails."

Under the astute guidance of Jiang Daxing, the inaugural Party secretary of Zhanqi Brigade, the brigade ardently pursued production growth as villagers threw themselves wholeheartedly into their work. Simultaneously, the transformation of agricultural water infrastructure was set into motion, fostering an appreciable enhancement in Zhanqi Brigade's farming prowess. To this end, Luo Huijin, the brigade's maiden leader, emerged as a beacon, galvanizing the villagers to orchestrate the systematic planning and reclamation of the brigade's land. His rallying cry of "Straight ditches, direct roads, orderly tree lines, and mechanized cultivation in the new farm" reverberated, fragmenting the land into coherent "blocks (条块化)," with each segment encompassing a two-mu plot, diligently tending to tasks irrespective of the weather's disposition. Over the course of approximately three years, Zhanqi Brigade's land had been seamlessly segmented into these cohesive blocks, with the irrigation ditches now flowing unswervingly.

Yet, the "blockization" of the land could not wholly metamorphose Zhanqi Brigade's production circumstances. Undeterred, the brigade's cadres persevered, inspired by Luo Huijin's visit to Dazhai, as they disseminated the spirit of the commune throughout the village, urging all to emulate Dazhai's triumph. Notably, in the spring of 1971, subsequent to the "Learning from Dazhai in Agriculture" conference convened by the Pixian County committee, Zhanqi Brigade's Party branch faithfully adhered to the directive and, buoyed by the benevolent guidance of the Wenjiang Military District's deputy commander, embarked on a monumental campaign of agricultural advancement baptized "Learning from Dazhai in Agriculture." From the winter of 1972 to the spring of 1973, Zhanqi Brigade wholeheartedly spearheaded an extensive endeavor, revitalizing terraced fields, ameliorating soil quality, and promoting water management. The entire brigade resolutely undertook the transformation of over 100 mu of terraced land, successfully rejuvenating a portion of the underperforming fields' fertility.

More crucially, the Party branch of the Zhanqi Brigade, through its unwavering focus on building the militia organization, propelled the agricultural irrigation efforts forward by transforming uneven, varied patches of land into perfectly standardized fields. Through the interconnectedness of ditches, channels, and roads, convenience permeated the irrigation and drainage systems, elevating the Zhanqi Brigade's proficiency in land cultivation and laying a steadfast foundation for increased food production.

Furthermore, driven by their pursuit of amplified harvests, the Zhanqi Brigade's Party branch garnered extensive expertise in early planning, meticulous field preparation, uniform seed sowing, diligent fertilization, and precise crop harvesting. Capitalizing on the fervent ambiance of the "Learning from Dazhai in Agriculture" movement, they galvanized the masses to engage in scientifically driven farming practices. As a notable example, to augment wheat yields, the entire Zhanqi Brigade rallied its cadres and populace, commencing in July 1972, to blueprint and actualize the production plan for the forthcoming spring season. By commencing with early planning, timely execution, and swift land cultivation, they bolstered bottom fertilizer application, securing immaculate field quality. Notably, the brigade achieved a remarkable feat by properly preparing approximately 80% of the wheat fields before the first frost, rendering them optimally dry, impeccably refined, and painstakingly raked to ensure an opportune sowing season, robust seedling growth, and flourishing foliage—a magnificent testament to their tenacious soil nurturing.

In their pursuit of enhancing rice production and addressing uneven terrain concerns, the Zhanqi Brigade orchestrated a collective labor-intensive offensive. Seamlessly merging the filling of high spots and excavation of low areas with judicious fertilization, they conscientiously leveled the land subsequent to plowing, facilitating shallow water irrigation. Vigilantly guarding against misapplication of fertilizers, they resorted to implementing basal fertilization (averaging 50 catties of phosphate fertilizer and 20 loads of manure per mu) and promptly supplementing it with additional fertilization (typically incorporating 5 catties of chemical fertilizer, 10 loads of manure, and 50 catties of oil within the first 15 days, followed by 100 catties of lime within 25 days).

Amidst the arduous winter and spring agricultural hustle, the Zhanqi Brigade harnessed the collective vigor of the masses, skillfully engaging a plethora of untapped laborers in land consolidation and production management endeavors. Consequently, the brigade witnessed a steady upsurge in their cumulative annual labor days, culminating in an impressive 1,221,666 person-days in 1973. With an average labor duration of 648 person-days per mu, this strikingly surpassed the 1966 figure by an astounding 367,369 person-days, reflecting an admirable growth rate of 43%, as eloquently portrayed in Table 3.

Therefore, the Zhanqi Brigade witnessed a remarkable surge in grain production within a mere few years. Despite the murmurs that the tremendous labor input had diluted the value of work points. In 1972, the worth of labor work points dwindled to a mere 0.43 yuan, plummeting over 50% from the 0.98 yuan recorded in 1966. By 1973, the rice cultivation area of the Zhanqi Brigade stretched over 1620.9 mu, boasting an average yield of 920 catties per mu. Notably, the eighth production

Table 3 Annual Accumulated Labor Days of Zhanqi Brigade, 1966–1967 and 1972–1973, Unit: Person-days

Year	*Accumulated labor days*
1966	854,297
1967	882,793
1972	1,212,614
1973	1,221,666

Year|Accumulated Labor Days.

Data Source: Same as Table 1. Notably, the original table erroneously presented the 1972 data, which has been accurately recalculated by multiplying the average labor days per person in the Zhanqi Brigade with the total number of individuals.

team achieved an impressive yield of 1016 catties per mu, marking an 80 catty surge from the previous year. This exponential growth resulted in an overall increase of 190,000 catties, establishing it as the Zhanqi Brigade's most prolific year in rice production.[23]

Concurrently, the wheat cultivation area expanded from 483.6 mu in 1972 to 505.4 mu in the same year, boasting an average yield of 520.2 catties per mu, resulting in a 13% increase from the preceding year.[24] Furthermore, the camellia oil yield flourished, reaching an impressive 248 catties per mu, while the corn yield achieved a commendable 580 catties per mu. Moreover, statistical data unveiled that in 1966, the Zhanqi Brigade's total grain output amounted to 1.2 million catties. Astonishingly, by 1975, the total grain output soared to an astounding 1.74 million catties, signifying a remarkable growth rate of 45%.[25]

4 Building the Militia Organization

The Zhanqi Brigade's swift mobilization of abundant labor, engaging them in agricultural production and the transformation of farming and water infrastructure, while maintaining exemplary order, owes its success to the robust establishment of their militia organization. **The disciplined and committed militia of this brigade dutifully answered every call, forging an almost military-like management system.**

Before 1970, the militia efforts in the Zhanqi Brigade were in their fledgling stage. Following the "Four Cleanups" campaign, they formed a militia platoon, with the party branch actively involved. However, prevailing sentiments at the time, such as dismissing the militia as outdated or irrelevant, hindered progress. Some party members regarded militia work as separate, believing it solely concerned the militia platoon leader, divorcing themselves from the cause. A prevailing sentiment even

[23] "Strive to go upstream and take big steps forward: The experience of the Pioneer Commune Zhanqi Brigade in increasing rice production in a large area" (September 20, 1973), Archives Collection of Pidu District, Sichuan Province, File No. 061-001-0025-007, Pages 17–23.

[24] "Experience of Xianfeng Commune Zhanqi Brigade with a Wheat Yield of 520.2 Catties per Mu" (June 29, 1973), Archives of Pidu District, Sichuan Province, Archive No. 061-001-0020-034, p. 207.

[25] "How did Xianfeng Commune Zhanqi Brigade's Pig Farming Develop" (July 1977), Archives of Pidu District, Sichuan Province, "Various Operations Office of Pixian County Revolutionary Committee," Archive No. 017-018-0019-019, p. 104.

dared to say, "Without the militia, progress remains unseen." Regrettably, inadequate attention, supervision, and support left the vital matter of "implementing the three requisites" in militia work unresolved.

In 1970, the Zhanqi Brigade underwent a revitalization of their militia efforts, undertaking three measures to reinforce the party's authoritative guidance, both ideologically and organizationally. The specific measures were as follows:

(1) Subjugating militia work under the dominion of the party branch, clearly delineating management rights and responsibilities. Among the seven party branch members, five were entrusted with positions in the militia platoon, gathering every fortnight to discuss militia work. To address the disarray arising from administrative and militia cadre asserting their own significance, an educational campaign promoting "the party's comprehensive focus on military affairs and universal conscription" was launched. Additionally, out of the eighteen platoon leaders across nine militia squads, eleven were appointed from the ranks of production team leaders or deputy team leaders. By adopting such measures, they seamlessly aligned militia work with other initiatives, guaranteeing the party's unified leadership.

(2) Setting an exemplary standard, with cadres leading the militia by personal example. The seven members of the party branch held themselves to strict standards, actively participating in militia activities without exception or favoritism. For instance, in 1971, during military training, the brigade's party secretary, Luo Huijin, missed the session due to attending a county meeting. Nonetheless, upon returning, he voluntarily sought supplementary lessons, diligently studying the prescribed subjects. Party committee member Dang Kaiying (党开炳), already in his fifties, relentlessly joined militia drills with the demeanor of a common soldier, never absent. Such acts of exemplary conduct resonated deeply, inspiring the vast militia membership.

(3) Emphasizing production and establishing a robust system for militia activities. Recognizing the militia organization as a mass armed entity, intrinsically linked to party leadership and inseparable from production, the party branch devised a judicious framework for scheduling militia activities. They adhered to the principle of prioritizing activities during agricultural lulls and reducing

> engagement during busy periods, striking a harmonious balance. Consequently, they established a necessary routine: morning military training and evening political education on the first and sixth of each month at the platoon level, monthly company-level drills and evaluations, biweekly meetings for cadre summaries and work arrangements beyond the platoon level, and a biweekly weapon cleaning schedule. Practiced and proven, this system effectively instilled a vigilant preparedness mindset among the militia at large.[26]

These measures firmly tethered the work of the militia within the grasp of the Party branch, allowing them to exert immense influence in upholding social order, safeguarding the brigade's authority, engaging in agricultural production, and revitalizing irrigation infrastructure. The Party branch wholeheartedly relied on and harnessed the backbone and assault units of the militia, skillfully altering the Zhanqi Brigade's initial course of diffuseness and stagnation.

Primarily, the militia company emerged as a formidable force in safeguarding the brigade's tranquility. In the early 1970s, the Zhanqi Brigade was plagued by fourteen consecutive instances of rampant timber theft, leaving the hearts of the people gripped with trepidation and severely compromising the brigade's productive endeavors. Swift to respond, the Party branch hastily rallied over 120 dedicated militiamen, who stealthily embarked on a nocturnal pursuit of the thieves. Traversing three counties and eight communes, and with the assistance of pertinent establishments, their relentless pursuit yielded astonishing results within a mere fortnight. They not only successfully unraveled the fourteen larceny cases afflicting the Zhanqi Brigade but also unearthed eighteen connected thefts and thirteen security breaches, managing to reclaim the lion's share of stolen goods. This exemplary feat garnered accolades from sister organizations such as Pengxian County and Guanxian County. In a display of indomitable spirit, Deputy Company Commander Yang Mingshu (杨明书) of the militia fearlessly disregarded personal safety to apprehend a

[26] Source: "Strengthen Party Leadership, Emphasize Line Struggle—The Zhanqi Brigade Militia Platoon Advances in the Three Revolutionary Movements" (May 25, 1972), Chengdu Pidu District Archives, "Xianfeng Township of Pixian County File," Document Number 061-001-0105-019, pages 125–130.

notorious perpetrator, Yi, residing in Xinsheng Commune. He unflinchingly concealed himself in Yi's woodland for an entire day and night, supported by local militiamen, until ultimately seizing Yi and bringing him to justice. Such gallantry exhibited by the Zhanqi Brigade's dedicated militiamen not only preserved local public order but also fostered an environment conducive to productive pursuits, earning the acclaim of esteemed superiors and the unwavering support of their fellow comrades.

Furthermore, the Zhanqi militia company emerged as an unwavering pillar during the brigade's arduous struggle against the perils of "public–private" interests. The Zhanqi Brigade had long been plagued by pernicious practices such as the encroachment upon communal lands, the expansion of terraced fields, intensive vegetable cultivation, and the abandonment of agricultural toil in favor of livestock rearing. With resolute determination, the Party branch rallied the militia, providing a platform to denounce fallacious ideologies like "self-interest" and "self-gain," thus ensuring the steady progress of the agricultural mass movement inspired by the illustrious Dazhai. Through widespread involvement and astute supervision, the Zhanqi militia company etched an indelible mark on the pursuit of the socialist path.

Lastly, the indomitable Zhanqi militia company stood as an unparalleled force in the brigade's agricultural productivity and the relentless pursuit of irrigation and water conservancy projects. Driven by an unwavering resolve to augment grain production in support of the nation's socialist development, the determined militiamen coined the rallying cry, "harvesting sustenance from fallow frontier embankments." With unwavering resolve, they converted over twenty mu (approximately 1.3 hectares) of the Zhanqi Brigade's erstwhile neglected riverbeds and uncultivated margins into flourishing paddy fields and fertile tracts, sowing rice and other vital crops. In their ceaseless march toward expansive agricultural progress since 1970, the militia company embraced scientific farming practices, establishing research groups at the company and platoon levels, and diligently cultivating model fields, seedbeds, and experimental plots. A remarkable testament to their unwavering commitment, a remarkable quintet of militiamen trudged over approximately 20 kilometers on foot, bearing an exorbitant load of fertilizers weighing in excess of ten thousand catties (approximately 5000 kilograms). By 1972, following the comprehensive involvement of the entire company, they proceeded to oversee meticulous spring field management operations, resulting in the bountiful sowing of vegetable seeds, some even sown thrice, the cultivation of wheat over a hundred mu (approximately 6.7 hectares), the removal of over two hundred stones, and the clearance of over sixty percent of rapeseed foliage. Such relentless endeavors laid a rock-solid foundation for the expansive growth of agricultural productivity.

The Militia Company of the Zhanqi Brigade played a formidable role, owed in part to its sheer numbers, the proportion of militiamen within the working class, the quantity of firearms, and the annual regimentation. In 1972, the brigade boasted 9 platoons and 37 squads, amassing a force of 480 militiamen, accounting for a staggering 37.7% of the brigade's overall populace. A dominant share of the labor force was also within their ranks. Their firearms arsenal was likewise bolstered under the guidance of the Zhanqi Brigade leadership. By 1975, they possessed an impressive arsenal of 32 firearms, outshining the Xianfeng Brigade by 24. Undeniably, the Zhanqi Brigade's militia prowess outshone that of other brigades within the Xianfeng Commune. Detailed data on the distribution of arms across the various brigades can be found in Table 4.

Table 4 Distribution of militia weapons in the Zhanqi Brigade, Xianfeng Brigade, and other brigades in 1975

Brigade	*Number of armed militia*	*Light machine gun*	*SMG*	*Rifle*	*Carbine*	*Remarks*
Zhanqi	144	33	–	29	–	The militia company of the Zhanqi Brigade usually studies proletarian theory and insists on practical training. The class, platoon, and company have a learning system and adhere to it all year round
Jinxing	37	1	1	4	2	
Dongfeng	31	1	–	–	6	
Xianfeng	34	1	–	–	7	

Source: "Statistics of the Distribution of Armed Militia Weapons in the Xianfeng Commune of Pixian County" (1975), Archives of the Pidu District Archives, File No. 152-001-0126-010, "Xianfeng Township File."

To sustain their combat effectiveness, the Militia Company of the Zhanqi Brigade owed much to the yearly reorganization and education diligently carried out by the Party branch. The militiamen's ideology and comprehension were honed to precision. Every year, the brigade conducted evaluations to select and reallocate personnel among the core militiamen, regular militiamen, and non-militiamen. The exceptional performers were rewarded with a place in the militia company or promotions, while those who fell short-faced demotions or expulsion. In 1972, for instance, the momentous reorganization unfolded under the watchful eye of Commissar Zhao of the People's Armed Forces. Together with the Work Group, they embarked on the pilot project for the 1973 militia regimentation at the Zhanqi Brigade, resulting in the integration of 10 new recruits, the transition of 40 regular militiamen to core militiamen, and 43 regular militiamen to core status. Consequently, the militia company was restructured into 9 platoons and 36 squads, with a formidable total of 490 militiamen. This constituted a remarkable 38.4% of the Zhanqi Brigade's overall populace, marking a noteworthy 0.7% increase from before the reorganization. The process of regimentation entailed organizing platoon-based studies on the nature, tasks, and criteria of the militia, followed by the announcement of enlistment, promotion, and demotion lists. The meticulous assignment of cadre members to squads, platoons, and militia positions hinged on the rigorous "five criteria for the successors of the revolutionary cause." Party branches submitted nominations, the masses deliberated, and the commune sanctioned. Adjustments were made to curtail the overextension of cadres, with particular emphasis on the deployment of deputy cadre members and female cadres. **Through the rigorous endeavors of militia education, the militiamen cultivated a love for learning, delving into the realms of Marxism-Leninism, Mao Zedong Thought, and the Party's fundamental principles. They experienced personal transformations, shedding ideological impediments along the way, thus fortifying their commitment to their duties.**

In addition, relying on the masses to embrace the path of open-door groupings becomes a vital cog in the machinery of the Zhanqi Brigade militia's collective efforts. As group education commences, the Zhanqi Brigade orchestrates joint learning sessions for the populace and the militia, fostering a shared growth. When summarizing their work and conducting assessments, they adopt a method where members evaluate the militia and vice versa, recognizing accomplishments while pinpointing shortcomings. By inciting member assessments of the militia and encouraging the militia to identify outstanding members supporting their cause, the brigade facilitates specialized discussions among the militia and the masses during departure, recruitment, and reassignment phases. Their focus: "How to be an exemplary militiaman" and "How to fortify the militia's endeavors." Guided by this elevated perspective, they deepen their understanding of the profound significance and indispensability of the militia's work.

Within their collective efforts, heartwarming scenes emerge—fathers aiding sons, mothers assisting daughters, brothers supporting sisters, husbands standing by wives. A testament to their devotion. Take, for instance, the resilient elder Su Dabo, a destitute farmer. At the sound of the militia's urgent assembly call, she promptly rises from slumber, urging the entire village's militia to gather. Or consider Uncle Chen, another impoverished farmer, who aids his son in recounting hardships and cherishing joys, hoping to secure his participation in the militia, even personally enlisting him.[27]

These examples prove pivotal in heightening the Zhanqi Brigade militia's consciousness. Their unwavering vigilance and shared wisdom cultivate an atmosphere teeming with optimism and progress. Not only do they ensure stability and bolster productive endeavors, but their tireless dedication serves as an invaluable blueprint for today's party on navigating the path of the masses.

In summation, against the backdrop of "Learning from Dazhai in Agriculture," the Zhanqi Brigade employs a multifaceted approach. They reshape the mindset of their cadres and populace, rallying countless women to transcend domestic confines and partake in agricultural and ancillary productions. Simultaneously, they refine the militia system and undertake transformative projects in agricultural and hydraulic infrastructure. Their unwavering commitment culminates in a consistent upswing in grain yields. Remarkably, their pursuit of agricultural abundance not only stems from extensive labor allocation but also from recalibrating incentives between agricultural and ancillary production, fostering the growth

[27] "Report on the Reorganization of the Militia Company of the Xianfeng Commune Zhanqi Brigade" (December 14, 1972), Archives of Pidu District, Sichuan Province, "Pixian County Xianfeng Township Archives", File No. 152-001-0105-018, No. Pages 117–124.

of pig farming, and enhancing soil fertility. Thus, they establish a virtuous cycle of agricultural progress.

5 Balancing Rationality Between Family and Collective: Achieving Side Business Prosperity

In the realm of side business endeavors, the Zhanqi Brigade boasts an array of productive resources such as swine, oxen, bees, oil mills, and grinding mills. Their operations are marked by diversification and a shrewd utilization of spatial resources, as exemplified by their astute beekeeping practices. Nonetheless, pig farming remains the prime side business pursuit for the Zhanqi Brigade. As the age-old adage goes, "Man tends to swine, swine cultivate the earth, and the land nurtures mankind." In an era devoid of chemical fertilizers and primarily reliant on agricultural income, the symbiotic bond between pig rearing and agricultural advancement was inextricable. Pig manure, a potent fertilizer, considerably bolstered grain production, thereby bolstering the supply of animal feed and propelling the growth of the pig farming trade.

During those times, side business endeavors were imbued with political significance, particularly pig farming, which thrived as a distinctive form of competition. In his missive titled "A Letter on the Development of Pig Farming (《关于发展养猪业的一封信》)" in 1959, Mao Zedong emphatically decreed the imperative for significant expansion in the pig farming domain. This directive reverberated as the guiding principle diligently upheld by grassroots organizations nationwide, assuming an indomitable role as a manifesto of sorts. When the Xianfeng Commune ranked its constituents based on per capita pig farming statistics, they posed the challenge, "Let's compare and observe, discerning the frontrunner: the Xianfeng Brigade hoists the crimson standard, standing tall in pig production. The Huohua Second Brigade, indomitable and ambitious, refuses to concede, ardently striving to seize the laurels. And the Huohua Third Brigade, a scholarly haven nestled in Dazhai, exhibits remarkable growth in pig farming, surging to secure third place within our commune."[28]

[28] Source: "The State of Pig Husbandry Development in the Xianfeng People's Commune at the End of February 1966" (February 26, 1966), Archives of Pidu District, Chengdu, Sichuan Province, "Pixian County Xianfeng Township Archive," File No. 152-001-0084-006, Page 14.

However, mere political mobilization alone failed to kindle the ardor within cadre ranks and commune members to raise pigs. Consider the case of the Xianfeng Brigade during the era of the "Great Leap Forward." Prior to the establishment of the People's Commune, the Xianfeng Brigade's livestock inventory boasted a grand total of 1844 porkers. Alas, following the Commune's inception in October 1958, a grim toll befell them, with 181 hogs succumbing within a mere two months, precipitating a simultaneous decline in both quantity and quality. Rooted in this predicament lay the post-Commune decree, wherein privately reared pigs and those nurtured within smaller communes were obligated to be relinquished to the larger commune at a diminished valuation. Feeding and oversight were centralized, and firmly held within the domain of production teams. "Such a directive spawned discord between former senior commune cadres and commune members concerning the pursuit of pig farming, thus stifling the boundless enthusiasm that could have been unleashed."[29]

Once upon a time, farmers deftly capitalized on the idle moments before and after meals, employing household provisions such as leftover rice and rice bran to nourish their porcine charges. However, this traditional method of family feeding gradually ceded ground to the commune's centralized approach, triggering a rapid surge in costs associated with feed and labor. As a consequence, the proactive leadership once embodied by cadres from smaller communes waned, and the communal populace displayed a diminished fervor for pig rearing, culminating in an all-encompassing setback for the porcine enterprise.

Political discourse must be melded with the actualities of rural society, striking a delicate balance between familial rationality and collective reasoning, to ignite the ardor of both members and cadre leaders within production teams. In the vernal month of 1959, the Sichuan Provincial Committee convened the Chongqing Level Six Cadres Conference, effecting swift adjustments to issues surrounding people's communes management. They decreed the devolution of swine ownership to the production brigades (management areas). The Xianfeng

[29] Source: "Report on the Progress of Pig Husbandry Development in the Xianfeng Management Area of Wanshou Commune, Pixian County" (June 18, 1959). Archives of Pidu District, Chengdu, Sichuan Province, "Pixian County Xianfeng Township Archive," File No. 152-001-0010-002, Page 9.

Brigade, teeming with over 500 households, compelled by the sheer magnitude of its numbers, further entrusted pig ownership to the production teams. The animals were tended and supervised by the unit, with the mess hall assuming custodial duties. To fortify these measures, they enacted "Five Fixations," "Five Combinations," competitive rewards, and a designated overseer for feeding management. **In the span of a mere four months, the Xianfeng Brigade had successfully transferred the reins of pig husbandry from the commune to the myriad production teams.** Nevertheless, beset by the pernicious throes of grain-feed competition and uneconomical private rearing practices, the Xianfeng Brigade's pig population experienced a sustained decline between 1959 and 1962. It wasn't until the promulgation of the "both public and private, with private farming as the crux" policy that the industry witnessed a revival, as denoted by Table 5.

How did the grassroots society astutely nurture the crucial ancillary profession of pig farming, deftly navigating the intricate waters between political discourse and economic exigencies? In the year 1965, a survey conducted within the Xianfeng People's Commune meticulously evaluated and compared the collective and individual gains pertaining to pigs reared under the aegis of "publicly owned, privately raised" provisions. Several production teams within the commune were the focus of this investigation. Class 1 bore a pernicious loss of 5.75 yuan per swine for the collective (sale proceeds—piglet expenditure—medicinal costs—remuneration for labor—fodder investment). Class 2 endured a loss of 15.5 yuan per pig for the collective. Meanwhile, Class 3 reveled in a profit of 2.75 yuan per pig, enriching the collective coffers. Refer to Table 6 for the precise balance sheet, illustrating the collective's inflows and outflows

Table 5 Xianfeng Brigade's Annual Swine Count

Year	Collectively owned sows	Collectively owned boar	Privately owned sows	Privately owned boar	Total Count

Data source: "Report on the Prodigious Advancement of Pig Farming within the Xianfeng Management Area of Pixian People's Commune" (June 18, 1959), Archives of Pidu District, Chengdu City, Sichuan Province, "Pixian County Xianfeng Township Archives," File Number: 152-001-0010-002, Pages 9–15; "Investigation Report on the Conundrum of Pig Husbandry Development in the Xianfeng Brigade (Amended Draft)" (May 21, 1961), File Number: 152-001-0013-002, Pages 4–10; "Statistical Table on the State of Pigs at the Conclusion of 1962 in Pixian Xianfeng People's Commune," File Number: 152-001-0016-004, Page 11; Zhao Renchun and Gao Guangjun's unpublished "Xianfeng Village Chronicles," Page 55.

Table 6 Collective Balance Sheet for "Publicly Owned, Privately Raised" Pigs in the Xianfeng People's Commune, 1965, Unit: Yuan

Name of production team	*Sales value*	*Cost of piglets*	*Cost veterinary drug*	*Member remuneration*	*Feed input*	*Collective profit and loss*
Shuguang Team 1	67.50	10.50	2	60.75	0	− 5.75
Shuguang Team 7	67.50	13.50	2	67.50	0	− 15.5
Huohua Team 2	67.50	10.50	2	47.25	5	+ 2.75

Data source: "Investigation Report on the Status of Developing Publicly Owned Pigs" (April 15, 1965), Archives of Pidu District, Chengdu City, Sichuan Province, "Pixian County Xianfeng Township Archives," File Number: 152-001-0038-019, Pages 82–85.

concerning "publicly owned, privately raised" porcine ventures in the Xianfeng People's Commune during 1965.

From the above chart, it becomes apparent that the greater the collective losses of a production team, the higher the remuneration for its members. However, this survey table fails to account for the investment value of each pig's manure, despite its significant impact. Based on estimated work points, the manure investment per pig amounts to approximately 25 yuan, representing the members' investment in the collective. In the absence of any collective feed input, the individual investment per pig in terms of dry and refined feed, rice bran, and the like, stands at approximately 35 yuan. Notably, within the table, Huohua Team Two benefits from a collective subsidy of 5 yuan toward the cost of feed. Consequently, the team members' investment per pig for rearing amounts to 30 yuan, resulting in a labor remuneration of 17.25 yuan after deducting costs from the total payment of 47.25 yuan. Taking into account the manure investment of 25 yuan, the members' actual income per pig—the total labor remuneration—amounts to 42.25 yuan, equivalent to the agricultural labor income for approximately 42.25 days.

The ultimate conclusion of this survey maintains that Huohua Team Two aligns with the principles of mutual benefit between the collective and its members. By no means does it exemplify a case of compromising the collective's welfare for individual gains. On the contrary, it fosters the development of collective pig farming while concurrently encouraging members to exploit communal resources for raising publicly owned pigs, ultimately bolstering their incomes. Notably, the state's purchase price for fattened pigs remains notably low. Even if we disregard the pivotal role of pig manure in boosting agricultural productivity, collective pig farming would yield minimal profit, regardless of any reduction in member remuneration by Huohua Team Two. For members, the path to increased earnings lies in capitalizing on their surplus labor and the affordable communal water supply for pig rearing.

Consequently, in such circumstances, a leader who comprehends the comprehensive returns of collective agricultural subsidiary industries would rationally advocate for the vigorous encouragement of communal or private pig-rearing practices. Conversely, leaders incapable of embracing the broader context would struggle to instill enthusiasm for pig farming among the members. As for member households, the sensible choice entails leveraging their spare time and the communal water supply to rear pigs, thereby securing additional income through work points and manure investments, effectively sustaining the well-being of their entire families. According to a 1964 briefing from the Xianfeng Commune on the development of collective subsidiary industries, 47.4% of production teams exhibited a favorable outlook toward pig farming. These teams' leaders were described as "clear-minded, with a defined direction, resolute in implementing the Party's policies," with the most notable illustration being the diverse production teams of the Pioneer Brigade.[30]

Therefore, led by the impoverished farmer Tang Sixue (唐思学), the Xianfeng Brigade emerged as a force to be reckoned with. They struck a delicate balance, aligning themselves with the political agenda of their superiors while also safeguarding their economic gains. Swiftly delegating the reins of livestock husbandry to the production teams through methods of collective contracting, individual household breeding, or individual household contracting and breeding, they achieved a remarkable feat. Even amidst a significant downturn in the profitability of the pig farming industry, the Xianfeng Brigade managed to minimize their losses, emerging as the pinnacle of pig farming excellence within the entire commune, county, and region. Like a scarlet banner fluttering proudly, they became the pride of Pixian County. Furthermore, the surplus organic

[30] Source: "Briefing on the Development of Collective Subsidiary Industries by the Party Committee of the Xianfeng Commune of the Communist Party of China" (January 21, 1964), preserved in the Archives of Pidu District, Sichuan Province, "Archives of Pixian Pioneer Township," Archive Number 152-001-0032-011, pages 48–50.

fertilizer derived from pig farming acted as a shield, shielding the Xianfeng Brigade's agricultural yield from the tumultuous tides of the "Great Leap Forward" movement.[31] By 1966, the Xianfeng Brigade reigned supreme, boasting the highest pig population and the greatest number of pigs per capita throughout the entire commune, averaging an impressive 1.06 pigs per person. It is worth highlighting that the destiny of the Xianfeng Brigade's pig farming industry, whether it continues its upward trajectory or ventures further into the realms of success, hinges greatly on the collective's ability to maintain rationality and strike a harmonious balance between collective reasoning and individual rationality.

Simultaneously, the fledgling Zhanqi Brigade had only just taken flight, barely a year since its inception. As of the end of February 1966, their pig population tallied a mere 806, amounting to a meager average of 0.83 pigs per person, relegating them to the fourth-lowest position within the commune's rankings. Thirteen households bore the burden of no pigs at all, among which forty sows loomed (five under collective ownership and thirty-five privately held). Nevertheless, the Zhanqi Brigade staged an astounding comeback, culminating in an impressive 1614 pigs by the close of 1972. This newfound prosperity translated into a remarkable average of 1.27 pigs per person, with a total of 114 sows (seventy-seven collectively owned and thirty-seven privately held). Their feat positioned them as the epitome of pig farming prowess, leading the commune's league tables in pigs per capita, as eloquently depicted in Table 7.

In '71, the Zhanqi Brigade outshone its '67 records, proudly standing as the beacon of the Xianfeng Commune and even Pixian County with its hefty hog population and impressive per capita pig count. Yet, the challenges faced in the swine industry after '66 were distinct from the tumultuous times of institutional reform. Philip C. Huang's study of the Yangtze River Delta region revealed a post-"Great Leap Forward" landscape where collectives solely tended to breed pigs: the commune overseeing boars, the brigade nurturing sows, and individual members raising fattening swine. Alas, the nation's meager pork prices rendered farming unprofitable, discouraging farmers from swine stewardship. The question then arises: how did the Zhanqi Brigade, in a mere four years, rally the masses to embrace porcine pursuits? And how did they deftly

[31] Source: "Investigation Report on the Development of Pig Farming in the Xianfeng Brigade (Revised Draft)" (May 21, 1961), held at the Pidu District Archives. Pixian County Xianfeng Township Archives, Document Number 152-001-0013-002, pages 4–10.

Table 7 Pig Farming Overview of Zhanqi Brigade in the Years 1966–1967 and 1971–1973, (Unit: number of pigs)

Year	*Total count*	*Pig count per capita*	*Publicly owned sows*	*Privately owned sows*
1966	806	0.83	5	35
1967	896	0.88	2	27
1971	1516	1.22	–	–
1972	1614	1.27	77	37
1973	1591	1.23	57	18

Data sources: "Status of Pig Husbandry Development in Xianfeng People's Commune by the End of February 1966" (February 26, 1966), Document Number 152-001-0084-006, page 14; "Allocation Table for Pixian County's 1967 Annual Settlement—Zhanqi Brigade" (Document Number 152-001-0089-011), pages 165–180; "Several Specific Opinions on Current Pig Husbandry Development" (December 25, 1971), Document Number 152-001-0099-004, pages 14–15; "Allocation Table for Zhanqi Brigade's 1972 Annual Settlement, Pixian County Xianfeng People's Commune" (Document Number 152-001-0107-002), pages 16–30; "Allocation Table for Zhanqi Brigade's 1973 Annual Settlement, Pixian County Xianfeng People's Commune" (Document Number 152-001-0112-003), pages 36–52.

navigate the conflicting interests between the collective and its members? Notably, the Xianfeng Brigade witnessed a dip in the growth rate of fattening pigs compared to the Zhanqi Brigade, as depicted in Table 8. The reasons behind this anomaly warrant exploration.

Historical accounts unveil the early years of the Zhanqi Brigade, mirroring the rise and fall experienced by their brethren, with pig production plateauing instead of prospering. As agricultural practices matured, fodder concerns became paramount. The party's branch within the Zhanqi Brigade launched an inquiry into the populace's disinclination to raise pigs. Their findings revealed a chorus of voices lamenting the arduous quest for quality feed: "We'd gladly nourish the swine, were it not for the insufferable fodder hunt." The party branch, determined to unearth the truth, embarked on earnest encounters with the masses, unearthing a disconcerting reality. Those cadres and members bemoaning the scarcity of sustenance were, in fact, peddling pig feed in the bustling marketplace. The allure lay in the exorbitant prices commanded by these provisions, where a modest sale of maize bran or rice bran translated to a profit akin to fattening a porcine specimen—a shrewd maneuver, saving both toil and time.

Table 8 A comparative snapshot of year-end pig statistics for Xianfeng Brigade and Zhanqi Brigade in 1971

Brigade	*Number of households*	*Population*	*Area of lands (mu)*	*Pig statistics*							
				Publicly owned			*Privately owned*			*Total count*	*Number of pigs per capita*
				Old sows	*Little sows*	*Boars*	*Old sows*	*Little sows*	*Boars*		
Xianfeng	689	3241	4096	108	10	68	226	17	2701	3130	0.97
Zhanqi	275	1238	1828	51	23	–	29	5	1403	1511	1.22
National Total	In 1970, the average number of pigs per capita in the country was 0.29; in 1973, less than 4% of the counties (cities) in the country met the requirement of "one pig per person, one pig per mu"										

Sources: "Several Specific Opinions on the Development of Pig Production" (Dec. 25, '71), preserved in the Pidu District Archives of Sichuan Province, "Archives of Xianfeng Township in Pixian County," Archive No. 152-001-0099-004, pp. 14–15; Bai Yunsong. Research on Pig Farming and Rural Society in Hebei Province during the Collective Era [D]. Baoding: Hebei University, 2017

"Feeding pigs falls short of selling pig feed," a clash between personal or familial gain and the collective interest. For the rational family, the allure of maximizing short-term profit reigns supreme. Yet, from a collective standpoint, selling more pigs, amassing fertile feed, and bolstering agricultural production serve as the driving force behind the comprehensive considerations of politics and economics. Society deems composting a collective responsibility, devoid of personal involvement. Thus, if the preceding phase of pig farming witnessed a struggle between communal and private husbandry, the Zhanqi Brigade now faces the battle of collective versus market dominance in the era of private ownership.

To confront this quandary, the Zhanqi Brigade commences by reshaping the mindset of its cadres. The party branch inaugurates a cadre training course to instill the essence of the party's fundamental course. Through this educational endeavor, certain cadres willingly admit their errors, offering self-reflections during the meetings with impoverished farmers. Concurrently, they renounce the lucrative gains obtained from exorbitantly priced sales. This method ensures the absence of clandestine pig feed transactions over the subsequent three years. Additionally, the entire brigade, including cadres and members alike, adheres to the breeding of robust swine in accordance with the prescribed plan. Neither sows carrying offspring nor piglets bred in personal quarters are sold independently. Instead, they are dutifully relinquished to the brigade for organized marketing, thereby securing the stable growth of pig farming throughout the entire brigade. Such efforts guarantee the supply of agricultural fertilizer and expedite the augmentation of the porcine population.

Beyond rectifying the cognizance of cadres and members, lies the quintessential imperative of bolstering the pig farming enthusiasm among the latter through institutional avenues. The Zhanqi Brigade's approach entails elevating pig numbers and enhancing soil fertility by optimizing feed grain allocation, regulating the piglet source, nurturing impoverished and lower-middle-class farmers engaged in pig farming, and meticulously coordinating feed cultivation.

Firstly, feed grain distribution encounters a transformative overhaul. While private farming predominates during this period, the brigade persuades its members to perceive pig manure as an investment toward the collective. Thus, each household quantifies its investment in the collective through pig farming, factoring in the volume of pig manure produced and its corresponding price per load, subsequently converting the amount into grain equivalent. As detailed in Table 9, the Zhanqi Brigade attained a yield of 1.24 catties of grain for each yuan invested in feed grains in 1966, soaring to an impressive 2.07 catties in 1972, before tapering down to 1.32 catties in 1973. In contrast, the feed grain allocation in 1972 for the entire Pixian County amounted to a mere 6% of the total grain allocation, yielding a paltry 1.19 catties of grain for every yuan invested—trailing behind the Zhanqi Brigade. Such adjustments in grain-to-feed grain investment ratios enable the fine-tuning of labor distribution within the brigade, with feed grain distribution surpassing work point allocation in 1972, ultimately kindling the members' ardor for pig farming.

Secondly, by grasping the origins of piglets and internalizing market risks, one effectively smoothens the undulations of the market. The Zhanqi Brigade's officers firmly believe that the fluctuating pig farming numbers of yesteryear were partly due to the sway of market prices. Therefore, it is imperative for the collective to possess the reins of pig farming authority to ensure a stable porcine supply. Only through unwavering adherence to the "dual-track" approach of pig farming can the acceleration of pig production be realized. The Zhanqi Brigade's Party branch assimilated historical lessons and substantiated, through practical evidence, the capacity of collective control over pig farming rights to insulate pigs from the caprice of market prices. Even when piglet prices reached exorbitant heights of over one yuan per catties in 1971, the brigade sold their porcine charges for a mere eight jiao per catties (10 jiao = 1 yuan), assuring the impoverished and middle-class peasants of their livestock sustenance. Similarly, during the market's plunge in 1973, with piglet prices decaying to a paltry three jiao per catties, the brigade's sales persisted at two jiao per catties, guaranteeing members' feeding requirements. A glance at Table 7 reveals that in 1966, a mere five publicly owned sows graced the Zhanqi Brigade, yet by 1972, their number skyrocketed to 77, rendering piglet supply nearly invulnerable to the swells of price fluctuations. In the face of dissenting cadres and members, who decried the futility of feeding sows and proposed their liquidation, the Zhanqi Party branch unwaveringly advocated for their perpetuation, supplementing select sow-feeders with an additional 45 points per month to safeguard their livelihoods, invigorating their dedication. This culminated in the enduring stability of publicly owned sow quantities.

Table 9 Grain allocation among Zhanqi Brigade members

Year	*Total allocation (Catty)*	*Basic grains*		*Work point grains*			*Grains for husbandry*		
		Count (Catty)	*Ratio (%)*	*Count (Catty)*	*Ratio (%)*	*Average Gain per day*	*Count (Catty)*	*Ratio (%)*	*Average Gain per yuan*
1966	515,953.8	411,285.8	80	822,273.0	16	0.98	20,123.0	4	1.24
1967	534,278.5	425,709.0	80	85,296.5	16	1	20,972.0	4	1.3
1972	660,719.5	527,401.5	80	53,402.5	8	0.43	78,570.5	12	2.07
1973	700,578.5	561,399.0	80	83,402.0	12	0.7	55,347.0	8	1.32

Source: "Pixian County 1966 Annual Final Distribution Table—Zhanqi Brigade," Document No. 152-001-0086-002, pages 20–38; "Pixian County 1967 Annual Final Distribution Table—Zhanqi Brigade," Document No. 152-001-0089-011, pages 165–180; "Pixian County Xianfeng Commune Zhanqi Brigade 1972 Annual Final Distribution Table," Document No. 152-001-0107-002, pages 16–30; "Pixian County Xianfeng Commune Zhanqi Brigade 1973 Annual Final Distribution Table," Document No. 152-001-0112-003, pages 36–52

Thirdly, the support for impoverished and lower-middle peasants, as well as underprivileged members, to engage in pig farming endeavors and expand the domain thereof. Since the inception of the "Four Cleans" campaign, the Party has espoused reliance on and assistance to impoverished and lower-middle peasants as the rural path to traverse, recognizing them as the vital force propelling collective economic growth and prosperity. By bolstering pig farming among this demographic, one strikes at the core of fostering the industry's advancement. Deprived of capital to procure pigs or erect swine dwellings, these individuals found themselves impeded in their porcine pursuits or bereft of porcine presence altogether. It is within this context that the Zhanqi Brigade, in a display of collective magnanimity, extended financial support and loans to a sum of 237 households, amounting to a grand total of 445 swine. Under the collective's benevolent guardianship, these stricken households succeeded in rearing fatted pigs, augmenting their earnings, and kindling a brighter existence. For instance, a destitute peasant named Meng Xiurong, a lone mother grappling with the responsibility of three young offspring, faced the onerous task of annually repaying the collective over 100 yuan, her daily life steeped in arduity. In 1971, the production team bestowed upon her a wooden enclosure and assisted in the construction of two earthen pigsties. Nurturing two publicly owned sows and procuring four piglets on credit, Meng Xiurong transformed her situation within a brief span of time. From a household in debt to one that reaped substantial profits, she pocketed a handsome sum of 230 yuan in cash over the course of a year, dramatically ameliorating her circumstances and even erecting a novel dwelling. **The measures undertaken by the Zhanqi Brigade to stabilize sow quantities and control the origin of piglets also fulfill the invaluable role of thwarting the insidious perils of internal wealth disparity within the village community—a quintessential attribute of the socialist creed.**

Fourthly, a rational arrangement of feed emerged as a pivotal pillar in the art of pig farming for the illustrious Zhanqi Brigade. Sky-high prices of sustenance constituted a vital adversary, afflicting the esteemed Xianfeng cooperative's porcine enterprise with grievous losses. Through tireless exploration spanning several years, the Zhanqi Brigade unearthed a stratagem that defied the grain's dominion: cultivating bounteous crops suited for fodder, embracing an assortment of green manure crops like cowpea seedlings and sweet potatoes, and transitioning to maize after the harvest of dual-season rice. The cultivation expanded, sowing autumnal scarlet sweet potatoes or cowpea seedlings following the rice's early and medium yield, later interposing with the burgeoning of spring. Seizing opportunities, they deftly interwove crops, surrendering the green manure fields entirely to the sowing of radishes and cowpea seedlings, with maize and Basan beans concurrently finding their roots. As the maize pits were unearthed, the Basan seedlings fed the swine, before the inclusion of sweet potatoes. Once the soybean-laden ridges were harvested, cowpea seedlings adorned the terrain, as all available crevices along ditches, riverbanks, and fallow lands were zealously seized. Resourceful deployment of agricultural by-products ensued, augmenting the fodder trove, aided by three dedicated feed crushers within the collective, pulverizing corn stalks, cobs, husks, pea stems, and vegetable scraps. Employing these very measures, each porcine inmate of the collective feasted on over 1800 kilograms of feed annually, accompanied by over 60 kilograms of processed dry materials gleaned from agricultural by-products, surmounting 70% of their yearly sustenance needs. Coupled with the personal allotments of the members and the opportune harvesting during agricultural lulls, the quandary of feed sourcing for swine reached its resolution.[32] Gleaned from the memories of certain brigade cadre, it became apparent that during that period, the collective furnished pig feed to each farmer at a significantly reduced price, a fraction of the outlay for procuring fertilizers, thus rendering pig farming a more judicious pursuit for agrarian folk.

Moreover, the triumph of the Zhanqi Brigade's swine husbandry was indissolubly tied to the exemplary conduct of its cadre, who took it upon themselves to guide the members by personal example. With a mere 41-strong contingent of the brigade's party branch tending to 54 hogs, an average of 1.3 swine were dutifully nurtured by each individual. Eventually, the Zhanqi Brigade soared to an average of 1.2 pigs per person, bestowing a yearly bounty of 130,000 loads of pig manure. In the vernal and festival seasons, the Zhanqi Brigade rallied the masses, beseeching them to retrieve over 200,000 catties of verdant grass from afar, while amassing an abundance of green manure, ash residue, clippings, and wild manure, thus augmenting their fertilizer stockpile while driving down expenditures. In 1971 alone, a staggering sum exceeding 4000 yuan

[32] From "Promoting the Development of Pig Production Direction" (June 19, 1974), Pidu District Archives of Sichuan Province, "Xianfeng Township File of Pixian County", File No. 152-001-0119-026, pp. 136–141.

was preserved in cash disbursements. The intricate apportionment of fertilization labor is eloquently illustrated in Fig. 1.

From the depicted graph, it becomes evident that the investment-to-work ratio in fertilizer surged to 2.59 times the figure in 1966. With the exorbitant prices of industrial fertilizers, resorting to natural fertilizers emerged as the most cost-effective solution. For instance, in 1972, the Xianfeng Brigade's cadre purchased copious amounts of ammonia water for field application. Yet, due to improper utilization, not only did it amplify cash expenditures, but it also hampered production. To rectify this predicament, the cadre organized study sessions, offering relevant education. Drawing lessons from this ordeal, they expressed their determination to acquire the expertise of the Zhanqi Brigade, striving for self-sufficiency and cost reduction.[33]

Undoubtedly, the low cost of natural fertilizers aligns with the nation's macroeconomic backdrop. During that era, a period marked by initial capital accumulation within industrialization, the collective organization

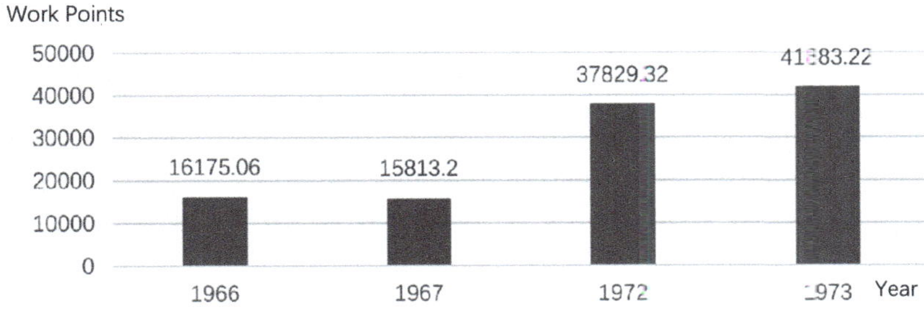

Fig. 1 Distribution of fertilizer labor in Zhanqi Brigade for the entirety of 1966–1967 and 1972–1973. *Source*: "Financial Allocation Table for Pixian County's 1966 Annual Settlement—Zhanqi Brigade", File No. 152-001-0086-002, pp. 20–38; "Financial Allocation Table for Pixian County's 1967 Annual Settlement—Zhanqi Brigade", File No. 152-001-0089-011, pp. 165–180; "Financial Allocation Table for Xianfeng Commune's Zhanqi Brigade in 1972", File No. 152-001-0107-002, pp. 16–30; "Financial Allocation Table for Xianfeng Commune's Zhanqi Brigade in 1973", File No. 152-001-0112-003, pp. 36–52

[33] "Brief Report on the Implementation of Rural Economic Policies and Cash Distribution in the Xianfeng Commune" (December 1, 1972), Pidu District Archives, Pixian County Pioneer Township File, Document Number 152-001-0105-010, pp. 47–50.

in rural regions functioned as the organizational conduit for state accumulation systems encompassing unified procurement and distribution of agricultural products, as well as centralized fiscal collection and support.[34] With industrial fertilizers commanding higher prices when dispatched to rural areas, juxtaposed with lower prices of agricultural products, the natural fertilizers' prices diverged significantly from their industrial counterparts.

In 1972, the Office of the Water Conservancy Bureau in Pixian County, Sichuan Province, disseminated literature such as "How did the Zhanqi Brigade tackle pig feed (《先锋公社战旗大队是怎样解决猪饲料的》)," showcasing the pig husbandry enterprise of the Zhanqi Brigade. From 1971 to 1973, the Zhanqi Brigade delivered a substantial 3771 fat pigs to the state, averaging more than three per household annually. Consequently, the Zhanqi Brigade gained a competitive edge in auxiliary production.

Upon contemplation of the aforementioned, it becomes apparent that pig farming indeed procured comprehensive returns through the integration of cultivation and animal husbandry within production teams. Admittedly, when assessing solely each household member's income, the profitability of pig rearing waned as piglet or pig feed prices ascended, making the individual sale of piglets and feed seemingly more lucrative. Nevertheless, from a holistic standpoint, pig farming not only bolstered members' immediate cash inflows, but, more importantly, the accumulated pig manure constituted a pivotal factor in enhancing soil fertility and agricultural output. Additionally, the quantity of fat pigs sold served as a significant avenue to heighten collective economic accumulation and attain political prestige.

Ergo, pig farming unveils a quintessential quandary within China's industrialization trajectory: the pursuit of short-term gains versus the enduring vision of comprehensive industrial accumulation. This quandary, pervasive during the collective era, partly accounted for the rise of socialist education and movements like "Learning from Dazhai in Agriculture." The battle and equilibrium between collective rationality and household rationality dictated the efficacy of such endeavors.

[34] Dong Xiaodan, Wen Tiejun. Macro Economic Fluctuations and Rural "Governance Crisis"—An Empirical Analysis of the Relationship between "Three Rural Issues" and "Three Lives Issues" since the Reform [J]. Management World, 2008(9):67–75.

When the Zhanqi Brigade first unfurled its banner, the swine industry had already embraced the principle of "a symbiotic blend of public and private, with private farming at the helm." Pig feed and piglets, having partially regained their place in the market, unraveled the growing tensions between the collective and the marketplace. Through ideological enlightenment, the Zhanqi Brigade tackled the members' quandaries, putting an end to the sale of pig feed and piglets. Augmenting the distribution ratio for feed grain boosted the members' fervor, while the collective's grasp over swine husbandry tamed the undulations of market prices, stabilizing production and fostering the relentless advancement of collective pig farming. Moreover, the collective's magnanimity shone as they extended substantial credit for piglets to the destitute and the struggling, leveraging prepayments to provide these impoverished households with the productive capital, a blow to the foundation of socioeconomic disparity. The collective's rational mastery became the lifeblood of the crimson flag that waved in the Western territories, while the Xianfeng Brigade, regrettably, failed to wield its critical role in the realm of collective reason.

In a capital-starved era, from 1965 to 1973, the Zhanqi Brigade marshaled internal labor, even the toil of women, rallying them under the militia system to partake in the bounty of agricultural and auxiliary pursuits. Swiftly, the agrarian output surged, and prosperity dawned upon the collective coffers. Upholding the credo of high accumulation, scant distribution, and parsimony in production costs, the Zhanqi Brigade amassed its primordial capital, hoisting the standard of the Western front.

Simultaneously, while attaining their internal capital accumulation, the Zhanqi Brigade upheld the sacred duty of securing the fundamental livelihoods of all farmers by tending to the destitute households (depleted in resources) and the disadvantaged. As discerned from Table 10, the proportion of the depleted households within the Zhanqi Brigade rarely surpassed 20%, momentarily spiking to 18.3% in 1972, driven by the capricious forces of calamity—an enviable figure when compared to the national average. Consider Hubei Province, where, during the 1970s, the depleted households commonly constituted around 30% of the total households.[35] Notably, the per capita population of the depleted households in the Zhanqi Brigade paled in comparison

[35] Yue Renchong. A Historical Probe into the Phenomenon of Depleted Resources in Xishui County during the 1970s [J]. Jianghan Forum, 2015(10): 87–92.

to that of the distributing households, signifying their meager labor force or the presence of frail elderly and infirm kin. Even the slightest mishap would plunge these households into a pit of fiscal ruin. It was during the era of the People's Commune that the distribution system, permitting loans (or depletions), assumed the role of safeguarding the essential lives of members. Simultaneously, the brigade's internal benevolence toward the beleaguered households mollified the repayment quandaries of the depleted, resolving the burdensome woes. Especially in the face of natural catastrophes, such as the ravages that befell the Zhanqi Brigade in 1972, leaving grain production in shambles, the brigade extended its benevolence by bolstering its provisions to the distressed households.

During that era, the Zhanqi Brigade extended explicit and covert support to its less fortunate members by tending to the "household enjoying the five guarantees,"[36] impoverished individuals, and managing excess resources. This internal adjustment within the village achieved the noble aim of uplifting the impoverished, thus fulfilling a vital social security role in rural regions and establishing the bedrock for the stable growth of the Zhanqi Brigade. In the epoch of collectivization, the distinguished hallmark of China's rural social security system resided in a framework that harmonized with the requisites of an industrialized accumulation under a planned economy. Embracing the collective economy as its cornerstone and collective welfare as its core, this system embodied not only relief measures targeting disaster-stricken and impoverished individuals but also provisions for the care and preferential treatment of military dependents and veterans. It even introduced novel elements such as the "Five Guarantees" support system and cooperative healthcare. The means and channels employed were multifaceted, encompassing production loans, resource allocation beyond means, grain repurchases, collective philanthropic aid, and essential national relief—all at the forefront of this explicit facade of social security. Concurrently, amidst the arduous rural economic conditions of yesteryears, the distribution system, with its semblance of egalitarianism in the rural collective economy, discreetly

[36] Translator's note: "Households enjoy the five guarantees" mainly refer to the rural elderly who are old and frail, unable to take care of themselves, have no children to support or cannot support their children. The five guarantees refer to the five safeguards provided by the state for this group of people, namely "food, housing, medical care, medicine, and burial.".

Table 10 Distribution outcomes of the Zhanqi Brigade in 1966–1967 and 1972–1973

Basic Demography			*Household with surplus*				*Households with deficit*				*Care situation*		
Year	*Number of households*	*Population*	*Number of households*	*Ratio (%)*	*Population*	*Money gained (yuan)*	*Number of households*	*Ratio (%)*	*Population*	*Money gained (yuan)*	*Number of destitute households*	*Money gained (yuan)*	*Grains gained (catties)*
1966	248	999	218	87.8	908	25,495	30	12.1	91	1630	28	1856	1580
1967	251	1013	207	82.5	855	28,603	44	17.5	158	1812	–	–	–
1972	300	1274	245	81.7	1085	25,386	55	18.3	189	4174	33	126	1344
1973	305	1298	259	84.9	1198	26,148	46	15.1	100	3673	21	261	363

Data sources: "Zhanqi Brigade, 1966 Annual Settlement and Distribution Table, Pixian County," document number 152-001-0086-002, pages 20–38; "Zhanqi Brigade, 1967 Annual Settlement and Distribution Table, Pixian County," document number 152-001-0089-011, pages 165–180; "Zhanqi Brigade, 1972 Annual Settlement and Distribution Table, Xianfeng Commune, Pixian County," document number 152-001-0107-002, pages 16–30; "Zhanqi Brigade, 1973 Annual Settlement and Distribution Table, Xianfeng Commune, Pixian County," document number 152-001-0112-003, pages 36–52.

Table 11 "Price scissors" in agricultural and industrial product prices of the Zhanqi Brigade during 1966–1967 and 1972–1973

Year	*Net production value of Zhanqi Brigade (yuan)*	*"Price scissors"*	*Estimated contribution of Zhanqi to industrialization (yuan)*
1966	37,791.38	0.19	7184.91
1967	44,162.43	0.14	6023.89
1972	59,368.78	0.17	10,272.64
1973	66,982.46	0.18	11,768.32
Total			35,249.76

Source: Yan Ruizhen, et al. "The Status, Development Trends, and Countermeasures of the Price Scissors Difference of China's Industrial and Agricultural Products." Economic Research, 1990 (2): 64–70. Ministry of Agriculture of the People's Republic of China. Statistical Data on China's Agriculture in the Past 60 Years of New China. Beijing: China Agriculture Press, 2009. "Financial Distribution Table of the Zhanqi Brigade for the Year 1966 in Pixian County," Archive No. 152-001-0086-002, pp. 20–38; "Financial Distribution Table of the Zhanqi Brigade for the Year 1967 in Pixian County," Archive No. 152-001-0089-011, pp. 165–180; "Financial Distribution Table of the Zhanqi Brigade in Xianfeng Commune, Pixian County for the Year 1972," Archive No. 152-001-0107-002, pp. 16–30; "Financial Distribution Table of the Zhanqi Brigade in Xianfeng Commune, Pixian County for the Year 1973," Archive No. 152-001-0112-003, pp. 36–52.

played an integral role in offering latent social security—an implicit undercurrent.[37] Therefore, the multi-tiered social security apparatus crafted by the state, collective entities, and individuals not only safeguarded the farmers' basic subsistence but also laid the institutional groundwork for nascent capital accumulation during the infancy of industrialization.

Moreover, beyond fulfilling the internal requisites of initial capital accumulation and ensuring fundamental survival, the Zhanqi Brigade consistently surpassed the state's grain procurement quotas. By capitalizing on the "price scissors" between industrial and agricultural prices, they made substantial contributions to the nation's industrialization endeavor, as exemplified in Table 11.

The data above, extrapolated from Professor Yan Ruizhen's calculation method on the "price scissors" between industry and agriculture, reveals a remarkable feat accomplished by the Zhanqi Brigade. In a mere four years, their contribution to industrialization exceeded a staggering sum of 35,000 yuan. This figure leads us to estimate that, between 1965

[37] Source: Song Shiyun. "Structure and Changes of China's Rural Social Security System (1949–2002)." Beijing: People's Publishing House, 2006.

and 1978, the Zhanqi Brigade's impact on the nation's industrialization amounted to no less than 100,000 yuan.

By 1974, the Zhanqi Brigade had achieved a commendable standard in pig farming and agricultural production, given the prevailing technological conditions of the time. The input–output ratio of labor and fertilizers had dwindled, leaving little room for further growth. The rewards reaped from continuous investments in labor and fertilizers had reached a plateau, while the efficacy of revolutionary rhetoric and political mobilization tactics had begun to wane. Contemplating their next move, the Zhanqi Brigade shifted their focus toward leveraging existing collective accumulation, aiming to transform their agricultural village into a thriving hub of agricultural, industrial, and ancillary pursuits. Simultaneously, they sought to secure external resources, aligning their strategy with a broader vision of progress.

PART II

1974–2003 The Gilded Zhanqi—The Dawn and Expansion of Village Industrialization

CHAPTER 5

The Arduous Genesis of Village Industry (1974–1977)

1 Core Thread: Local Government Corporatism

Recalling the intricate dance between the central and local authorities from the 1950s to the 1990s, one could argue that it was a process of the central power relinquishing its grip to empower the localities. Curiously enough, each instance of devolution seemed intrinsically linked to China's cyclical economic perils. The initial delegation of authority occurred between 1958 and 1960, when Soviet investment in China halted, causing an abrupt decline in fiscal resources. The ensuing fiscal deficits spiraled, surpassing 10% of revenue in both 1959 and 1960. Consequently, the national economy took a severe blow, with GDP sliding in 1960 and plummeting by a staggering 27.3% in 1961. A subsequent wave of decentralization emerged in the late 1960s and early 1970s, paralleling intensified geopolitical tensions in China's neighboring territories. This period saw the birth of indigenous fiscal deficits, reaching a staggering 2.048 billion yuan in 1967. Coupled with a substantial drop in fiscal revenue, China experienced another economic setback. Three more rounds of ostensible fiscal reforms between 1980 and 1993 aimed to redress the situation, employing the mantra of "Fiscal Responsibility System (财政包干)." Notably, the impetus behind the 1980 reform stemmed from a financial crisis triggered by heightened investments in industrial construction and increased spending to uplift living standards. By 1979, the fiscal deficit had surged to a formidable 135.41 billion yuan, devouring 11.8% of total revenue. Likewise, the reform of 1988

© Peking University Press 2024
X. Dong, *Zhanqi Village Over Fifty Years*,
https://doi.org/10.1007/978-981-97-5426-7_5

materialized as China grappled with its inaugural stagflation crisis since the nation's inception, witnessing an alarming fiscal deficit equivalent to 14.8% of revenue in that year and soaring to a daunting 25.1% in 1989.

From the retrospective panorama painted above, a certain empirical understanding emerges: **throughout the years spanning the 1950s to the 1990s, whenever economic crises loomed, the central government instinctively sought solace in devolving power to stimulate local development and weather the storm.**

Opinions diverge on the nature of China's planned economic system, often seen as a realm where comprehensive government intervention prevails. Although the tides of the market economy have gradually reshaped China's industrialization process since the 1980s, the government has remained an "intrinsic participant" in economic affairs. Characterizing both the planned economy and the market economy stages as facets of "government corporatism (政府公司主义)" would not be an overstatement. Regardless of the rhetoric surrounding government-market relations, the indelible truth remains the government's unwavering grip on economic life. The distinction lies in the era-specific nature of this corporatism. **During the planned economy era, it embodied a "central government corporatism," whereas since the 1980s, it has been predominantly shaped by the tenets of "local government corporatism."**[1]

The birth of the "local government corporatism" model stems from profound economic structural reasons. In the midst of fiscal reform, the delayed division of powers between central and local governments, coupled with the labyrinthine government budgeting channels, have left local government budgets reliant on precarious finances. It's a hand-to-mouth existence, with administrative expenses and personnel costs often left unguaranteed, rendering the government unable to fulfill its rightful duties. Consequently, fiscal power and administrative authority have been torn asunder. To ensure the smooth functioning of governance, the faithful execution of responsibilities, and the completion of assigned tasks, local governments at all levels have had to resort to extralegal

[1] "Local government corporatism" emerged as a concept coined by Professor Jean C. Oi of Stanford University, who observed the dynamics of township enterprises in the Southern Jiangsu model. See Jean C. Oi, 1992, "Fiscal Reform and the Economic Foundations of Local State Corporatism in China", World Politics (1992), World Politics, 45 (Oct.).

fiscal revenues (off-budget income and self-raised funds) as a means of sustaining operations.

The pivotal source of such off-budget revenues lies in the remittance of profits from township enterprises, particularly those industrious endeavors meticulously overseen by local authorities themselves.[2]

From 1979 to 1992, the total output value of township enterprises surged at an annual average pace of 28.2%. By 1994, these ventures accounted for half of the nation's industrial output value, providing gainful employment to a staggering 110 million individuals. Notably, the calculated marginal labor productivity of township enterprises was sevenfold that of agriculture, further inciting labor migration. As we contemplate regional distribution, the labor force in the eastern coastal areas has predominantly gravitated toward non-agricultural sectors, leaving the untapped potential of substantial marginal labor productivity in the central and Western regions.[3]

The corporate competition system adopted by local governments has undoubtedly played a pivotal role in propelling economic growth at an astonishing pace over the past three decades. However, like the dual nature of all things, this system has also spawned a series of grave consequences. On one hand, we witness the perils of excessive economic intervention, such as rampant overproduction, intensified macroeconomic turbulence, the emergence of regional protectionism leading to fragmented economic fiefdoms, and the insidious breeding of rent-seeking behaviors.

On the other hand, the corporatization of local governments has resulted in a dearth of responsibilities concerning the welfare of the populace and provision of public services, thereby exacerbating societal conflicts, inadequate supply of public goods and services, wanton resource wastage, and environmental degradation. The far-reaching impact of this corporatized competitive system lies in the transformation of local governments from purportedly unlimited entities burdened with "governing" responsibilities to entities with limited liability, or even as power-hungry entities absolving themselves of any accountability—a "power company" devoid of even the slightest sense of responsibility. In tandem with the

[2] Wen Tiejun, et al., Deciphering Southern Jiangsu, 2011.

[3] Lin Qingsong, Du Ying. China's industrial reform and efficiency—a comparative study of state-owned enterprises and non-state-owned enterprises [M]. Kunming: Yunnan People's Publishing House, 1997.

escalating corporate rivalry witnessed since the 1980s, local governments have increasingly embraced limited liability, albeit without the requisite institutional regulations. Consequently, such limited liability local governments frequently evade the burden of risks, instead transferring all potential hazards to the central authority.

It is crucial to note that even conventional limited liability companies engaging in market competition are obligated to assume liability within their limited scope, only shifting societal burdens when their losses surpass their assets.

2 Political Dividends for Internal Accumulation

In 1974, Zhanqi Brigade's pig and agricultural production soared to impressive heights, given the technological constraints of the time. With labor and fertilizer inputs optimized and growth potential limited, they pondered a shift from an agrarian village to an integrated development of agriculture, industry, and ancillary occupations, leveraging existing collective accumulation.

"Experience taught us that until agricultural science and technology made significant breakthroughs, the key to progress lay in drastically increasing yield per unit area. However, this pursuit came at a cost—as yield improved, fertilizer usage surged, and grain production expenses skyrocketed. The outcome? High-yield, impoverished teams where productivity didn't align with income."[4] Such limitations on production growth began to erode the mobilization capability of the Zhanqi Brigade's militia, and even their steadfast company faced performance setbacks and failed assessments during the 1977 "Small Rectification (小整风)" campaign. Observing this, the higher-level party committee unearthed a blind optimism and laxity among the ranks of the militia company.

"Comrades revealed that loose thinking led to a decline in enthusiasm among a minority of cadres and members for organizing and excelling in militia activities. Some even set production at odds with militia affairs,

[4] Source: "Path to Rapid Agricultural Development: Embracing the Integrated Development of Agriculture, Industry, and Ancillary Occupations—The Xianfeng Commune's Zhanqi Brigade" (July 22, 1979), "Archives of the Social Enterprise Bureau of Pixian County," Pidu District Archives Collection, File No. 046-001-0031-003, p. 24.

fearing that the latter would impede progress. Looseness in work style resulted in a few comrades dragging their feet during assemblies, meetings, and lectures, lacking the earlier seriousness. At times, they even shunned gatherings altogether. Laxity in adhering to regulations allowed a few comrades to slack off... and they regarded training as a burdensome chore." The repercussions soon became evident in their training performance. During two live ammunition shooting assessments held in 1977, the militia company of the Zhanqi Brigade fell short. Even at the county-level competition on September 29, their shooting and bombing results failed to impress.[5] These issues weren't confined to the militia alone; there was a general slackening of spirit among the cadre ranks. Thus, the "Small Rectification" movement focused on rectifying the leadership core of the militia company.

The emergence of such phenomena wasn't solely the fault of the cadres or the masses; it stemmed from the inherent limitations of agricultural production under prevailing circumstances. Prior to this, the Zhanqi Brigade's cadres had already begun exploring external avenues for development.

In July 1974, they forged an agreement with the Provincial May 7th Cadre School to maintain roads. In response to the pressing need to transport construction materials to the site, which required substantial volume and improvements in local transportation infrastructure, the May 7th Cadre School collaborated with Zhanqi Brigade's party branch leaders, Luo Huijin and Yang Zhengzhong (杨正忠). They devised a plan to maintain the Hongbao Road, ensuring its unimpeded flow. This road stretched from Hongwei Town to Baoguang Temple, spanning 5 kilometers. The responsibility for its maintenance was entrusted to the Zhanqi Brigade of the Xianfeng Commune in Pixian County. The brigade shouldered the organization, management, and upkeep of the road, with the understanding that one person would oversee maintenance per kilometer, amounting to a team of 5 individuals. At the end of each month, the Cadre School would disburse road maintenance fees to the Zhanqi Brigade. The remuneration was calculated on the basis of workdays, with 155 for longer months and 150 for shorter ones, each valued at 1.15

[5] Source: "Militia Work Report (No. 8): Identifying Discrepancies in Performance, Shattering Complacency, and Striving for Renewed Progress" (October 22, 1977), Pidu District Archives Collection, "Archives of the Xianfeng Township of Pixian County," File No. 152-001-0132-03, pp. 70–75.

yuan. Accordingly, the Zhanqi Brigade's yearly income would exceed 2000 yuan, allowing them to transfer five laborers.[6]

According to Luo Huifu's oral account, the Zhanqi Brigade, as per the contract, undertook the construction of roads for the May 7th Cadre School, earning a total project fee of 26,378 yuan. Consequently, a connection between the Zhanqi Brigade and the Provincial May 7th Cadre School was established.

Moreover, the Zhanqi Brigade seized opportunities to generate cash income by organizing and hosting various activities. In 1974, they took on the task of accommodating and feeding militia platoon leaders and higher-ranking officers (a total of 151 individuals) during their local training from July 6 to 15, organized by the Xianfeng Commune. This venture provided a much-needed infusion of scarce cash resources.[7]

3 Collective Enterprise Chronicles: Zhanqi Brick Factory

"The government dispatched an envoy to accompany me on a quest to Chengdu, seeking a brick-making machine from the Logistics Department Commander of the Military District. We scoured the city for over a month, relentlessly inquiring from every corner until we stumbled upon his hidden trove of machines. However, our elation was short-lived. The contraption we acquired turned out to be undersized, incapable of birthing bricks. Desperate, we returned to him, and he graciously granted us a larger contrivance. He had originally placed an order with Guanghan Machinery Factory. Thus, we embarked on a pilgrimage to the factory, only to discover it entangled in the throes of the 'Cultural Revolution,' crippled in its manufacturing endeavors. To surmount this setback, we hastily assembled a makeshift task force in tandem with the county government, laboring diligently to resurrect the dormant contraption. It consumed a tedious month, but eventually,

[6] Source: "Agreement: Delegation of Maintenance Responsibilities for the Hongbao Road (Hongwei Town to Baoguang Temple) in Pixian County, Entrusted by the Construction Office of the Provincial May 7th Cadre School" (July 24, 1974), Pidu District Archives Collection, "Archives of the Xianfeng Township of Pixian County," File No. 152-001-0119-022, pp. 98–99.

[7] Source: "Report on the Training of Militia Platoon Leaders and Higher-Ranking Officers by the Party Committee of the Xianfeng Commune" (July 16, 1974), Pidu District Archives Collection, "Archives of the Xianfeng Township of Pixian County," File No. 152-001-0120-001, pp. 1–3.

the machine was resuscitated, and we triumphantly transported it back for deployment."

Source: Interview record with Luo Huifu, November 2019.

The interviewee, Luo Huifu (罗会富), held the mantle of the brick factory' director at Zhanqi, the pioneering village-owned enterprise. The interview log vividly portrays his relentless pursuit and the arduous ordeals endured to acquire machinery during those formative years.

Born in 1969, the Zhanqi Brick Factory (Xianfeng First Brick Factory) evolved alongside advances in brick-making techniques, traversing the eras of earthen kilns (affectionately dubbed "jar kilns") from 1969 to 1976. Zigzag kilns (曲线窑, known as "shuttle kilns") from 1976 to 1979, and the zenith of tunnel kilns (轮窑) from 1979 to 2003. From these kilns emerged green bricks, exclusively fashioned for the community's edification: constructing schools, auditoriums, brigade offices, dispensaries, and retail establishments. The advent of curved kilns allowed for the expansion of this purview, catering to the burgeoning needs of new villages while entertaining external trade. Astutely, Luo Huifu reveals that only 40% of our output sufficed for the new village's construction, while the remaining 60% found eager buyers. Our piece de resistance manifested as a state-of-the-art tunnel kiln, a quintessence of modernity, magnitude, and scientific ingenuity—a grandeur unparalleled in Pixian County, with an annual yield of 10 million resplendent red bricks. In those times of dearth, when merchants reigned and resources were scarce, our kiln thrived amidst insatiable demand, bestowing prosperity that served as the bedrock for Zhanqi's second collective enterprise. The Xianfeng brick factory, having achieved resplendent heights, bowed out gracefully in 2003, bequeathing an indelible legacy to Zhanqi's industrial tapestry.

1975 marked the ascendance of Li Shibing (李世炳), who assumed the mantle of the Party Branch Secretary at Zhanqi. Inspired by his visit to Dazhai, he championed the adoption of the collective abode model, thus the clarion call for "building the new village" resonated throughout our domain. To erect this new abode, bricks were indispensable, prompting Luo Huifu, having returned from his sojourn to Dazhai, to remark: "I beheld a metamorphosis—a seamless transition from stone-strip homes of yore to brick-laden abodes." Luo Huifu recognized the laborious toil of our comrades who, in yesteryears, braved the mountains, armed with dry provisions, to procure the necessary stones for our nascent village. The exigencies of constructing the new village far surpassed the meager supply of green bricks, hence our unanimous resolve to build a Zigzag kiln.

Li Shibing's visionary pursuit of the Dazhai model, fostering communal cohesion through concentrated habitation, spurred the ambitious endeavor of constructing the new village. This noble quest resonated deeply with our shared existence, igniting a harmonious convergence of collective rationality and domestic equilibrium, as the collective's accrued agricultural and subsidiary incomes were judiciously deployed to erect the Zigzag kiln—an emblem of progressive aspirations amidst the convulsive struggle for balance.

Li Shibing chose to study the concentrated living model of Dazhai and construct a new village. His aim was to tackle the intricacies of daily life intertwined with the members and rally the entire team of cadres and members to invest the collective agricultural and sideline income into building the Zigzag kiln. This phase marked the resurgence of the struggle and equilibrium between collective rationality and familial rationality.

The genesis of building the new village served as a catalyst for the industrialization development of the Zhanqi Brigade. Though the brigade possessed a traditional earth kiln, its output was lackluster, occupying a mere 4 mu of land. The impetus for erecting this kiln originated from Luo Huijin, the then secretary of the Zhanqi Brigade, who sought bricks and tiles for the construction of a brigade hall and a primary school. Thus, as early as 1969, Zhanqi embarked on the construction of the earth kiln. Guided by Luo Huifu, a 26-year-old at the time, a group of eight individuals ventured to the neighboring Yuanyi Village (now Hengshan Village) to excavate kilns on the earthen mound, molding brick and tile blanks. The production of these clay-fired bricks primarily facilitated the establishment of the brigade's primary school, hall, office, medical station, and sales outlets, resulting in substantial savings of liquid capital during the Zhanqi Brigade's developmental phase.

During the initial stages of Zigzag kiln construction, the brigade cadres held divergent opinions. A minority deemed the brigade to be lacking in capital, machinery, technology, and workshops, making the establishment of such a factory fraught with complexities and difficulties. Addressing these concerns, the brigade branch conducted meticulous analysis and research, unanimously concluding that "material sourcing for this enterprise is accessible... requiring minimal investment, yielding rapid results, and accumulating substantial gains. Coupled with the resolute demand from the masses to establish cooperative enterprises, foster rapid agricultural advancement, and swiftly transform the brigade's countenance, expeditious and proficient implementation of the Zigzag kiln is imperative to contribute to agricultural mechanization. It serves as the fundamental pathway to both provide a means for surplus labor and fortify the collective economy."[8]

Consequently, Secretary Li Shibing and Luo Huifu first achieved a unified understanding within the party branch. Simultaneously, they persuaded the majority of the members by emphasizing the substantial requirement for new bricks in constructing the new village. In terms of site selection, they reached an agreement with the neighboring Hengshan's Yuanyi Brigade, securing 10 mu of hilly clay land through a mutually beneficial exchange of paddy fields. This locale was deemed optimal for launching the Zigzag kiln.

However, achieving unanimity within the brigade's ranks was merely the initial hurdle as acquiring a brick-making machine posed a formidable challenge during that era. Consequently, with the recommendation of the county's Armed Forces Department, the Zhanqi Brigade established contact with the logistics department of the former Chengdu Military Region. Notably, the Zhanqi Brigade's commendation by the county's Armed Forces Department was intrinsically tied to its outstanding militia efforts mentioned earlier. This clandestine social capital enabled the Zhanqi Brigade to access such resources, a feat that proved arduous within the contemporary social milieu.

In the 1970s, a brick machine fetched a hefty sum of 40,000 yuan. The valiant Zhanqi Brigade found itself in need, and it was the benevolent Armed Forces Department of Pixian County that extended a helping hand, providing the necessary funds. As per the archives, the brigade secured a loan of 60,000 yuan from the credit union to procure the coveted machinery. With this infusion of capital, the brigade's industrial progress took flight. And in addition to the formidable backing from the Armed Forces Department, the brigade ingeniously capitalized on its collective past, harnessing the fruits of its agricultural toils, auxiliary

[8] "Path to Rapid Agricultural Development—Embarking on the Comprehensive Development of Agriculture and Side Industries—Zhanqi Brigade, Xianfeng Commune" (July 22, 1979), "File of the Social Enterprise Bureau of Pixian County," Archives of Pidu District, File Number 046-001-0031-003, pp. 23–29.

occupations, and service ventures. They traded the annual yield of approximately 110,000 kilograms of reserve grain for an equivalent of 110,000 work points, which were diligently invested in subsequent factory infrastructure. Factor in the construction expenses, including the indispensable building materials, and the total expenditure came to an impressive sum of 72,636 yuan. Moreover, the resourceful production teams also lent a hand, contributing tables, benches, and other essentials. To ensure technical finesse, the Sichuan Institute for Building Materials Industry provided invaluable guidance to the Zigzag Kiln's evolution.

The era presented daunting challenges in procuring essential elements such as funds, equipment, and technology. In a 1980 report submitted by the Liming Brigade of the Xianfeng Commune, they appealed to the County Committee of Pixian County for assistance in establishing a rotary kiln brick factory. The ambitious venture necessitated a considerable cash injection, estimated at 241,500 yuan, to yield an annual output of 10–12 million bricks. Alas, the brigade's modest means could only muster 20,000 yuan, and the credit union extended a loan of 30,000 yuan. Despite the labor deductions made by various production teams, an unfilled void of over 100,000 yuan remained, beseeching the county committee for a generous loan.

A comprehensive breakdown of the budget can be observed in the illustrious Table 1.

Henceforth, it becomes evident that the intrepid Zhanqi Brigade, even prior to the dawn of 1980, harnessed its internal and external resources judiciously, fashioning the Zigzag Kiln into a resounding success. Armed with indomitable spirit and a dearth of funds, the brigade discovered

Table 1 Construction Budget for the Liming Brigade Rotary Kiln Brick Factory in 1980

Item	*Count*	*Value (10,000 yuan)*	*Item*	*Count*	*Value*
Brick machine	1	5	Electrical appliances	–	1
Cement	100 tons	1	Stone	150 m3	0.15
Steel	24 tons	1.5	Sand	–	0.8
Wood	100 meters	2.5	Tiles	–	1
Brick	1,200,000	3.6	Lime	–	0.4
Salary	–	7.2	Total	–	24.5

a savior in the form of the unwavering Armed Forces Department and the benevolent credit union, propelling them toward the acquisition of machinery and equipment. In their quest for kiln sanctuaries, the resourceful brigade rallied their collective might investing in trees, bamboo, and wheat straw. Equipped with rudimentary tools, they took to the task with unwavering resolve. And when expertise seemed elusive, they summoned wisdom from afar or dispatched their own ranks for skill enhancement.

In under six months, the resplendent Zigzag kiln, with an awe-inspiring capacity to yield two million standard bricks per annum, proudly emerged from its crucible in April 1977. These machine-crafted marvels fulfilled the village's housing requirements while reserving a portion for commercial transactions, their proceeds devoutly channeled back into the collective. In a testament to their unwavering dedication, the Zhanqi Brigade erected four magnificent tile-roofed edifices, comprising 64 enclaves and spanning 15,000 square meters, each square meter commanding a dignified price of 25 yuan. This momentous endeavor bore fruit as 32 households eagerly embraced their newfound abodes, each relishing a generous living space of 20 square meters.

A pertinent point to underscore is the southwest region's humid climate, which, when contrasted with its northern counterpart, fosters an ardent yearning for improved living conditions through technological advancement. The intricate process of brick drying, an arduous feat requiring abundant manpower, witnessed revolutionary strides as the transition unfolded from earthen kilns to Zigzag Kilns, ultimately culminating in the illustrious rotary kilns. This relentless march toward drying perfection catapulted production quantities to unprecedented heights, truncated manufacturing cycles, and slashed costs. Thus, it comes as no surprise that Zhanqi Village, well-endowed with technological precedence, outpaced its counterparts in the 1970s, reigning supreme as a formidable machine brick factory.

* * *

The Craft of the Brick Factory

The brick factory's craft can be classified into three: earth kilns, Zigzag kilns, and tunnel kilns.

The earth kiln technique, also known as the "Pot Kiln," involves the meticulous production of handmade bricks, crafted one by one, then fashioned into small rectangular units—typically arranged in sets of four. The name "Pot Kiln" derives from its shape: narrow at the base, expanding in the middle, and tapering toward the top. At one-fifth of its height, a furnace bridge is positioned, facilitating airflow during charcoal combustion, while the bricks find their place in the middle. A skilled artisan named Luo Huifu, once a carpenter, adeptly commanded the art of firing bricks in earth kilns.[9]

The Zigzag kiln, also referred to as the "Shuttle Kiln," bears a striking resemblance to its pot kiln counterpart externally. However, its interior boasts transformative modifications. Standing tall, the Zigzag kiln displays a gracefully curved base and a flat upper surface, the latter housing a capacious groove adorned with an impressive aperture. Applying pressure from above, the bottom end simmers until the bricks are thoroughly baked. Consequently, driven by the interplay of heat expansion and contraction, the bricks nimbly emerge, as if propelled by their own volition, leaving space for new ones above. The traditional method demands a subsequent process of sun-drying and subsequent firing, while the shuttle kiln's bricks undergo an all-in-one journey, encompassing both drying and firing—a commendable advancement.[10] In 1990, the Vanguard Brick Factory contributed a remarkable 11.277 million crimson bricks.[11]

Nonetheless, it merits clarification that although the Zigzag kiln technique constituted considerable progress over its earth kiln predecessor, the contractor of the brick factory, Yang Zhongmo (杨忠模), expressed reservations regarding the quality of its output. Lamentably, the absence of drying chambers compromised its excellence, rendering it more akin to an outcome of scientific experimentation. Supporting documentation from the Office of the Social Enterprise of the County Revolutionary Committee attests to this: "The brigade machine brick factory emerged as a nascent entity, and the Zigzag kiln method represented a novel technique. Yet, due to insufficient proficiency in its operation and the

[9] Source: Interview transcript with Feng Zhonghui, February 10, 2020.

[10] Ibid.

[11] Summary of Enterprise Work in 1990, Archives of Pidu District, Sichuan Province, File No. 152-001-0291-015, Page 2.

substantial initial start-up costs, compounded by other factors, the realization of unified national pricing proved challenging. In order to foster the development of brigade enterprises, following thorough deliberation, the three-hole red bricks manufactured by your brigade can presently be sold at 8.5 fen per brick. However, it is imperative that the bricks conform to the established national standard, measuring precisely 11.5 centimeters in height. Our sincere hope is that you will embrace the primacy of class struggle, dedicating yourselves to elevating technical prowess, reinforcing managerial acumen, and gradually reducing costs."[12] Consequently, the Zigzag kiln's tenure lasted a mere three years. Although fleeting, its contributions were not to be understated. The bricks birthed by the Zigzag kiln were already ripe for external trade, far exceeding the quantity required for the construction of burgeoning settlements.

The tunnel kiln, distinguished by its unceasing cycle of smelting, constitutes a notable improvement over the earth kiln's practice of firing one batch at a time. Divided into multiple sections, the tunnel kiln orchestrates simultaneous production, boasting vast throughput, heightened efficiency, abbreviated processing periods, and swift turnover. Under ordinary circumstances, each kiln section could yield an impressive tally of 60,000 bricks per diem.

To build a new village, merely relying on machine-made bricks is not enough. In 1976, adjacent to the brick factory, the Zhanqi Brigade forged ahead by establishing a prefabricated component factory. Their aim? To fulfill the demands of new village construction and cater to the aspirations of villagers seeking new homes.

This prefabricated component factory*, under the stewardship of Jiang Anyong, faithfully served the Zhanqi Brigade's Jianxin Village and the progressive development of rural areas. Though modest in size, with a workforce barely exceeding a dozen, it stood shoulder to shoulder with the brick factory, shouldering the weight of the Zhanqi Brigade's residential and communal enterprise construction. The factory operated under a tenancy system, faithfully remitting an annual rent of ¥7000–¥8000 to the village collective.*

[12] "Reply on the Price of Three-hole Bricks of the Xianfeng Commune Zhanqi Brigade" (April 30, 1977), Archives Collection of Pidu District, Sichuan Province, File No. 046-001-12-009, page 90.

Simultaneously, steadfast in their commitment to simplicity, self-reliance, and grassroots ingenuity, the entire brigade successfully established eight enterprises encompassing agriculture, secondary industry processing, construction, cotton processing, hairstyling, slaughterhouses, and tailoring. By 1979, a noteworthy 110 members of the community served as both industrial and agricultural laborers. However, in the ensuing years, the brick factory's income emerged as the primary industrial revenue stream for the Zhanqi Brigade.

By 1979, the Zhanqi Brigade's fixed assets amounted to a commendable ¥1.03 million. The combined output value of agriculture and secondary industries reached a noteworthy 991,000 yuan that year, contributing to 54.3% of the brigade's overall income and yielding tax payments of ¥50,000. The brigade's workforce boasted 247 members engaged in off-farm labor, accounting for 37.5% of the total labor force, with their earnings soaring to 299,770 yuan.[13] The brigade's enterprises achieved an impressive output value of ¥175,000, with the brick factory's contribution alone amounting to ¥92,000. In comparison to 1977, the output value of brigade-run enterprises burgeoned by 1.2 times, with per .capita output value skyrocketing by 120%. The cumulative profit stood at a remarkable ¥158,000, among which the brick factory reaped ¥99,000 in profit over a span of three years.[14]

As they advanced industrially, the Zhanqi Brigade wisely allocated funds from their communal enterprises to fuel agricultural mechanization. A sum of 42,000 yuan facilitated the acquisition of two Dongfeng (东风) 40 trucks, a Fengshou (丰收) 35 tractor, and a Gongnong (工农) 12 tractor. Mechanized farming soared to encompass over 90% of the brigade's cultivation area, manifesting in irrigation and drainage, grain threshing, and feed processing. Moreover, 1000 yuan procured an electric welding machine, serving as a boon for agricultural machinery repairs. A sum of 3500 yuan facilitated the construction of a kindergarten, while 4700 yuan brought forth a 2.5-kilometer-long high-voltage

[13] Source: "Introduction to the Collective Industrial and Subsidiary Industries Development of Zhanqi Brigade in Pixian County," Archives of Pidu District, Sichuan Province, File No. 005-005-0076.

[14] Source: "High-Speed Development of Agriculture Path—Taking the Road of Comprehensive Development of Agricultural and Subsidiary Industries—Zhanqi Brigade in Pixian County" (July 22, 1979), "Files of the Social Enterprise Bureau of Pixian County," Archives of Pidu District, Sichuan Province, File No. 046-001-0031-003, pp. 23–29.

line, illuminating the five production teams within the brigade. Not only did this solve the brigade's power supply woes, but it laid a foundation for electrification, endowing over 200 households with electric lights. An investment of 20,000 yuan secured the necessary equipment for enterprises, nurturing conditions to alleviate labor intensity and foster expanded production.

According to Li Shili's (李世立) account, the Zigzag kiln underwent a transformative change, evolving into a tunnel kiln after a mere three years of operation. Despite its relatively short production tenure, the Zigzag kiln garnered substantial profits for the Zhanqi Brigade amidst a market characterized by insatiable demand. Its success laid a vital groundwork for the subsequent development of village-level enterprises. Following the brick factory's newfound profitability, starting in 1983, the Zhanqi Brigade judiciously allocated funds through loans and investments to township enterprises such as Xianfeng Brewing Factory, distilleries, cultural courtyards, compound fertilizer factories, honeycomb coal factories, and bean paste factories. Profits from the honeycomb coal factory directly fostered the inception of the Huifu Bean Paste Factory (会富豆瓣厂), presently known as the venerable Fuyou Green Seasoning Company (富友绿色调味品公司). It can be said that the fledgling and flourishing township enterprises in Zhanqi shared a profound interconnection with the brick factory—an essential mother figure ceaselessly channeling funds to other township enterprises, providing primordial capital during establishment and safeguarding their welfare in times of bankruptcy.

In conclusion, during the years 1974–1979, the Zhanqi Brigade embarked on a transformative journey, shifting its focus from agrarian villages to a comprehensive development of agricultural and industrial endeavors. This marked their transition toward industrialization. Capitalizing on various forms of social capital that had materialized around 1973, the Zhanqi Brigade gained a competitive advantage, enabling them to swiftly acquire equipment and funds compared to their counterparts. With remarkable swiftness, they established curved kilns, effectively seizing the early stages of industrial development. Moreover, the brick factory, constructed during the era of collectivization, utilized the proficient labor force of trained militia members. Wages were paid via a work points system, signifying the collective investment of the Zhanqi people in the construction process. Additionally, the purchase of machinery was facilitated by surplus grain from the collective, showcasing the collective enterprise's initial capital accumulation through self-sacrifice. This effective internal mobilization was a testament to the organizational strength fostered through earlier emphasis on production, militia construction, and socialist education. In the 1960s and 1970s, the outstanding political performance of Zhanqi forged social relationships that extended beyond their immediate region. These relationships, in turn, were transformed into social capital during the industrialization process, providing a solid foundation for Zhanqi's collective industrial development in the 1980s.

* * *

A Comparison Between Xianfeng Township and Zhanqi Village—The Case of the Brick Factory

In 1986, Liang Quanyi (梁全义), the director of the enterprise office and the militia brick factory manager in Xianfeng Township, offered insight into the brick industry within Xianfeng Township. With a tone tinged with disappointment, he recounted the challenges faced by these enterprises. The lack of technical expertise resulted in collapsing kilns and substandard brick production, despite the futile attempts of inviting outside technicians to supervise operations. However, amidst these failures, a glimmer of hope emerged through the assistance of skilled technician Master Deng. It was Deng's technical prowess that breathed new life into the struggling brick factory. The third brick factory in Xianfeng faced a different predicament; while technical personnel were exchanged with the township brick factory, the managerial positions were filled by individuals with no prior enterprise experience. This knowledge gap hindered effective production processes, technological advancements, and overall command, ultimately pushing the third factory to the brink of collapse. Only with the arrival of Comrade Fang Hongkang (房洪康) did the situation experience a positive turnaround. His expertise in the field bore remarkable fruit within a short span of time. On the other hand, the militia brick factory showcased youthful vigor but suffered from a lack of both technical knowledge and management acumen. Despite being in operation for over two years, the personnel, from the factory manager to the workshop director, struggled to grasp the intricacies of the technology and failed to provide adequate command, resulting in exorbitant costs and meager output for the entire brick factory.

To address these issues, Liang Quanyi proposed merging the militia brick factory and the township brick factory, creating two distinct workshops with separate profit and loss calculations. This arrangement would foster healthy competition between the workshops and allow for the flexible allocation of personnel and technological resources. Recognizing the insurmountable challenges faced by a single bulldozer in accomplishing the earthwork tasks, Liang proposed the addition of another bulldozer to overcome the difficulties. While this would increase the workload for the factory-level cadres, the benefits outweighed the drawbacks. Both workshops produced products of the same specifications, ensuring consistency in quality and treatment. Despite the increase in responsibility for factory-level leaders, this harmonious arrangement presented a viable solution. These proposals were put forward against the backdrop of a 1985 State Council notice, which imposed strict regulations on loans to township enterprises. Enterprises were required to possess a substantial percentage of self-owned funds for loan applications, failing which, loans would be denied or existing loans would require the supplementation of self-owned capital.

Analyzing the loan and working capital situations in 1987, the joint brick factory, the third brick factory, and the Zhanqi Brick Factory had varying degrees of financial pressure. The joint brick factory held a considerable loan amount, supplemented by a moderate working capital. In contrast, the third brick factory faced a significant loan burden with no working capital. Remarkably, the Zhanqi Brick Factory stood apart, unaffected by loan repayments and boasting the most abundant working capital among the three. This surplus allowed the Zhanqi Brick Factory to extend financial support to other enterprises within Zhanqi Village. In comparison, the opportunity cost savings were substantial, particularly when considering the stringent regulations imposed by the State Council on loans to township enterprises.

The absence of loan repayment pressure for the Zhanqi Brick Factory shared a profound connection with Luo Huifu's stringent management practices. The financial management of the brick factory remained rigorous, with even minor expenses requiring proper documentation for accountability. In the arduous phase of constructing the new village, the brick factory faced financial challenges. Proceeds from surplus bricks were reinvested in purchasing materials for building construction, leaving the workers with limited meal options. During times of financial strain, workers' wages were delayed by a month, yet understanding prevailed among them. Luo Huifu, adamant about avoiding loan reliance and minimizing collective burdens, expressed a resolute stance. Even in the face of hardships, he remained steadfast in his commitment.

4 Management System: Work Point System (1974–1982)

In assessing the relationship between Zhanqi Village's collective and its collective enterprises, we observe a journey spanning four distinct phases from 1974 onwards: the work point system, contract system, share cooperation system, and leasing system.

4.1 Political Landscape

The genesis of rural township enterprises in the 1980s sprouted from the limitations imposed by preceding policies, which forbade social teams from engaging in commerce and service sectors of lesser thresholds, confining their activities solely to industry. However, in 1965, the Party Central Committee and the State Council acknowledged the possibility of production teams and township enterprises undertaking collective sideline businesses, granted such endeavors maintained a balance of human resources, finance, and materials.

4.2 Village Situation and Land Conditions

Foundational to the work point system was the pivotal role of land. Before delving further, it is pertinent to outline Zhanqi Village's circumstances during that period. In 1975, Zhanqi transitioned from accounting at the small team level to large team accounting, necessitating the acknowledgment of disparities in land fertility. Zhanqi's categorization of land quality into nine distinct grades, with a grain differential of 50 kilograms per grade annually, underscored this shift. During the same year, a comprehensive assessment of the village's population and collective assets was conducted for the construction of a new village. The population totaled 1403 individuals, cultivated land covered an area of 1709 mu (approximately 113.9 hectares), grain reserves amounted to 116,890 kilograms. Once the collection task was accomplished, each member received an annual ration of 600 kilograms of grain. Furthermore, the village boasted seven tractors and 311 public houses distributed among its small teams.

Zhanqi comprised nine production teams, with the highest-earning team generating up to 1.8 yuan per day, culminating in an annual income of 657 yuan. By contrast, in that same period, the average monthly wage for ordinary workers in Pixian County stood at a meager 30 yuan. Zhanqi's main sideline business was vegetable cultivation, primarily catering to neighboring villages. During 1980 and 1981, Zhanqi's per mu production levels reached the county's pinnacle.[15]

4.3 *Implementation of the Work Point System*

In the phase of collective ownership, Zhanqi Village's primary enterprises were the Xianfeng Brick Factory and the Xianfeng Brewing Factory, both falling under the purview of the collective. Profits were subsequently distributed among the collective, with the Xianfeng Brewing Factory established utilizing surplus profits from the brick factory. During this period, the two collective enterprises embraced the work point system as their mode of distribution. Through unified accounting at the large team level, work points were allocated to production teams, fostering internal differentiation in distribution. This approach served to invigorate farmers' motivation while ensuring collective benefit. Initially, a team reward system governed affairs within the enterprises. However, as the enterprises matured structurally and divisions of labor grew increasingly intricate, with an expanding workforce, individual rewards were introduced for the factory director.

The work point system, prevalent within China's rural collective economic organizations, serves as both a quantitative gauge of farmers' labor involvement and a means to calculate labor remuneration. Also referred to as the labor-day system, it embodies a form of labor management practiced by rural collectives, encompassing three layers of significance. Firstly, as an organizational embodiment of labor management, the work point system facilitates the collective allocation of members' labor resources. Secondly, work points function as units of measurement for labor quantity, offering a tangible representation of individual labor's quantity and quality within the collective framework. Lastly, as a metric for labor remuneration, work points become a pivotal criterion in the equitable distribution of collective labor achievements.

[15] Source: Interview record with Li Shili on January 11, 2020.

Essentially, the work point system manifests as an organizational and management apparatus, a system governing agricultural production, as well as a mechanism for resource allocation. By quantifying labor and allocating labor resources, it establishes a hierarchical structure within and among groups, fostering division of labor across the industry chain. As a distribution system, it forges links between income and individual work points and group productivity, creating incentives that propagate technological dissemination and labor competition throughout the production process. Drawing upon the social fabric of rural communities, the work point system operates as an organizational framework, allocating labor while leveraging the intrinsic advantages of familiar social connections, thereby enabling cost-effective internal supervision and benefiting from robust external oversight. The confluence of these mechanisms galvanizes collective productivity.

Indeed, it was the implementation of the work point system that empowered Zhanqi Village to embrace both industry and agriculture, utilizing agricultural produce to fuel industrial growth and foster the development of public services and essential infrastructure within the village. This system, in conjunction with their exemplary militia training, resulted in the seamless integration of the village collective's financial and administrative authority. Demonstrating remarkable organizational and mobilization capabilities, the village collective adeptly managed their collective enterprises with remarkable efficiency.

CHAPTER 6

Changing Institutional Environment and the Structural Expansion of Village Industries (1978–1987)

1 Township and Village Enterprises: Their Essence and Objectives

Township and Village Enterprises (TVEs), unlike common conceptions of ownership or geographical boundaries, embody a unique breed of enterprises, founded by individuals with peasant roots, operating predominantly in non-agricultural sectors within rural areas.

1.1 The Essence of Township and Village Enterprises

Township and Village Enterprises (TVEs), first and foremost, possess a communal essence, assimilating the goals of the community into their very fabric. Secondly, they are bound by ties of kinship and locality, a social tapestry where familiarity breeds trust, requiring no prior agreement. Thirdly, the "minimum wage" sets them apart; their employees wear the dual hats of workers and farmers, mitigating risk and profit expectations. In essence, akin to rural households, these enterprises solely account for material consumption, disregarding labor costs. As long as their investments can be recouped, ensuring employee income surpasses the opportunity cost of engaging in domestic labor, their existence finds a reason. Fourthly, burdened by a high debt-to-asset ratio, it is a defining feature of township and village enterprises, where liabilities pave the path for initial investments and the expansion of overall assets. Lastly, they occupy an extrinsic sphere, independent of plans. In stark contrast to

© Peking University Press 2024
X. Dong, *Zhanqi Village Over Fifty Years*,
https://doi.org/10.1007/978-981-97-5426-7_6

state-owned counterparts, township and village enterprises emerge within an unplanned realm, wholly reliant on the capricious whims of the market. During the period of economic reformation and restructuring from 1989 to 1990, an irrevocable force caused 300,000 township and village enterprises to succumb, leaving them no recourse but to vie for survival amidst cutthroat market competition. This union of stringent constraints and the "minimum wage" positions township and village enterprises on a pedestal, surpassing state-owned enterprises both structurally and operationally.[1]

1.2 Township and Village Enterprises' Objectives

According to Wen Tiejun, the driving force behind the establishment of township and village enterprises lies in maximizing rural community employment and welfare, rather than the typical profit-centric pursuit of general businesses.[2]

Lin Qingsong and Du Ying posit that township and village enterprises embody a "trinity" of objectives, involving the government, community, and the enterprise itself. In this intricate dance, the enterprise and the government engage in a transactional relationship, albeit one that eludes the confines of a formal contract. This transaction encompasses two dimensions: on the one hand, the government, leveraging its authority, provides the enterprise with an array of tangible and intangible services, including resource amalgamation, safeguarding of enterprise rights, and liaising with other governmental bodies; on the other hand, the enterprise assumes, to a certain extent, the responsibilities of the community government, striving to achieve the very goals it demands. In exchange, the enterprise must, to a certain degree, relinquish a portion of its net income and corporate ownership. Although this transaction exacts a toll on the enterprise's profitability, such losses are not irredeemable. Compensation takes two forms: firstly, the transaction itself substantially curtails the costs associated with direct involvement in an imperfect market, alleviating myriad challenges encountered during inception and operation; secondly, it affords access to non-monetary capital and low-cost capital

[1] Lin Qingsong, Du Ying. China's Industrial Reform and Efficiency: Comparative Research on State-Owned and Non-State-Owned Enterprises. Kunming: Yunnan People's Publishing House, 1997.

[2] Wen Tiejun, "The Origin of Township Village Enterprise Assets and Relevant Principles in Restructuring," Zhejiang Social Sciences, 1998(3): 39–42.

within the institutionalized monetary market. Ultimately, this transaction begets an ambiguous demarcation of corporate ownership, thereby birthing a multifaceted trio of objectives encompassing the government, community, and enterprise. As a consequence, the enterprise finds itself compelled to simultaneously maximize profits while fostering employment growth, enhancing per capita income within the community, and meeting the fiscal demands of the government. In essence, the trinity of enterprise objectives manifests itself through this transaction.[3]

1.3 *Origins of Assets in the Initial Accumulation Phase of Township and Village Enterprises*

In the realm of township and village enterprises, capital's initial accumulation usually occurs under the weight of substantial indebtedness. Adhering to the notion that the definition of corporate property rights hinges solely on the initial investment and employing an analogous approach to dissect the issue, we can discern four primary sources from which township and village enterprises draw their assets.

Firstly, there lies the transfer of land capital gains. Urban enterprises allocate 30–40% of their investments toward land occupancy expenses. Presently, struggling urban businesses seize the opportunity to reverse their misfortunes through the strategy of "withdrawing from second industry and entering into third industry," effectively capitalizing on the enhanced value of land capital as it transitions from the secondary to the tertiary sector. In the 1980s, when township and village enterprises were founded, the escalated value of rural land's conversion from primary to secondary and tertiary industries was predominantly and gratuitously claimed by these enterprises. Consequently, the profits derived from this portion of land capital perpetually fuel enterprise accumulation. Therefore, 30–40% of the investments made during the establishment of township and village enterprises should rightfully belong to the rural landowners in the vicinity, in other words, the collective economic organizations formed by members of the community.

[3] Lin Qingsong, Du Ying, "China's Industrial Reform and Efficiency: A Comparative Study of State-owned Enterprises and Non-state-owned Enterprises," Kunming: Yunnan People's Publishing House, 1997.

Secondly, there exists the conversion of welfare and social security. In rural areas, surplus funds from employee welfare and social security expenditures can be channeled into corporate accumulation. Urban enterprises allocate 30–40% of their investments toward non-productive expenses like canteens, dormitories, and office buildings, as well as social security costs including labor protection, welfare benefits, medical care, retirement, and unemployment provisions. The absence of these social expenditures in township and village enterprises arises from the "excessive surplus" of labor stemming from rural populations and the safety net furnished by land ownership following the transition to household-based farming. In such distinctive circumstances, divergent from urban settings, loss-making township, and village enterprises can halt operations or even refrain from remunerating farmers during periods of unemployment. This elucidates how, within rural communities, the risks undertaken by entrepreneurs can effortlessly be shifted onto farmers and land. Consequently, the accumulation of corporate assets emerging from the conversion of unspent social security funds should rightly be apportioned to the community or the enterprise's employees, with employees entitled to ownership based on their length of service and contributions during the restructuring process.

Thirdly, we encounter the phenomenon of negative interest rates and tax exemptions. During the 1980s, bank credit interest rates plummeted below the inflation rate, thereby establishing a realm of "deeply negative interest rates." Under the policy landscape of that era, access to bank loans was limited to entities affiliated with collective economic organizations, leading to a scenario in which most corporate loans were shouldered and jeopardized by rural entities. Moreover, township and village enterprises, owing to their capacity for resolving rural employment issues and shouldering the responsibility of "supporting agriculture with industry," enjoyed favorable tax exemptions that culminated in accumulated corporate assets over the years. Therefore, the assets possessed by township and village enterprises as a result of negative interest rates and tax exemptions are not products of entrepreneurial ingenuity. This segment of assets typically accounts for approximately 10% of total corporate assets. If these enterprises are relieved of the aforementioned obligations following restructuring, then the net assets of 10% should rightfully belong to the local government or the rural collective.

Lastly, we encounter the assets forged through the amalgamation of entrepreneurial risk-reward and managerial surplus labor. This component occupies approximately 10–20% and should be bestowed upon enterprise management and key technical personnel.

To summarize, when township and village enterprises undergo restructuring, a comprehensive assessment of assets should be undertaken. Proceeding in accordance with the principle of "investment equates ownership," the allocation of equity primarily takes the form of quantified distribution of shares. Thus, the notion of "unconditional" possession of collective assets is inexistent. Entrepreneurs and technical experts should be granted 10–20% of the equity. Comparatively, this proportion suffices to motivate entrepreneurs in the framework of a standard market economy. Common laborers (namely farmers and enterprise employees) should be entitled to 70–80% of the equity, while the remaining 10% should be held by local government or rural collective organizations. As for the manner in which laborers and their collective hold shares and distribute profits, it is a matter to be pragmatically addressed during the restructuring process. Additionally, if we base our analysis on the aforementioned premises, it becomes comprehensible why individuals tend to disregard the cost of investing in community public welfare facilities and essential agricultural irrigation infrastructure in developed areas flourishing with a collective economy. Similarly, the phenomenon of a relatively substantial proportion of "non-productive occupation" by townships and villages in heavily indebted township and village enterprises becomes more easily fathomable.

2 Expansive Factory Construction amid Capital Surge

In 1980, the Party Central issued Document No. 75, granting recognition to the household responsibility system. By the end of 1981, a staggering 99.5% of production teams in the region adopted the sweeping contracted responsibility approach. In the "Chronicle of Zhanqi Village's Transformation,"[4] it is recounted that when village officials presented their work report to the county in 1981, a mere three households agreed to and signed the household responsibility contracts. Secretary Li Shili, in an interview, revealed, "Thirty households declined to sign the contracts."

[4] Qu Xihua, et al. Chronicle of Zhanqi Village's Transformation[M]. Chengdu: Sichuan University Press, 2014.

Herein lies the discrepancy. Zhanqi Brigade Party Branch Secretary Yang Zhengzhong (杨正忠) and Village Director Yi Fengxian (易奉先), during their report to the county, requested a postponement of the household responsibility system, which the county leaders begrudgingly granted. However, by 1982, the county leaders ceased to approve such deferment requests, compelling the Zhanqi Brigade to embark on the path of household contracted production, gradually paving the way for the emergence of township and village enterprises.

Examining the landscape of township and village enterprises, the phase of industrial competition in the era of capital expansion can be divided into two distinct periods. The initial stage, spanning the 1980s to the early 1990s, witnessed a fervent wave of large-scale factory establishments fueled by capital. Leveraging its preexisting industrial foundation, Zhanqi Village initially enjoyed a modicum of economic advantage. Over the course of the first 10 years since the inception of township and village enterprises in the 1980s, an impressive dozen factories took shape. The latter stage, spanning the 1990s to the twenty-first century, witnessed a shift in the trajectory of capital expansion. Though entrenched in path dependence, external changes in the macro environment compelled a delicate balancing act between capital expansion and debt burden, leading to the unfortunate demise of select enterprises.

More precisely, during the 1980s and 1990s, despite the overarching objective of establishing new enterprises and expanding existing ones, Zhanqi Village managed to sustain its prior competitive edge. This period witnessed a notable transformation of the village's brick and tile factory, evolving from a zigzag kiln to a tunnel kiln, thus substantially augmenting its production capacity. Sprouting like fresh spring blooms, numerous new enterprises took root. The first collective enterprise of the 1980s, known as the Xianfeng Brewery, commenced operations in 1980. By 1983, its fixed assets had swelled to an impressive 41,500 yuan. The second collective enterprise, Fengguan Distillery, thrived during its heyday, boasting ten sprawling workshops, each accommodating up to 82 fermentation pits. The third collective enterprise, a resin factory established in 1982, flourished in its early years, profiting from the innovative appeal of resin as a novel material, outperforming its counterparts in the collective enterprise realm. As the late 1980s transitioned into the early 1990s, Zhanqi Village birthed additional enterprises, including flour mills, compound fertilizer factories, bean paste factories, and honeycomb coal factories. Naturally, these ventures confronted a more intricate market landscape compared to their counterparts established in the early 1980s, which shall be examined more closely in the subsequent phase.

Under the auspices of a market-driven economy, the various enterprises of Zhanqi Village embraced Deng Xiaoping's pragmatic philosophy of "it doesn't matter if a cat is black or white, as long as it catches mice," unearthing their individual prowess and initiating the process of initial accumulation. Some enterprises relied on established counterparts to attain their initial accumulation goals. Notably, the construction of the flour mill and the modernization of machinery drew funds from the preexisting brick and tile factory and brewery in Zhanqi Village, with the collective land serving as the foundation for their physical structures. The compound fertilizer factory adopted an even more intricate joint venture model, bringing together the village collective, state-owned enterprises, and a chemical research institute, thereby facilitating the mobilization of working capital from within the collective.

By 1987, Zhanqi Village boasted a constellation of collective enterprises, encompassing the brick and tile factory, bean paste factory, precast component factory, trade company, Fengguan Distillery, resin factory, orchard, foundry, agricultural machinery factory, and more. By 1992, the village boasted over a dozen collective enterprises, simultaneously witnessing closures and new ventures, with a maximum of twelve enterprises coexisting. Arranged chronologically, the vital statistics and assets of key enterprises are meticulously captured in Tables 1 and 2.

1. Xianfeng Brewing Factory: In 1980, a mere 4500 yuan from a brick factory fueled the birth of the Xianfeng Brewing Factory. With humble beginnings, they acquired square tables, bamboo baskets, and raw materials. Those bamboo baskets served both as production tools and office chairs, while transportation relied on a lone yellow ox. Soy sauce and douban production marked their early endeavors, yielding an annual output of over 10,000 catties of soy sauce. By 1983, their fixed assets skyrocketed to 41,500 yuan, a staggering growth of 9.2 times their initial capital! Today, the Xianfeng Brewing Factory proudly stands as the Sichuan Xianfeng Ecological Seasoning Park Co., Ltd.
2. Resin Factory: Established in 1982, the Resin Factory emerged from a collective effort, as the village pooled together 5000 yuan for working capital. After 8 months of toil, it fell under the capable management of Li Shili. Gao Demin (高德敏), the current secretary

Table 1 Basic information of Zhanqi village enterprises in 1987 *Source* "Contracting and Leasing Operations of Xianfeng Township and Village Enterprises" Appendix "Economic Performance of Rural Enterprises in 1987 (Part V)" and "Basic Information of Contracting and Leasing Operations of Township and Village Enterprises (Part III)" (January 10, 1988), archived at the Pixian County District Archives, Sichuan Province, File No. 152-001-0265-051

Name of enterprise	*Form of responsibility system*	*Contractor/ lessee*	*Number of employees*	*Output*	*Output value (yuan)*	*Income (yuan)*	*Profit (yuan)*	*Floor area (m^2)*
Fengguan Distillery	Contractor	Yang Mingshu	24	126 tons	253,400	229,400	21,956	3,333
Pioneer Brewing	Contractor	Yao Chongqing	25	495 tons	144,700	226,041	14,284	3,666
Resin Factory	Contractor	Li Shili	21	14,729 tons	207,200	154,743	201	1,133
Zhanqi Brick Factor	Contractor	Luo Huifu	169	10,000,000 units	435,000	514,000	12,600	66,660
Foundry	Contractor	Xie Guangcheng	42	–	100,000	–	–	1,000
Prefabricated Component Factory	Lease	An Yongjiang	10	313 m^3	200,000	53,000	-6,600	1,333
Trade and Commerce Company	Lease	Wang Ligang	18	–	55,000	–	–	–

of Zhanqi Village, honed his craft as a technician at the New Resin Decoration Factory in Pixian County, mastering the art of the trade. Upon returning to the village, he assumed the role of a technician at the resin factory. A versatile substance, resin found its way into glass-making and car parts, distinguishing the Zhanqi Village resin factory as the top performer among collective enterprises. With Li Shili's ascent to a village cadre, he handed over the reins to his nephew. However, the factory's ill-fated transition into a furniture enterprise in the late 1980s marked the beginning of its decline. Eventually, the resin factory halted operations, allowing the Xianfeng Brewing Factory to claim its premises.

3. Trade and Commerce Company: Born in the mid-1980s, the Trade and Commerce Company traces its roots back to the Zhanqi Brigade

Table 2 Assets of Zhanqi Village Enterprises in 1988, Unit: Yuan *Source* "Contracting and Leasing Operations of Xianfeng Township and Village Enterprises" Appendix "Basic Information of Contracting and Leasing Operations of Township and Village Enterprises (Part III)" (January 10, 1988), archived at the Pixian County District Archives, Sichuan Province, File No. 152-001-0265-051

Name of enterprise	*Fixed assets*	*Current assets*	*Loans*	*Total assets*	*Ratio of fixed assets to total assets (%)*	*Ratio of current assets to total assets (%)*	*Ratio of loans to total assets (%)*
Fengguan distillery	244,891	32,658	292,500	277,555	88	12	105
Pioneer brewing	125,580	23,034	30,000	148,614	85	15	20
Resin factory	50,467	10,000	–	60,467	83	17	–
Zhanqi brick factor	406,450	34,900	–	441,350	92	8	–
Foundry	240,000	260,202	232,500	500,202	48	52	46
Prefabricated component factory	15,717	1000	19,000	16,717	94	6	114
Trade and commerce company	5500	16,269	230,000	21,769	25	75	1057[a]
Total	1,088,611	378,063	804,000	1,466,674	74	26	55

[a]The high loan amount of the commercial trading company is related to its retail nature, as it requires quick turnover of goods

Purchasing and Sales Store, established in 1971. This humble establishment found its new lease on life under the capable management of Wang Ligang, orchestrating the wholesale fabric business.

4. Foundry: In 1987, Zhanqi Village joined hands with the Chinese People's Liberation Army 5719 Factory to forge a unique venture—the foundry specializing in exceptional civilian castings. As a collectively owned township enterprise, it stood independently, guided by the financial system of its kind. The grand total of 300,000 yuan was invested, with the 5719 Factory contributing 30,000 yuan toward equipment and Zhanqi Village offering the factory building, valuing 70,000 yuan in the form of a discounted liquor factory

edifice. The remaining 200,000 yuan was secured through a loan from a bank. During operations, the 5719 Factory provided technical expertise and sales channels. Upon completion, the foundry boasted a projected output value of 800,000 yuan and a profit margin of 100,000 yuan. In terms of profit distribution, Zhanqi Village and the 5719 Factory settled for a 70:30 ratio. In 1990, constrained by military enterprise regulations, the 5719 Factory withdrew from Zhanqi Village. Nevertheless, it left behind a cadre of skilled technicians and lucrative sales channels. Consequently, the foundry transitioned into the sole proprietorship of Zhanqi Village. By 1991, market forces dictated its cessation.

5. Flour Mill: In 1989, orchestrated by the resourceful Yi Fengxian, the Flour Mill took shape within the remnants of an old liquor factory. Guided by Yi Fengxian's son-in-law, it flourished. Luo Huifu, the esteemed director of the brick factory, extended a loan of 80,000 yuan to Yi Fengxian's son-in-law. Out of this sum, 40,000 yuan fueled machinery acquisition, while the remaining 40,000 yuan facilitated the flow of operations. As the winds of change blew, transferring Yi Fengxian to the town in 1995, it was Yang Kaifu (杨开富) who rallied to manage the Flour Mill, assuming control in 1996.[5] Faced with the need to upgrade machinery, Yang Kaifu secured a loan of 100,000 yuan from Gao Yuchun (高玉春), the venerable director of the Xianfeng Brewing Factory. During its heyday, the Flour Mill commanded unrivaled profitability. Alas, its doors closed in 2007, succumbing to market forces.
6. Honeycomb Coal Factory: In 1989, under the visionary leadership of Luo Huifu, the Honeycomb Coal Factory came into existence. Braving the scarcity of resources, Luo Huifu and the Pixian County Coal Construction Company ventured to the Songzao Coal Mine, negotiating a deal with the Wenjiang Coal Construction Company. Caravanning back with 1200 tons of coal, they allocated 200 tons, valued at 200 yuan/ton, to the cement factory. The remaining 1000 tons fuelled the production of honeycomb coal. The coal factory thrived, amassing a profit exceeding 300,000 yuan. A portion of this bounty, 200,000 yuan, bolstered the establishment of the Huifu Douban Factory and the acquisition of its equipment. It's important

[5] Source: Interview record with Luo Huifu on February 19, 2020.

to note that this factory solely belonged to the indomitable Luo Huifu, independent of collective enterprises.

3 Case Study of Collective Enterprise: Fengguan Distillery

This case study focuses on the intriguing journey of Fengguan Distillery, which stands out amidst a multitude of enterprises. It delves into the tumultuous development of township businesses during the fiercely competitive market of the 1980s.

Established in the latter half of 1979, Fengguan Distillery commenced production in the first half of 1980. The decision to launch the distillery stemmed from its status as a planned commodity, guaranteeing a steady demand, and the existence of brewing expertise in Xianfeng Township. Spearheaded by Luo Huifu, the construction of the distillery neared completion. However, as Luo Huifu still had managerial responsibilities at the brick factory, he handed over the reins of the distillery to Yang Mingshu (杨明书), the head of the Supply and Marketing Section, in 1983. Notably, Yang Mingshu had previously served as the director of public security in the village, renowned for his astute mindset, which deemed him fit for the role of supply and marketing chief. Within this narrative, Feng Zhonghui, the interviewed individual, initially served as a technician in the distillery. Subsequently, he assumed various roles, including workshop director, salesman, and deputy factory director overseeing supply and marketing.

With substantial investment in its construction, the distillery erected two fermentation rooms and later added a koji room and storage facility, occupying a sprawling 40-acre expanse. Its production capacity witnessed rapid expansion. During its zenith, the grandeur of the distillery encompassed ten colossal workshops, each housing up to 82 cellars. Even the smallest cellar boasted a voluminous capacity of 12 cubic meters. Master brewers from Jiannanchun Liquor Factory were engaged to provide technical guidance. Alas, the production of fine liquor demanded an extensive timeframe. The prolonged production cycles, coupled with the accumulation of loan interest, financial constraints, and a myriad of other predicaments such as late payment penalties, compelled the distillery to seek loans from the brigade. The escalating loan costs diluted the business profits, eventually plunging the establishment into insurmountable debt.[6]

In 1985, Yi Fengxian, the village director at the time, reported the burgeoning issues to Yang Zhengzhong, the village party secretary. Consequently, the village cadres proposed a transformation for the distillery, transitioning it into a contract-based system. This gradual shift aimed to regain collective control while concurrently decelerating the pace of the distillery's expansion. However, at that juncture, the distillery was already engrossed in its expansion endeavors. Regrettably, the brigade's reserves of 200,000 kilograms of grain were inadvertently diverted to the "abyss" of the distillery. Additionally, Feng Zhonghui candidly shared a common adage, "People from Henan deceive Sichuan, people from Sichuan deceive Shanxi, but in the end, if it turns into money, it's mine." He shed light on the speculative behavior that unfolded amidst the cutthroat market competition. Sichuan relied heavily on Shanxi's sorghum as the primary grain for liquor production. A mere introduction letter facilitated the acquisition of copious amounts of grain on credit, thanks to the low prices Shanxi offered. Liquor production commenced, and the repayment for the sorghum procurement was structured as a gradual settlement. Subsequently, the excessive number of distilleries in Sichuan intensified competition, driving down liquor prices. Simultaneously, operational risks metamorphosed into moral hazards, gradually transforming the outstanding debts owed to Shanxi for sorghum into irrecoverable losses. As Sichuan's liquor prices plummeted, the liquor market in Henan thrived. Some individuals from Henan would purchase bulk liquor from Sichuan and manipulate it through adulteration or counterfeiting, rebranding it as their own. These Henan merchants merely made advance payments, leaving the bulk liquor from Sichuan to accumulate as bad debts. Initially, Fengguan Distillery specialized in kiwi liquor, known as "kiwi liquor." It employed kiwi juice for fermentation, employing a distinctive liquid fermentation technique prevalent in the Dujiangyan area. However, the factory's production of kiwi liquor witnessed a decline in quality over time. Subpar kiwis became the new raw materials, blended with sugar, essence, water, and colorants, leading to a gradual deterioration in the liquor's overall caliber.

[6] Source: Interview with Feng Zhonghui, February 10, 2020.

The years 1986 and 1987 bore witness to a nationwide trend in product returns, instigated by quality issues plaguing Sichuan liquor, consequently tarnishing its reputation. Coupled with the constraints imposed by tight working capital, Fengguan Distillery found it arduous to persevere.[7] Desperate for funds, the distillery sought loans totaling 100,000 yuan from the brick factory and secured a bank loan of 200,000 yuan. Originally intended for the acquisition of grain for liquor production, these funds were later diverted toward constructing the distillery's office and crafting trademarks. Subsequently, another loan was procured from the credit union to support working capital. Alas, the inability to meet repayment obligations left the distillery no choice but to succumb to bankruptcy. Two decades later, the former bank president jestingly remarked, "We loaned you money to purchase grain, but we never had the chance to savor the liquor you produced."

The fortunes of Fengguan Distillery hinged on the vicissitudes of the liquor market. Figure 1 illustrates the fluctuations in retail prices of renowned liquors in Chengdu. From 1981 to 1987, liquor prices experienced a dramatic surge compared to the preceding decades, offering lucrative opportunities for substantial gains. During this period, Fengguan Distillery reveled in the bountiful dividends derived from soaring liquor prices, thus embarking on an ambitious expansion endeavor. However, by 1987, liquor prices began their descent, prompting Fengguan Distillery to lease portions of its premises to a foundry. Subsequently, in 1989, the liquor market suffered a severe downturn, significantly impacting Fengguan Distillery, and eventually driving it to bankruptcy.

The journey of Fengguan Distillery is not an isolated tale. Xianfeng Township, its home, responded to the deteriorating external environment by encouraging the growth of village-run enterprises and formulating numerous regulations. For instance, "For villages with village-run enterprises that achieve an output value of 2 million yuan, a reward of 500 yuan will be bestowed; for villages with an output value of 2.5 million yuan, a reward of 1000 yuan will be granted; for villages with an output value of 3 million yuan, a reward of 2000 yuan will be conferred; and for villages whose village-run enterprises generate profits (as per the accounts) surpassing 100,000 yuan, a reward of 1000 yuan will be presented." Despite these endeavors, the inexorable decline could not be masked.

[7] Source: Interview with Feng Zhonghui, February 10, 2020.

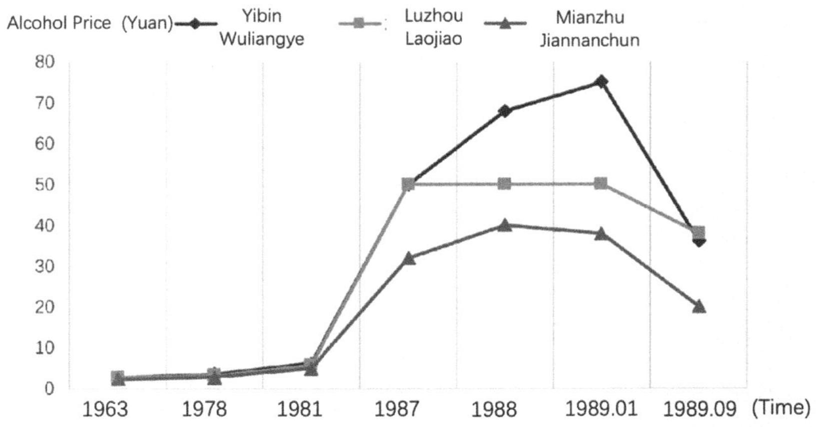

Fig. 1 Changes in retail prices of famous liquors in Chengdu (Liquor price, unit: yuan), Yibin Wuliangye, Luzhou Laojiao, Mianzhu Jiannanchun. *Source* Chengdu Local Chronicles Editorial Committee. Chengdu Chronicles Price Chronicles [M]. Chengdu: Sichuan Lexicography Publishing House, 1998

* * *

Regulations for Enterprise Growth and Economic Excellence (1988)

To propel our township's businesses to new heights, effectuate a strategic paradigm shift, participate in the global economic cycle, and stride alongside enterprise evolution, the ensuing regulations for fostering economic prosperity and nurturing enterprise development have been meticulously crafted.

Firstly, extend a warm invitation to both provincial and non-provincial factories, research institutions, and other external entities to forge alliances in matters of commerce, technology, resources, capital, and expertise. Establish symbiotic "windows" or bespoke partnerships, with collaboration methods of the host's choosing. They may opt for an exclusive proprietorship or collaborative ventures, product diffusion or stock dividends, compensation trade or technology transfers, joint operations or contracted undertakings, or propose alternative collaborative modes. In the pursuit of economic parity and mutual benefit, offer preferential treatment by extending economic incentives. Projects that exhibit remarkable economic viability shall be accorded superior consideration in profit distribution.

Secondly, irrespective of whether they are local or external officials, employees, or rural constituents, those instrumental in furnishing intelligence, forging connections, or introducing projects conducive to our township's economic advancement shall receive a service remuneration equal to 0.3% of the project's output value upon the successful signing of contracts. Should the enterprise yield tangible economic benefits within the first 12 months of production, they shall be duly rewarded with 10% of the after-tax profit. Township officials and enterprise management personnel involved in project introductions shall receive half of the aforementioned remuneration benchmarks.

Thirdly, extend preferential treatment to newly relocated scientific and technological personnel. Those willingly committed to advancing our township's economy and fostering product innovation, while retaining their position without salary, shall be entitled to the treatment prescribed in the eight measures for external economic and technological cooperation established by the County Party Committee and County Government.

Fourthly, existing enterprises that expand their operations and augment investments, while meeting the contracted project targets, shall be exempted from remitting the post-tax profits obtained within 2 years. In the initial year, retain 40% of the profits as an incentive (30% in the subsequent year), allocating the remaining amount toward loan repayment and as a development fund. Concurrently, contingent upon the enterprise's profit performance, and subject to approval from the enterprise office, management personnel may enjoy an increase in wages.

Fifthly, augment the remuneration for the developmental strides of enterprises existing below the village level. Building upon the 1987 baseline, villages that accomplish a mid-year performance value increment of ¥10,000 for village-operated enterprises shall be awarded ¥20. A ¥5 reward shall be conferred for a ¥10,000 increase in output value for "the last three rounds" of enterprises. A ¥150 reward shall be bestowed for a ¥10,000 increase in village-operated enterprise profits (based on recorded accounts). Half of the aforementioned bonuses shall be disbursed by the township, while the remaining half shall be sourced by the village.[8]

Sixthly, institute the Xianfeng and Innovation Award to kindle the growth of village-operated enterprises. Villages achieving an output value of 2 million yuan shall receive a 500 yuan reward, while those reaching 2.5 million yuan and 3 million yuan shall be granted 1000 yuan and 2000 yuan, respectively. Villages with village-operated enterprises yielding 100,000 yuan in profits (as per recorded accounts) shall be awarded 1000 yuan. The aforementioned rewards shall be shared evenly between the township and the village, with each bearing half of the costs.

Seventhly, cultivate a culture of motivation through incentives for enterprises beneath the village level to fulfill their management fee obligations. Enterprises faithfully adhering to the stipulated regulations by duly reserving and regularly submitting management fees shall be rewarded 5% of the total amount remitted to the key officials of village-operated factories. For villages exhibiting proactive diligence in ensuring timely fee submissions, the principal officials of the village shall be entitled to a 5% reward of the total amount remitted. Commencing in 1988, villages unable to fulfill their remittance obligations shall face a proportionate deduction from comprehensive rewards, equivalent to the total outstanding amount.

By Xianfeng Township Vanguard Party Committee

Xianfeng Township People's Government

Source: "Regulations for Enterprise Growth and Economic Excellence" (March 14, 1988), archived at the Pidu District Archives, Sichuan Province, "Xianfeng Township File," Archive Number 152-001-0266-002.

4 Administrative System–Contract System (1982–1994)

1. Policy Background

In 1978, the 3rd Plenary Session of the 11th Central Committee of the Communist Party of China brought forth the land contracting policy. By 1982, Zhanqi had implemented the land contract system. As land was distributed among households, the

[8] Note: It is not specified whether this reward is per individual within the enterprise.

labor point system naturally vanished within the Zhanqi collective. The village branch swiftly shifted focus from grain production to collective enterprises, avoiding animal husbandry due to its inherent disease risks. Village director Yi Fengxian and accountant Luo Huiping (罗会平) meticulously audited the assets of the previous village collective. Guided by the principle of "grasping the large and releasing the small," management under the contract system was allocated to larger enterprises, while smaller ones fell under the leasing system. By 1983, Zhanqi permitted farmers to acquire large-scale production assets, followed by the allowance for farmers to fund enterprises and settle in townships for self-sustenance in 1984. In Document No. 4, the central government explicitly outlined the significance and role of township enterprise development, laying out guidelines and the historic mission to revolutionize township and village enterprises. Policy-backed, township and village enterprises embarked on a fresh wave of industrial competition. The 1988 constitutional revision acknowledged private enterprise as a valuable supplement to the socialist economy. The flourishing of township and village enterprises was an outcome of progressive policy liberalization.[9]

2. Implementation of the Contract System

Under the contract system, management operated under the "wage + bonus" model. Factories adhered to predetermined production and profit targets, with standards tailored to previous years' operational performance. Ideally, targets escalated annually, and, in practice, most factories met the requirements. Surpassing the set tasks warranted rewards, while failure to meet goals theoretically merited deductions, although none were practically implemented.[10] Management personnel received three times the salary of regular workers, with additional rewards for profits exceeding 100,000 yuan. Factory directors, management personnel, and ordinary workers shared the spoils, each group with its designated proportion. Take, for instance, the brick factory, where Luo Huifu

[9] Lin Qingsong, Du Ying. Industrial Reform and Efficiency in China: Comparative Study of State-owned Enterprises and Non-state-owned Enterprises. Kunming: Yunnan People's Publishing House, 1997.

[10] Source: Interview records with Gao Demin on October 2, 2019.

and Yang Zhongmo assumed the role of contractors. Their agreement entailed an annual contribution of 80,000 yuan to the village, while the brick factory bore its own fortunes. Excess profits were divided, with 20% allocated to the collective and 80% to the factory. Within the factory's 80% share of profits, the director received 40%, and the remaining 60% was reinvested for expansion purposes. Figure 2 depicts the contractual agreement for the management and operation of the brick factory.

社队企业联产责任制

承包合同

在党的十二大精神指引下，为了进一步搞活经济，致富农民，充分调动社队企业职工的积极性，改革企业经营管理，提高经济效益，开创社队企业新局面，从一九八三年起，实行集体所有制企业承包给个人经营，包干上交收益的大包干责任制，现签订企业承包合同如下：

承包企业名称：

出包单位（甲方）

承包人（乙方）

承包时间从198 年 月 日起198 年 月 日止共 年

（一）乙方承包项目

1. 产值年

2. 经营收入（营业额）年

3. 上交甲方：

Fig. 2 Contractual agreement for the joint production responsibility system in the village collective enterprise

Alongside the contract system, the leasing system ran parallel, with its own assigned tasks. Completion of these tasks granted the enterprise full ownership of the remaining profits, albeit without wages or bonuses. These enterprises, the "small" ones released under the principle of "grasping the large and releasing the small," deserve clarification. It is important to note that in the evolutionary process of Zhanqi's collective economic system, large and small enterprises were governed by distinct approaches. The contract system of 1982 and the shareholding system of '94, previously mentioned, were applicable to larger enterprises and held no bearing on smaller ones.[11]

[11] Source: Interview records with Li Shili on January 11, 2020.

CHAPTER 7

Macroeconomic Waves and the Evolution of Collective Economic Systems (1988–1994)

1 Background: Township and Village Enterprises Restructuring

In the realm of geography, the strategy of opening-up to the world was subject to regional disparities due to varying geographic tiers. The coastal cities in the east were the fortunate beneficiaries of policy advantages. Renowned scholars such as Hu Angang emphasized in their "Regional Disparity Report of China" that the fundamental cause for the striking gap in per capita GDP between developed and underdeveloped regions lay in the substantial disparity in per capita investment. Two factors contributed to this divergence: firstly, since the 1980s, the central government pursued an imbalanced development strategy, diverting central investment projects toward coastal areas; secondly, the prosperous coastal regions took the lead in implementing reforms, diversifying their sources of investment and swiftly diminishing the share of non-state-owned economy in total investments.[1] The primary reason behind these discrepancies was the expansionist development of capital, which fueled regional development disparities. In the 1980s, Zhanqi Village, located in the rural Western region, confronted the challenge of single-source investments, a

[1] Hu Angang, Wang Shaoguang, Kang Xiaoguang. Regional Disparity Report of China. Shenyang: Liaoning People's Publishing House, 1995.

© Peking University Press 2024

X. Dong, *Zhanqi Village Over Fifty Years*,
https://doi.org/10.1007/978-981-97-5426-7_7

significant share of non-state-owned economy in total investments, and consequently, scarcity of capital.

Following the mid-1980s, China entered a phase dominated by local governments in the realm of industrial capital, where industrial capital development was propelled through competitive corporatization.

On one hand, due to the dearth of non-market institutional resources and an unfavorable macroeconomic environment, and on the other hand, due to the geographical alignment of market resources and capital distribution with stark urban–rural disparities and regional discrepancies, Zhanqi Village, situated in the rural Western region, almost inevitably suffered operational losses as it expanded its debt under the strain of extreme capital scarcity. Unfortunately, during the national fiscal deficit crisis, the government implemented the stockization reform, with all village members collectively holding shares. This marked the pinnacle of collective economy, which later faced criticism for its systemic "incomplete reform" when the costs of crisis were shifted.

In 1994, amid a macroeconomic crisis, the central government implemented a series of intensive regulatory measures. Building upon the foundation of the "Sixteen Ironclad Measures (铁血十六条)" introduced in 1993, the fiscal system reform was set in motion in 1994, abolishing tax benefits for township and village enterprises. This reform was accompanied by banking and exchange rate system reforms, objectively leaning toward a strategy favoring coastal areas and urban centers. Regions below the county level were severely affected by loan contraction and liquidity shortage. The Western regions witnessed a massive exodus toward the southeast, thereby exacerbating serious "Three Rural Issues" and imposing dual institutional cost pressures on Zhanqi Village.

The year 1993 cast a dark cloud over the city, as Western sanctions and capital withdrawal thrust China into the throes of three major crises. Small and medium-sized banks collapsed one after another, rendering capital an exceedingly scarce resource, township and village enterprises, which relied on loans to sustain their growth, suddenly found themselves devoid of any loan sources, exposing all past debts. In other words, restructuring initially severed the lifeline of loans to township and village enterprises. Consequently, the debt ratio of township and village enterprises surged, leading to widespread restructuring as an ensuing consequence. However, before the crisis of 1994 was resolved, the market and policies faced a dual challenge emanating from the 1997 Asian financial crisis. The financial crisis erupted, burdening banks with a high volume of bad loans, and thus forcing all township and village enterprises to undertake thorough privatization reforms. Over twenty million township and village enterprises underwent an almost instantaneous transformation into private ownership. Our analysis of "Understanding Southern Jiangsu" shed light on the impact of the macroeconomic environment on the micro-level operations of township and village enterprises post-1997, as well as the government's logic of "embracing the large and releasing the small" in promoting the restructuring of township and village enterprises. Further research conducted in Daqiuzhuang Village around 2012 elucidated the catalytic role of banking commercialization reforms in the split and privatization of Daqiuzhuang Village Enterprise Group under the pressures of the 1997 Asian financial crisis. The financial system, in its pursuit of ascribing clear responsibility for loan recipients, exerted pressure through the administrative system, necessitating a complete "privatization reform" for township and village enterprises, a direction in stark contrast to that taken a few years earlier. All of these elements to some extent indicate a "compulsory institutional transformation." Many regions explicitly emphasized the need for restructuring in a "privatization without joint-stock" direction. In 1997, the "Law of the People's Republic of China on Township and Village Enterprises" was enacted, finally granting legal status to township and village enterprises. While they attained legal recognition, at the end of the year, the government issued policy documents for the restructuring of township and village enterprises, and the supervisory department actively aligned itself with international practices by dissolving the "Division of Township and Village Enterprise."[2]

Since 1998, the economy has been gripped by a recession, which further deteriorated in 2003. Global industrial realignments prompted multinational corporations to shift their production bases to China, giving precedence to the developed coastal regions. Consequently, the Eastern economy burned bright while the Western regions experienced a chilling decline, leading to economic disparities and a marked dichotomy between the East and West. In the 1980s, township and village enterprises had the ability to alleviate rural issues and generate export revenues. However, by the 1990s, regional development increasingly manifested as stratified growth under distinct geopolitical policies, placing Zhanqi Village at a relatively lower point during this period. Hence, beneath the macro

[2] Source: Discussion records of Wen Tiejun, Dong Xiaodan, and others on June 8, 2019.

crisis of the late 1990s, institutions permitted "leveraged" privatization, enabling acquirers to purchase enterprise equity with a cash offer as low as 20% discount. According to official statements, the comprehensive restructuring of township and village enterprises was accomplished in 2001. This signified that the true embodiment of the "collective attribute" of township and village enterprises existed merely for 4 years within the realm of the law. Subsequently, the "township" in "township and village enterprises" became a mere geographical epithet.

2 Collective Industries Struggle to Sustain Operations

At this juncture, industrialization competition blazes with intensity. If we dare say that the mid-1980s witnessed the onset of unfavorable conditions, with growth pursued through indebtedness and scale expansion, following the well-trodden path of industrialization, then the fiscal, monetary, and foreign exchange reforms of 1994, coupled with the crippling blows of a late-stage economic crisis, steered the national policy environment inexorably toward coastal regions and the pursuit of export-led prosperity. Bank loans were targeted at entities beyond the county level, leaving the township and village enterprises, below the county threshold, bereft of their former privileged environment, both in terms of loan quotas and fiscal incentives. This unmistakable regional bias in the policy environment casts a shadow over Zhanqi's fortunes in the latter half of the industrialization competition, namely the waning years of the 1990s.

For Zhanqi, "collective economic efforts to sustain operations" entail a period bereft of the exuberant progress enjoyed in previous stages. Nonetheless, fortified by the foundations laid in preceding years, their overall performance remains commendable. In 1994, the village's combined industrial and agricultural output soared to a staggering 75 million yuan.[3] Zhanqi's "two committees" rallied behind the development objectives of "integrating industry, agriculture, commerce, and tourism; fostering enterprise growth and group formation; elevating farmer livelihoods to prosperity; and adorning the new village with a

[3] Source: "Advanced Materials of Zhanqi Village Party Committee" (April 5, 2000), Archives of Pidu District, Sichuan Province, File No. 149-001-0548-024, Page 1.

garden-like ambiance."[4] By 1996, the village's combined industrial and agricultural output surged to a remarkable 141 million yuan, with village-level enterprises boasting net assets worth 10 million yuan, collective disposable income reaching 560,000 yuan, and the per capita annual net income of farmers hitting 2974 yuan.[5]

Zhanqi soared to the second position in terms of income among the 260 villages within the county, two years ahead of schedule in joining the ranks of prosperous villages. By the first half of 1997, Zhanqi revised the overall social output value of the village, downsizing it from a staggering 105 million yuan to a more modest 63.12 million yuan. During that same year, the collective's net income reached 380,000 yuan, the village's industrial total income amounted to 59.88 million yuan, tax profits stood at 1.2764 million yuan, and the per capita net income of farmers settled at 1785 yuan, with an overwhelming 99.8% of households surpassing the 1800 yuan mark.[6]

In the tranquil hamlet of Tangchang Township, Pixian County, as depicted in Fig. 1,[7] Zhanqi claimed two spots out of thirteen in the esteemed roster of 1994's economic commendations. Xianfeng Brewing Factory and Xianfeng Casting Factory, both emblematic enterprises, stood tall. Among the thirty-five individuals honored, Luo Huifu (director of the mechanical brick factory and Huifu Broad Bean Paste factory), Yang Zhongmo (one of the contractors at the mechanical brick factory), Feng Zhonghui (director of the compound fertilizer factory), and Wang Ping (director of Xianfeng Brewing Factory) garnered well-deserved recognition as outstanding contributors.

Amidst these years, the grandest event that unfolded in Zhanqi's chronicles was the establishment of the Chengdu Jifeng Industrial Corporation (hereinafter referred to as Jifeng Corporation).

In 1994, Zhanqi earned its stripes as a restructuring pilot project in Pixian County. Jifeng Corporation, serving as a managerial platform,

[4] Ibid., p. 2.

[5] Source: "Advanced Deeds of Zhanqi Village" (November 5, 1997), Archives of Pidu District, Sichuan Province, File No. 149-001-0490-010, Page 1.

[6] Source: "Main Economic Indicators of Zhanqi Village in the First Half of 1997," Archives of Pidu District, Sichuan Province, File No. 149-001-0490-009.

[7] On October 27, 1992, Pixian County underwent administrative restructuring, leading to the abolition of Xianfeng Township, with its jurisdiction transferred to the administration of Tangchang Township.

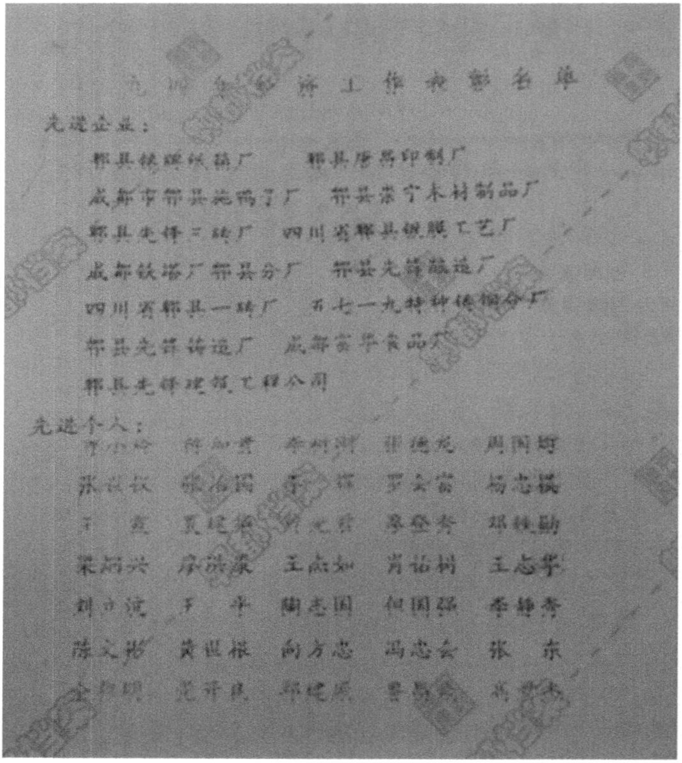

Fig. 1 Commendations for economic work (1994) [*Source* "Decision of the Tangchang Town Committee of the Communist Party of China and the People's Government of Tangchang Town, Pixian County, Regarding the Holding of the Annual Rural Economic Work Summary and Commendation Conference for 1994" with Annex "List of Advanced Enterprises and Individuals" (January 14, 1995), Archives of Pidu District, Sichuan Province, File No. 149-001-0455-015.]

wielded dominion over five enterprises. Each entity retained its financial and operational autonomy, yet donned the shared mantle of distinction. These five illustrious enterprises comprised Xianfeng Brewing Factory, Xianfeng Brick Factory, Chengdu Pixian Compound Fertilizer Factory, Huifu Broad Bean Paste Factory, and Xianfeng Flour Processing Factory. In an audit report from Pixian County's Audit Office dated November 21, 1994, the total assets of these esteemed establishments amounted to a staggering 9,360,938 yuan. Fixed assets tallied 2,116,376 yuan, while net assets reached an impressive 3,066,690 yuan.[8] *In 1995, following comprehensive evaluation by provincial authorities, Zhanqi Village earned the prestigious designation of a "prosperous village" within Sichuan Province. Gao Yuchun, Chairman and General Manager of Jifeng Corporation, emerged as a celebrated rural entrepreneur in Chengdu and was honored as one of Pixian County's distinguished talents in the second batch, reaping a monthly stipend of ten yuan. At its zenith, Jifeng Corporation boasted a remarkable dozen subsidiary enterprises. However, not all twelve existed concurrently, as the ebb and flow of opening and closing enterprises dictated their numbers. By 1999, a comparison with the state of affairs 5 years prior revealed a 1.12-fold increase in production output, a 1.36-fold surge in operating income, a 1.19-fold boost in profit, and an impressive capital return rate of 94.4%.*[9] *However, from 2003 to 2004, the five major enterprises relinquished their shared "hat" and embarked on individual pursuits.*[10]

Within Jifeng Corporation, a rewarding system took hold. For instance, the production plan formulated in 1995 aimed at achieving 2000 tons of soybean paste, 100 tons of condiments, and 55 tons of pickled vegetables, with projected sales revenue of 4.08 million yuan and a profit target of 220,000 yuan (aiming for 300,000 yuan). The baseline profit for 1994 stood at 161,000 yuan. Those who achieved a score of 95 or higher in the assessment were entitled to a factory director's salary twice that of the average worker's earnings. Upon meeting the profit target, the factory director could claim 30% of the allocated bonus fund. If the profit target was surpassed, the "2–3–5" reward system was set into motion, entailing 20% remitted to the parent company, 30% bestowed upon the enterprise's director, and the remaining 50% allocated for internal distribution.[11]

[8] Source: "Assessment Report on the Assets of Five Enterprises in Zhanqi Village, Pixian County" (November 21, 1994), Archives of Pidu District, Sichuan Province, File No. 149-001-0445-015.

[9] Source: "Advanced Materials of Zhanqi Village Party Committee" (April 5, 2000), Archives of Pidu District, Sichuan Province, File No. 149-001-0548-024, pp. 2–3.

[10] Source: Interview Record with Li Shili on January 11, 2020.

[11] Source: "1995 Factory Director's Target Responsibility Letter of Chengdu Jifeng Industrial Corporation," Records.

Among the quintet of enterprises, Huifu Broad Bean Paste Factory, though fashioned later, flaunts remarkable prowess.

In 1992, the factory's foundations were laid, and by 1993, it sprang forth, fueled by a modest capital of roughly 510,000 yuan. The brickyard contributed bricks worth 113,000 yuan for the construction of the factory premises, featuring a kitchen, warehouse, fresh pepper chamber, small tile abode, and a machinery repair space. In total, the structure spanned 2942.71 square meters. Additionally, the brickyard invested nearly 400,000 yuan in ancillary building materials and labor costs.[12] *Come 1994, Huifu Broad Bean Paste Factory's total assets tallied 1.7155 million yuan, liabilities reached 1.6122 million yuan, with an owner's equity amounting to 103,200 yuan.*[13]

In 1993, the Economic Committee of Tangchang Town People's Government dispatched a communiqué to Sanlian Plastic Compression Factory. The directive stipulated a demand that the latter allocate 4–6% of their sales revenue as operating expenses and other fees, entrusted to the factory director for business expansion and venturing into novel avenues. On one hand, this notice hints at the fervor of market competition, necessitating specific provisions of sales revenue to satiate the exigencies of further business growth. On the other hand, any economically savvy individual knows that 4–6% is the customary profit margin for economic entities. By designating these funds as business expenses, the enterprise's profits are severely diluted, hampering further development.

In the crucible of cutthroat market competition, the liquor and compound fertilizer factories fall short of the Broad Bean Paste Factory's asset exclusivity. The former succumbs to the influence of speculative machinations, compelled to compromise the quality of its in-house libations. Meanwhile, the compound fertilizer factory, drowning in a sea of counterfeit and subpar products, conspires with supply and marketing cooperatives and fertilizer suppliers, engaging in illicit procurement or selling of quotas, capitalizing on the specialized fertilizer loophole.

During the mid-1990s, spurred by a confluence of market economics and internal organizational constraints, a quintet of collective enterprises shuttered their doors. The compound fertilizer factory serves as a salient exemplar, undergoing visible debt burdens brought about by grandiose

[12] Source: Interview record of Luo Huiyou on November 3, 2019.

[13] Source: "Summary and Detailed Report of 1994 Asset Assessment Declaration."

expansion, encumbered by stringent market oversight, and ensnared in the predicament of "Gresham's law (an inferior currency to drive a superior currency out of circulation)" amid fierce market competition.

As counterfeit wares proliferate unchecked, regulatory bodies tighten the noose around enterprises producing such goods. The administrative oversight measures engender direct consequences in the form of fines and supplementary taxes. The more calamitous effect, however, arises from the dearth of timely returns on previous massive investments, precipitating a rupture in the financial lifeblood and an insufficiency of liquidity. Compounded by stringent financial policies, the dearth of liquidity remains unmitigated. Scores of rural enterprises find themselves ensnared in the vice of both amplified external regulation and insufficient liquidity, culminating in a surfeit of closures and decline. The tale of Fengguan Liquor Factory and Compound Fertilizer Factory of Zhanqi serves as but a minuscule microcosm of this somber reality.

3 Case Study: Compound Fertilizer Factory

Not far from the entrance of Zhanqi Village, a plume of smoke rises from a stately Western-style house by the roadside. Feng Zhonghui and his kinfolk are preparing for a meal, and the patriarch, a sprightly 60-year-old, is in high spirits as he personally takes charge of the kitchen.

Within this abode dwells a harmonious clan spanning four generations, encompassing seven souls. Feng Zhonghui shares his dwelling with his parents, his wife, his son and daughter-in-law, and a vivacious 10-year-old granddaughter. Prior to the eve of the Spring Festival, a serendipitous encounter took place between General Secretary Xi Jinping and this very family, who were at the time immortalizing their kinship with a heart-warming photograph. When inquired about the contentment of Feng Zhonghui's father, Feng Jiaxiang, General Secretary Xi was met with a multitude of approving nods. True happiness, indeed, originates from the depths of one's heart. The blissful existence of Feng Zhonghui's kin stands as a vignette of the bustling rural life that permeates the sprawling landscapes of Chengdu.

Source: Chengdu Business Daily, March 7, 2018

Feng Zhonghui,[14] as mentioned in the narrative, not only embodies a paragon of contentment in the village of Zhanqi during this era, but also holds a significant role in the illustrious history of the prosperous compound fertilizer factory that graced the village's soils in the vibrant 1990s. His tumultuous journey of ups and downs remains intrinsically intertwined with the destiny of Zhanqi's communal enterprises.

Located in the Western outskirts of Tangchang Town, the Chengdu Pixian Compound Fertilizer Factory (henceforth referred to as the "Compound Fertilizer Factory")[15] is an innovative chemical enterprise that sprouted its roots in 1991. Situated a mere six kilometers from the illustrious National Highway 317, three kilometers from Pengwen Road, and eight kilometers from the Tanjiachang Railway Station, it boasts a highly advantageous geographical position.

Originally, the inception of the compound fertilizer factory was not anticipated within the pioneering Xianfeng Township. According to Feng Zhonghui, it was Yang Zhengzhong who clandestinely absconded with the project upon catching wind of its potential. Serendipitously, the Sichuan Institute of Chemical Industry had recently devised a groundbreaking patent involving the production of nitrogenous fertilizers using ammonium chloride—a revelation that set the compound fertilizer domain ablaze. Thus, in 1991, under the auspices of the

[14] Feng Zhonghui: worked as a technician in a winery and was later promoted to deputy director. After the winery closed, he worked as a mobile wine seller for a year. Worked as a salesperson in the supply and marketing department of a compound fertilizer factory, and later as the factory director. After that, he worked as the production director of a factory in Guanghan for two years. After the leasing system was implemented, he worked under the new director of the compound fertilizer factory and helped the fertilizer factory straighten out its sales channels and the relationship with law enforcement agencies. Now Shibafang in Zhanqi Village operates a Fuxing mash shop, selling online and offline.

[15] Since its establishment, Chengdu Pixian Compound Fertilizer Factory has always adhered to the business purpose of "quality first, service first, and integrity first." The "Wangcong" brand series of compound fertilizers produced are based on the needs of different regions, different soil qualities, different crops, and the needs of different crop growth points in my country, using high-quality raw materials and scientific formulas to develop various high, medium, and low concentrations. Compound fertilizers and special fertilizers. It is not only suitable for the planting of more than 20 crops such as rice, wheat, rape, corn, cotton, fruit trees, watermelon, peanuts, tobacco, tea trees, etc., but also plays a positive role in improving soil, serving ecological agriculture, and developing green agriculture. In addition to selling well in this county and surrounding Dujiangyan City, Chongzhou City, Pengzhou City, and Wenjiang County, our products are also exported to Shandong, Shaanxi, Jiangxi, Chongqing, and other places.

Armed Forces Department of Pixian County, the factory was conceived through a trifecta collaboration among Zhanqi Village, Xianfeng Township Economic Commission, and Dayi County Agricultural Materials Corporation. Regrettably, before its realization, the three entities parted ways due to inadequate funding, ultimately leaving Zhanqi as the sole proprietor. Zhanqi Village provided the land, factory buildings, and circulating capital, while Xianfeng Township Economic Commission dispatched personnel for management, and the Sichuan Institute of Chemical Industry lent its technical expertise as a shareholder.

In the nascent stages of the factory's operation, antiquated equipment, sourced through the Sichuan Institute of Chemical Industry, was employed—a consequence of their upgraded machinery becoming obsolete. The initial round of loans secured a modest working capital of a mere ten thousand yuan, with Yi Fengxian shouldering the responsibility of coordinating bank loans, and the town government providing the necessary guarantees. Additional funds were procured through internal channels within the brick factory, where interest rates proved more favorable than those of traditional loans. However, the start-up capital allocated for the acquisition of raw materials amounted to a mere ten to twenty thousand yuan.[16] Toward the end of 1991, procuring raw materials proved to be an arduous task, with Feng Zhonghui, responsible for procurement, making personal appeals to the sales department of the raw material factory.

During its embryonic phase, the compound fertilizer factory occupied an expanse of land spanning over ten mu (approximately 6666 square meters), with an employee's monthly wage amounting to a meager seventy yuan. Subsequently, it expanded its reach, acquiring the derelict factory building of a foundry, thereby extending its footprint to twenty mu (around 13,333 square meters). Boasting an annual production capacity exceeding ten thousand tons, the factory abided by a sales principle that dictated proximity over distance. Sales personnel diligently navigated the grassroots supply and marketing cooperatives and agricultural machinery stations, only proceeding once obtaining their unanimous approval. Over time, the compound fertilizers forged new avenues, being dispatched to neighboring regions such as Wenjiang, Chongzhou,

[16] Source: Interview record with Feng Zhonghui on February 10, 2020.

and Dujiangyan, and even stretching their influence beyond provincial borders.[17]

In 1992, the fertilizer factory fell under the management of the town's enterprise. However, Zhanqi Village wasn't convinced. They suspected the appointed managers (village cadres from nearby villages, who had previously ruined their own cement factory) of engaging in kickbacks during equipment purchases and lacking adequate management skills. So, they took matters into their own hands and reassigned Su Yuntian (苏运田), the former Minister of the Xianfeng Township Armed Forces, to lead the charge. Su, highly qualified both militarily and intellectually, along with Zhanqi Village, assumed responsibility. By year's end, the village committee awarded the compound fertilizer factory to the Guiyang Normal College in Guizhou Province, with the specific task of managing the facility. Their agreement centered on performance assessments, where the benchmark was profitability. From the day of operation, the annual profit target was set at 80,000 yuan. According to the profit distribution principle, surplus profits beyond the contract would be allocated as follows: 50% to be retained for enterprise development, 40% to the Zhanqi Village Committee, and 60% to the research institute. The village committee guaranteed an annual profit of 40,000 yuan, while the research institute secured 40,000 yuan. In the unfortunate event of operating losses, the research institute would bear the burden.

Come 1994, Su Yuntian was no longer at the helm as the compound fertilizer factory underwent restructuring. Feng Zhonghui, a sales representative, took over as the factory director. At this juncture, the factory saw a collective ownership split: 50% belonged to the workers, while the other half rested with the collective. The staff numbered around 30 to 40 individuals. Technological upgrades boosted the factory's annual production from a mere 10,000 tons to an impressive 30,000 tons. Riding on success, director Feng Zhonghui treated himself to a sleek sedan worth 120,000 yuan, leaving the compound fertilizer factory basking in glory. Even the head of the credit union tagged along to select his own wheels.

By 1995, the compound fertilizer factory hit its pinnacle, raking in millions. The net profit handed over to the village collective exceeded a hundred grand, with tax revenues nearing the 200,000 yuan mark. Employee salaries swelled to an impressive 1000–2000 yuan. Lin Genzhi,

[17] Source: Interview record with Lin Genzhi (林根志) on October 3, 2019.

a former worker, recollected, "Back then, folks around these parts were green with envy, all clamoring for a spot at the compound fertilizer factory." However, the market had reached saturation, and competition turned fierce. To counter the challenge, the factory delved into producing specialized fertilizers, tailored for rice, wheat, and other crops. Essentially, these new concoctions shared the same formula as the regular compound fertilizers, merely donning different labels. It was nothing more than a case of "new name, same game."

Fast forward to 1996, and the compound fertilizer industry's declining product quality had caught the watchful eye of regulators. The root of the problem was the unholy alliance between supply and marketing cooperatives and fertilizer suppliers. Collaboratively, they smuggled subpar products into the hands of unsuspecting farmers by acquiring or selling quotas illicitly. The regulators struggled to untangle the web woven by the cooperatives and fertilizer factories. Farmers, however, experienced a slump in crop yields after using the compound fertilizer. Sensing trouble, the authorities cracked down on quality control. The Pixian County compound fertilizer factory discreetly recalled their sold products, plunging into a period of production downturn. In the same year, the government launched an investigation into tax evasion, slapping the compound fertilizer factory with a fine of over 200,000 yuan. Thus, the factory began keeping two sets of books.[18]

By 1998, the village collective reclaimed the compound fertilizer factory, enduring a loss of approximately 200,000 yuan.

In 1999, the factory underwent a transformation, investing 480,000 yuan in overhauling the production facility. The previous single-line production system, capable of churning out a paltry 10,000 tons annually, specializing in low-concentration ammonium chloride-based compound fertilizers, underwent an ambitious conversion. It morphed into a cutting-edge production line, boasting a yearly capacity of 30,000 tons, generating high-concentration urea-based specialized fertilizers for tobacco, fruit trees, and other crops.[19]

A report from 2000 titled "Application for the Extraction and Development Fund and Exemption of Value-Added Tax from

[18] Source: Interview records with Feng Zhonghui on February 10, 2020.

[19] Source: "Advanced Materials of Zhanqi Village Party General Branch, Tangchang Town" (April 5, 2000), stored in the Pidu District Archives in Sichuan Province, File No. 149-001-0548-024, pp. 2–3.

Profit Calculation by Chengdu Pixian County Compound Fertilizer Factory (《成都郫县复合肥料厂关于提取开发基金和减免增值税不作利润计算的申请报告》)" revealed that "from 1992 to 1996, the factory faced five consecutive years of losses. The resilient staff explored every avenue, cutting costs and streamlining operations. By the end of 1997, income and expenses had leveled out, and after another year of tireless effort, positive results finally materialized by the close of 1999." The report further stated, "In the cutthroat market, the factory grappled with challenges like limited warehouse space and cramped production workshops. Being an agricultural enterprise, it operated at a loss, relying on the state's value-added tax exemption policy and social fundraising to stay afloat amid intense market competition. In anticipation of the grand Westward Development and in an effort to secure a brighter future for the fertilizer factory, preventing its demise, we humbly request preferential policies that allow our company (the compound fertilizer factory) to access development funds and exempt the reduced value-added tax portion from taxable profits."

* * *

Contract for Contracted Operation of Chengdu Pixian Compound Fertilizer Plant (1992)

Contractor (Party A): Mr. Yi Fengxian, Legal Representative of Zhanqi Village Villagers' Committee, Xianfeng Township, Pixian County, Sichuan Province.

Contracting Party (Party B): Research Institute of Guiyang Normal College, Guizhou Province.

In accordance with the spirit of the "Regulations on Rural Collective Ownership Enterprises of the People's Republic of China" and the "Provisions on Contracted Operation Responsibility System for Township and Village Enterprises," and in order to revitalize the enterprise, leverage technological advantages, achieve profitability, and cross-regionally contract and operate the Chengdu Pixian Compound Fertilizer Plant, a collectively owned unit, the Research Institute of Guiyang Normal College (Party B) has engaged in multiple consultations with Party A and hereby enters into the following contract:

1. At the time of contracting, the enterprise's existing fixed assets have an original value of ______ yuan, a net value of ______ yuan, current assets of ______ yuan, and borrowed funds of ______ yuan. After inventory and registration, they shall be transferred to Party B for use. Upon the expiration of the contract period, the residual value of fixed assets shall belong to Party A, and the current funds shall be fully returned to Party A. In the event of any shortfall, Party B shall be liable for compensation. In the event that Party B needs to invest in the acquisition of fixed assets for expanding the operating projects (such as diversified and efficient micro-fertilizers) after the contract period expires, Party B shall raise the necessary funds independently, and the fixed assets purchased with the investment shall belong to Party B.
2. The assessment of contracted indicators shall focus on profitability. Starting from the date of production, the annual profit target is 80,000 yuan. Profit distribution shall follow the principle of a guaranteed minimum share, wherein Party A is guaranteed an annual profit of 40,000 yuan. Any additional profit beyond the contracted portion shall be allocated as follows: 50% shall be used as an enterprise development fund for expansion and reproduction, and the remaining 60% shall be distributed in a 40–60% ratio, with Party A receiving 40% and Party B receiving 60%. Party B shall bear the responsibility for operational losses. Profit-sharing shall be realized after the year-end settlement.
3. Rights and Responsibilities of Party A and Party B:
    1. Within the scope prescribed by national policies and laws, Party B shall have autonomy in production, supply, marketing, and finance (production and operation). Party B shall have the right to decide on the establishment of internal institutions, recruitment of cadre employees, reject unauthorized personnel placement, unauthorized fees, and unauthorized assessments. Party B shall also have the authority to administer penalties to employees and determine the forms of employment and wage payments.
    2. Party B shall willingly accept supervision, inspections, and guidance from relevant departments, ensuring the correct implementation of national policies, laws, and financial accounting systems.

3. Party A shall actively provide business guidance and information transmission, coordinate local relationships, provide various services, and create a favorable external environment for the normal production of the enterprise.
4. Party A shall assist Party B in applying for loans for working capital, up to a maximum of 1 million yuan.
5. In the event of losses caused by poor management or administrative negligence that cannot be compensated for, Party A, in conjunction with the relevant departments, shall have the right to terminate the contract in advance and hold the responsible person liable for economic responsibilities.

4. Other Matters to Be Clarified by Both Parties:

1. Financial management shall follow the financial management system of township and village enterprises. Various reserves shall be withdrawn according to the proportions stipulated by township enterprise regulations.
2. Except for the listed fixed assets, the use of the original distillery warehouses and hydroelectric facilities, as well as the leased land used as a site by farmers, shall all be governed by lease agreements. An annual rent of ______ yuan shall be paid, which shall be included in the cost.
3. Party B shall continue to bear the expenses related to the use of patented technology for compound fertilizer production and the supervision mark by the Chemical Research Institute.
4. If it becomes necessary to change the enterprise name, scope of operations, or the legal representative due to the expansion of production projects or the signing of the contract, the enterprise shall make the necessary applications, and Party A shall provide assistance in the process.
5. Party B shall fulfill the existing rights and obligations, and any uncollectible amounts due to bad debts shall be borne by Party A and shall have no bearing on Party B.

5. Contract Period:

The contract period is 10 years, starting from December 1992 and ending in December 2002.

6. Breach of Contract Responsibilities:

1. Both parties shall diligently fulfill the contract. In the event that one party is at fault, causing the contract to become unenforceable or unable to be fully performed, the party at fault shall bear the liability for breach of contract. The non-defaulting party shall not only have the right to claim compensation from the defaulting party but also have the right to terminate the contract in advance.
2. If the enterprise is unable to produce due to force majeure, rendering it impossible to continue performing the contract, both parties shall engage in negotiation and find a mutually agreeable solution.

   Note: The details of the receivables from the chemical factory are as follows: usage fees of 18,000 yuan in 1992, depreciation fees of 17,790.17 yuan in 1992, overall planning fees of 8696 yuan in 1992, and material receivable fees of 8,942.03 yuan. The bank interest payable for 1992 is also included. The total amount is 53,428.20 yuan (excluding bank interest) (February 13, 1993).

Source: Contract for Contracted Operation of Chengdu Pixian Compound Fertilizer Plant (1992), Chengdu Pixian County Archives, "Xianfeng Township File," File No. 149-001-0429-007.

Note: Some values in this column are blank due to missing information in the original archives.

After the compound fertilizer factory shifted to a leasing system in 2004, the collective promptly reclaimed the cash value of workers' personal shares. The motive behind the restructuring was the meager management fees the collective received each year, a mere pittance compared to the bountiful harvest enjoyed by outsiders. The workers, recognizing the dearth of profit and dividends in personal ventures, embraced the conversion to a leasing system. By surrendering their shares to the collective, they could realize their worth with direct immediacy. A single share, initially valued at one yuan, would metamorphose into three yuan in cold, hard cash.

This restructuring, however, concealed a clandestine contest between the factory chief and the village collective. Feng Zhonghui, the former factory director, disapproved of the shift to leasing, perceiving it as an affront to his personal interests. In response, the village collective initiated an examination of the books, revealing a quartet of discrepancies. Firstly, completed sales were recorded at the original price; secondly, external inventory remained unaccounted for in sales records; thirdly, the entirety of revenue manifested as advanced payments; and fourthly, pricing was reserved until the year's conclusion. The inquiry unraveled off-the-books assets amounting to eight hundred thousand yuan, humorously dubbed the "small treasury" by village officials, with five hundred and ten thousand yuan constituting a deficit. Feng Zhonghui conceded the existence of this 510,000 yuan loss, attributing it to the pervasive sway of the economic climate. Village officials, cunningly prepared for such an eventuality, employed two strategies. Initially, they privately approached Feng Zhonghui, conveying the potential legal consequences should he withhold the 800,000 yuan from the collective. Subsequently, if negotiations with Feng Zhonghui faltered, they intended to summon the Economic Investigation Brigade from Pixian County to scrutinize the affairs of Zhanqi Village. Faced with the ominous prospect of imprisonment, Feng Zhonghui reluctantly remitted the entire sum to the collective. Though he steadfastly maintained that the 510,000 yuan loss was a casualty of the macroeconomic landscape, he "voluntarily" relinquished his post.

On February 26, 2004, Feng Zhonghui relinquished the accounts and seals to the village collective, momentarily succeeded by the stewardship of Gao Demin for a fleeting 2-month interim. Subsequently, on April 26, that same year, Feng Zhonghui's official designation was rescinded, while Qin Xiangbin (覃祥斌) ascended as the anointed legal representative. Total assets were evaluated at one million yuan. The compound fertilizer factory, through auction, found itself leased to a shrewd building materials magnate from Chongqing, the fortuitous encounter facilitated by a local compatriot who chanced upon knowledge of the factory's staff during a rendezvous at the cadre training institute in Sichuan Province. An overt business alliance between this magnate and Qin Xiangbin further solidified the transaction, consummated for a contract fee of fifty thousand yuan.

As the twenty-first century materialized, Zhanqi emerged as a sanctified water source sanctuary, prioritizing society's clamor for verdant well-being over pecuniary pursuits. In 2014, the compound fertilizer factory emigrated to the industrial part of Meishan City. Accompanied by seventy administrators and workers, this collective exodus extended opportunities to those disinclined to partake, with prospects of employment awaiting them in Zhanqi's neighboring enclaves. Gradually, the relocation endeavor reached its culmination, casting an equalizing pall on the prefabricated component factory and resin factory, ultimately leading to their complete cessation. In 2015, the compound fertilizer factory gracefully bowed out of Zhanqi Village's historical stage. The dismantled edifice fused with adjacent parcels, forming a unified collective construction land, its inaugural presence in Sichuan's market for collective construction. Thus, it commenced a fresh chapter, revitalized in this nascent epoch.

CHAPTER 8

The Secondary Restructuring of Collective Economy: Analysis from the "Rent Theory" Perspective (1995–2003)

1 Management System: Joint-Stock Cooperative Era (1995–2003)

1.1 Policy Background

On a frosty December day in 1992, the Ministry of Agriculture issued a document titled "Notice on Promoting and Perfecting the joint stock cooperative system in Township and Village Enterprises" [Agri. (Ent.) No. 24]. It aimed to address the blurred lines between government and enterprise in most township and village enterprises. The underlying concern was that the collective wielded excessive power, which could hinder efficient business operations by requiring enterprises to surrender a significant portion of their earnings.

Then, on a similar December day in 1993, the National People's Congress approved and enacted the "Company Law of the People's Republic of China" (hereinafter referred to as the "Company Law"). It provided a legal framework for the joint-stock cooperative system and served as a reference for its development and regulation. In March 1994, the Ministry of Agriculture circulated the "Opinions on the Reform of Property Rights System in Township and Village Enterprises (《乡镇企业产权制度改革意见》)." It emphasized the significance of property rights reform in these enterprises, outlining its guiding principles, objectives,

© Peking University Press 2024
X. Dong, *Zhanqi Village Over Fifty Years*,
https://doi.org/10.1007/978-981-97-5426-7_8

and challenges. It emphasized that implementing the joint-stock cooperative system (股份合作制) was the primary and most effective form of property rights reform in township and village enterprises.

1.2 The Restructuring Process

In the mid-1980s, as villages and towns across the nation birthed enterprises, an excess of goods saturated the market. The government sought to remedy the situation, thus birthing the concept of "restructuring." Previously, they suggested making minor adjustments when faced with challenges, but during the restructuring, they advocated for robust alliances among enterprises. It was not an overnight transformation but rather commenced with experimental initiatives and gradually expanded. Pixian County became a testbed for enterprise restructuring, and within its borders, Zhanqi Village and another neighboring village were selected for the trial run.

Source: Excerpted from interview record of Li Shili in July 2019.

In 1994, Zhanqi Village was handpicked as a restructuring pilot in Pixian County. The Township Enterprise Bureau of Pixian County offered guidance, dispatching personnel from the enterprise office to facilitate the intricate operational aspects. They cautiously initiated the share system on a modest scale. Four state-owned enterprises and two villages, including Zhanqi Village and Juancheng Village, underwent the restructuring process. Finally, on December 1, 1994, Zhanqi Village submitted a formal request to the People's Government of Tangchang Town, seeking approval for the transformation from the contracted system to the share system. The metamorphosis was ultimately accomplished in 1996.

The restructuring encompassed sizeable establishments such as brick factories, bean paste factories, brewing factories, flour mills, and compound fertilizer plants. The foundry, despite its substantial stature, abstained from the restructuring due to its participation in joint operations.

The first stride involved amalgamating the five aforementioned enterprises into Chengdu's Jifeng Industrial Corporation referred to henceforth as Jifeng Corporation. A board of directors and supervisory board were instated, with the five enterprises operating as subsidiaries. The subsequent phase entailed conducting a thorough inventory of assets and quantifying shares after acquiring a comprehensive understanding of their worth. The assessment involved employing both the cost reset method and the historical cost method.

Under the contracted system, all assets belonged to the collective. However, with the advent of the share system, profit distribution was split equally between the collective and the enterprise. Within the enterprise's share, 30% was designated as corporate shares for development and reinvestment. The remaining 20% became employee shares, allocated based on factors such as tenure, contributions, and hierarchical positions. The concept of "corporate legal entity" referred to the organization serving as the enterprise's legal representative, while "corporate shares" denoted the collective shares, albeit the distinction remained somewhat ambiguous. To subscribe to employee shares, workers were required to have served in the company for over a year, with shares varying based on job positions. For instance, factory managers were entitled to shares five times greater than the average employee. Shares were purchased at a ratio of 1:3, meaning that for every yuan invested, three yuan worth of shares were allotted. When the conversion culminated in 2003, shares were redeemed following the same 1:3 ratio.

In practice, the restructuring encountered challenges. Gao Demin summarized the situation, stating, "In theory, it was a share cooperative enterprise. However, some village cadres treated it more like a private enterprise or a contracted venture. They deviated from the prescribed management and operational regulations of a share cooperative enterprise. Moreover, unlike the present times, financial management was rather chaotic, and an abundance of cash transactions occurred beyond the scope of supervision. Consequently, a substantial loss of collective assets ensued." Regrettably, many interviewees perceived this restructuring endeavor as unsuccessful. Despite the transformation, the village collective retained fixed expenditures, continuing to levy fixed rent on the enterprise annually. The essence of the share system is primarily manifested in the relationship between the enterprise and its employees. For instance, even during lean times, the company was obligated to provide monetary contributions to the village, albeit employees might no longer partake in dividends as per the share system.

1.3 Restructuring Consequences

Firstly, the company's asset share dwindled. Looking at the asset changes of Jifeng Corporation post-restructuring (1995–1999) in Table 1, the total assets rose from 9.41 million yuan in 1994 to 15.89 million yuan in 1999. However, the increase was sluggish between 1995 and 1997, climbing only from 11.82 million yuan to 12.54 million yuan. For a sizable enterprise, this pace was rather lethargic. A closer examination of the financial data reveals a consistent upward trend in inventory turnover rate, indicating that inventory growth outpaced the growth of primary business revenue, resulting in increased inventory costs. Conversely, the company's current asset turnover rate declined annually, primarily due to a notable decrease in operating income, signifying deteriorating business conditions. In 2003, substantial cuts were made to ongoing projects and long-term investments, causing a shrinkage in asset share. Additionally, with a significant surge in operational income, the overall asset turnover rate experienced a considerable rise (Fig. 1).

Secondly, collective assets were lost. During the period of 1994–1997, the enterprise maintained a semblance of normal functioning. However,

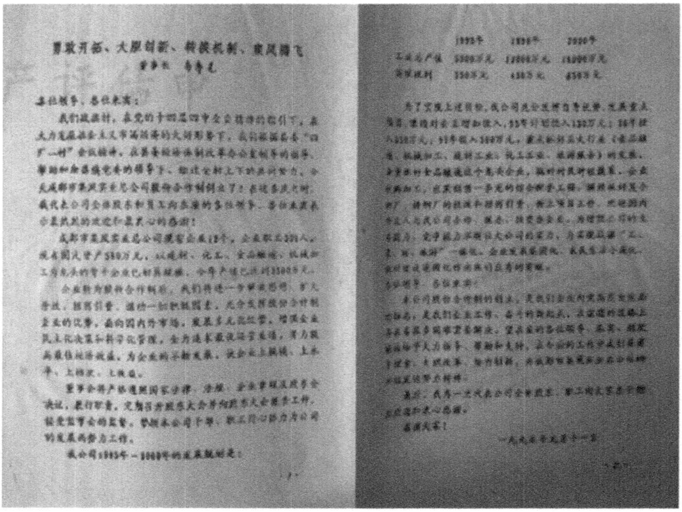

Fig. 1 Excerpt from the speech "Brave Exploration, Bold Innovation, Mechanism Transformation, and Ji Feng's Takeoff". *Source* Speech manuscript titled "Brave Exploration, Bold Innovation, Mechanism Transformation, and Jifeng's Takeoff" by Yi Fengxian, Chairman of Jifeng Corporation (January 11, 1995), Zhanqi Archives

as the restructuring extended beyond the pilot phase, the situation gradually worsened, particularly after 1998 when the profitability of various factories plummeted drastically. In the early stages of the joint-stock cooperative system, operators held shares at an average ratio five times higher than that of employee shareholders, accounting for a mere 3% to 4% of the company's total shares, falling short of the 5% mark. Nevertheless, in the late 1990s, as the restructuring deepened, Pixian County adopted a policy that allowed factory employees to purchase company shares with a 20% discount, along with an additional 20% discount for full upfront payment. Coupled with the initial 40% discount, the Office of System Reform even proposed further concessions, resulting in an overall discount of 50%. In other words, acquiring the company required only half the capital investment. This stark contrasted with the factory directors who held less than 5% of the shares.[1] As the mindset of management personnel became imbalanced, the efficiency of operations gradually declined, leading to a substantial loss of collective assets. By 1999, the village collective had accumulated debts of 2 million yuan.[2]

Thirdly, the ownership structure became chaotic. In private conversations, factory directors admitted to holding a mere 3% to 4% of the shares. For a company with assets worth 1 million yuan, they could acquire it by investing only 500,000 yuan. As the operators' mindset underwent a transformation, it wielded a significant influence on the company. Some factory directors boldly asserted, "Why should the company be collective? It ought to be my personal possession. Initially, the collective invested 50,000 yuan in the enterprise, and now I have transformed it into 500,000 yuan or even 1 million yuan, owing to my astute management. I need only return the original 50,000 yuan to the collective." Driven by such notions, management issues surfaced, resulting in diminished profitability. Certain companies even went 2 years without issuing dividends, triggering dissatisfaction among employees. Additionally, during interviews, it came to light that the credibility of the village secretary was feeble, with several factory directors disapproving of his role as the chairman of Jifeng Corporation due to his dual role of managing both the village collective enterprises and his personal venture. Of course, this was merely one of the factors. Under the joint-stock cooperative system,

[1] Source: Interview record with Li Shili on June 7, 2019.

[2] Source: Meeting minutes of Zhanqi Village on March 3, 1999.

the dividends allocated to factory directors were insufficient, and their autonomy diminished, exerting a substantial impact. For instance, the meager shareholding percentage among management personnel led to their reluctance to make long-term investments in fixed assets of the company. Although this impact remained inconspicuous in the short term, its long-term consequences manifested as reduced profitability. Similarly, within this process, there exist instances where collective entities possessed shares but failed to contribute adequate investments. For example, Luo Huifu, director of Brick Factory and Huifu Broad Bean Paste Factory, openly criticized this situation during a meeting: "The village only concerns itself with the village, neglecting the factories. If we adopt a joint-stock cooperative system, should the collective not inject funds? If we were to purchase a 500,000 yuan machine, should the village not contribute 250,000 yuan?".[3] The unreasonable distribution of shares during the pilot restructuring phase resulted in a prisoner's dilemma between the collective and the factory directors, with neither party inclined to undertake long-term investments. Consequently, the enterprise evolved into a hybrid entity, featuring characteristics of both collectivism and shareholder ownership, while being muddled by a mix of paternalistic and familial management styles.

To address these aforementioned issues, the joint-stock cooperative system was transitioned to a "lease system (租赁制)" in 2003.

2 Management System: Lease System (2003–2020)

The key to the transition from the joint-stock system to the lease system lies in determining who has absolute control over the enterprise, the collective or the contracted operators.

For the collective, the ownership structure of the five enterprises under the Jifeng Corporation is as follows: 50% owned by the village collective, 20% by the operators and employees, and 30% by the corporate legal entity. According to the Company Law of the People's Republic of China, the equity of enterprises implementing the joint-stock cooperative system can be adjusted internally and can be transferred or donated. By repurchasing the 20% of shares held by individual operators and employees,

[3] Source: Meeting minutes of Zhanqi Village on November 17, 2002.

the village collective obtains absolute control over the enterprise, as the collective holds the majority 50% of shares.

For the contracted operators, the gap in ownership was opened during the restructuring in 1994 when 30% of the corporate legal shares were reserved for the second-stage reform of equity. As early as 2001, the contracted operators requested to be awarded the 20% of corporate legal shares that the collective used for development and reproduction, thus gaining absolute control. Li Shili, the former village committee director, proposed that it must be approved by the shareholders' meeting, which prevented the operators from achieving their goal and was one of the reasons why Li Shili failed to be re-elected in the subsequent village committee elections.

The conversion to the lease system began in 2003,[4] and was completed in 2010.[5] According to the description by village cadres, this conversion is also referred to as "contracting." Current assets and fixed assets are leased to individuals, while the collective retains ownership of the fixed assets. In fact, under the contracting system in 1982, after the factories paid the contracting fees, they did not distribute dividends to the collective.

2.1 *Restructuring Process*

Firstly, preparations for the conversion were made. In the second half of 2002, relevant officials began visiting Nanjie Village, Liuzhuang Village, and Huaxi Village to learn from their experiences. The two committees actively studied theoretical knowledge and continuously practiced to prepare for the restructuring. In 2003, Zhanqi spent 3,000 yuan to invite professors from the School of Economics Research at the Southwestern University of Finance and Economics to teach courses on ownership and operational rights. The professor's lectures were recorded, and if they couldn't understand them on the spot, they could replay them for further study.

Secondly, obstacles to the conversion were promptly cleared. Only Gao Demin and Li Shili believed that the "turnaround" to reclaim the enterprises for the collective was achievable, while others did not believe it.

[4] Source: according to the statement of Yang Yong, the village director, it started as early as 1998.

[5] Source: Interview record with Gao Demin on October 2, 2019.

The restructuring of the enterprises required a vote by the board of directors, but there were many dissenting voices among the board members who were former factory directors. So the village collective changed its approach and began to repurchase the villagers' shares at a high price. According to Li Shili, the money spent by the village was essentially the villagers' money, so different negotiation policies should be adopted for different contracted operators. For example, negotiate with the factory directors that if they sell their personal shares now, the village collective will buy them. However, if they sell their shares later, the collective will not repurchase, and the shares they hold will become "empty shares." Alternatively, if they disagree with collective purchase, pressure can be applied by raising land fees since the land occupied by the factory belongs to the collective. In the end, the village committee repurchased 20% of the shares owned by the operators and employees for about 700,000 yuan.[6]

In February 2003, the conversion was officially implemented, and fixed assets and intangible assets were leased for operation. Based on the serious loss of liquid assets in the past, the village collective conducted a one-time auction of the liquid assets, selling them to the operators for immediate cash realization. One key point here is how the collective priced the liquid assets. The village collective set a basic price for each factory, taking into account the contributions of the contracted individuals, and prioritized the original legal persons. If the enterprise operators did not accept the price, an open tender would be conducted within the village, and competitive pricing would be implemented, with the highest bidder winning. The specific operation involved having the original legal persons reconfirm the value of the accounts, and the collective then priced the assets based on the original cost of the accounts (Yang Zhongmo believed it was market value, not purchase value[7]). For example, for soybeans and chili, the accounted value was 50 cents per catty, excluding the cost of labor, but only accounting for 50 cents. The actual price might be 70 or 80 cents. In other words, all the prices set by the factories were lower than the market price (but only applicable to raw materials).

The pioneering enterprises in the conversion were Huifu Bean Paste Factory and Machine Brick Factory. The lease contract for Huifu Bean

[6] Gao Jikai. The "Bull" Strength of "Old Scalpers"[N]. Chengdu Evening News, 2010-04-23 (4).

[7] Source: Interview record of Yang Zhongmo on December 25, 2019.

Paste Factory's fixed assets was signed every 3 years, and the estimated value of the liquid assets was over 700,000 yuan, but the actual value was around 800,000 yuan or even over 1 million yuan. The operators believed that there would be no one bidding, so they set the prices of raw materials relatively low and did not accept the collective's pricing. When Luo Huifu's son-in-law offered 700,000 yuan, it was unsuccessful, and Yang Kui (杨奎) won the bid with 720,000 yuan, resulting in the failure of Luo Huifu's family's bidding. There is also a saying that Luo Huifu's son-in-law was busy with other business and did not even register for bidding.

On April 19, 2003, the liquid assets of the Machine Brick Factory were auctioned, with a deduction of 5% for waste for brick blanks, 8 fen for clay blanks, and 9.5 fen for red bricks. The starting price was 40,000 yuan, and four villagers competed in bidding, with villager Wen Chaoming (文朝明) winning the bid at a price of 61,000 yuan. The land fees remained unchanged.

On June 8, 2004, the raw materials of the Xianfeng Brewery were priced based on the accounting value for unprocessed materials and the market value for processed ones. For example, the price for water beans (i.e., broad beans) was 0.7 yuan/jin for members, 0.9–1 yuan/jin on the market, and the negotiated price was 0.8 yuan/jin. Considering that a new round of macroeconomic prosperity began in the second half of 2002, with rising prices, the conversion took place during an economic upturn, and the collective benefited from a wave of price increases. The total value of the liquid assets of the factory was 3.88 million yuan, and the new factory director paid in installments. The village collective converted the funds from the auction of liquid assets into debts and lent them to the new factory director at an interest rate of 10%. After the liquid assets were auctioned, they realized 4.2 million yuan, which was used for further production and development. Secretary Gao Demin later reviewed that the village collective received over 5 million yuan in income after the conversion!

2.2 *Impact of the Restructuring*

Firstly, the village collective finally halted the bleeding of their assets, witnessing a surge in collective profits.

The initial chunk came from the liquid asset auction, amassing a total of 4.2 million yuan (according to the words of Li Shili).

Subsequently, rental income played its part. Prior to 2004, the village collective raked in an annual contract income of 285,000 yuan (land + fixed assets + liquid assets combined). However, with fixed assets and land fetching a rental income of 325,000 yuan, an extra 40,000 yuan was added to their coffers.

The third boon arrived in the form of interest income. The aforementioned 4.2 million yuan could be further capitalized on through interest earnings. After allocating a fraction for expenses and future ventures, the remaining funds (approximately 3 million yuan) were entrusted to the new factory director, yielding an annual interest income of 300,000 yuan. Risk mitigation measures required the "two committees" to convene and grant their consent. Moreover, the funds were only extended to enterprises, with their liquid assets serving as collateral. Perusing the meeting records reveals that the compound fertilizer factory borrowed 250,000 yuan, while the brewery and flour mill secured loans of 300,000 yuan and 200,000 yuan, respectively, the latter using liquid assets as collateral. Additionally, the foundry procured 100,000 yuan for their workshop expansion.[8]

Secondly, the power of the Party branch was invigorated. The advent of the joint-stock cooperative system severely restrained the effectiveness of the Party branch. Hindered and helpless, their influence waned while the profits plummeted. Consequently, the Party branch bore the brunt of the blame. To counteract this slide, the villagers closely scrutinized the monetary distributions made by the branch secretary during their tenure. This created a ripple effect, compelling each successive village branch leader to fervently pursue economic growth. Under the leasing system, the authority of the branch flourished, as it allowed for adaptable solutions that didn't merely retrace previous steps. Secretary Li Shili astutely observed, "A driver proficient in cars insisting on piloting an airplane can only expect faltering progress" (the joint-stock cooperative system is akin to an airplane, while the leasing system is likened to a car).

Thus, the bond between the village collective and the contracted operators weathered an unprecedented deterioration. In the deluge of privatization, why did the village collective steadfastly seek control over the enterprise? Village officials were inclined to depict collectivization as

[8] Source: Minutes of the Zhanqi Village meeting on February 21, 2004.

a seamless continuation of institutional norms, but practical implementation proved arduous. Even in the predominantly individualized rural regions of southern Zhejiang, the village officials innately possessed a proclivity for bolstering the collective economy, driven by their inherent position. Alas, the development of collectivization proved to be an uphill battle. In this light, Zhanqi Village boldly defied the current, propelled by the universal impetus to fortify the collective economy. As all village officials harbored an innate inclination to strengthen the collective economy, Zhanqi's stalwart cadre withstood the tidal wave of privatization while most others reluctantly capitulated to the prevailing winds.

3 Macro and Micro Factors in Township and Village Enterprise Restructuring

Township and village enterprises, the epitome of China's rural industrialization, emerged and flourished under unique historical and policy circumstances. Their development, surpassing the general patterns of industrialization seen in other nations, bore the unmistakable imprint of "Chinese characteristics."[9]

From a broad perspective, the original equipment of these enterprises primarily comprised second-hand and low-grade machinery. However, the price they paid for such equipment was far from low. Moreover, the restructuring process exposed the depreciation of aged machinery, necessitating support from rural cooperative finance to facilitate equipment upgrades. For township and village enterprises, rural cooperative finance served as a crucial funding source. However, the financial crisis that erupted in 1997 led to the prohibition of rural cooperative finance. Overnight, the financial system that had been operating became illegal, transforming all loans into illicit debts. Unwilling to repay, numerous individuals defaulted, ushering in a wave of debt evasion. This credit default, caused by an abrupt institutional shift, ultimately resulted in bad debts for rural credit cooperatives and agricultural banks. Furthermore, exacerbated by prior government policies aimed at tightening the economy and curbing overheating, small and medium-sized township

[9] Lin Qingsong, Du Ying. China's Industrial Reform and Efficiency: A Comparative Study of State-Owned Enterprises and Non-State-Owned Enterprises [M]. Kunming: Yunnan People's Publishing House, 1997.

and village enterprises were the first casualties. The deteriorating external conditions further intensified internal conflicts within these enterprises.

In this narrative, the very act of restructuring represents a micro-level mechanism undergoing transformation amidst the pressure of deteriorating macro external conditions. The altered micro-mechanism is characterized by a sudden elevation in the bargaining power of labor factors such as technology, managerial capabilities, financial capacity, and talent. Simultaneously, the bargaining position of the heavy asset investments (subject to depreciation) declines, resulting in a widespread phenomenon of state-owned enterprises being sold at meager prices. Compounded by an unfavorable financial climate, the restructuring process itself becomes an inadvertent consequence of macroeconomic regulatory policies aimed at short selling.

Delving into the micro factors, Say's Law[10] posits that the value of a commodity is synergistically created by three production factors: labor, capital, and land. These factors can partially substitute for one another, with scarce elements multiplying to replace others. Although restrictions on land were relatively limited in the 1980s, we shall refrain from discussing the land factor here.

Regarding labor, once the subjective initiative of labor assumes a significant organizational scale within the original agricultural production mode, it triggers a tremendous multiplier effect on labor input. Harnessing this effect, Zhanqi Village formed rural collective enterprises, which later blossomed into township and village enterprises. While labor's role as a source of initial accumulation remained crucial, the advent of industrialization placed higher demands on capital, technology, management, and other factors. Industrialization's regulatory demands on these factors far surpassed those of agriculture, creating a divergence in the requirements for these elements based on business models.

[10] Translator's note: In classical economics, Say's law, or the law of markets, is the claim that the production of a product creates demand for another product by providing something of value which can be exchanged for that other product. So, production is the source of demand. In his principal work, A Treatise on Political Economy (Traité d'économie politique, 1803), Jean-Baptiste Say wrote: "A product is no sooner created, than it, from that instant, affords a market for other products to the full extent of its own value." And also, "As each of us can only purchase the productions of others with his own productions—as the value we can buy is equal to the value we can produce, the more men can produce, the more they will purchase."

Considering the capital factor, as agriculture transitioned into an industrial form, the multiplier effect of labor input was supplanted by the multiplying influence of capital input, precipitating institutional changes. During the restructuring process, the scarcity of capital assumed greater prominence. Particularly in the 1980s, exorbitant price levels characterized a state of negative interest rates. Amidst this negative interest rate environment, Zhanqi Village ingeniously transformed the social resources acquired during militia training into capital in the economic realm. Consequently, Zhanqi Village secured a portion of the benefits derived from inflation and interest on funds, gaining an advantage over other villages. The substantial disparity between the scarcity of capital and the inflation rate forged an external condition that precipitated the institutional reform in Zhanqi. For example, while establishing a compound fertilizer plant, Zhanqi Village received insider information about investment attraction and secured government-provided loans.

Moreover, it is essential to acknowledge that the cognizance and traditional customs of relevant interest groups wield influence over the restructuring process. Firstly, the village collective, as a mediator between local governance and villagers, plays a pivotal role in shaping the restructuring decisions. The degree of decision-making autonomy granted to village collectives determines the diversity of shareholding cooperative models across regions.[11] Consequently, it also influences the core principles most likely to be embraced during regional restructuring endeavors. Secondly, the perception of asset originators regarding collective assets significantly impacts the reform of collective asset shareholding cooperatives. This perception directly shapes the core principles most likely to be selected during the restructuring of collective assets, serving as a wellspring for disparities in the core distribution logic within the reform of the collective asset joint-stock cooperative system.

The focus of the 1994 shareholding cooperative reform rested upon asset liquidation and confirmation criteria. Over a decade of development, enterprise dimensions transcended their original boundaries. The earlier nature of collective enterprises rendered many contributions challenging to classify accurately. When crises or risks erupted, implicit contributions naturally metamorphosed into explicit entities, catalyzing a game-like process. Additionally, the 1994 shareholding cooperative reform was a

[11] Jin Wenlong. Social construction of property rights: Research on the reform of rural collective asset cooperative system [M]. Beijing: Social Sciences Literature Press, 2019.

top-down pilot endeavor, lacking autonomy and deviating significantly from local cognizance of the origin of collective assets, intertwined with habits, traditions, and other factors. Hence, this complexity contributes to the multifaceted evaluation of the 1994 share reform by Zhanqi Village officials.

4 Township and Village Enterprise Restructuring: From a Rent Theory Perspective

Rent studies in economics originated from the division of land benefits. The Physiocrats believed rent to be the surplus gained by landowners beyond their necessary expenses. Thomas Robert Malthus defined rent as "the portion of all produce left to the landowner after deducting production costs and other necessary charges."[12] Further exploration was conducted by David Ricardo, William Petty, James Anderson, and their contemporaries.[13]

Alfred Marshall's study of "quasi-rent," John Bates Clark and Paul Anthony Samuelson's research,[14] and Robert D. Tollison's examination of "economic rent" propelled the concept of rent forward, completing its evolution from a specific category to a general one. Marshall, for instance, expanded the concept of rent to include remuneration for temporarily inelastic production factors known as quasi-rents. Rent gradually encompassed payments made for land, labor, equipment, money, and even institutional resources—an aggregation of payments for various elements contributing to production. It became "the balance of actual returns on factors of production minus opportunity costs." I align with Adam Smith's view that rent, in its true sense, represents the surplus obtained by owners through their monopolistic positions.[15]

[12] Malthus, T.R. Inquiring Into the Nature and Progress of Rent. Baltimore: John Hopkins Press, 1903.

[13] Spiegel, Henry W. The Growth of Economic Thought, Englewood Cliffs, NJ: Prentice-Hall Inc, 1971.

[14] Samuelson, Paul A. 1971. Economics, 3rd Canadian edition (corresponding to 8th American edition). Toronto: McGraw-Hill of Canada, Ltd.

[15] Dong Xiaodan. Organizational Rent and Governance Costs: Rural Conflicts and Local Governance Issues in the Process of Modernization. Beijing: Renmin University of China, 2009.

Figures 2 and 3 depict shifts in enterprise profits under diverse macroeconomic circumstances and alterations in anticipated profits for operators within a fixed rent system framework. Figure 2 illustrates profit distribution during a period of macroeconomic growth, while Fig. 3 portrays profit distribution during a period of economic downturn.

In these figures, Q*u and Q*d represent the market sales volume required to pay fixed rent to the collective, while u and d denote the growth and depression periods, respectively. During macroeconomic growth, an operator's profit takes the shape of area S_{ABCD}, as depicted in Fig. 2. Conversely, during a depression, a decline in marginal revenue (MR) leads to a decrease in marginal costs (MC), an increase in base sales volume Q*, and an operator's profit resembling area S_{ABCD}, as illustrated in Fig. 3. If Q*d surpasses Qm, the operator incurs negative profits.

The principle of restructuring involves exchanging the original fixed rent and profit-sharing rent through a one-time cost. If this fixed cost is significantly lower than the initial investment, it implies an increase in the enterprise's risk-free assets, a crucial optimization of asset allocation during times of economic downturn.

Consequently, after restructuring, the change in fixed costs (FC) becomes insignificant, with only marginal costs (MC) increasing as shown

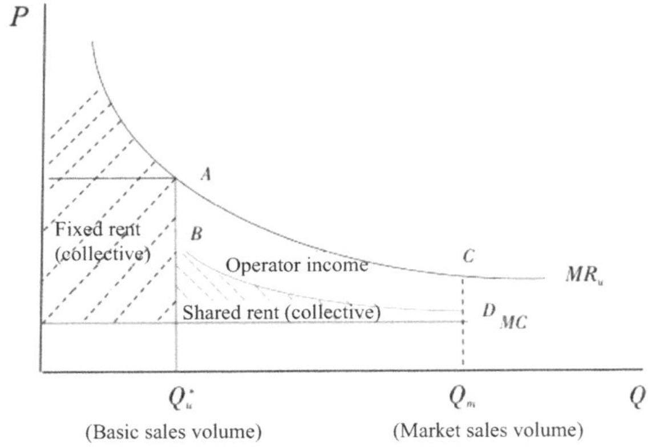

Fig. 2 Profit distribution of enterprises during macroeconomic growth. 固定租（集体）Fixed rent (collective), 经营者收益Operator income, 分成租（集体）Shared rent (collective), 基础销量Basic sales volume, 市场销量Market sales volume

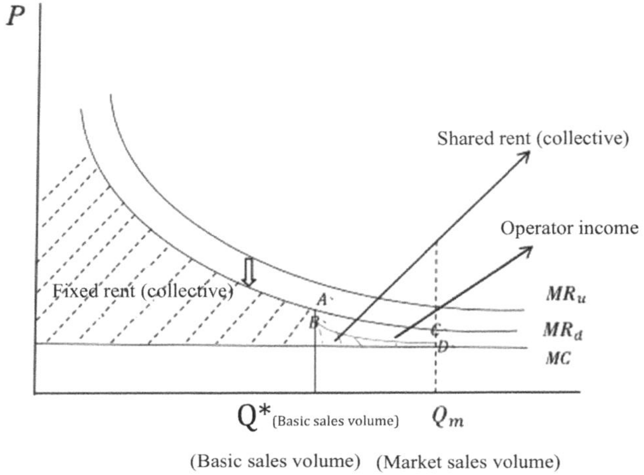

Rising period: $Y_{up} = f_u(Q) = \int_0^Q (MR_u - MC_u)\, d_q$

Falling period: $Y_{down} = f_d(Q) = \int_0^Q (MR_d - MC_d)\, d_q$

Pay rent (fixed rent + share rent): $R_T = R_F + R_P$

Operator income: $P = Y - R_T$ (Shared income between Q* and Qm)

Fig. 3 Profit distribution of enterprises during macroeconomic depression. 上升期间rising period, 下降期间falling period, 上交租金 (固定租 + 分成租) Pay rent (fixed rent + share rent), 经营者收益Operator income, (Q*到Qm之间的分成收益) (Shared income between Q* and Qm)

in Fig. 4. The daily operational profit then encompasses the area of 1 + 2 + 3, highly advantageous for maintaining the enterprise's cash flow.

Considering the macroeconomic situation, it becomes apparent that during a growth period, the marginal revenue, marginal costs, and market capacity all exceed those during a depression. In a growth period, the sales volume required to cover fixed rent falls below that of a depression period. In a depression, if the sales volume necessary to cover fixed rent exceeds the contracted market capacity, it implies the operator will experience a loss. However, in the case of fixed rent coupled with profit-sharing rent, the fixed rent receives priority in distribution. Thus, the contractor becomes the primary risk-bearer, with risks and rewards moving in the direction of increased risk. At this point, if there is an

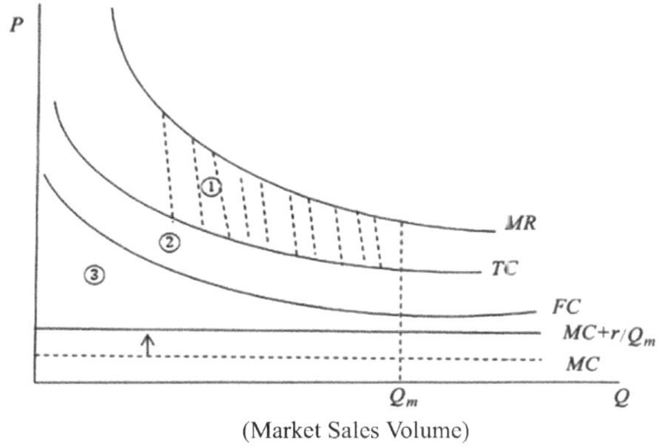

Fig. 4 Profit distribution of enterprises after restructuring. 市场销量Market Sales Volume

opportunity for acquiring the enterprise, the transaction shifts from a rent payment to a one-time payment, allowing for a comparison of the price-to-rent ratio against annual land rent. If institutional preferential policies enable low-cost acquisitions, it signifies the acquisition of a risk-free asset, thereby greatly optimizing resource allocation. Hence, restructuring becomes a demand for institutional transformation driven by the economic rationality of operators during times of economic downturn.

To delve deeper, under the work points system, the value of rent is internalized as institutional rent. "Institutional rent" can also be viewed as a form of "power rent," resulting in inequality and asymmetry in the distribution of institutional benefits and costs within the organization. Through organizational internalization, institutional rent can be allocated and retained, ensuring rent value remains intact and promoting production development.

Under the contracting system, the value of rent is externalized as institutional rent. Contracting transforms previously internalized rent value into distinct levels of capital intensification, with heavy capital and light capital exhibiting different rental rates. The contracting system evolves collective internalized institutional rent into latent rent, which is then captured by contractors. This transition from internalization to externalization of institutional rent in the contracting system leads to contractors individually claiming latent rent while transferring negative externalities to the collective. Moreover, when contractors possess latent rent, they perceive it as personal income. Once personal ownership of latent rent is established, rent value dissipates, prompting the shift from a leasing system to a restructuring system. For example, externalities such as pollution caused by a brick factory or water source occupation by a Broad Bean Paste Factory, which was concealed when these enterprises were collectively owned, become apparent after implementing the contracting system.

In essence, the leasing system manifests latent rent as explicit rent. Activities such as assessment, disposal, and auctions of liquid assets transform latent rent into visible rent. The first round of restructuring converted institutional rent under the work points system into latent rent under the contracting system, resulting in the externalization of institutional rent and the emergence of negative externalities. In the second round of restructuring, the collective regained rental value, transforming the organization into a leasing system and generating rental income. This intricate process signifies the complete journey of township enterprise restructuring in Zhanqi Village.

PART III

2003–2019: The Verdant Zhanqi: A Tale of Reshaping Collective Economy and Ecological Transformation

Part Three: 2003–2019

Verdant Zhanqi: A Tale of Reshaping Collective Economy and Ecological Transformation

The "Three Rural Issues," born out of an agricultural nation grappling with population growth and limited resources while pursuing industrialization, has a twist of fate awaiting.

Over the past century, China, compelled to follow the Western-dominated path of industrial civilization, found itself entangled in the "Three Rural Issues" of agriculture, rural areas, and farmers. The establishment of the New China marked a time of revival, with a dire need for progress. Yet, faced with the blockade imposed by Western nations, China could only amass the initial capital for industrialization through agriculture. Following the era of reform and opening-up, urbanization and the market-driven push for industrialization continued to siphon land, labor, and capital from rural areas, perpetuating the net outflow of these vital elements. In addition, misguided policies like "capital going to the countryside" and "agricultural industrialization" resulted in surplus agricultural production and widespread pollution plaguing the rural landscape. In summary, the "Three Rural Issues" worsened to an alarming extent, witnessing unprecedented levels of large-scale security incidents in rural communities.

The beginning of the twenty-first century witnessed a gradual shift in the developmental narrative, focusing on sustainable growth

and resolving the pressing "Three Rural Issues." Recognizing its paramount importance, the Party Central Committee, in 2002, initiated policy adjustments, elevating the issue to a national priority in 2003. The subsequent introduction of the New Rural Construction initiative in 2005 reflected the nation's commitment to prioritize the "Three Rural Issues." Financial estimates indicate that from 2003 to 2012, the central government's investment in this sector exceeded a staggering 6 trillion yuan. These strategic adjustments continued, culminating in the establishment of the ecological civilization strategy in 2012, the proposal of the "new normal" by the new government in 2013, and the subsequent structural reform on the supply side of the industry. By 2014, the emphasis shifted toward equal exchange of urban and rural factors and balanced allocation of public resources. The comprehensive reform for ecological civilization was introduced in 2015, coinciding with the implementation of targeted poverty alleviation strategies aimed at rebalancing wealth disparities and the ambitious goal of eradicating poverty by 2020. In 2016, structural reforms on the supply side of agriculture were proposed, promoting the dual-driven development of new urbanization and new rural area construction. Finally, the 19th National Congress of the Party, in 2017, unveiled the rural revitalization strategy, prioritizing the development of agriculture and rural areas, heralding an era where ecological civilization took precedence over industrialization and urbanization. **These transformative shifts, fundamentally improving the plight of the "Three Rural Issues," paved the way for its resolution and rejuvenated the non-industrial and non-economic realms.**

With previous collective accumulation falling short as a viable investment, the resurge of Zhanqi in the early twenty-first century, capitalized on the opportune historical moment of national strategic transformation and relied on fortuitous institutional dividends. The 19th National Congress of the Communist Party of China proclaimed the dawn of a socialist new era, shifting the nation's primary contradiction from imbalanced and inadequate development to the ever-growing aspirations for a better life. This necessitated supply-side structural reforms and an all-encompassing optimization of industrial structure. **A response to the array of opportunities and challenges that surfaced in early twenty-first-century China demanded seizing the moment while confronting the obstacles.** On one hand, China, boasting a comprehensive range of industries and formidable manufacturing capabilities, emerged as the world's leading industrial powerhouse in the early twenty-first century. The previously contentious supply-demand imbalance, resulting from insufficient production, had been fundamentally resolved, laying a solid foundation for industrial upgrading. On the other hand, China boasted the largest middle-income population globally, unlocking immense market potential with their purchasing power. The convergence of these factors created a scenario where seizing market opportunities and upgrading industrial structures held immense promise. **Concurrently, challenges emerged:** China grappled with surplus supply since 1998, increased economic dependence on external demand, unparalleled environmental pollution due to leading global emission levels, and a workforce of monumental proportions, engendering unprecedented governance challenges.

The convergence of opportunities and challenges signaled a divergence among interest groups tethered to the archaic reform and institutional adjustment framework. Most, hindered by their innate conservatism, struggled to keep pace with the central government's realignments. Those agile enough to synchronize with the baton of central command, embracing timely structural adjustments, reaped institutional rewards. This, precisely, forms the bedrock upon which Zhanqi Village, poised for a fresh start in the ecological competition of the new era, unfurls its institutional acumen.

Digging deeper, the rise of the middle class, propelling green consumption demands, and the fusion of urban and rural spheres through "urban dwellers venturing countryside," catalyzed the transformation of agriculture, rural areas, and farmers into green production. This paradigm shift rendered the developmental pursuit a vital conduit for the national ecological civilization strategy, unlocking avenues to mitigate the environmental pollution that plagued previous agricultural and industrial practices. Moreover, it presented an opportunity for rural China to leap onto the fast-moving train of twenty-first-century development. In this context, China's social structure underwent significant transformations since the new century dawned, ushering in the rise of the middle class. Empowered by formidable purchasing power, a considerable segment of this group embraced activities aligned with green production, where environmental considerations stood as a pivotal facet of their consumption patterns. Aligning rural communities with these evolving demands translates into an excess return, capitalizing on both policy incentives and market dynamics. Zhanqi Village stands as a testament to this approach.

Located in Chengdu, a Western mega city that experienced a resurgence under the auspices of regional rebalancing, Zhanqi Village harnesses the radiating consumption power of the middle class, sculpting a development strategy that intertwines agriculture, culture, and tourism.

Unlike the colossal negative externalities wrought by the industrialization of agriculture over the past two decades, green production harbors substantial positive externalities. However, it necessitates a sizable indivisible space as a foundational requirement. This unveils the enigma behind Zhanqi Village's resplendent triumph in the ecological competition of the new era—its ability to deftly integrate space within the village. By surmounting fragmented spaces, expanding the planar reach and vertical dimension of the environment, and augmenting economic and social spatial capacities, the village accommodates diverse ecological spaces and fosters a multidimensional ecological development. Grounded in the enhancement of natural ecological spaces, the village propels the amelioration of industrial and social ecological spaces. From the vantage point of political economy, **Zhanqi Village secures the coveted "space rent."**

It must be acknowledged, however, that only grassroots collective economic organizations in rural areas possess the potential to effectively consolidate the fragmented spaces within their entire domain. Leveraging their unique institutional advantages, these organizations harness internal mobilization to handle transaction costs, facilitating the low-cost integration of ecological resources such as mountains, forests, water bodies, land, lakes, and grasslands. This symbiosis engenders a comprehensive, multidimensional developmental strategy founded on ecological principles. In contrast, entities governed by the market economy logic tend to engage in one-dimensional, flat integration, seeking market opportunities in specific sectors, often at the cost of substantial negative externalities on the ecological environment.

Nonetheless, the question remains: How can the majority of grassroots collective economic organizations in rural areas, grappling with fragile foundations, spearhead spatial integration and construction? **To unravel this enigma, a comprehensive examination of Zhanqi Village's collective economy is necessary.** It chronicles the village's extraordinary journey from near obscurity at the turn of the twenty-first century to its gradual expansion, bolstered by the winds of policy, culminating in the accumulation of over 60 million yuan in collective assets and an estimated valuation of over 200 million yuan for collectively developed land.

CHAPTER 9

Land Re-concentration and the Rejuvenation of Collective Economy (2003–2010)

In 2002, a new era dawned in Zhanqi Village. Li Shili took charge as the Party branch secretary, and Gao Demin assumed the role of village director. Alongside this political shift came a reevaluation of the village's economic structure and direction.

Enterprises underwent a significant change as the joint-stock cooperative system gave way to a leasing system, granting the collective renewed ownership and control. This shift was pivotal in the village's rejuvenation. By restructuring collectively, the loss of assets was prevented, and the village's income surged. Auction proceeds, interest income, rental earnings from fixed assets, and land all contributed to the growing collective wealth. This bolstered the foundation for subsequent actions, including the concentration of land and the establishment of cooperatives to strengthen the collective economy. The restructuring of enterprises also enhanced the new village leadership's organizational capacity and credibility, crucial in rallying the villagers' support for land concentration.

The re-concentration of land emerged as a vital facet in the reconstruction of the collective economy. It served as the linchpin in rebuilding a new economic landscape in Zhanqi Village, where land value had dwindled to near insignificance.

Land concentration entails a continuous discovery and realization of its value. In the initial stages, land value is predominantly derived from agricultural production during times of political competition. However,

© Peking University Press 2024

X. Dong, *Zhanqi Village Over Fifty Years*,
https://doi.org/10.1007/978-981-97-5426-7_9

as industrialization takes hold, land assumes the role of a resource base for industrial capital. Industrial operations become the primary source of wealth for a village, with land playing a relatively diminished role. Yet, at the turn of the twenty-first century, an opportunity arose for land value to be rediscovered in rural areas. The realization of land value was no longer confined to traditional means, but rather through the three-dimensional development of rural spatial resources. While the new leadership team may not have fully grasped this concept during their initiation of land concentration in 2003, they did recognize that the benefits from previous land development were plateauing, and industrial overcapacity loomed as a risk. Consequently, the village collective shifted its strategy towards a land-focused approach. Initially, land concentration yielded differential ground rent from large-scale operations, eventually leading to the realization of "space rent" through comprehensive three-dimensional development.

The discovery and realization of land value were closely intertwined with national strategic transformations and macroeconomic and social developments.

In the wake of the twenty-first-century's dawn, China underwent a strategic transformation that would redefine its urban and rural landscapes. This transformation, pivoting towards regional equilibrium and harmonious urban–rural development, opened up a pivotal opportunity for the conspicuous valorization of rural land values across the nation's Western frontiers. In 2003, Hu Jintao introduced the concept of "scientific development," placing a resolute emphasis on a people-centric approach. This visionary perspective underscored the imperative of holistic, coordinated, and sustainable development. It sought to foster comprehensive progress in economics, society, and individual well-being, all while seamlessly orchestrating urban–rural growth, regional advancement, socioeconomic harmony, and a balanced coexistence with nature. This paradigm shift became a cornerstone of the Party's strategic ideology.

Fast forward to December 8, 2006, when the State Council convened to endorse the "Eleventh Five-Year Plan for Western Development (《西部大开发"十一五"规划》)." This ambitious blueprint aimed to propel the Western regions towards economic prosperity and elevate the living standards of its inhabitants. **With this new developmental phase came an unprecedented surge in land valuation, prompting a pressing need to devise complementary policies and explore institutional avenues for rural communities to partake in the burgeoning land appreciation.**

Consequently, the cities of Chengdu and Chongqing were designated as national pilot zones for comprehensive urban–rural reform (全国统筹城乡综合配套改革试验区). These cities, emblematic of the "big cities with big rural areas" archetype prevalent in the Western regions, grappled with pronounced urban–rural dualism. The selection of these urban centers as focal points for national urban–rural reform underscored the nation's resolve to expedite the development of its central and Western regions, foster regional cohesion, and harmonize the urban–rural continuum in this new epoch. This strategic move was not only a response to the need for dismantling the prevailing urban–rural dualism but also a crucial exploration of novel developmental paradigms tailored to the central and Western regions.

Zhanqi Village, situated within Chengdu's urban embrace, stands as a quintessential case in point, reaping the benefits of this strategic metamorphosis that has led to the materialization and appreciation of land values.

In parallel, another pressing conundrum emerged—how to perpetuate rural areas as viable conduits for absorbing financial capital within the context of global financial capital globalization. The imperative to utilize rural land assets, natural resources, and even ecological ecosystems to engender conditions conducive to currency absorption loomed large. Post-2002, local governments, spurred by a burgeoning fiscal revenue appetite, found themselves steeped in an unprecedented fervor for land development, infrastructure investments, and the expansion of local construction initiatives.

Yet, as urbanization necessitated vast capital infusion, local governments grappled with mounting deficits. In a landscape where financial capital had assumed a posture of autonomy, the era of relying solely on banks for investment was in the rearview mirror. In this milieu, local governments leveraged their monopoly on land resources, engaging in a practice whereby they acquired land from farmers at remarkably low prices. Subsequently, they used these lands as collateral to secure loans from financial institutions, with the resulting capital injections being channeled into infrastructural development. This marked the genesis of a development paradigm that defined the twenty-first century—characterized by "soaring debts + exponential investments = commensurate economic growth."

In the midst of this land acquisition surge, masterminded in concert by local authorities and financial capital, land emerged as an asset class endowed with unparalleled appreciation potential. However, the distribution of these land appreciation dividends among farmers, local governments, and developers remained strikingly asymmetrical. **Thus, the quest for effective pathways for rural areas to harness their own land value appreciation, and fortify their collective economic foundations, became an endeavor that beckoned further exploration.**[1]

Once more, within the comprehensive urban planning framework of Pidu District, the promotion of land consolidation emerges as a pivotal strategy, aimed at unlocking the latent value of land and effecting a transformative shift in the rural landscape. This strategic endeavor assumes paramount significance, not only in mitigating the perennial conundrum of urban and rural land allocation but also in propelling the metropolis towards a renaissance in economic dynamics.

As the wheels of productivity continue to turn, and the drumbeat of urbanization quickens, a conspicuous array of challenges comes to the fore. These span a worrisome dependence on land-based fiscal mechanisms, the ebbing vitality of the secondary sector, and an overreliance on external investments. Concurrently, the district grapples with an escalating urban–rural land disparity, a dearth of arable land reserves, and the sharpening contours of human-land conflicts.

A retrospective glance at the "Pidu County Land Consolidation Planning Description (2011–2015) (《郫县土地整治规划说明 (2011–2015年)》)" divulges a deliberate effort, dating back to 2006, whereby Pixian County—now rebranded as Pidu District—embarked on a staggering 20 land development and consolidation projects. These endeavors encompassed 17 agricultural land consolidation initiatives, accounting for a sprawling 116,633.85 mu of terrain. In this ambitious endeavor, a noteworthy 8403 mu of arable land were incrementally cultivated, boasting a salient uptick in the new arable land rate to the tune of 7.20%. Simultaneously, three construction land consolidation ventures were undertaken, entailing 1266.9 mu of correlated transferable indices and amassing substantial savings to the tune of 825.45 mu in construction land.

This meticulous land consolidation process unveiled a set of outcomes: a burgeoning arable land expanse, augmented efficiencies in arable land

[1] Yang Shuai and Wen Tiejun. "Economic Fluctuations, Fiscal and Tax System Changes, and Land Resource Capitalization—An Empirical Analysis of the 'Three Enclosures' Issues in China since the Reform and Opening Up." Management World, 2010(4): 32–41, 187.

utilization, an equitable equilibrium in land acquisition and compensation, the optimization of land utilization structures, and a remarkable elevation in the parsimonious deployment of construction land. These outcomes collectively laid the bedrock for an ecologically sound terrain—a sine qua non for the modern agricultural renaissance envisioned.

Fast forward to 2018, and the unveiling of "Pidu District Land Consolidation Planning (2016–2020) (《郫都区土地整治规划 (2016–2020年)》)" underscored an overarching strategy. This strategy sought to orchestrate rural land consolidation, harmonize urban and rural construction land fluctuations, and breathe new life into derelict industrial and mining terrains. The ultimate goal: an adept orchestration of urban and rural land configurations that would not only safeguard arable land but also refurbish the rustic domiciles and grassroots infrastructure. In parallel, it aspired to kindle a land-saving ethos, allay the burgeoning urban–rural land frictions, sculpt the urban–rural ecological tapestry, and accelerate the sweeping tide of urbanization.

In the broader panorama, Chengdu City envisaged itself as a vanguard, buttressing the historical destiny of a "world-class modern eco-park city." The city harnessed the periphery's prowess as a crucible for the city's economic mettle, channeling its influence and radiance. Simultaneously, it preserved spaces for the germination of agriculture and the nurturing of rural dreams. Against this overarching tableau, the proliferation of land consolidation on a grand scale in villages responded keenly to the clarion call of the higher echelons of governance, drawing down additional dividends from the institutional edifice.

In this intricate weave, rural hamlets found themselves at a moment of serendipity. As urban and rural residents calibrated their consumption matrices towards an ascending arc, the gamut of opportunities for agriculture and rural expansion burgeoned. Shifting from the domain of land consolidation to the crucible of tertiary industry development, the inexorable march towards the valorization of spatial resources offered the sole viable route in a landscape marked by "deindustrialization."

In closing, viewed through the microcosmic lens, the villages of Pixian County have notched remarkable success by adroitly steering land operations and development, effectively crystallizing land value appreciation and galvanizing collective incomes. The archives of the "Investigation on the Current Status of Collective Disposable Income in Pixian County Villages (《关于郫县村集体可支配收入现状的调查》)" for December 1999 offer poignant testament to this journey. In Huayuan

Town's Tongchun Village, astute exploitation of the local floral industry's vantage led to the adoption of a "company + farmers" paradigm. This catalyzed the expansion of planting scales and, in turn, propelled collective disposable incomes from a modest tally to commanding figures in the tens of thousands of yuan.

Yongdu Village in Anjing Town leveraged the advent of central village construction in 1998 as a golden opportunity. They embarked on the development of 18,000 square meters of land, attracting an infusion of capital exceeding 6 million yuan. This fortuitous endeavor swelled the village's collective disposable income by a substantial 20,000 yuan. Concurrently, Huangyan Village in Ande Town judiciously seized the strategic moment presented by the central village construction in the township. Vigorously delving into the realm of real estate development, this initiative efficaciously augmented the village's collective disposable income. Remarkably, from 1995 to 1999, a commendable tally of 46 villages across the county, through an array of land operations and development stratagems, accomplished the remarkable feat of doubling their collective disposable incomes.

In the macro and micro context of increasing land value, Zhanqi Village, driven by factors such as safeguarding village resource rights and maximizing sustainable income for households, initiated the process of land consolidation after 20 years of household contract-based land operation reform.

For the village collective, on the one hand, when enterprises transitioned to a leasing system, their growth faced limitations, and the village collective could only secure fixed rental income at this point. Looking at the longer term, fixed rental income only represents immediate benefits; to achieve continuous growth in income, resources need to be under the village's control. For a village, the most important and fundamental resource is land. As Gaodemin puts it, "Land is the fundamental resource, all resources are attached to the land; once land ownership is clarified, everything becomes clear."

On the other hand, when the village wants to establish new factories or expand existing ones, it requires land resources. By that point, the existing land resources have already been fully utilized, and further developable land resources can only be obtained through land consolidation. Therefore, the new leadership team must break through the limitations of individual groups, consolidate land throughout the entire village, and transfer group authority to the village collective. This is the consideration of the new leadership team.

For villagers, land consolidation also aligns with their considerations for the economic interests within their households. As villagers increasingly find employment both within the village's enterprises and outside, working off the land offers more income and less risk compared to farming, leading to a gradual reduction in villagers' dependence on land. Many villagers are no longer willing or able to continue farming, and during the agricultural tax phase, some even leased or gave away their land to others for cultivation. According to Li Shili's recollection, around 2000, in Zhanqi Village, out of more than 1600 people, over 400 worked in the village's enterprises, and it was quite common for people to lease their land to others.

Land consolidation is a key step in Zhanqi Village's gradual development and growth in the new era of ecological competition, as well as the foundation for the village to establish and maintain a long-term resource rights mechanism. On one hand, land consolidation achieves the integration and restructuring of the village's spatial environment, laying the spatial foundation for future ecological layout and comprehensive development of resources throughout the region, as well as obtaining "space rent." On the other hand, land consolidation is also a reorganization of rural society and a reshaping of the "new collective." The "collective economy" serves as an important intermediary variable that can effectively reduce transaction costs for any external entity, including the government, to establish contractual relationships with scattered small-scale farmers. At the same time, organizing farmers is a basic condition for forming reasonable contracts through equal negotiations, enhancing the ability of farmers to express and protect their legitimate interests.

In summary, the transformation of transferring enterprise management authority to the collective and promoting land consolidation began almost simultaneously. These two factors together led to the transformation of Zhanqi Village's grassroots collective economic organizations from a weak foundation to becoming a key player in spatial integration and development, gaining "opportunistic institutional benefits" in the national strategic transformation. Specifically, after implementing the household responsibility system for 20 years, the land consolidation in Zhanqi Village mainly went through the following stages.

1 Initial Venture into Land Concentration in 2003

Zhanqi Village had adhered to the household responsibility system for farming since the 1980s. In September 1980, the Central Committee of the Communist Party of China affirmed the household contract responsibility system in its directive titled "Notice on Further Strengthening and Improving the Agricultural Production Responsibility System (《关于进一步加强和完善农业生产责任制的几个问题》)." By 1981, the system had been widely implemented in rural areas across China, but the majority of Zhanqi's villagers were reluctant to divide the land. In 1982, with county leaders no longer granting extensions, Zhanqi embarked on the path of household contracting, leasing the collectively cultivated land to individual farmers for cultivation. As the 1990s unfolded, Chengdu's rural economy transitioned to a market-driven model, witnessing the emergence of "company + household" operations and a focused effort to develop a "dual-operating system" in the countryside. Correspondingly, Chengdu's rural areas gradually saw the development of moderate-scale land management and transfer mechanisms. In 1998, the first round of contracts expired, prompting Zhanqi Village to embark on the second round of land contracting at the year's end. Adhering to the principles of "maintaining stability with minor adjustments" and "clear ownership, stable contracting rights, and flexible usage rights," the contracting period was extended to 30 years.

During the 1990s, there were occasional instances of land transfer among villagers for vegetable cultivation in Zhanqi Village. However, these endeavors were primarily driven by individual initiative and involved relatively small areas. In 2002, with the arrival of Li Shili and Gao Demin, land transfer and centralized management became prominent tasks for the village collective.

Back in the 1960s, Li Shibing of Zhanq Brigadei (then a part of the Jinxing Brigade), paid a visit to Dazhai for learning and inspiration. He actively responded to the national call for the "Learn from Dazhai in agriculture" movement, achieving remarkable success in agricultural irrigation, militia construction, and transforming the mindset of cadres and the masses. Through self-reliance and unwavering determination, Li successfully altered the fundamental conditions of agriculture, leading to significant increases in rice and wheat yields within a few short years.

In a similar vein, in August 2003, Li Shili and Gao Demin embarked on a week-long study trip to Huaxi Village, Nanjie Village, and Liuzhuang Village, prominent examples of advanced collective economic powerhouses in the new era. Huaxi Village, for instance, initially thrived on agriculture and subsidiary industries, eventually transforming into an industrialized village. It later focused on diversified industrial development and comprehensive village growth, thereby nurturing a robust collective economy. Notably, the pursuit of knowledge differed from the past "Learning from Dazhai in agriculture" movement. It no longer solely emphasized the tenacity required to overcome agricultural production challenges but also aimed to rebuild a new form of collective economy in this fresh developmental phase. Following their investigations, the duo reached a resounding conclusion: villages with thriving collective economies generally eschewed individual land management, instead opting for the integration and centralized administration of land resources at the village level. Li Shili remarked, "Huaxi Village had already established a substantial collective economy prior to the implementation of household contracting. Such a system would have hindered its economic progress, thus emphasizing the continuation of a collective economy. In 1981, Nanjie Village adopted household contracting, only to reclaim the land in 1984 and establish communal enterprises, embracing a 'communist' approach. Those who independently initiated enterprises were promptly expelled from the village. Both villages have flourished economically." However, it was understood that although Xiaogang Village witnessed heightened agricultural productivity and increased grain yields after adopting household contracting, it faced limitations in overall village development and construction.

Nonetheless, the drive for land concentration was not an impulsive decision made after a mere study trip. Considering the historical context, Chengdu City had already pioneered institutional explorations of urban–rural coordination and the promotion of land concentration, preceding other regions in the country. In 2003, Chengdu City implemented a strategic vision of "coordinating urban and rural economic and social development and promote urban and rural integration (统筹城乡经济社会发展、推进城乡一体化)." In early 2003, building upon the experiences gained from Shuangliu County's **"Three Concentrations"** (industrial concentration in parks, rural population concentration in towns, and land concentration in scaled operations), the newly elected Chengdu Municipal Party Committee and Municipal Government decided to initiate an "urban–rural integration" reform with the promotion of the "Three Concentrations" as its central tenet throughout the city.

Internally, within the village, the promotion of centralized land operation stemmed from two principal motivations. Firstly, land concentration offered advantageous prospects for both the village collective and individual households as the village assumed responsibility for agricultural tax payments. Secretary Gao Demin revealed that collecting "public grain" tax was a crucial task occupying a significant portion of the village cadres' time and energy. By centralizing land operation, village cadres could be relieved of this burdensome duty, devoting their efforts to other village development initiatives. Moreover, moderate-scale cultivation and centralized administration facilitated improved agricultural yields, propelling advancements and endeavors towards excellence. Simultaneously, for villagers who increasingly relied less on agriculture for their livelihoods, land cultivation burdens could be alleviated. **Secondly, land concentration facilitated the development of village-operated enterprises or the introduction of external enterprises by freeing up space.** Li Shili noted that the initial plan entailed each group collectively contributing 3 fen (equivalent to 66.7 square meters) of land, which would then gradually be centralized at the village committee level through adjustments. Ultimately, this consolidated land would serve as the foundation for new factories. Although this plan proved challenging to implement and remained unrealized, it effectively epitomized Zhanqi Village's exploration of novel collective economic avenues during that era.

After this field study trip, both Li Shili and Gao Demin became more determined to promote land consolidation and strengthen the collective economy, a goal they had already in mind. Of course, this does not mean copying the development experiences of other villages, but rather, building upon the lessons and experiences of other villages, and combining them with the specific circumstances of Zhanqi Village to find its own path to development. However, it is clear that consolidating land resources within the village is a necessary and essential task.

After their return to the village, the two embarked on a spirited mobilization effort. From late September to the year's end, Zhanqi Village engaged in its annual land redistribution, wherein land was transferred from "decreasing" households to those in need of "increasing" their holdings. Their plan, devised to ensure uninterrupted agricultural production the following year, called for the completion of the centralized land work before September 25, 2003. Throughout September, a series of meetings were organized. The village committee convened to chart the path of development most suitable for Zhanqi. Subsequently, a general assembly of party members representing the entire village was held to discuss and dissect the proposed implementation plan. Captain meetings, internal team gatherings, and village representative assemblies ensued, rallying village officials, party members, and team leaders to lead the charge, comprehend the desires of the villagers, and devise an effective execution strategy. Finally, individual team leaders were tasked with mobilizing their respective group members, convening meetings to gage each household's circumstances.

Zhanqi Village's original land distribution method had long maintained a relatively equitable per capita arable land area within the groups, a vital advantage when it came to implementing centralized land management. Following the second round of land contracts, Zhanqi Village mirrored other villages across the nation, as each group shared an equal per capita muage. However, one distinction lay in the fact that the southern Sichuan region, characterized by its hilly topography and sparse population, fostered a tradition of annual land adjustment in numerous villages. Zhanqi was no exception; during the fallow period each year, land would be reconfigured, allocating plots previously owned by deceased or married-out individuals to newborns or newlywed women. With the exception of cases where additional population awaited land distribution or instances of certain individuals excessively occupying land, this practice upheld a consistent per capita land area within the groups. Consequently, compared to the prevailing norm of significant per capita muage disparities resulting from the household-arranged land distribution model of "no land increase when the population grows, no land decrease when the population shrinks," Zhanqi's approach significantly mitigated the mobilization challenges during land consolidation and redistribution.

Furthermore, the diminishing significance of agricultural income in Zhanqi eased the burden of land consolidation. During the 1980s and 1990s, as village enterprises underwent structured expansion, the three elements of production—land, labor, and capital—gradually tilted towards the secondary sector. Agricultural land was transformed into industrial space, and a considerable labor force transitioned into the industrial and other sectors. A new breed of farmers emerged, combining agricultural pursuits with non-farming occupations, thereby reducing the intensity of capital investment in agriculture. The rapid growth of village enterprises further marginalized the relative importance of agricultural output and income. A glimpse at the "Rural Economic Income Distribution Record for Pixian County (《农村经济收益分配情况记录表》)" in 1986 reveals that Zhanqi Village boasted a collective fixed asset value of 520,000 yuan, surpassing other villages which remained below 100,000 yuan. Employment in village-owned enterprises exceeded 300, far surpassing the sub-100 employee count in other villages. The average wages and bonuses per person in Zhanqi Village soared to 85 yuan, while neighboring villages scarcely reached 10 yuan. Hence, in comparison to other villages, Zhanqi's agriculture assumed a lesser role, and the dependency of its farmers on land decreased, thereby facilitating a smoother integration of land resources.

Although the waning reliance on land by farmers persisted, the burden of agricultural taxes still loomed. However, this predicament created an opportunity for collective-villager transactions. The village pledged that the profits derived from the consolidated land would aid farmers in meeting their agricultural tax obligations. Since the establishment of the People's Republic of China, agricultural taxes were levied once a year, divided into two collections. Summer saw the collection of wheat, while autumn entailed the surrender of millet or rice. Tax rates commenced at 5%, with an upper limit of 30%. Additionally, an irrigation grain levy of 20 catties per mu was imposed. Commencing in 1950, there was no distinction between public grain, self-sufficient grain, and irrigation grain. The produce from every household was pooled together and allocated by the county authorities. In 1954, a unified purchase and sale policy was enacted, obligating each household to sell surplus grain to support national development alongside fulfilling the delivery quota for various grains. Starting from May 17, 1985, when the Ministry of Finance received and endorsed the inquiry regarding the adoption of a "reverse 3–7" ratio for agricultural tax payment in grain equivalent, farmers were allowed to substitute cash for physical grain during the remittance of "public grain." As evidenced in Table 1, the average agricultural tax payment in Group 2 in 2004 stood at 37.49 yuan per mu, with individual households contributing a minimum of 43.49 yuan and a maximum of 303.31 yuan. According to data from the National Bureau of Statistics, the per capita net income of rural households in Sichuan Province in 2004 amounted to 2518.9 yuan.

Table 1 List of land area and agricultural tax for each household in Group 2 in 2004

Number	*Area (mu)*	*Basic tax (yuan)*	*Addition tax (yuan)*	*Total tax (yuan)*	*Defaulted payment (yuan)*	*Total count (yuan)*
1,002,045	3.47	108.42	21.68	130.1	0	130.1
1,002,046	2.31	72.17	14.43	86.6	0	86.6
1,002,047	4.63	144.66	28.93	173.59	0	173.69
1,002,048	4.63	144.66	28.93	173.59	0	173.69
1,002,049	4.63	144.66	28.93	173.59	0	173.69
1,002,050	4.63	144.66	28.93	173.59	0	173.69
1,002,051	6.17	192.78	38.56	231.34	0	231.34
1,002,052	6.17	192.78	38.56	231.34	0	231.34
1,002,053	4.63	144.66	28.93	173.59	0	173.59
1,002,054	5.78	180.59	36.12	216.71	0	216.71
1,002,055	5.78	180.59	36.12	216.71	0	216.71
1,002,056	2.31	72.17	14.43	86.6	0	86.6
1,002,057	6.94	216.83	43.37	260.2	0	260.2
1,002,058	6.94	216.83	43.37	260.2	0	260.2
1,002,059	8.09	252.76	50.55	303.31	0	303.31
1,002,060	3.47	108.42	21.68	130.1	0	130.1
1,002,061	1.16	36.24	7.25	43.49	0	43.49
Summary of 2 groups	81.74	2553.88	510.77	3064.65	0	3064.65

Despite the minor role agricultural taxes played in per capita income, the prospect of exemption remained an appealing transaction condition for the frugal villagers. Moreover, by relinquishing this portion of land, they could sidestep the inherent natural and market risks associated with agricultural production, as these uncertainties would be borne by the collective. The village guaranteed that the income generated from land consolidation would cover the farmers' agricultural tax liabilities, and any shortfall resulting from inadequate transfer revenue would be absorbed by the collective. Additionally, with Zhanqi's industrial development commencing in the 1980s, an array of village-owned enterprises emerged. The influx of internal and external migrant workers gradually diminished the proportion of income derived from farming, thereby reducing the villagers' dependency on land.

Consequently, considering the aforementioned factors, an average contribution of one-third of a plot per person to the collective remained an enticing proposition for the farmers.

Here's the English translation of the provided Chinese text:

In addition, during the mobilization process, the external experiences and information gained by village cadres through learning trips also effectively contributed to the formation of the village's ideology, promoting the optimistic expectation among villagers that they can lead a better life through centralized land ownership. During the mobilization meetings, village cadres showed DVDs of Huaxi Village and Nanjie Village, illustrating how these villages achieved a prosperous life, similar to that of urban residents, by concentrating land resources and developing collective economies. Extensive propaganda and mobilization efforts encouraged villagers to unify their thinking, reinforcing the concept that "agriculture must be developed through large-scale farming."

This expectation also revived the collective memory deeply ingrained in the hearts of Zhanqi Village residents. Since its establishment as an independent village, the eighth village party secretary consistently followed the path of collectivization for development. During the militia period, the Zhanqi Brigade was recognized as advanced and set as an example. Even when land was distributed to individuals in 1982, village-owned enterprises remained in collective hands. Therefore, the collective consciousness of "coming together to accomplish tasks (集中起来干事情)" had long been imprinted in the minds of every Zhanqi Village resident, especially the older generation. It is precisely due to this history that villagers have a stronger sense of trust in the collective and a higher level of acceptance for centralized land management.

However, they faced formidable challenges during the mobilization. One significant hindrance stemmed from the crude execution of land family contracting reforms over the past two decades, resulting in an uneven distribution of vested interests. In the past, due to factors such as soil quality and location, less fertile farmland could be counted as one and a half or two mu per mu, leading to an inequitable land possession issue. Some individuals exploited this loophole, occupying more resources, while others retained more land than specified in their contracts. Consequently, the process of land consolidation necessitated a leveling of land ownership, compelling those benefiting from the status quo to relinquish their surplus land. Predictably, this gave rise to substantial resistance.

Furthermore, villagers harbored concerns regarding the potential complications of land concentration, particularly the difficulties in land circulation and the possibility of corruption among village officials. As a result, the village actively sought prosperous farmers willing to lease the land and established meticulous financial management procedures. However, discrepancies in the mobilization abilities of elite members within the groups and conflicting interests impeded progress, resulting in varying degrees of difficulty across each group. Although the initial objective was to implement internal land concentration across all nine village groups, after the first round of mobilization, only Groups 5, 7, and 9 expressed willingness to embark on this endeavor. Notably, Li Shili belonged to Group 6, but deep-seated internal conflicts prevented their successful mobilization. Conversely, Gao Demin exhibited remarkable leadership, not only mobilizing Group 5 but also inspiring Groups 7 and 9.

Groups 7 and 9 were led by capable individuals who possessed strong mobilization skills. Ultimately, under the guidance of Secretary Gao Demin and the elite members within the groups, Groups 5, 7, and 9 successfully accomplished the mobilization task. However, just as victory seemed within reach, Group 9 encountered disagreements during the land adjustment process, stemming from conflicts between a family member of a village cadre within the group and the Group 9 leader. Consequently, only Groups 5 and 7 reached a resolution for land concentration, blazing the trail as pioneers in the village's land consolidation journey and serving as a tentative "trial run."

Liao Daijian (廖代建), who was the leader of Group 5 at the time, detailed the process of land consolidation as an eyewitness. After the village held a meeting of group leaders, Liao Daijian organized a meeting for the villagers of Group 5 and selected two or three villagers as representatives. The group leader and representatives then held meetings to discuss the specific situations of each household in the group, potential issues they might encounter, and corresponding solutions. They started their mobilization work with the villagers' representatives, village officials, party members, and their friends and family, going door-to-door within each courtyard. Many factors played a crucial role in this process.

Firstly, starting from the 1960s and 1970s, the elites of Zhanqi Brigade began leading the villagers in hard work, building a strong political trust within the village towards the village collective. This early trust formed a deep social foundation for the land consolidation. From the establishment of the village to the mid-1990s, Zhanqi Village first increased grain production and solved the villagers' food and clothing issues by taking advantage of the opportunity for military-civilian cooperation in agricultural and water conservancy construction. Then, they established village collective enterprises to develop the collective economy and increase villagers' income. The village collective led the villagers from nothing to prosperity, filling their stomachs and making money. As a result, the villagers developed strong political trust in the village collective. This was not something that every village could easily achieve, as it was the result of several village party secretaries leading the villagers towards a common goal, and the villagers benefited from the system's dividends. Not to mention whether other villages had such a policy environment, even just having multiple village party secretaries with the same goal was difficult to achieve. Although around the year 2000, Zhanqi Village's collective economic income fell to almost zero, the village collective reversed the situation by reforming the collective economy, preventing individuals from taking over the accumulated resources. This "revived" the political trust that had been accumulated in the past and shifted the focus of interests from a minority of elites to the overall development of the village.

Apart from leading the villagers from scratch, the village-run enterprises were also managed by individuals with "high political consciousness, practical work abilities, and a strong sense of mission." Therefore, from the stage of collective labor in the political competition phase to the structured expansion in the industrial competition phase, the process of selecting village leaders took place under the condition of abundant information about collective labor. The abilities and moral standards of the village elites were scrutinized by the villagers, further strengthening the villagers' political trust in the village collective.

In 2003, the strong mobilization for this small-scale consolidation was made possible by the efforts of Li Shili and Gao Demin, who led the village collective. Gao Demin, as the village director and a crucial representative of Group 5, led the mobilization efforts in Group 5, Group 7, and Group 9, among others. In addition, the persuasive power of the group leaders, their understanding of the issues, and their willingness to solve them were also crucial. Li Shili specifically mentioned that the group leaders in Group 5 and Group 7 were relatively convincing and forward-thinking, and they understood and were willing to promote this matter. Therefore, the progress in Groups 5 and 7 was relatively fast. From a micro perspective, even if villagers have good relationships with relatives and village officials, they will not agree to land consolidation if they do not trust the village collective. Conversely, when villagers have strong political trust in the village collective, as long as their interests are not significantly compromised, they are willing to support the work of the village collective. In some cases, even when collective interests outweigh personal interests, they may accept persuasion from friends, relatives, and village officials. It is based on a strong trust in the village collective that villagers believe in the village collective's expectations and are willing to surrender their land first and enjoy the benefits later, thus achieving a level of organization that is difficult for other villages to achieve.

Next, the Linpan settlements in Western Sichuan,[2] characterized by a scattered living pattern based on surnames or clans, significantly reduced the difficulty of mobilization. Liao Daijian took full advantage of this aspect during his mobilization efforts. Taking 5 groups as an example (see Fig. 1), at that time, there were 49 households in 5 groups, with more than 200 people in total. Among them, the Wu family had 10 households (Yang Yong, a capable individual from 5 groups, later became a small-scale land contractor, and his mother's surname was Wu), the Gao family had 9 households (the family of Gao Demin), the Wang family had 7 households (the Wang and Gao families had marital ties), and the Liao family had 3 households (the family of Liao Daijian, the leader of 5 groups). Under the influence of village representatives and village cadres, over half of the households (29 households) agreed and signed. Some conforming households (a total of 10 households) were in a wait-and-see state, but they signed one by one after seeing that most households had already signed. The remaining 10 households, who were more "stubborn," had

[2] The Linpan in Chengdu Plain, also known as Linpan settlements (林盘) are traditional rural communities in the Chengdu Plain, Sichuan. They are characterized by small-scale farming, rectangular fields, and natural elements such as water, trees, and bamboo, all of which are supported by the ancient Dujiangyan Irrigation System. Linpan settlements adhere to traditional farming practices and culture, playing a crucial role in the preservation of the Chengdu Plain's natural environment. The main structures of the human environment include patches (vast plains of farmland), corridors (roads and irrigation canals), and matrices (small matrices consist of thousands of Linpan villages, while large matrices consist of towns), all of which contribute to the beauty and uniqueness of the Chengdu Plain's rural landscape.

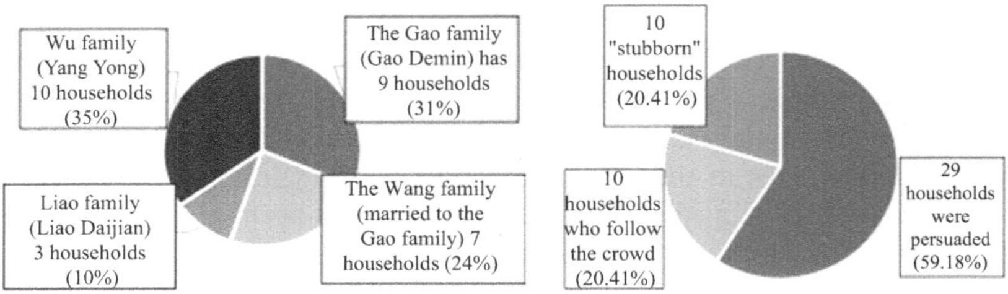

Fig. 1 Attitudes of Group 5 family clans and members towards land consolidation in 2003. 吴氏家族 (杨勇) 10户 Wu family (Yang Yong) 10 households, 廖氏家族 (廖代建) 3户 Liao family (Liao Daijian) 3 households, 高氏家族 (高德敏) 9户 The Gao family (Gao Demin) has 9 households, 王氏家族 (与高氏联姻) 7户 The Wang family (married to the Gao family) 7 households, "顽固"的农户10户 10 "stubborn" households, 从众的农户 10户 10 households who follow the crowd, 带动的农户 29户 29 households were persuaded

concerns, and the mobilization team addressed their concerns one by one, depending on each household's specific situation.

For individual villagers who were reluctant to participate in the land consolidation because they had occupied more land, the village collective would request them to present their land lease certificates, present the facts and reason with them, explaining that the actual land area they possessed exceeded the muage stated on the certificate. The additional land should rightfully belong to the village collective, and the collective had the right to demand land occupation fees from them. Through these efforts, land consolidation eventually gained the approval of all 5 groups' villagers.

In addition, compared to other groups, the poorer land quality and location of groups 5 and 7 were also important factors that made it easier for these two groups to form collective actions. Looking at the entire village, groups 2 and 8 had the best soil quality, while groups 5, 6, 7, and 9 had poor soil quality. As shown in Fig. 2, these four groups had the lowest per unit tax production yield. In terms of per capita tax production yield, groups 5 and 7 were significantly lower than the other groups. According to Gao Demin, one significant factor that only groups 5 and 7 succeeded in this endeavor was that these two groups had a high water table, resulting in very wet fields, making their land relatively barren compared to other groups. The other groups could yield up to

1200 jin per mu, while groups 5 and 7 had an average yield about 300 catties lower per mu. Li Shili also mentioned in an interview that the land consolidated by groups 5 and 7 was farther from the villagers' residential courtyards and was in a less favorable location. For the villagers of groups 5 and 7, who had weaker land conditions, giving up 30% of their land in exchange for exemption from agricultural taxes was obviously more beneficial to themselves. The gap between the organizational benefits brought by collective actions and the benefits of individual actions was larger for these two groups than for other groups, which was also one of the reasons why mobilization work was easier to carry out.

In the end, only groups 5 and 7 completed the mobilization. In order not to disrupt agricultural production, both groups quickly began the work of land surveying, consolidation, and redistribution. Group 5 had over 210 people, with an average of about 1.3 mu of land per person, plus some additional land, totaling nearly 300 mu of land. With the villagers'

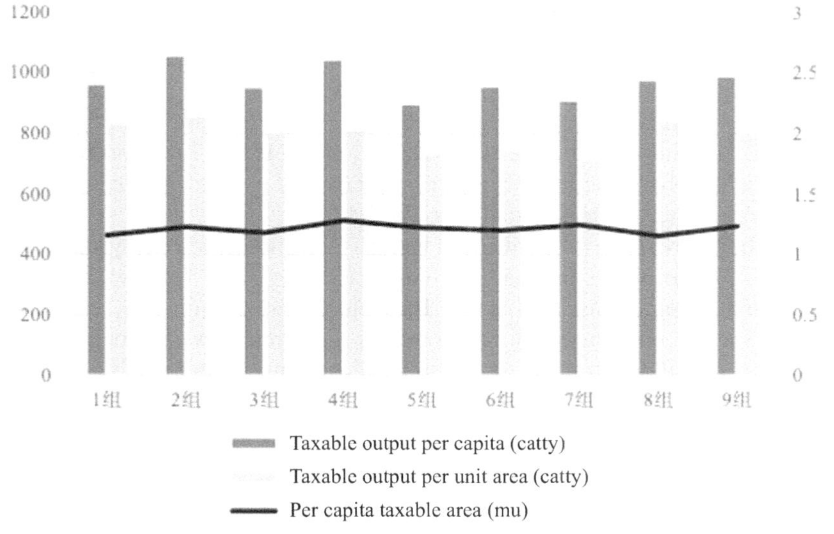

Fig. 2 Comparison of land tax situation in different groups of Zhanqi Village in 1985 (in terms of rice). 人均计税产量 (斤) Taxable output per capita (catty), 单位面积计税产量 (斤) Taxable output per unit area (catty), 人均计税面积 (亩) Per capita taxable area (mu)

consent, they re-measured the land area (including terraces) and assessed the fertility of the land. Each person contributed 0.21 mu of land, eventually setting aside about 50 mu of the poorest land for collective operation by the village. Group 7 had about 180 people and about 200 mu of land, of which about 50 mu were consolidated. The remaining land of the two groups was redistributed based on the current population, regardless of the number of mu on the land lease certificates or the actual occupied area at the time. Newborns and newlyweds who had not received land before were also eligible for land distribution.

During the process of redistributing land, the absence of significant conflicts was mainly attributed to the rational internalization mechanisms formed by the village community, which had a relatively fair overall distribution. This achieved a comprehensive balance across various dimensions and made the land redistribution process, which could have resulted in a series of conflicts, proceed very smoothly, greatly reducing internal transaction costs.

Firstly, when allocating land, factors such as soil fertility, plot size, and proximity to residential land were considered comprehensively. The land was divided into two grades, and each household received land of different grades. At the same time, efforts were made to ensure that the newly allocated land matched the originally contracted land, with priority given to allocating land close to residential plots. If two households were interested in the same plot, a lottery system was used to ensure fairness and transparency throughout the process.

Furthermore, land redistribution was carried out at the courtyard level, initially redistributing land at the courtyard level and later within the courtyard at the household level. In a close-knit community, personal interests were influenced by relationships with relatives and neighbors, as well as moral constraints. As a result, villagers no longer solely pursued maximizing individual benefits in land distribution but considered factors such as soil quality, size, and distance within their courtyards.

Throughout the process, the village collective took responsibility for guiding and coordinating the centralized land work, leading efforts in land improvement, road construction, and ditch digging, and providing financial support. For example, after about 50 mu of land were centralized by two groups, the village took the lead in field renovation, road construction, and deep ditch digging during the low-precipitation winter season. In addition to improving the centralized area, the village also carried out infrastructure development, including paving asphalt on existing roads, totaling 2–3 kilometers, at a cost of tens of thousands of yuan (mainly for materials), with some policy subsidies. Villagers who were willing to participate could do so, and the village primarily subsidized labor costs at 10 yuan per person per day.

The village also took responsibility for finding and connecting with the contracted operators after land was centralized. Through the village collective transfer, approximately 50 mu of land centralized by Group 5 were eventually contracted to Yang Yong (杨勇), a local agricultural expert and village director.[3] Before cultivation, Yang Yong spent his own money on road repairs and deep ditch digging. In the first year, he planted vegetables (such as Chinese cabbage), and the annual rent was 380 yuan per mu. However, due to high costs and market saturation, vegetable cultivation resulted in losses, so he later switched to flower cultivation. Approximately 50 mu of land centralized by the Group 7 were contracted to Li Yongchang (李永昌), a large-scale farmer from a neighboring town. Before handing it over to Li Yongchang, the village spent tens of thousands of yuan on land improvement and ditch drainage, so the rent was slightly higher at 480 yuan per mu annually. This additional 100 yuan was due to land improvement and infrastructure enhancement.

As the supporting infrastructure gradually improved, the rent increased to 500–600 yuan per mu annually in the second year.

The village kept its promises and used the land rent collected from Yang Yong and Li Yongchang to pay agricultural taxes on behalf of all the farmers in the Groups 5 and 7. This served as a guaranteed transfer fee for the farmers, while also covering the natural risks of agricultural production and the transaction costs of market access. The income generated from renting out the land at 380 yuan or 480 yuan per mu, after deducting agricultural taxes and other management costs, was managed by the village on behalf of the group. In addition to paying agricultural taxes on behalf of the farmers, the village also covered fees such as the one-child policy fees for the households within the group. With the rent increase in the second year, the surplus also increased accordingly.

In 2006, the Pixian County Government announced the complete abolition of agricultural taxes and agricultural tax surcharges, marking the era when farmers no longer had to provide grain or pay taxes for farming. After the abolition of agricultural taxes, the land rent received from these

[3] Source: Interview record with Gao Demin on October 2, 2019.

two plots was distributed equally on a per capita basis within Group 5 and Group 7.

* * *

The Village's Leading Steward of Land Transfer: Yang Yong

Yang Yong, once a member of Group 5, assumed the role of village director for Zhanqi Village in 2010.

Upon completing high school in 1988, Yang Yong found employment at the village's Broad Bean Paste Factory.

Between 1993 and 2000, while venturing beyond the village boundaries, Yang Yong donned many hats—a radio repairman, agricultural institute trainer, spring mattress technician, handicraft restorer, factory overseer, salesman, and storekeeper. These ventures cultivated his expertise and bestowed him with a wealth of managerial acumen.

In 2000, Yang Yong returned to the village, leasing 20 mu (roughly 1.3 hectares) of land in Group 4 to nurture floral seedlings. The initial 3 years proved arduous, with profitability only gracing his endeavors in 2003.

With the village's internal land consolidation effort in 2003, Yang Yong undertook the leasing of 50 mu (about 3.3 hectares) from Group 5, at an annual rent of 380 yuan per mu. Acquiring the necessary advance payment demanded resourcefulness, prompting Yang Yong to approach the credit society for a loan. During 2003 and 2004, he sowed crops like corn and bok choy. Yet, formidable challenges in the form of mounting land rent, extensive investments in road repairs and trench digging, market saturation, and erratic vegetable prices impeded financial gains. Faced with persistent losses, Yang Yong shifted his focus to cultivating lawns. However, after 6 months, the meager returns prompted him to pivot towards nurturing floral seedlings.

In 2006, as the village underwent a large-scale land consolidation, Yang Yong pressed on with land leasing, expanding his purview to encompass 300 mu (around 20 hectares) from Groups 4, 5, and 6. His cultivation of floral seedlings on this vast expanse continues to this day. Presently, land rent is calculated based on the market price of approximately 450 kilograms of rice, fetching about 2000 yuan per mu, with annual settlements. In 2006, his total sales eclipsed one million yuan, with nursery stock claiming an 80% share and flowers making up the remaining

20%. Yang Yong makes annual sojourns to survey and appraise, ensuring timely adjustments to his floral seedling varieties.

According to Yang Yong, between 2003 and 2010, he actively facilitated employment for 50–60 individuals within the village. At present, tending to the 300 mu of floral seedlings necessitates close to 30 permanent laborers, incurring an annual workforce expenditure of 700,000–800,000 yuan. Fertilizer, film, and other agricultural machinery costs amount to approximately 200,000 yuan per year. One-time expenses for acquiring seedlings sum up to 200,000 yuan, while land rent reaches a substantial 6 million yuan. Consequently, yearly costs surpass 1.6–1.7 million yuan, leaving Yang Yong with meager profits that barely balance the books.

Beyond cultivating the 300 mu of floral seedlings within Zhanqi Village, Yang Yong received an invitation in 2014 from the town authorities. They sought his assistance in developing 200 mu of fallow land, planting ornamental peach blossoms. The barren land had long been neglected, and finding someone willing to undertake its transformation proved challenging. However, planting peach blossoms held the promise of attracting tourists and fostering growth in local businesses and tourism. Consequently, the land was handed over to Yang Yong free of charge, exempt from any land rent obligations. Yang Yong and his team invested over half a year and more than 3 million yuan in reclaiming the land, planting, and sculpting picturesque landscapes. The peach trees finally burst into bloom in 2015, attaining their zenith in 2016 Typically, the months of March and April witnessed the resplendent display of flowers, coinciding with the bustling spring travel season. The resulting influx of visitors propelled the flourishing of neighboring eateries and tourism ventures. However, the substantial initial investment has yet to be recouped, as Yang Yong shared.

Source: Interview transcript with Yang Yong, October 6, 2019.

2 "2006 New Policies" Drive the 500 mu of Farmland Concentration into Cooperative

In 2003, after conducting pilot tests with around 50 mu of land concentrated in Groups 5 and 7, the plan was to continue promoting land concentration in other groups the following year. However, until 2005, the area of concentrated land in Zhanqi Village had remained largely unchanged, with only a few instances of land exchange between villagers for vegetable and flower cultivation. The momentum for land concentration had slowed down. Meanwhile, the village faced the dilemma of further developing village-run enterprises, hindered by constraints such as limited land availability, fragmented agricultural plots, and low productivity. How to advance land consolidation became a vexing problem.

Then came a series of policies in Chengdu, exploring the path of coordinated urban–rural development, which provided a timely opportunity for Zhanqi Village to push for greater land concentration. These policies, coupled with increased subsidies, raised the income prospects for villagers, fostering the concentration of 500 mu of land into cooperatives. This consolidation marked a transitional phase, extending the previous small-scale concentration within groups and laying the groundwork for a comprehensive consolidation of arable land throughout the entire village, utilizing residential land as the foundation.

In July 2005, the Pixian County Government issued interim measures and implementation rules for land acquisition, compensation, and resettlement, setting the stage for rural "consolidating and rebuilding courtyards (拆院并院)" pilot projects. Subsequently, in August of the same year, they released guidelines on promoting the concentration of farmers into towns, aiming to advance the "three concentrations" initiative. The Tangchang Town Government also published implementation opinions emphasizing the need for further urban–rural integration, with a focus on planning the construction of new villages, particularly prioritizing Zhanqi Village. They aimed to bolster the development of agricultural professional cooperative organizations, uniting individual farmers under the "Party branch + association + households" model within 3 years, covering all 27 villages in the town. The policies further aimed to concentrate land into leading enterprises and strategic projects, fostering the growth of modern and large-scale agriculture. Building upon existing vegetable and flower planting bases, high-quality rice fields, and pickled vegetable farms, their objective was to establish three to five high-quality pollution-free agricultural product bases by 2005, driving the cultivation of premium pollution-free vegetables.

Guided by these policies, and considering their specific circumstances, Zhanqi Village sought assistance from Chengdu Institute for Rural Design to devise an overarching village plan. Their aim was to reconfigure agricultural land, residential plots, and operational areas, all in preparation for large-scale land management and concentrated living. Although the initial budget was set at 90,000 yuan, by 2006, only a portion of the plan had been realized, with an actual expenditure of 50,000 yuan.[4] Nonetheless, this period marked the beginning of Zhanqi Village's consideration for village-wide spatial planning, highlighting the pressing need for further land concentration.

Simultaneously, Chengdu was gradually refining its system to promote moderate-scale land management while introducing encouraging policies. These policies were centered around stabilizing the rural household contract system and, in accordance with the principles of legality, voluntarism, and compensation, encouraging subcontracting, leasing, and equity participation. Such measures aimed to facilitate the concentration of land into agricultural leading enterprises, new collective economic organizations, professional cooperative economic organizations, and large-scale farming, ultimately achieving scaled and efficient operations. By concentrating industrial development in designated areas, industrialization would stimulate urban and tertiary industry growth, thereby providing conditions for farmers' migration. Similarly, by concentrating farmers in residential areas, population density would create business opportunities, fostering further industry and urban development, and concurrently facilitating large-scale land management. By consolidating land for scaled operations, agricultural production methods could be transformed, promoting the development of modern agriculture. Strengthening rural land consolidation efforts and effectively utilizing the differences in land value between urban and rural areas, as well as land occupation and compensation balance policies, would contribute to raising funds for rural development.

Driven by these policies, the city had achieved a total of 1.6 million mu of land under scaled operation by the end of 2006. Zhanqi Village also experienced a significant acceleration in land transfer during this period. From 2005 to 2006, external individuals increasingly approached Zhanqi Village to lease land, mainly for large-scale vegetable and flower seedling cultivation. The annual transfer fees for vegetable cultivation averaged around 600 yuan per mu, while flower seedlings commanded higher fees, reaching a maximum of 780 yuan per mu.[5]

Under the influence of supportive policies and the appeal of external transferees, the value of land became more apparent. This realization

[4] Source: Interview record with Gao Demin on October 2, 2019.

[5] Source: Interview record with Gao Demin on October 2, 2019.

served as a vital catalyst in persuading villagers to accept land concentration and paved the way for the establishment of a land cooperative. The village recognized that forming a cooperative would not only break the boundaries imposed by group-based land ownership but also enable large-scale operations and prepare for concentrated living. Additionally, the cooperative could apply for government subsidies to enhance agricultural production conditions, improve village infrastructure, boost agricultural rent differentials, and further facilitate land consolidation. Consequently, land concentration began to gain momentum.

Between 2003 and 2006, the restructuring of collective enterprises boosted the village collective's income by 5–6 million yuan, providing a **financial foundation** for promoting cooperative establishment and refining village planning.

In the latter half of 2006, the village collective planned to establish a land cooperative and developed statutes, land valuation methods, and other necessary procedures. However, due to policy restrictions, the cooperative had not yet been officially registered. Consequently, the speed of land concentration did not experience a dramatic surge. **At that time, only 500 mu of land were concentrated, involving Groups 2, 3, 4, and 8.**[6] These particular groups were selected because the land formed a contiguous tract, had fewer courtyards, higher elevation, and better overall conditions, resulting in relatively lower transformation costs.

The process of land concentration this time went much smoother than before. Village officials began rallying the villagers in the first half of 2006. Dealing with the diverse interests and demands of the villagers posed a challenge for the village collective during the land consolidation process. Different villagers required different approaches to mobilize them.

Certainly, there were villagers who adamantly refused to transfer their land. For this handful, the village officials endeavored to accommodate them by reallocating land, striking a balance between their personal interests and the necessity of land consolidation. Of course, those unwilling to adjust their land were not coerced; they could continue tending to their own plots. This highlighted the virtually non-existent

[6] The claim that 500 mu of land were concentrated involving Groups 2, 3, 4, and 8 originates from Li Shili, while Gao Demin suggests that 600 mu of land were concentrated involving Groups 3, 8, and 9.

cost of withdrawal for villagers during the land adjustment and consolidation. Villagers could opt out at any time should they wish to cultivate their own land, and the collective would honor their decision rather than resorting to hardline tactics. Paradoxically, this method of upholding the villagers' right to till their own land alleviated concerns among other villagers about entrusting their land to the collective, making them more inclined to relinquish their plots.

> *Some people dissented (regarding land transfer). The lack of uniformity in the tools used to measure land area in the past—a mishmash of rulers and sundry objects—prompted us to introduce a standardized measuring apparatus. Yet, it got smashed three times. Some were reluctant to adjust their land. I told them, 'Your certificate is akin to a deposit, while the collective functions as a bank. Deposit your money here, and I will lease you whichever plot you choose, as long as the quantity and quality remain unchanged.'*
> *Source: Interview record with Gao Demin on December 26, 2019.*

On the whole, the mobilization efforts proceeded rather smoothly for the following reasons:

Firstly, the consolidation of land in Groups 5 and 7 in the past bolstered the villagers' trust in the village collective, thereby fostering further land concentration. Concerns about the generation of increased value from land consolidation, fair distribution of benefits, and the village collective's ability to safeguard the collective assets against loss all influenced the villagers' political trust in the village collective. Following the land consolidation in 2003, the village underwent land improvements, resulting in improved soil quality, reduced cultivation costs, and increased land revenue. Honoring their commitment, the village collective covered agricultural taxes for the villagers in Groups 5 and 7 and still managed to generate a surplus. **These tangible benefits reinforced the trust between the villagers and the village collective and heightened expectations of increased profits from land concentration, thereby mitigating resistance during the mobilization process.**

Moreover, the establishment of cooperatives enabled applications for government subsidies and infrastructure development projects for large-scale land operations. This created a strong anticipation of land value appreciation within the village collective. By implementing a distribution model that combined a guaranteed minimum rent of 800 yuan per mu with a 50% additional dividend, the villagers developed a keen expectation of profitability. This became a pivotal factor in enticing them to transfer their land to the cooperative. Minutes from village committee meetings elucidated, "Land concentration is entirely voluntary. It is the prevailing trend. Only through land concentration can land value increase, garner government support, and benefit farmers. We hope everyone can properly grasp the relationship between the overall situation and individual interests, as well as the collective and personal perspectives. A self-centered focus does not yield fruitful results." However, whether the risks were borne by the cooperative and fixed rent was provided to the villagers, or the villagers assumed all the risks, neither option garnered the villagers' agreement. The former failed to secure future appreciation gains, while the latter contradicted the rationality of risk-averse small-scale farmers. The distribution model of "guaranteed minimum rent + dividend" not only bestowed stable income upon the villagers through minimum rent but also ensured their ongoing participation in future land appreciation. Initially, the guaranteed minimum income was set at 720 yuan per mu per year. However, in response to numerous villagers expressing dissatisfaction with the low guarantee, the village officials raised the annual minimum income to 800 yuan per mu in 2008—an amount exceeding the highest transfer fee within the village by 20 yuan. Furthermore, this prepayment allayed the villagers' concerns and minimized risks. Deducting the cost of the premium (800 yuan) from the land transfer fee pledged by the village collective, the remaining amount was split equally between the villagers and the village collective. Grounded in this distribution model, the villagers gained confidence in augmented profits, rendering them more willing to transfer their land to the village collective and significantly mitigating conflicts during the land consolidation process. Simultaneously, the villagers could secure employment in the cooperative, providing them with an additional source of income. Given the concurrent plans for concentrated housing construction, this employment initiative of the cooperative aligned with the farmers' desire for stable income.[7]

Furthermore, considering the prevalence of non-agricultural employment, the diminished role of agriculture as a fundamental

[7] It can be seen from the "Zhanqi Village Chronicle" (unpublished manuscript) that more than 200 people in the village became agricultural workers. In 2008, the per capita net income of farmers in Zhanqi Village reached 7,133 yuan.

means of subsistence, and the land being transferred to the collective through basic land rent, the impact on villagers' essential survival was relatively minimal. Consequently, resistance to land concentration diminished. During that period, not only did many villagers work in village enterprises, but the number of villagers seeking employment outside the village also surged. The village officials quantified this situation for the villagers: "Two individuals cultivating 3 mu of land would earn an annual net income of 2400 yuan. However, by going out to work in 2006, they could earn around 30–40 yuan per day, equivalent to over 1000 yuan per month, totaling more than 10,000 yuan per year."[8] Therefore, transferring land to the cooperative for operation also aligned with rational expectations of augmenting income and reducing risks within families.

Formal land concentration commenced after the autumn harvest. Land transfer contracts previously inked between villagers and large-scale farmers were rendered null and void, supplanted by agreements with the village collective. Accordingly, the village collective, rather than individual farmers, consolidated the land held by villagers and subsequently transferred it to large-scale farmers (predominantly non-village residents) through the cooperative for the cultivation of vegetables and rice. This not only reduced the cost of small-scale farmers searching for information but also curtailed the transaction costs incurred by large-scale farmers in coordinating land transfers with numerous small-scale farmers. Simultaneously, this approach proved instrumental for the cooperative in enhancing land utilization efficiency, promoting land value appreciation, and pursuing policy subsidies—a true win–win situation. Additionally, the village officials had previously "agreed" with the large-scale farmers that if the village were to implement concentrated housing, the lease contracts would automatically be invalidated. Naturally, some villagers believed that operating through the cooperative would diminish their rental income. Consequently, they were disinclined to transfer their land to the cooperative for management by the large-scale farmers. In such cases, the village officials duly respected their wishes.

After the cooperative was formed, the county's agricultural development department allocated over **three million yuan to construct essential infrastructure such as ditches, roads**, and bridges in Zhanqi

[8] Source: Interview with Gao Demin on December 26, 2019.

Village. This development covered the land of the original Groups 3, 8, 9, and parts of Group 2, benefiting nearly half of the village's agricultural territory.[9] The government, with its financial support, provided water, electricity, and even greenhouses, improving the fundamental conditions for agricultural production. **Consequently, the village effortlessly acquired its initial share of land rent, virtually cost-free.**

Additionally, the facilities on the transformed agricultural land provided a favorable environment for capital-intensive farming practices. Following an adjustment in the agricultural industry structure, **the village encountered a second wave of differential land rent.** As the conditions for agricultural production improved, the annual rent, calculated based on the market value of rice, climbed to a range of 900–1000 yuan per mu. By 2008, it had reached a staggering 1200 yuan per mu, subsequently escalating each year. The zenith peaked at over 2200 yuan per mu, and presently, it stabilizes at approximately 2150 yuan per mu annually.[10]

During the early years of prosperous operations, the rent was paid upfront. However, as the flower and nursery market experienced a downturn in 2015 and 2016, numerous prominent cultivators adopted a deferred rent payment approach. **The cooperative's distribution method, characterized by a "minimum guarantee + bonus," facilitated the secondary allocation of the generated differential land rent, allowing for the payment of village insurance, agricultural land and water conservation maintenance, and cooperative management expenses. Ultimately, the remaining profit underwent a secondary distribution between individual villagers and the village collective.**

Undoubtedly, policy subsidies have expanded the operational capacity of the village collective, elevating the income expectations of its inhabitants and catalyzing the consolidation of land resources. Moreover, the policy subsidies for land possess an inherent indivisibility, given the scale requirements. This reality propelled Zhanqi Village to seize the advantageous external conditions bestowed by supportive policies, initiating a process of spatial reconstruction within the village's geographical boundaries, anchored in agricultural and residential land.

By harmonizing scattered plots into an integrated whole, the government subsidies and the returns garnered from industrial upgrading

[9] Source: Interview with Gao Demin on October 2, 2019.

[10] Source: Interview record of Yang Yong on October 5, 2019.

constitute what can aptly be described as "space rent." Subsequent experiences have consistently demonstrated that this "space rent" serves as the primary source of collective economic gains and communal accumulation for Zhanqi Village in this modern era.

* * *

The Journey and Status of Zhanqi Vegetable Cooperative

To achieve a grand scale of land operation, in 2006, Zhanqi Village conceived a plan: guide farmers to invest their land rights and infuse village funds, thereby forming the Zhanqi Land Cooperative. However, due to policy constraints, registration as a land cooperative was not permitted initially. It wasn't until November 7, 2008, that official registration took place under the name "Pixian Zhanqi Edible Mushroom Professional Cooperative." On September 2, 2009, it was further renamed "Pixian Tangchang Town Zhanqi Vegetable Professional Cooperative." Its registered capital amounted to 100,000 yuan. Notably, in 2013, to meet the criteria of being a national demonstration cooperative—requiring a capital of one million yuan and more than 100 members—the registered capital of Zhanqi Vegetable Professional Cooperative increased to 1.06 million yuan. The village committee contributed 500,000 yuan, and 104 representatives were elected to symbolize all members, with the land's equity converted into intangible assets valued at 560,000 yuan.

In August 2014, Pixian County issued the "Key Points for the Pilot Work of Stock Cooperative of Agricultural Land in Zhanqi Village (《战旗村农用地股份制合作试点工作要点》)," necessitating modifications to the cooperative's articles of association. Key revisions included provisions for the establishment of land shares after farmers invest their land rights in the cooperative, as well as the management and distribution of equity. While Zhanqi Village aspired to convert the vegetable cooperative directly into a land cooperative, policy restrictions prevented it. Consequently, on August 28, 2014, a land cooperative was established, despite having no significant operations. The operational cooperative within the village continued to focus primarily on vegetables. Subsequently, on October 27, 2017, due to administrative changes, the name transformed to Chengdu's Pidu District Zhanqi Vegetable Professional Cooperative, formerly known as Pixian Tangchang Town Zhanqi Vegetable Professional Cooperative.

From 2006 to 2007, the cooperative paid farmers an annual minimum land rent of 720 yuan per mu. This figure increased to 800–900 yuan per mu from 2008 to 2010, surpassing the general rate of 600–700 yuan per mu prevalent in other villages at the time. In 2011, the rent elevated further to 1200 yuan per mu, subsequently remaining relatively constant. Each quarter, the rent was disbursed by the 15th day preceding its conclusion. Apart from the minimum rent, dividends from the previous year were also distributed in January of the subsequent year. Dividends per person amounted to 200 yuan from 2010 to 2012, 300 yuan from 2013 to 2014, 350 yuan from 2015 to 2017, and 400 yuan in 2018. Dividends experienced a slight annual increase. During the initial stages of cooperative development, when profits were meager, the village committee compensated for the difference.

The cooperative fulfilled multiple roles. First, as a land manager, it facilitated large-scale land transfers by liaising with prominent farmers and external agricultural enterprises. This reduced transaction costs for investors engaging with numerous small-scale farmers, effectively harnessing the advantages of land scale. Second, it assumed the role of coordinating planting varieties, thereby controlling the selection of crops within the park to prevent cutthroat competition. Third, it served as a remarkable financing platform, capable of securing agricultural policy subsidies and preserving the village committee's developmental funds. Additionally, it functioned as an implementing or intermediary body for agricultural policies.

Moreover, the cooperative endowed the village with flexibility concerning land utilization. At its zenith, the cooperative managed close to 500 mu of land, dwindling to approximately 100 mu during quieter times. In 2017, as part of an effort to promote the smooth implementation of the comprehensive rural revitalization plan, the town revised its land use plan. The transformation replaced flower and seedling cultivation with a rotational system of rice and vegetables. Adhering to government standards, the cooperative undertook a self-operating approach. By the end of 2019, the cooperative independently managed over 300 mu of land. Roughly 150 mu comprised woodlands that could not be connected to other parcels, leading the cooperative to assume their care. With infrequent maintenance requirements, annual weeding and fertilization sufficed. These woodlands served the dual purpose of afforestation and potential external sales. Furthermore, over 150 mu of land were allocated for rice cultivation, necessitating significant labor input and responsibility for sales. In 2019, after consulting with village leaders, it was decided to forgo external sales, instead processing the rice into rice and distributing it as welfare to villagers, roughly amounting to 30 catties per person.

Presently, the cooperative's income structure primarily relies on land transfers. Therefore, efforts to diversify income streams are being explored. In 2019, the cooperative initiated plans to construct a controlled atmosphere storage facility. The core storage area would encompass approximately 10 mu, with an additional peripheral area, collectively covering around 20 mu. Estimated construction costs range between 4.5 and 5 million yuan, with a portion of the funds self-generated. The remainder is projected to be acquired through an application for a subsidy from Chengdu's municipal finance, amounting to approximately 3 million yuan. Completion of the project is anticipated by the end of January 2021, subsequently providing fruit and vegetable preservation, packaging, and distribution services to neighboring areas in exchange for rent or service fees.

Currently, the cooperative employs only three permanent staff members: an accountant, a cashier, and a technician. Temporary workers fulfill the remaining labor requirements.

Source: Interviews with the cooperative's accountant, Fang Lei, Li Shili, and others, along with "Zhanqi Village's 2010 Work Summary and Next Year's Work Ideas."

3 2007–2011: Homestead Consolidation Spurs Land Concentration in the Entire Village

On the 2nd of July 2007, Zhanqi Village was handpicked as a pilot project for the "New Rural Community Construction." All nine village groups rallied together for the "demolition and relocation" initiative. Remarkably, this endeavor resettled a staggering 96% of the village's population, effectively transforming 208 mu of construction land into agriculturally zoned parcels linked to urban utilization. By cleverly hitching expectations of revenue growth to the comprehensive land consolidation project, the village leveraged the benefits of concentrated farming, cultivating an environment primed for cooperative land management and scaled agricultural operations. In September 2009, the cooperative system successfully amassed 1097 mu of land. By the end of 2010, that number swelled to approximately 1600 mu. Come year-end 2011, the cooperative had successfully amassed a remarkable 1820 mu, accounting for an impressive 95% of the village's arable land.

3.1 Pioneering the Pilot Project for "New Rural Community Construction"

On the 19th of July 2005, the Pixian County Government unveiled its "Opinions on Initiating Pilot Projects for 'Demolition and Relocation' in Rural Areas (《关于开展农村"拆院并院"试点工作的意见》)." The document underscored the necessity to uphold the "State Council's Decision on Deepening Reforms and Stringent Land Management (《国务院关于深化改革严格土地管理的决定》)." With resolute determination, the county aimed to forge ahead with the "Three Concentrations" strategy and expedite the process of urban–rural integration. The plan also ambitiously sought to explore viable avenues for the utilization of rural collective construction land, breathing life into these dormant resources and substantially improving the living and working conditions of farmers. The key directive entailed rallying dispersed rural residents into meticulously planned towns, central villages, or settlements through the "demolition and relocation" campaign. This revolutionary undertaking successfully centralized farmland operations, facilitated the consolidation of replaced construction land within urban areas and industrial development zones, and mitigated the stress associated with land scarcity for developmental purposes. A crucial provision enabled the legally sanctioned transfer of increased agricultural land for ambitious agricultural industrialization projects, with the collective proceeds benefiting the farmers, provided such decisions garnered the consent of over two-thirds of the members of the rural collective economic organization or the village representatives, subject to the scrutiny of the township government.

In 1996, Zhanqi Village committed an investment of 420,000 yuan to erect a multifaceted edifice spanning two floors, boasting a generous architectural footprint of 876 square meters. Buoyed by this success, the village collectively injected 3 million yuan into the construction of a new village area by 1999. This pristine development warmly welcomed nearly one hundred households, primarily from Groups 4 and 8, representing around 20% of the village's populace. Unfortunately, other farming households remained scattered, far removed from this centralized haven. As the year 2005 unfurled, Zhanqi Village conscientiously undertook comprehensive village planning, diligently paving the way for a future characterized by consolidated living arrangements on a grand scale. Regrettably, the nascent plan languished due to the absence of cohesive support policies.

It wasn't until the twilight of April 2006 that the Ministry of Land and Resources designated Sichuan Province, Shandong Province, Jiangsu Province, Hubei Province, and Tianjin as pioneering locales for the inaugural wave of urban–rural land consolidation pilot projects. Seizing the coveted honor of being the country's first pilot unit, Sichuan province initiated the "Land Consolidation Project in Urban and Rural Areas (城乡建设用地增减挂钩项目)" during the first half of 2006. Chengdu City assumed the vanguard role in piloting this audacious endeavor, selecting Tangyuan Town's Changlin Village as its proving ground. Embracing a land expanse of 2294 mu, a quarter of which comprised rural construction land, Changlin Village boasted an average of 0.382 mu (255 square meters) of construction land per villager. In a remarkable coup, the diligent implementation of the "demolition and relocation" process yielded three resplendent residential enclaves sprawled across 112.26 mu of land, effectively increasing the village's agricultural land stock by a net gain of 263 mu. Furthermore, the surplus rural construction land relinquished through "demolition and relocation" found a new home in the proximity of Pixian County, specifically Xipu Town and You'ai Town, reaping a remarkable monetary reward of 135 million yuan.[11]

In the latter half of 2006, Zhanqi Village's cadre ventured forth to Changlin Village, their eyes transfixed on the project's execution, eager to glean insights that could illuminate their own path towards the realization of "demolition and relocation" and concentrated living. This unsanctioned excursion, devoid of formal organization, witnessed an exchange of wisdom and a candid reflection on the challenges confronted by Changlin Village during its pursuit of consolidated living arrangements. Struggles concerning housing allocations and construction planning served as potent reminders for Zhanqi Village's ambitious quest.

[11] National School of Development, Peking University. "Empowering through Land Transfer: Establishing a Reliable Foundation for Long-Term Development—Investigation Report on Chengdu's Land System Reform" [R/OL]. (2009-06-24) [2021-01-2_]. nsd.pkv.edu.cn/rzyj/kyxm/tdzdyj/252840.htm.

"Our visit to neighboring Changlin Village was an ordinary affair, bereft of grand orchestration. Mere murmurs of their successful implementation of concentrated living prompted our curiosity to ascertain the truth. Yet, the quandaries besetting Changlin Village's experiment in concentrated living served as a stark admonition, one that would indelibly shape Zhanqi Village's endeavor. It became abundantly clear that drawing lots for housing assignments and meticulous planning were indispensable."

Source: Interview record with Li Shili on January 11, 2020.

* * *

Land Consolidation Starting from Here: Changlin Village in Tangyuan Town

"Terraced fields remain, ponds for farming still exist; in the tranquil woods, conversations about farming leisure float in the air." Strolling through Changlin Village, Tangyuan Town, Pidu District, Chengdu City, one witnesses the meandering stone paths, nestled between vegetable gardens and shaded havens. A serene creek flows silently beside the village, while the single family houses, adorned in the distinctive style of Western Sichuan architecture, stand proudly against the mountains, embraced by the bamboo groves.

However, before 2006, the village bore a different visage: adobe huts were the prevalent abodes, scattered and dilapidated, with haphazard layouts and rugged dirt roads. The farmland was sporadic, and the utilization of land was abysmal. What brought about the transformation of this once dirty, backward rural setting? And what turned these rural areas into the idyllic havens sought after by urban dwellers in search of nostalgia and a slower pace of life? The key lies in the integration of urban and rural construction land—the secret code to unlocking the metamorphosis of a beautiful countryside.

1. Transforming a Village: Land Consolidation Unleashes Development Potential

   Before 2006, Changlin Village covered a sprawling expanse of 2299 mu, with a per capita land allocation of 1.61 mu. However, arable land accounted for a mere 1699 mu. Due to fragmented cultivation practices, the village was riddled with 21 ditches, spanning nearly 40 mu. Terraced slopes occupied 49 mu between the scattered farmlands, while 358 mu accommodated 39 farmhouse settlements. Neglected independent factories, desolate lands, and grassy patches accounted for 77 mu, resulting in a woefully low land utilization rate.

But change was on the horizon. In 2006, Sichuan Province decided to initiate a pilot project for the consolidation of urban and rural construction land in Chengdu City, choosing Tangyuan Town's Changlin Village as the testing ground. At this pivotal moment, the town's party committee and government hesitated: Would the villagers, accustomed to their dispersed rural lifestyle, willingly relocate to centralized dwellings? Could the adjustment of land ownership following integration provoke new conflicts? Many grassroots officials likened it to disturbing a "hornet's nest."

Should the pilot proceed or not? The power to decide was placed in the hands of the villagers themselves. Through rounds of extensive propaganda, the policies of land integration became deeply entrenched in the collective consciousness. Gathering together, the villagers of Changlin Village astonishingly displayed over 80% support for the integration initiative.

Jiang Zitong, a 67-year-old resident, declared, "This is the best decision I have ever made in my lifetime." Recalling the past, he described a time when his family of six squeezed into a brick and tile house left by their forefathers, toiling from dawn till dusk, with an annual income barely exceeding 10,000 yuan. Today, they not only reside in a new two-story house spanning over 180 square meters but have also leased their land following comprehensive land improvement, reaping an annual income exceeding 20,000 yuan.

Ma Deru, the secretary of Changlin Village's Party branch, remarked that land integration had unleashed the development potential of the rural areas, liberating farmers from the constraints of land ownership and facilitating the transition from traditional single-agricultural production to diversified rural economic development. A total of five professional cooperatives were established in Changlin Village, propelling the per capita income from 4000 yuan to 23,000 yuan in 2017.

2. Transforming a City: Rural Villages Blossom into Picturesque New Communities

The successful pilot project in Changlin Village infused vitality into the land of Chengdu, sparking a new era of comprehensive land improvement. Orchestrated by the municipal government and executed in harmony by various departments, this endeavor hinged on farmers' aspirations, resource integration, and the paramount goal of fostering coordinated urban and rural development. Gradually, this initiative flourished, akin to a vibrant tree with bountiful branches.

To convert land into capital and stimulate the capitalization of rural assets, as well as the unrestricted circulation of production elements, Chengdu Rural Property Exchange emerged in 2008. "Through land integration, the cleared indicators can be listed for trading on the rural property exchange, or serve as collateral for financing," elucidated a staff member from Chengdu Rural Property Exchange.

By June 2010, Chengdu City had issued 33,000 collective land ownership certificates to village groups, along with 1.78 million land contract and operation right certificates, 649,000 forest rights certificates, 1.657 million collective land use certificates, and 1.571 million house ownership certificates.

In the aftermath of the 2008 Wenchuan earthquake, Chengdu City transcended regional restrictions on indicator utilization, merging land integration with comprehensive land improvement. This fusion birthed a novel mechanism for streamlining agricultural land consolidation and construction land organization—where unified planning, separate project proposals, synchronous implementation, and separate acceptance converged. Consequently, the implementation of this mechanism not only expedited post-disaster reconstruction but also enabled numerous farmers to reap the benefits of land appreciation resulting from the transfer of collectively owned construction land.

From 2014 onwards, the construction of new villages in land integration project areas began to exhibit distinct features, fostering the development of small-scale, clustered, eco-friendly, and idyllic rural complexes. The decision-making process embraced a philosophy of "Let the villagers decide whether to build, and let them have a say in how to build," according to an official from Chengdu Land and Resources Bureau. During the project's inception, the village held numerous meetings, empowering the farmers to determine their participation in the land integration project, select new village plans and locations, design house types, and choose construction teams. This democratic decision-making mechanism, guided by governmental direction, expert consultations, and villagers' involvement, was established.

Throughout the project's implementation, the integration of land and the promotion of agricultural industrialization proceeded hand in hand. Property owners, large-scale farmers, and leading enterprises were encouraged to invest and develop, with farmers being guided towards transitioning into agricultural industry workers or shifting from agriculture to the secondary and tertiary sectors. This shift fostered diversified sources of income, ranging from land-dependent cultivation to rental income, wage-based employment, and dividends from shareholdings.

Over the past 12 years, one village after another has metamorphosed into joyful and picturesque new communities. From the front yards to the fields, from town streets to village paths, Chengdu has painted vibrant and captivating pictures of rural revitalization. With an investment totaling 60 billion yuan since 2006, Chengdu City has completed 770 land integration projects, with nearly 400 projects successfully concluded. Approximately 250,000 mu of land has been consolidated, while over 2000 centralized residential areas have been constructed, providing homes for more than 600,000 residents.

3. Paving a Path: Promoting Urban–Rural Integration through Land Consolidation

In Wuxing Village, Baitou Town, Chongzhou City, the landscape reveals rows of harmoniously arranged buildings, boasting white walls and gray tiles, as visitors meander through the thriving community surrounded by sprawling rice fields. As one of the key villages in the third phase of rural poverty alleviation and development, Wuxing Village, through the implementation of land integration policies, allows the natural beauty of the village to shine, while the annual per capita income of its residents has soared from 4000 yuan to 18,000 yuan.

Embracing the land integration policy as its cornerstone, Mingyue Village in Pujiang Ganxi Town, once an obscure and nameless hamlet, has transformed into a featured town covered by the CCTV Evening News and the People's Daily, capitalizing on the development approach of "agricultural innovation + cultural creativity."

In Ranyi Town, Qionglai City, the land integration project has created space for the construction of tens of thousands of mu of high-standard farmland. With the establishment of ten specialized land cooperatives, land circulation has been achieved, effectively resolving the question of who would cultivate the high-standard farmland after its construction. The formation of a land cooperative association has facilitated large-scale and standardized production, while the "Ranyi Royal Rice" brand has been established, earning market recognition through its commitment to high-quality products.

In the Dujiangyan City Qipan Village residential area, nestled within the enchanting valleys of pristine beauty, villagers no longer fret about muddying their feet or the perils of geological disasters. Today, they enjoy the convenience of amenities such as running water, electricity, natural gas, broadband, and telephone services. The community is further adorned with fitness equipment, basketball courts, community activity centers, newspaper stands, and libraries.

Over the past 12 years, Chengdu has embarked on a journey of urban–rural integration, with land integration serving as the driving force, cementing the foundation for rural development and fortifying the bond between the city and the countryside. By undertaking comprehensive improvements in agriculture, water resources, transportation, forestry, and villages, Chengdu has achieved homogeneity in the lives of urban and rural residents. Infusing the principles of "innovation, coordination, greenness, openness, and sharing" into land integration, the city has granted its residents the sight of mountains, the serenity of water, and the remembrance of cherished hometowns.

For the past 12 years, Chengdu's land integration policy, starting from Changlin Village, has steadily extended its reach. Hundreds of thousands of households residing in adobe houses across the vast land of Sichuan have found solace in the integration of land, dwelling in their own "little mansions." Endless green fields, interlacing rivers and canals, thriving crops, and greenhouse structures veiled amidst lush foliage—Sichuan, propelled by land integration, moves forward, ever guided by determination and adherence to the law.

> "Nowadays, the lives of many farmers are truly enviable, their yearning for nostalgia grows stronger," remarked a representative from the Sichuan Provincial Department. "This nostalgia is born out of farmers' gratitude for their lives and their longing for a better future."

In 2007, both the nation and the city of Chengdu unveiled comprehensive policies to synchronize urban and rural development, propelling the swift execution of "linking urban and rural construction land increase and decrease" projects. On June 7 of that year, the notification approving the establishment of national comprehensive pilot reform zones for coordinating urban and rural development in Chongqing and Chengdu was released by the National Development and Reform Commission (《国家发展改革委关于批准重庆市和成都市设立全国统筹城乡综合配套改革试验区的通知》).

The directive mandated both cities to pragmatically advance systemic reforms across various domains, encompassing theoretical research and innovative practices concerning rural property rights systems, including national and collective land ownership, state-owned and collective land use rights. The objective was to lead by example and provide a nationwide demonstration. Consequently, the Chengdu Municipal Party Committee and Municipal Government subsequently introduced the "Opinions on Promoting the Construction of Comprehensive Pilot Reform Zones for Coordinating Urban and Rural Development (《关于推进统筹城乡综合配套改革试验区建设的意见》)," stipulating the exploration of a unified urban and rural land market. This would facilitate autonomous transactions and transfers of collective construction land within the tangible land market, aligning it with state-owned land in terms of location, value, and rights. This initiative aimed to achieve "two types of ownership, one market" and serve as a vital measure to guide the adjustment of urban and rural land structures, optimize their layout, and promote efficient and harmonized urban and rural development.

To address the scarcity of funds for urban development and establish a financing platform for modern agriculture and new rural construction, Chengdu officially sanctioned the formation of Chengdu Small Town Investment Co., Ltd. on March 26, 2007, with a registered capital of 100 million yuan. Additionally, Chengdu Huinong Investment Construction Co., Ltd. was established on July 10, 2007, as a wholly state-owned subsidiary of the Chengdu Pixian County State-owned Assets Supervision and Administration Office.

Inspired by external experiences and motivated by relevant policies, Zhanqi Village voluntarily stepped forward to become a pilot for reform, implementing comprehensive land treatment projects through market-oriented mechanisms. On July 2, 2007, fourteen rural new community construction projects submitted by nine districts and counties, including Pixian County, Xinjin County, and Chongzhou City, became the inaugural projects initiated by the Small Town Investment Company. Among them, the pioneering rural new community construction projects in Zhanqi Village of Tangchang Town, Pixian County, Xinping Town of Xinjin County, and Qiquan Town of Chongzhou City took the lead as pilot projects.

Zhanqi Village's successful application for the project owed much to the heightened visibility it gained from the previous "University Students Visiting Rural Families" campaign. In the first half of 2006, Pixian County launched an "Cultural experiment between urban and rural interaction" to propel the "University Students Visiting Rural Families" initiative. The endeavor aimed to establish enduring mechanisms for the interactive development of "universities—party branches—rural families," "universities—party branches—enterprises," and "universities—party branches—agricultural industrialization." Despite the county's extensive search for pilot villages, the progress had remained stagnant. In truth, when policies descended to the rural areas for implementing specific tasks in education, healthcare, culture, and other sectors, the challenge of high transaction costs loomed, amplified by the "de-organization" of previous efforts. The "University Students Visiting Rural Families" initiative faced a similar obstacle. Numerous villages aspired to be selected as pilot sites to reap the benefits of institutional advancement. However, most lacked the necessary mass foundation and operational capacity to undertake such endeavors. Yet, even though Zhanqi Village was still in the early stages of collective economic reconstruction and relatively unknown, it possessed a robust collective economic foundation and political mobilization capabilities. For the grassroots governmental departments, it presented a pivotal lever to swiftly achieve tangible outcomes at minimal cost. Consequently, the Tangchang Town Government recommended Zhanqi Village as a pilot project to the county government.

For Zhanqi Village, the experiences of studying DaZhai and organizing militia work during previous politically charged competitions taught them to align themselves with the policy direction and leverage the system. They swiftly recognized the opportunity to transform the villagers' mindset and promote the village's reputation. They understood the profound significance it held for pursuing advantageous political opportunities in the village's future development. In the minutes of the village committee meeting on April 28, 2006, Li Shili asserted, "This activity will play a tremendous role in constructing a socialist new rural area, generating a considerable impact throughout the village, particularly in terms of ideology and culture." Recalling his interview with Gao Demin, Li further shared, "The leaders asked me if we wanted to organize the 'University Students + Party Branches + Farmers' initiative to propel the development of the new rural area. More than 300 people participated. I replied affirmatively, recognizing the significant impact that over 300 individuals would have on Zhanqi Village. They inquired about the subsidy required for the initiative, to which I responded that none was needed." The village cadres of Zhanqi Village comprehended that the promotional benefits derived from this activity surpassed what could be achieved with a substantial advertising budget. Subsequently, the village cadres convened meetings with team leaders, party members, and villagers to prepare for accommodating university students in rural homes.

During the Labor Day holiday in 2006, 365 college students from institutions such as Xihua University and Sichuan Normal University Chengdu College resided with rural households in Zhanqi Village, sharing meals, accommodations, and labor for 5 days. On average, each household in Groups 1–9 hosted two university students. Throughout the activity, the students toured five village-owned enterprises, diligently maintained daily diaries, performed meaningful tasks for the farmers each day, captured a photograph alongside their paired farming families, and diligently completed social practice activity logs. They also motivated the farmers to participate in radio calisthenics, aided in tidying the environment within the households' yards, and assisted in tutoring children. Through their actions and presence, they served as guides, encouraging the farmers to cultivate civilized habits and lifestyles. The university students organized diverse training activities, including dance, calligraphy, English, Mandarin, and even driving lessons. They held debates with the theme of "Which holds greater importance, promoting civility or achieving prosperity," prompting profound contemplation among the villagers regarding their lives and production. Simultaneously, the students offered consultation services on law, animal husbandry, computers, and distributed over 1000 informative materials. The director of the Chengdu Municipal Party Committee's Propaganda Department arranged for Sichuan's "comedian" Li Boqing to perform alongside the villagers, enriching the cultural lives of the rural community. Amidst this open exchange, the university students learned firsthand about the farmers' industriousness, kindness, and simplicity, fostering their practical skills while basking in the villagers' authenticity and warmth.

Praise poured in from all quarters for this event, hailed as an "cultural experiment in urban–rural interaction." The County Committee Propaganda Department lauded the "university + party branch + rural household" approach as a tangible and vibrant embodiment of urban support for rural areas, a crucial step towards seamless urban–rural integration. It even garnered recognition as one of the top ten innovative initiatives in national governance. With each passing day, the villagers felt like they were celebrating the New Year, their spirits uplifted. Experts, too, openly expressed their admiration, delving into the theoretical and practical facets of the event, leaving no stone unturned.

Since its inception, save for an interruption in 2008 due to an earthquake, Zhanqi Village has witnessed an annual influx of 60–100 college students during summer vacations. They immerse themselves in the rural lifestyle for approximately twenty days, living and dining alongside the local farmers. The village provides financial support, granting each household a subsidy ranging from 200 to 300 yuan. As the year 2010 marked the villagers' consolidation in one area, the college students no longer resided in their homes. Alternative accommodations were arranged within the village, ensuring their continued presence.

The impact of this endeavor extends in two directions. Firstly, within the village, it stimulated a remarkable transformation in the mindset of its inhabitants, laying the foundation for the implementation of the "demolishing and rebuilding courtyards" initiative. The college students infused the villagers with novel knowledge and ideas, fostering improved lifestyles and cultural enrichment. Consequently, the chasm of ideological, spiritual, and cultural disparities between urban and rural areas narrowed. Notably, the village's environmental hygiene witnessed a marked improvement. Li Shili, too, attested to this transformative change, stating, "The village's 'three concentrations' implementation has greatly increased the villagers' acceptance and enthusiasm for 'demolishing and rebuilding courtyards.' It has propelled the development model of interactive operations between the village, enterprises, and farmers in Zhanqi Village, bolstering the organizational efficiency of agricultural production."

Secondly, the endeavor reverberated beyond the village, igniting a surge of support. Although the activity did not directly align with the "demolishing and rebuilding courtyards" project, it propelled Zhanqi Village to the forefront, resuscitating its illustrious reputation and laying the groundwork for its designation as a pilot demonstration area. Leveraging the village's newfound prominence, the government seized the opportunity to amplify the influence of this pilot project. According to an interview with Li Shili, high-ranking officials, including the Secretary of the Chengdu Municipal Party Committee, visited Zhanqi Village before the 2007 Spring Festival. Li Shili presented a comprehensive village plan based on previous unfinished blueprints, outlining strategies to address employment and income concerns following the "villagers move upstairs" initiative. The utilization of existing village enterprises and the introduction of external businesses aimed to reduce the institutional costs associated with "demolishing and rebuilding courtyards" and land consolidation. The officials expressed satisfaction with Zhanqi Village's diligent preparations for this endeavor.

Post the Spring Festival of 2007, on the first working day of the Chengdu Municipal Party Committee and the Municipal Government, a rural work conference was convened. Zhanqi Village was selected as a pilot site for the "new rural community construction project." Thus, the "demolishing and rebuilding courtyards" work commenced that same year. Notably, in 2016, the Pixian County was dissolved, and the Chengdu Pixian District was established, as per the announcement on the website of the Sichuan Provincial People's Government.

From January to August 2007, Zhanqi Village embarked on propaganda, mobilization, housing preference surveys, design plan development, and planning. The majority of the villagers resided in dilapidated houses, yearning for the affordable luxury of modern residential areas. Some hesitated, approximately 20% of rural households, due to concerns such as the recent construction of their own homes, apprehensions regarding inconveniences in agricultural activities, or the high cost of housing. In response, the village provided economic compensation, implemented centralized land management, and introduced external companies to address employment challenges. With the collective effort of numerous villagers and village cadres, the concerns of this hesitant group were eventually resolved.

In August 2007, the "new rural community construction" project in Zhanqi Village commenced officially. It received approval and implementation from the Provincial Land and Resources Department. All nine village groups participated in the ambitious "demolishing and rebuilding courtyards" endeavor. The project focused primarily on constructing low-rise residential buildings in a self-built neighborhood, complemented by multi-story apartment buildings. Commencing in August 2007, extensive consultations were held with villagers to determine the ideal sites for the new community. Ultimately, the decision was made to construct the new community on the elevated and easily accessible lands of Groups 2, 4, 8, and a portion of Group 3. Compensation was provided to farmers within the designated construction areas, adhering to stipulated guidelines. Farmers who opted for multi-story apartments received a transitional allowance until the handover of their new homes, while those who chose self-built houses received a monthly stipend for 6 months. Throughout the transition period, farmers were responsible for resolving their housing and related living issues. The majority negotiated with the village, finding temporary accommodation in vacant houses within the village.

The project faced a temporary setback in 2008 due to the devastating "5.12" earthquake. Construction came to a halt for 2–3 months, resuming only in March 2009. Eventually, the splendid Zhanqi New Community, spanning an area of 91,000 square meters, was completed. Following the previously agreed-upon allocation plan, villagers drew lots for their new residences starting in April 2009. By the end of that year, the majority had settled into their new homes. A total of 469 households (1655 people) found solace in the community, achieving a remarkable 96% concentration rate. It is worth noting that the remaining households were located on the outskirts of the community, along the adjacent roads, falling outside the scope of land consolidation.

The project resulted in the consolidation of the villagers' original residential lands and courtyards, securing an additional 440.8 mu (29.39 hectares) of construction land indicators. Following rigorous scrutiny by the Provincial Land and Resources Department, 215 mu (14.33 hectares) were allocated for the construction of the Zhanqi residential area and its accompanying infrastructure. An additional 208 mu (13.87 hectares) were designated as arable land. Once the inspection and acceptance were completed, these construction land indicators were seamlessly linked to urban use, generating a staggering land transfer revenue of 130 million yuan. After repaying financing costs amounting to 115 million yuan, the remaining 15 million yuan was predominantly allocated to the construction of the necessary infrastructure in the Zhanqi Modern Agricultural Industrial Park, facilitated through government subsidies and other means.[12] However, according to Gao Demin's interview on October 2, 2009, referencing the approximate price of 1.8 million yuan per mu in certain villages, the 208 mu of construction.

land indicators should have yielded approximately 360 million yuan in land transfer revenue. Regrettably, Zhanqi Village only received slightly over 90 million yuan.

In addition to Changlin Village and Zhanqi Village in Pixian County, statistics reveal that between 2006 and 2008, Chengdu City embarked on 15 linked projects, collectively applying for 6980.23 mu (465.35 hectares) of linked transfer land indicators. Among these, 1649.01 mu (109.94 hectares) were dedicated to rural resettlement areas, while 5331.22 mu (355.41 hectares) were allocated to replacement areas. These linked projects facilitated the migration of 7578 rural residents (totaling 24,869 people) to new communities. The cumulative investment in these 15 linked projects within rural areas amounted to 800 million yuan, averaging 150,000 yuan per mu of increased urban land usage. The highest price per mu reached 600,000 yuan, while the lowest stood at 120,000 yuan. On average, each farmer reaped a profit of 32,000 yuan from the appreciation of land values. Although six of these projects remained confined within the administrative boundaries of a single town, and none extended beyond the limits of a single county, they achieved significant differentials in land rents within a limited geographic scope. This approach represents one of the most effective ways for Chengdu City to actively share the benefits of urbanization land with rural areas and farmers, operating within the framework of the prevailing land expropriation system. Not only does it align with the central government's policy directives in recent years, but it also serves as a practical starting point for Chengdu's comprehensive reform efforts and the harmonization of urban–rural development.

Figure 3 visually illustrates the operational process of the new community project.

12 Source: Tangchang Town People's Government of Pixian County Document (Tang Govt. [2014] No. 78): "Report on the Construction of New Rural Community in Zhanqi Village."

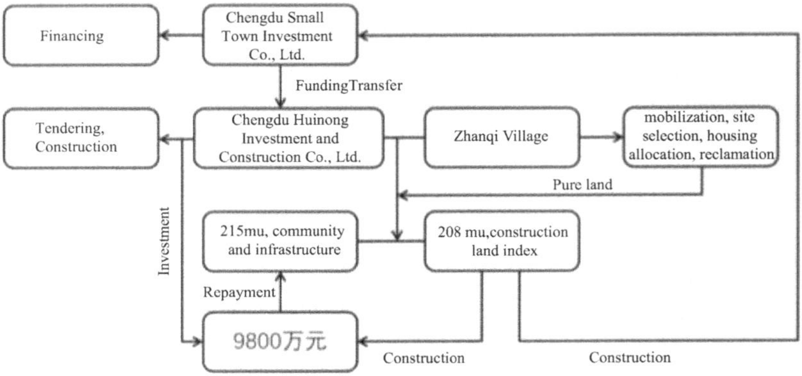

Fig. 3 Operational process of the new community project. 融资Financing, 成都市小城镇投资有限公司Chengdu Small Town Investment Co., Ltd., 划拨资金Funding Transfer, 招标、建设Tendering, Construction, 成都市惠农投资建设有限责任公司Chengdu Huinong Investment and Construction Co., Ltd., 战旗村Zhanqi Village, 215亩, 小区及基础设施215 mu, community and infrastructure, 208亩, 指标增减挂钩208 mu, construction land index, 投资Investment, 动员、选址、分房、复垦mobilization, site selection, housing allocation, reclamation, 净地Pure land, 偿还Repayment, 建设Construction

* * *

Zhanqi Village: The Project for a New Rural Community

The responsibility of investing in the "New Community Construction Project" falls upon Chengdu Small Town Investment Co., Ltd. (referred to as Small Town Investment Company), while the project owners are the respective branch institutions in each district (city) and county, with Chengdu Huinong Investment Construction Co., Ltd. (referred to as Huinong Company) acting as the project owner for Zhanqi Village. Small Town Investment Company allocates funds to Huinong Company in stages, and it is the latter's duty as the project owner to handle the tendering process and oversee the construction of the new district.

The estimated total cost of the "Demolition and Reconstruction of Courtyard Houses" project in Zhanqi Village amounts to 95.518 million yuan, expecting to yield an additional 244.7 mu of arable land. For each mu of newly acquired land, an investment of 390,300 yuan is required. The budget is outlined as follows:

1. In accordance with the implementation of Document No. 45 issued by the county government in 2005, the cost for demolition subsidies of rural courtyard houses and attached structures is estimated at 29.871 million yuan. On average, each household will receive a subsidy of 63,700 yuan, with a per capita subsidy of 19,100 yuan. Regarding the demolition of rural houses, the self-demolition method is adopted, and the standards for demolition subsidies for houses and attached structures are in line with the regulations set forth in Document No. 45 issued by the county government in 2005. Firstly, concerning the housing aspect, subsidies for building demolitions require the dismantling of 33,080 square meters of buildings. Based on a subsidy rate of 280 yuan per square meter, the financial demand amounts to 9.2624 million yuan. As for single-story house demolitions, it is necessary to dismantle 63,324 square meters of such houses. With a subsidy rate of 240 yuan per square meter, the funds needed reach 15.1978 million yuan. For demolishing general houses, covering an area of 7278 square meters, the subsidy standard of 100 yuan per square meter calls for a budget of 727,800 yuan. Additionally, concerning attached structures and seedlings, a total subsidy of 4.683 million yuan is required, calculated at 3000 yuan per person.
2. The total cost for constructing new community housing and providing subsidy funds is estimated at 11.57 million yuan. The calculations are based on the following factors: one-person households, two-person households, and 50% of three-person households will reside in multi-story apartment buildings, while four-person households and those with more than four members will occupy low-rise attached buildings. The per capita floor area for low-rise attached buildings is calculated at 45 square meters, and the government subsidizes 80 yuan per square meter (floor area) for architectural style development. Multi-story apartment buildings, on the other hand, have a per capita floor area of 40 square meters. The unified construction cost for multi-story apartments is estimated at 700 yuan per square meter, whereas farmers purchase at a rate of 300 yuan per square meter. According to the data provided by Zhanqi Village, there are 40 households in multi-story apartment

buildings, including 1-person households (40 households), 2-person households (80 households), and 3-person households (185 households). Consequently, approximately 480 individuals will reside in multi-story apartment buildings, necessitating a government subsidy of 7.68 million yuan [(480 × 40 × (700–300))]. At that time, with a total population of 1561, the cost for low-rise attached buildings amounted to roughly 3.89 million yuan [((1561–480) × 45 × 80)]. Thus, the grand total reaches around 11.57 million yuan.

3. The construction of internal roads, supporting facilities, and the reclamation of courtyards within the community requires approximately 21.887 million yuan.
4. External infrastructure development, such as village roads and water conservancy, and other financial needs amount to around 32.19 million yuan. In accordance with the regulations stated in the Chengdu Municipal Bureau of Land and Resources' "Opinions on Regulating the Consolidation and Concentrated Use of Non-Urban Construction Land in the Central Urban Area," the land released by Zhanqi Village can only be used within the range of Tangchang Town. However, due to the land prices in Tangchang Town in 2007, it is challenging to achieve a balance between land index benefits and investment funds. Consequently, Tangchang Town has adopted a phased implementation approach. Priority is given to the construction of internal infrastructure within the new community, while other basic facilities in the village are gradually improved after a specific amount of special funds become available.[13]

From 2007 to 2009, Zhanqi Village received a total investment of 98 million yuan in batches from Small Town Investment Company. This capital was employed to implement comprehensive land improvement and construct the new community. Expenditures primarily consisted of a 52.9 million yuan construction cost for the new community (300 yuan per square meter for apartments and 480 yuan per square meter for villas), nearly 20 million yuan for supporting infrastructure construction, 29.02 million yuan for farmers' relocation compensation (with a maximum

[13] Source: Tangchang Town People's Government of Pixian County Document (Tangfu Fa [2007] No. 23): "Tangchang Town People's Government's Request for the Demolition and Relocation Plan of Zhanqi Village's 'Demolition and Reconstruction of Courtyard Houses'."

compensation rate of 280 yuan per square meter for their original houses), and 2.99 million yuan for land reclamation and consolidation (once the land was reclaimed and assessed by a third-party organization, reclamation fees were then paid).

The construction of the new community commenced in August 2007, focusing on the independent construction of low-rise attached buildings (villas) as the primary housing option, with multi-story apartment buildings as secondary. Villagers were free to choose their preferred housing types and collectively registered with the village committee, determining the allocation proportion of low-rise attached buildings and multi-story apartment buildings based on the number of registrations. Farmers independently constructed their new houses by building or designated areas. Relevant households established "homeowners' committees" and acted as the construction parties, signing agreements with construction units to undertake the building process. Each household was also required to provide a deposit of 2000 yuan. Simultaneously, efforts were made to engage and persuade a portion of the population while construction progressed, adhering to the principle of "repairing one building after convincing one household."

After a construction halt of over 2 months following the Wenchuan earthquake in 2008, thorough technical surveys were conducted on all buildings. Any structures failing to meet the requirements were demolished and reconstructed, resulting in a significant increase in construction costs.

By March 2009, the new community was essentially completed, resulting in the establishment of the 91,000-square-meter Zhanqi New Community. It encompassed 401 sets of standardized self-built low-rise attached buildings (villas) with a total floor area of 76,200 square meters. These included three household types:

5-person households (260 square meters), 4-person households (220 square meters), and 3-person households (170 square meters). Farmers purchased the houses at a rate of 400 yuan per square meter, while the government subsidized 80 yuan per square meter (floor area) for architectural style development. Moreover, 171 sets of standardized multi-story apartment buildings were constructed, with a total floor area of 14,200 square meters. These consisted of two household types: 2-person households (80 square meters) and 1-person households (40 square meters). Farmers acquired these houses at a rate of 300 yuan per square meter. Following compensation for demolition and relocation, farmers' income and expenses were effectively balanced. Approximately 10% of families (primarily the elderly) chose apartments, while the remaining 90% opted for villas. Among those who chose villas, 80% of farmers selected the 3-person household type. After the earthquake, construction costs increased by 50 yuan per square meter, but the amount paid by the farmers remained unchanged. In theory, each permanent resident was entitled to a housing index of 35 square meters. Any excess area was evaluated based on the comprehensive cost per unit area of the apartment buildings. However, due to varying economic capacities and housing needs among households, indices could be traded internally between families. Over a dozen households engaged in index trading, starting at 10,000 yuan per square meter and eventually reaching 13,000 yuan per square meter. Furthermore, Secretary Li Shili foresaw the future rise of car ownership among the younger generation, even though few villagers owned cars at the time. Consequently, each villa included a garage.

Once the community was completed, the house allocation process began in April 2009 (the discussion on allocation methods had commenced in 2008). To ensure unanimity among household members and achieve fairness, justice, and transparency, each household was required to provide a receipt proving that 40% of the construction payment had been made. The allocation order was determined through a lottery system, and specific house positions were assigned based on newly drawn lot numbers. For three-person households (two-story) and four-person households (two-story), distribution occurred within designated concentrated areas. Other household types were uniformly allocated throughout the entire community. The house allocation process concluded on April 10, 2009.

On January 11, 2020, Li Shili remarked during an interview, "When organizing the house allocation, the rule was that you had to pay the money in full before being eligible for the lottery. The lottery took place on the stage in the cultural courtyard, and we had representatives from the notary office to supervise the process. Seven boxes represented different types of houses. When it was your turn, the designated person would guide you to participate in the lottery, and after drawing, you would accompany the staff to the finance department for registration. Only during the registration process could the number be revealed."

Source: interview record with Li Shili on January 11, 2020.

However, various circumstances, including the devastating Wenchuan earthquake, exerted their influence on on-site construction, leading to additional unforeseen expenses for the construction companies in each section. Initially, the winning bid for self-built houses stood at 480 yuan per square meter. However, factors such as material price hikes resulted in an additional 58.49 yuan per square meter. Moreover, there were additional costs of 1.5 million yuan for deepening the foundations, soil backfilling, repairing earthquake-damaged firewalls, and implementing "three connections and one leveling." The construction companies repeatedly sought a clear payment method for this portion of funds. After negotiations, Zhanqi Village managed to raise over 700,000 yuan, while the remaining amount was invested by Huinong Company. Unfortunately, as the contract did not account for risks arising from force majeure, the implementation proved to be a formidable challenge. Zhanqi Village had made substantial contributions to the new rural construction, leaving them incapable of bearing this financial burden. Moreover, it was not feasible for the community homeowners to gather the necessary funds. The town faced significant financial constraints and was unable to resolve the issue promptly, resulting in delayed responses to the construction companies. Consequently, the companies reported losses, hindering their cooperation in the subsequent handover and rectification processes. This, in turn, caused a delay in the fulfillment of the demolition compensation, as per the agreement, leading some farmers to resort to petitioning the town.

Following the distribution of houses, there remained 14 unoccupied apartments, all of which belonged to Huinong Company, the project owner.

Zhanqi Village invested 430,000 yuan in constructing a cultural courtyard in 2006, while an additional 350,000 yuan went towards greening and appearance transformation. Furthermore, the relocation and construction of a new brewery within the new community site required a substantial investment of 1.89 million yuan. In March 2007, the village incurred various expenses, amounting to a total of 780,000 yuan, for planning and designing the new community, conducting surveys to gage villagers' preferences, sealing off houses for inspection, and demolishing courtyards within the construction site. Regrettably, both companies and the cultural courtyard suffered damages due to the Wenchuan earthquake. Reconstructing the cultural courtyard alone required a staggering sum of over 2 million yuan. Additionally, substantial funding was necessary for public services and social management after the residents moved into the new community. The total required funds surpassed 5.5 million yuan, leaving a substantial shortfall. Consequently, on May 6, 2009, the village committee applied to the Tangchang Town People's Government, requesting that the remaining apartments be transferred to the village and managed as collective assets. The generated income would then be utilized to address the village's funding gap.

During the house distribution, some dwellings were not yet fully renovated. Consequently, the earliest move-ins occurred within a month. For others, occupancy was delayed until the second half of 2009, with most residents settled by the end of that year. A small number of households only managed to move in at the beginning of 2010.

Farmers within the new community site were required to relocate by June 30, 2007, as stipulated in the agreement. Farmers outside the construction site commenced the demolition of their old houses only after the distribution of houses in the new community. Their relocation period was set at 3 months from the date of handover. Farmers failing to complete the relocation within the specified timeframe would face the village committee's intervention for demolition, which would be organized according to village rules and regulations. The costs incurred would be borne by the farmers, calculated at a rate of 10 yuan per square meter based on the total area of the demolished houses. This amount could be offset against the unpaid portion of the total demolition compensation. Alternatively, if affected individuals completed the demolition and relocation within the agreed timeframe or agreed in writing to relinquish their property to the town government without compensation, they would receive a one-time demolition fee reward of 500 yuan per household, subject to acceptance inspection. Nonetheless, due to personal reasons, some farmers were reluctant to relocate, resulting in a nearly year-long delay in the demolition process.

The project successfully fulfilled the farmers' aspiration for affordable housing. Each household paid the actual construction cost of 34.41 million yuan, with 29.02 million yuan deducted as demolition compensation. Consequently, the average payment per household amounted to approximately 1.15 million yuan [(34.41 − 29.02) ÷ 469]. In terms of housing expenses, farmers' investments constituted a mere 5% of the total investment. The completed houses were minimally furnished with basic fixtures, including wall finishes and kitchen and bathroom facilities. For villagers residing in multi-story apartment buildings, a personal investment of a few thousand to tens of thousands of yuan was sufficient to furnish their homes. As for villagers who constructed low-rise attached houses following uniform standards, the housing payments they made and the subsidies received (with a maximum compensation of 280 yuan per square meter for the original houses) offset each other. In summary, one-third of households had to contribute tens of thousands of yuan from their own pockets, while one-third managed to break even. Regarding decoration and furniture, villagers allocated their investments based on their economic circumstances and personal preferences. Some villagers chose not to invest or made minimal contributions, whereas others, with better income, spent over ten thousand yuan to enhance their living environment.

As the land utilization pattern underwent changes, the village's organizational structure was also adjusted. Following the concentration of residences, villagers were regrouped based on proximity for the sake of effective management. Previously, groups had rights pertaining to land operation. However, these rights were now centralized under the village, with group powers transitioning towards public affairs such as community management, policy promotion, environmental sanitation, and conflict resolution. Additionally, before 2009, surplus income generated by each group was handled and distributed within the group. However, starting in 2009, a unified accounting system for village-wide income and expenses was implemented, eliminating the limitations imposed by groups.

The project further enhanced various supporting infrastructure facilities. It encompassed 1200 square meters of green space, 6 kilometers of hardened roads with delineated lanes, 10 kilometers of asphalt roads, and an 8-kilometer standardized canal system. Main roads throughout the village were equipped with streetlights and traffic signals. Public busses now traversed the new community, showcasing a renewed appearance characterized by cleanliness, accessible roads, clean water, and picturesque scenery. Concurrently, the new community witnessed the construction of complementary facilities such as kindergartens, supermarkets, convenience service centers, and health stations, spanning over 2000 square meters. Villagers gained access to clean energy sources, including fiber optics, tap water, and natural gas, while enjoying convenient services such as kindergartens, markets, supermarkets, and public transportation. Furthermore, post-disaster reconstruction efforts encompassed the construction of fundamental infrastructure, including the cultural courtyard. The "Three New Homes" demonstration project significantly narrowed the gap in public services between urban and rural areas, promoting the simultaneous transformation of farmers' living and production methods. It marked an initial step towards achieving urban–rural integration and substantially increased the property value within the village, thereby strengthening the political trust of villagers in their collective community.

Source: Tangchang Town People's Government, Pixian County, Documents (Tangfu [2014] No. 78): "Report on the Construction of New Rural Areas in Zhanqi Village by Tangchang Town People's Government"; Tangchang Town People's Government, Pixian County, Documents (Tangfu Fa [2007] No. 23): "Request for Approval of the Demolition and Resettlement Plan for 'Demolish Courtyards and Combine Houses' in Zhanqi Village by Tangchang Town People's Government"; "Demolition Compensation and Housing Placement Agreement for Zhanqi Village's New Community Demolition and Relocation"; Tangchang Town People's Government, May 21, 2009: "Report on the Factors Affecting the Stability of Zhanqi New Community Housing Distribution"; Interviews with Gao Demin and others.

* * *

The Five Major Investment and Financing Platforms in Pixian County

1. Chengdu Huinong Investment Construction Co., Ltd.

   In 2010, Chengdu Huinong Investment Construction Co., Ltd. (referred to as Huinong Company) established seven departments, including the General Department, Finance Department, Project Department 1, Project Department 2, Contract Department, Engineering Department, and Insurance Department, with a total of 32 staff members. Huinong Company's wholly-owned subsidiary, Chengdu Huinong Property Rights Transfer Guarantee Co., Ltd., was renamed Chengdu Huinong Property Rights Transfer Financing Guarantee Co., Ltd. (referred to as Guarantee Company) in December 2010, approved by the Financial Office of the People's Government of Sichuan Province. The two companies operate under the model of "two brands and one team." Since their establishment, under the leadership of the County State-owned Assets Administration, Huinong Company and Guarantee Company have strictly followed the requirements of the County Agricultural Investment Construction Project Investment Review Committee, promoting the construction of the comprehensive demonstration belt of urban and rural integration in Pixian County.

Huinong Company and Guarantee Company held two County Agricultural Investment Review Committee meetings in 2010, reviewing and approving a total of 19 agricultural projects involving Huinong Company and Guarantee Company, with a total amount of 605.787 million yuan. On July 28, 2010, the ninth meeting of the County Agricultural Investment Review Committee was held, reviewing and approving 14 sub-projects of two major categories of agricultural investment, including six financing, guarantee, entrusted loan, and investment projects of Huinong Company, and eight guarantee projects of Guarantee Company. On November 16 of the same year, the tenth meeting of the County Agricultural Investment Review Committee was held, reviewing and approving five agricultural guarantee projects.

In response to the financing situation, Huinong Company has innovated its work measures and adopted an operating model of "project + village-level asset management company + district (city) county guarantee network + bank." It fully utilizes the results of the rural reform and uses rural collective construction land and other rural property rights as collateral for financing. At the same time, it continues to strengthen cooperation with municipal-level platform companies and financial institutions, actively packaging projects in accordance with the modern agricultural development plan of Pixian County, and strives to obtain funding from various sources to support agricultural projects related to the construction of a new rural area, agricultural industrialization, and comprehensive improvement of agricultural land in Pixian County. By the end of 2010, Huinong Company had raised a total of 392.27 million yuan through direct financing, guarantee loans, and other methods.

Huinong Company has raised funds through cooperation and coordination with municipal-level platform companies and financial institutions, using various methods such as credit, direct investment, and guarantee. It has raised a total of 223.4 million yuan for high-quality agricultural projects in the "Shaxi Line" and IT industries, as well as for the land comprehensive improvement projects of Tangchang Town's Zhanqi Village and Xinminchang Town's Yunling Village, the construction of large-scale grain and oil demonstration bases in Pixian County, comprehensive improvement of rural land in the Shaxi Line, rural specialized cooperatives, and loans for farmers' independent entrepreneurship.

In 2010, Huinong Company completed a total fixed asset investment of 45.396 million yuan. Firstly, the construction project of the new community in Yunling Village, Xinminchang Town, with an investment of 18 million yuan, was completed. Secondly, the construction project of the new community in Yongquan Village, Huayuan Town, with an investment of 15 million yuan, was completed. Thirdly, the standardized construction project of grass-roots agricultural service stations, with an investment of 12.01 million yuan, has been completed, and the agricultural service stations in Tangyuan, Xinminchang, Sandaoyan, Gucheng, Deyuan, Hongguang, and You'ai towns have been transferred to the Agricultural Development Bureau. Fourthly, the road infrastructure construction project of Phase III of the park in Xinminchang Town was completed with an investment of 386,000 yuan.

In addition, in accordance with the spirit of relevant documents from the central government, province, and city regarding tight monetary policies and strict control of government debt, the company adheres to the principle of "government promotion, financial subsidies, market operation, voluntary participation by farmers, and shared responsibility." It carries out policy agricultural insurance work for sow breeding, market hogs, rice, and rapeseed. In 2010, a total of 101,357 mu of rice, 55,825 mu of drought-prone areas, 34,424 mu of rapeseed, 24,292 market hogs, and 7031 sows were insured in the county.

2. Chengdu Pixian State-owned Assets Investment and Operation Co., Ltd.

In 2010, Chengdu Pixian State-owned Assets Investment and Operation Co., Ltd. (referred to as Pixian State-owned Assets Company) as a wholly state-owned company performing the responsibilities of the capital contributor of the Pixian State-owned Assets Administration, completed a financing task of 870.4 million yuan. It has four departments: Finance Department, Project Department, Asset Operation Department, and General Department, with 32 employees. The company has effectively performed its role in capital aggregation and made positive contributions to the construction of infrastructure, public welfare facilities, and public facilities throughout the county.

The company adheres to the "three cores" approach (with "courage" as the core, it is good at investing tomorrow's money in the construction of infrastructure, exchanging today's development; with "innovation" as the core, it forms a virtuous cycle of project resource lock-in, resource-to-fund conversion, and fund-driven project construction; with "approach" as the core, it establishes a financing platform, improves the legal person governance structure, and strengthens the regulatory system) and operates in accordance with the requirements of the modern enterprise system, adapting to market-oriented operation, and advancing project investment and financing work in accordance with the law and procedures.

In terms of investment, the company completed fixed asset investments of 823 million yuan in 2010. The main projects include Pixian Hospital, Ande Tap Water Plant, Pixian Second Hospital, Jiaxiang Foreign Language School Pixian Branch, Pixian No. 4 Middle School, Chengxi Road reconstruction, small watershed pollution control, Wangcong resettlement garden in Pitong Town, Tangchang Town Mingfeng resettlement community, Hongyang Road, Xili Road, and affordable housing.

3. Chengdu Xihui Urban Construction Co., Ltd.

In 2010, Chengdu Xihui Urban Construction Co., Ltd. (referred to as Xihui Company) continued to serve as the main urban investment and construction entity and investment and financing platform enterprise. It operated in accordance with the state-owned system and market mechanisms, guided by the ideas of "government guidance, market mechanisms, and enterprise operation." It earnestly implemented the investment and construction of resettlement housing, affordable housing, and low-rent housing within Pixian County, as well as the investment and construction and management of urban infrastructure and public welfare facilities, investment and construction of sewage treatment plants and drainage networks, and investment and construction of urban service projects (such as hospitals, archives, etc.), as well as land development and commercial housing development projects.

By the end of 2010, Xihui Company's assets exceeded 10 billion yuan, with five subsidiary companies: Chengdu Beikong Shudu Investment Co., Ltd., Sichuan Huimei Real Estate Co., Ltd., Chengdu Cooperation Sewage Treatment Co., Ltd., Pixian Xihui 398 Hospital Co., Ltd., and Pixian Chengjiao Investment Co., Ltd.

The company earnestly implemented the major decisions and work arrangements of the county party committee and county government, carried out the strategic approach of "project-driven and investment-led," and made unremitting efforts to promote the construction of Pixian County as a "demonstration county for one city, two belts, and three bases, an ideal livable and business-friendly modern countryside." At the same time, the company adheres to the core values of "doing things well," seizes opportunities, strives hard, builds core competitiveness, promotes the healthy and sustainable development of the company, and actively contributes to the construction of a livable and business-friendly modern countryside and the economic and social development of Pixian County.

In the context of the tightening of national monetary policy and strict control of government debt, the company adheres to the innovative financing approach of "walking on multiple legs." It has established a multi-level financing structure and diversified financing channels, enhances communication and coordination with various financial institutions, and has successfully cooperated with provincial and domestic financial institutions such as Bohai International Trust, China Railway Trust, Jilin Bank, Zhejiang Merchants Bank, Chengdu Agricultural Commercial Bank, and Chengdu Bank in trust products, trust loans, and other business cooperation.

In 2010, the company completed a financing of 1.46 billion yuan, meeting the funding needs of the company's land consolidation, resettlement housing construction, and infrastructure construction, providing financial support for the urban construction of Pixian County. It completed fixed asset investments of 934 million yuan, completed the construction of 227,500 square meters of housing (including Xichi Community, Juancheng Community, and Jinyuan Phase II projects), completed 380.86 mu of land consolidation, and exceeded the targets set by the county party committee and county government. At the same time, the company actively sought support funds, obtaining 10 million yuan in central government financial support for the second phase of the cooperation sewage treatment plant project and 8 million yuan in support funds for the comprehensive archives building project in the central and Western regions.

In addition, the company invested in land consolidation and sporadic land development. As of December 2010, the company had completed a total of 3566.78 mu of land consolidation. The company also invested in the construction of urban infrastructure and public welfare facilities (such as the Zitong Road in Longzi District and Chengdu Cooperation Sewage Treatment Plant), and new housing projects.

4. Chengdu Gangtong Investment and Development Co., Ltd.

Chengdu Gangtong Investment and Development Co., Ltd. (referred to as Gangtong Company) has developed over the past 5 years. By the end of 2010, its total assets had exceeded 3.9 billion yuan. The positioning of Gangtong Company's functions by the Pixian County Party Committee and County Government is to serve the promotion of the "new industrial base." Its main responsibilities include the collection and storage of industrial land in the industrial harbor park, real estate development, assisting the Industrial Harbor Management Committee in clearing idle land and factories in the park, venture capital investment in leading industrial projects in the industrial harbor park, as well as building a financing and guarantee platform for enterprises in the industrial harbor park, integrating Chengdu Shudu Small and Medium Enterprises Financing Guarantee Co., Ltd. and Chengdu Shuxi Small and Medium Enterprises Investment Co., Ltd. It is also responsible for the investment and financing management of infrastructure and living supporting areas in the industrial harbor park and the responsibilities of the industrial harbor park property management company, as well as the management and operation of state-owned assets in the industrial harbor park. It implements the model of "two brands and one team" with Chengdu Shudu Small and Medium Enterprises Financing Guarantee Co., Ltd. and Chengdu Shuxi Small and Medium Enterprises Investment Co., Ltd.

The company has innovatively adopted a work approach of "locking resources with projects and exchanging resources for funds," and has raised funds through various channels, providing solid financial support for the rapid development of the industrial harbor. It meets the enormous funding needs in the process of industrial harbor development and construction and makes due contributions to the rapid economic development of Pixian County. In 2010, the company completed a financing of 850 million yuan and completed the auction of the second phase of the land consolidation project for the "1519" project.

In terms of infrastructure construction investment, the company strictly follows the national management standards for engineering projects, adheres to the bidding procedures, organizes carefully, coordinates comprehensively, scientifically manages, and promotes the construction of infrastructure in the industrial harbor park. In 2010, the company completed the construction of the planned roads and supporting facilities for the Western Sichuan International Road and the demolition of parts of the relocated industrial park roads, as well as the rectification work of the cooperation sewage treatment plant and supporting pipelines. The company completed a fixed asset investment in infrastructure of 351.24 million yuan in 2010.

Regarding new housing projects, the "Xincheng Jiayuan" project is a major livelihood project in Pixian County and one of the key municipal projects undertaken by Gangtong Company. The project has an investment of 712 million yuan and a construction area of 239,244.5 square meters. After completion, it will solve the housing resettlement needs of 3005 households and 5480 displaced people.

5. Chengdu Shudu Sichuan Cuisine Industry Investment and Development Co., Ltd.

   Chengdu Shudu Sichuan Cuisine Industry Investment and Development Co., Ltd. (referred to as Shudu Sichuan Cuisine Company) was formally established on January 12, 2010. Shudu Sichuan Cuisine Company is a wholly state-owned company with a registered capital of 125 million yuan. It is a financing and investment platform and implementation entity established by the Pixian County Party Committee and County Government for projects such as new rural construction, infrastructure construction, resettlement housing construction, agricultural product standard demonstration bases, land consolidation, and comprehensive agricultural development within the scope of the Sichuan Cuisine Industry Functional Zone.

By the end of 2010, Shudu Sichuan Cuisine Company had raised a total of 309 million yuan in financing, laying the foundation for the implementation of government investment projects within the functional zone, active service in the “two belts” and the demonstration zone for new rural areas in the Shaxi Line.

During the construction of infrastructure projects, the company strictly follows the national management standards for engineering projects, adheres to the bidding procedures, carefully organizes, coordinates comprehensively, scientifically manages, and vigorously promotes the construction of infrastructure in the Sichuan cuisine industrial park. By the end of 2010, the company had completed the construction of a 3.2-kilometer main road and a 5.4-kilometer industrial plantation road in the Sichuan cuisine industrial park, as well as a 515-meter road in the urban–rural demonstration belt and other supporting infrastructure projects, with a total investment of approximately 41 million yuan.

The company actively implemented comprehensive land consolidation projects, actively sought support from provincial and municipal land and planning departments, explored the use of rural collective construction land, and maximized the market's allocation of resources to expand industrial development and urban construction land space, improving rural production and living conditions. By the end of 2010, Shudu Sichuan Cuisine Company had fully launched the land consolidation projects in Tianxing Village, Tangyuan Town, and Mingfeng Village, Jinning Town, with a total investment of 260 million yuan. The company has completed the implementation plan, general layout design, floor plan design, and infrastructure construction of the Tianjin Road section of the Jiucai Base Project in Tangyuan Town. It has integrated and promoted the development of modern agriculture and the construction of new urban–rural communities, initially forming a demonstration project that utilizes land intensively, accelerates industrial development, builds new residential areas, and improves the development environment.

The company also actively implemented the construction of the Shaxi Line New Rural Demonstration Zone in accordance with the requirements of the county party committee to speed up its construction. It conducted in-depth investigations of the construction of new rural areas in Jingju Village, Xinminchang Town. Based on the "striving for excellence" activities and the actual development of Jingju Village, the company raised and self-raised a total of 250,000 yuan in county policy subsidies, actively participated in the paired construction work, and supported the construction of 81 greenhouses in Jingju Village, creating a 60 mu greenhouse vegetable planting base and employing 35 workers. This has changed the traditional assistance approach of mainly providing financial support with supplementary technical concepts and further clarified the focus of support in terms of funding, technology, personnel, industry cultivation, and concept transformation. At the same time, the park enterprise purchased vegetables from the greenhouse for driving the development of the vegetable industry in the whole village, effectively improving the production and living standards of farmers and receiving high praise and promotion from the county leadership.

Source: Pixian County Local Chronicles Compilation Committee. Pixian County Yearbook 2011. Chengdu: University of Electronic Science and Technology Press, 2012.

3.2 "Anti-Anticipation Gains" Drives Concentration of Arable Land in the Village

The "Rural New Community Construction" project in Zhanqi Village held significant political weight for the local government. It marked the city's inaugural implementation of grassroots governance mechanisms in rural areas, embodying an exemplary model that honored the will of the masses and harnessed their essential role in shaping the new countryside. Moreover, it stood as the city's pioneering initiative in employing market-driven mechanisms for comprehensive land consolidation, establishing a centralized residential zone for farmers. Additionally, it served as a prototype project for the construction of "1 + 23" standard configurations for village (community) public services and social management.

Seizing the opportunity provided by the urban–rural coordination experimental zone, Zhanqi Village also reaped the benefits of land indicators being priced according to urban standards. However, such claims may prove unconvincing at first glance, for they underscore the correlation between external policies and village actions, simplifying the entire affair into a mere cause-and-effect scenario, as if favorable policies alone could instantaneously ignite a swift response from the village. Yet, those acquainted with rural grassroots realities are well aware that rural development has never been a simplistic affair.

Reinserting the situation into the context of the village's bygone era offers a more three-dimensional reconstruction of the event's progression. Soon after the project's implementation, on September 11, 2007, the Pixian County Committee issued the "Opinions on Advancing the Concentration of Agricultural Land for Facilitating Rapid Agricultural Industrialization through Scale Operation (Trial Implementation) (《关于推进农用地向规模经营集中促进农业产业化快速发展的意见（试行）》)." This document underscored the imperative of furthering the "three concentrations," with a foundation based on the objectives of modern urban agriculture. It called for advancing the concentration of agricultural land through scale operation, expediting rural economic development and agricultural industrialization, propelling urban–rural integration, diligently augmenting farmers' incomes, comprehensively constructing a new socialist countryside, and continuing the agricultural industry's overarching layout encompassing "one park, three belts, and four major bases." The plan aimed to cultivate four advantageous industries—pollution-free vegetables, flowers and seedlings, rare edible mushrooms, and high-quality grains and oils—striving to transform Pixian County into a modern agricultural demonstration hub. The county committee further introduced a land transfer incentive policy, encouraging village and community organizations to mobilize farmers to form specialized cooperative economic entities through land shares, thus enabling the transfer of land on a large scale. For land transfers exceeding 1000 mu and lasting over 3 years, forestry economic organizations would receive rewards ranging from 50,000 to 100,000 yuan.

Within the context of continuous policy encouragement and support for land concentration, buoyed by the impetus of the county's comprehensive agricultural industry layout, the village collective persevered in driving the concentration of agricultural land by consolidating and centralizing homesteads, rapidly expanding from 500 mu to over 1820 mu—occupying a staggering 95% of the village's arable land—and greatly accelerating the pace of land resource consolidation.

Subsequent to the widespread relocation of villagers to their new dwellings in 2009, the old residences were self-demolished, setting Zhanqi Village's efforts in motion to reclaim and till the land. Simultaneously, villagers were mobilized to transfer their land for centralized operation by Zhanqi Vegetable Professional Cooperative Society. According to the cooperative's management personnel, after the demolition of the villagers' former abodes, repeated clearing of small and large stones cluttering the yards became a necessity. Many fields remained fallow for 1 or 2 years before the completion of the meticulous reclamation and restoration work, eventually earning the seal of approval.

With the transition to centralized living, the radius of cultivation expanded for many villagers, while the increasing employment opportunities provided by village enterprises significantly dampened their inclination to personally cultivate the land. Consequently, the village collective, utilizing the project as an impetus, capitalized on extensive adjustments to villagers' land holdings, successfully mobilizing the vast majority to transfer their reclaimed land to Zhanqi Vegetable Professional Cooperative Society, enabling unified management.

It was not until 2009 that the cooperative society truly embarked on its operational journey. In September of that year, the society centrally transferred 1097 mu of land, encompassing roughly 60% of the village's arable land. To align with the county's grand plan for establishing a modern agricultural industrial park, the cooperative society leased 700 mu of land to large-scale cultivators, while the remaining 397 mu underwent meticulous reclamation and restoration, exclusively designated for cultivating high-end vegetables. To finance these endeavors, the cooperative society secured a loan of 1.3 million yuan from Tangchang Town Rural Commercial Bank in Pixian County. The loan, disbursed in two installments—800,000 yuan and 500,000 yuan—benefited from interest subsidies of 110,000 yuan and 70,000 yuan, respectively. The ultimate interest payments were subsidized by the county government to facilitate supporting infrastructure development. The 397 mu of land featured a 15 mu seedling center, entirely encompassed by steel-framed greenhouses, employing the floating culture method utilizing liquid nutrient media. The seedlings nurtured therein sufficiently met the vegetable cultivation demands spanning over 3000 mu in the vicinity with Zhanqi Village at its core. As for the 380 mu vegetable planting center devoted to new varieties, it accommodated simple greenhouses primarily fostering bitter melon, winter melon, cabbage, and other premium vegetables, employing intercropping and interplanting techniques. The Zhanqi Vegetable Professional Cooperative Society in Tangchang Town, Pixian County resolved the employment quandary for over a hundred locals, propelling the prosperity and augmented income for local farmers.

On August 21, 2010, Zhanqi Village released the "Implementation Measures for Land Concentration (《土地集中实施办法》)" (hereinafter referred to as the "Measures"). The "Measures" declared that, upon the village's inhabitants settling in the new community, the imperative of land concentration became a pressing issue to resolve. To maximize the economic benefits generated by the land, propelling Zhanqi Village towards greater development, the Village People's Congress deliberated and resolved upon the "demolition and consolidation" of courtyards. Once the homesteads were consolidated into arable land, the original occupants forfeited their usage rights, which were subsequently collectively integrated into the contracted land area. Ensuing rights distribution for the contracted land was executed uniformly on a per capita basis for the entire village.

The "Measures" also stipulated that following the establishment of land rights through contracting, the villagers, guided by principles of legality, voluntarism, and remuneration, would contribute their contracted land (including homesteads after reclamation) and self-retained land to Zhanqi Village Agricultural Cooperative Society (Zhanqi Vegetable Professional Cooperative Society) for unified management, fostering a benefit distribution framework embracing the "minimum guarantee + bonus" approach. Farmers opting not to contribute shares would have their land separately allocated based on the contracted area, forfeiting the benefits arising from land utilization. For villagers relocating to the community and fully incorporating their family's land shares (including households with single elderly residents and children), a monthly retirement allowance of 30 yuan would be disbursed commencing from January 2011, when they reached 60 years of age (supplanting the previous 160 yuan allowance tied to the Double Ninth Festival 重阳节). However, those whose land shares were not entirely incorporated would receive the retirement allowance only upon the complete incorporation of their family's shares, albeit subject to a postponed timeframe.

The nuanced differentiations established within the "Measures" regarding the income and welfare distribution among farmers who elected to contribute shares or not played a robust motivational role for the majority of villagers. By the end of 2010, the cooperative society had successfully concentrated approximately 1600 mu of land, accounting for 80% of the village's arable land. This encompassed 495 households, constituting a collective sum of 1551 individuals. Among these figures, 1420 mu of land had been transferred to large-scale cultivators, yielding rental income of 1.87 million yuan. Meanwhile, the cooperative society directly operated 320 mu of land. Due to the impoverished nature of the reclaimed farmland, entailing considerable investment and modest output, by December 2010, the cooperative society had invested a total of 96,000 yuan in soil improvement expenses.

By the conclusion of 2011, the cooperative society had amassed over 1820 mu of concentrated land, representing a staggering 95% of the village's arable land. This was accomplished through three distinct modes of operation: firstly, the cooperative society collectively managed 90 mu, erecting a modern vegetable seedling center spanning 15 mu, thereby bolstering the demonstration of novel varieties; secondly, it enticed the involvement of 16 property owners and leading enterprises, leasing 1740 mu of land to foster the development of modern agriculture; and thirdly, it augmented the growth of collective enterprises within the village to invigorate the collective economy. As a result of these endeavors, a 400 mu pollution-free vegetable planting base was constructed within the park's confines; standardized and regulated modern agricultural sight-seeing greenhouses spanning 320 mu were established; a 160 mu standardized edible mushroom planting base yielded an annual output value of 90 million yuan; and a 600 mu Mom's Farm was established, cultivating organic vegetables over an expanse of 600 mu. Furthermore, active exploration of collaboration with the Fifth Season Vegetable Production and Marketing Company, employing a 40–60 profit-sharing model, served to enhance the income of the cooperative society and farmers, thereby elevating the transformative power radiating from Zhanqi Industrial Park for Modern Agricultural.[14]

Zhanqi Village Agricultural Cooperative Society strategically consolidated land and expanded its operations, reaping a plethora of policy incentives and subsidies. In 2011, their exemplary efforts were recognized at the provincial level in Sichuan Province, entitling them to a handsome reward of 100,000 yuan. Subsequently, in 2015, the cooperative society secured a grant of 450,000 yuan for the development of an ecological canal project, primarily utilized for constructing canals in their flourishing blueberry fields. The following year, an additional funding of 250,000 yuan was acquired from the district government, designated for the construction of agricultural pathways and scenic lanes in their winter strawberry domain. Moreover, in 2017, another grant of 250,000 yuan was obtained for the creation of an ecological canal, connecting Lü's Residence (吕家大院) to the vibrant site of Eighteen Rural Workshops. Remarkably, the final say in welcoming major projects to Zhanqi Village rests with the district government, while the village diligently collaborates with the park to facilitate water management and other related tasks. Once projects are established, the district government extends policy-based financial support tailored to the prevailing circumstances.

[14] Pixian County Tangchang Town People's Government Document (Tangfu [2014] No. 78): "Report on the Construction of Zhanqi Village's New Rural Development Situation."

By the close of 2019, the cooperative society successfully administered and cultivated a substantial expanse of 1937 mu of agricultural land, with 1670 individuals joining its ranks, encompassing a remarkable 98% of the village's total rightful landholders (1704 individuals), while the remaining inhabitants independently managed their lands, catering to their distinct requirements.

The cooperative not only centralized land holdings but also embraced an equitable "guaranteed income + dividends" system, allowing the farmers to metamorphose into diligent agricultural workers, basking in the fruits of their labor and securing a stable source of income. This transition also ensured a reliable revenue stream for the rural households residing in robust structures.

Furthermore, addressing concerns such as increased living expenses for villagers inhabiting these modern dwellings and the rise in surplus labor following land consolidation, the village collectively responded to the county's comprehensive agricultural industry layout of "one park, three belts, and four major bases." Consequently, they commenced attracting enterprises to tackle the rising issue of employment within the village post land consolidation. According to Gao Demin, under similar circumstances, the village would unequivocally favor enterprises that offer a greater number of employment opportunities.

To expedite the progress of modern agricultural development and fortify the industrial foundation for Zhanqi's burgeoning new rural area, in March 2007, the vibrant Tangchang Town of Pixian County introduced Chengdu Rongzhen Mushroom Industry Co., Ltd. (hereafter referred to as Rongzhen Mushroom Industry), a prominent agricultural industrialization enterprise in Pixian County, to set up shop within the realms of Zhanqi Industrial Park for Modern Agricultural. The grand scheme entailed a total investment of 80 million yuan, with a sprawling planned area of 1000 mu. The initial phase, occupying 300 mu, involved an investment of 40 million yuan, envisioning the creation of Southwest China's most expansive standardized and mechanized production base for delectable rare mushrooms. This ambitious endeavor anticipated a daily mushroom yield of 40 tons, generating an annual output value exceeding 60 million yuan, while providing gainful employment for over 800 industrious agricultural workers, amassing labor income in excess of 6 million yuan. Moreover, it promised to invigorate land circulation within the park, actively propelling the momentum towards large-scale agricultural operations and promoting the advancement of agricultural industrialization.

Subsequently, on August 3, 2007, Rongzhen Mushroom Industry officially established its roots within Zhanqi's Modern Agricultural Park, commanding an impressive expanse of 301.5 mu (lying outside the confines of the urban planning area). By mid-March 2008, the primary phase, covering 300 mu, witnessed significant strides in construction, amounting to a substantial investment of over 40 million yuan. By late March of the same year, the facility commenced full-scale production. Zhanqi Village predominantly witnessed the cultivation and growth of coveted mushroom varieties, including shiitake mushrooms and enoki mushrooms, courtesy of Rongzhen Mushroom Industry. Given the prolonged production cycle of shiitake mushrooms, which persistently thrived throughout the year, yielding an average of 50 tons of mushrooms daily, the entire process, from bagging and inoculation to harvest, trimming, packaging, and sales, demanded meticulous manual labor, necessitating a consistent influx of diligent workers.

At present, the company proudly employs approximately 350 staff members, of whom nearly 60% hail from Zhanqi Village. Additionally, villagers from neighboring communities such as Jinxing Village and Hengshan Village have joined their ranks. These committed workers earn an average monthly wage of 3500 yuan. In an effort to bolster facility agriculture projects, the government extends preferential treatment to Rongzhen Mushroom Industry, offering the lowest agricultural production electricity rates for their mushroom production. Furthermore, 50% of the rental costs for the transferred agricultural land are subsidized. Moreover, an array of subsidies amounting to over 10 million yuan is provided, including 8.1858 million yuan for facility support, 1.7014 million yuan for equipment, 0.257 million yuan for production management facilities, and 1.222 million yuan for interest subsidies on loans. The government holds this project in high regard, chiefly due to its labor-intensive nature, effectively absorbing the surplus rural labor force and enhancing the economic standing of local farmers.

* * *

Back to the Roots: Li Zongtang, the Maestro of Chengdu's Fungal Fortune

Li Zongtang (李宗堂), the man behind Chengdu's esteemed Rongzhen Mushroom Industry Co., Ltd., hails from the tranquil town of Tangchang in Pixian County. Armed with a diploma in intermediate agricultural techniques and a degree in economics and management from the Sichuan University, this visionary entrepreneur embarked on a mushroom odyssey in 1983, amassing a remarkable 26-year cultivation legacy that has garnered him an illustrious reputation within China's edible mushroom sphere. Leading the vanguard, Li Zongtang adroitly capitalized on the region's lofty altitude and climatic conditions to pioneer off-season production techniques for golden needle mushrooms, a triumph that birthed a comprehensive, standardized, and mature cultivation methodology. This ingenious approach has since been adopted by countless off-season growers, positioning Li Zongtang as the progenitor of Sichuan's off-season mushroom industry. Additionally, he serves as the manager of Chengdu Green Source Mushroom Industry Co., Ltd., further bolstering his influence in driving Sichuan's mushroom sector towards prosperity and elevating the livelihoods of rural communities.

In 2007, fueled by an unyielding entrepreneurial spirit, Li Zongtang spearheaded an expedition to the hamlets of Zhanqi and Jinxing, nestled within the picturesque enclave of Tangchang. Subsequently, he invested in the establishment of Chengdu Rongzhen Mushroom Industry Co., Ltd., a stronghold committed to the industrialization of edible mushrooms, amalgamating production, processing, and trade under one roof. Spanning an impressive expanse of 300 mu, with 180 mu dedicated to state-of-the-art infrastructure, the company's ambitious blueprint began to materialize. By June 2008, the initial phase of infrastructure construction had reached fruition, yielding an annual output value of 360,000 yuan. The subsequent year witnessed the realization of complete infrastructure construction, propelling the annual output value to an impressive 7.2 million yuan. Li Zongtang's entrepreneurial ethos remains deeply rooted in the principle of "developing the mushroom industry, serving the nation and its people, self-actualization, dream realization, and mutually beneficial triumph." Harnessing the company's specialized production capabilities, he diligently established the Tangchang Town Mushroom Association, fostering close collaborations with provincial, municipal, and county-level mushroom associations to propagate advanced production techniques while supporting the endeavors of professional growers. Moreover, his benevolent approach welcomed disenfranchised farmers into his fold, facilitating the seamless transition of rural labor and effectively addressing the employment concerns of over one hundred individuals. This symbiotic alliance ultimately engendered a two-million-yuan boost in farmers' earnings, culminating in a resounding win–win for both the enterprise and its agricultural counterparts.

Li Zongtang navigates the intricate labyrinth of mushroom cultivation by heeding the guiding star of technology, trailblazing a path towards scientific entrepreneurship and sustainable efficacy. Traditionally, mushroom production has remained shackled by stringent temperature and climatic prerequisites, limiting the possibilities within greenhouse cultivation. Ever the visionary, Li Zongtang skillfully integrates cutting-edge domestic and international technologies, nurturing the proliferation of production facilities centered around temperature-controlled edifices. This strategic pivot equips him with an unparalleled advantage, enabling year-round mushroom yields untethered from the shackles of external climatic constraints. As a testament to his unwavering pursuit of excellence, Li Zongtang incessantly delves into the realms of research and development, cultivating over ten varieties of off-season mushrooms that have blossomed into bountiful economic rewards, heralding a transformative era for Pixian County's mushroom products and rippling across the expanse of Sichuan Province.

In his relentless quest to unravel the untapped potential of the mushroom industry, Li Zongtang spearheaded a collaborative initiative with the esteemed research institutions of Sichuan Agricultural University and Southwest Minzu University. By the conclusion of 2008, they unveiled a preliminary study on the metamorphosis of mushroom remnants into premium fodder and organic fertilizers, swiftly transitioning into the production phase of these newfound resources come early 2009, effectuating the auspicious renaissance of biological resource exploitation.

Li Zongtang ardently champions a "people-centric, collective prosperity" ethos, instilling a profound commitment to knowledge-sharing among not only his enterprise's staff but also the farmers of Tangchang Town and aspiring cultivators who flock from distant corners. In 2009, he inaugurated the grandiose "Rongzhen Mushroom Industry Production Knowledge Dissemination" event, attracting a staggering 800 participants. As the year progressed, six training sessions had been successfully conducted, enlightening and empowering over 2000 individuals. These invaluable training endeavors served as a potent catalyst, harnessing the demonstrative influence of the company while galvanizing the engagement of more than 220 pioneering souls from 46 agricultural households in Tangchang Town, generating an impressive output value of 600,000 yuan.

Embracing a holistic approach that transcends mere economic imperatives, Li Zongtang bestows equal weight upon the construction of political, governmental, and social organizations. Consequently, he established the company's party branch, trade union, and Communist Youth League branch, assiduously safeguarding the legitimate rights and interests of employees. This concerted effort harnesses the full potential of labor, youth, and women's organizations, epitomizing the harmonious development and proactive participation within the enterprise.

Li Zongtang's accomplishments have not gone unnoticed. In 2006, he was lauded as a national "Mushroom Industry Figurehead," an exemplary individual in Sichuan Province. In 2007, he was celebrated as the vanguard of rural youth entrepreneurship and wealth creation nationwide, a luminous beacon illuminating the Chinese mushroom industry. Simultaneously, he assumed the role of vice chairman in the Sichuan Edible Mushroom Industry Technical Innovation Alliance, while Chengdu City bestowed upon him the honorary titles of a scientific and technological trailblazer among party members and cadres, an outstanding youth of the eighth magnitude, a paragon of youthful excellence in Pixian County, and the pioneering figurehead for scientific and technological strides towards prosperity and rural affluence. In 2008, he proudly clinched a position among Sichuan Province's top ten outstanding young farmers, a testament to his unwavering commitment to agricultural excellence. These accolades bear testament to his unwavering commitment to the industry, and he has been the recipient of multiple awards at the county, municipal, provincial, and industry levels.

The year 2010 witnessed Li Zongtang receiving high praise from provincial and municipal leaders. Chengdu Mayor Ge Honglin and other esteemed figures engaged in multiple fruitful exchanges with Li Zongtang, touring Chengdu Rongzhen Mushroom Industry Co., Ltd., to seek inspiration and offer their invaluable guidance.

Source: Relevant documents provided by Pixian Archives.

Looking back, reflecting upon the entire process of implementing the "Rural New Community Construction" project and the subsequent hastening of land consolidation, along with the establishment of agricultural industrial parks, one can discern a pattern. In 2006, when the cooperative was formed, amalgamating 500 mu of land, the pace of land circulation accelerated. This surge was fueled by the continuous surge in the expected appreciation of arable land, spurred on by policy subsidies. However, the dispersion of homesteads became an objective barrier to land consolidation. The scattered nature of the villagers' dwellings inadvertently led to the fragmentation of cultivated land.

To achieve the concentration of cultivated land, it became imperative for the villagers to reside together. Inextricably linked, the organization of homesteads and cultivated land were interdependent. Sensing this, Zhanqi Village proactively petitioned to initiate the "Comprehensive Land Consolidation Project." Their objective was to exploit the anticipated benefits derived from land consolidation, thereby propelling the streamlining of homesteads throughout the village and facilitating the standardized management of farmland. The conjecture posited by the research team was intriguing: the dispersed nature of homesteads objectively impeded the consolidation of cultivated land. Yet, the appreciable gains stemming from land consolidation played a pivotal role in fostering the concentration of homesteads. This, ultimately, proved to be a decisive factor behind Zhanqi Village's proactive application for and successful implementation of the "Rural New Community Construction Project." Remarkably, Zhanqi Village adroitly aligned with the policy of land linkage, revealing the subtle mastery concealed beyond the realm of written verse. Deceptively separate in name, the "Comprehensive Land Consolidation Project" was, in essence, a cohesive entity.

In a daring inference, the research team ventured further: grateful that Zhanqi Village embarked upon the consolidation of homesteads in 2007, a period when the latent value of rural construction land had yet to fully manifest. At that time, the villagers had yet to harbor expectations of profit from their homesteads, enabling the integration of construction land resources to proceed unhindered. Had the value materialized completely, the task of integration would have presented formidable challenges! This aligns harmoniously with the research team's proposal regarding the functioning of the primary market within the village's "three-tier market": setting modest prices to effectively cultivate the villagers' aspirations for resource appreciation, thereby fostering the transfer of operating rights and resource integration. Curiously, the narrative framework embedded within the confines of "external policies-village actions" adhered to a paradoxical sequence.

Ordinarily, the anticipated returns from construction land surpass those of agricultural land. However, in this case, the circumstances were inverted. The anticipated profits from homesteads had yet to materialize, while the gains from land consolidation had already crystallized. Thus, leveraging the future appreciation income of agricultural land to stimulate the reorganization of seemingly inconsequential homesteads and subsequently auctioning the restructured indicators proved remarkably lucrative, owing to the unceasing ascent of market prices. During this extraordinary era, the captivating dynamics of "reverse expected income" between agricultural land and construction land conjoined to forge an impressive tapestry of spatial integration for Zhanqi Village. As a result, both cultivated land and homesteads were consolidated on a comprehensive scale throughout the village. If, initially, every plot of land had been unambiguously priced and fixed in value, the village collective would have found the task of integrating construction land significantly more arduous.

4 Experience Summary: Rationalizing the Land Concentration in Village Communities

Zhanqi Village's decade-long process of land concentration embodies a multidimensional internalization mechanism, formed by the village's complex structure. This mechanism serves as the institutional foundation of China's grassroots governance structure, which has remained stable for thousands of years. After observing and reflecting on these phenomena, our research team has conjectured a theoretical explanation called the "rationality of the rural community" from an institutional economics standpoint. This theory explores how the domain and methods in which village rationality operates vary across different stages.

In 2003, when the village contemplated implementing small-scale land concentration within its boundaries, it faced the challenge of revitalizing its collective economy, which had previously undergone a phase of relative privatization during industrialization and competition. Mobilizing the villagers became a crucial consideration, demanding an exploration of the tools and mechanisms at their disposal.

At the time, village leaders sought to address the fundamental issue affecting farmers' livelihoods—agricultural taxes. Land remained the cornerstone of their existence, while agricultural taxes directly impacted every farmer's well-being. With agricultural taxes transitioning to cash payments, farmers had to sell their grain in the market to secure monetary income, exposing them not only to the inherent risks of agriculture but also to market volatility in grain supply and prices. Moreover, the lack of well-established social services in agricultural production resulted in substantial transaction costs for farmers in various activities such as seed and fertilizer purchases, hiring mechanized farming teams, and selling their crops. Sensing an opportunity, the village made a promise: after the land was collectively concentrated, the resulting income from its transfer would be used to pay agricultural taxes. If the income fell short, the village collective would shoulder the remaining burden. For the villagers, surrendering a portion of their land to the collective proved to be a shrewd decision, shifting some of the natural and market risks, as well as transaction costs, onto the village collective. This practice was especially appealing to those in Group 5 and Group 7, where land resources were relatively scarce. Evidently, leveraging the rational choices made by villagers to mitigate risks became an effective means of facilitating land concentration, aligning with the low transaction costs associated with the rationality of rural community.

During the internal mobilization process within Group 5, social capital was skillfully employed to bolster the villagers' trust in the village collective. Constructing an environment where the villagers anticipated the benefits of land concentration became another manifestation of the village's rationality. Leveraging the strong foundation of political trust accrued through the village's historical development and establishing networks based on surnames or clans as communal units, village cadres and elites became pivotal intermediaries, effectively tapping into the power of kinship and friendship. This concerted effort ensured a successful collaboration within the entire group.

The generation of increased value post land concentration, the fair distribution of profits, and the village collective's capacity to safeguard communal property all influenced the villagers' political trust in the collective. The outcome—whether positive or negative—determined whether political trust was reinforced or weakened. Following the land concentration in 2003, the village collective not only assumed the burden of agricultural taxes for villagers in Groups 5 and 7 but also generated surplus income. This surplus was allocated towards agricultural land transformation and road construction, elevating the differential land rent. These achievements further cemented the villagers' political trust in the village collective and solidified their expectations of the benefits arising from land concentration.

Additionally, the remaining land within Groups 5 and 7 underwent a redistribution process that embraced a relatively equitable allocation scheme. This mechanism, fostering fairness within the village community, represented the fundamental embodiment of members' rights and constituted a vital aspect of the village's rationality. Distribution occurred at the courtyard level, considering factors such as soil fertility, plot size, and proximity to residential land. Achieving a comprehensive balance encompassing kinship, friendship, and geographical ties, this process minimized potential internal conflicts, to the extent that a method of drawing lots was even implemented in cases where two households expressed interest in the same plot of land. Such measures effectively mitigated internal transaction costs, ensuring the smooth progress of the land distribution process, which, otherwise, could have been marred by numerous conflicts.

In summary, during the phase of small-scale concentration within the team, the value of land remained inconspicuous. It was imperative to start from the farmers' core needs, swiftly leveraging the village's internal structural relationships in the initial stages of collective economic revitalization. Although the area of concentration may have been modest, the value of land concentration gradually emerged, engendering initial mobilization among villagers and rekindling collective memories within Zhanqi Village. Moreover, this period honed the political mobilization abilities of the newly appointed leadership. Most importantly, this undertaking served as a "pilot," exploring the viable and effective mechanisms for a reinvigorated collective economy.

In 2006, the phase of concentrating 500 mu of land under the cooperative society emerged. In addition to applying previously successful methods, this phase enjoyed a more favorable external institutional environment. Leveraging policies promoting land circulation and the establishment of cooperative societies to facilitate large-scale land operations, the village collective pledged to distribute profits within the cooperative society using a "minimum guarantee + profit-sharing" approach. This instilled strong profit expectations among the villagers, becoming the primary incentive to persuade them to entrust their land to the cooperative society.

After the cooperative was established, the government stepped in to construct essential water and electricity facilities, even greenhouses, thereby enhancing the fundamental conditions for agricultural production. Consequently, the village obtained its initial slice of differential ground rent at virtually no expense. Moreover, the structured agricultural land proved conducive to the advancement of capital-intensive farming, resulting in a second portion of differential ground rent after the adjustment of the agricultural industry. These accumulated ground rents were subsequently distributed between farmers and the village collective through the cooperative's "guaranteed income + profit-sharing" model, allowing the villagers to relish tangible gains. Such actions fortified the political trust of the villagers in the village collective.

Furthermore, the previous land transfer contracts between villagers and prominent landowners were rendered null and substituted with agreements with the village collective. In simpler terms, the cooperative enabled significant farmers to connect with numerous small-scale farmers, thereby diminishing the information retrieval costs for the latter while concurrently reducing the transactional expenses involved in coordinating land transfers between influential farmers and the smaller ones. This transition also served as an indispensable means for the cooperative to heighten land utilization efficiency, promote land appreciation, and secure policy subsidies. Truly, a mutually beneficial arrangement.

Between 2007 and 2011, through the consolidation of residential plots via the "demolition and reconstruction of homesteads," the land holdings underwent a further consolidation from 500 mu to an impressive 1820 mu. This stage served to strengthen the farmers' anticipation of augmented earnings through the continued provision of policy subsidies, facilitating subsequent land concentration. During this phase, the land's value became strikingly apparent. Consequently, by harnessing the expected returns yielded by extensive land concentration, either through the infusion of external industrial capital or the village's independent land development endeavors (encompassing guaranteed rent, dividends, increased welfare benefits, and employment opportunities), farmers were galvanized into action. This approach, of course, hinged upon the establishment and reinforcement of prior political trust.

Upon reflecting upon the aforementioned stages, one discerns that the mobilization of villagers in each instance derived from the rational conduct of the village collective across multiple dimensions. These encompassed historical traditions, the bedrock of trust in the village collective, sanguine prospects for the village collective, the village's intricate social network, and inherent mechanisms of equity. When these factors converged with external policies, the process of land and homestead consolidation unfolded organically within the village, unfurling seamlessly, with minimal institutional costs and relative stability. Not once did it succumb to the pressure of government intervention, the prodding of village cadres, or the impatience of external investors to hastily execute a "rapid mobilization" of rural areas. In contrast, many other villages grappled with upheaval and disputes over vested interests as land acquisition and rural transformations transpired. As land values surged and collective economic development surged forward, contradictions surrounding the rights and interests of members within collective economic organizations escalated, triggering collective petitions and even appeals to higher authorities. By comparison, the process in Zhanqi Village progressed serenely, unburdened by the governance predicaments and conflicts that afflict social stability. Through the deployment of a repeated game mechanism and a multidimensional structure of associations between the collective and individual farmers, the village achieved ample, cost-effective information sharing within its confines and relatively equitable distribution of interests. This harmonious resolution effectively defused latent tensions, skillfully navigating the transactional costs inherent to cooperative endeavors and the transformation of property relations.

Beyond its role in fostering land concentration, the rational conduct of the village collective serves a second function: mobilizing internal resources for capital accumulation through the medium of the collective organization. For instance, the cooperative reserves 50% of its dividends, while a subsequent collective asset management company earmarks 10% for statutory public funds and 20% for capital reserves, thereby facilitating expanded reproduction. When confronted with the question of whether the village's profits should be more inclined towards the collective or the individuals, the leader of Group 7 opined, "We are presently in a developmental stage, necessitating the retention of substantial funds within the collective to ensure future growth. It is impractical to distribute all the funds immediately. If we were to do so, how would we sustain progress in the future? It is far better to entrust the funds to the village, enabling everyone to comprehend this rationale." Gaodeming echoed the sentiment, stating, "Why squander the dividend distribution? A mere thousand yuan per year fails to fulfill one's needs. However, through accumulation, we can accomplish grand endeavors."

The village collective represents a geographical entity, formed on the foundation of shared lineage and geographic ties, harmoniously unifying production, livelihood, and ecology. Naturally, such a collective possesses innate problem-solving capabilities. Once this approach is embraced, the village collective can navigate this process with minimal transactional hurdles, ensuring efficiency and elegance in their endeavors.

CHAPTER 10

Property Rights Reformation and Market for Collectively Owned Land Parcels (2008–2015)

In the early days of 2008, the curtains were drawn on Chengdu's rural property rights reformation. Zhanqi Village emerged as the testing ground for this endeavor, anointed by the county committee and government. They set in motion the registration and certification of rural land and housing rights, culminating in the establishment of a collective economic organization on April 20, 2011, boasting 1704 members. A total of 1937.448 mu of arable land was subsequently distributed equitably among these members from the village's 1938.36 mu. The unified management and operation of this land were entrusted to the Zhanqi Vegetable Cooperative in Tangchang Town, Pixian County. As for the collectively owned land parcels (集体建设用地), Chengdu Jifeng Investment Management Co., Ltd. took the reins, ensuring the village's land was managed, transferred, and allocated uniformly. By elucidating property rights, Zhanqi Village laid the foundation for forthcoming asset appraisals and the establishment of a collective asset management firm, all in preparation for the market exchange.

Come February 2015, Pixian County was among the select few chosen nationwide to partake in the experiment of bringing the rural profit-oriented land (集体经营性用地) into the market. From March to August 2015, under the watchful gaze of the county and town governments, Zhanqi Village diligently prepared for this momentous event. Asset appraisals and the formation of a collective asset management company were top priorities. Finally, the maiden blow resounded: Maigao

© Peking University Press 2024

X. Dong, *Zhanqi Village Over Fifty Years*,
https://doi.org/10.1007/978-981-97-5426-7_10

Company acquired the 40-year land usage rights for this collectively owned land parcels, offering a handsome sum of 525,000 yuan per mu. Thus, the transaction marked the "first gavel" in the province's annals of collectively owned land parcels transactions. Yet, the significance transcended the mere plot of land auctioned; it was the discovery of asset prices through such transactions that ignited fervor. Other residual collectively owned land parcels in the village could now reference these valuations. The impact reverberated on three fronts: firstly, it ameliorated the village collective's creditworthiness for securing bank financing; secondly, it fortified the villagers' faith in the village's collective economic organization, easing the transactional burdens of integrating resources across the entire village; and lastly, it elevated the village collective's status in external negotiations, rendering capital a tool rather than a master. Indeed, this "first gavel" not only showered Zhanqi Village with renewed acclaim but, more crucially, empowered them through the discovery of prices, while simultaneously reaping institutionalized benefits from their foray into the market.

1 Reforming Property Rights: Clarifying Ownership for Market Foundations

In tandem with the "Rural New Community Construction Project," an equally crucial endeavor took shape—determining the membership qualifications of collective economic organizations.

To effectively address the "Three Rural Issues" at their core, it becomes imperative to rouse the slumbering capital within rural areas, affording farmers the same property rights and developmental prospects as their urban counterparts. On January 16, 2008, the Chengdu Municipal Party Committee and Municipal Government set forth the "Opinions on Strengthening the Protection of Cultivated Land, Further Reforming and Improving the Rural Land and Housing Property Rights System (Trial)" (Chengfa [2008] No. 1) (《关于加强耕地保护进一步改革完善农村土地和房屋产权制度的意见 (试行)》(成发〔2008〕1号)). This directive emphasized deepening the reform of rural land and housing property rights, focusing on the registration of collective land and housing rights in rural areas, and propelling the rights of land contract management and rural collectively owned land parcels utilization. Thus, the curtains were raised on Chengdu's rural property rights reform, aiming to establish a rural property rights system embodying clarity of ownership, well-defined rights and responsibilities, stringent protection, and unhindered circulation. Capitalizing rural assets, facilitating the free movement of production factors between urban and rural domains, and prioritizing the empowerment of rights formed the core of this endeavor. Consequently, the registration and certification of collective land ownership (农村集体土地所有权), collectively owned land parcels (homestead) usage rights (集体建设用地 (宅基地)使用权), land contract management rights (土地承包经营权), forest rights (林权), and housing ownership (房屋所有权) unfolded.

On November 7, 2008, Pixian County convened a work conference on the reform of rural property rights, imposing a 4-month deadline for completing registration and certification efforts across all agricultural areas within the county. Each rural household would obtain three certificates: the "Land Contract Management Right Certificate (《土地承包经营权证》)," the "Collective Land Usage Right Certificate (《集体用地使用权证》)," and the "Housing Ownership Certificate (《房屋所有权证》)." Designated as an expanded pilot village for the "rural property rights system reform," Zhanqi Village finalized the issuance of these "three certificates" to its villagers in February of the following year (2009). However, a fundamental pillar of rural property rights reform lay in the recognition of membership qualifications within collective economic organizations, which presented a certain contradiction when juxtaposed against Zhanqi Village's existing village community membership qualifications. Policy guidelines stipulated a fixed definition for the membership qualifications of collective economic organizations, contrasting significantly with membership recognition that fluctuated with population changes. This issue grew more apparent as Zhanqi Village witnessed the continuous manifestation of land value, the gradual fortification of the collective economy, and the subsequent appreciation of member statuses. Solidifying membership qualifications would bar future newcomers from reaping the rewards of the collective economy's value appreciation. Nevertheless, Zhanqi Village, as a pioneering hamlet, could not act against policy guidelines. Moreover, the village genuinely yearned for a precise delineation of property boundaries. At that time, the new community construction project in rural areas had mostly concluded, leaving the village to face challenges of consolidated land across village groups and consequent changes in village governance structures. Simultaneously, a comprehensive asset cleanup of the entire village loomed, as collective assets continued to appreciate. The question of determining who belonged to the collective economic organization of the village, possessing land contract management rights, and holding the distribution rights to future collective asset value increments, as well as the rights of village self-governance, became an inescapable quandary.

Taking into account policy guidance and the village's internal dynamics, Zhanqi Village promulgated the "Measures on the Definition of Members in the Zhanqi Village Collective Economic Organization (《战旗村集体经济组织成员界定办法》)" in 2010. These measures established that collective membership qualifications operated on a household basis, remaining unaffected by births or deaths. However, prior to the final determination of collective economic organization membership qualifications, villagers who had relocated their household registrations away from Zhanqi Village due to marriage or educational pursuits, for instance, were at liberty to decide whether to return their household registrations to Zhanqi Village. By completing the requisite registration procedures at the local police station and garnering the agreement of two-thirds of the village members, they could attain membership in the collective economic organization. Additionally, new residents could also be defined as members of the collective economic organization. These regulations not only adhered to policy requirements but also granted the village a modicum of maneuverability.

Initially, the village had aimed to determine the collective economic organization's membership qualifications by September 30, 2010, as the registration deadline. However, due to the protracted negotiation process, a definitive resolution remained elusive. It was not until the spring of 2011, around March or April, that the anticipated property rights of newly added residents were adequately addressed, gradually fostering unanimity among the village members. Ultimately, following collective consultation and discourse, April 20, 2011, emerged as the pivotal date marking the identification of 1704 collective economic organization members.

> "Our annual property rights registration and adjustment spanned from September 30 to December 30. This timeframe coincided with the autumn harvest, rendering the fields vacant. Consequently, our original deadline for property rights registration had been September 30, 2010. However, during the membership determination process, some individuals contemplated events such as marriage, the imminent arrival of grandchildren,

or personal commitments in December. These circumstances impeded progress, postponing the final resolution until April 2011. At that point, with no objections raised, I unequivocally declared April 20 as the definitive date, thereby initiating our property rights registration efforts."
Source: Interview record with Gao Demin, December 26, 2019.

As the shifting demographics unfolded, the entrenched nature of membership qualifications foreshadowed a cascade of predicaments. In response, the village devised the "Supplementary Opinions on the Definition of Members in the Zhanqi Village Collective Economic Organization (《战旗村集体经济组织成员界定办法补充意见》)," enshrining a periodic adjustment for membership eligibility. Due to the constraints on expanding residential land, while agricultural land could be reallocated, future additions to the collective economic organization would solely partake in the distribution of its economic benefits and hold the corresponding contractual rights, relinquishing their entitlement to residential plots.

Following the completion of land consolidation through the New Community Construction Project in 2010, the village's entirety became coalesced under the stewardship of cooperatives. To ratify membership qualifications, an assembly of village representatives was convened, culminating in the unanimous adoption of the "Zhanqi Village Collective Land and Housing Rights Confirmation Plan (《战旗村集体土地及房屋确权方案》)." This comprehensive strategy established joint ownership of collective land for all members within the village, facilitating the issuance of collective land ownership certificates. The management and operation of arable land and collectively owned land parcels were entrusted respectively to the Zhanqi Vegetable Professional Cooperative in Tangchang Town and Chengdu Jifeng Investment Management Co., Ltd., ensuring unified administration, streamlined circulation, and equitable allocation of the village's land.

Moreover, a fair redistribution of all arable land, including both preexisting and newly cultivated plots, was effectuated. However, before the definitive delineation of membership qualifications, Zhanqi Village convened a meeting of villagers on March 25, 2011. Subsequently, on April 6, a momentous resolution addressing the implementation of "long-term stability of rural land contract rights" was enacted, receiving the resounding approval of two-thirds of the members. The resolution stipulated the following:

1. An overview of the village's contracted land: 529 households (comprising 1704 individuals) were engaged in agricultural contracts. The actual surveyed area of collective arable land stood at 1938.36 mu, all of which were contracted and duly conferred to individual households, leaving no remaining idle land.
2. The commencement of the policy ensuring the enduring stability of land contracting rights: Starting from April 20, 2011, contracted land would remain unaltered, implementing a principle of "no land adjustment with population increase or decrease." Contracts would be automatically renewed upon expiration, precluding any repossession by the collective economic organization or land readjustments due to natural disasters.
3. Determination of land compensation through collective deliberation by farmers.
4. Voluntary land transfers, mortgage loan applications, one-time transfers, inheritances, and donations were all permissible.

Upon the completion of membership qualification determination on April 20, 2011, the village committee assumed responsibility for land distribution. Out of the 1938.36 mu of arable land, an equitable allocation of 1937.448 mu was apportioned among the 1704 members of the collective economic organization, equating to an average allocation of 1.137 mu per individual. On July 15, 2011, land contracting agreements were formalized, accompanied by the issuance of operating certificates on a household basis.

This groundbreaking land redistribution initiative shattered the confines of existing factions, harmonizing the per capita allocation of arable land throughout the entire village. Although initial disparities in arable land ownership within Group 7 amounted to 1.3 mu per individual, while Group 5 had a mere 0.8 mu, the consolidation process encountered relatively little resistance, as fluctuations in population naturally gave rise to undulations in land apportionment. Moreover, once united under the village's collective banner, the notion of average distribution became an organic reality, prompting minimal dissent among the villagers. Presently, farmers' concerns gravitate more towards their income, employment opportunities, and the like, rather than the land itself.

Sources: Interview records with Group 7 leader on October 4, 2019.

During the village's comprehensive integration in 2009, I initially sought to resolve internal conflicts within each group before addressing the tensions between them. For instance, in the case of Group 1, which possessed a relatively higher per capita land share, the consolidation effort necessitated dismantling the group boundaries, much to the chagrin of Group 1. I proposed communal living arrangements, where it was plausible for Group 1 residents to inhabit Group 8s land. While Group 8 possessed a lesser expanse of land, it begged the question—what warranted the right to occupy their land? Thus, in the spirit of communal unity, I implored all to relinquish their grievances...

Source: Interview records with Gao Demin on October 2, 2019.

This comprehensive village-wide land redistribution not only entailed an equitable reassignment in terms of area but also adhered to the Ministry of Land and Resources' directives by precisely defining plot locations and boundaries. Moreover, to preempt future challenges related to industrial land, the village ingeniously partitioned the land into several fields, each subdivided into eight portions and distributed among individuals. As a result, every individual acquired a minimum of ten plots, thereby diluting the influence of any single villager over a vast tract of land. Consequently, the transaction costs during the land acquisition process diminished, fostering smoother negotiations with the villagers. Given that the land was solely contracted and not actively cultivated by the villagers, this process unfolded without any conflicts. Post-consolidation, the cooperative employed two operating models: Firstly, the cooperative independently managed 90 mu of land, including 15 mu dedicated to the establishment of a state-of-the-art vegetable seedling center, fostering innovation in crop varieties. Secondly, they collaborated with 16 homeowners and leading enterprises, leasing 1740 mu of land to bolster the development of modern agriculture.

Similarly, collectively owned land parcels (excluding homesteads designated for farmers) underwent unified management overseen by Chengdu Jifeng Investment Management Co., Ltd., facilitating the streamlined administration, circulation, and fair distribution of the village's land. Subsequently, any accrued appreciation benefits would be equitably divided among the members of the collective economic organization.[1]

[1] Source: "Report on the Construction of New Rural Areas in Zhanqi Village by Tangchang Town People's Government." Tangfu [2014] No. 78.

2 Marketization of Collectively Owned Land Parcels: Self-Empowerment through "One Gavel Striking Three Gongs"

In the wake of the People's Republic of China's establishment, our nation set a unilateral system for acquiring collective land essential for urban planning. For years, collective land could only enter the market after being requisitioned as state-owned or undergoing a change in its nature. Yet, at the grassroots level, rural areas across the country embarked on autonomous exploration of transferring collectively owned land parcels into the market. The earliest traces of this practice can be traced back to the 1990s in Guangdong Province's Nanhai District, with subsequent appearances of rural collectively owned land parcels marketization observed nationwide.

In 2004, the State Council introduced the "State Council's Decision on Deepening Reform and Strict Land Management (《国务院关于深化改革严格土地管理的决定》)." Then, in 2005, the Ministry of Land and Resources issued the "Opinions on Regulating Pilot Projects Linking Urban Construction Land Increase with Rural Construction Land Decrease (《关于规范城镇建设用地增加与农村建设用地减少相挂钩试点工作的意见》)." These regulations legally paved the way for indirect market entry of rural collectively owned land parcels. By 2008, with the global financial crisis making its impact, land requisition escalated, fueling conflicts surrounding it. That year, during the Third Plenary Session of the 17th CPC Central Committee, the need to "establish a unified market for urban-rural construction land," "narrow the scope of land requisition," and "ensure equal rights between collectively owned land parcels and state-owned land, based on compliance with planning" was emphasized, setting the overall direction for rural collectively owned land parcels marketization reform.

Then, at the Third Plenary Session of the 18th CPC Central Committee in 2013, the central government announced the implementation of the "Three Uses of Land" reform[2], forging a unified market for urban-rural construction land. This reform allowed rural collective

[2] Translator's note: The "Three Uses of Land" reform ("三块地"改革) refer to the three major institutional reforms for the use of rural land: (1) rural land expropriation, (2) marketization of collectively owned land parcels, and (3) homestead management system.

operating construction land to be transferred, leased, and invested in, enabling it to enter the market on par with state-owned land in terms of rights, equality, and pricing. On February 27, 2015, the National People's Congress Standing Committee passed the "Decision of the NPC Standing Committee on Temporarily Adjusting the Implementation of Relevant Legal Provisions in 33 Pilot Counties (Cities, Districts) including Daxing District, Beijing (《全国人民代表大会常务委员会关于授权国务院在北京市大兴区等三十三个试点县（市、区)行政区域暂时调整实施有关法律规定的决定》)." Beijing's Daxing District, Haicheng City in Liaoning Province, Songjiang District in Shanghai, Yucheng City in Shandong Province, Changyuan County in Henan Province, Yicheng City in Hubei Province, Pixian County in Sichuan Province, and other pilot areas were selected as the testing ground for rural collective operating construction land reform. This milestone marked the substantial implementation phase of the pilot project for marketizing collective operating construction land.

After completing the land rights confirmation for arable land and collective operating construction land, Zhanqi Village initiated a comprehensive evaluation of its collective assets. The plan involved quantifying the entire collective assets into shares, establishing a joint-stock company, and transforming villagers into shareholders. However, progress was slow, hindered by internal resistance arising from the rapid appreciation of collective assets and the increased value of membership status.

Only in February 2015, when Pixian County became part of the pilot project for rural collective operating construction land reform, did a breakthrough occur. The publication of the "Implementation Plan for the Pilot Reform of the Rural Collectively Owned Land Parcels Marketization in Pixian County (《郫县农村集体经营性建设用地入市制度改革试点实施方案》)" presented a turning point. As soon as Secretary Gao Demin learned about the policy for the pilot reform, he swiftly applied for Zhanqi Village's inclusion, recognizing the exceptional opportunity it posed to unearth and realize the value of their land. Situated on the outskirts of Pixian County, Zhanqi Village suffered from an unfavorable geographical position that failed to showcase any land value advantage. At that stage of development, the need to discover asset prices grew strong. The land plots previously occupied by the village collective for fertilizer and precast component factories were rented out, generating annual rent of less than 100,000 yuan. The factories violated environmental standards and marred the village's aesthetics, leading to their gradual closure. Once the land was available, a development predicament ensued. In 2014, a Chengdu-based enterprise saw the potential of these collective operating construction lands, with plans for long-term investments in rural tourism. They even deposited 1 million yuan, but due to procedural difficulties, the venture eventually fell through. Zhanqi Village harbored many such construction land opportunities, calling for the realization of land value and the establishment of the village's reputation.

Nonetheless, according to the "Land Administration Law of the People's Republic of China (《中华人民共和国土地管理法》)," certain conditions had to be met for a village to qualify as a pilot project:

1. Compliance with the overall land use plan, township (town) and village construction plans, and annual land use plans.
2. The land must be either rural collective stock construction land or agricultural land legally approved for construction purposes, with planned usage for business-related activities such as industry or commerce. Collective land for nonprofit public facilities (集体公益性建设用地) and homesteads (宅基地) cannot be traded.
3. The collective operating construction land must be duly registered, with clear and legal ownership, well-defined boundaries, and no disputes.
4. The consent of over two-thirds of the collective economic organization members or over two-thirds of the village representatives was required.
5. In practice, preference was given to economic entities or organizations with legal personality, authorized by the ownership body, demonstrating higher levels of marketization. This facilitated the progress of market entry-related work.
6. Sound financial systems and well-defined profit distribution plans for market entry were necessary.

In line with the pilot project, Pixian County issued the "Opinions on Conducting Pilot Projects for the Transformation of Rural Collective Economic Organizations into Joint-stock Companies (的《关于开展农村集体经济组织股份制改造试点的意见》)," encompassing all collective economic organizations involved in rural collective operating construction land marketization.

In Pixian County, only a few villages met all the requirements for market entry, capable of offering substantial land plots. Most of the suburban lands had been requisitioned or occupied, making it difficult to find plots with clear ownership and no historical burdens that could participate in the collectively owned land parcels marketization policy. Alternatively, lands had already been leased out at exorbitant rents, lacking the impetus for market entry. According to Secretary Gao Demin, at that time, Zhanqi Village was almost the sole village that met the market entry conditions to a relatively full extent. This was mainly due to the village's thorough and solid preparatory work. The restructuring of enterprises granted the collective significant control over the land occupied by the enterprise. "Demolition and consolidation" efforts extensively tidied up farmland and construction land throughout the village, eliminating the issue of scattered plots. In 2013, land use rights certificates for over 60 mu of land designated for the old factory site were successfully obtained. These plots would later become part of the market entry.[3] In 2015, the revised "Chengdu Drinking Water Source Protection Regulations" came into effect, leading to the demolition of the old factory and freeing up additional construction land for Zhanqi Village. After the land plots entered the market, they were allocated for commercial development and upgrading the village's industrial structure. Additionally, Zhanqi Village defined membership qualifications for collective economic organizations and clarified property rights, while ongoing asset inventory work continued.

According to the 2014 survey data, Zhanqi Village possessed a total of 699.9 mu of construction land. Among them, state-owned construction land accounted for 11.94 mu, roughly 1.71% of the total collectively owned land parcels. This land was primarily utilized for roads and independent construction purposes. The remaining land consisted of collectively owned land parcels, totaling 687.96 mu. The village area accounted for 475.65 mu, approximately 69.14% of the total collectively owned land parcels. Other independent construction land covered

[3] Yang Yong mentioned in an interview on October 6, 2019: "Construction land formed before 1999 had historical solidification and required no expenditure. Starting from 1999, it demanded payment, with each mu of land costing 125,400 yuan as a quota fee, along with a fine of 20,000 yuan and a processing fee of 500 yuan. Therefore, the 60 mu of land obtained without cost were processed first. There is also another 70–100 mu of land acquired after 1999, which remains unprocessed. They will be handled once funds become available."

103.32 mu, around 15.02% of the total collectively owned land parcels. Furthermore, transportation, water conservancy, and other construction land occupied 108.99 mu, accounting for roughly 15.84% of the total collectively owned land parcels, as indicated in Table 1.[4]

The rural village of Zhanqi possessed ample resources of collectively owned land parcels, with a significant portion occupied by village factories, leaving "other independent construction land" at the villagers' disposal. With the establishment of a collective asset management company, the village collective gained substantial control over the utilization of this land, presenting vast potential for exploration and ensuring

Table 1 Zhanqi village's collectively owned land parcels in 2014, (Unit: mu)

Names the of land owners	*Land of public road*	*Land for rural residence*	*Other independent construction land*	*Land for special purpose*	*Total*
Zhanqi Village Group 1	28.47	16.76	0	0	45.23
Zhanqi Village Group 2	0	101.62	42.25	2.1	145.97
Zhanqi Village Group 3	0	16.83	28.3	0	44.86
Zhanqi Village Group 4	28.16	87.82	0	0	115.98
Zhanqi Village Group 5	0	0	0	0	0
Zhanqi Village Group 6	0	0	0	0	0
Zhanqi Village Group 7	43.02	0	0	0	43.02
Zhanqi Village Group 8	7.24	228.82	31.17	0	267.23
Zhanqi Village Group 9	0	23.8	1.87	0	25.67
Total	106.89	475.65	103.32	2.1	687.96

[4] According to the "Land Use Plan of Zhanqi Village, Tangchang Town, Pixian District, Chengdu City (2006–2020)" issued by the Tangchang Town People's Government of Pixian District in May 2017 (based on the 2014 survey data supplemented by subsequent investigations, covering all land within the village boundary of Zhanqi Village, including 9 village groups, with a jurisdiction area of 1.95 square kilometers).

resource security for the entry of collectively owned land parcels into the market.

However, Zhanqi Village does not completely meet the various requirements for entering the market. For example, both Chengdu Jifeng Investment Management Co., Ltd. and the "Land Shareholding Company" in Zhanqi Village lack the operating permits for land market entry. The village committee is a grassroots self-governing organization and not an economic entity. In accordance with the legislative proposal "Clarify the Legal Market Entity Status of Collective Economic Organizations (明确集体经济组织合法市场主体地位)" put forward by Pixian County, and following the separation of land ownership and land use rights concept, Zhanqi Village has innovatively designed an organizational structure of "property subject + implementing subject." The village committee represents the collective farmers in exercising collective rural construction land ownership. They have established the "Pixian County Tangchang Town Zhanqi Asset Management Co., Ltd." with 1704 members of the locked Zhanqi Village collective economic organization as shareholders. This company serves as the implementing subject for collectively owned profit-oriented land, authorized to carry out land market entry and represent the collective farmers in exercising land use rights, as well as the corresponding operating rights and income rights. This system design effectively safeguards and maintains the land rights of the members of the collective economic organization. Pixian County's proposal to "Clarify the Legal Market Entity Status of Collective Economic Organizations" has been absorbed and adopted in the revision of the "General Provisions of the Civil Law of the People's Republic of China (《中华人民共和国民法总则》)."

The "Pixian County Rural Collective Asset Inventory and Quantification Operation Rules (《郫县农村集体资产清产核资和股份制量化操作规程》)" stipulate that the detailed inventory and balance sheet must be publicly disclosed for 15 days, and the list of participants in the share quantification must be publicly disclosed for 15 days after discussion at the village assembly. The collective asset share quantification to individuals plan also needs to be publicly disclosed for 15 days. Even if other work is carried out concurrently during the public disclosure period, it still takes at least 45 days to complete the procedure. In order to strive for the "first gavel" for rural collective profit-oriented land market entry, from March to August 2015, following the relevant requirements of the county and town governments, the village worked diligently on market entry preparations.

As early as 2008, Zhanqi Village issued the "Collective Economic Organization System Reform Plan," which comprehensively sorted out profit-oriented assets and nonprofit assets of the collective economic organization. Profit-oriented assets were entrusted to Chengdu Jifeng Investment Management Co., Ltd. for management, while nonprofit assets were managed by the village collective asset management committee. It was required to clarify property rights and solidify quantification to individuals. On August 6, 2015, the Zhanqi Village Committee once again issued a more detailed "Implementation Plan for the Pilot Work of Collective Economic Demutualization Reform in Tangchang Town, Pixian County (《郫县唐昌镇战旗村集体经济股份化改造试点工作实施方案》)." It quantified all collective assets, and the participants in the share quantification were based on the definition of Zhanqi Village collective economic organization members as of April 20, 2011. This resulted in a resolution to solidify shareholding rights, ensuring that the members of the collective economic organization held their collective asset shares unchanged for the long term. In principle, only individual shares were issued, and no collective shares were retained. Shareholders have ownership, disposal, and profit distribution rights over their shares, which can be inherited, gifted, and transferred, but shares cannot be withdrawn or cashed out.

On August 10–11, 2015, the village committee held a meeting to discuss matters related to the pilot reform of collective economic shareholding.

On August 12, 2015, a village representative assembly was held, and the decision to "Carry out the Pilot Work of Collective Economic Demutualization Reform in Zhanqi Village (《在战旗村开展集体经济股份化改造试点工作》)" was passed.

On the evening of August 15, 2015, a village representative meeting was held, and a work group for the entry of profit-oriented land into the market was established in Zhanqi Village. During this meeting, the initiators of Zhanqi Village Collective Asset Management Company, the distribution of shares, personnel allocation, board members, and supervisors were determined. The meeting also discussed and defined the scope of assets for Zhanqi Village Collective Asset Management Company. It was proposed that a comprehensive audit of the collective assets, resources, and funds of the entire village be conducted by the Asset Evaluation and Verification Working Group. After confirmation and approval by the village representatives, the funds would be injected into the Zhanqi Village Collective Asset Management Company.

On August 17, 2015, Zhanqi Asset Management Co., Ltd. in Tangchang Town, Pixian County was registered and established. It was designated as the entity for collectively owned land parcels entering the market, and the villagers became shareholders to increase their property income. The company had 35 members from the Village Council as initiators, with Yang Yong, the village director, serving as the legal representative. The registered capital was 17.04 million yuan, and it locked in the 1704 members of the collective economic organization as shareholders, each with 10,000 yuan in shares. Shares were held by households, were indivisible but inheritable within households (with exceptions for a few households that no longer exist, whose shares were returned to the collective).

On August 20, 2015, a shareholders' meeting of Zhanqi Asset Management Co., Ltd. in Tangchang Town, Pixian County was held, where they discussed and approved the "Zhanqi Village Collectively Owned Profit-oriented Land Transfer Plan (Draft) (《战旗村集体经营性建设用地出让方案 (草案)》)." This plan involved transferring a land parcel of 8964.43 square meters (approximately 13.45 mu), which was collectively owned by Zhanqi Village residents, to the Zhanqi Asset Management Co., Ltd. as part of the collective investment in the company. On August 19, 2015, the land use certificate was changed to the name of Zhanqi Asset Management Co., Ltd. The land was designated for other collective construction purposes, with the right to use allocated land and had undergone verification and certification. According to the "Tangchang Town Zhanqi Village Village Planning (2011–2020)," the nature of the land was for village commercial service facilities, with a 40-year lease term and a reserve price auction method for sale. The floor area ratio was ≤ 2.0, building density $\leq 50\%$, and the building height was generally 4 floors, with some areas allowing 5 floors. Green space requirements complied with relevant regulations, and other land use requirements followed the "Planning Conditions Notice for Collectively Owned Profit-oriented Land" issued by Pixian County Planning and Management Bureau on August 19, 2015.

The meeting also discussed and approved the "Income Distribution Plan (Draft) for the Asset Management Company." After extracting

40% for the surplus reserve fund (used for further company development), 30% for public welfare funds (used for collective public welfare and charity projects), and 10% for the risk reserve fund (used to cover company losses), the remaining 20% of net income would be distributed to the 1704 shareholders of the company according to their shares. The "Distribution Plan" was further detailed in accordance with the company's articles of association and shareholder meeting resolutions: 10% of annual earnings went into the statutory reserve fund, 20% into the capital reserve fund for business expansion, 20% into village public welfare (since 2009, the village had been providing unified medical insurance for villagers and elderly subsidies, with subsidies of 50 yuan/month for those over 60 and 100 yuan/month for those over 70. After the company was established, these benefits continued, with medical insurance rising from 10 yuan/year in 2009 to 220 yuan/year in 2019, with annual welfare expenses exceeding 300,000 yuan); 15% for community public management (including community security, environmental improvement, and community hygiene); 15% for community and village infrastructure construction and maintenance (including water, electricity, gas, communication, roads, and greenery); 20% distributed to collective economic organization members.[5]

After the successful entry of land into the market, in early 2016, all members of the Zhanqi Village collective economic organization received cash dividends of 520 yuan each. Throughout 2016, a total of 206,670 yuan was spent on villagers' medical insurance. From October 2015 to September 2016, subsidies totaling 262,500 yuan were distributed to elderly residents aged 60 and above. In early 2019, each shareholder of Zhanqi Asset Management Co., Ltd. received a dividend of 95 yuan from the previous year.

At that time, in Zhanqi Village, there were collectively owned land parcels totaling nearly 600 mu (approximately 40 hectares). The question was how to determine which lands could be brought to the market, which became a pressing issue for the villagers. Originally, Zhanqi Village had planned to use a plot of land on the north side of Shaxi Road, measuring a total of 65.51 mu, as a pilot project for market entry. They intended to develop the "18 Rural Workshops" tourism and commercial service

[5] Document of the Tangchang Town People's Government of Pixian County (Tangfu [2014] No. 78): "Tangchang Town People's Government Report on the Construction of New Rural Areas in Zhanqi Village."

complex, including elements such as "Rural Hotels" and an "Intangible Cultural Heritage Exhibition Area for Pixian Broad Bean Paste."

Later, under the guidance of the district committee and district government, they applied the "Three Determinations" principle, which involves setting a base number, determining the land plots, and specifying the scale. They carefully reviewed the land parcels within the village that were in line with the "Overall Land Use Plan," the "Zhanqi Village Village Plan," and the industrial development plan. Eventually, they identified the land parcels belonging to the village's former compound fertilizer plant, precast component plant, and the old village committee office building. These parcels were granted land rights certificates by the village committee in 2012, ensuring clear ownership, favorable terrain, and full compliance with the conditions for collectively operated profit-oriented land to enter the market.

On August 26, 2015, Zhanqi Village listed a total of 13.447 mu of collectively owned land, which included the former compound fertilizer plant, precast component plant, and the old village committee office building, on the Pixian County Public Resources Trading Center for public auction. The listing period was from August 26, 2015, to September 7, 2015. Based on land valuation results, benchmark land prices, government industrial policies, and the land market situation, the starting price for this collectively owned land was set at 495,000 yuan per mu, with an incremental increase of 10,000 yuan per mu for each bid. In addition, the winning bidder was required to pay a bidding deposit of 1.33 million yuan (20% of the bidding price multiplied by the land area) to the Pixian County Public Resources Trading Service Center on behalf of Zhanqi Asset Management Co., Ltd.

On September 7, Maigao Company secured a 40-year land use right for this collectively owned land at a price of 525,000 yuan per mu, marking the "first gavel" in the province's market entry transactions for collectively operated profit-oriented land. The total auction price for the land entering the market was 7.06 million yuan. According to the "Notice on the Sale of Collectively Owned Profit-Oriented Land Use Rights (《集体经营性建设用地使用权挂牌出让竞买须知》)," the winning bidder had to pay 30%, 40%, and 30% of the land price within 10 days, 50 days, and 90 days, respectively, from the date of signing the "Pixian County Collectively Owned Profit-Oriented Land Use Rights Sale Contract." The bidding deposit of 1.33 million yuan was converted into the final installment of the land price. Additionally, the land value increment adjustment fee was paid separately by the winning bidder at a rate of 15% of the transaction price. Within 5 working days from the day of the first land transfer payment, the winning bidder had to transfer the land based on the current infrastructure and natural conditions and commence construction within 6 months, completing all planned projects within 18 months within the red line boundary of the land.

After negotiations between Zhanqi Village and Maigao Company, both parties decided to cooperate by establishing a joint operating platform. They planned to continue the development of the Zhanqi Village AAA scenic area in line with the concept of "tourism promotes the village." On December 14, 2012, the Zhanqi Village's Fifth Season Flower Resort (第五季香境, hereinafter refer as "Fifth Season Resort") welcomed an inspection and acceptance team from the national AAA scenic area review.

Minutes from a village committee meeting on July 13, 2016, state: "Yesterday, Maigao Company and the village had preliminary communication and intend to establish a platform company to manage the scenic area in a standardized manner. Village Director Yang Yong believes that establishing a platform company will help upgrade tourism, and the purpose of establishing the platform company is to promote Zhanqi Village and regulate the management of the scenic area. Our cooperation aims to guide villagers in orderly operations, maximizing the collective assets' operational benefits." On July 21, another village committee meeting recorded: "Regarding the establishment of the platform company, the town suggested that we proceed with caution, exchange management personnel, each bear their own costs, establish fixed positions and staff management, and allocate a portion of the revenue to development funds." On July 25, the village committee meeting minutes stated: "Personnel costs for the platform company are shared by both sides, with each providing subsidies." On August 24, the village committee meeting minutes stated: "In order to unify management, we have established a cooperation platform with Maigao Company to comprehensively manage the scenic area. The specific situation of the cooperation is that the village holds 49% of the shares, while Maigao holds 51% of the shares, forming a villagers' agreement to regulate the operation of the scenic area."

After about a year of negotiation and preparation, on November 7, 2016, both parties jointly invested and registered the village's scenic area operating platform—Sichuan Huayang Zhanqi Tourism Xiangjing Management Co., Ltd. The name "Huayang Zhanqi" was based on the positioning Maigao Company had done for Zhanqi Village at the time—a vibrant Zhanqi with unique experiences. The registered capital of the company is 1 million yuan, with Maigao Company and Chengdu Jifeng Investment Management Co., Ltd. (a subsidiary of Zhanqi Asset Management Co., Ltd.) contributing 510,000 yuan and 490,000 yuan, respectively, holding 51% and 49% of the shares. As of 2020, the only facilities operated by this platform are the "Fifth Season Resort" and a parking lot in the village. The name "Fifth Season" was chosen because Mama Farm had previously established the "Fifth Season" brand in Zhanqi Village, and Maigao Company believed that using the same theme would be beneficial for regional brand consistency. Therefore, at that time, after contacting Mama Farm, it was decided to jointly develop the "Fifth Season" brand for Zhanqi Village. "Fifth Season" refers to weekends and holidays as the fifth season apart from the four traditional seasons. Maigao Company eventually invested over 70 million yuan to create the "Fifth Season Resort" commercial complex, which officially started operations in April 2018 and includes businesses such as folk snacks and hotels.

In fact, the work of clearing property rights and assets was not completely finished when collectively owned land parcels entered the market. On August 27, 2015, Zhanqi Village held a meeting of the Property Rights Clearance and Valuation Working Group. Starting on September 11, a professional asset assessment team hired by the working group conducted a comprehensive measurement, survey, and audit evaluation of all collective resources, assets, and funds, except for contracted land and villagers' homesteads, based on the 2011 baseline. They clarified ownership of various types of assets, established accounting records, and involved processes such as collective asset identification, drafting of valuation schemes, and soliciting opinions. Collective resources included all unregistered agricultural land, profit-oriented collectively owned construction land, nonprofit public facility land, collective water, electricity, transportation, and other productive facilities, as well as public facilities for education, culture, health, and welfare. Collective assets included tangible and intangible assets, debts, and credits, while funds included the village collective's cash and bank deposits. Specifically, unregistered agricultural land and other unused land were valued at 2150 yuan per mu, referring to the price of agricultural land circulation within the village; construction land was valued at 46,000 yuan per mu, referencing the government acquisition price for neighboring village construction land. Structures such as factories, bridges, and trees were priced based on construction or planting costs.[6]

On January 20, 2016, Zhanqi Asset Management Co., Ltd. held a shareholder meeting to summarize the results of asset evaluation and clearance. After review by the village representative assembly, the results were posted publicly and confirmed by the members of collective economic organizations (or representatives of household heads). The final total assets of the entire village were determined to be 46.07 million yuan, with a receivable land payment of over 7.05 million yuan (which was still in the process of being processed at that time). If a comprehensive clearance of all resources is required, an additional expenditure of 200,000 yuan would be needed. The board of directors suggested not assessing it for now and to evaluate the actual transaction objects if necessary.

Following the asset evaluation and clearance, the property rights of all collective resources, assets, and funds, including agricultural land, collectively owned land parcels, real estate, roads, water channels, and more, were clearly defined. Secretary Gao Demin mentioned that Zhanqi Village had been more thorough in this regard compared to other villages. The reason for emphasizing the definition of land property rights was that land is the most fundamental resource, and all other resources are attached to it. By clarifying land ownership, everything else becomes clear. In comparison to Zhanqi Village, many villages have seen a fading collective concept, weakened collective capacity, unclear collective property rights, and a gradual trend towards "privatization," making it difficult for the village collective to enter the market. Although Zhanqi Village had not completed its asset evaluation and clearance at the time of entering the market, the village collective still had a relatively high degree of autonomy over collectively owned land and village collective enterprises. This allowed Zhanqi Village to enter the market with a total of 13.447 mu of collectively owned land that included the original village-owned compound fertilizer factory, prefabricated component factory, and the old village committee office building.

In response to the policy of concentrating collectively owned land into the market, Zhanqi Village, as one of the pilot projects, took advantage of the opportunity provided by the national land system reform pilot in Pixian County. They sold 13.447 mu of idle collectively operated

[6] 18 Rural Workshops invested 11 million yuan, and as of the end of 2019, there were a total of 57 million yuan in asset stock.

construction land, originally owned by the village collective and housing the compound fertilizer factory, prefabricated component factory, and the old village committee office, to Sichuan Maigao Tourism Resource Development Co., Ltd. for 52.5 thousand yuan per mu. The village earned over 7 million yuan from this transaction, marking the "first gavel" for the entry of profit-oriented land into the rural market in the province. By the end of 2019, the village had cleared nearly 200 mu of collectively owned construction land, with collective assets valued at over 200 million yuan. They developed projects such as the Rural Revitalization College and the 18 Rural Workshops through stock operation, independent development, direct listing, and more. Among these, the cultural and tourism complex in western Sichuan, with an investment of 70 million yuan by Maigao Company, has been completed and opened. Zhanqi Village also used various types of property rights, such as land contract rights, construction land use rights, and ownership of production facilities, to mortgage financing of over 60 million yuan. In the case of the "first gavel" market entry project, collective construction land was used as collateral, securing a 15 million yuan credit line from Chengdu Rural Commercial Bank, with an actual loan of 4.1 million yuan.

Source: Zhanqi Village Work Report "Remembering the Entrusted Task, Forging Ahead, and Accelerating the Construction of Rural Revitalization Demonstration Zone."

As is well-known, in rural areas, the current maximum income comes from the development of collectively owned land parcels, given the shadow prices set by urban external markets. Zhanqi Village gained an income of 7.06 million yuan by entering the market with collectively owned construction land, earning the title of "first entry" into the market. Why are they still holding nearly 200 mu (approximately 13.3 hectares) of construction land?

The answer is quite clear. Although Zhanqi Village obtained over 500,000 yuan per mu of land, compared to the profits from urban land development, this amount is insignificant. The income gained from land auctions is one-time only, and once the land is sold, the village loses its reserve resource for future development. Therefore, self-development is the key to maximizing the value-added benefits of land.

The direction of the national land system reform is to ensure equal rights and benefits for urban and rural land. However, the problem lies in the severe financial constraints in rural areas, which prevent them from engaging in self-development and achieving equal rights and benefits. In such a situation, the significance of the "first entry" into the market is not just about the land being auctioned, but it also sets a pricing reference for other collectively owned construction land within the village. In other words, its primary function is to discover asset prices through transactions. The larger significance is that the unsold land also holds this value ("the entire village has cleared nearly 200 mu of collectively owned construction land, with a collective asset valuation exceeding 200 million yuan"), thus laying the groundwork for future self-capitalization development. This point is also supported by the interview with Gao Demin.

I own more than 20 mu of land in total. I don't want to sell it all at once. I've only sold over 13 mu, and I want to develop something on my own. More land is certainly better, but I want to create a supporting project. Rural land has no value; the purpose of selling more land is to enter the market and transform resources into capital to maximize their value. One of the key focuses of the reform is to ensure that collectively operated construction land in rural areas has the same location, price, rights, and responsibilities as state-owned construction land. How attractive is that!

Additionally, I really want to earn the title of the "first" to enter the national market with land. If I achieve the "first," the central government will publicize it, and people from all over the country will come. Think about the advertising effect (how significant) that would have! Even if I spend all the money from the land on promotion, I still wouldn't achieve this effect!

Furthermore, this auction has set a price, and if we cooperate with external partners in the future, all land transfer prices will not be lower than this price. After President Xi came, the land price doubled to 1 million yuan per mu. Now, many people come to negotiate with the village, and it's not about whether he wants it or not, it's about whether I give it to him or not.

Source: Interview records with Gao Demin on October 2, 2019.

During the process of asset verification, the price of construction land was 46,000 yuan per mu. In a village committee meeting on June 24, 2015, discussing the introduction of a water recreation project, it was suggested that construction land should be valued at 250,000 yuan per mu for shareholding purposes. In September 2015, Maigao Company acquired this land at a price of 525,000 yuan per mu. Currently, Zhanqi Village can demand a price of 1 million yuan per mu, as seen in negotiations with Mama Farm for the right to use construction land at 1 million yuan per mu. This effectively serves as a pricing standard, with no current cooperation below the price of 525,000 yuan per mu, although whether actual cooperation occurs is another matter.

As Zhanqi Village led the way in entering the market with profit-oriented rural collective construction land, dormant land resources in various villages were gradually awakened. Taking the rural land system reform pilot project in Pixian County as an opportunity, various land policies were integrated and applied, continuously revitalizing idle land resources and transforming them into capital. As of July 2018, a total of 42 transactions involving rural collectively operated construction land were completed, totaling 542 mu, with land transfer income of 380 million yuan, adjustment funds of 80 million yuan, and equivalent deed tax adjustment funds of 10.02 million yuan.

Profit-oriented land in rural areas is the most important component of collective assets, with approximately 40 million mu (about 2.67 million hectares) of such land nationwide. These collectively owned land parcels have long suffered from issues like dispersed layouts and extensive utilization. Through the reform of entering the market using collectively owned land, Zhanqi Village has revitalized rural land resources, improved land resource utilization, and unleashed the vitality of rural land resources, thereby realizing the value of rural land resources.

The role of discovering transaction prices through land auctions can be likened to "striking three gongs." First, it has improved the credit conditions for village collectives to obtain financing from banks. One systemic reason why it is difficult to combine finance with rural areas is the lack of bank-recognized collateral. Most of the resource-based assets owned by rural areas are challenging to market and, consequently, difficult to assess and pledge.

Taking this reform as an opportunity, Pixian County has innovated market financing models, paving the way for enterprise financing and social capital injection. It has included the use rights of rural collective profit-oriented land in the risk fund protection scope for rural property rights mortgages. The risk fund at the municipal and district levels shares the net losses from acquisition and disposal at a ratio of 4:6. They also provide special incentives and credit incentives to financial institutions engaged in rural collective profit-oriented land use rights mortgage loans.

After this land auction, Zhanqi Village obtained over 60 million yuan in financing through various property rights mortgages, such as land contracting rights, construction land use rights, and ownership of production facilities. For the "first auction" market entry project, they used collectively owned land as collateral and obtained a credit line of 15 million yuan from the Chengdu Rural Commercial Bank, with an actual loan amount of 4.1 million yuan. This established the collateral right for profit-oriented land.

However, the future of profit-oriented land mortgage loans remains uncertain. While the national policy encourages it, specific policies and operational methods are still lacking. For example, the specific terms to be used, the forms of collateralization, and the interest rate standards for different projects are not very clear.

In addition, a notice from the State Council's Office in 2007 strictly prohibited collective-owned construction land use rights owned by rural collectives from being used for commercial residential development after entering the market. Therefore, how to operate to generate income to repay the loans is still under exploration. In this situation, many banks are hesitant to lend, making it difficult for entities with rural collective profit-oriented land use rights to solve their financial problems through land mortgage financing. This also hinders the promotion of profit-oriented land entry into the market and the full and effective use of land resources after entering the market.

Second, it has increased villagers' confidence in village collective economic organizations and laid a good foundation for absorbing surplus funds from villagers, reducing the transaction costs of integrating resources within the village.

Only when there is an internal transformation of funds into shares within the village can surplus funds within the village be mobilized, reducing the dependence on external funds and reversing the general position of capital owners. Whether villagers are willing to invest in shares depends on their expectations of future returns. The "first auction" clarified the market valuation of collective assets, which helps to boost villagers' confidence in the collective economy and their desire to invest in it. In 2019, the village began to establish a capital cooperative, participating in the self-capitalization of village land resources to obtain income through "capital into shares." The village plans to build a youth hostel through special capital fundraising as the first project. This is the village's first attempt at financing, starting with low-risk projects to gradually build villagers' confidence.

Furthermore, compared to land requisition, farmers' income from entering the market with profit-oriented land is significantly higher than land compensation. For a long time, China has implemented a low-price land requisition policy based on agricultural per-acre income multiples, resulting in low compensation for farmers in land requisition. However, with collective construction land entering the market, the distribution ratio of income obtained by village collectives and villagers has significantly increased. After entering the market, farmers can continue to receive land value-added income distribution. In order to ensure the continuous growth of collective assets, long-term guarantees for villagers' interests, normal operation of village public welfare projects, and the smooth operation of village affairs, Pixian District has formulated a "two-tier adjustment" for external distribution and a "Pareto principle" for internal distribution. After deducting the land value-added income adjustment fund, the remaining net income is distributed according to the "Pareto principle." Twenty percent of the net income is used for cash dividends to collective members, while 80 percent goes to the village collective reserve fund and public welfare fund, ensuring the long-term livelihood of villagers and promoting the sustainable development of the collective economy.

Third, it has elevated the village collective's position in external negotiations, making capital a tool rather than the master.

When village collectives cooperate with external investors based on resource-sharing, the appreciation of construction land resources enhances their negotiation position. In attracting investment and foreign cooperation, local governments often make significant concessions to capital, partly due to the scarcity of local capital and the difficulty in pricing resources properly. However, for the cooperative venture of Zhanqi Village and Maigao Company, called "Colorful Zhanqi," the positions of both parties are basically equal, with the village collective holding 49% of the shares and Maigao Company holding 51%. Moreover, according to the profit distribution agreement, Maigao Company actually receives only about 1/4 of the premium income, with about 3/4 going to the village collective and villagers. Starting from 2017, when it began developing "Xiang Cun Shi Ba Fang," Zhanqi Village has gained full control over the development, from initial investment and construction to subsequent management of businesses in the area. This means that investors cannot participate in investments in the same way as Maigao Company.

The elevation of the village collective's negotiation position is also reflected in the increasing land rents charged to external companies as land prices and construction land prices rise, the overall commercial atmosphere in villages is created, and the number of tourists continues to grow. For example, Manjianghong Condiment Food Co., Ltd., which entered Zhanqi Village in October 2010 to lease 15 mu of land for building a chili sauce processing factory, paid an annual land rent of 70,000 yuan in the first year, equivalent to about 4667 yuan per mu. Starting in 2015, the rent for the same 15 mu of land rose to 10,000 yuan per mu per year, while during the same period, Fuyou Green Condiment Co., Ltd., also in the village producing chili sauce, paid only 3650 yuan per mu per year for land rent. It can be seen that the village collective's bargaining power is continually increasing when attracting external enterprises, and they can use their gradually enhanced negotiation position to favor village-based enterprises in terms of land rent, thereby to some extent maintaining the development advantage of village-based enterprises.

In this context, the "first gavel" not only brought the "star effect" back to Zhanqi Village but, more importantly, served to "discover prices" through transactions, thus achieving "self-credit-enhancement," "self-confidence," and "self-empowerment." For many scholars, these basic principles of institutional economics are often considered somewhat obscure and are usually overlooked in academic discussions, with the emphasis being placed on "privatization." It's surprising to see Zhanqi Village applying them effectively, which is truly commendable!

Looking at the process before and after collectively owned land parcels entered the market, both Zhanqi Village and Maigao Company took advantage of the policy to profit from collectively owned land entering the market.

Firstly, Zhanqi Village seized the opportunity of the "first gavel" for collectively owned land entering the market, gaining political premium income higher than the normal land market price. After Xi Jinping's visit to Zhanqi Village on February 12, 2018, the village increased its asking price for collectively owned land to 1 million yuan per mu, doubling the previous price and aligning it with state-owned land prices, thus benefiting from a political premium income.

The reason Zhanqi Village was able to sell land at a high price of 525,000 yuan per mu, totaling 7.06 million yuan, despite its unfavorable location, and why the starting price of 495,000 yuan was significantly higher than the market price, is that Zhanqi Village was one of the few villages that could provide the amount of land required for entry into the market. As the "first gavel" in the province, it needed to have a sizable land parcel to set the benchmark, provide a more reliable reference, and take the lead among many pilot projects nationwide. Therefore, Zhanqi Village had some negotiating power during the bidding process.

In contrast, in Meitan County, Guizhou Province, the "first gavel" for profit-oriented collectively owned land entering the market was struck on August 27, 2015, and a land parcel of 3332 square meters, approximately 5 mu, was auctioned for 800,000 yuan. The average price per mu was only 160,000 yuan, which can be partly attributed to the small size of the land parcel. Meitan County's investigation revealed that there were 3.0833 million square meters (4624.95 mu) of collectively owned land for profit-oriented use, with only 123,500 square meters (185.25 mu) eligible for immediate entry into the market and 1.0507 million square meters (1591.05 mu) eligible for adjustable entry. However, these lands were distributed among 120 villages, and many of them were not concentrated, making it difficult for entry into the market and subsequent development, which ultimately hindered the increase in auction prices.

Although entry prices are not solely determined by land parcel size, the fragmented and dispersed distribution of collectively owned land parcels into the market can indeed be detrimental to raising entry prices for development. Zhanqi Village, due to its thorough preparations, was able to merge three pieces of land, including the former village-owned compound fertilizer factory, prefabricated component factory, and village committee office building, into a single parcel of 13.447 mu of collectively owned land, showcasing the advantage of the village in collectively utilizing land at scale. This allowed them to achieve the political effect of the "first gavel" and reap high political premium income.

Even though Zhanqi Village was able to offer a substantial amount of land that met entry requirements, considering the unique nature of rural development, it was still a risky investment. With no takers initially, the government negotiated with Maigao Company to persuade them to take over at a final price of 525,000 yuan per mu.

In summary, while market-driven value discovery is the nominal explanation for this institutional change, in practice, it is not entirely market-driven pricing but rather the advertising effect brought about by the "first gavel" that stimulated various stakeholders' interests. Under the influence of various factors, Zhanqi Village was able to gain a significant opportunity income advantage due to the scale of its land, which became an important foundation for its subsequent development of the 18 Rural Workshops.

For Maigao Company, although they spent 7.06 million yuan to acquire this piece of land, they also seized the opportunity to hitch a ride on various convenient factors.

Firstly, they hitched a ride on existing village industries represented by Mama Farm. When Maigao Company entered in 2015, Mama Farm was already established, and the village had a good foundation in the tertiary sector and a large customer base. This was a significant factor that attracted Maigao Company. Mama Farm had invested significant costs in creating agricultural tourism attractions and other tertiary sector developments, which became concepts and usable resources that Maigao Company could promote. In this sense, Maigao Company benefited from Mama Farm's spillover effects.

Mama Farm can be seen as a strategic investor in Zhanqi Village because it bore the initial investment and ongoing losses, helping with the foundational development of the entire village area. However, many of the subsequent tertiary sector development benefits did not internalize within Mama Farm but spilled over. Of course, Mama Farm also benefited because after President Xi Jinping's visit, Zhanqi Village received political and economic resources, which also accelerated Mama Farm's tertiary sector development.

In addition to Mama Farm, Maigao Company also hitched a ride on the industrial foundations created by the blueberry and strawberry farms. However, the latter also benefited from the influx of resources after collective land use entered the market. Overall, the various entities in Zhanqi Village have a mutually supportive structural relationship, and in general, profits and costs are relatively balanced. These entities enriched the village's business landscape, brought positive externalities and spillover effects to other entities, and also rode the wave of Zhanqi's overall business environment and reputation.

Secondly, Maigao Company hitched a ride on the existing infrastructure construction, spatial development, industrial foundation, and village governance structure of Zhanqi Village. After entering Zhanqi Village, Maigao Company created the "Fifth Season Resort" commercial complex, which relied not only on the village's existing infrastructure and landscaping but also on the village's industrial foundation, especially in the tertiary sector. This included the later development of the "18 Rural

Workshops" by the village collective, and also relied on the village's governance structure to avoid disputes and conflicts.

Maigao Company applied the Maigao model to Zhanqi under these basic conditions and benefited from the strong reputation of Zhanqi Village after President Xi Jinping's visit. This is why Maigao Company was willing to spend 7.06 million yuan to acquire this land and accept only 1/4 of the premium income in the Colorful Zhanqi platform. Additionally, although the "Fifth Season Resort" project invested over 70 million yuan and is currently not performing well in terms of returns, all the shops have been transferred to a light asset model, significantly reducing operational risk. This further demonstrates that Maigao Company is seizing opportunity-based income.

In a sense, Maigao Company can also be considered a "strategic partner" of Zhanqi Village. Unlike Mama Farm, which strategically redirected the village's development in another direction, Maigao Company has a strategic impact on Zhanqi Village by opportunistically choosing to cooperate with it, which is strategic for Maigao Company itself. This can be seen in the significant transformations Maigao Company has undergone since its establishment. In March 2015, Maigao Company expanded its business scope to include tourism-related businesses, and its name changed to "Sichuan Maigao Tourism Resource Development Co., Ltd." In December 2017, it further expanded its scope to include management consulting, corporate image planning, creative planning, and tourism consulting (excluding travel agencies). In November 2018, it expanded its scope to include business consulting (excluding securities, futures, financial, and investment consulting). It is evident that Maigao Company's business transformation and involvement in Zhanqi Village's business occurred in parallel. Maigao Company leveraged its cooperation with Zhanqi Village to complete its own business transformation and upgrade. As Maigao Company executives put it, Maigao Tourism, as a village development service provider, has participated in Zhanqi Village's projects and has become a milestone in Maigao Company's participation in rural revitalization services.

CHAPTER 11

Ecological Transformation and Industrial Ecologization in the New Era (2011–2019)

The 19th National Congress of the Communist Party of China declared the arrival of a new era of socialism with Chinese characteristics, necessitating structural reform on the supply side and comprehensive optimization of industrial structure. China found itself at the crossroads of opportunities and challenges, urging the need to seize the former and confront the latter.

1 Macro Context and Epochal Traits of Ecological Transformation

In the realm of opportunities, the world has transitioned from an era dominated by industrial capital to one ruled by financial capital. China, possessing the largest accumulation of industrial capital and a robust array of industries, now faces the inevitability of fierce international competition. The transformation of China's twenty-first-century ecological civilization strategy and the establishment of Xi Jinping's thought on socialism with Chinese characteristics for a new era bear immense significance in addressing the persistent imbalances and inadequacies of social development. The critical challenges of disorderly rural governance, industrial decline, cultural degradation, and environmental destruction necessitated the formulation of the "rural revitalization" policy, characterized by "thriving industries, livable ecology, civilized rural conduct, effective governance, and prosperous livelihoods (产业兴旺、生态宜居、

© Peking University Press 2024
X. Dong, *Zhanqi Village Over Fifty Years*,
https://doi.org/10.1007/978-981-97-5426-7_11

乡风文明、治理有效、生活富裕)." The historical quandaries of supply–demand imbalances resulting from insufficient production have been largely resolved, laying a material foundation for industrial upgrading. Moreover, China's profound socioeconomic transformation has cultivated the world's largest middle-income population, placing China in the esteemed ranks of upper-middle-income countries. The liberation of this substantial consumer potential promises immense market opportunities for China's structural advancement.

However, as challenges loom, China has encountered a period of supply surpassing demand since 1998, with dwindling industrial profits reaching unsustainable lows. The overreliance on external demand as the driving force for consumption has escalated the risks of economic externalization. Furthermore, China's vast workforce has given rise to mounting social contradictions, intensifying the urgency of effective governance.

Throughout the twentieth century, China's agricultural development aimed to provide the necessary primitive accumulation for industrialization. The industrialization of agriculture predominantly focused on workshop-style secondary industry farming, leading to detrimental externalities inflicted upon the environment. The 17th and 18th National Congresses of the Communist Party of China advocated for expeditious shifts in economic development patterns while emphasizing the paramount importance of ecological civilization. The development of the tertiary sector within agriculture aligns harmoniously with these aspirations, promoting environmentally friendly production methods, enhancing the value-added nature of spatial resources, and propelling the modernization of agriculture.

The ecologization of industries represents an intrinsic imperative in realizing supply-side structural reform and achieving high-quality economic development in the present phase. Converging with international standards, it diligently safeguards against trade barriers and reduces trade frictions. Since the 1990s, society at large has wholeheartedly responded to the guiding policies of "clean production," "circular economy," "sustainable development," and "green growth." As a testament to this commitment, ecological industrial parks and green circular parks have proliferated nationwide, effectively curbing industrial waste emissions while simultaneously fostering economic growth. Particularly noteworthy is the substantial progress achieved in the ecologization of industries since China's accession to the World Trade Organization in

2001, a period marked by the dual pressures of domestic and international demands. However, both material industries and overall social circulation remain wanting. The modest increase in the comprehensive utilization rate of solid waste (from 45.9% in 2000 to 62.1% in 2014) coupled with the subsequent downward trend since 2010 signifies the existence of untapped potential in achieving comprehensive societal waste recycling. Moreover, the rational reutilization or degradation of accumulated industrial waste assumes paramount importance, serving as an imminent challenge amidst the realm of opportunities.

2 Spatial Reconstruction: Integration and Transformation

Zhanqi Village's triumphant performance in the ecological competition of the new era can be attributed to two key factors. Firstly, the village proactively consolidated its land resources, creating a surplus platform for future spatial utilization. This empowered the village collective to assert its influence when engaging with external enterprises. Secondly, the village swiftly aligned itself with the central government's ecological development policies, leading to a transformation of the local enterprise structure.

2.1 The Role of Collective Economic Organizations

Ecological transformation represents the manifestation of ecological civilization's values, and the dormant assets must be reinvigorated. By converting a portion of the national investments in rural areas into productive assets within the new collective economic framework, the total assets of village-level collective economies received an instantaneous boost. Consequently, village-level cadres assumed the responsibilities of managing these assets, effectively acting as custodians of their communities' financial well-being.

While comprehensive development of spatial resources is essential, over 90% of rural areas consist of small-scale farmers, resulting in fragmented property boundaries that hinder the formation of a cohesive spatial landscape. Therefore, improving rural governance becomes crucial in fostering harmonious relations between cadres and the masses, thereby facilitating comprehensive spatial development. Only through such comprehensive development can monetary circulation be realized. By stimulating government finance and credit expansion, a significant number of high-income individuals can be cultivated, who will contribute to rural consumption and investments. In turn, this creates an opportunity for the accumulation of wealth in rural areas.

In 2009, Zhanqi Village successfully concentrated its territorial resources, shielding the village's resource assets from external influences. Led by the village collective economic organization, the process involved democratic consultations with the villagers to determine the pricing and realization of resource assets through monetization or capitalization. The profits were distributed back to the collective through share returns from the cooperative, ensuring that resource asset owners enjoy long-term, stable, and sustainable benefits. This approach not only enables resource integration under limited financial resources but also allows the collective economic organization to repurchase and subsequently sub-lease. Moreover, it provides an opportunity to gain greater premium returns in secondary and tertiary markets.[1] This innovative practice, which employs finance as a substitute for fiscal measures, prevents excessive government debt and leverage while efficiently leveraging surplus financial capital to ensure the green, safe, high-quality, and sustainable development of agriculture.

Zhanqi Village's resource integration has yielded several advantages for enterprise development. Firstly, due to meticulous prior mobilization efforts, the village repossessed the land allocated to individual households, centralizing it under the village collective. As a result, Zhanqi Village stands as the sole region in the surrounding villages with favorable conditions for development. Enterprises can directly negotiate land transactions with the village and cooperative, thus streamlining communication and reducing associated costs. Secondly, the process of land concentration empowered the collective economic organization with a monopolistic hold on regional resources, bolstering their bargaining power in market negotiations. This enabled the establishment of equitable and trust-based transaction relationships with foreign investors. Furthermore, the village ensured the comprehensive improvement and maintenance of

[1] Tang Li, Liu Yahui, Dong Xiaodan. Analysis of the innovative mechanism of land rights confirmation and "citizens going to the countryside" [J]. Journal of Fujian Agriculture and Forestry University (Philosophy and Social Sciences Edition), 2018 (2): 1–5.

surrounding roads and canals during the land concentration process. Once cooperation agreements are reached, enterprises can readily access these existing resources. Consequently, through early land concentration efforts, the village collective accomplished internal reconfiguration, transforming the resultant internalization of external costs into a competitive advantage for enterprises. This symbiotic relationship between the village and enterprises promotes a mutually beneficial dynamic.

2.2 *Transformation Driven by Water Source Protection Policies*

In 2010, a pollution survey report released by the State Council revealed that agriculture had overtaken industry and urban life, emerging as the primary source of non-point source pollution in China. Consequently, addressing agricultural pollution assumes paramount importance when discussing agricultural modernization.

As the conflict between industrial development and environmental pollution intensifies, sustainable environmental protection becomes a focal point for development. China's total freshwater resources amount to 2.8 trillion cubic meters, with a per capita availability of only 2100 cubic meters, representing 28% of the global average. Consequently, as the accelerated construction of new urbanization unfolds, water resources protection and management must be reinforced, particularly in densely populated cities and those grappling with ecological deficits. Measures encompassing robust water environmental planning, systemic reforms in water resource management, effective control of water pollution, and safeguarding water sources become imperative in curbing the issue's escalation.

In 2015, Chengdu implemented the "Chengdu Drinking Water Source Protection Regulations." This legislation introduced a series of measures designed to fortify water source protection, ensuring the safety of drinking water and the well-being of urban and rural residents. The Baitiao River, meandering through Zhanqi Village, became a designated protected area. Chengdu Water Plant Six, positioned over 20 kilometers downstream, exemplifies the significance of the river. Subsequently, in the latter half of 2016, Chengdu Water Plant Seven was constructed in close proximity to the Baitiao River, further underscoring Zhanqi Village's status as a crucial water source protection zone. In response to these municipal water source protection policies, the village collective conducted consultations in 2016 and proceeded to close eight enterprises that posed a threat to water source security. Among these businesses were several highly profitable ones, such as the steel foundry, which generated tax revenues amounting to millions annually for the village. Nonetheless, due to their high levels of pollution and energy consumption, these enterprises faced substantial opposition from the public and failed to meet the construction standards for water sources. Consequently, considering the future direction of green industry development, the village bravely opted to shutter these enterprises.

With the previous work on the concentration of village collective land resources completed, the closure of the old factories in 2016 proceeded smoothly. Negotiations involved solely the enterprises and the village collective, minimizing communication costs. Village Director Li Guangju (李光菊) noted that although some of the closed factories did not directly contribute to water source pollution, they were shut down as they violated Zhanqi Village's industrial development plan by generating dust and air pollution. This short-lived pain endured during the transformation and development of the village collective economy ushered in an era of upgraded industrial standards. Following the closure of multiple enterprises, Pioneering Ecological Seasoning Co., Ltd., Fuyou Broad Bean paste Factory, Pixian Manjianghong Seasoning Food Co., Ltd., and "Grandpa Lang" Farm and Sideline Product Processing Enterprises emerged as the backbone of Zhanqi Village. Aligning with the contemporary trend of ecological development, Zhanqi Village imposed higher requirements on the production and operation of these enterprises, establishing a standardized development environment within the village. Consequently, ample space was freed up for the construction of the "Fifth Season Fragrance Resort" leisure tourism industry and the training business of the Rural Revitalization Institute. Zhanqi Village, by deftly surmounting spatial fragmentation, achieved increased planar extension and vertical dimensionality. Consequently, economic and social space capacity expanded, accommodating diverse ecological spaces and fostering diverse industrial ecologies. By harnessing the improvement of natural ecological spaces as a foundation, Zhanqi Village bolstered the enhancement of industrial ecological spaces and social ecological spaces.

3 The Ecological Transformation of Zhanqi Village: Harnessing Space Resources for Sustainable Development

3.1 Cultivating a Harmonious Coexistence of Industry and Nature

As GDP rises and society flourishes, the desires of individuals transcend mere subsistence, expanding to embrace the beauty of nature and a green, low-carbon lifestyle. Ecological agriculture has emerged as a response to these evolving consumer demands, satisfying not only the leisure pursuits of residents but also embodying the essence of green development.

Ecological agriculture, a form of agriculture that aligns with the upward shift in consumer preferences, holds a superior position in terms of needs hierarchy and consumption patterns compared to conventional agriculture. By appealing to higher levels of human needs, it transcends the constraints of traditional farming practices. Psychologist Abraham Maslow's hierarchy of needs theory supports this idea, suggesting that once lower-level needs are met, higher-level needs come to the fore. In the context of agricultural consumption, as income levels increase, people shift their focus from quantity to quality, seeking unique experiences in social interactions and aesthetics.

(1) Rongzhen Mushroom Industry Company

In the face of modern economic development, ordinary agricultural products are no longer sufficient. The standards have been raised to demand high-quality produce that is free from pollution and compatible with the environment. Against this backdrop, Zhanqi Village embraced innovation, coordination, openness, greenness, and sharing as guiding principles to accelerate the transformation of its agricultural sector. The village sought to improve the structure of agriculture, enhance its role in daily life, and establish a new paradigm by shedding traditional agricultural perspectives and ushering in novel industries.

Relying solely on nature is insufficient when it comes to cultivating mushrooms. Situated in Chengdu, an area with distinct seasons, relying on traditional methods of planting and waiting for suitable temperatures on a three-acre plot is inadequate to guarantee mushroom yields. Moreover, the labor and resources expended on shuttling between mountainous and high-altitude regions do not yield commensurate returns.

The partnership between Zhanqi Village and Rongzhen Mushroom Industry Company (hereinafter refer as "Rongzhen Mushroom") emerged in 2007. At that time, Zhanqi Village took the pioneering step of land consolidation in Pixian County, facilitating concentrated living arrangements and preparing for the village's industrial transformation by collectively pooling over 98% of its land. As an integrator of internal resources, Zhanqi Village elevated its standing in external negotiations by establishing an initial valuation for internal resources, thereby attracting external investors to participate in the "secondary market" and recalibrate rural resource prices. Seizing the opportunity, Li Zongtang, an experienced edible mushroom grower in Pengzhou City, envisioned breaking free from nature's whims by embarking on modern agriculture.

In August 2007, Chengdu Rongzhen Mushroom Industry Co., Ltd. was established on nearly 200 acres of land in the original Zhanqi Village, with an additional 100 acres from Jinxing Village. Here, the process of cultivating shiitake mushrooms, including mixing, sterilization, seeding, and low-temperature cultivation, took place. Leveraging the abundant edible mushroom resources in Western China, the company assumed the mission of revitalizing the edible mushroom industry in the region. By integrating resources through modern business practices, it became the core platform for the edible mushroom industry in Western China. With the introduction of large-scale production lines and the implementation of standardized processes and stringent quality management systems, it established the first standardized, large-scale, year-round edible mushroom factory in Western China.

In the subsequent stages of development, Rongzhen Industry forged collaborations with Xihua University, Sichuan Agricultural University, and others. They delved into key technologies related to edible mushroom cultivation and microbial fermentation, successfully completing 42 research cooperation projects. Their achievements include 20 projects focused on technology transfer, the development of 82 new varieties, and breakthroughs in utilizing by-products from edible and medicinal mushroom processing. Not limited to traditional agriculture, the modern agricultural industry, leveraging the power of "Internet+ ," also found fertile ground in Zhanqi Village.

"In 2007, when we first started cultivating shiitake mushrooms in Zhanqi Village, each mushroom weighed a mere 200 grams. According to industry standards, an average weight of 450 grams was considered acceptable," lamented Wang Deyong (王德勇), the director of Rongzhen

Mushroom in Zhanqi Village, as he marveled at the transformative impact of modern technology. By 2018, Rongzhen Mushroom Industry had established four branch factories nationwide. The Zhanqi Village branch alone boasted an annual output value of 100 million yuan, commanding a market share of 60% to 70% in the southwestern region of China.

(2) Mama Farm

In the midst of urban congestion, the allure of rural landscapes becomes apparent. As "urban diseases" spread and property prices skyrocket, urban space has become increasingly scarce. The vast vistas and natural beauty of rural areas, which offer respite for flora and fauna, have become sought-after havens for urbanites lacking living space. These natural landscapes, infused with cultural customs and human spaces, provide profound consumer benefits. Their economic value goes beyond aesthetics, encompassing tourism, leisure, education, wellness, and other tertiary services. When the luxuries of gazing at the moon, opening one's doors to panoramic views, and admiring unpolluted skies become distant dreams in urban locales, rural areas that retain pristine environments and free themselves from light and atmospheric pollution find opportunities to engage in tourism, farmhouse accommodations, and nature-based education for families.

Mama Farm serendipitously encountered the beginnings of Zhanqi Village's ecological transformation. In the wake of overheated investments in the real estate industry in 2007, the first half of 2008 witnessed a continued year-on-year growth rate of over 30% in national real estate development investments, placing significant pressure on the overall real estate market. Seizing the opportunity, Sichuan Dahang Hongye Group Co., Ltd. (四川大行宏业集团有限公司), a real estate developer, decided to transform into rural tourism, tapping into the abundant space resources and stable, long-term returns offered by countryside attractions in the Bazhong region.

"I told him I didn't want to deal with farmers because it can be quite cumbersome. He replied that they already had cooperatives established in their area, and it was that simple. Thus, he enticed me to come over.

Our land ownership is straightforward. We just need to sign an agreement with the village, and you'll have it tomorrow. The land is managed by the cooperative, not individual farmers. It will be swiftly transferred to you."

Source: interview record with Mr. Li from Mama Farm on October 5, 2019.

With a single business card and numerous invitations, Zhanqi Village possessed the unwavering determination to concentrate its valuable land resources. By 2010, Zhanqi Village had completed the integration of its territorial resources. Guided by Gao Demin, the former director of Zhanqi Village, the village embarked on a plan for industrial transformation, utilizing unused land for higher value-added endeavors to stimulate collective economic growth. During a joint trip to Beijing with the Pixian County Investment Promotion Bureau, Gao Demin established contact with the chairman of Dahang Hongye Group, who expressed interest in investing in rural tourism. Through multiple exchanges, Dahang Hongye Group gained a comprehensive understanding of the resource integration in Zhanqi Village, recognizing that the village had successfully resolved the typical concerns associated with businesses venturing into rural areas. Firstly, Zhanqi Village had already achieved concentrated living arrangements, and its land ownership structure was straightforward. This circumvented the issue of excessive transaction costs resulting from fragmented land ownership by individual farmers. The assets management company directly liaised with the collective, ensuring the timely acquisition of land for construction. Secondly, Dahang Hongye Group was captivated by the expansive riverbank wasteland in Zhanqi Village, as well as the available residential land and courtyard structures, which mitigated investment costs during the construction phase. Lastly, due to the relatively recent Wenchuan earthquake, tourists were somewhat hesitant to visit Dujiangyan City. Zhanqi Village, situated at the intersection of Dujiangyan, Pengzhou, and Pixian, enjoyed a humid climate similar to Dujiangyan and was a mere 40 kilometers away from Chengdu City, ideally meeting the weekend sightseeing needs of urban residents.

After reaching a mutual cooperation agreement, Zhanqi Village, in 2010, contributed agricultural land as equity at a rate of 1600 yuan per mu. This partnership led to the establishment of the Fifth Season Asset Management Company, in which Dahang Hongye Group held a 95% stake. Another account suggests that Zhanqi Village priced its collectively owned construction land at 5 million yuan per mu, based on the pricing of surrounding state-owned land.[2] Zhanqi Village primarily assumes responsibility for the management of the park.

Mama Farm primarily focuses on rural sightseeing agriculture, encompassing elements such as hotels, dining, conference facilities, wedding preparations, and leisure activities in the countryside. By 2012, they had completed a 20-mu facility for sightseeing agriculture, a 30,000 m2 leisure club, a rural hotel, and other interactive primary and tertiary sector projects. Mama Farm's project was divided into two phases: the first phase comprised hotels, dining, conference rooms, and leisure areas, covering an area of 600 mu acquired through leasing for a period of 50 years. The second phase primarily consisted of flower greenhouses, providing the collective with an annual revenue increase of over 300,000 yuan.

Thus, the barren land sprouted a new chapter in industrial transformation, and Zhanqi Village became home to Sichuan's first lavender flower field. Leveraging its geographical advantage alone, Mama Farm was merely one among numerous rural tourism enterprises across the expansive land, insufficient to captivate passersby. Consequently, the investor adopted a new approach to attract visitors, driven by a commercial perspective. In 2011, Zhanqi Village unveiled its first iconic attraction—the Lavender Garden. It marked the village's inaugural ecological transformation and Sichuan's first lavender estate. Even before its official opening, the Lavender Garden attracted 50,000 visitors per day to Zhanqi Village. Quick to capitalize on the transformation dividends, Zhanqi Village invested in road repairs within the village and purchased seedlings from villagers to support Mama Farm's landscape resources. These efforts maximized the quality of leisure and sightseeing experiences for visitors. By March 2012, when Mama Farm officially commenced operations, it had evolved into a fully developed ecological hotel estate.

3.2 Exploring Opportunities: Cultural Renaissance Fueling Ecological Industrialization

The essence of ecological transformation lies in the metamorphosis of environmental prowess into thriving domains like ecological agriculture, industrial prowess, and enchanting eco-tourism. In the tapestry of rural renaissance, lies the key to revitalize dormant ecological treasures that,

[2] Internal report of the Agriculture, Rural and Forestry Bureau of Pixian District. Case Collection of Pixian's Experience in Rural Revitalization [R], 2018.

for far too long, remained bereft of valuation. Through ingenious means of valorizing these resources, urban and rural elements can harmoniously intertwine, igniting a virtuous cycle of investment and benefit. As the sunlit fields of Rongzhen Mushroom Industry breathe life into primary agriculture, and the allure of Mama Farm kindles the flames of cultural tourism, the entrance of eco-centric enterprises breathes a new lease of life into the fabric of Zhanqi Village. Hence, even amidst the forced closure of enterprises that fell short of the green development mandate, Zhanqi Village finds solace in a sustainable wellspring of progress.

United by purpose, Rongzhen Mushroom and Mama Farm have planted the seeds of ecological awakening, thereby etching Zhanqi's rural tourism onto the map. While seeking shade beneath the boughs, Zhanqi Village never forgets the art of planting, ensuring an enduring verdant legacy.

(1) The Enigma of Zhanqi's 18 Rural Workshops

As collective economic organizations, custodians of ecological wealth, embrace equitable transactions with external capital, a market emerges, where interplay between internal and external forces fuels sustainable growth. This catalytic fusion unlocks latent local resources, fostering urban and tertiary industry development, thereby accentuating their intrinsic value. Substantial gains further nourish the collective economic organism, fostering public services and the amelioration of rural governance, thereby fortifying the bedrock of regional prosperity.

Zhanqi's 18 Rural Workshops (乡村十八坊) symbolize a momentous juncture, where the collective steps forth from the shadows of ecological transformation. Mama Farm, Blue Rainbow Picking Garden, and their ilk have metamorphosed Zhanqi into an esteemed brand, fusing agriculture, culture, and tourism, transcending the shackles of mere cultivation. Yet, the full potential of this brand remains untapped, as collective investment merely graces the realm of land leases, untethered from operational involvement and the realization of land's inherent value. In the nascent stages of ecological metamorphosis, the collective assumed a passive stance in the background. The genesis of Zhanqi's 18 Rural Workshops finds its roots in the 11th National Forum of Village Director in 2011, where the visionary concept of agricultural parks, espoused by Mr. Shen Zejiang (沈泽江), ignited the curiosity of Secretary Gao Demin. In the throes of industrial transformation, Zhanqi Village yearned for a transformative endeavor, one that could infuse spatial resources with tangible value. Alas, due to financial constraints and spatial limitations, the vision distilled into the singular concept of "Zhanqi's 18 Rural Workshops."

The early-stage odyssey, where external enterprises found solace in Zhanqi's ecological bosom, not only relieved the village from the onus of solo transformation but also harnessed the brand's gravitational pull to secure financial support from banking institutions. Seizing the auspicious moment when Pixian County was anointed one of the nation's 33 pilot counties for rural land system reform, Zhanqi Village showcased its dormant village-run enterprise land, spanning 13.447 acres, at 495,000 yuan per acre, culminating in a sale to Sichuan Maigao Tourism Company at 525,000 yuan per acre. This transaction heralded a windfall of 7.06 million yuan, kindling the embers of Zhanqi's 18 Rural Workshops. With an investment surpassing 30 million yuan, bank loans accounted for over 70% of the financial infusion. The sterling reputation built during the initial ecological transmutation, spanning the realms of agriculture, culture, and tourism, fortified Zhanqi's rapport with several banks, paving the path for loans at lenient interest rates. Additionally, the village harnessed the capital mobilization prowess of asset management firms, captivating party members, cadres, and villagers with alluring interest rates, amassing over 500,000 yuan in social capital.[3] Construction commenced in March 2017 on Phase 1 of Zhanqi's 18 Rural Workshops, at a cost exceeding 900 yuan per square meter. The advent of Phase 2, on September 2, 2018, saw the outlay escalate to approximately 1100 yuan per square meter.[4] By December of the same year, meticulous tourism blueprints for the cultural courtyard were drafted, paving the way for prospective investments from January 2019 onward.[5]

Drawing inspiration from Yuanjia Village's model, Zhanqi's 18 Rural Workshops crafted a unique deposit collection system. Diverging from the cooperative approach dependent on capital infusion, Zhanqi Village embraced a unified investment structure through collective economic organizations. Deposits levied upon merchants were contingent on

[3] Source: Interview record of Lin Genzhi, Zhanqi's 18 Rural Workshops representative, on October 5, 2019.

[4] Construction costs encompass material and labor expenses, with the 2018 price surge attributable to raw material inflation.

[5] Source: Interview record of Gao Demin on October 2, 2019.

their tenure and shop area. The inaugural phase (August 8, 2018) favored merchants with a reduced deposit rate of 600 yuan per square meter, gradually ascending to 1000 yuan per square meter during the second phase (January 2019). Lin Genzhi, the vanguard of Zhanqi's 18 Rural Workshops and director of Zhanqi Village's Comprehensive Office (Public Service Center), elucidated, "Deposits primarily serve to steady merchants, ridding the landscape of volatile elements." The accumulation of deposits unfurls a gradual refund process, unfurling three years hence. The first year bequeaths a 30% refund, followed by another 30% in the second year, culminating in a final 10% restitution in the third year. The remaining corpus forms the bedrock of an assurance fund dedicated to the upkeep of the premises. Merchants are typically bound by a three-year lease, with those departing within the first year eligible for a 90% deposit refund, allocating the remaining 10% for maintenance costs. Entrepreneurs exiting between the first and third years receive an 80% refund. Collected deposits assume an investment mantle for the collective's developmental ventures.

(2) Pixian County Broad Bean Paste (Douban) Museum

Manjianghong Food Technology Co., Ltd. (hereafter referred to as Manjianghong Company), a latecomer transitioning towards the tertiary industry, hitched two rides on the "bandwagon" of Zhanqi Village.

In 2009, Foxconn inked a deal with Chengdu City to set foot in Sichuan, appropriating vast tracts of land in Deyuan Town for a residential project. Seeking a fresh location for their operations, Manjianghong Company, which once occupied a factory in Deyuan Town, found a promising prospect in Zhanqi Village—a product of resource integration. This village possessed prime positioning, offering more favorable rents than the Sichuan Cuisine Garden District and boasting dormant factory spaces. Consequently, Manjianghong Company saved on construction costs when establishing their broad bean paste (douban豆瓣) processing plant. Furthermore, Zhanqi Village had a precedent of housing Broad Bean Paste Factories, shouldering the initial costs of market risks, organizational structures, and product research and development for the latecomer, Manjianghong Company. Capitalizing on acquaintances and a network of geospatial information, on October 1, 2010, Manjianghong Company and Zhanqi Village sealed a 20-year contract, with the village leasing its formerly owned Xianfeng Brewing Factory and Shudu Packaging Factory's fixed assets to Manjianghong Company.

Table 1 illustrates the fluctuations in Manjianghong Company's land lease in Zhanqi Village.

As Zhanqi Village's agricultural, cultural, and tourism development embarked on the right path, Manjianghong Company, attuned to the trend of industrial integration, broadened its scope of operations. They reaped the dividends of Zhanqi Village's transition to the tertiary industry while enjoying favorable land prices, courtesy of the trust costs accumulated during their early factory operations. On February 25, 2018,

Table 1 Changes in Manjianghong company's land lease in Zhanqi village

Year	*Original use of land*	*Area (mu)*	*Rent*	*Purpose*
2010	Xianfeng brewing factory Shudu packaging factory	15	Starting from 70,000 yuan[6]	Douban processing
2015	Xianfeng brewing factory Shudu packaging factory	15	Starting from 150,000 yuan	Douban processing
	Prefabricated component factory	Factory building plus 1 mu of land	Starting from 100,000 yuan	
2018	Xianfeng Brewing factory Shudu packaging factory	15	Starting from 150,000 yuan	Douban processing
	Prefabricated component factory	1	Starting from 100,000 yuan	
	Cultural courtyard	A comprehensive building plus 1 acre of land	1300 catties of rice/mu House rent: 100,000 yuan	Establishing Pixian Douban museum

[6] Original Contract: Rent of 70,000 yuan from 2010.10.01 to 2011.09.30. From the second year onwards, an annual increment of 20,000 yuan until reaching a ceiling of 150,000 yuan per year. Subsequent rent adjustments occur every five years based on the prevailing economic conditions.

Manjianghong Company and Zhanqi Village signed a 20-year lease contract for the construction of broad bean paste Lane, one of the "18 Rural Workshops" in the rural area, and the Pixian Douban Intangible Cultural Heritage Traditional Production Exhibition Base. Zhanqi Village leased 10 mu of land within the Cultural Courtyard and a comprehensive building in the same compound to Manjianghong Company. The land rent was determined based on the guiding price of 13 million jin of rice per mu per year, while the house rent amounted to 100,000 yuan.

The design of the Pixian Douban Museum primarily fell within the realm of the Manjianghong Company, with external decoration companies lending a hand in refining the design. The design expenses totaled approximately 140,000 yuan, and the museum's construction demanded a grand sum of 10 million yuan, entirely borne by Manjianghong Company. Drawing inspiration from Pixian Douban's unique regional environment and embracing local cultural, geographical, and historical elements, the designers adhered to the principle of "promoting traditional culinary culture, showcasing the profound history of broad bean paste, and fashioning a distinctive museum image." Their efforts yielded a culturally rich museum that seamlessly integrated exhibition, collection, and promotion, transforming it into a renowned cultural emblem of Pixian County. Following several comprehensive revisions, Pixian Douban Museum officially opened its doors on September 30, 2018.[7]

Since its inauguration, Pixian Douban Museum has welcomed an average of approximately 3000 visitors daily. People from all corners of the country have immersed themselves in the essence of Sichuan cuisine, experiencing firsthand the enduring heritage and magnificence of Pixian Douban—"the ancient art of sauce-making and the craftsmanship of nature."[8]

[7] Sichuan News Network. Unveiling the Legend of broad bean paste, Exploring broad bean paste Production: Pixian Douban Museum Commences Today [EB/OL]. (2018-09-30) [2021-01-21]. http://scnews.newssc.org/system/20180930/000911830.html.

[8] Chengdu All-Search News Network. Constructing Museums to Enrich and Exalt the Billion-dollar Douban Industry [EB/OL]. (2019-02-12) [2021-01-21]. http://news.chengdu.cn/2019/0212/2032150.shtml.].

4 Rural Revitalization: Novel Resources, Boundless Value

4.1 *"Lucid Waters and Lush Mountains Are Invaluable Assets"*

The rural revitalization strategy, a paramount endeavor introduced during the 19th National Congress, stands as a seminal tactic for the transformation of China's ecological civilization. By harnessing external capital, it seeks to imbue ecological resources with value through the prism of eco-industrialization and industrial ecology. Thus, it caters to the welfare of the local community, the idyllic countryside, encompassing mountains, rivers, forests, lakes, and even the essence of pristine air.

Zhanqi Village boasts a bountiful tapestry of soil, climate, and water, endowing it with unparalleled ecological advantages. Firstly, the village serves as a vital water source preservation zone for Chengdu City, safeguarded by stringent ecological policies that uphold the pristine quality and safety of its primary industries. Secondly, its advantageous geographical position provides a fertile ground for secondary industries, such as the production of delectable bean paste crafted from the region's remarkable water, enabling enterprises to fashion exceptional products, cultivate reputation and brand, and enhance profits. Lastly, the village's natural resources form the bedrock of the tertiary sector's development, as the flourishing purple floral fields of Mama Farm, the tranquil murmur of water meandering beside Phoebe zhennan forests, and the tantalizing aroma emanating from the Pixian Douban Museum's brimming fermentation vats stand testament to the rediscovered bounties of nature.

(1) Regional Uniqueness

Geographic peculiarities define agriculture as distinct from its industrial counterparts, epitomizing the diverse kaleidoscope of ecological splendor. Variances in topography and landforms engender divergent hydrothermal conditions, while natural elements like slopes, altitudes, and soils yield dissimilar product qualities. Hence, even with cutting-edge techniques, precisely catering to the environmental requisites of agricultural produce remains an arduous endeavor.

Endowed with the stewardship of nature, Zhanqi Village revels in an unprecedented advantage, where the art of brewing bean paste embodies the adage of "seizing opportune moments, capitalizing on favorable terrain, and fostering amicable relations." Luo Yanhua (罗艳华), the Deputy General Manager of Manjianghong Company, lauds the production superiority of Zhanqi Village's water quality: "Take the water used for crafting Pixian Douban in other regions. Although we have produced Broad Bean paste elsewhere, it lacks the authentic zest found here."[9] Situated at the heart of Chengdu Plain, Pidu District enjoys well-defined seasons, perennial moisture, an extended frost-free period, an average annual temperature of 15.7 °C, 1264.7 hours of annual sunshine, and an average relative humidity of 84%. These optimal conditions foster the proliferation of diverse microorganisms and enable comprehensive enzymatic breakdown by various molds. The water quality of Dujiangyan undergoes natural softening and flows to Zhanqi Village in impeccable measure, forging a favorable natural setting for the meticulous processes of fermenting, sun-drying, and exposure that underpin the creation of Pixian Douban.

Pidu District, nestled within the Dujiangyan irrigation area upstream of the Minjiang River, boasts uncontaminated water sources of pristine quality. Falling within the ambit of the Chengdu Municipal Water Source Protection Zone, this locale is replete with diverse minerals, especially a plethora of trace elements. Such natural endowments provide the stable, high-quality brewing water indispensable to the craft of Pixian Douban. The surface soil, arising from Quaternary sediments, is endowed with profound depth and predominantly comprises paddy soil, boasting excellent fertility, permeability, and cultivability. Its richness in minerals, including phosphorus, potassium, calcium, magnesium, manganese, and others, complements its natural fecundity, fostering the flourishing growth of crops such as chili peppers and fava beans. Thus, it offers an abundance of premium raw materials for the production of Pixian Douban.[10]

(2) Ecological Panoramas Unveiled

[9] Science and Technology Daily. "Green Development": Zhanqi Village Transforms "Weakness" into "Advantage." (2018-12-05). Retrieved from http://news.sina.com.cn/o/2018-12-05/doc-ihmutuec6270309.shtml.

[10] China News Network. "Chengdu Pidu District: Blueprint for a Billion-yuan Industrial Cluster to Elevate Sichuan Cuisine's Aroma Globally." (2019-03-15). Retrieved from https://cbgc.scol.com.cn/news/124663?app_id=cbgc&from=timeline.

"Everywhere, poetic realms unfold, nature's bounty ever at hand." Amidst the urban cacophony, people's yearning for poetry and distant horizons finds solace here. The countryside, cradled by majestic mountains and serenaded by meandering waters, greets each day with the melodic chorus of birdsong and a delicate mist that adorns the morning. As dusk descends, a cascade of sunset hues bathes the rustic rooftops and verdant fields. Spring's cultivation, summer's tending, autumn's harvest, and winter's respite—traditional agriculture's livelihood finds its essence within these four simple seasons. Bestowing newfound purpose upon agriculture, the leisurely allure of rural tourism defines not only productivity but also an ecological tapestry.

During its nascent stage, Mama Farm prioritized stabilizing visitor flow. Despite incurring three consecutive years of losses, it chose to sacrifice ticket revenues, seeking to cultivate a stream of patrons. Most tourists arrived with a sightseeing agenda, immersing themselves in the ethereal landscapes, capturing vibrant windmills against the cerulean sky, yet often departing without partaking in even a sip of water, carrying solely the indelible memories of these panoramas. Mama Farm, employing landscape ecology as its visual marketing strategy, understood that sight shapes our initial perception of the world. Similarly, in the realm of consumerism, visual stimuli serve as the gateway to product cognition. By offering a captivating, sensorial experience, latent intrigue in potential customers can be kindled, facilitating the impetus for promotional engagement. Much like Starbucks coffee, which conquered the world without pervasive television advertisements, it became an emblematic scene to witness office workers cradling coffee cups—a symbol of cozy contentment. Visual marketing transmits messages that ignite swift consumer interest, and Mama Farm artfully choreographed its approach. Perhaps on a post-rain sunny day, when the sky unveils its unblemished azure canvas, visitors amble into Zhanqi Village. Rays of sunlight delicately spill over the eaves of courtyard houses, caressing the expansive asphalt road below. Aromatic wisps of vegetation, saturated with a hint of moisture, permeate the air, while lavender and verbena exhibit newfound vibrance after their rejuvenating shower. Towering windmills peek from within the floral seascape, inviting one to meander amidst the idyllic pastoral setting or tread the adjacent path, all the while immersed in the captivating splendor of the rural panorama. Reflecting the essence of ecological resources unto the beholder's gaze is the epitome of resource monetization, especially within the communal fabric of village life, where word-of-mouth serves as the ultimate conduit of advertisement. Through meticulous cultivation of early acclaim, Mama Farm transformed its fortunes, pivoting from losses to profits, heralding a path of triumphant trajectory by the year 2015.

4.2 *The Passing of Time, Elevated Value in Resources*

The interplay between old and new enterprises in Zhanqi Village represents a conversation between the "pioneers" and the "followers" in their journey of ecological transformation. Consolidating the village's resources demanded its due negotiation costs, but Zhanqi Village, after careful selection, welcomed several new enterprises. In compliance with Chengdu's strict water source protection policies, Zhanqi Village bid farewell to numerous high-polluting companies, their idle factories and production equipment becoming capital for the village's transformative expansion.

The premise of sustained industry lies in the torchbearer propelling the successors. Old enterprises bear the brunt of market exploration costs for the newcomers, providing a sturdy platform for development with their surplus resources. The Douban industry has long thrived in Zhanqi Village, with the Pioneer Brewery commencing production in 1981 and claiming second place in the 1990 Pixian County broad bean paste evaluation competition. The brewery's stellar reputation swiftly opened doors in the market, granting Fuyou Douban Factory and Manjianghong Company, as the subsequent enterprises, advantageous conditions to address market risks, organizational structure, research and development of production technology, and product innovation costs. Upon joining the village, besides paying land rent to the collective, Manjianghong Company required no additional capital for constructing factory buildings. A simple revamp of the former Xianfeng Brewery's dormant workshops allowed them to set forth in production, skillfully capitalizing on the favorable winds and waters of Zhanqi Village.

The pioneers forge ahead, exploring uncharted territories. Tales of thriving industries must be woven anew by the followers, akin to a manor's flower field blossoming with a swarm of butterflies in an arid landscape, breathing new life into the dormant cultural enclave. Truth be told, Sichuan's climate is less suited for cultivating lavender, yet from a tourism development perspective, the "Fifth Season Resort" dared to venture forth into this fresh experiment. Mr. Li ventured to Provence, immersing himself in learning and consulting with experts to master breeding techniques. Ultimately, through the combination of sagebrush and lavender, a 600-acre lavender estate emerged, a resplendent testament to ecological aesthetics. Thus, the once-fallow wasteland experienced a rebirth, witnessing an increase in its intrinsic value, while fostering enhanced reputation through word-of-mouth in cultural tourism, further propelling the appreciation of village land. As an integral part of the ecological transformation, the collective of Zhanqi Village can rightfully claim their place among the ranks of the successors. Following resource integration, they stand more self-reliant, having weathered the trials and tribulations during the early stages of transformation, silently supporting other enterprises from the shadows. Accumulating invaluable experience, they have finally emerged from the shadows to take center stage. In 2015, Zhanqi Village identified the land housing the village-owned compound fertilizer factory, prefabricated component factory, and the old village committee office building for market auction, eventually concluding the transaction at a total price exceeding seven million yuan at the Pixian District Public Resources Trading Center. A portion of these funds served as the launch capital for the "18 Rural Workshops" project. Moreover, the cultural enclave at the village entrance functions as the face of Zhanqi Village, its enviable location endowing it with the role of a welcoming ambassador. Capitalizing on the industrial reputation cultivated during the earlier stages, the "18 Rural Workshops" project has united the distinctive regional products, harnessing collective strength to ignite a renewed flame of western Sichuan's folk culture in Zhanqi Village. It has emerged as a new cornerstone of cultural tourism, irresistibly beckoning curious travelers.

Transitioning is no facile task, and sustaining progress poses an even greater challenge. The burgeoning successors must embrace the mantle of responsibility inherited from the pioneers, ensuring the continued diversity of industries. In the course of Zhanqi Village's industrial exploration, enterprises such as the Pioneer Brewery and the brick factory have made monumental contributions to the village's economic growth. Now, in sync with the spirit of the times, the industrial village seeks sustainable development through ecological transformation. The emerging enterprises within the village deftly leverage the factories and spatial framework bequeathed by their predecessors, seamlessly transitioning their operations while harmonizing with Zhanqi Village's development rhythm, thus embracing the third industry. Manjianghong Company, employing a fusion of the secondary and tertiary sectors, has fashioned the Pixian Douban Museum, promoting immersive experiential marketing that revitalizes intangible cultural heritage. The year 2018 witnessed their turnover soar to six million yuan, setting a model for sales bolstered by tourism. The visit of President Xi Jinping infused fresh energy into the "18 Rural Workshops" project. Endowed with distinct western Sichuan characteristics, traditional handmade products experienced an upsurge in reputation and value owing to President Xi's favor, triggering an upswing in both tourist footfall and sales. This consolidation solidifies the proactive significance of cultivating locally distinctive brands. Mama Farm, at the vanguard of the successors, has traversed the arduous path of operational fatigue amidst interactive collaboration with diverse enterprises. Though the novelty of lavender may have waned, the lavender flower fields have nurtured a sense of renewal, birthing blueberry and strawberry gardens, as well as the "18 Rural Workshops" project. Simultaneously, this perpetual sense of freshness has transformed Zhanqi Village into a beacon on the road to rural revitalization, propelling the formation of the Zhanqi Red Brand. Mama Farm, mired in the throes of transformation, has finally hitched a ride on the favorable winds. Having tasted the dividends of cultural resources, Mama Farm has expanded its conference and training business, centering on red education and transforming Zhanqi Village's localized culture into rural education. The existing hotel within the park conveniently accommodates the needs of study groups, offering sustenance and shelter.

4.3 Crafting Profound Rural Heritage

Agriculture, culture, and tourism suffer from an inherent imbalance, with the cultural preservation aspect of agriculture gradually fading amidst the onslaught of the market economy, while leisure tourism experiences a sudden surge. Most folk culture villages, regrettably, offer nothing more than superficial tourist attractions, fixating on shallow sightseeing, fruit-picking, rustic accommodations, and a superficial fusion of agricultural and cultural elements. This shallow approach lacks the depth necessary to sustain long-term development. Consequently, despite ample material provisions, most rural areas remain languishing in desolation.

In November 2012, at the onset of a new historical chapter, the 18th National Congress of the Communist Party of China made a strategic decision to "vigorously advance the construction of ecological civilization." The objective of rural revitalization lies in the renaissance of rural civilization, breathing new life into withering countryside landscapes. Culture serves as the bedrock for rural rejuvenation, a scarce resource sought after by rural communities for their industrial development. The revitalization of rural areas through culture should primarily focus on unearthing the indigenous cultural treasures, employing local spatial resources in a manner that upholds the fundamental principle of preserving authentic local culture. Only then can folk villages avoid transient existence, marred by haphazard influxes of external capital.

Within specific geographic enclaves, the broad bean paste industry acts not only as an economic powerhouse but also as a vessel and guardian of agrarian cultural heritage. Pixian County's broad bean paste, hailed as the "essence of Sichuan cuisine," boasts nationwide acclaim. Yet, such accolades were not hastily won; as early as the 1980s, Pixian County's broad bean paste advertisements adorned busses and billboards, as captured in Fig. 7.1. A single fava bean, stripped of its skin, soaked, blended with wheat flour, and fermented using rice koji, metamorphoses into sweet broad bean paste through natural fermentation. Superior-quality, naturally curled Erjingtiao chili peppers (a variety native to Sichuan) are salted, crushed, and placed in vats to ferment, forming chili embryos. The amalgamation of sweet broad bean paste and chili embryos, left to mature through a series of processes including flipping, sun-drying, and exposure, ultimately yields the indispensable broad bean paste sauce adorning Sichuanese dinner tables. Wandering through the halls of the Pixian Douban Museum, the tapestry of broad bean paste's history and flavors unfolds serenely, embodying the museum's initial mission: to showcase China's most historically cherished condiment.

Industrial tourism constitutes the pièce de résistance of the Pixian Douban Museum. The initial integration of broad bean paste processing facilities bestowed an intrinsic foundation upon the museum, whereby the public display of secondary industry production scenes morphs into a tourist spectacle within the tertiary sector. The spirit of craftsmanship reverberates throughout. During the factory's formative years, Chairman Luo Zunrong (罗遵荣) paid multiple visits to Master Zeng Zhengyun (曾正云), the inheritor of broad bean paste's intangible cultural heritage, seeking collaboration to safeguard the authentic essence of Pixian Douban. Zeng Zhengyun stipulated a prerequisite for such cooperation: "To delve into genuine techniques, one must possess a thousand traditional sun-drying vats."[11] After extensive exploration throughout Sichuan, Luo Zunrong discovered the suitable clay in Hengshan Town, essential for crafting the sacrosanct sauce vats. Standing atop the sauce-dripping platform in the museum, gazing downward, a succession of colossal vats brimming with crimson elixir comes into view. Amidst this panorama, workers from Manjianghong Company intermittently lift the lids, inspecting the fermentation progress of each vat—an exquisite spectacle encapsulating the broad bean paste sauce production process.

The Pixian Douban Museum orchestrates its itinerary according to the time-honored brewing process of broad bean paste. Visitors, led by their olfactory senses, gradually detect the alluring fragrance permeating the air, gradually unraveling the enigmatic origins of broad bean paste, until they themselves become acquainted with its irresistible essence. The museum, designed in the architectural style of western Sichuan, houses a collection of over 3000 historical tools, artifacts, and more. It encompasses the Shu Sauce Workshop, the Pixian Douban Chinese Intangible Cultural Heritage Impression Theme Hall, the Pixian Douban Traditional Production Display Base, the Shufu Cellar 1393, the Pixian Douban Innovation Hall, the Fermentation Workshop, the Traditional Sun-drying Field, and the Experience Hall.[12] Embarking on a journey through the 18 Rural Workshops of rural areas, visitors traverse the Pixian Douban Museum, bearing witness to a grand expanse of sauce vats. Initially, most tourists marvel at the spectacle and revel in its opulent flavors. However, upon entering the museum's inner sanctum, they encounter elucidations of broad bean paste's cultural origins adorning both flanking walls. The narrative unveils the fortuitous genesis of broad bean paste sauce, hinging upon the favorable climate of the Shu region for brewing and the ingenious substitution of chili peppers for Juncus effusus by the denizens of Shu during the late Ming and early Qing dynasties. Progressing through the production workshop, visitors glimpse rudimentary millstones, sieves, and processing machinery such as elevators and blanching drums. The seamless fusion of ancient Shu sauce culture with the brewing techniques

[11] Chengdu Municipal People's Government website. Pixian Douban Museum opens in Zhanqi Village [EB/OL]. (2018-10-01) [2021-01-21]. http://www.chengdu.gov.cn/chengdu/home/2018-10/01/content_2b0d6ca78a7e467a811aa09913d79bb3.shtml.

[12] Chengdu Municipal People's Government Website. Pixian Douban Museum Opens in Zhanqi Village [EB/OL]. (2018-10-01) [2021-01-21]. http://www.chengdu.gov.cn/chengdu/home/2018-10/01/content_2b0d6ca78a7e467a811aa09913d79bb3.shtml.

of Pixian Douban resonates vividly, encapsulating a microcosm of historical reverence. Imbued with the lingering aroma of sauce permeating the halls, visitors traverse the Flavor Corridor, where they learn that Pixian Douban has garnered the recognition of esteemed leaders, both domestic and foreign, evoking a profound sense of pride.

As a bridge between yesteryears, the present, and the future, culture derives its significance from enlightenment, contemplation, and innovation. The Shufu Museum hosts a digitalized production process, unveiling the modus operandi of Manjianghong Company. During broad bean paste sauce's nascent stages, to surmount the challenges posed by traditional craftsmanship's protracted timelines and the impediments to mass production, Manjianghong Company collaborated with Sichuan University and Xihua University, embarking on research and development. By employing a multi-strain fermentation method, they successfully addressed issues pertaining to prolonged production cycles and compromised flavor profiles, striking an exquisite balance between traditional artistry and contemporary market demands. This emblemizes the progressive spirit of Manjianghong Company and the reverential preservation of broad bean paste culture. Following a stroll through the annals of the sauce garden, tracing its trajectory from the "front shop" to the "back workshop," visitors once again ascend the sauce-dripping platform. Within the confines of the vats lies not merely sauce but also the essence of the western Sichuan region's natural climate and the venerable craftsmanship of koji-making and sauce brewing.

Adjacent to the museum lies an experiential hall, adorned with numerous hotpot tables, inviting visitors to partake in the art of broad bean paste creation and sample various renditions of broad bean paste sauce. The Pixian Douban Museum compels patrons to invest in non-utilitarian values such as cultural identity, deftly implementing a marketing strategy that harmoniously combines tourism with sales, thus contributing a vital, transformative touch to the cultural ambiance permeating the 18 Rural Workshops of rural areas.

In a serendipitous convergence, nestled approximately 20 kilometers from Zhanqi Village, lies Qinggangshu Village, where Sichuan embroidery culture, employing "Water Conceals Mulberry Fields" as its picturesque backdrop, thrives as an agricultural, cultural, and touristic tapestry, eloquently weaving the narrative of beauty as a conduit for harmonious coexistence.

* * *

Water Conceals Mulberry Fields, an Exquisite Homestead

Sichuan embroidery (Shu Xiu 蜀绣), as the name suggests, is the art of needlework unique to the Western plains of Sichuan. The"Shu Records (《华阳国志·蜀志》)" of the Jin Dynasty proudly proclaims Sichuan embroidery, along with jade, gold, silver, tin, and brocade, as treasures of the Shu region. Thus, it becomes evident that Sichuan embroidery culture holds a significant place within the realm of Ba-Shu heritage.

Qinggangshu Village, hailed as one of China's ten most beautiful villages in 2015, orchestrates the fusion of its forests, waterways, and farmlands into a harmonious tapestry of livelihood. Enamored with the pursuit of a picturesque new village, they embrace the concept of "beauty" as their developmental ethos, positioning grain cultivation and rural tourism as their prevailing industries. In their commitment to preserve traditional culture and enrich the village's tapestry of offerings, Qinggangshu Village joined hands with Cai Shimin (蔡世民), Chairman of the Chengdu Embroidery Cultural Development Co., Ltd., and invested 250 million yuan to establish a Sichuan embroidery workshop and exhibition center within the village.

On the momentous day of March 10, 2019, the "Water Concealing Mulberry Fields—Embroidery Village (水隐桑田·绣里)" project unfurled its doors, inviting guests with open arms. Water Concealing Mulberry Fields, Embroidery Village stands as a pioneering immersive cultural and tourism complex, uniquely intertwining the essence of mulberry silk culture, the intangible heritage of Sichuan embroidery, the development of cultural tourism products, and the dissemination of educational knowledge. Within its premises, a captivating panorama of clothing culture, leisurely pursuits, immersive experiences, and cultural exhibitions seamlessly merge.

Unlike the Pixian Douban Museum, which draws upon the existing industrial scenes and shares the landscape of the tertiary sector, Embroidery Village capitalizes on its inherent natural advantages. It ingeniously weaves together the scenic attractions by harnessing the flow of the Xuyan River, in perfect harmony with Qinggangshu Village's ecological wetlands. The waters from the Shu prefecture nourish all living beings. Thus, nearly 30 varieties of mulberry saplings thrive within the threefold boundaries of the mulberry grove. On a sun-kissed day, one can revel in the ethereal fragrance of mulberry leaves and bask in the cascading splendor of the distant Changchun Waterfall. After savoring the abundance of silkworms and mulberry trees, the "Ten Acres ("十亩之间")" and the ecological museum ingeniously converge to breathe life into the intricate beauty of every embroidered stitch. The museum vividly narrates the epic journey of Sichuan embroidery, unraveling its historical tapestry through displays of exquisite and peerless works. Each masterpiece pulsates with a vibrant zest for life. Meanwhile, "Ten Acres" embraces interactive experiences, fostering a deeper connection between visitors and the intangible heritage of Sichuan embroidery, woodcarving, bamboo weaving, and other cultural treasures, thereby enriching their understanding of the agrarian heritage.

During the early months of 2018, General Secretary Xi Jinping embarked on an auspicious visit to Zhanqi Village, where Sichuan embroidery took center stage among a collection of distinctive exhibits. Among the treasures showcased were a replica of Han Dynasty Shu brocade armguards, bearing the auspicious pattern "Five Stars Rising from the East, Benefiting China (五星出东方利中国)," unearthed in Xinjiang in 1995. Additionally, a Sichuan embroidery masterpiece inspired by Luo Zhongli (罗中立)'s renowned painting "Father" was on display. This masterpiece, meticulously crafted over the course of a year by two skilled embroiderers, elicited resounding praise from Xi, attesting to the remarkable artistry of Sichuan embroidery. As a carrier of ancestral culture, Embroidery Village, much like the Pixian Douban Museum, shoulders the mantle of enlightenment and education. By harnessing the rich tapestry of Sichuan embroidery culture in western Sichuan, the exhibition center fosters a continuous stream of local talents well-versed in the art of Sichuan embroidery, thus perpetuating the splendor of exceptional traditional culture. Moreover, it guides village residents towards flexible employment within the comforts of their homes, while simultaneously igniting the flames of creativity within the surrounding regions, nurturing a community of skilled embroiderers, numbering in the hundreds.

: Internal report of the Agriculture, Rural, and Forestry Bureau of Pixian District. Collection of case studies on the rural revitalization experience in Pixian [R]. 2018:26.

Beyond the fiery allure of their famous hot chili sauce, the Chengdu Plain embraces a world of vibrant customs and daily existence. Pixian Douban, a renowned product of traditional craftsmanship produced on a grand scale, embellishes the landscape by nurturing the intangible heritage culture, adding depth and value to the essence of broad bean paste. Amidst the rustic charms of rural tourist areas, one can stumble upon traditional handicraft shops, each a humble corner preserving the ancient trades. However, amidst the mingling throng, some lose sight of their authentic origins, detached from the local traditions, merely capitalizing on the tidal wave of rural tourism. Over time, the tapestry of folk customs loses its original flavor, entangled in the monotony of roadside stalls, and the intrinsic meaning behind the landscape becomes obscured, resulting in the forfeiture of its cultural and tourism value.

On the pivotal day of February 12, 2018, General Secretary Xi Jinping embarked on a voyage to Zhanqi Village to assess the progress of rural revitalization efforts. The "Splendid Zhanqi" online service hall played host to an array of captivating agricultural products and handicrafts, including the illustrious Yunqiao radishes and handcrafted cloth shoes. Each distinctive folk tradition caught the discerning eye of Xi, who bestowed his heartfelt praise upon the collective achievements. The spotlight illuminated these showcased products, elevating their status, while the affirmative nod of Xi conveyed a message of endorsement, captivating the masses. Thus, during the festive Spring Festival holiday, Zhanqi Village bustled with the ebb and flow of eager visitors, transforming into a coveted hotspot for tourism. The local snack stalls, anticipating a modest five-day demand, were promptly depleted within a single day. Meanwhile, the cloth shoes, which had captured Xi's personal interest, swiftly became an internet sensation, with sales multiplying several-fold.[13]

The 18 Rural Workshops of the countryside shoulder the noble responsibility of resurrecting the ancient folk culture, gathering scattered fragments of traditional crafts and transforming them into tangible treasures of commercial value. To ensure the preservation of the "authentic" folk essence within their storefronts, the 18 Rural Workshops conducted a comprehensive evaluation of merchants during the initial stages of investment, taking into account their entrepreneurial prowess, craftsmanship, and the sustainable development of their commercial enterprises. By doing so, they ensure the preservation of the rich flavors of traditional western Sichuan folk customs.

[13] Sichuan Daily. Zhanqi Village in Pixian District, Chengdu City: Striving to Lead Rural Revitalization [EB/OL]. (2018-02-27) [2021-01-21]. http://sc.cnr.cn/sc/2014cd/20180227/t20180227_524145561.shtml.

5 The Positive Externality of Ecological Transformation

5.1 Sustaining Ecological Harmony, Where Green Flourishes

The urgency for ecological transformation becomes starkly evident as the scourge of ecological pollution looms larger. Riding the wave of rapid agricultural modernization, China's total grain production surged from 325 million tons in 1981 to a whopping 618 million tons in 2017, surpassing global averages per capita. However, this success story carries its own set of drawbacks: rising agricultural production costs, underutilized agricultural resources, and the lurking hazards of compromised quality and safety in agricultural products due to ecological contamination.

Though recent years have witnessed a decline in the growth rate of fertilizer usage, thanks to the "one control, two reductions, three basics" policy, the per-mu fertilizer consumption of Chinese crops still outpaces that of developed nations. The excessive use of fertilizers not only burdens farmers with inflated production costs but also corrodes soil health, jeopardizing the delicate equilibrium of the agricultural ecosystem. Consequently, the need to boost organic fertilizer usage becomes an undeniable imperative.

Zhanqi Village's ecological journey has birthed an industry system of ecological economic value tailor-made for the Chengdu Plain, embracing production, consumption, and restoration. Rongzhen Mushroom has graced the village with ecological products, deftly transforming the production process to yield premium, high-quality ecological goods while mitigating pollution. Traditional edible mushroom production, plagued by limitations on scale and the challenge of secondary utilization of mushroom residue, had been beset by quality concerns. Rongzhen Mushroom, inspired by the tenets of "circular agriculture," harnesses materials like soybean meal, bran, and sugarcane residue. Through the alchemy of microbial technology, organic matter in these raw materials undergoes lactic acid fermentation, birthing mushroom residue brimming with abundant carbon and nitrogen. This processed residue, after secondary treatment, emerges as a valuable resource, serving as fertilizer and fodder, thus nurturing a virtuous cycle. Additionally, the mushroom factory generates around 36 tons of discarded mushroom bags daily, yielding approximately 13,000 tons of mushroom bran residue annually. These bags, blended with human and animal manure, wheat bran, rice bran, and more, constitute compost, while coupling them with microorganisms produces about 15,000 tons of high-quality organic fertilizer. In a scenario devoid of animal husbandry, a prevalent reality on the Chengdu Plain, this solution triumphantly resolves the scarcity of organic fertilizer in agricultural production, steering agriculture towards verdant pastures.

Ecological transformation heralds a step-by-step, upward march—a paramount move to fortify the bedrock of the ecological environment, faithfully executing the precept that "lucid waters and lush mountains are invaluable assets." The ethereal lavender flower fields not only ushered Mama Farm into a bustling market but also ignited the beacon of ecological revitalization in Zhanqi Village. Swarms of tourists graced the village, their footsteps revealing the promising vista of rural cultural transformation. Seizing the moment, the village collective purchased an abundance of seedlings from the villagers, adorning the park with indigenous flora as a complementary landscape. By internalizing resources, the village generously covered the cost of upgrading the scenic resources, an earnest investment in Mama Farm.

The beauty of ecology lies in the symphony of holistic harmony—where mountains, waters, forests, fields, lakes, and grasslands unite in seamless harmony. The interdependence of ecological elements holds true even within a petite environment, intertwining rural landscapes with the very fabric of rural life. Enhancing the infrastructure of the ecological environment manifests as a pivotal measure, breathing life into General Secretary Xi Jinping's aphorism that "lucid waters and lush mountains are invaluable assets," knitting together the smaller realm with the grander ecosystem. As tourists flock to savor the scenic splendors, their journey through the village blends seamlessly with their exploratory odyssey.

Even before Mama Farm's official inauguration, hordes of visitors flocked in its wake. A testament to the unyielding commitment towards sustainable development and the quest for greater influence in the village's industrial metamorphosis, Zhanqi Village took the initiative to fund the refurbishment of roads and canals surrounding the estate. The neighboring ambiance aligned harmoniously with the genteel allure within Mama Farm, heightening the overall visual aesthetics of the scenic area while refurbishing the village's infrastructure. Upon Mama Farm's grand opening, the park's functional zones radiated sophistication, while the village's pathways leading to the scenic area offered a smooth and spacious passage, engendering a heightened sense of artistic allure in rural tourism.

Moreover, the village's consolidated resources granted Zhanqi Village the prerogative to attract investment. Encountering the demands of water source protection policies, Zhanqi Village navigated the realm of action, armed with experience gleaned from the trials and tribulations of prior ecological transformation and business closures. Mama Farm's fledgling operations bore the brunt of an environmental trial and error, as the village's foundry, still operational during the initial stages, employed volatile ammonium chloride for casting. While the park's landscape construction captivated the eye, the pungent and intrusive odors marred the enchantment of many visitors, igniting a sense of concern within the village. As Mama Farm gradually found its stride, the brand effect of rural tourism kindled the value of Zhanqi Village's land, bolstering confidence in external investment. Consequently, in 2014, the village collective made the resolute decision to shutter the foundry.

In 2015, the water source protection policy was officially enacted, epitomizing a new chapter in Zhanqi Village's journey. The early ecological transformation and enterprise closures cushioned the village against the throes of economic downturn, while the subsequent ecological transformation stood armed with more stringent environmental protection requisites. Prior to the arrival of merchants in the 18 Rural Workshops, their product craftsmanship underwent rigorous screening, harmonizing the authenticity of folk handicraft with the imperatives of ecological sustainability. For instance, the profusely profitable barbecue industry, tainted by its pollutive production process, failed to meet the stringent requirements of Chengdu's Water Source Protection Policy, consequently, subjecting it to restrictions. Nature preceded humanity's advent, and therefore, our approach to managing natural resources necessitates a holistic perspective, embracing the intrinsic laws governing these resources. By conscientiously preserving the self-purifying function of the ecosystem, we embark on a journey of deliberate intervention, ushering in a comprehensive elevation of multifaceted ecological functionality.

5.2 *Fostering Surroundings, Crafting an Emerald Haven*

With the dichotomy of urban–rural systems and the taut rapport between humanity and land deeply ingrained in our national fabric, coupled with the lackluster comparative efficiency of agriculture, despite incremental strides in productivity, we remain unable to stave off the erosion of agriculture's standing, the exodus of farming populace, the degradation of farming environments, and the gradual decay of rural landscapes. Particularly distressing is the pervasive "elderly agriculture" phenomenon that has taken root as young rural laborers seek greener pastures elsewhere. The consolidation of village resources has shattered traditional small-scale farming models, ushering in newfound avenues for farmers to augment their income, beyond the realm of agriculture itself. The villagers now partake in tangible benefits, basking not only in the dividends reaped from land, but also in the prospects of gainful employment within enterprises. The erstwhile predominant reliance on farming income has gradually given way to diverse revenue streams, primarily through labor or other entrepreneurial ventures, effectively diversifying the earnings structure for farmers.

The most conspicuous manifestation of this industrial metamorphosis lies in its role as an employment catalyst, as villagers transition from a rustic agrarian identity to that of industrious workers. The amiable sentiments exuded by the revamped Zhanqi Village, as espoused by Mama Farm's formidable matriarch, Su, stem from the rejuvenated entrepreneurial landscape that has taken root within the village's environs. This metamorphosis has laid the groundwork for robust industrial development, affording villagers the opportunity for stable employment right on their doorstep. At Rongzhen Mushroom, approximately two-thirds of its frontline workforce hails from Zhanqi Village, resolutely addressing the employment conundrum faced by nearly 500 villagers. The Village 18 Rural Workshops, when pursuing investment prospects, gives due precedence to budding entrepreneurs within the village, with almost 80% of its merchants boasting local origins. Thus, the villagers' entrepreneurial fervor ignites, as their influential voice kindles a fiery passion for business pursuits.

In our nation's traditional societal fabric, agricultural production has long been intricately interwoven within the village communities. These communities, serving as both production collectives and communal dwellings, are bound by a network of social ties, where cooperation and interaction among villagers are tethered to the ebbs and flows of human connections. Hence, the social benefits stimulated by external enterprises extend beyond the confines of the village, not only boosting local employment but also fostering a palpable elevation in work enthusiasm, as individuals strive to measure up against their acquaintances. Moreover, Zhanqi Village's strategic investment approach, bolstered by resource concentration, involves direct engagement with enterprises. As an integral cog in the contractual machinery, the village collective assumes the dual role of guaranteeing and overseeing the villagers' work, thereby alleviating the burden of staff screening costs for incoming enterprises. To enhance the villagers' vocational aptitude, Rongzhen Mushroom collaborates closely with the village's governing bodies, utilizing workshops as training grounds to regularly organize mushroom production tours and educational sessions on cultivation techniques. These initiatives equip villagers with an array of specialized skills beyond mere farming, facilitating their transformation into accomplished new-age farmers. The allure of such technically demanding "dignified" work beckons a fresh wave of youth to forsake their wanderlust, choosing to stay and actively contribute to their ancestral abode.

As previously mentioned, the ecological transformation sets forth a propitious cycle, not only through the gradual refinement of fundamental ecological construction but also in the interplay between neighboring villages. By enlivening spatial resources, Zhanqi Village seizes the opportunity to embrace diverse developmental pathways, establishing itself as a bastion of successful experiences. In 2015, the output value of Rongzhen Mushroom soared to an astonishing 100 million yuan. Capitalizing on this achievement, Li Zongtang, in a gesture of remarkable magnanimity, transferred the enterprise to shareholders within Zhanqi Village, subsequently founding Chengdu Huiguyuan Biological Technology Co., Ltd. in the nearby enclave of Pingle Village. While venturing forth into novel enterprises, the invaluable wisdom gleaned during the establishment of the factory in Zhanqi Village cascaded into neighboring realms. Many laborers at Huiguyuan were once self-reliant mushroom cultivators. The triumphant operation of Rongzhen Mushroom's factory in Zhanqi Village unveiled a shimmering vista of fresh prospects, disabusing these erstwhile subsistence farmers of their age-old reliance on nature alone. It became abundantly clear that agricultural pursuits thrive when fortified by technology and scalable operations. The achievements and wisdom amassed by external enterprises ultimately permeated the very essence of the village's brand, attenuating the credit costs incurred during subsequent investment solicitations by the village collective. Consequently, this fruitful convergence spurred an upsurge of collaborations between enterprises and Zhanqi Village, fortifying the bedrock of industry, magnifying the collective's clout, and assuming the mantle of a proactive guardian, shouldering the social responsibility of propelling the neighboring villages' growth. Owing to the village's robust industrial infrastructure, the pressing conundrum of employment had been substantially mitigated several years prior, resulting in a surplus of available positions to be extended to the outlying villages.[14]

Heightened prominence inexorably begets augmented social obligations, and Zhanqi's metamorphosis into an ecological haven has acquired a didactic purpose. At present, the art of Pixian Douban production has ascended to the coveted echelons of the second batch of national intangible cultural heritage list. The Pixian Douban Museum, nestled in Pixian County, astutely leverages its educational prowess, actively fostering cultural exchange exhibitions, thereby providing an engaging nexus for the masses and connoisseurs alike to commune, safeguarding and perpetuating the cultural legacy of Pixian Douban. On November 8, 2018, Tangchang Linsheng Elementary School orchestrated a captivating educational sojourn, leading students on an enlightening pilgrimage to the hallowed precincts of the Pixian Douban Museum. Against the cultural tableau adorning the museum's walls, the children marveled at the tapestry of Shu Kingdom's heritage and the storied evolution of Pixian Douban. As the docents expounded upon the intricate craftsmanship, quality, and accolades bestowed upon broad bean paste, the children absorbed a profound comprehension, acquainting themselves not only with their homeland's gastronomic gem but also honing their faculties of observation, collaboration, communication, and information gathering. Simultaneously, the children imbibed the diligent spirit of laborious toil, engendering a profound ardor for their native soil. Furthermore, the nascent phase of the Village's 18 Rural Workshops project has tantalizing prospects of incubating educational escapades, envisaging the formation of a tourism service company in a collective guise, poised to forge alliances with neighboring schools. This enterprise aspires to orchestrate distinctive research-based activities centered around red-themed education, the inimitable charm of intangible cultural heritage, and the edification of agrarian customs. The accrual of the brand's preexistent influence has garnered the

[14] Source: Interview records of Boss Su from Mama Farm on October 2, 2019.

resolute support of Pixian District government, facilitating fruitful partnerships with numerous primary and secondary educational institutions within the district.[15]

[15] Source: Interview records of Village 18 Rural Workshops' representative Lin Genzhi on October 5, 2019.

PART IV

Monographic Studies

CHAPTER 12

The Intersection of Social Capital and Land Value Appreciation: Examining Land Concentration and Development since 2003

1 The Macro Context of Rural Land Value Appreciation

In 2018, the No. 1 Central Document emphasized the need to promote the integrated development of the third industry in rural areas as a crucial element in driving modern agricultural progress. This integration of the first, second, and third industries not only serves as a vital component of the rural revitalization strategy but also acts as a catalyst for enhancing agricultural productivity, rural prosperity, and farmers' income. By embracing this paradigm, rural areas can transform low-value industries into high-value ones, leading to increased land value. Additionally, the consolidation of land, with the village collective taking the lead, reduces land transfer costs for businesses, attracting investments and facilitating industrial rejuvenation. Furthermore, fragmented land ownership poses challenges for functional appreciation, as highlighted by Zhao Yanjing (赵燕菁). In his view, transitioning from dispersed to centralized land ownership, developing supporting infrastructure, aligning land use with its intended purpose, and conducting transactions with the principle of maximizing interests all contribute to maximizing benefits.[1] Zhao also underscored the potential devaluation of land and natural resources

[1] Zhao Yanjing. "The Optimal Proportion of Different Land Uses in Cities." Beijing Planning and Construction, 2018(4):150–152.

© Peking University Press 2024

X. Dong, *Zhanqi Village Over Fifty Years*,
https://doi.org/10.1007/978-981-97-5426-7_12

resulting from fragmented property rights.[2] Therefore, to enhance land value through the development of the tertiary industry, the first step is to integrate land resources. Nevertheless, integrating land resources and achieving land value appreciation pose significant challenges for villages. Since agricultural development serves as the foundation for industrial progress, the outflow of rural labor, coupled with non-agricultural development and capital inflow to urban areas, impedes efforts to centralize land and rally farmers' cooperation.

While China's rapid economic development and population mobility since the twenty-first century have led to a transition from closed, self-sufficient villages to semi-open rural areas, influential figures, and prominent families have experienced a diminished impact on village governance. As a result, rural society has been subject to external disruptions and challenges.[3] Nevertheless, the fabric of rural society, rooted in kinship-based social networks, continues to play a vital role in driving village development and reaping the rewards of collective action. Social capital, the resources acquired through interpersonal relationships and social networks,[4] facilitates trade, cooperation, and individual gains among organizational members. In essence, land concentration represents the process by which the village collective reclaims land contracts and leases. While villagers weigh the costs and benefits associated with their decisions, their choices are profoundly influenced by the social capital shared between villagers and the village collective. Moreover, a broader sense of social capital also acts as a catalyst for land appreciation.

Drawing on the preceding analysis, this study focuses on elucidating how Zhanqi Village leverages social capital to promote land concentration and enhance land value. From the perspective of political trust, institutional fields, kinship networks, and interconnected networks, this study encapsulates the impact mechanisms of Zhanqi Village's social capital on land appreciation, as depicted in Fig. 1.

社会资本 social capital.

[2] Zhao Yanjing. "The Basic Framework of National Spatial Planning." Urban Planning, 2019, 43(12):17–26, 36.

[3] Zhao Quanmin, Li Yi. "Network Relationships and Cooperative Economy in Chinese Rural Society: A Perspective of Social Capital." Agricultural Economic Issues, 2007(8):40–44.

[4] Zhang Wenhong. "Social Capital: Theoretical Debates and Empirical Studies." Sociological Research, 2003(4):23–35.

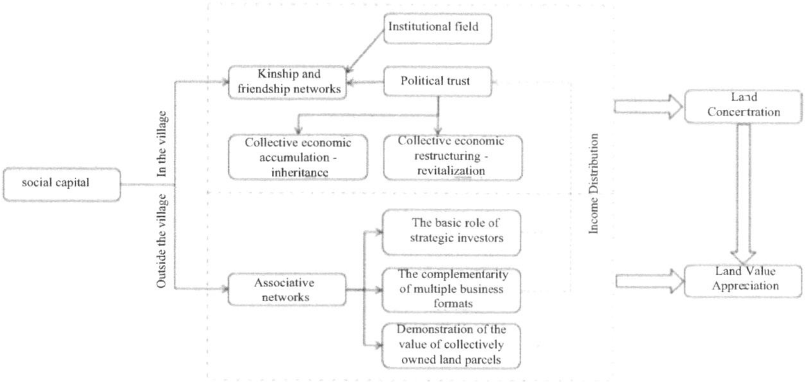

Fig. 1 The role of Zhanqi Village's social capital in land appreciation mechanisms

村内|亲友缘网络|制度场|政治信任|集体经济积累——继承|集体经济改制——盘活 In the village | Kinship and friendship networks | Institutional field | Political trust | Collective economic accumulation—inheritance | Collective economic restructuring—revitalization.

村外|链接型网络|战略性投资者的基础作用|多元业态的互补性|建设用地价值显化.

Outside the village | Associative networks | The basic role of strategic investors | The complementarity of multiple business formats | Demonstration of the value of collectively owned land parcels.

收益分配 Income Distribution.

土地集中|土地增值 Land Concentration|Land Value Appreciation.

2 The Foundation and Strengthening Power of Political Trust

2.1 Political Trust: The Bedrock for Concentrated Land Ownership

Political trust, in simple terms, is the faith villagers place in their village collective. The initial surge of political trust served as the bedrock upon which kinship and friendship networks thrived, establishing a solid foundation for the subsequent consolidation of land. But how was this formidable trust forged? The macro backdrop of the 1960s and 1970s can be distilled into four key facets: first, unresolved subsistence issues, which even impeded progress; second, a nationwide focus on "learning from Dazhai in agriculture" movement; third, the early 1970s marked the meticulous implementation of the "three aspects" of militia work at both central and local levels, encompassing organizational, political, and military dimensions; fourth, the prevailing era of people's communes, wherein communal ownership extended to public properties, including land. Zhanqi Brigade, during its fledgling years, was indigent and lacking.

At the time, the girls from neighboring villages shunned the idea of marrying into ours due to the harsh living conditions. Farmers toiled for over 12 hours a day, cultivating their own plots and distributing crops. Back then, the laborious hours stretched to thirteen or fourteen. There even existed a rhyme illustrating the adverse soil conditions: "Plant not in Jiangjiawan, a year-round plight; one season's labor yields but a morsel."

Source: Interview record of Li Shili on June 7, 2019.

Amidst this grand panorama, under the guidance of the first and second village branch secretaries, Jiang Daxing and Luo Huijin, and with the support of the county armed forces, Zhanqi Brigade resolved the team's subsistence problems by optimizing land utilization to increase grain production. In the span of nearly a decade, Zhanqi Brigade, once impoverished, metamorphosed into an exemplar of advanced brigades, boasting some of the highest grain yields in the county. This triumph precluded any lingering concerns for subsequent industrial development.

Given that many brigades nationwide operated under similar macro conditions, what propelled Zhanqi Brigade to excel? Zhanqi Brigade's remarkable achievements in areas such as agricultural water management owed much to its quasi-military mobilization strategies and the synergy of military and civilian efforts. In the 1970s, the deputy commander of Wenjiang Military Division, leading an inspection team, marveled at Zhanqi Brigade's exemplary militia work. Subsequently, the county armed forces regarded Zhanqi Brigade as the epitome of military-civilian collaboration, stationing a dedicated task force to provide ongoing assistance in the militarization training of the militia. Unlike other brigades, whose militia activities encroached upon productive labor, Zhanqi Brigade astutely implemented the "support farming through military endeavors, bolster farming through military influence" strategy, deftly sidestepping any overlap between training and labor. Additionally, the militiamen imbued their swift and resolute combat spirit into agricultural production.

By prioritizing militia work and farmland development, Zhanqi Brigade amplified agricultural productivity and reaped bountiful harvests.

After the Third Plenary Session of the Eleventh Central Committee of the Communist Party of China, the party's focal point shifted towards economic development. Subsequently, Zhanqi Village recalibrated its growth strategy. Yang Zhengzhong, the fourth village branch secretary, established the village's first collective enterprise, a brick factory born from humble origins. Profits in hand, he ventured to create multiple village collective enterprises. During his tenure as village director and village branch secretary, Yi Fengxian, the fifth village branch secretary, birthed eleven enterprises in total. Zhanqi Village's annual net income soared to several hundred thousand yuan. The surge of village collective enterprises not only bolstered the communal economy but also significantly augmented villagers' incomes.

> "In ordinary villages, workers received monthly wages ranging from 30 to 40 yuan, and securing 50 yuan was considered a highly desirable job. With a single family member employed, life improved. In our village, one person could earn 1.8 yuan per day, with excellent attendance... In the 1980s, the Luo family, with an ample labor force, received over 3000 yuan in year-end distributions, exerting a profound influence at the time."

Source: Interview record of Li Shili on June 7, 2019.

From its inception to the mid-1990s, Zhanqi Village initially leveraged the military-civilian collaboration to boost grain production through agricultural water management, addressing villagers' subsistence concerns. Subsequently, through the establishment of village collective enterprises and the expansion of communal economy, the village augmented the villagers' incomes. The village collective, leading the villagers from rags to riches, satiated their hunger and amassed wealth. Thus, the villagers developed an unwavering political trust in the village collective. Such an accomplishment is not easily attained in ordinary villages but rather a testament to the successive village branch secretaries diligently guiding the villagers towards a unified goal, reaping the benefits of an advantageous system. Leaving aside the question of whether other villages enjoy a similar policy environment, the convergence of multiple village branch secretaries' lofty aspirations is an extraordinary rarity.

How does the foundational role of political trust manifest? The political trust accumulated during the collectivization era laid a solid groundwork for concentrated land ownership. Though Zhanqi Village experienced a precipitous decline in the collective economy around 2000, the deep reservoirs of political trust allowed the village collective to revive through the restructuring of the communal economy, reversing the previous trend of extensive individual appropriation of collective accumulation. It is this trust that convinced the villagers that the anticipated benefits offered by the village collective could be realized, making them willing to surrender their land upfront in exchange for future gains. Thus, Zhanqi Village achieved an organization of villagers that other villages find arduous to replicate. Political trust, therefore, forms the bedrock for the effective functioning of kinship and friendship networks and fosters land concentration.

2.2 *The Unyielding Growth of Political Trust Fuels Land Concentration*

The aftermath of land concentration brings forth questions of whether it generates increased profits, if the distribution of these gains is equitable, and whether the village collective possesses the capacity to safeguard the preservation of its communal assets. These elements significantly influence the political trust vested by villagers in their local community. The outcome, be it positive or negative, serves as an indicator of whether political trust has been fortified or eroded.

Following the land concentration in 2003, the village collective assumed responsibility not only for paying the agricultural taxes of residents in Groups 5 and 7, but also for implementing innovative reforms to enhance the quality of the consolidated land. Differential ground rent was heightened, ensuring the absence of instances where villagers were left to bear the burden of unpaid agricultural taxes. Subsequently, in 2006, the village collective exhibited an exemplary credit history. Departing from the initial phase, the abolition of agricultural taxes facilitated farmers' participation in cooperative ventures, wherein they were entitled to a guaranteed minimum of 800 yuan, supplemented by dividends. However, due to the cooperative's nascent stage, profits were lackluster, with dividends only materializing in the third phase. During this period, the cooperative undertook the vital task of developing agricultural and water infrastructure associated with the land, thereby further augmenting the allure of differential ground rent. Around 2010, after the completion of land concentration, the village collective transferred the land to the cooperative, affording villagers a minimum guaranteed sum of 1200 yuan, supplemented by dividends. Furthermore, elderly individuals aged 60 and above received a monthly subsidy of 50 yuan. Meanwhile, the cooperative dedicated two years to streamlining the land and elevating the status of differential ground rent. This chronicle illuminates that throughout every stage of land concentration, the village collective exhibited an outstanding credit history, bolstering not only differential ground rent but also the financial welfare of villagers. Consequently, political trust was ceaselessly fortified, fostering the progression towards the subsequent phase of land concentration.

3 The Power of Institutional Field

3.1 The Force of Formal Institutions

Examining the various stages of land concentration, one cannot deny the intertwined relationship with state policies. In 2003, Zhanqi Village seized 50 mu of land from Group 5 and Group 7, under the condition of exempting agricultural taxes. However, after the abolition of agricultural taxes in 2005, the leveraged approach of using taxes to consolidate land could no longer be pursued, leading to a temporary suspension of the land concentration plan. It was in the latter part of 2005 that Pixian County issued relevant land reorganization documents. Zhanqi Village embarked on village planning, preparing for centralized living, and initially concentrated 500 mu of land, which was temporarily leased to two prominent operators for rice and vegetable cultivation. Furthermore, to capitalize on the policy subsidies for large-scale land operation, Zhanqi Village established a professional vegetable cooperative, managing the centralized 500 mu of land. The year 2007 witnessed Zhanqi Village being chosen as a pilot project for "new community construction." Subsequently, in 2009, as villagers moved to new dwellings, the demolition of old homes and the reclamation of homesteads commenced. By 2010, Zhanqi Village had centralized 80% of the entire village's land, and in 2011, following the confirmation of membership qualifications, the consolidated land reached an impressive 98% of the village's total.

(1) Policy as a Lever: Small-Scale Concentration in 2003

Since Zhanqi Village's industrial development in the 1980s, numerous village-operated collective enterprises provided employment for some villagers. Simultaneously, with the growth of township enterprises, adjustments in the household registration system, and the shift of manufacturing industries to coastal regions, the number of migrant workers increased. Consequently, land revenue accounted for a modest proportion of total household income, leading to a limited dependency on land among villagers. Moreover, agricultural taxes were still obligatory during that period. Although these taxes only comprised 1% of per capita income, when villagers contributed 30% of their land, the village collective assumed the responsibility of paying the entire agricultural tax. This arrangement proved beneficial to the villagers. For those who continued to cultivate the land, the surplus income from cultivating approximately one mu of land belonged solely to them, while also sparing them the time and energy spent on tax payments. For those who left their land uncultivated, they were relieved of the burden of allocating a portion of their household income for agricultural taxes, thereby enjoying peace of mind and ease. Zhanqi Village effectively leveraged these circumstances to consolidate 50 mu of land from Group 5 and Group 7. However, simply assuming the responsibility of paying agricultural taxes was insufficient to achieve small-scale consolidation. Only Group 5 and Group 7 successfully completed the consolidation. On one hand, the group leaders played an active role in promoting this endeavor, utilizing personal connections to their advantage. On the other hand, to avoid the desolation resulting from extensive land concentration and with the village collective's original intent to test the waters without hampering regular agricultural production, the land concentration came to a halt on September 30 of that year.

(2) Fostering Large-Scale Concentration: The "Demolition and Consolidation Project"

Visualizing the "demolition and consolidation" project within the village's context allows for a more comprehensive understanding of the process, as homestead consolidation and land concentration were inherently interlinked. The scattered residential areas of the villagers inevitably fragmented the land. Complete land concentration could only be achieved when villagers resided in centralized areas, making the dispersion of homesteads a genuine hindrance. In response, Zhanqi Village was designated as a trial project for the "new rural community construction." The implementation entailed land comprehensive management and urban–rural land conversion through market mechanisms. By capitalizing on the anticipated increase in land value due to policy subsidies, the speed of land transfers accelerated, and the increased value resulting from land concentration contributed to the concentration of homesteads.

3.2 *The Harmonious Union of Formal and Informal Institutions Reduces the Difficulty of Land Concentration*

(1) The Informal Operation of Formal Institutions Alleviates Consolidation Obstacles

The village collective utilized the land contracting system as a means to regulate villagers within the institutional framework, successfully resolving issues arising from uneven land distribution that hindered consolidation. During the second round of land contracting in 1998, uniform per capita land allocations were established within the same group. Hence, during the land concentration process in 2003, for those reluctant to participate in small-scale consolidation due to excess land occupation, the village collective required them to surrender their land contracting certificates. Consequently, the portion of land exceeding the documented acreage on the certificates was returned to the collective, with the collective having the authority to demand land occupation fees.

(2) The Influence of Informal Institutions on Land Concentration

Following the second round of land contracting, Zhanqi Village, like countless villages across the nation, maintained equal per capita land distributions within each group. However, the distinction lay in the customs prevalent in the southern Sichuan region, characterized by hilly landscapes and sparse population. Many villages embraced the annual practice of adjusting land distribution during the vacant period in August and September. This tradition involved transferring the land of deceased or married-out individuals to newborns or newlywed women. Unless additional population awaited land allocation or cases of excessive land occupation arose, this custom ensured consistent per capita land distribution within each group. In contrast to the significant disparities in per capita land distribution resulting from the general land allocation practices coordinated within families, wherein land remained unchanged despite population fluctuations, Zhanqi Village's informal institution greatly alleviated the challenges of motivating small-scale consolidation and subsequent land redistribution within the groups.

4 The Facilitating Power of Kinship and Friendship Networks

In 2003, Zhanqi Village achieved the consolidation of 50 mu of land from 5 groups, and the linchpin behind this success was the operation of the kinship networks. During the mobilization process for land concentration, the functioning of these networks played a crucial role, built upon a foundation of political trust and supported by enabling institutional conditions. The kinship networks provided unwavering support to each member of the family, fostering an intimacy that transcended ordinary relationships and engendered a robust social trust among the villagers. As a result, the challenges of mobilization were diminished. Acting as a lever, the institutional framework secured the family members' support only for transactions that were profitable or, at the very least, not detrimental. Furthermore, with the kinship networks in motion, the majority of the farmers agreed to consolidate their land, and through the friendship networks, the village leader successfully persuaded the remaining households to join the land concentration efforts. In essence, driven by individuals of high repute and a willingness to consolidate land, the seamless progress of land concentration was achieved through the operation of kinship networks, bound by ties of blood and marriage, supported by a backdrop of robust political trust and favorable institutional conditions.

Similarly, the friendship networks operated on the bedrock of trust and institutional facilitation, further catalyzing the process of land concentration. However, they differed from kinship networks in two distinct ways: friendship networks represented weaker connections compared to the strong bonds found in kinship networks, and while the establishment of kinship networks proved challenging, friendship networks could be cultivated and nurtured.

In 2006, Zhanqi Village unveiled its cultural haven, boasting facilities such as basketball courts, table tennis rooms, gyms, libraries, electronic reading rooms, and leisure venues like tea houses, cafes, dance rehearsal halls, movie theaters, and an open-air stage. The village's collective spirit flourished as various groups, including the village youth league branch, elderly sports association, and entrepreneurs, rallied the entire community to form reading groups, fitness teams, and performance troupes. Particularly, the creation of the renowned "Zhanqi Performing Arts Team" ensured the celebration of variety shows during festive occasions. The cultural haven became the breeding ground for the blossoming of friendship networks among villagers, bridging the divide between village officials and residents, and propelling the third phase of land concentration.

The effective functioning of kinship and friendship networks in promoting land concentration stemmed from the collective reconfiguration of land functions within the village. In the era of planned economy, where market-oriented land benefits were absent, governmental requisition of land resolved the employment predicaments faced by those who depended on the land for their sustenance. Consequently, land requisitioning proceeded without friction, with farmers readily relinquishing their land in exchange for state provisions. However, as land became the last bastion of security for farmers when capitalization extended its reach into rural areas, villagers became reluctant to part with their land unless they could secure enduring wage-based income or social safeguards. Zhanqi Village's collective leadership astutely met the villagers' longing for land security, instilling the conviction necessary for land concentration. For villagers, especially the elderly, land held a vital role as a safeguard. Through land concentration, the introduction of enterprises, and bolstering collective income, the village collective fulfilled the villagers' longing for security that was once fulfilled by the land, distributing dividends, providing employment opportunities, and contributing to pension plans. Consequently, the villagers willingly embraced the concentration of their land.

5 The Power of Associative Networks in Boosting Land Value

Michael Woolcock and his team, following James Coleman's groundwork, precisely defined the concept of "associative networks." These networks signify the establishment of social capital among individuals from different social strata through interaction. In this regard, the operation of associative networks exhibits a structured characteristic when it comes to promoting land appreciation. While the network of kinship and friends revolves around building relationships within the village, these connections are hereditary and focus on how to invigorate and strengthen existing ties. On the other hand, associative networks manifest themselves more prominently in external relationships, demanding greater effort to construct.

Figure 2 visually illustrates the underlying mechanism of structured associative networks. Mama Farm, represented by 1, serves as the bedrock of strategic investors. Entities such as Blueberry Base and Winter Strawberry Base (symbolized by 2) joined Zhanqi Village later, following the establishment of rural tourism infrastructure by Mama Farm. Their entry adds complementary elements to the tourism resources already in place. Value realization of construction land, indicated by 3, involves projects such as the new community development initiative supported by the municipal government, as well as the collective operation and market entry of construction land facilitated by Maigao Company and the government. The concentrated appreciation of land value is most apparent in the case of collectively owned profit-oriented land entering the market. While 1 and 2 mainly focus on agricultural land for tourism development, 3 represents the tertiary development of construction land, resulting in complementary business formats between the two.

农用地 agricultural land.

互补 complementary.

基础 Foundation.

增值收益(主要) Value Appreciation (main).

建设用地 Collectively owned land parcels.

Fig. 2 Intrinsic mechanism of structured associative networks

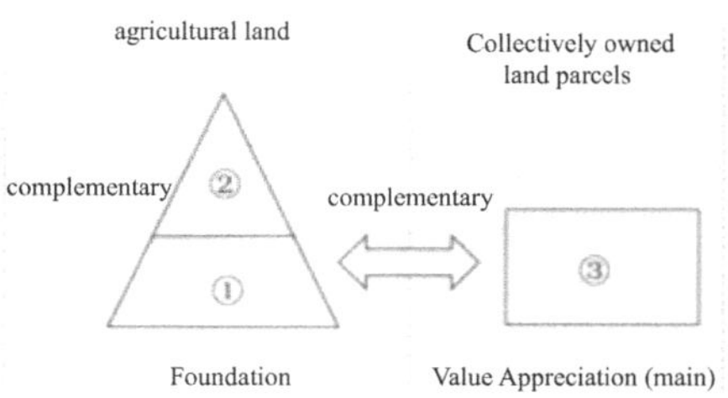

Table 1 Key Events Promoting Land Appreciation and Construction Directions of Associative Networks

Year	*Builder of the associative networks outside Zhanqi Village*	*Key driving events*
2006	Pixian County Propaganda Department	New community construction project
2007	Party Secretary of the Chengdu Municipal Committee	
2008	A senior executive of Sichuan Dahang Hongye Group Co., Ltd	Building "Mama Farm"
2013	Sichuan Blue Rainbow Ecological Agriculture Co., Ltd	Establishing the "Blueberry Base"
2014	Chengdu Yufengxiang Agricultural Technology Co., Ltd	Establishing the "Winter Strawberry Base"
2015	Pixian County Government, Maigao Company	Sichuan Province's "first gavel" into market transactions of collectively owned land

Source: Relevant materials from the District Archives of Pixian and interviews with relevant personnel

During the process of land resource integration, Zhanqi Village fortified its land value by establishing associative networks beyond its borders. Table 1 presents the key events contributing to land appreciation in Zhanqi Village and the corresponding construction directions of associative networks.

5.1 *Associative Networks Drive the Tertiary Development of Agricultural Land*

As previously mentioned, Mama Farm's arrival marked Zhanqi Village's transition from developing the primary industry to fostering the tertiary sector. Gao Demin proactively forged an associative network with a senior executive from Sichuan Dahang Hongye Group Co., Ltd. (referred to as Dahang Hongye Group). Coupled with Zhanqi Village's preexisting consolidated land resources, this collaboration enabled the introduction of Mama Farm.

But how did these two parties establish their associative network? It all began at a trade fair in Beijing, where Gao Demin took the initiative to connect with a senior executive from Dahang Hongye Group. Through regular private interactions, they developed a solid rapport. During their exchanges, Gao Demin expressed his desire to introduce a project that would facilitate the transformation of rural industries, aligning with Dahang Hongye Group's inclination towards transitioning into the tourism sector. Subsequently, representatives from Dahang Hongye Group conducted numerous visits to Zhanqi Village. After approximately 50 inspections, a unanimous agreement was reached with the village collective.

So, how does this associative network operate? With the consolidation of spatial resources within the village, Zhanqi Village sought external collaborations to strategically invest and develop these integrated resources. Mama Farm emerged as the strategic investor after Zhanqi Village's land concentration efforts. To attract Mama Farm, Gao Demin proactively established an associative network with high-level executives from the company. The effectiveness of this network relied on resource exchange. On one hand, Zhanqi Village made economic concessions, offering construction land shares in exchange for participation. Mama Farm only needed to pay an annual usage fee of approximately 2200 yuan per mu, while the surplus value of the construction land, as determined by a third-party evaluation, would be deducted from Mama Farm's net profit annually. The annual land circulation fee for agricultural land amounted to 1575 yuan per mu. On the other hand, thanks to Zhanqi Village's land concentration efforts, Mama Farm could lease contiguous agricultural land through the cooperative society, eventually securing around 400 mu of agricultural land and 23 mu of construction land. This scale is rarely achieved in ordinary villages. Li Wenge, the current chairman of Mama Farm, cited four reasons for choosing Zhanqi Village: first, through multiple interactions with Gao Demin, his unwavering dedication left a lasting impression on Dahang Hongye Group's management; second, Zhanqi Village's prime geographical location within the Dujiangyan Water Source Protection Zone, boasting a favorable ecological environment, is conducive to tourism development; third, the group was undergoing a transformation, aiming to shift its focus to rural tourism; and fourth, Zhanqi Village had successfully consolidated its collective assets, allowing for direct coordination without the need to engage with individual villagers.

Leveraging its pristine ecological environment, Zhanqi Village embarked on localized tourism, offering an accessible entry point for various industries. The interplay between diverse formats not only propelled the development of Zhanqi Village's tourism sector but also generated external effects through complementary business operations.

Following Mama Farm's settlement, their Lavender Festival became a local sensation, leading other enterprises to actively seek collaborations with Zhanqi Village. Similarly, village officials utilized associative networks to introduce other businesses. In 2013, Sichuan Blue Rainbow Ecological Agriculture Co., Ltd. cooperated with the village collective, leasing 160 mu of land for blueberry cultivation, primarily focusing on sightseeing and picking activities. The blueberry base connects with Mama Farm, creating a contiguous tourist route. In 2014, Chengdu Yufengxiang Agricultural Technology Co., Ltd. leased over 60 mu of land from the cooperative society for winter strawberry cultivation. In 2015, Sichuan Manjianghong Food Technology Co., Ltd. established the Pixian Douban Museum, fully exploring the cultural value of Pixian Douban. This diverse and complementary development approach not only stimulated Zhanqi Village's tourism industry but also manifested in external effects such as increased collective dividends and rental income. Since the introduction of Mama Farm in 2010, Zhanqi Village has raised the land dividend for farmers every 1–2 years (ranging from 50 to 100 yuan). Additionally, the village collective contributes to the minimum standard of pension insurance for villagers, providing monthly subsidies of 50 yuan, 100 yuan, and 150 yuan to individuals aged 60, 70, and 80, respectively. These distribution methods further strengthen the political trust of villagers in the collective, promote land concentration and other internal affairs within the village, and create a virtuous cycle.

Through land concentration, Zhanqi Village effectively integrated its spatial domain, overcoming the fragmentation of land and enhancing its horizontal and vertical spatial capacity, thereby expanding its economic and social space to accommodate diverse ecological and industrial sectors. Zhanqi Village, with relatively low costs, consolidated agricultural land and residential land under collective ownership, continuously attracting investment and engaging in negotiations. During the initial negotiations, Zhanqi Village quoted relatively low prices. However, by capitalizing on enterprises' sensitivity to negative feedback, Zhanqi Village gradually improved its negotiation skills.

5.2 *The Operation of Associative Networks Enhances the Value Manifestation of Construction Land*

In 2006, the Propaganda Department of Pixian County and Zhanqi Village established a associative network during the "Cultural Experiment of Urban–Rural Interaction." Through this network, they cooperated by leveraging their respective resources to achieve their goals. For Zhanqi Village, they gained publicity and expanded their influence, while the Pixian County Propaganda Department found a willing participant in their experimental activities. Although seemingly insignificant, this activity became the foundation for Zhanqi Village's further development. The "College Students Going to the Countryside" activity, thanks to the Propaganda Department's coverage, increased Zhanqi Village's prominence. Coupled with the village's existing groundwork, it became an exemplary model in the county. In early 2007, following the county's recommendation, the Secretary of the Chengdu Municipal Committee and others visited Zhanqi Village. Since 2003, Zhanqi Village had been consolidating land resources and had initially met the conditions for concentrated living, both in terms of land planning and farmers' intentions. Consequently, after the Spring Festival of 2007, Zhanqi Village was designated as a pilot village for the construction of a new type of community. The injection of government project funds and policy guidance significantly accelerated the integration of land resources in Zhanqi Village and promoted comprehensive planning and layout. This greatly reduced transaction costs for enterprise settlement and development, while also revealing the immense potential of Zhanqi Village to enterprises like Mama Farm. The kinship network played a crucial role in this process.

Firstly, the strong associative network between Zhanqi Village and Pixian County was forged through long-standing interactions. On one hand, Pixian County aimed to create a flagship model for promotional purposes. On the other hand, despite Zhanqi Village's previous struggles due to the reformation of township enterprises around 2000, its collective economic income remained significantly higher than that of other villages in the county. Moreover, Zhanqi Village actively concentrated land for development. The convergence of interests allowed for mutually beneficial cooperation. Zhanqi Village consolidated resources internally, and the county government provided phased policies and financial support.

Secondly, the robust associative network created conditions for establishing new associative networks. Zhanqi Village gained the opportunity to showcase itself to the Secretary of the Chengdu Municipal Committee and others through the county's recommendation. The associative network established between the Chengdu municipal government and Zhanqi Village resembled the previously mentioned two-tier associative networks: Zhanqi Village had essentially met the conditions for concentrated living through its independent development, and after the Chengdu municipal government became aware of its situation, it offered policy and financial support. Thus, it is evident that establishing a associative network alone is insufficient to promote resource integration and enhance land value. The effectiveness of the network lies in the exchange of resources between the parties. The previous section described the operation of the associative network, and the following section will elucidate how the operation of the associative network enhances the value of land.

In 2015, the policy on collective-operated construction land entering the market was announced, and Pixian County was designated as a pilot area for collectively owned profit-oriented land entering the market. Following the national policy announcement, Zhanqi Village promptly conducted a comprehensive assessment of all its assets and established a company to prepare for the entry of collectively owned profit-oriented land into the market. Simultaneously, the local government aspired to secure the first transaction of collective-operated construction land and persuaded Sichuan Maigao Tourism Resources Development Co., Ltd. to acquire the construction land in Zhanqi Village. Taking political factors and the foundation of tourism resource development in Zhanqi Village into account, Maigao Company agreed to cooperate. Thus, based on the associative network, the three parties engaged in resource exchange to achieve their respective goals. Maigao Company acquired 13.447 mu of construction land in Zhanqi Village for 525,000 yuan per mu, marking the inaugural transaction in Sichuan Province's market for collectively owned profit-oriented land. This became the most significant appreciation of land value in Zhanqi Village, with the proceeds from the auction primarily used for further village development and a small portion distributed to villagers, further reinforcing their trust in the collective. Simultaneously, Maigao Company and Zhanqi Village collaborated to establish Sichuan Colorful Zhanqi Tourist Area Management Co., Ltd. Maigao Company utilized its light assets to centrally develop the land acquired through the auction, while property owners who purchased shops could provide physical services such as catering and accommodation through business or self-operation. This formed a complementary business format with the tertiary development initiated by Mama Farm, the blueberry plantation base, the winter strawberry plantation base, and other endeavors.

Additionally, the realization of value through the tertiary development of collectively owned profit-oriented land includes the acquisition of monopolistic institutional benefits. Under the influence of institutional arrangements, the land appreciation benefits obtained by Zhanqi Village were monopolistic. Initially, Zhanqi Village occupied construction land intended for the secondary industry using the cost of the primary industry. As the secondary industry's capacity phased out due to water source protection measures, Zhanqi Village seamlessly transitioned to the tertiary sector. This not only saved costs but also gained significant institutional benefits. In 2009, indicators for the collectively owned profit-oriented land in rural areas became stringent, and most regions no longer possessed the conditions to develop the tertiary sector using their own land. However, Zhanqi Village was one step ahead, reaping monopolistic returns. Not only did it have high economic rents, but there were no competitors of the same caliber in the vicinity.

6 Conclusion

This chapter's discoveries can be summarized as follows.

Firstly, within the village, the kinship and friendship networks, rooted in political trust, acts as a catalyst for land concentration within the institutional realm. Over time, the collective economic growth has fostered a deep sense of political trust, and the restructuring of the collective economy has revived this trust, forming the foundation for land concentration. The institutional realm, by influencing individual or collective behavior within its domain, facilitates land concentration. It encompasses both formal and informal institutions, with the informal exploitation of formal systems playing a significant role. Notably, the leveraging effect of formal institutions is evident in the manipulation of agricultural taxes to drive small-scale concentration and the unforeseen benefits of "demolishing and consolidating courtyards" that promote land concentration. Moreover, the functioning of the kinship and friendship network directly propels land concentration, as witnessed through the kinship network's influence on the friendship network, ultimately fostering land concentration. It's worth noting that while the friendship network primarily relies on weak ties, it can be cultivated over time.

Secondly, to actualize land appreciation based on land concentration, an expansion of the kinship and friendship network is necessary, giving rise to a associative network structure conducive to land capitalization and development. Land concentration serves as the bedrock for achieving development-oriented land appreciation in the tertiary sector. Through the effective integration of spatial resources within the village, land concentration bolsters the bargaining power of the collective in external negotiations and gradually unlocks the potential for land appreciation. On one hand, the comprehensive nature of spatial resources necessitates a holistic approach to their development, with land serving as the carrier of these resources. On the other hand, fragmented property rights can devalue land and other natural resources. Additionally, the functioning of an associative network structured around connections exhibits distinct characteristics. Once internal resource integration within the village is accomplished, collaboration with a strategically invested enterprise becomes imperative, as it attracts further corporate participation and facilitates the emergence of diverse industries when tertiary sector development reaches a certain scale. Concurrently, the development of construction land within the tertiary sector also represents a form of diversified industry, while its entry into the market signifies a concentrated realization of land appreciation.

Thirdly, land appreciation inherently entails income distribution, which further solidifies the existing pattern of land concentration. The book primarily examines three facets of land appreciation. Firstly, the elevation of differential land rent, sourced from collective inputs, policy funding support, and enterprise investments. Secondly, the shift of agricultural land from low-value primary food crops to high-value cash crops and the exploration of tertiary sector potential, such as agritourism and pick-your-own farming. Lastly, the visualization of construction land value, encompassing the correlation between land appreciation and reduction, as well as the integration of collective-operated construction land into the market. Income distribution resulting from land appreciation provides benefits to villagers, while the enterprises introduced during this process create opportunities for villagers to earn wage income. These factors collectively strengthen the villagers' trust in the village collective, thereby promoting land concentration and enhancing land value.

Fourthly, whether through the kinship and friendship networks or the associative networks structured around connections, their effectiveness lies in the economic considerations of all parties involved. The kinship and friendship network's promotion of land concentration originates from the village collective's utilization of land appreciation income as a substitute for land's protective function for villagers. Likewise, the associative network structured around connections drives land concentration and enhances land value through resource exchanges among the village collective, enterprises, and local governments, each pursuing their respective objectives.

Lastly, apart from the direct or indirect role of social capital in promoting land appreciation, the achievement of development-oriented land appreciation in the tertiary sector also hinges on obtaining monopolistic institutional benefits.

CHAPTER 13

"Village Enterprise Development: The Confluence of Opportunity, Location, and Harmony—A Case Study of Xianfeng Brewing Factory"

In Xunzi's "Wang Ba" chapter (《荀子·王霸篇》), it is written, "Farmers, with their humble strength and limited abilities, remain attuned to the opportune time above, the favorable conditions below, and achieve harmony with people, ensuring the prosperity of all endeavors (农夫朴力而寡能，则上不失天时，下不失地利，中得人和，而百事不废)."

In today's Pidu District, there exists a simple yet rewarding commodity that enriches the lives of villagers through honest toil and unwavering dedication—Douban. This fermented broad bean paste, a result of cultural integration and population fusion in the southwestern region of China, has a rich history. Legend has it that during the late Ming and early Qing dynasties, Chen Yixian (陈逸仙) migrated from the town of Xiaogan in Fujian Province to Pixian County. There, he mixed chili peppers, salt, and sun-dried broad beans, laying the foundation for Pixian Douban. In the Xianfeng era, Chen's descendants took inspiration from tofu fermentation techniques, using wheat bran, Douban, and salted chili peppers to create Douban. Thus, the "Yifenghe (益丰和)" sauce garden was established, bearing the symbol "Yi (益)" to mark its inception, "Feng (丰)" to represent the Xianfeng (咸丰) era, and "He (和)" to incorporating the harmony of heaven, earth, and people, it flourished. Subsequently, other sauce brands such as "Shuntianhao (顺天号)," "Yuanfengyuan (元丰源)," and "Shaofenghe (绍丰和)" emerged (Fig. 1).

© Peking University Press 2024

X. Dong, *Zhanqi Village Over Fifty Years*,
https://doi.org/10.1007/978-981-97-5426-7_13

Fig. 1 "Yifenghe" Sauce Garden

In 1915, the Sichuan Military Government sought Pixian Douban to reward its stationed troops in Tibet. They ordered 20,000 kilograms from the renowned "Yifenghe" and "Yuanfengyuan (元丰源)" sauce brands. After a three-month journey, meticulously packed in lotus leaves, oiled paper, and bamboo baskets, the Douban arrived at the snowy plateau, unspoiled and vibrant. The Sichuan Military Government commended this exceptional quality, honoring the gardens with plaques as a token of appreciation. During the 1920s–1940s, both "Yuanfengyuan" and "Yifenghe" sauce brands thrived, boasting expansive drying fields, thousands of fermentation jars, and a dedicated workforce of craftsmen. Their annual production of Douban reached an impressive 400,000 catties.

In the 1950s, the amalgamation of "Yifenghe," "Yuanfengyuan," and "Shaofenghe" birthed the state-owned Pixian Douban Factory. Supported by local authorities, it flourished and expanded. In 1981, it proudly registered the "Juan Cheng" brand and the "Yifenghe" trademark. The Sichuan Provincial Government honored it with the prestigious "High-Quality Product" title in 1983, and the Ministry of Light Industry recognized it in 1985. The factory achieved further acclaim by winning the gold award at the inaugural China Food Expo in 1988. With a plethora of accolades, Pixian Douban products found their way into households across the nation.

Unlike the aforementioned state-owned enterprises, the Pixian Douban Factory discussed in this book is a village-owned enterprise known as "Xianfeng" in Zhanqi Village. Established in 1980 and operational the following year under the name "Zhanqi Douban Factory," it was the village's pioneering Douban enterprise. Besides Douban production, it also ventured into soy sauce brewing. In 1990, it adopted the name "Xianfeng Brewing Factory," and in 2004, following a transition to a leasing system, it transformed into the "Sichuan Xianfeng Ecological Park Condiment Co., Ltd." For most of its existence, the factory was helmed by Gao Yuchun (高玉春). However, after 2004, Gao Lin (高林), Gao Yuchun's son, assumed the role of legal representative, with a registered capital of 5 million yuan. The "Xianfeng" trademark, under which their products are sold, received recognition as a "Famous Trademark of Chengdu" and a "Famous Trademark of Sichuan." Such honors were bestowed upon it in 1998 and 2005, respectively, as documented in the "Zhanqi Village Chronicle." Praised as the soul of Sichuan cuisine, Pixian Douban truly embodies the spirit of "Xianfeng (meaning 'vanguard' in Chinese)."

The evolution of this village-owned enterprise can be delineated into three distinctive stages. In the initial phase, leveraging the opportunities arising from agricultural collectivization and rural industrialization, the enterprise capitalized on the resources accumulated within the village community and its localized advantages. It embraced the fortuitous timing. During the subsequent market-oriented transformation, the enterprise, buoyed by its capabilities and managerial expertise, expanded its presence from Pidu District to the entire nation. It fully embraced its advantageous location. In the third stage, distinguished from resource-capitalized enterprises burdened with environmental externalities, which faced closure or transformation, the Xianfeng Brewing Factory embraced the guiding principles of "ecological industrialization" and "industrial ecologicalization." Consequently, it emerged as one of the few surviving enterprises in the village. Through restructuring and realigning the interests between the enterprise and the village, it fostered a harmonious and mutually beneficial governance relationship. Indeed, it exemplified the essence of harmony.

The founding story of the Xianfeng Brewing Factory is not an isolated incident. While such examples may be scarce in Western regions, they are relatively common in the east. Notably, the four renowned township and village enterprises in the 1980s—Eastern Shandong, Eastern Liaoning,

Southern Jiangsu, and Northern Zhejiang—emerged by harnessing internal village resources to attract urban industrial capital. Among them, the Southern Jiangsu model stands as a representative example. Under the internalization mechanism of village communities, Southern Jiangsu township and village enterprises swiftly accumulated capital and evolved. During this period, Zhanqi Village resonated with Southern Jiangsu, albeit in distinct spatial contexts.

1 Leveraging Village and Community Assets: Seizing the Opportune Moment

1.1 Inception: The Collective Framework's Primitive Capital Accumulation

Marx's discourse on economic development and the process of societal reproduction suggests that "both social and individual endeavors demand monetary capital as the primary impetus and sustained driving force behind every nascent business." This unveils the inherent necessity for industrial sectors, irrespective of their form, to undergo primitive capital accumulation, establishing a universal cycle of capital circulation revolving around monetary assets. The capital cycle, driven by monetary capital, involves the procurement of labor and production materials through currency, their amalgamation in the production process to generate surplus value, and the eventual sale of commodities to attain increased monetary capital. Thus, currency initiates and perpetuates this process.

Hence, comprehending the mechanisms of primitive capital accumulation becomes the logical starting point for our theoretical interpretation.

Conversely, China's rural industrialization, in its nascent stages, encountered a microcosmic entity—township and village enterprises—that emerged within institutional crevices, lacking the necessary conditions for monetary capital formation. In the 1970s, as the nation's industrial capital accumulation reached its preliminary completion, the opportunity arose to restore diplomatic ties with Western countries, resulting in a phase of large-scale importation of foreign equipment and subsequent structural adjustments in the national industrial landscape. However, the "43 Plan (四三方案)" and the subsequent "82 Plan (八二方案)" led to fiscal deficits in 1974 and 1978, culminating in two economic crises within the process of national industrialization.

In 1981, the fourth economic crisis erupted, triggering the implementation of the Household Responsibility System, known as "large-scale contracting," in rural areas. This momentous change unleashed productive forces, stimulated internal demand with farmers at its core, and gradually rejuvenated the macroeconomic landscape. Subsequently, starting from 1982, the government released five consecutive "Number One Documents," advocating for the widespread adoption of the household contracting system in rural areas, thereby granting collective-owned industries the autonomy to flourish. Despite the government's imposition of increased taxes on enterprises and tightened credit while favoring urban industries during this crisis, collective-owned enterprises swiftly captured the consumer goods market due to their low reliance on state financial loans.[1] In 1983, after Deng Xiaoping listened to a report on rural development in Suzhou and discovered the developmental trajectory of Huaxi Village's small hardware industry, he exclaimed, "Never did I imagine the sudden rise of township and village enterprises." Consequently, in the same year, Lü Guanqiu of Xiaoshan City, Zhejiang Province, took charge of a farm machinery repair factory, initiating a legendary transformation from a modest workshop to a thriving private enterprise. Over the span of a dozen years, township and village enterprises emerged as a silent storm, springing into existence, expanding exponentially, and capturing over half of the industrial added value. Significantly, the majority of these enterprises were rural industries operating below the county level.

Our inquiry arises from a retrospective exploration of the aforementioned macro and micro backdrop. Within the dual constraints of scarce capital and financial limitations imposed by the government, how did township and village enterprises embark on their initial steps towards capitalization? The recollections of those involved offer a glimpse into the transformative potential hidden within China's rural landscape.

At that time, if you needed equipment for work, it was as simple as utilizing bamboo baskets, typically employed for storing broad bean paste, which could be ingeniously reversed to serve as stools. The capital for establishing the factory, amounting to 4500 yuan, originated from the brick factory. With the purchase of raw materials, soy sauce was still transported using oxen. An elderly gentleman would lead an ox and sell the soy sauce in the Dujiangyan area.

[1] Wen, Tiejun, et al. "Eight Crises: China's Real Experience 1949–2009." Beijing: Dongfang Publishing House, 2013.

Source: Interview record of Gao Yuchun, October 31, 2019.

These seemingly modest recollections furnish us with vital information. Firstly, village-owned enterprises can markedly reduce the costs of industrialization by capitalizing on internal factors that are either unpriced or priced at a minimal level within the community. Secondly, the most scarce resource during the inception of township and village enterprises was capital. Yet, the internalized mechanisms of fund circulation and utilization within the village substantially mitigated the costs associated with acquiring capital. The Zhanqi Broad Bean Paste (Douban) Factory, financed with an investment of 4500 yuan from the village's pioneering collective-owned enterprise, the Xianfeng Brick Factory, commenced operations in 1981. Through the deployment of initial capital, they procured bamboo baskets and raw materials, producing bean paste and soy sauce. Under the collective framework, the Zhanqi Douban Factory only required the procurement of specialized fermentation materials. As a venture collectively owned by all village members, the demand for land could be seamlessly accommodated within the framework of the collective, thus minimizing costs. Initially spanning an area of approximately one mu, the Zhanqi Douban Factory employed five workers. Their remuneration was not dispensed as wages, but rather in the form of labor allocation, akin to how fellow members toiled within the production team. Year-end calculations were unified and subject to comprehensive scrutiny by the production team, reducing the need for interim funds and consequently lowering capital costs. Furthermore, the final income received by laborers was contingent upon the realization of the year-end work allocation value established by the entire production team, with no separate accounting conducted within the enterprise. This not only indicates that the enterprise was established through collective investment, thereby entitling the collective to reap the benefits, but also underscores the collective's assumption of entrepreneurial risks. Expanding further, this collective responsibility implies that all members collectively bear the risks associated with enterprise operations. In essence, it exemplifies an internalized mechanism within the collective, one that leverages agriculture and diversification to mitigate enterprise risks. While discussions often revolve around profitable enterprises employing strategies such as reducing the value of work allocation, as practiced in regions like southern Jiangsu to increase enterprise accumulation—whereby "earning 2 yuan within the enterprise translates to receiving 1.6 yuan (or 1.8 yuan) when collected from the production team"[2]—rarely do we acknowledge that if an enterprise fails, the remuneration paid to laborers originates from the value created by other members in different fields (primarily agriculture).

Evidently, the conversion of scarce rural surplus into the initial capital for collective-owned industrial development is facilitated through the rationality of village communities—a mechanism internalized within the collective framework. Cost-effective land and labor contribute as significant elements to the process of primordial capital accumulation. Through the surplus generated by the brick factory, the collective establishes initial capital. This method, characterized by the internal allocation of land, money, goods, and labor within the collective, constitutes the principal path for the capitalization of rural resources. Subsequently, observing the structured expansion process of village enterprises, we ascertain the perpetuation of internalized mechanisms within the village community through self-deprivation. This process nurtures over ten enterprises, laying the foundation for Zhanqi Village's advantageous position in local assessments such as "meeting standards and striving for excellence" during the industrial competition stage in the 1990s.

1.2 *Management: Institutional Dividends Empower a 100% Gross Profit Margin*

Zhanqi Douban Factory's operational journey after its inception entails a shift from monetary capital to productive capital. The production process of its primary products, Douban and soy sauce, follows a path of low-cost and high-profit, intimately intertwined with the macro-policy environment.

The first, second, third, fourth, fifth, and sixth factories in Chengdu are all state-owned enterprises, operating within a planned economy. They relish the advantage of inexpensive national grain supplies and affordable semi-finished goods. We, as a business (representing the company), procure some semi-finished products from them, perform simple processing, and venture forth to make sales.

Regardless of whether the peppers are priced at a modest one fen, two fen, or eight fen per catty, I merely charge you (the supply and marketing cooperative) a mere 8% management fee. If you purchase 100,000 catties

[2] Source: Interview record of Li Shili, June 7, 2019.

from me, the total cost amounts to 6000 yuan, of which I allocate 480 yuan as a handling fee. For as long as my costs remain low, my profits soar high.

Source: Interview record with Gao Yuchun, December 26, 2019.

The interview record reveals two sources of raw materials for Douban: firstly, the procurement of semi-finished Douban and broad beans from state-owned enterprises in Chengdu, and secondly, commissioning the supply and marketing cooperative to purchase nearby peppers, while remunerating them with a procurement management fee. Under the planned economy, national grain supplies come at a bargain price of 0.36 yuan/catty for Douban and a mere 0.06 yuan/catty for peppers. When producing Douban, the ratio of the two ingredients maintains at 4:6. One catty of finished Douban necessitates 4 liang of Douban, 6 liang of peppers, and 2 liang of salt. The raw material cost approximately amounts to 0.2 yuan, while the market's wholesale price stands at 0.39 yuan/catty, yielding a profit of around 0.2 yuan/catty. Considering price fluctuations, the gross profit margin occasionally scales a staggering 100%.[3]

For an enterprise like Zhanqi Douban Factory, operating with minimal investment in machinery and capital, how is it possible to achieve a resounding 100% gross profit margin? One reason lies in the village-based enterprises enjoying the spoils of the macro institutional arrangement.

To unravel this, a brief exploration into historical context proves indispensable.

In the 1950s, China embraced a planned economy with a distinct objective: extracting surplus value to fuel capital primitive accumulation for the nation. The ensuing price structure showcased two distinctive features: firstly, the "price scissors" between industrial and agricultural products, whereby rural areas sold agricultural produce at lower prices while procuring industrial goods at higher prices, thereby channeling surplus to urban industries. Extensive theoretical research exists in this realm.,[4,5] Secondly, the concentration of value-added predominantly

[3] At this point, the gross profit margin signifies the profit gained per unit cost, i.e., the cost-profit ratio, utilizing the same calculation method throughout.

[4] Yan, R., Gong, D., Zhou, Z., et al. (1990). The Current Situation, Development Trend, and Countermeasures of Price Scissors Difference between China's Industrial and Agricultural Products. Economic Research, 2, 64–70.

[5] Kong, X., & Cheng, S. (1997). Economic Analysis of China's Rural Economic System Transition and Its Performance. Teaching and Research, 10, 25–30.

manifested at the terminal sales stage, with settlements between production stages based on cost price, reducing the capital utilization across the entire production system. However, the pricing at the sales stage targeting end consumers witnessed a steep surge, allowing for the accumulation of profits from all preceding stages in one fell swoop. Given the supply side's monopoly control from production to sales, alongside the state serving as the primary subject for capital primitive accumulation, such an institutional arrangement exhibits logical coherence. Throughout most periods, the state strictly constrained the production and operational endeavors of non-state-owned units in urban and rural areas to sustain the closed-loop operation of the aforementioned value chain, ensuring that the benefits of value-added remained firmly within the state's grasp. Naturally, exceptions occurred during economic crises.

Between 1958 and the first half of the 1960s, amidst exceedingly challenging economic circumstances, the state eased restrictions on rural industries, encouraging the establishment of "Five Small Industries" within rural areas. However, commercial and service industries remained subjected to stringent limitations. From 1979 to 1984, under the weight of economic crises and severe fiscal deficits, the government stimulated the development of rural collective enterprises (later renamed "township and village enterprises") and granted farmers the freedom to engage in commercial and service industries controlled by state monopolies. Zhanqi Douban Factory emerged in 1981, a year enveloped by the nationwide eruption of an economic crisis. On one hand, national policies relaxed, enabling village-based enterprises to directly face the market. On the other hand, society grappled with a glut of commodities, causing state-owned enterprises to grapple with market contraction and financial hurdles. Under such circumstances, village-based enterprises seized the opportunity to collaborate with urban state-owned enterprises

The partnership between Zhanqi Douban Factory and the supply and marketing cooperative operates under the same premise. Possessing institutional and social network advantages in the domain of circulation, the supply and marketing cooperative amalgamates administrative circulation entities with enterprise-based economic organizations.[6] It renders services to village-based enterprises, evading capital entrapment, augmenting business revenue, and fostering the social exchange

[6] Huang, S. (1988). General Laws of Cooperative Economy and the Reform of Supply and Marketing Cooperatives in China. China Rural Economy, 07, 24–27.

of commodities, thereby resolving the inherent contradictions between agricultural product production and sales.

In a price system where all profits amass solely at the sales terminal, unreformed yet liberated market entities, Zhanqi Douban Factory establishes connections with upper-level state-owned units while catering to the end consumer market. Essentially, it partakes in the full spectrum of industry chain benefits once monopolized by the state, encompassing the journey from raw material processing to sales. Village-based enterprises merely bear the costs associated with entering a single segment of the industry, while the state shoulders the entire cost of constructing the entire industry chain, spanning from economic infrastructure to superstructure. When compared to urban industrial sectors, rural commerce, and industry boast higher returns on marginal investment. Consequently, the independent development of village-based enterprises propels urbanization and industrialization, allowing them to secure a stronghold in the general consumer goods market at minimal cost, emerging as the driving force behind national economic resurgence throughout the 1980s.

A simple economic assessment of Zhanqi Douban Factory's other product, soy sauce, further corroborates the comparative advantage of early entry into the existing price system for township and village enterprises. Chengdu's soy sauce and vinegar brewing industry flourish, boasting a lengthier brewing history than Douban. The production process and product quality sufficiently cater to consumer demands, with local brands commanding a market share exceeding 80%. Taking the soy sauce production in 1981 as an example, the main raw materials—soybeans and wheat—were priced at 0.345 yuan/catty and 0.155 yuan/catty, respectively. Calculations based on the traditional process's raw material ratio reveal a production cost of 0.074 yuan/catty for brewing soy sauce, while the contemporaneous selling price reached 0.24 yuan/catty, resulting in a profit margin exceeding 300%.[7] For rural communities newly embarking on industrialization, this represents an invaluable opportunity. Subsequently, the market environment diverged significantly from this period: by 1989, soybean prices soared to 1.2 yuan/catty, witnessing

[7] The primary raw material ratio for traditional soy sauce consists of 600 catties of soybeans and 360 catties of wheat. On average, each catty of blended raw materials produces 3.7 catties of standard soy sauce. With 960 catties of raw materials, 3552 catties of soy sauce can be produced, amounting to a total cost of $0.345 \times 600 + 0.155 \times 360 = 262.8$ yuan, and a sales revenue of $3552 \times 0.24 = 852.48$ yuan.

a staggering 247% growth compared to 1981, while contemporaneous product prices ascended to 0.48 yuan/catty. Although experiencing a 100% increase, it paled in comparison to the escalating production costs, rendering it a meager gesture in the face of mounting challenges.

* * *

Fluctuating Soy Sauce Prices: A Possible Background for Xianfeng Brewing Factory's Transformation

Through interviews, we gleaned that in the twilight of their business, the enterprise transitioned its main focus from soy sauce production to the realm of douban, leaving the former behind. This column compiles records of soy sauce retail prices and changes in raw material costs, shedding light on the objective factors guiding the company's product selection.

According to records from the Sichuan Agricultural Improvement Institute, back in 1937, a catty of soy sauce in Chengdu, our setting, cost a mere 0.143 Chinese currency units. However, by the time Japan surrendered in 1945, its price surged to an astonishing 203.73 currency units, an astronomical increase of approximately 1425 times compared to its 1937 value. In 1948, it skyrocketed further to 1345 currency units, marking an exponential surge of about 9040 times compared to the original price.

Following the establishment of the People's Republic of China, during the 1950s, soy sauce prices remained relatively stable, with retail prices for unpackaged soy sauce hovering between 0.24 and 0.28 yuan. Amid the trying times of the three-year hardship, the price of soy sauce saw a surge. In 1960, it rose to 0.50 yuan, roughly double that of an ordinary year. Sensing the burden on the people, the government took action and classified soy sauce as one of the "18 essential daily necessities," effectively freezing its price. As the national economy adjusted and supply conditions improved, prices gradually returned to the levels witnessed in the 1950s.

In the era of the "Cultural Revolution," prices remained stagnant while soy sauce prices remained stable, despite a notable hike in the prices of raw materials. The primary ingredient, soybeans, witnessed a price increase from 0.324 yuan per kilogram in 1983 to 0.432 yuan in 1986, and a staggering 2.4 yuan in 1989, marking a surge of roughly 6.4 times compared to its 1983 value. The price of wheat bran witnessed an even more dramatic increase. Coupled with escalating fuel prices, higher interest rates on loans, mounting labor costs, and miscellaneous expenses (such as retirement pensions for retired employees), product prices remained unchanged for many years, resulting in widespread losses and rendering production unsustainable for most enterprises. In order to safeguard market supply, the municipal government summoned relevant departments to deliberate and eventually decided to grant businesses exemption from the business tax prior to adjusting product prices (spanning from January to May 1986), providing a lifeline to help them navigate the difficult period.

From May 1986 onwards, soy sauce prices gradually rose, ascending from 0.24 yuan to 0.34 yuan, and eventually reaching 0.48 yuan in 1989.

Source: Chengdu Local Chronicles Editorial Committee. Chengdu Chronicles · Price Chronicle [M]. Chengdu: Sichuan Lexicographic Press, 1998.

One could assert that the institutional benefits garnered by villages and communities were fleeting and opportunistic. At such times, the village's foundation played a defining role in seizing these opportunities. Despite embarking on a low-cost venture, the Zhanqi Village found itself compelled to allocate 4500 yuan in liquid funds for procuring indispensable production equipment. In an era of unparalleled financial scarcity, the purchase price for dried chili peppers lingered at a paltry 0.06 yuan per catty, rendering the sum of 4500 yuan tantamount to a staggering 75,000 jin of this fiery commodity! Only villages with relatively substantial collective assets, such as Zhanqi, possessed the requisite wherewithal to grasp such prospects. Consider this: if other villages had only begun accumulating funds upon discerning the allure of monetary gain, they would find themselves arriving late to the party, for that window of opportunity may have slammed shut. Within the same institutional milieu, disparate villages exhibited contrasting aptitudes for seizing opportunities, thereby birthing profound disparities in subsequent growth.

It bears mentioning that, within the confines of the contemporary institutional space, rural collective economic organizations, state-owned enterprises, and supply and marketing cooperatives were all units within the "system," facilitating transactions among themselves with relatively low associated costs. Conversely, individuals scarcely possessed the means to align themselves with state-owned enterprises. Ergo, the fortuitous dividends reaped by the Zhanqi Douban Factory belonged not to an individual, but rather to the entirety of the village's denizens.

2 Embracing Geographical Gains: One End Inside and One End Outside

2.1 Capital Expansion Amidst Macro-Economic Crisis

> "Capital, driven by an insatiable desire to obliterate all barriers to exchange, strives to conquer the entire globe as its marketplace. Simultaneously, it seeks to diminish space through time, minimizing the duration required to transport goods between locations. As capital evolves, the market through which it circulates expands, paving the way for its spatial growth, fueled by the relentless quest to annihilate space with time."

Source: Marx, Engels. Marx and Engels Collected Works: Volume 46 (Part I) [M]. Compiled and translated by the Marx, Engels, Lenin, and Stalin Institute of the Central Committee of the Communist Party of China. Beijing: People's Publishing House, 2009.

According to classical political economy theory, enterprises that have achieved the primitive accumulation of capital strive to expand their financial prowess through internal growth, additional investments, and the assimilation of external resources. This pursuit stems from their intrinsic need for survival and development.

As the local contractor put it, "To ensure our factory's survival and growth beyond mere task completion, we must expand our operations. We employ the additional earnings to fund expansion, while the remaining funds bolster our fixed assets." Following the challenging process of national industrialization, the 1980s witnessed a phase of industrial capital expansion. Village-run enterprises, having successfully amassed their initial capital, naturally harbored aspirations for further growth.

Driven by the allure of industrialization and urbanization opportunities since the 1980s, rural enterprises across the nation made conscious investments, targeting a booming consumer market. Consequently, they achieved an average annual output growth rate surpassing 30%, outperforming state-owned industries by a margin of 10 percentage points, thus becoming the primary catalyst for economic recovery and renewed prosperity. Rural industrialization propelled rapid economic growth, commencing in 1983, wherein the country experienced five to six consecutive years of demand-driven expansion. Notably, rural household incomes outpaced their urban counterparts for four years preceding the economic crisis of 1988.[8]

Yet, the government's unwavering preference for urban industries, persisting like the proverbial "sword of Damocles," cast a shadow over village-run enterprises. Coupled with the market-oriented reforms aimed at stimulating growth, these policies inadvertently triggered numerous institutional costs. Consequently, village-run enterprises that relied on internal mechanisms faced the imperative of fostering comparative advantages and business acumen to withstand risks and sustain progress.

For instance, the outbreak of the second economic crisis between 1988 and 1990 served as a formidable test for village-run enterprises.

During the 1980s, rural industrialization fueled robust consumer demand and heightened investment opportunities, exposing the inherent flaws of an irrational price system. In response, the government embarked on comprehensive market-oriented price reforms, abolishing the unified procurement and distribution system for agricultural and sideline products. Apart from a few select commodities subject to contractual and guided pricing, the majority enjoyed liberalized pricing, leading to an observable upward price trend. In 1988, authorities adjusted grain and oil procurement prices, transforming covert subsidies for major food items (meat, eggs, vegetables, sugar) into overt subsidies. Additionally, they liberated the prices of renowned tobacco and alcohol brands while raising the prices of premium cigarettes and grain-based spirits.

Though market activities thrived, a new issue emerged—soaring prices and arbitrary fees. In the first half of the year, prices surged by an average of 1.4 percentage points monthly. The ensuing "price frenzy" triggered a nationwide buying spree, catapulting July and August price increases to 16.5% and 19.3%, respectively. Despite rectification measures taken in September, the national retail price index still soared to 18.5% that year. The purchase prices of industrial raw materials and fuel rose by 19%. In Chengdu, for instance, the retail price index surged by 25.7% in 1988, with a staggering 41.1% increase recorded in October alone.[9] From a macro perspective, monetary expansion outpaced overall economic growth starting in 1986. In the same year, the government's fiscal deficit,

[8] Wen Tiejun et al. Eight Crises: China's Real Experience 1949–2009 [M]. Beijing: Eastern Publishing House, 2013.

[9] Chengdu Local Chronicles Compilation Committee. Chengdu Chronicles·Price Chronicles [M]. Chengdu: Sichuan Lexicographical Press, 1998.

calculated on a comprehensive basis, surpassed 20 billion yuan, ultimately exceeding 30 billion yuan in 1988.

To curb pernicious inflation, the government implemented policies such as price controls, investment restraint, and credit tightening. Consequently, bank deposit and loan interest rates rose, increasing the cost of capital utilization for enterprises. Combined with restricted product sales and mutual debts among enterprises, a nationwide cascade of liabilities unfolded, heralding a cyclical economic crisis characterized by both inflation and stagnant production. This crisis dealt a severe blow to village-run enterprises, burdened with outdated technology, limited funds, and a scarcity of management talents. Numerous enterprises became ensnared in debt, and some even succumbed to bankruptcy.

Amidst this macroeconomic backdrop, the Zhanqi Douban Factory continued to thrive, expanding its reach from a confined regional domain to a national scale. By the mid-1990s, it had surpassed the industrial benchmark with annual revenue exceeding 5 million yuan. We attribute the transformation of crisis into opportunity to the reliance on path dependence, whereby human capital played an instrumental role. Market expansion unfolded nationwide, leveraging regional advantages and local raw materials to lower production costs—embodied in the development model of maintaining one foot inside and one foot outside.

This notion of path dependence finds its foundation in the developmental journey of Zhanqi Village. At each stage, the presence of high-caliber human capital fueled sustained progress, empowering the village to navigate political, industrial, and ecological competitions. Since the implementation of the contract system in 1983, the village witnessed a union between labor endowed with managerial abilities and village-run enterprises, truly birthing entrepreneurs. Previously, such managers relied on the village's collective platform to exert influence, sharing returns among all members and collectively bearing risks—a form of human capital collectively owned by the village. Under the contract system, individual entrepreneurs leveraged their managerial prowess to confront market risks, reaping corresponding rewards. This transition, made possible by village-run enterprises that had completed the primitive accumulation of capital through internal mechanisms, brought about a shift in income distribution from the collective era's unified management and allocation to a distribution format of "fixed targets + surplus sharing."

* * *

The Institutional Evolution

In 1983, Zhanqi Douban Factory hoisted a new flag—shifting from collective operation to contracted management. The Contractual Agreement on Collective Enterprise Joint Production Responsibility System (《社队企业联产责任制承包合同》see Fig. 2) inked between the contracting party and the collective left no room for ambiguity. The terms were crystal clear: A total annual output value of 150,000 yuan in 1983 demanded a contribution of 12,000 yuan to the collective's coffers. This included a management fee of 1500 yuan, fixed asset depreciation of 4150 yuan, a profit of 2900 yuan, equipment loan interest of 2950 yuan, and land rent of 500 yuan. Payments were to be made quarterly, with 3000 yuan in the first quarter, 2000 yuan in the second and third quarters, and a final sum of 5000 yuan in the fourth quarter. Once the delivery targets were met, the collective claimed 50% of the surplus profit, while the contracting party retained the other half for their own allocation.

By 1985, a new agreement (see Fig. 3) was sealed between the contracting party and the collective. Between 1985 and 1988, with a

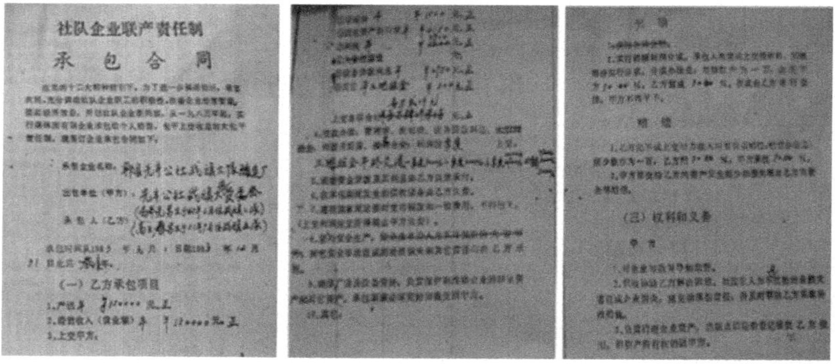
社队企业联产责任制
承 包 合 同
（一）乙方承包项目
（三）权利和义务

Fig. 2 Contractual Agreement on Collective Enterprise Joint Production Responsibility System (January 1983–December 1983). Note: Management fees refer to various fees collected by the management office, fixed asset depreciation is approximately 10%, and equipment loan interest rates are a few cents to one percent

production value of 197,100 yuan, the contracting party was bound to contribute 14,000 yuan to the collective. This amount encompassed management fees, fixed asset depreciation, profits, and sundry expenses, all paid in quarterly installments. After fulfilling the contractual obligations, the collective's share in the excess profit dwindled to 20%, allowing the contracting party to retain a hefty 80% for their own discretion. Within this 80%, the contracting individuals held onto 40%, while the Zhanqi Douban Factory allocated the remaining 60% to fuel its expansion plans.

Fast forward to 1991, the contracting party and the collective penned the "Contractual Agreement on Township Enterprise System Contracted Operation in Pixian County" (《郫县乡镇企业系统承包经营合同》, see Fig. 4). The pact laid out the blueprint for the next three years (1991–1993). The enterprise's total output value skyrocketed, reaching 900,000 yuan in 1991, 1,000,000 yuan in 1992, and soaring to 1,100,000 yuan in 1993. The contracting party dutifully paid their dues, relinquishing 40,000 yuan in 1991, 50,000 yuan in 1992, and a sizable 60,000 yuan in 1993 to the first party. In return, the factory acquired the privilege of utilizing 40% of the net profit earned through meticulous accounting.

Data source: "Contractual Agreement on Collective Enterprise Joint Production Responsibility System" 1983, 1985–1988, 1991–1993, Zhanqi Village Archives.

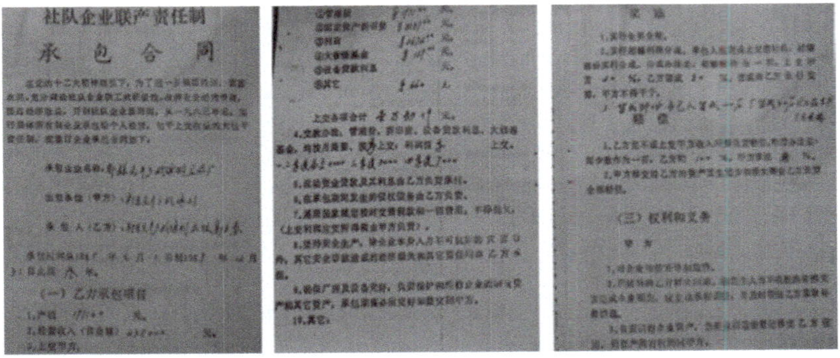
社队企业联产责任制
承 包 合 同

Fig. 3 Contractual Agreement on Collective Enterprise Joint Production Responsibility System (January 1985–December 1988)

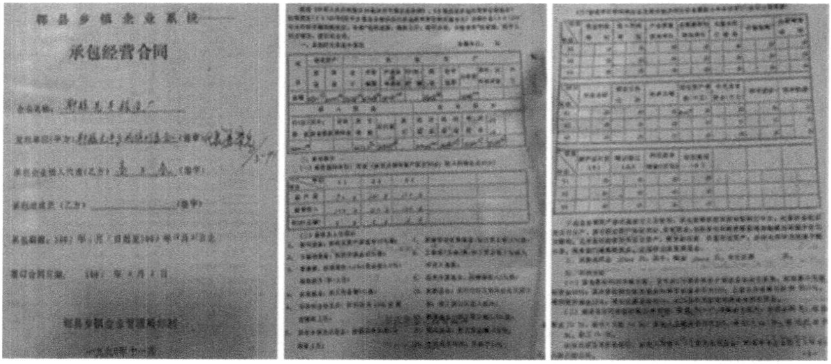

Fig. 4 Contractual Agreement on Township Enterprise System Contracted Operation in Pixian County (January 1991–December 1993)

Gleaning through the three contracts, one can discern the shifting tides of profit distribution between the collective and the enterprise. Assuming a 10% depreciation rate, the metamorphosis of fixed assets becomes apparent. In 1983, the enterprise's fixed assets amounted to 41,500 yuan—an impressive ninefold increase from the initial capital of 4500 yuan. By 1985, fixed assets swelled to 85,400 yuan. Astoundingly, by 1991, the net worth of fixed assets stood at a staggering 300,000 yuan, a monumental surge of 67 times the initial capital. Clearly, the enterprise's operation burgeoned in scale. Analyzing the proportion of income contributed by the enterprise to the collective in relation to the annual output value reveals the collective's return on investment during different contracting periods. In 1983, the collective enjoyed an 8% return (1200/15,000), which slightly diminished to 7.1% during the 1985–1988 timeframe (1400/19,710). Subsequently, the collective's return continued to taper off, reaching 4.4% in 1991 (4000/90,000), 5% in 1992 (5000/100,000), and peaking at 5.5% in 1993 (6000/110,000). In terms of distributing surplus profits, the collective's share plummeted from 50% in 1983 to a mere 20% in 1985. Evidently, as the management system underwent adjustments, the once-shared model of reaping rewards and bearing risks among all members of the village collective metamorphosed into a paradigm where the collective and the enterprise formed distinct boundaries of interest.

Gao Yuchun, the venerable director of the Xianfeng Brewery, fondly recollected the profit distribution during the contracting era. He reminisced, "After paying the contracting fee and national taxes, the remaining profits were not channeled to the collective. Instead, they constituted bonuses for workshop directors and indispensable personnel. Once salaries were disbursed, I even set aside extra money for them. And when fortune smiled, I indulged myself, purchasing cars like the sleek Santana, prestigious Hongqi (红旗), and 131 Beijing–Santana was for customers while 131 Beijing for transportation."[10] It is worth elucidating that, following the customary practice of cost accounting in industrial enterprises, the welfare expenses and bonus funds for mid-level managers are incorporated into product costs. Ergo, an increase in such expenses inversely diminishes the total profit base, subsequently curtailing the net profit available for distribution.

In essence, the manner in which benefits were allocated among different stakeholders during the contracted system, and whether the distribution of increased value resulting from resource inputs abided by the principle of equivalent contributions and returns, represents a pivotal clue for deciphering the trajectory of enterprise development.

2.2 *Maximizing the Advantage of National Spatial Resources*

> "Sales hold the key to production speed. Sell fast, produce fast. As the tanks rotate by the thousands, as long as you can sell them, they can be replaced swiftly. The sales team in the factory attends the sugar and liquor expos every year, and those are vital opportunities that must be seized."

Source: Interview record with Yang Hongfu (杨洪福) on December 25, 2019.

This worker's remark reveals the pivotal role of sales in the brewing industry, where swift production cycles and rapid rotation are paramount. Douban Factory tackles its sales challenges through conventional means such as expanding their customer base and product differentiation. For instance, the factory director enrolls in sugar and liquor expos in cities like Shijiazhuang, Zhengzhou, and Xi'an annually, striving to establish

[10] Data source: Interview record with Gao Yuchun on December 26, 2019.

the brand and generate publicity. They also participate in the anonymous evaluation competition for Douban in Pixian County. In 1989, utilizing personal social resources and employing consignment methods, they successfully dispatched products worth over 300,000 yuan in six train carriages to Beijing, thereby penetrating the Beijing market. From that moment, their product distribution continued to flourish, and by the 1990s, they had achieved nationwide sales coverage.

This seemingly unremarkable phenomenon merits profound contemplation: how does a village-based enterprise manage to conquer the national market? To comprehend this, we must grasp the monopolistic advantages of Pixian Douban from a geographical standpoint.

Pixian Douban, an essential seasoning for Sichuanese cuisine, is widely known. Its distinctively spicy flavors make it stand out among the eight major Chinese culinary styles. Locals even proclaim, "In China, one eats, in Sichuan, one tastes, and in Pixian resides the soul (食在中国，味在四川，魂在郫都)." However, Pixian Douban's recognition as the "soul of Sichuanese cuisine" is not a mere coincidence. It is generally attributed to Pixian County's geographical attributes. Situated on the Western plains of Sichuan, Pixian County enjoys a humid climate, long springs, rainy autumns, and foggy winters. The movement of moist air, propelled by winds, fosters an optimal environment for cultivating diverse microbial communities. The locals have honed their production techniques in accordance with the shifting climate, employing methods such as sun-drying on clear days, covering during rain, turning during the day, and exposing to dew at night. The resulting Douban exhibits the distinctive qualities of being vividly red, lusciously oily, spicily balanced, and indulgently flavorful—a testament to the region's unique essence.

The northern Minjiang River, a northern tributary of the mighty Yangtze River, courses untamed and free. Ever since Li Bing's masterful construction of the Dujiangyan Irrigation System, which bifurcated the Minjiang into the Inner River and Outer River, effectively implementing automatic water diversion based on volume, the waters from the Inner River flow into the Chengdu Plain through the Bottle-Neck Channel (宝

瓶口),[11] bestowing upon the land the designation of the "Land of Abundance," where hunger is an alien concept. From a broader geographical perspective, this region assumes a pivotal role in shaping China's political landscape, as the saying goes, "Gain Sichuan, gain dominion." Simultaneously, the convergence of diverse cultures across China has engendered the iconic Pixian Douban. Along the Indian Ocean's warm and humid airstream, scaling the roof of the world, ice and snow form at the lofty elevation of 4,000 meters. Under the radiant plateau sunlight, this frozen artistry dissolves into water, cascading through valleys, flowing into the Dujiangyan, and traversing the Baopingkou like a splendid fan, dividing into multiple river channels that grace the vast Chengdu Plain. Nurtured by an intricate network of ditches and canals, interwoven with human industry and abundant resources, it weaves a tapestry of the "Land of Abundance." The Pidu District, situated at the first juncture of the golden water network between the Minjiang River and the Chengdu Plain, holds the advantageous position of being bathed in favorable winds and waters. Zhanqi Village, located at the confluence of Dujiangyan, Pidu District, and Pengzhou, thrives in the art of brewing, nourished by the Baitiao River, one of the four main channels of the Inner River in Dujiangyan.

Distinct waters and soils yield distinct flavors. This distinctive spatial and geographical resource constitutes a partial utility of Pixian Douban as a commodity and serves as a vital factor contributing to product differentiation. When Pixian Douban transcended its regional confines and expanded nationwide, the regional characteristics imbued within naturally extended into a broader geographical expanse, solidifying their product's comparative advantage amid the relentless "siege" by various condiments.

2.3 *Localization for Cost-Effective Production*

Even in the presence of a market and established sales channels, numerous enterprises confronted mounting pressures during the extraordinary period of soaring prices and rigorous regulatory control by relevant authorities (1988–1990). Material shortages, escalating production costs, arduous debt recovery, and severed financial lifelines stymied productivity.

[11] Translator's note: which was gouged through the mountain, is the final part of the system. The channel distributes the water to the farmlands in the Chengdu Plain, while the narrow entrance, that gives it its name, works as a check gate, creating the whirlpool flow that carries away the excess water over Flying Sand Fence, to ensure against flooding.

Under the auspices of the "coastal economic development strategy," the government mandated coastal towns and enterprises to prioritize overseas resources and markets, relinquishing domestic assets. Zhanqi Douban Factory deftly circumvented material shortages by adopting a shrewd approach—introducing external seeds and nurturing them within local confines, yielding substantial savings in production costs.

In 1990, poised to expand their business scope, Zhanqi Douban Factory underwent a transformation, rebranding as Xianfeng Brewing Factory. Expanding their product portfolio, they unveiled a series of salt-pickled vegetable delicacies, including salted garlic, pickled vegetables, winter vegetables, fermented black beans, and pickled chili peppers. The factory director proactively imported mustard green seeds from distant regions, disbursing them free of charge to village households, thereby inspiring over a thousand farmers to engage in mustard green cultivation. The factory procured the harvest at a protective price of 0.08 yuan per kilogram. By embracing a "company + farmers" development model, Zhanqi Village cultivated approximately 500 mu (33.3 hectares) of land for mustard greens by 1994. They ventured into northern and Sichuan-style pickled vegetables, with an impressive production volume of 1.5 million catties (750,000 kilograms). This engendered a per capita income increase of 586 yuan, while the enterprise accrued profits amounting to 392,000 yuan. Not only did this uplift the farmers' livelihoods, but it also alleviated the material scarcity predicament, facilitating cost-effective local procurement, thus bolstering the product's competitive edge. In the same year, Xianfeng Brewing Factory submitted a request to the county government for agricultural development funds to finance a technological transformation project, aiming to expand their vegetable product production capacity by 1200 tons per year. They appealed for the resolution of a funding shortfall amounting to 600,000 yuan, aspiring to foster symbiotic growth between the enterprise and agriculture, hastening the journey towards prosperity.

In 1992, Xianfeng Brewing Factory leased land from farmers at a rate of 700 yuan per mu, expanding their factory premises to over 20 mu (1.33 hectares). Annual output surged beyond one million catties, accompanied by an increase in the workforce to over 60 individuals, each earning a monthly wage averaging 200–300 yuan. Over the period from 1992–1994, Xianfeng Brewing Factory amassed an impressive output value of 14.6 million yuan, generating revenue of 8.8 million yuan, and securing a profit and tax amounting to 1.23 million yuan. It emerged as an undeniable pioneer amid the fierce industrial competition. Xianfeng Brewing Factory's factory director, Gao Yuchun, earned esteemed accolades during this phase, attributed to his astute management acumen, receiving the titles of "Entrepreneur of Township and Village Enterprises" and "Model Worker of Chengdu City."

Within this narrative lies an intriguing episode. In 1995, Gao Yuchun assumed the position of Party Branch Secretary of Zhanqi Village while concurrently serving as the General Manager of Jifeng Industrial Corporation. Between 1994 and 1996, the contracting and operational agreements between the village collective and Xianfeng Brewing Factory designated Wang Ping as the legal representative of the enterprise, rather than Gao Yuchun. In August 1995, Wang Ping (王平) was relieved of his duties as factory director and redirected to oversee supply and marketing operations for the parent company, allowing Gao Yuchun to assume complete responsibility for managing Xianfeng Brewing Factory.

Unraveling the intricacies of the governance structure adjustment between the parent company and the brewing factory and the entangled responsibilities, rights, and interests remains a challenging endeavor. Nonetheless, during the 1980s and 1990s, the economic bedrock of enterprise development underwent a transformative shift, diverging from its nascent stage. The enterprise's returns increasingly mirrored the risks and rewards of the market environment. Amidst their expansive market outreach, Xianfeng Brewing Factory adroitly capitalized on their spatial and geographical advantages while leveraging localization to ensure cost efficiency. Through a harmonious amalgamation of internal and external elements, they derived the utmost advantage from their favorable geographical position.

3 Reconstructing Village Enterprise Governance: A Human Endeavor

In the 90 s, China braved two economic crises, gleaning wisdom from each and embarking on an ecological transformation in the twenty-first century. Representative of this era, village-operated enterprises, led by Xianfeng Brewing Factory, underwent two adjustments: first, a shift from the contract system to joint-stock cooperation in 1995, and later, a transition from joint-stock cooperation to leasing in 2004.

3.1 *Stagflation Crisis and the Rise of Demutualization*

The lingering stagflation crisis from 1988 to 1991 prompted an open-door strategy, aimed at augmenting exports and resolving the foreign debt predicament. However, due to the rapid monetization by the central government and the liberalization of the stock market, futures market, and real estate market—pillars of the capital economy—money surged forth, unleashing an investment frenzy. Not only did government entities establish sprawling enterprises, but societal investment desires swelled, with individuals eagerly participating in investment and fundraising endeavors. Bond and token interest rates skyrocketed to 20% to 40%, while savings grew sluggishly. This economic fervor birthed what was succinctly dubbed the "Four Heats," "Four Highs," "Four Strains," and "One Chaos."[12] Unprecedented money supply growth, coupled with fiscal deficits and mounting trade imbalances and debts, culminated in a joint eruption of fiscal, financial, and foreign exchange deficits in 1993. Consequently, the CPI surged by a staggering 24.1% in 1994. In response, reform measures were implemented, including currency devaluation to spur exports, the adoption of a "tax-sharing system" to alleviate central fiscal woes, cuts in public sector expenditure for education and healthcare, downsizing and streamlining state-owned enterprises, and curbing interregional credit to ease the financial quagmire. The repercussions of these policies were acutely felt by small and medium-sized enterprises, leading to a scarcity of funds and mounting financing costs. Despite a nominal loan interest rate of 10% in 1994, enterprises effectively faced a burdensome rate of 20%. The unrestrained credit expansion by banks exacerbated interlocking debts and inventory pressures among enterprises, ultimately stagnating production.[13]

During this critical juncture, Zhanqi Village emerged as a pioneering pilot for enterprise restructuring. Asset assessments were conducted by the Pixian County Auditing Office, while equity divisions and quantifications unfolded within the village. On January 11, 1995, a reorganization

[12] The "Four Heats" encompassed real estate, development zones, fundraising, and stocks; the "Four Highs" comprised inflationary investments, industrial growth, monetary expansion, and price hikes; the "Four Strains" referred to transportation, energy, essential materials, and capital shortages; the "One Chaos" represented anarchy in economic order.

[13] Wen Tiejun. What Do We Really Want? [M]. Beijing: Huaxia Publishing House, 2004.

conference convened in Zhanqi Village, culminating in the establishment of Jifeng Industrial Corporation, jointly formed by five collective enterprises. The equity structure allocated 50% to the village collective, 20% to employees, and 30% to the enterprise. Notably, employees were granted a share quantification system, apportioning shares based on headcount (30%), seniority (30%), position (20%), professional title (10%), and contributions (10%). Employees entitled to share quantification subscribed to individual shares, based on a ratio of 1:3 (where one yuan purchased three shares), effectively becoming shareholders in the company.[14] Xianfeng Brewing Factory's total capital amounted to 2.039 million shares, with collective capital accounting for around 39.47% (approximately 804,900 shares), and individual employee capital totaling about 466,500 shares.[15] Through this arrangement, the entire workforce of Xianfeng Brewing Factory enjoyed full ownership, reaping dividends in proportion to their shareholdings (Table 1).

* * *

Table 1 Chengdu Jifeng Industrial Corporation's Xianfeng Brewing Factory Share Percentage and Allocated Amounts in 1995

	Number of shares	*Share proportion (%)*	*Amount payable (10,000 yuan)*
Village collective shares	804,893	39.47	12.38
Corporate legal person shares	273,741	13.43	4.21
Common shares of the enterprise	445,623	21.85	6.85
Individual shares of employee	466,455	22.88	7.18
Shares of village committees	48,300	2.37	0.74
Total	2,039,012	100	31.36

[14] Excerpt from Xianfeng Brewing Factory's "Records of Major Events"

[15] Calculated based on the "Supplementary Table for Profit Distribution of Chengdu Jifeng Industrial Corporation in 1995".

Report on the Asset Evaluation of Five Enterprises in Zhanqi Village

This column compiles the complete contents of the 1994 "Report on the Asset Evaluation of Five Enterprises in Zhanqi Village, Tangchang Town, Pixian County," offering readers insight into the asset and liability status of collective enterprises. The original text is as follows.

Zhanqi Village People's Committee, Tangchang Town, Pixian County:

Under the endorsement and commission of Tangchang Town People's Government, our office formed an evaluation team comprising registered auditors, engineers, economists, and asset evaluation professionals to conduct asset evaluations of the five village-owned enterprises. After one month of work and with the support and collaboration of the village committee and enterprises, the asset evaluation was successfully completed. We now present the evaluation report of the results.

(1). Enterprise Overview:

The five enterprises, including Sichuan Pixian Xianfeng Brewing Factory, Pixian Xianfeng First Brick Factory, Chengdu Pixian Compound Fertilizer Factory, Pixian Huifu Douban Factory, and Pixian xianfeng Flour Processing Factory, are all village-operated enterprises affiliated with Zhanqi Village in Tangchang Town. As of the benchmark date, the total assets amount to 9,360,938 yuan, with the original value of fixed assets at 2,116,376 yuan and net assets at 3,066,690 yuan. With the approval of the County Economic Restructuring Commission, they were included in the demonstration villages for the reform of village-level economic organizations in Pixian County, aiming to promote the overall development of village-level economic organizations and accelerate the reform process.

(2). Evaluation Purpose:

To transform the operating mechanism and implement shareholding reform.

(3). Benchmark Date of Evaluation:

November 20, 1994.

(4). Principles and Basis of Evaluation:

This evaluation is based on the notice from the State-Owned Assets Management Bureau and the State Assets Administration [Document No. 36, 1992, "Notice on the Issuance of the Implementation Rules of the Management Measures for State-Owned Assets Evaluation"], as well as the evaluation standards and recognized criteria of the Chengdu Asset Evaluation Management Center.

The evaluation team adhered to the principles of objectivity, fairness, and independent evaluation throughout the assessment process, guided by the principles of objectivity, fairness, and truth-seeking in their professional practices. They were free from interference or intervention by the asset evaluation client (or the asset occupier), their supervisory unit, government departments, or other economic actors, ensuring the authenticity and accuracy of the asset evaluation conclusions.

(5). Scope and Types of Evaluation:

The overall evaluation of all assets lawfully occupied and legally owned by the five enterprises.

(6). Standards and Methods of Evaluation:

The evaluation adopts the national-prescribed replacement cost standard, the net present value standard, and corresponding methods.

(7). Asset Inventory:

Inventory and verification of the assets of the five enterprises were conducted simultaneously on the unified benchmark date. The accounting treatment of the inventory results and the clearance of debts were adjusted in the accounting statements for the benchmark date. Therefore, in the adjustment column, only accounting items were adjusted, and there were no changes in the total assets.

(8). Evaluation Conclusion:

Based on the benchmark date and the evaluation standards and methods, the evaluation of the assets of the five enterprises affiliated with Zhanqi Village concluded that the total assets amounted to 9,360,938 yuan, with an evaluated value of 10,271,968 yuan, resulting in a net increase of 911,030 yuan and an appreciation rate of 9.73%. The total liabilities were 6,294,248 yuan, and the owner's equity was 3,066,690 yuan, resulting in an evaluation increase of 911,030 yuan.

(9). Evaluation Qualifications and Legal Liabilities:

Our office has obtained the qualification for asset evaluation, granted by the Chengdu Municipal State-owned Assets Bureau, in accordance with Document No. 18, 1993, "Approval of Asset Evaluation." Our office assumes responsibility for the authenticity of the evaluation conclusions mentioned above.

Pixian County Audit Office.

November 21, 1994.

Source: Pixian County Audit Office, "Report on the Asset Evaluation of Five Enterprises in Zhanqi Village, Tangchang Town, Pixian County".

It is noteworthy that, in the face of rising funding costs amidst the surge of the three deficits, the adoption of new management systems and the development of shareholding economies became a crucial avenue. It not only harnessed internal village funds but also rallied local residents and factory workers for capital mobilization, effectively replacing exorbitant bank loan interests and mitigating financial constraints. Meanwhile, state-owned enterprise reforms compelled employees to buy out their years of service, downsizing the surplus workforce. Some township and village enterprises sought loans by transitioning into private entities, albeit failing to concurrently shoulder the social security burdens, which triggered a series of mass incidents.

Zhanqi Village's innovation in equity allocation lay in the introduction of employee shares, granting villagers the right to partake in the fruits of enterprise development. This recognition honored the labor contributions of employees, safeguarding their assets derived from labor and land as an alternative to capital investment. Although the relationship between the village and enterprises had transformed from close interdependence during the collectivization era to a deeper level of detachment, the fact that the enterprises hadn't completely severed ties with the rural collective economy granted them legitimacy to engage in market activities under the collective enterprise banner. Simultaneously, rents and management fees collected by the collective were allocated to social public expenses. Early profits sustained high levels, with employee share purchases offsetting their expenses through dividends in preceding years. The enterprises also absorbed surplus labor from the village, forging a symbiotic bond with the villagers. Consequently, villagers gained dividends from shares, wages, bonuses, and diverse income channels, which alleviated the institutional costs associated with restructuring to a certain extent.

Through restructuring and the consolidation of internal funds and personnel, Xianfeng Brewing Factory remained primed to enhance its market competitiveness through capital densification. Subsequent investments, such as constructing a storage facility capable of accommodating one million catties of fermented bean paste, as well as the acquisition of material storage pools, drying rooms, ball mills, and elevators, bolstered Zhanqi Village's industrialization efforts.[16] Zhanqi Village surged ahead on its path of industrialization, ranking 10th among 261 grassroots units in Pixian County for industrial output value in 1996–1997, achieving an output value of 73.78 million yuan. By 1997, village enterprises boasted a total output value of 65.92 million yuan, securing the 7th position.

3.2 *Surplus Production and the Second Revamping*

Amidst the previous crisis, village-owned enterprises deftly resolved the capital scarcity by consolidating resources and labor into financial assets. Yet, when confronted with the deflationary gloom cast by the East Asian financial tempest, individual enterprises found themselves at the mercy of dire circumstances. Truly, when the nest is overturned, how can one safeguard the fragile eggs?

The stagflation crisis of the early 1990s left an indelible mark on economic development, leaving two distinct impressions. Firstly, the three-year span from 1994 to 1997 witnessed macroeconomic regulation, which burdened both urban and rural communities with institutional costs. As a result, domestic demand significantly dwindled from the vibrant days of the 1980s, with exports becoming the paramount driver of economic growth. China's economic interdependence with the world

[16] According to the "1999 Work Report of Chengdu Jifeng Industrial Corporation" and the "2000 Work Report of Chengdu Jifeng Industrial Corporation".

surged, rendering it increasingly susceptible to the ebbs and flows of the global economic cycle. Secondly, industrial capital gradually slipped into surplus, while profit-driven financial capital divorced itself from tangible industrial assets. The East Asian financial crisis stands as a testament to the ramifications of these two ailments.

In 1997, East Asia was engulfed by a financial maelstrom that directly crippled China's exports. The export growth rate in 1998 plummeted to a mere 0.5%, a drastic decline from the previous year's 4.2%. As external demand contracted, economic growth subsided, amplifying the pressures of unemployment. The ensuing period from 1999 to 2001 witnessed a deflationary depression, shrouding the underlying contradictions of domestic supply and demand that were masked by the growth in net exports. In response, the central government implemented a series of measures, such as commercializing banks, issuing long-term national bonds for infrastructure development, and unveiling strategic initiatives to address regional and urban–rural disparities. This governmental intervention served as the primary means to sustain a decade of high economic growth throughout the twenty-first century.[17]

In the current crisis, numerous domestic scholars contend that China is transitioning from scarcity to surplus. However, the extensive development model, which relies on government-led investment to spur economic growth, has inadvertently exacerbated overproduction. In the wake of global industrial capital reshuffling and China's integration into the international economic cycle, surpluses have emerged in the realms of industrial capital, commercial capital, and financial capital.

* * *

The Dawn of the Twenty-First Century: The Growth of the Pixian Douban Industry

The phenomenon of overproduction finds glimpses of revelation in the development of the Pixian Douban industry.

In 2001, the Pixian County government unequivocally set its sights on constructing a colossal Pixian Douban industry, envisioning the creation

[17] Wen Tiejun, et al. Eight Crises: China's Real Experiences 1949–2009. Beijing: Oriental Publishing House, 2013.

of the nation's largest condiment base. Through astute capital management, it endeavored to erect a vast douban conglomerate, fostering large-scale, industrialized enterprises. By 2004, the number of douban production enterprises within Pixian County had surpassed 160. These enterprises primarily dotted 19 townships, including Tangchang, Huayuan, Xinsheng, Ande, Tangyuan Township, and You'ai Township. The county's annual average douban production reached an impressive 70,000 tons, generating an annual sales revenue of over 200 million yuan, and contributing more than 10 million yuan in tax revenue.[18] This endeavor birthed distinctive brands such as Juancheng, Chuan Lao Hui, Dan Dan, Chuan Pixian, Lao Ji Shi, and Hengxing.

The downturn in business operations triggered by external crises has shattered the fragile foundations of transactional relationships within village-owned enterprises, becoming the pivotal catalyst for the reconfiguration of mutual interests.

Since 1999, village committees and enterprise operators have convened multiple meetings to address the developmental challenges faced by share cooperative enterprises. Discussions encompassed the need for improved cooperatives, enhanced management practices, a comprehensive understanding of subsidiary companies, rewarding factory directors with salaries three times higher than employees, providing annual bonuses, and establishing a well-managed financial system for companies. The objective was to rectify the loose and imperfect organizational structure of companies, and to clarify the roles and responsibilities of enterprise operators, producers, and owners.[19]

In 2001, recognizing severe losses within the parent company, the village collectively employed the reserve funds of Jifeng Corporation to facilitate distribution. According to the "Annual Report on the Work of Jifeng Industrial Corporation in 2001," the accumulated reserved funds were disbursed, with employees receiving their entitled amounts fully transferred to individual shares for participation in that year's distribution. The collective shares and individual shares of the village and the "two committees" were allocated a total of 610,000 yuan. Of this sum,

[18] Yang Jianwei. Chengdu City Pixian County Food Industry Association Contributes Strategies to Revitalize the Pixian Douban Industry. Rural Economy, 2004(1): 43–44.

[19] Information sourced from the "Meeting Records of Zhanqi Village Committee" in the Zhanqi Village Archives.

460,000 yuan was disbursed, while 300,000 yuan was utilized to settle outstanding debts, leaving a surplus of 160,000 yuan. As one former village cadre recollected, "At that time, the village committee was penniless. The exact amount of debt eludes my memory. The village was bereft of funds. With 50% of the reserve funds, we distributed 460,000 yuan. After settling the previous debt of 300,000 yuan, we were left with 160,000 yuan. The village transformed from indebtedness to financial solvency."[20] Xianfeng Brewing Factory amassed reserve funds totaling 507,000 yuan, distributed at a rate of 0.25 yuan per share. This allowed employees to receive a share totaling 116,613.75 yuan. Following the stipulations, individual shares for employees increased to 583,068.75 shares in 2001, granting them participation in that year's distribution.

Furthermore, in collective enterprises, the measurement of profit growth resulting from additional investments made by business operators has remained ambiguously defined since the advent of the self-contracting system. In 2001, following the regulations set forth in Document No. 13 issued by the Pidu Committee, village-run enterprises rewarded their business operators with all the collectively owned shares. The Xianfeng Brewing Factory, for instance, saw a transformation of its 446,273 collectively owned shares into shares granted to the operators as rewards.[21] In 2002, a total of 583,143 shares from reward shares and accumulated shares were distributed to the operators, with 291,571 shares allocated as reward shares and the remaining 291,572 shares reinstated as collectively owned shares, as indicated in Table 2. While this restructuring objectively increased the operators' income, subsequent interviews revealed that the realization of the reward shares, for various reasons, did not materialize.

From an objective standpoint, the operational performance of the Xianfeng Brewing Factory, as depicted in Table 3, experienced a substantial decline in 2003. Compared to 1999, the total annual profit plummeted by 73%, and collective dividends dwindled from 130,200 yuan to a mere 28,500 yuan in 2003, marking a significant decline of 78.1%.

In 2004, Zhanqi Village's collective spearheaded the reform of leasing within their village-run enterprises. Repurchasing employee shares, the collective sought expert guidance to elucidate the intricate relationship between "operating rights and ownership." Given the employees' limited

[20] Information sourced: Interview record with Li Shili on January 6, 2020.

[21] Based on "Chengdu Jifeng Industrial Corporation's 2001 Work Report.".

Table 2 Changes in Xianfeng Brewing Factory's Share Structure from 2000 to 2003

Equity situation		*2000*	*2001*	*2002*	*2003*
Amount of participation in distribution (10,000 yuan)		17.92	11.66	9.16	6.53
Total share amount		2,038,705	2,154,474	2,154,474	2,154,474
Distribution per share (10,000 yuan)		0.0879	0.0541	0.0425	0.0303
Village collective shares	Share amount	941,764	941,764	941,764	941.764
	Apportionment (10,000 yuan)	8.2781	5.0949	4.0025	2.8535
Common shares of the enterprise	Share amount	446,273	–	291,572	291,572
	Apportionment (10,000 yuan)	3.9191	–	1.2392	0.8835
Individual shares of the two village committees	Share amount	48,300	48,300	48,300	48,300
	Apportionment (10,000 yuan)	0.4241	0.2613	0.2053	0.1463

Source: "Chengdu Jifeng Industrial Corporation's Profit Distribution Plan (2000–2003)."

Table 3 Xianfeng Brewing Factory's operational performance from 1999 to 2003, Unit: 10,000 yuan

Operating conditions	*1999*	*2000*	*2001*	*2002*	*2003*
Operating income	464.98	440.03	361.73	366.23	418.78
Operating cost	357.31	344.42	279.96	249.57	299.98
Operating expenses	33.85	33.88	34.63	61.72	62.03
Business tax	1.22	1.55	1.44	1.11	0.73
Management costs	30.19	30.30	31.90	37.83	42.05
Financial expenses	7.11	7.16	1.57	0.28	2.52
Operating profit	42.14	29.88	12.23	15.72	11.47
Non-operating income	0.63	0.29	0.80	0.37	–
The total profit	0.53	2.35	–	–	–
Profit to be distributed	42.51	27.82	13.03	16.09	11.47
Collective dividends	28.26	17.92	11.66	9.16	6.53
	13.02	8.28	5.09	4.00	2.85

Source: Compiled from the 1999–2003 "Chengdu Jifeng Industrial Corporation Income Statement."

individual shareholdings and their fragmented entitlements, devoid of the capacity to augment income through equity, the collective's repurchase initiative secured prompt cash inflows. Simultaneously, the operators grappled with the constraints imposed by imminent increases in future operating costs. Consequently, the synergistic alignment of the collective and the villagers corresponded harmoniously with the overarching imperatives of restructuring the village's collective interests. On May 29, 2004, the village collective reacquired personal shares of the Xianfeng Brewing Factory, remunerating the employees at a nominal price of 1 yuan per share, in cash. This transaction witnessed the transfer of 581,267 shares among 49 employees, as illustrated in Fig. 5.

Having regained control of the enterprise, the collective conducted a comprehensive assessment and verification of the factory's assets, eventually leasing the enterprise, with preference given to the original operators, by divesting fixed assets and auctioning off current assets. On June 10, 2004, the total value of the Xianfeng Brewing Factory's fixed assets amounted to approximately 1.18 million yuan, with current assets totaling about 4.62 million yuan and long-term investments reaching 250,000 yuan.[22] Subsequently, on June 18, 2004, the village collective and the former director, Gao Yuchun, finalized the "Agreement on the Purchase and Redemption of Current Assets of Xianfeng Brewing Factory." The village collective sold the enterprise's current assets to Gao Yuchun

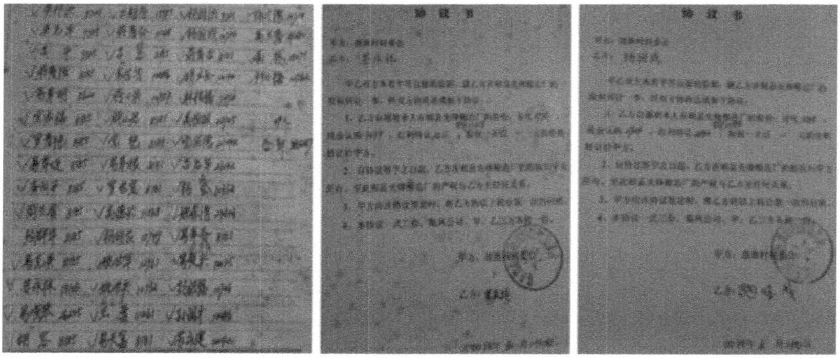

Fig. 5 Roster of Employee Share Transfers at Xianfeng Brewing Factory

[22] Compiled based on the "Xianfeng Brewing Factory's 2004 Balance Sheet.".

for an estimated value of around 4.89 million yuan. After deducting taxes, wages, personal loan principals and interests amounting to roughly 470,000 yuan, as well as enterprise shares (including reward shares for the business operators) valuing about 520,000 yuan, the remaining cash payable stood at approximately 3.88 million yuan. Pursuant to the agreement, Gao Yuchun was expected to remit 2.59 million yuan by the end of June 26, 2004, while the remaining 1.29 million yuan would be borrowed from the collective, with a stipulated three-year repayment period and annual installments of 430,000 yuan commencing on July 14, 2005, inclusive of interest.[23]

The valuation of current assets hinged on the book value for unprocessed raw materials and market estimations for processed products, all of which were subsequently sold to the lessee. Amidst the economic upswing commencing in the latter half of 2002, raw material prices witnessed an ascent. For instance, the factory price for semi-finished water chestnuts hovered around 0.7 yuan per catty, while the market price ranged from 0.9 to 1.0 yuan per catty. Ultimately, the village enterprise negotiated a compromise, settling on a price of 0.8 yuan per catty. [Based on the meeting minutes of June 8, 2004, the final confirmed prices for Xianfeng Brewing Factory's raw materials were 0.8 yuan per catty for water chestnuts, 0.75 yuan per catty for dried chili embryos, and 0.85 yuan per catty for fresh chili embryos.] We ascribe the 0.1 yuan per catty price increment to a natural reflection of the prevailing circumstances, thereby enabling the collective to reap the benefits of this price surge. Consequently, it becomes comprehensible why the former director contested the pricing methodology for current assets: "I pay 0.52 yuan for sea peppers, and with additional expenses and interest, it amounts to 0.62 yuan. Yet, they (alluding to the collective) sell them to me for 0.82 yuan, pocketing a profit of 0.20 yuan! If you're not interested, so be it. Frankly, I can't fathom (this pricing method)."[24]

The auctioning of current assets infused a revitalizing force, akin to "living water," into the transformation and development of the village. This can be gleaned from the multiple summaries and reports summarizing the prevailing situation. The August 2004 "Summary of the

[23] Compiled based on the "Agreement on the Purchase and Redemption of Current Assets of Xianfeng Brewing Factory.".

[24] Source: Interview record with Gao Yuchun on December 26, 2019.

Situation of Enterprise Change in Management Mechanism" emphasized that the enterprise's nature had become lucid and the asset attributes discernible. The enterprise assumed a collective ownership nature, while operationally functioning as a leasing entity. The report underscored the greater benefit accruing from value addition. Refraining from effecting the change would have led to the enterprise's demise within three years, rendering the three to four hundred employees bereft of employment prospects—an unimaginable consequence. Concurrently, as the enterprise underwent restructuring, the village collective diligently orchestrated land consolidation efforts. The funds recovered from the current assets served as a financial resource for the village's socio-cultural development and public welfare expenditures, ultimately acting as a lever for facilitating the ecological transformation ushered in by the new era.

The disposal of fixed assets necessitated adjusting rental prices every three years, with payments due by the end of each December. A ground-level investigation revealed that in March 2008, in response to the concentrated residency of village inhabitants, the Xianfeng Brewing Factory relocated to the vicinity of the Shaxi Road (opposite the road at Zhanqi Village's entrance). The compensation for the old factory building, attached objects, and relocation expenses amounted to 1.42 million yuan in total. The collective invested 1.89 million yuan to facilitate the relocation and construction of the new factory building, ensuring that the new and old structures maintained roughly the same area, spanning approximately 20 acres. The annual rent for land and the factory building ranged from 400,000 to 500,000 yuan.

This form of the collective collecting fixed rent and the enterprise utilizing land for construction necessitates contextualizing it against the backdrop of macro and micro factors. The revised "Land Administration Law of the People's Republic of China" in 2004 imposed rigorous constraints on enterprises occupying land for developmental and productive purposes. Concurrently, Chengdu City introduced and executed a development strategy centered on the concept of "concentration," encouraging the aggregation of industries within parks, moderate-scale land utilization, and concentrated residential areas for farmers. The government even provided fiscal subsidies to support the consolidation of land resources, thereby heightening their value. Zhanqi Village experienced land consolidation alongside infrastructure development, consequently witnessing a surge in land costs for newly established industrial enterprises. A village resident voiced his thoughts during an interview, stating, "For construction land, for example, the listed price at the Chengdu Pidu District Exchange stands at 800,000 yuan per mu, yielding a return of 0.4%. If I were to charge rent based on the bank interest rate, you would owe me 3000 yuan per month."[25] By comparison, the collective collected a monthly rent of 1670–2080 yuan per mu from village-run enterprises, thus underscoring the rent's divergence from market-based pricing. The collective retained certain powers concerning resource allocation throughout the village, thereby ensuring the seamless relocation of enterprise sites.

Moreover, the collective continued to nurture enterprises, exhibiting an enduring role. Extending loans to local enterprises at an interest rate of 10%, the collective enabled the generated value increment to flow back into the village, expanding its collective reserves and establishing a virtuous cycle within the village enterprise ecosystem. For instance, in November 2004, the "Summary of the Situation of Enterprise Change in Management Mechanism" referenced the Xianfeng Brewing Factory's requirement to pay over 3.88 million yuan for current assets. Although the contract stipulated that two-thirds should be paid upon signing, the factory, in practice, disbursed only 1.5 million yuan that year, with the outstanding 1.2 million yuan remaining unrealized. Subsequently, through consultations, both parties concurred that "if there are difficulties in paying salaries by the end of January 2005, the village will lend (the enterprise) 200,000 yuan to cover employee salaries (a short-term loan, with further loans contingent upon the enterprise's ability to pay salaries)."

Taken as a whole, against the backdrop of an unstable economic environment and intensifying competition, the strategic reconfiguration of transactional relationships and governance boundaries between village-run enterprises and the village itself, aimed at achieving "harmony among people," bestowed the enterprises with a competitive edge, fostering their sustained development in the new era.

[25] Source: Interview record with the director of Mama Farm on October 3, 2019.

4 Conclusion

Born in adversity, bred in hardship. The fate of township and village enterprises remains entwined with the ever-present specter of the external macrocosm. Yet, they are not mere adherents to the prescribed contours of their surroundings, merely treading the beaten path. This enigma has long beguiled the minds of scholars, casting a curious allure over township and village enterprises.

Within the realm of this discourse, Xianfeng Brewing Factory stands as an exemplar of collective enterprise. It traversed the arduous stages of inception, contracting, restructuring, and leasing, ultimately converging upon collective ownership. Blessed with the serendipity of opportune circumstances, fortuitous geographical placement, and harmonious human synergy, it weathered the storm. The crux of its resilience lies in the deep-rooted interconnection it forged with the village collective from its very genesis. The enterprise leaned upon the bedrock of the village community, fostering primal capital accumulation. As the institutional landscape evolved, it yielded to the inertia of historical contingency. Moreover, the tapestry of distinctive climatic patterns and geographical endowments conspired to bestow upon this brewing establishment a singular spatial advantage, enabling its survival despite tribulations endured.

CHAPTER 14

A Village Enterprise in the Macroeconomic Cycle—The Decade of Zhanqi Village's Broad Bean Paste Factory

Chengdu's Fuyou Green Seasoning Co., Ltd. (aka Fuyou Green Seasoning Company) occupies a humble corner of Zhanqi Village's Group 2. Nestled on approximately 12 mu of land, it employs a loyal crew of 36. Their craft revolves around crafting fiery concoctions like red oil bean paste, traditional bean paste, and the beloved hot pot bean paste. This enterprise's annual revenues dance in the realm of 50–60 million yuan. Trace back to its origins, and you'll find the roots of Hui Fu Bean Paste Factory, which officially sprang to life in 1993, pioneering the art of bean paste production in Zhanqi Village. The year 2003 witnessed a transformation, with Yang Kui taking the reins as the company's legal representative. With a modest registered capital of 1 million yuan, the venture underwent a rebirth, assuming its new identity as Chengdu's Fuyou Green Seasoning Co., Ltd.

1 Emerging Amidst Macroeconomic Surge (1992-1993)

In 1992, Deng Xiaoping's Southern Tour Speech propelled China's reform and modernization into uncharted territory, affirming the significance of township enterprises as part of our socialist economy. It was a political nod that elevated their standing and opened doors to new horizons. In 1993, the State Council issued a decisive decree, fueling the

© Peking University Press 2024
X. Dong, *Zhanqi Village Over Fifty Years*,
https://doi.org/10.1007/978-981-97-5426-7_14

development of township enterprises in the central and Western regions. This macro policy backdrop birthed Huifu Douban Factory.

Luo Huifu, the founder and former director, was a carpenter born in '49. Back in the early days of New China, skilled craftsmen were rare commodities, both in urban and rural landscapes. Unfortunately, the natural flow of talent was severed in Zhanqi Village.

I found work in Guanxian County in '65, assisting the Supply and Marketing Cooperative as a carpenter. After about a year, the director took a liking to me and urged me to return after settling the relocation formalities. However, the branch team secretary, Jiang Daxing, disagreed, and I went back to work. But within a fortnight, my elder brother Luo Huichang, representing the village, summoned me, insisting I help with the brigade's development. I faced a dilemma. On one side, the Cooperative offered better prospects, but my family struggled, and I had just tied the knot with nothing to my name. Yet, my brother promised to wait if I didn't return. The next day, I followed him back home.

Source: Luo Huifu's interview record, December '19.

Zhanqi Village, in a bid to retain talent, employed political tactics and personal networks, resisting the market's role in optimal resource allocation. It safeguarded its reservoir of skilled labor, accumulating premium human capital for the village's future. Technical talents, with Luo Huifu at the helm, laid the groundwork for Zhanqi Village's infrastructure, gradually igniting its industrialization. Luo's Pioneer No.1 Brick Factory became an incubator for collective enterprises, birthing a series of township ventures like Douban Factory, Liquor Factory, Flour Factory, Prefabricated Component Factory, Fertilizer Factory, and Honeycomb Coal Factory. Huifu Douban Factory emerged as one of the enterprises nurtured by the brick factory's investment.

Recalling 1992, Luo Huiyou (罗会友), who was then teaching at Pioneer Middle School, was summoned by his brother Luo Huifu (罗会富) to establish Douban Factory in Zhanqi Village. Hence, "Fu (富) You (友) Douban" acquired its name.

Much like other township enterprises, Huifu Douban Factory transcended from nothing to something, relying on the collective economy.

First, let's examine the capital element. The factory's initial capital amounted to roughly 510,000 yuan, with the brick factory allocating 110,000 yuan worth of red bricks for the construction of the factory premises. Huifu Douban Factory boasted a kitchen, warehouse, fresh pepper room, small tile room, machinery repair room, and more, encompassing a total area of 2942.71 square meters. Additionally, the brick factory invested close to 400,000 yuan in other construction materials and worker wages.[1] Once Douban Factory commenced operations in 1993, it encountered the common hurdle of funding shortages. Given the difficulty in securing bank loans for township enterprises, the factory director rallied more than 20 Douban Factory employees and over 80 brick factory workers to pool funds. They pledged to repay within a year, with a mere 1-cent interest. Ultimately, they accumulated over 1 million yuan in cash to sustain the first year's production, resolving the funding shortfall. Herein lies the inherent advantages of township collective economic enterprises. With both the director and employees being local villagers of Zhanqi Village, the enterprise boasted a robust social fabric. This embedded social network within the rural community empowered township enterprises, affording them access to all favorable resources within the village society at minimal cost, an advantage urban capital sorely lacks. Of course, we mustn't overlook the intangible assets entrepreneurs invest, such as personal reputation, influence, authority, and extensive labor contributions.

Next, we delve into the land element. In the initial stages of township enterprise development, the collective ownership nature justified the rationality and legality of utilizing collective land for industrial expansion, obviating the need for corresponding land use or transfer fees. In 1992, the enterprise inked an agreement with Zhanqi Village's Group 2 residents, leasing over 10 mu of land for factory construction. The annual land fee amounted to a modest 1200 yuan per mu. During this phase, Huifu Douban Factory benefited from policy and institutional dividends. However, the 1998 revision of the "Land Administration Law of the People's Republic of China" ushered in national monopolization of the primary land market. Consequently, costs for enterprises acquiring and occupying rural land skyrocketed, eradicating any dividends.

Now, let us focus on the labor element. During the early stages, Huifu Douban Factory recruited 15 employees, all relatives of brick factory workers, predominantly local villagers ranging from 40 to 60 years old. Given the unique nature of Douban Factory's product production, a piece-rate wage system prevailed, devoid of a minimum wage.

[1] Source: Luo Huiyou's interview record, November 3, 2019.

The workers were part-time farmers, tending to agricultural duties during peak seasons and engaging in factory work during lulls. The farmers not only made valuable contributions to the enterprise by accepting lower wages but also alleviated the burden of fixed costs. Notably, during the nascent phase of Huifu Douban Factory, the principal executives received meager salaries, while the factory director forfeited any remuneration. The employees, in turn, contributed their unused property to the enterprise's operations. In essence, township enterprises seized an abundance of surplus labor at an extraordinarily low cost, free from the corporate culture and individual incentive quandaries that plague urban capital. All these distinctive attributes stem from the social effects unique to township enterprises.

Lastly, we scrutinize the distribution method employed by Huifu Douban Factory. Founded on the cusp of the shareholding system reform, the factory initially adhered to the contracting model. Each year, the enterprise remitted a contract fee of 50,000 yuan to the village collective, absolving the collective of any loss risks or involvement in surplus profit sharing. In the inaugural year, a significant portion of Huifu Douban Factory's profits was allocated to settling debts owed to employees.

2 Corporate Restructuring and Management during Economic Excess and Recession (1994-2002)

External shifts in institutions always intertwine with macroeconomic fluctuations. In 1993, a trifecta of fiscal, financial, and foreign exchange deficits hit, triggering a debt crisis in township enterprises. To tackle this, the government pursued a demutualization reform strategy as their means of "withdrawing" heavily indebted township enterprises.

In 1994, the nation initiated a pilot program for corporate demutualization, and Pixian County was handpicked as a trial county for enterprise restructuring, with Zhanqi Village among the chosen test sites. Answering the call, the village collective merged Chuanfu Douban Factory with four other thriving ventures in 1995, birthing Chengdu's Jifeng Industrial Corporation (known as "Jifeng Corporation")—a pinnacle of entrepreneurial reform. Jifeng Corporation established a board of directors and a supervisory board, overseeing these five enterprises as subsidiaries. To ascertain their financial footing, a thorough examination of their assets was carried out by certified evaluators.

The evaluation of Chuanfu Douban Factory revealed a total asset worth of 1,715,456 yuan, liabilities amounting to 1,612,248 yuan, and owner's equity reaching 103,208 yuan. In line with directives from the Township Enterprise Bureau, the enterprises devised a shareholding reform plan: 50% of the shares belonged to the collective, 30% to enterprise development stock, dedicated to reinvestment and excluding private quantification, while the remaining 20% was quantified and distributed among employees and the factory director. Personal shares from this 20% portion required subscription, with each share valued at one-third of the individual's contribution. The number of shares allotted to individuals hinged upon comprehensive assessments of personal contributions, tenure, positions, and other factors. Notably, the factory director's allocation could not surpass five times the average employee's shares, and the director's ownership could not exceed 5% of the company's total shares. Figuring in Fig. 1a, Jifeng Corporation's profit and loss statement for the years 1994–1999, post-shareholding reform, exhibited an upward trajectory in business performance. In 1995, revenue rose by 5,326,936 yuan compared to 1994. However, by 1997, Chuanfu Douban Factory's profitability dipped considerably, and Jizhuan Factory, an affiliated enterprise, plunged into losses amounting to 165,210 yuan. Responding to the crisis, Jifeng Corporation allocated a portion of Chuanfu Douban Factory's interest and profits to alleviate Machine Brick Factory's losses. Both factories suffered losses amounting to 43,693 yuan in 1998. Concurrently, Jifeng Corporation implemented a capital expansion plan, illustrated in Fig. 1b, by introducing an additional 214,200 shares of personal stock.

However, the shareholding reform caused Chuanfu Douban Factory to transition from an enviable high-profit model to a liability-driven paradigm, influenced by a confluence of factors. The join-stock system, regarded as an exogenous institutional arrangement, incurred negative externalities due to exorbitant transaction costs within the village's unique operational milieu.

Given the advanced nature of the stock cooperative system, it necessitated a higher caliber of managerial personnel. However, the management staff of township enterprises primarily hailed from lowly educated farming backgrounds, ill-equipped to navigate the intricacies of the joint-stock mechanism. Consequently, the enterprises evolved into an amalgamation of incongruous management styles, including elements of demutualization, contracting, leasing, and private individual endeavors. The ethos of paternalistic governance and familial management permeated the

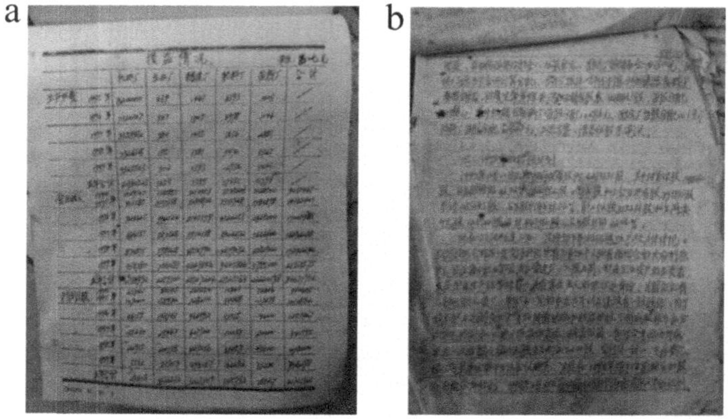

Fig. 1 **a** Jifeng Corporation's Profit and Loss Statement (1994–1999). **b** Jifeng Corporation's Capital Expansion Plan in 1998. *Source* Zhanqi Village Archives

company's operations. While the enterprises initially functioned relatively smoothly, cracks started to appear in later years.

Source: "Chronicle of Zhanqi Village's Evolution."

Moreover, due to fixed village expenditures, the original contracting system persisted alongside the implementation of the stockholding system, with the stockholding system predominantly influencing the relationship between the enterprises and their employees. For instance, during periods of poor business performance, the enterprise still had to contribute financially to the village, potentially depriving employees of dividends based on stockholding. Throughout this period and subsequent rounds of restructuring, the village continued to reap rent from production houses and fixed assets. Recalling those times, Luo Huifu disclosed that Chuanfu Douban Factory was burdened with a yearly management fee of 50,000 yuan. Additionally, dividends were distributed based on stockholding, diminishing the distributable profits for operators. Simultaneously, alterations occurred in the profit distribution model of the village's collective economy. Pre-shareholding reform and Jifeng Corporation's establishment, all management fees were fully surrendered to the village collective. Post-reform, the management fees paid by the enterprise were evenly split between Jifeng Corporation and the village collective. The obscure allocation mechanism bred opportunities for rent-seeking, sapping the vigor that once thrived from an originally equitable and inclusive distribution system.

Simultaneously, owing to Zhanqi Village's premature adoption of institutional transfer, the shares allotted to collective enterprise operators paled in comparison to the later stages of stockholding reform in other township enterprises. This created negative incentives for Zhanqi Village's collective enterprise operators. Gradually, the operators' mindset shifted, leading to instances of asset diversion. In 2000, Zhanqi Village initiated an investigation into Chuanfu Douban Factory's losses, depicted in Fig. 2. Although the factory reported a loss of 24,094.19 yuan in 2000, the actual investigation revealed a profit of 12,952.80 yuan. A portion of the income remained unaccounted for, including rental income of 13,880 yuan, interest income of 13,209.95 yuan, electricity fee income of 9818.84 yuan, pumping fee income of 128.80 yuan, water fee income of 122.50 yuan, and income from the sale of waste materials, totaling 886.90 yuan. With the exception of a 1000 yuan Spring Festival subsidy, 37,046.99 yuan went unrecorded in the income calculation.

Naturally, we cannot overlook the prevailing macroeconomic backdrop. By the late 1990s, township enterprises underwent extensive expansion amid an economic crisis. The competition between township enterprises, fueled by excess production capacity, coupled with a contracting consumer market, inevitably resulted in a deteriorating business environment for enterprises. The inherent transaction costs, compounded by the macroeconomic downturn, perpetuated Chuanfu Douban Factory's shrinking profits, with employees deprived of company dividends for years. The distribution and asset fluctuation of Chuanfu Douban Factory during this period are depicted in Table 1 and Fig. 3.

3 Enterprise Transformation and the Resurgence of Village Collective Economy (2003)

Zhanqi Village's enterprise restructuring in 2003 followed the natural course of institutional change. With Gao Demin assuming the role of village director, the enterprise contractors saw an opportunity for privatization reform. Under pressure from the economic elites and the need for collective economic control, Zhanqi Village embarked on its second phase of restructuring.

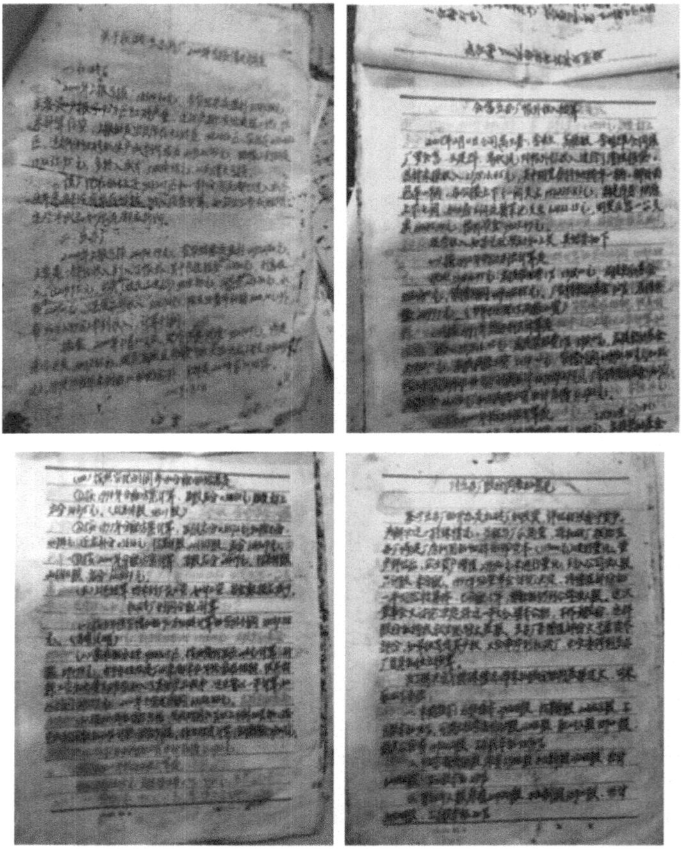

Fig. 2 Investigation into Machine Brick Factory and Douban Factory's Losses in 2000. *Source*: Compiled based on Jifeng Corporation's distribution records

At that time, conforming to prevailing principles meant succumbing to the wave of privatization sweeping the nation. But Zhanqi Village stood apart. They faced a crucial question: Should they follow the herd and let their enterprise wither away? They couldn't bear to see the hard-earned assets of over a thousand villagers go to waste. They were determined not to become the culprits responsible for the village's downfall. It was a difficult decision, for the path forward seemed uncertain.

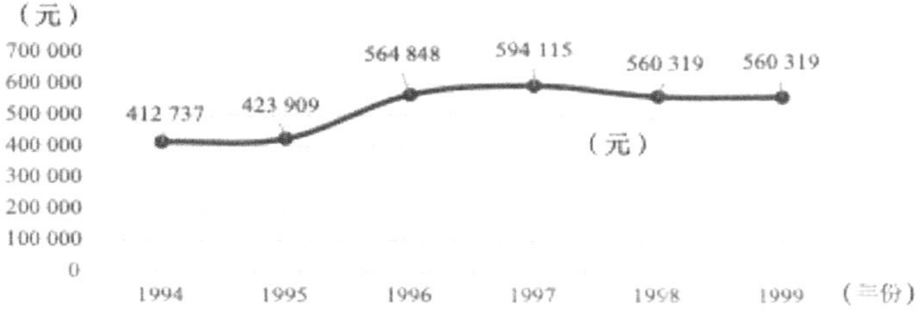

Fig. 3 Net Asset Changes of Chuanfu Douban Factory (1994–1999). *Source*: Compiled based on Jifeng Corporation's distribution records

Table 1 Distribution Situation of Chuanfu Douban Factory (1995–1999)

Distribution Situation	*1995*	*1996*	*1997*	*1998*	*1999*	*Total*
Number of employees	14	19	23	21	13	18
Salary (yuan)	37,382	47,980	58,112	27,445	30,000	200,919
Bonus (yuan)	8	32,249	–	–	–	41,020
Income per capita (yuan)	3296	4222	2526	1016	2307	–

Source: Compiled based on Jifeng Corporation's distribution records

They considered various options. First, they sought to improve the internal mechanisms of the joint-stock system, strictly adhering to government regulations. However, the reality proved unyielding. The older, less educated operators couldn't be expected to undergo a transformative shift in their thinking and embrace modern management practices. Change their minds? It seemed implausible. Replacing them wasn't a viable solution either. These operators had been there from the start, birthing and nurturing the enterprise. How could they be replaced? The first path proved impassable.

The second option entailed reverting the joint-stock enterprises back to collective ownership. Yet, this presented a significant challenge. Zhanqi Village had already left behind the era of communal resources and returning to it wasn't readily acceptable. However, if they didn't act, the enterprise would perish. They had no choice but to return it to the collective. It was in this moment that the role of the party branch resurfaced. This became the basis for their reform.

Zhanqi Village's actions were perceived as unconventional amidst the broader environment. Nevertheless, it is essential to recognize the village committee's inherent drive to strengthen the collective economy. By bolstering the collective economy, the party branch could regain its influence.

Others, including the town leaders, deemed their approach unsound. Yet, in line with tradition, Zhanqi Village was granted the freedom to try. It embodied the party's respect for grassroots innovation, harnessing the creative force of the people.

To reclaim control over the enterprise, Zhanqi Village began by transforming the operators' mindset. They sought the guidance of a professor from Southwest University, who shed light on matters of management rights and ownership for the villagers. Subsequently, they selected pilot projects and gradually expanded their efforts. The brick factory and bean paste factory under Luo Huifu's stewardship were early subjects of restructuring.

After the transformation, the enterprise's equity structure comprised 271,528 shares, with the village collective holding 76% and individual employees holding 24%. The latter included quantified individual shares for workers, quantified shares for the village committee, subscribed shares, and incentive shares for the operators.

Upon regaining control, Zhanqi Village quantified the enterprise's assets in 2003. The evaluation posed a unique challenge since the bean paste factory had been an investment of the brick factory, resulting in no net assets. To address this, they reached an agreement with the factory director, converting the red bricks used for the bean paste factory's construction into capital for quantification. The quantification process revealed an asset appreciation of 299,734 yuan, with the unquantified portion incorporated into the corporate legal shares.

Following capital quantification, the village committee swiftly initiated an open bidding process. While their principle was to prioritize the original operators and minimize conflicts, Luo Huifu found the bidding price exorbitant and abstained from the bean paste factory bidding. Ultimately, Yang Kui secured the leasing rights for the factory with a bid of 760,000 yuan. The village committee leased the factory buildings and remaining raw materials to Yang Kui for 600,000 yuan. Yang Kui was to pay annual land rent and factory rent, contributing directly to Chengdu Jifeng Industrial Corporation. To encourage enterprise development, the

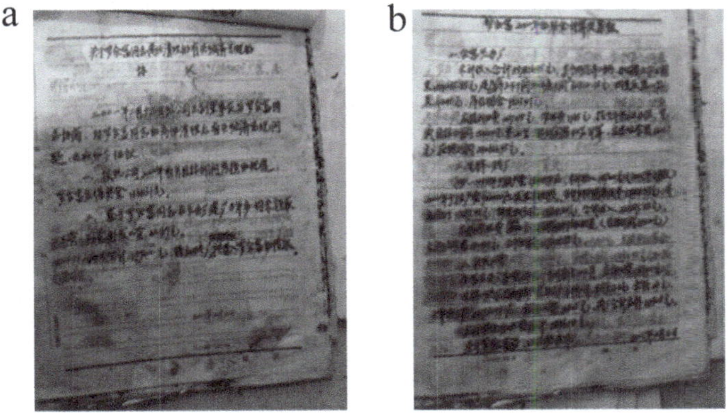

Fig. 4 **a** Relevant resolutions regarding Comrade Luo Huifu's resignation and cleanup. **b** Agreement on the final economic payment of Luo Huifu's bonus in 2000

village collective provided a 260,000 yuan loan to the bean paste factory, with an annual interest rate of 10% (Fig. 4a, b).

In 2017, Fuyou Green Seasoning Company, with an output value of 50-60 million yuan, paid a total of 451,624 yuan in fees to the village. Employee numbers increased from 14 to 36, and average monthly wages rose from 2493.57 yuan to 4500 yuan.

The enterprise's cost and revenue structure for 2018 are detailed in Table 2.

Table 3 presents a comparison of the bean paste factory's operating conditions before and after the restructuring.

The second round of enterprise restructuring necessitated acknowledging the role played by informal organizations. These unwritten rules, shaped by long-term social interactions, encompassed values, ethics, cultural traditions, customs, and ideologies. By quantifying and leasing assets, the bean paste factory safeguarded collective assets. The concealed rent within the contracting and joint-stock systems was laid bare, augmenting the village collective's disposable assets. Simultaneously, restructuring expanded the scope of management rights, providing clarity in property ownership, and enabling the enterprise to endure the cutthroat market competition. This not only ensured future income for the village collective but also mitigated the social costs associated

Table 2 2018 Cost and Revenue Structure of Fuyou Green Seasoning Company

Items		*Amount (yuan)*	*Ratio to total income (%)*
Cost	Raw materials	3500	70
	Financial expenses	150	3
	Marketing expenses	750	15
	Labor expenses	100	2
Gross profit (= operational income − operational cost)		1500	30
Net profit (= gross profit − Financial expenses − Marketing expenses − Labor expenses)		500	10
Total income (= Cost of raw materials + Gross profit)		5000	100

Table 3 A comparative analysis of pre- and post-restructuring operating conditions of the bean paste factory

Asset	*2002*	*2003*	*2018*
Total assets (yuan)	218,0032.27	1,881,210.06	Missing financial data of enterprises after restructuring
Total liabilities (yuan)	1,383,851.99	1,019,589.06	Missing financial data of enterprises after restructuring
Owner's equity (yuan)	796,180.28	861,351	Missing financial data of enterprises after restructuring
Operating income (yuan)	978,455.07	850,207	5000–6000
Total profit (yuan)	33,414.82	50,000	Missing financial data of enterprises after restructuring
Covered area (mu)	13	13	12
Number of employees	14	14	36
Total monthly salary (yuan)	32,259.26	34,910	162,000
Average monthly salary (yuan)	2304.21	2493.57	4500

with mass unemployment resulting from enterprise closures. Nonetheless, leasing was merely a stopgap measure to safeguard the collective economy, limiting future growth potential. In other words, the restructuring was an ongoing process. Today, Zhanqi Village continues to explore the path forward for the collective economy.

CHAPTER 15

Innovative Integration: Maigao Company and Zhanqi Village's Collaborative Exploration in Spatial Resource Development

1 Introduction

Maigao Company, a specialist in village development services situated in Pidu District, Chengdu, has embarked on a remarkable journey of rural revitalization. Formerly a village-run enterprise, it transformed into a private entity, evolving from a humble liquor factory to a diverse portfolio that includes alcohol production and valuable fixed assets like gas stations. Since the 90 s, their focus gradually shifted towards rural development, aiding villages in fundamental infrastructure construction.

Maigao Company has unveiled an inventive model for rural collective economic growth—a model encapsulated in the Maigao Model of "1–2–3–4." At its core lies the philosophy of "complementary strengths, aligned responsibilities, equitable treatment, and collaborative construction for shared prosperity." By constructing a robust platform to foster convergence, propelling the impetus of "two separations," instituting effective mechanisms through the "three pillars," and orchestrating transformative processes for development, Maigao paves the way for a new era of cooperative village enterprise synergy.

This case study delves into the intricacies of Maigao's visionary approach, illuminating their quest for an elegant fusion of resources and the boundless potential it holds for both company and village alike.

© Peking University Press 2024
X. Dong, *Zhanqi Village Over Fifty Years*,
https://doi.org/10.1007/978-981-97-5426-7_15

2 Maigao Company and Its Operating Model: A Concise Overview

2.1 Introduction to Maigao Company

Maigao Company emerged on November 2, 2005, with an initial name, Sichuan Maigao Real Estate Co., Ltd., and a capital of 8 million RMB. Zeng Xudong (曾旭东), the company's charismatic figure, held 75% of the shares, simultaneously serving as the executive director and general manager. The corporation nurtured three subsidiaries: Sichuan Colorful Zhanqi Tourism Scenic Area Management Co., Ltd., Sichuan Yanyun Business Service Co., Ltd., and Sichuan Yuansxiang Agricultural Technology Service Co., Ltd. Prior to its official establishment, Maigao primarily engaged in the rustic territory, where construction adhered to no fixed norms. To circumvent high establishment costs, villages and towns would typically outsource their ventures to companies with superior credentials and established brands.

Since its repositioning as a rural service provider in 2002, Maigao Company has actively participated in the development of various rural landscapes, including Sandaoyan Huili Commercial Street, Qinggangshu Village, and Zhanqi Village in Chengdu's Pidu District. Its influence in promoting collective economic growth spans approximately one-third of the district's towns. Noteworthy accomplishments include Qinjiamiao Village in Sandaoyan Town, Zhanqi Village in Tangchang Town, and Hengshan Village. Today, Maigao's endeavors extend into the Ande region. The company's modus operandi varies across different villages, ranging from offering planning and design assistance to fully managing three villages: Guyan Community in Sandaoyan Town, Qinggangshu Village, and Zhanqi Village.

Maigao Company operates with eight hierarchical levels, each further divided into four tiers. Typically, newcomers commence at Level 2, while graduate recruits join at Level 3. Those capable of managing an entire village occupy Level 4, and overseeing a region like Pidu District requires attaining Level 5, and so forth.

Based on a 2019 interview with Maigao Company's top executives, the company is in the midst of planning a conglomerate, overseeing all subsidiary entities, namely Sichuan Maigao Yuanxiang Construction Engineering Co., Ltd., Sichuan Maigao Tourism Resource Development Co., Ltd., Sichuan Bingzuo Garden Greening Engineering Co., Ltd., and Chengdu Happy Agriculture Development Co., Ltd. Three platform companies, namely Sichuan Yanyun Business Service Co., Ltd., Sichuan Xiangcaohu Tourism Scenic Area Management Co., Ltd., and Sichuan Colorful Zhanqi Tourism Scenic Area Management Co., Ltd., also fall under the conglomerate's control. The establishment of this umbrella entity serves two purposes: to effectively coordinate the multitude of subsidiaries and to foster clarity in each subsidiary's functions and business orientation. Formerly, sectors handling substantial business volumes will transition into independent subsidiaries, encouraging team motivation through enhanced efficiency.

2.2 The Maigao Model[1]

Collective economic growth and the integration of commercial interests into rural areas confront formidable challenges. The emergence of novel collective economic models encounters hurdles such as scarce resources but abundant potential, infrastructural development without operational means, and the presence of various elements lacking human capital. Simultaneously, the urban integration of commercial investments into rural spheres contends with the precarious balance between soaring costs and meager returns, enduring high risks with minimal rewards, and limited involvement despite potential gains. In this landscape, Maigao Company courageously embarks on an innovative route for rural collective economic advancement. Anchored in fundamental principles and inherent patterns, the Maigao Model epitomizes "complementary strengths, matched responsibilities, equitable partnerships, and shared construction and rewards." It forges a robust foundation through the "1–2–3–4" Maigao Model, fostering unification through a grand platform (一大平台), invigorating progress through dual separations (两大分离), enhancing effectiveness through triumvirate mechanisms (三大机制), and fostering development through quadruple transformation (四个再造). This path paves the way for a new era of village enterprise collaboration within the collective economic landscape.

[1] Information derived from interviews with Maigao Company's directors and managers, and internal documents titled "Innovative Practice of Complementary Co-construction of Village Enterprise for the Development Path of Collective Economy—Maigao Company's '1–2–3–4' Model".

(1) Building the "Grand Platform": Consolidating urban and rural resources. The operational rights or usage rights of marketable assets such as dispersed dwellings, lands, agricultural facilities, and ancillary structures are entrusted to village collective economic organizations. Maigao Company injects capital, collaborating with these organizations to establish comprehensive professional operation firms. These entities cater to market demands, proficiently steering scenic areas towards commercial prosperity. Collective economic organizations contribute by relinquishing property rights at a reduced price or through capital investment. Tasked with managerial responsibilities, the professional firms co-manage and supervise communities (districts, scenic zones) alongside personnel deployed from collective economic organizations and Maigao Company.
(2) Spearheading "Dual Separations": Cultivating rural developmental impetus. On one hand, the model advocates for separating collective land and housing assets from ownership constraints. The initial step involves separating rural contracted land rights, homestead ownership, and the usage rights of agricultural dwellings. All such rights amalgamate within village collective entities. Collaboratively, these entities join forces with Maigao Company, establishing versatile professional platforms that integrate and harmonize fragmented operating and usage rights. Subsequently, a secondary separation and transfer of operational rights and usage rights ensue. Platform entities, through mutual agreements, reassign these integrated rights to businesses, granting them the autonomy to operate under specified terms. The platforms retain supervisory privileges, reclamation rights, and a portion of revenue rights while collecting management and leasing fees. On the other hand, the model advocates for segregating front-end managerial functions (business entities) from back-end operational service functions (platform companies).
(3) Constructing "Triumvirate Mechanisms": Fostering shared development dividends. Primarily, a mechanism of shared construction and consensus formation takes root. Platform co-construction and collective decision-making form the bedrock of this mechanism. Furthermore, a mechanism of synergistic operations emerges, leveraging the collaborative potential of village committees, collective

officials, local governments, platform companies, villagers, homeowners, and businesses. Lastly, a mechanism for equitable profit distribution materializes, ensuring stakeholders, including villagers, collective entities, Maigao Company, businesses, and governmental bodies, partake in a "guaranteed price + surplus sharing" system, fostering a multifaceted network of shared interests.

(4) Achieving "Quadruple Transformation": **Initially, spatial forms** undergo an uplifting metamorphosis. Robust infrastructure emerges, dilapidated structures receive a facelift, distinctive character flourishes, and ecological sanctity finds protection. **Simultaneously, industrial forms** witness rejuvenation. With platform companies at the helm, regional agricultural sectors undergo holistic optimization, fostering a transition towards higher-end industries. This propels the fusion of agriculture, commerce, culture, and tourism, manifesting novel industries, formats, and models encompassing leisure tourism, sporting encounters, wellness agriculture, and cultural innovation. **Operational forms** undergo a renaissance. Platform companies undertake unified planning, utilization, operation, and management of collective resource assets, culminating in a transformation from dispersed deployment and fragmented ownership to centralized operation. **Lastly, governance forms** experience rebirth. The entrance of platform companies encourages a shift in grassroots social governance from conventional single-center models to inclusive multi-center frameworks. Government entities, village committees, grassroots officials, business operators, and farmers all assume roles within this diverse social fabric.

This model has successfully spread to Liangxiang Town in Beijing's Fangshan District, where it revitalized collective property rights and instigated collective economic development, yielding significant outcomes. Multiple regional governments and enterprises, including Hainan Baisha Farm, Guizhou Baili Dujuan Tourism Group, and Hebian Town in Mianyang City, have expressed intentions to adopt this model, currently engaging in concrete negotiations. This attests to the Maigao Model's profound conceptual underpinnings, organizational structures, and systemic designs, which hold substantial merit and universal applicability across the nation.

3 A Fortuitous Alliance: When Maigao Company Met Zhanqi Village's Monetization of Collectively Owned Land Parcels

Maigao Company found a golden opportunity to collaborate with Zhanqi Village when Sichuan Province introduced the policy of collective profit-oriented land entering the market back in 2015. As one of the pioneering trial areas, Pixian County attracted significant attention.

Initially, Maigao Company showed no interest in bidding, letting other more formidable contenders take the stage. Zhanqi Village engaged in talks with multiple potential investors who proposed constructing hotels spanning five to six floors to align with their investment and operational needs. Yet, the local regulations stipulated that commercial buildings in rural areas should not exceed three floors. With Zhanqi Village lacking an ideal location for developing the tertiary sector, along with height limitations and soaring auction prices, the interested companies ultimately abandoned their bidding endeavors.

However, the local government was determined to claim the title of "Sichuan's first (and potentially the nation's first) collective profit-oriented land entering the market." This led them to approach Maigao Company, persuading them to participate in the land auction.

From August 26 to September 7, 2015, Zhanqi Village put forth 13.447 mu (approximately 8.965 hectares) of collective profit-oriented land, including the existing village-owned compound fertilizer plant, prefabricated component factory, and the old village committee office building, with an initial auction price of 495,000 yuan per mu. Eventually, Maigao Company secured the 40-year land-use rights for this plot at a price of 525,000 yuan per mu, marking the province's inaugural transaction of rural collective profit-oriented land entering the market. The auction total reached a staggering 7.06 million yuan. As outlined in the "Notice on Listing and Bidding for the Transfer of Collective Profit-oriented Land Use Rights in Pixian County (《集体经营性建设用地使用权挂牌出让竞买须知》)," the successful bidder had to pay 30% of the land price within ten days, followed by 40% within fifty days, and the remaining 30% within ninety days after signing the "Pixian County collective Profit-oriented Land Use Rights Transfer Contract (《郫县集体经营性建设用地使用权出让合同》)." The bid deposit of 1.33 million yuan would then be converted into the final payment. Once the transfer formalities were completed, Maigao Company obtained the certificate granting them the right to utilize the land for construction purposes.

According to the accounts of Maigao Company's veteran, Zeng Xianyong (曾贤勇), and other senior executives, the decision to invest a hefty sum of 7.06 million yuan was not solely influenced by the government's "persuasion" tactics. Rather, the corporation meticulously evaluated multiple factors before making a rational choice.

Firstly, the project carried substantial political significance. Pixian County aspired to become the frontrunner in collective profit-oriented land entering the market within Sichuan Province, a direction aligned with Maigao Company's focus on rural town services. Furthermore, venturing into the development of collective profit-oriented land was an area of exploration for the corporation. Thus, acquiring this land held profound implications for Maigao Company's brand positioning, augmenting its influence and the eminence of the Maigao model. Since Maigao Company targeted the entire market of Pixian County, aiming to create and manage a comprehensive brand encompassing all rural areas, the region's strategic location and promising market prospects added weight to the decision. Consequently, building trust and establishing a cooperative relationship with the government became imperative, streamlining the cost of acquiring information across various villages while facilitating cross-village integration.

Secondly, Zhanqi Village demonstrated early resource consolidation before the policy on collective profit-oriented land entering the market was unveiled. Through the village-level platform, Zhanqi Village unified its resources under collective ownership, including agricultural land and collective construction land. The village successfully achieved what they referred to as the "dual separations"—a fundamental prerequisite for the village collective to unite operating rights during the initial stages of village development. Thus, the crucial factor contributing to Maigao Company's collaboration with Zhanqi Village lay in the fact that, compared to other villages, Zhanqi Village possessed a distinct outline of collective economy. Seizing the opportunity presented by collective profit-oriented land entering the market, Maigao Company forged a partnership with Zhanqi Village's collective asset management company, gaining operational rights over the entire village.

Thirdly, Zhanqi Village boasted a robust industrial foundation. Maigao Company had long been attentive to the growth trajectory of villages, particularly those dedicated to advancing the collective economy. As early as 2007, Zhanqi Village embarked on new village construction, industrial upgrades, and the enlargement of their collective economy through land increment and decrement-linkage projects. This initiative facilitated new housing arrangements and allocated collective profit-oriented land, enabling the village to attract secondary and tertiary industries. The endeavor not only addressed the concerns of local employment and income for villagers but also fostered the expansion and development of the collective economy and assets. Prior to Maigao Company's involvement, the village had consolidated agricultural land under cooperatives, while also establishing solid foundations in sectors such as chili bean paste, fermented bean curd, soy sauce, and more. In the realm of the tertiary industry, Zhanqi Village had proactively embarked on development, creating a 3A-rated scenic area centered around Mama Farm.

Fourthly, Maigao Company identified with the philosophical outlook and capabilities of the village's "two committees," particularly Secretary Gao Demin. Earlier collaborations in projects such as the construction of new housing and the development of the 3A-rated scenic area had established a certain level of rapport between Maigao Company and the village committee. Notably, the project involved Mama Farm, which required significant funding to transform into a 3A-rated scenic area. Upon completion, the village aimed to secure a 5-million-yuan reward from provincial and municipal governments. Maigao Company bore the upfront costs of construction, and once the village acquired the reward, the sum would be allocated to reimburse Maigao Company. In addition, Maigao Company assisted the village by constructing a visitor center and road signs, among other amenities. Through these collaborations, Maigao Company gained insights into Zhanqi Village and Secretary Gao, recognizing that Secretary Gao transcended the role of a mere secretary and exhibited the spirit of a pragmatic entrepreneur. This realization formed the bedrock of trust and amicable relations between the parties, substantially reducing frictions and conflicts, minimizing transaction costs, and laying the groundwork for the subsequent establishment of a joint platform company to operate the scenic area.

Fifthly, the two parties possessed a shared vision for Zhanqi Village's future, encompassing industrial development, resource integration, and the bolstering of the collective economy. On one hand, Maigao Company observed Zhanqi Village's resolute commitment to developing the collective economy. While most rural areas prioritized administrative governance, Zhanqi Village had already set its sights on collective economic growth, treating the village collective as an operational entity rather than a purely administrative one. Notably, in previous land increment and decrement-linkage (增减挂钩) projects, Zhanqi Village reserved certain land assets under collective ownership. This foresight not only paved the way for the debut of the "Fifth Season Fragrant Resort" plot of collective profit-oriented land but also showcased the village's expanding governance mechanisms for connecting with the market, particularly concerning resource pricing. On the other hand, Maigao Company proposed a market-driven approach to integrate and manage rural resources, aiming to realize comprehensive three-industry development throughout the entire village. By leveraging Mama Farm's configuration and existing foundations in the tertiary industry, they aspired to forge a regional exemplar while refining the village's governance structure. Secretary Gao also aligned with this vision. Both parties recognized that to embark on a new wave of industrial upgrades, Zhanqi Village required resource synergies and cohesive management. With ample space for operational industries, coupled with a unified and specialized industrial operation service platform, the village possessed the opportunities and prerequisites for industrial transformation.

Lastly, Maigao Company's extensive experience in rural town services and profound understanding of rural operations rendered them more competitive than other bidders.

In conclusion, despite Zhanqi Village's absence of an optimal location for tertiary industry development and the region's relatively weak foundation in this sector, Maigao Company devoted 7.06 million yuan to acquire the land after a comprehensive evaluation.

4 The Maigao Model in Zhanqi Village

Maigao Company reckoned Zhanqi Village lacked inspirational projects to stir progress. They aimed to galvanize the entire village by utilizing its resources and establish a model project for the region. Secretary Gao embraced the idea, leading to a joint investment decision. Together, they formed an operating platform named "Fifth Season Fragrance Land" as the focal point for development.

4.1 *Scenic Area Operating Platform Company—Sichuan Colorful Zhanqi Tourism Scenic Area Management Co., Ltd.*[2]

After securing the land, Maigao Company engaged in discussions with the village on the collaboration approach. Eventually, they decided to establish a joint operating platform. Following a year of negotiations and preparations, on November 7, 2016, Maigao Company and Zhanqi Village jointly invested in the registration of Sichuan Colorful Zhanqi Tourism Scenic Area Management Co., Ltd. The aim was to create a village-wide operating platform. Maigao Company obtained a 40-year land-use right for this collectively operated land. However, forming the Colorful Zhanqi Platform Company with the village collective was crucial to avoid segregating commercial activities from village governance. Moreover, the utilization of village assets for operation was pre-funded by Zhanqi Village. Without this shared platform, conflicts between the company's interests and the villagers' and village collective's interests were likely to arise, posing governance challenges within the village. Hence, both parties entered into numerous contracts and took preventive measures.

Maigao Company held the majority shares in Colorful Zhanqi Platform Company. Their rationale was that Secretary Gao and the village "two committees" had significant administrative responsibilities in rural governance, making it challenging for them to focus on the market. On the other hand, Maigao Company excelled in business operations, allowing them to concentrate on their expertise. Therefore, the division of labor was established, with the enterprise taking the lead in operations and market coordination, while the village collective assumed responsibility for village governance and resource coordination. Notably, the scenic area operating platform did not possess ownership of the assets; it merely held the operating rights. The ownership of village assets remained with the members of Zhanqi Village's collective economic organization.

The board of directors comprised five members, appointed through delegation. Maigao Company appointed three members, and Chengdu Jifeng Investment Management Co., Ltd. appointed two. Each member had one vote during board meetings, and resolutions required the consent

[2] [Information mainly comes from interviews with Maigao Company's directors and managers, as well as the articles of association of Sichuan Colorful Zhanqi Tourism Scenic Area Management Co., Ltd.].

of a majority of directors. The chairman of the board was selected from the directors appointed by Chengdu Jifeng Investment Management Co., Ltd., while the legal representative was chosen from the directors appointed by Maigao Company. In 2019, Gao Demin, the village branch secretary of Zhanqi Village, assumed the role of chairman in Colorful Zhanqi Platform Company. Li Songman from Maigao Company served as a director, general manager, and legal representative. The company also appointed one supervisor from Chengdu Jifeng Investment Management Co., Ltd.

Initially, the company's vision was to consolidate Zhanqi Village's idle assets and resources suitable for tertiary industry development onto the collaborative platform. Based on the existing 3A-grade scenic area, their plan was to upgrade and operate it as a 4A-grade scenic area through market-oriented means. The operating company devised strategies for Colorful Zhanqi's 4A-grade scenic area, utilization of idle resources, and the organization of public resources. Zhanqi Village, as the implementing entity, commenced construction of the "18 Rural Workshops," with the village collective taking the lead. However, they later recognized that achieving a 4A-grade scenic area required specialized expertise. As a result, Zhanqi Village invested over 400,000 yuan to enlist Chengdu Pingge Feiyang Tourism Planning and Design Co., Ltd. for designing and planning the 4A-grade scenic area (including the "18 Rural Workshops"). In the first half of 2019, Zhanqi Village successfully obtained 4A-grade scenic area status, with the village investing over 10 million yuan, supplemented by government subsidies of approximately 1.6 million yuan. The 18 Rural Workshops and the "Fifth Season Fragrance Resort" primarily focused on local specialty cuisine as their main business ventures. The management personnel of Maigao Company emphasized the projects' minimal overlap, highlighting their complementary nature. As a pilot project for rural land reform in China, the initiative garnered substantial attention and support from the higher-level government and various functional departments. Support included expediting administrative procedures, providing bank loans, and coordinating investment promotion.

Whether it be vacant homes belonging to locals or agricultural land and collectively operated construction land, once entrusted to the platform, a minimum guaranteed income was assured. The surplus generated through platform operations was shared between the platform and the village collective, proportionally distributed to the villagers by the collective.

This approach revitalized the village's resources through the operating platform, facilitating sustainable independent operation within the region.

Following General Secretary Xi Jinping's visit to Zhanqi Village on February 12, 2018, government leaders recognized Zhanqi Village's significance, leading to increased attention and resources. Consequently, the collaboration between Maigao Company and Zhanqi Village slowed down, and Maigao Company's plans for the comprehensive operation of Zhanqi Village were temporarily shelved. During that time, the only operations under the platform company were the "Fifth Season Fragrance Resort" and a village parking lot.

4.2 *"Fifth Season Fragrance Resort" and the Franchise Operation Model*

Maigao Company acquired the land and proposed the development of the "Fifth Season Fragrance Resort." Recognizing the lack of a commercial street in Zhanqi Village and the ongoing construction of the Zhanqi's 18 Rural Workshops, the company decided to construct a commercial complex. The choice of "Fifth Season Fragrance Resort" as the theme was influenced by the previous success of Mama Farm in establishing the "Fifth Season" brand in Zhanqi. Maintaining thematic consistency for regional branding, Maigao Company and Mama Farm joined forces to create the Fifth Season brand in Zhanqi.

With an investment of over 70 million yuan, Maigao Company successfully built the "Fifth Season Fragrance Resort" commercial complex. The planning, construction, and investment attraction processes were synchronized, with 70% of the investment attraction work completed by the time the project was completed. The first floor introduced specialty tourist products, snacks, and other shops, while the second and third floors featured the Tujia Sweetome Hotel. Considering the return on investment, the company constructed a relatively large building with a plot ratio of around 1.0, resulting in a total construction area of nearly 10,000 square meters for the commercial complex. By February 12, 2018, before General Secretary Xi Jinping's visit to Zhanqi Village, the "Fifth Season Fragrance Resort" was mostly completed. In March 2018, the tourism and commercial street area, showcasing the distinctive style of western Sichuan rural residences, was fully completed and operational, exuding an authentic and pleasant spatial experience.

Fifth Season Fragrance Resort adopted a enclosed commercial form. Unlike ordinary community storefronts, this type seamlessly integrates living, commercial, leisure, and entertainment spaces within the district. Drawing inspiration from the spatial organization of traditional villages and combining the centrality and multilevel courtyard spaces of primitive villages, this form connects various singular functions, supplemented by "passages" to create a strong impression of an ecological environment and a pleasant spatial experience. Through this commercial district form, Fifth Season Fragrance Resort effectively utilizes limited ground space while maintaining an open and uncluttered appearance. The storefronts are surrounded by glass rather than reinforced concrete, providing an open and non-oppressive atmosphere. The design of the district incorporates traditional western Sichuan and Anhui architectural styles, featuring curved corridors as passages. These corridors also increase the time visitors spend, which is beneficial for boosting consumption. Although it is a commercial development space, the overall style harmonizes with the cultural essence of Zhanqi Village.

After the completion of Fifth Season Fragrance Resort, it was entrusted to Colorful Zhanqi Company for operation, following a franchise operation model. This involved three steps: property rights transfer, franchise operation, and investment attraction to the outside, involving three entities: property owners (small owners), platform companies, and actual operators.

(1) Property Rights Transfer

Firstly, Maigao Company transferred the property rights (40-year ownership) of the shops in "Fifth Season Fragrance Resort" to the property owners, thus recouping the construction costs. The transfer process began around mid-2017 (before the completion of the resort) and was mostly completed by the end of that year.

The total area of the first floor was approximately 3500 square meters. Initially, the villagers believed that the construction cost should be around 2000 yuan per square meter. However, due to the company's high standards and insistence on maintaining quality, the expected price kept rising. Eventually, the price reached around 7000 yuan per square meter, approaching 10,000 yuan per square meter by 2017. The village residents had priority in purchasing, and they received a discount of one to two thousand yuan per square meter compared to external owners. Ultimately, 30–40% of the shops were purchased by residents of the village, while 60–70% were purchased by outsiders.

The total area of the second and third floors was approximately 5000 square meters. The furnished rooms were priced at around 5000 yuan per square meter, while the bare rooms (unfinished) were priced at around 4000 yuan per square meter. Most of these rooms were purchased by Tujia Online Information Technology Co., Ltd. (hereinafter referred to as Tujia) to operate the Sweetome Hotel. The "Fifth Season Fragrance Resort" project was Tujia's first investment in a rural hotel project. Maigao Company had multiple rounds of communication with Tujia's senior management during the process. In addition to Tujia, several rooms on the second and third floors were purchased by residents from other villages who settled in Zhanqi and by visitors from outside the area for vacation purposes. Sweetome Hotel does not need to pay rent to the platform but only needs to pay a commercial management fee of 1.9 yuan per square meter. After collecting the commercial management fee, the platform company is responsible for back-end operations, including providing operational space to businesses in the scenic area (commercial district), property management, environmental improvement, regional marketing, and other supporting services.

The fourth floor consists of six conference rooms with a total area of approximately 1000 square meters. Maigao Company had previously intended to cooperate with Zhanqi Village to develop a training project. Before the establishment of Zhanqi College, the personnel for the training institute were mostly in place, and the original plan was to use all the conference rooms as training classrooms. However, after Zhanqi College was established, Maigao Company did not continue with the training project. When Zhanqi Institute was established, the State Development Investment Group Co., Ltd. had considered partnering with Maigao Company to establish the college. However, Maigao Company believed that training should be operated in a market-oriented manner and should not be burdened with too many political tasks, so they did not agree to the cooperation. Currently, the conference rooms serve as office spaces and are mostly idle, occasionally used for Sweetome Hotel conferences.

Currently, except for the conference rooms on the fourth floor, all the necessary procedures for property rights transfer have been completed, but the owners have not received the property ownership certificates. These certificates were originally issued by the Housing Management

Bureau, similar to purchasing a house in the city. However, the policy regarding collectively operated construction land is not yet complete, and the detailed implementation rules of the policy have not been released. Therefore, Maigao Company is unclear whether the certificates should be issued by the Housing Management Bureau, the Natural Planning Bureau, the village collective, or other entities. For now, they can only wait for the policy to be clarified.

(2) Franchise Operation

The property owners entrusted the property management rights to Colorful Zhanqi Platform Company (operating platform). Along with signing the purchase contracts, the property owners also signed franchise operation contracts, entrusting Colorful Zhanqi Platform Company with unified investment attraction and operational management. As a professional operation company, the platform company enhances operational stability through fixed rents, lease terms, selecting high-quality merchants, and standardized daily management. This preserves the commercial order and value of the commercial street district, ensuring the sustainable development of the investment projects for the property owners.

The property owners also have the option to operate their businesses independently, such as the Guangming Supermarket and braised food stores on the first floor. However, they must comply with the requirements of the platform company, including conforming to the overall business format planning and refraining from subleasing the shops.

Most of the property owners on the first floor chose the franchise operation model. At the time, there were a total of 71 shops on the first floor, with an area of approximately 3500 square meters. Only six of them (around 500 square meters) were operated by the property owners themselves, while the remaining 65 shops (around 3000 square meters) were all entrusted to the platform.

(3) Investment Attraction

Once the property owners entrusted their shops to the platform company, Colorful Zhanqi Platform Company did not operate them directly. Instead, they priced and attracted external businesses to rent the shops and operate them as the actual operators. In 2018, "Fifth Season Fragrance Resort" officially commenced operations.

During the industrial implantation phase, various parties promoted investment attraction through word-of-mouth among friends and spreading investment news in government groups, among other methods. The coverage was extensive. As the village was simultaneously applying for a 4A-level scenic spot status and improving some basic infrastructure, the investment attraction and industrial implantation processes were delayed. The village intended to wait until the basic infrastructure and demonstrative projects, including the Zhanqi's 18 Rural Workshops invested by the village collective, were complete and presented before introducing other industries. Thus, investment attraction and industrial implantation lagged behind. However, after General Secretary Xi Jinping's visit to Zhanqi Village in early 2018, a significant influx of capital and forces entered the village, leading to significant changes in the village's development focus. As of the end of 2019, there had been no further progress in the cooperation between Maigao Company and the village.

All the first-floor shops have been fully rented out or operated by the property owners themselves, mainly for shopping and dining purposes. For self-operated shops, the platform company does not collect rent. For shops under franchise operation, the platform company charges the actual operators a monthly rent of 35–40 yuan per square meter. Additionally, they provide different preferential policies (such as rent waivers and discounted commercial management fees) or adjust the rent (such as renting to a bank at a rate of a few hundred yuan per square meter) based on the leased area, time, scale, and business format.[3] Furthermore, among the 65 shops entrusted to the platform, nine shops (approximately 500 square meters) are leased by the government for exhibition platforms, cinemas, rural loans service stations, and the Youth League Committee's innovation center, with rents the same as other shops. For all the first-floor merchants, Colorful Zhanqi Platform Company also charges a commercial management fee of 5 yuan per square meter.

* * *

[3] This is Maigao Company's approach elsewhere. According to Maigao Company, if a new business format enters without creating additional value but benefits from the regional footfall dividend, it should pay higher rent. If they disagree with the rent, they can choose not to settle.

The Exotic Inn in the "Fifth Season Fragrance Resort"

The Exotic Inn, a humble abode, commenced operations on May 10, 2018, encompassing a modest expanse of 295 square meters. Hailing from the city of Neijiang in Sichuan Province, the innkeeper forged a familial alliance with a household from Zhanqi Village, embarking on a shared enterprise to run this establishment.

Before inaugurating their venture, an investment of around ¥400,000 was funneled into refurbishment, fixtures, and tableware. Presently, the inn's predominant costs encompass the following: (1) a monthly rent of ¥35 per square meter, with a merchant-enticing perk of rent exemption for the initial half-year; (2) a property management fee of 5 yuan per square meter per month; (3) a team comprising five individuals, including chefs and servers. The culinary artisans were enlisted from Neijiang, earning a wage of 6400 yuan per month, while the managerial and service personnel hailed from the village, garnering monthly wages ranging from 2000 yuan to 4800 yuan. Cumulatively, the labor expenses amount to approximately 24,000 yuan per month; (4) utility expenses encompassing water, electricity, and distribution costs. Once the rent exemption period elapses, the monthly operational expenditure of the inn will hover close to 40,000 yuan.

Regrettably, the inn's current revenue performance is lackluster. During the peak season (which unpredictably transpires once or twice a year, spanning a mere two to three months), the net monthly income eclipses 20,000 yuan. Conversely, the sizzling August and frigid January represent the nadir, rendering the inn bereft of clientele and incurring monthly losses ranging from 40,000 yuan to 50,000 yuan. At other times, a delicate equilibrium is maintained between income and expenses. Notably, there exists no exigency to further infuse working capital, as the meager profits scarcely suffice.

Residing within the Zhanqi enclave, the extended family secures a modest two-bedroom domicile, obliging them to disburse a nominal monthly rent of ¥400. Given their predilection for partaking in the inn's repasts, their personal living expenses dwindle. Endurance becomes their modus operandi, fervently awaiting the influx of visitors that shall inevitably amplify their accrued gains.

Source: An empirical expedition undertaken by a research cohort, ascertained during face-to-face interviews over the course of the 2019 National Day holiday.

(4) Profit Distribution Model

The essence of rural collective-operated land lies in its dual nature of "business-oriented" operations and its belongingness to the village collective. Thus, as Maigao Company diligently pursues industrial attraction, it concurrently collaborates with the local community to enhance public services and facilities, fostering an equitable scheme that shares benefits among the village collective, small property owners, industrial stakeholders, and the operational platform.

In respect to the profits acquired from operating "The Fifth Season Fragrance" on the Colorful Zhanqi Platform, the company allocates 10% annually to statutory reserves. Withdrawals cease once these reserves exceed 50% of the registered capital. The purpose of these reserves encompasses compensating for past losses, expanding production and operations, or bolstering the company's capital. Nonetheless, they are not to be employed in mitigating losses. Once losses have been offset and statutory reserves withdrawn, the remaining after-tax profits are distributed proportionately according to shareholders' contributions, as outlined below.[4]

After deducting the guaranteed rental fees (ranging from 6.8 to 12.75 yuan per square meter) disbursed to property owners,[5] and accounting for a 5% maintenance fund,[6] the surplus proceeds are divided between the collective economic organization and the villagers, each receiving 50%. The surplus income of 50% garnered by Colorful Zhanqi Company is then distributed according to the respective shares held by the village's collective economic organization and Maigao Company, as depicted in Fig. 1. Here, the term "collective economic organization" refers to Chengdu Jifeng Investment Management Co., Ltd. (overseen by Zhanqi Asset Management Co., Ltd. in Tangchang Town, Pixian County), whereby

[4] This allocation method is derived from information documented in the July 2016 topic titled "Collaborative Establishment of a Commercial Service Platform Company by Chengdu Jifeng Investment Management Co., Ltd. and Maigao Company." Moreover, provisions ensure that the dividend ratio of the platform company's annual profits does not exceed 50% to foster future growth.

[5] AS exemplified by Maigao Company's practices in the management of Sichuan Xiangcao Lake Tourist Area, situated in Qinggangshu Village, Sandaoyan Town, Pixian County, Chengdu.

[6] Which accumulates over time and is settled every five years, its percentage serving as a relative indicator, subject to actual expenses.

the accumulated income is retained by the village collective at a predetermined ratio, with the remaining portion apportioned among the villagers based on their respective shares. In this distribution model, Maigao Company effectively receives a mere quarter of the surplus income, while the remaining three quarters belong to the village collective and its inhabitants.

At that time, this distribution methodology solely applied to the income generated by the ground-floor shops in "The Fifth Season Fragrance" on the Colorful Zhanqi Platform. The upper-floor shops were responsible solely for the payment of commercial management fees, with the profits being shared directly between the owners and Sweetome Hotel. Following a deduction of approximately 30% from the turnover for operating expenses (comprising labor costs, utilities, materials, and commercial management fees, among others), the remaining 70% was divided equally between the hotel and the owners.[7] Notably, the commercial management fee for the hotel was 3.1 yuan per square meter cheaper than that of the ground-floor shops, reflecting a divergence in the distribution approach. This disparity emerged due to the hotel's operational oversight of the upper floor, with Maigao Company solely lending support in management. Additionally, given Zhanqi Village's less favorable location, this arrangement aimed to entice businesses to establish a presence in the vicinity.

税后利润 After tax profit.

扣除5%维修基金 Deduct 5% maintenance fund.

保价收益 Insured income.

集体、村民 collective, villagers.

溢价收益 Premium income.

集体经济组织和村民 Collective economic organizations and villagers.

按比例(资产) By asset ratio.

平台管理公司 Platform management company.

村集体经济组织|企业 Village collective economic organization|Enterprise.

[7] This distribution approach between Sweetome Hotel and the owners was instituted in April 2019.

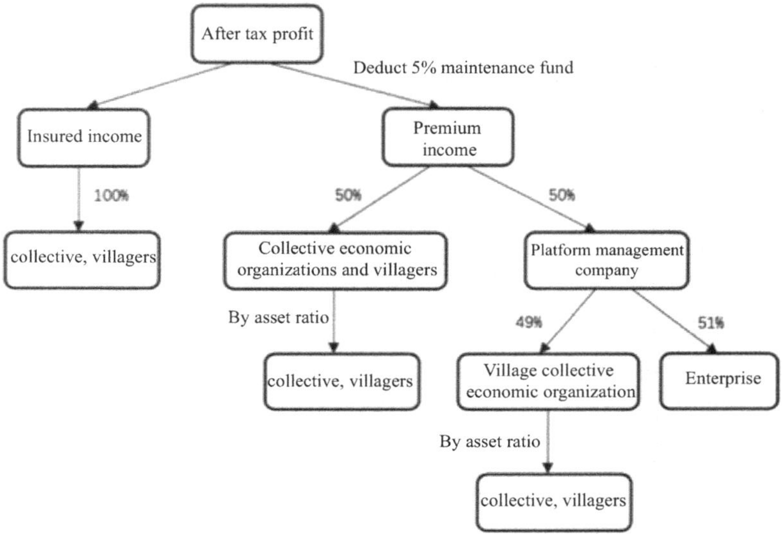

Fig. 1 Profit allocation model of colorful Zhanqi platform company

4.3 *Parking Lot Business*

Parking lots sprouted during the flourishing years of Zhanqi Village, between 2012 and 2013, as a distinguished fragment of the majestic 3A-grade scenic haven. Spanning across 13 acres of coveted land, it stood as a companion facility for the resplendent realm. When the platform company emerged, the village entrusted this very parking lot to its vigilant care.

With over 230 parking spots at its disposal, each vehicle seeking refuge was asked to part with a meager sum of 10 yuan. During peak seasons, the cash register swelled with an astonishing daily revenue of two or three thousand yuan, while in the tranquil lulls of the off-season, the modest figure dwindled to a mere few hundred yuan. Human resources accounted for the primary operational costs, embracing the employment of four guardians who were duly compensated with a monthly wage hovering around 2500 yuan. Given its role as a caretaker, the platform company, in its benevolent might, spared the village the burden of rental fees. The spoils were to be divided, with the village collective claiming a lion's share of 70% while the platform company contented itself with the remaining 30%.

4.4 *Evolution of Collaborative Prospects*

According to the original blueprint, the esteemed Colorful Zhanqi platform company assumed responsibility for the comprehensive management of Zhanqi Village's vast wealth. However, by the latter half of 2017, the village grew disenchanted with the tardy pace of progress. Consequently, in 2018, they embarked on a quest for collaboration and serendipitously found a suitor in the form of Tianfu Tourism Resort Development Co., Ltd. The following year, a pact was sealed, birthing aspirations to jointly shepherd the Zhanqi culinary sanctuary and conceive a new abode of repose. Zhanqi Village, tendering 6.5 acres of fertile collective land as an offering, secured a stake in the enterprise. On the other hand, Sichuan Tianfu Tourism Resort Development Co., Ltd., a paragon of financial prowess, fortified the partnership with their monetary infusion. Thus, the Sichuan Zhanqi Piaopiai Operation and Management Co., Ltd. emerged into existence, with Zhanqi Village and Sichuan Tianfu Tourism Resort Development Co., Ltd. sharing the mantle of ownership, occupying 49% and 51% of the domain, respectively.

Ever since General Secretary Xi Jinping graced Zhanqi Village with his noble presence on the illustrious date of February 12, 2018, the sociopolitical and economic tapestry of the village underwent a profound metamorphosis. The overarching authority embraced Zhanqi Village with a newfound reverence. On that momentous February day in 2019, the inaugural ceremony of the Zhanqi Training Institute for Rural Revitalization unfurled its grandeur in the heart of Zhanqi Village, nestled within the hallowed precincts of Pidu District, Sichuan Province. This heralded the dawning of an establishment ardently dedicated to cultivating erudite and pragmatic champions for the reawakening of rural realms across the nation.

PART V

The Illuminations from Zhanqi Village

CHAPTER 16

Internalizing Costs: The Rural Bedrock of National De-dependency

In 1965, as the Zhanqi Brigade broke free from the Jinxing Brigade, China found itself embroiled in the grueling process of "de-dependency."

In the early 1950s, with the eruption of the Korean War, New China, against a complex backdrop, forged a strategic alliance with the Soviet Union, reaping a total of 5.4 billion dollars' worth of industrial equipment and technological investments between 1950 and 1959. This robust infusion of foreign capital swiftly extricated China from its economic doldrums of the 1950s, propelling it into a headlong sprint towards industrialization, while simultaneously cementing a system of collectivization in the rural domains.

Yet, by the late 1950s, Sino-Soviet relations plunged into an abrupt deterioration, compelling China to sever its bonds entirely. The People's Communes emerged from this economic crisis, seeking to address the turmoil and perpetuate the trajectory of industrialization.

From 1959 to 1961, China was beleaguered by extensive spells of droughts and floods, resulting in a drastic deceleration in agricultural output growth. Crop yields dwindled year after year, and per capita grain consumption in rural areas plummeted from 409 catties in 1957 to a meager 312 catties in 1960. Insufficient fiscal revenue, coupled with the onus of repaying Soviet debts, inexorably exacerbated the dearth of domestic agricultural supplies, plunging some farmers into the clutches of poverty.

© Peking University Press 2024
X. Dong, *Zhanqi Village Over Fifty Years*,
https://doi.org/10.1007/978-981-97-5426-7_16

To alleviate the institutional costs birthed by breakneck industrialization, the state embarked on a dual path. On one hand, urban labor forces were streamlined, triggering the repatriation of a significant number of urban dwellers to their rural origins. On the other hand, an all-out mobilization of cadres, intellectuals, and the populace at large was undertaken, immersing them in the crucible of national primitive accumulation for industrialization. By channeling a concentrated torrent of labor inputs, the long-standing scarcity of capital was supplanted, with substantial investments being poured into the colossal edifice of infrastructure, vital for state-led industrialization and agricultural development.

Against such a macro backdrop, the Zhanqi Brigade assumed the mantle of shouldering not only the institutional costs of national "de-dependency," including the integration of educated youth into rural life, but also the role of providing surplus agricultural and ancillary products to the nation. Through the internalization of costs, it gradually realized the primitive accumulation of capital for industrialization, all the while charting a course towards agricultural village industrialization post-1973. Since the 1960s, commencing with the slogan "Learning from Dazhai in agriculture, Wavering the Battle Flag (Zhanqi) in the West," the Zhanqi denizens have weathered numerous tribulations, repeatedly surging forth to eventually blossom into a shining exemplar of rural revitalization. The annals of the Zhanqi Brigade not only epitomize the microcosm of the national "de-dependency" process but also furnish a distinguished and enduring case study in the arduous voyage of national industrialization. The ability of the Zhanqi Brigade to triumph over manifold hardships stems from the catalytic "external" influences of the macro environment. Gradually, these influences converged to forge an intrinsic spiritual nucleus within the Zhanqi, permeating its developmental mechanisms. Unfazed by adversity, the resilient people of the Zhanqi have fearlessly forged ahead, ultimately furnishing an indomitable impetus that unfurls the Zhanqi's glorious past, present, and future. These indomitable spirits comprise the lodestars of party leadership, dauntless responsibility, collective primacy, unity and mutual assistance, unflagging toil, audacious innovation, progressive adaptation, astute policy utilization, and above all, the relentless spirit of struggle, placing the "common good" concept at its zenith.

1 Guided by Party Building, Embracing Courageous Responsibilities

Gao Demin, the current secretary of Zhanqi Village, recalled the origin of the name "Zhanqi" and mentioned that it was precisely because "every Party member in Zhanqi (战旗, meaning "battle flag" in Chinese) is like a battle flag." This fully embodies the crucial role of party building leadership in the development of Zhanqi Village. The consolidation of this spirit has also laid the foundation for the formation of other spirits in Zhanqi. Once the system and path are determined, the abilities and qualities of party and government officials determine the development of an organization. Zhanqi Village has cultivated a group of young and proactive individuals with integrity and honesty, injecting fresh vitality into the Party.

The first secretary of Zhanqi Brigade was Jiang Daxing, and at that time, Luo Huijin served as the director. They led the entire party and government leadership collective of Zhanqi Brigade and started from scratch. Luo Huifu, who was a carpenter at the time, responded to the brigade's call and returned to the village to engage in construction work. He led a group of skilled workers to build a series of infrastructure such as water turbines, brigade offices, medical stations, and retail stores. In 1969, Luo Huijin became the second secretary of Zhanqi, and Yang Zhengzhong and Li Shibing served as deputy secretaries. Under their leadership, the militia construction in Zhanqi achieved outstanding results. They brought the efficient and disciplined style of the militia into production, improved production efficiency, completed the transformation and construction of a series of agricultural water conservancy facilities, and increased grain and sideline production. Zhanqi Brigade continuously transformed the appearance of the village and the spirit of the villagers, and completed the original accumulation of internal capital, gradually entering the industrialization stage. In 1975, Zhanqi Brigade built the first concentrated residential area for farmers in Pixian County. Zhanqi's industry sprouted and grew from the curve kiln that provided machine bricks for the new village, realizing the transformation from agriculture to industry. Since then, the desire for a better life has taken root in the hearts of the people of Zhanqi, which is also the spirit of forging ahead inspired by party building leadership. After Yang Zhengzhong became the fourth secretary of Zhanqi Village, he led everyone to build the Pioneer No. 1 Brick Factory and Huifu Douban Factory, accumulating a considerable amount of funds, and Zhanqi Village began to stride towards modernization.

The ability of several party branch secretaries and directors of Zhanqi Brigade to continuously lead cadres and the masses in their struggle and progress is inseparable from their work style. After the establishment of the brigade, the party branch of Zhanqi Brigade established the development policy of "self-reliance and hard work" based on the actual situation. Once the direction was clear, the cadres of Zhanqi Brigade took the lead in every aspect and always looked for problems within themselves when encountering difficulties, and earnestly rectified the leadership team.

As a result, none of the 13 brigades in Zhanqi misappropriated any public funds or encroached on any property of the brigade. They actively participated in labor, reduced the collective management costs and production costs, reduced collective and personal consumption, non-productive expenses, etc., internalized costs, and quickly completed the capital accumulation of the village.

In the twenty-first century, under the circumstances of slow economic development in the village, the prevalence of private enterprises, and the outflow of labor force, Secretary Li Shili and Director Gao Demin played the role of party building leadership, leading the village onto a new era of "Long March." In terms of industry, they restructured enterprises, not only preserving the accumulated efforts of generations of people but also earning capital for economic development. In terms of agriculture, village cadres centralized more than 100 mu of land under the condition of paying agricultural taxes, and after the state exempted agricultural taxes, Zhanqi Village established a professional cooperative for the cultivation of shiitake mushrooms, consolidating 600 acres of land in the village... Through several years of land consolidation practice, large-scale operations have gradually achieved economies of scale, laying the foundation for the subsequent entry of collective operational construction land into the market, which also embodies the spirit of party and government, laying the foundation for cultivating the spirit of keeping pace with the times and making good use of policies in the later stage.

The global financial crisis, the Wenchuan earthquake, and other difficulties have not been able to stop the progress of the people of Zhanqi. After the completion of projects such as "demolishing and rebuilding courtyards" in 2007, Mama Farm in 2012, blueberry picking in 2013, and cooperation with Maigao Company in 2015... The people of Zhanqi fully realized that party leadership must be put in the first place. To make the spirit of party and government effective, it is essential to unite the people. The people of Zhanqi have continuously developed Zhanqi under the leadership of the Party, gradually accumulating more trust and reliance on the Party and the village collective in the process, greatly reducing the transaction costs that hinder the development of the village, and laying the foundation for future development. The traditional spirit of party building leadership and the soaring spirit of Zhanqi have not been abandoned with the change of leadership, but have been passed down from generation to generation, continuously consolidating into a new spirit of party building leadership.

2 Collective Primacy, Forging Unity through Mutual Support

The collectivization of rural China gained strength during the arduous process of breaking away from Soviet assistance in the late 1950s. On one hand, the nation required political means to mobilize its labor force for economic production, replacing the invisible hand of the economy, rendered ineffective due to the scarcity of capital, with a politically visible alternative. On the other hand, the collectivization of rural areas, under the dichotomy of urban and rural systems, proved advantageous for absorbing unemployed urban youth into the countryside and facilitating the unified transfer of agricultural surplus to urban industries. In a realm where each household constituted a separate entity, how could educated urban youth be allocated? The collective organization served as a conduit, effectively reducing the two-way costs of communication between urban and rural domains.

The spirit of prioritizing the collective emerged amidst the labor-intensive process, where an abundance of labor replaced capital in production. Against the backdrop of the agricultural revolution in Dazhai, the Zhanqi Brigade harnessed the power of its labor force, including militias and women, to embark on endeavors such as drainage systems and land improvement. Through these labor processes, a formidable organizational force arose, remolding both the physical landscape of Zhanqi's village and the spiritual character of its members in a remarkable and efficient manner.

The relentless pursuit of being the first further solidified the spirit of collectivism within the Zhanqi Brigade, firmly embedding the collective mindset in the hearts of its inhabitants.

The spirit of collective prioritization blossomed within an atmosphere of shared labor and competition, gradually becoming an intrinsic part of the Zhanqi Brigade's developmental journey, amidst the perpetual struggle between collective and individual interests. Guided by this spirit, the Zhanqi Brigade reduced individual allocations while increasing collective distributions, leading to substantial accumulation within the collective economy. In terms of distribution, the state's portion remained relatively stable (with a temporary decline in 1972 due to poor harvests), while the collective's retained share progressively increased, and individual allocations grew at a modest pace. This equilibrium fostered a climate of high accumulation and restrained consumption. By 1973, Zhanqi Brigade's collective retention accounted for 15.34% of total food distribution, marking a 6.16% increase from the 9.18% in 1966. It was this relentless drive for accumulation that propelled the Brigade's public funds to surpass 200,000 yuan, with grain reserves exceeding 200,000 catties.

The ability of the Zhanqi Brigade to achieve such high accumulation in the collective economy through self-deprivation and internalization of costs stemmed not only from the collective ownership of the three essential production factors by the village, but also from the cohesive system of unity and mutual assistance within the collective. During the latter phase of the people's commune, distribution largely adhered to a system where 70% or 80% was allocated as basic grain rations and 30% or 20% as work points. Basic grain rations guaranteed the livelihood of the majority, while the Zhanqi Brigade implemented explicit and implicit subsidies for members with lower living standards through support for the impoverished and excessive distribution. These internal mechanisms of the village acted as a safety net, alleviating poverty and providing social security in the rural landscape, establishing a solid foundation for the stable development of the Zhanqi Brigade.

Thus, the multi-tiered social security system built between the state, the collective, and the members safeguarded the basic survival of the farmers, facilitating the realization of the collectivist spirit and constructing the institutional framework for the primitive accumulation of capital during the early stages of industrialization.

In the wake of the 1980s, as the process of nurturing "market-oriented reforms" and establishing a foundation for resource allocation based on the market gained momentum, the collective economy of Zhanqi Village transitioned from a state of high work-point allocation to operating under a burden of debt. The 1990s witnessed an extreme scenario, where town and township enterprises, under the pressure of macroeconomic crises, embarked on a restructuring guided primarily by privatization. By the turn of the century, the collective economy of Zhanqi Village had all but vanished, and the spirit of collectivism waned. Nonetheless, through the restructuring of the collective economy, Zhanqi managed to reverse the trend where collective accumulation, resulting from labor contributions, was predominantly appropriated by individuals. This revitalized the collective spirit during the ecological competition of the twenty-first century, empowering it to reclaim its significant role.

Although the spirit of collectivism first may not have been explicitly manifested during the phase of industrial competition, it served as a fundamental prerequisite for the development of Zhanqi Village during this period. In the mid-to-late 1970s, seizing the opportunity presented by the "Building a New Village" campaign, the Zhanqi Brigade ventured into industrial development by establishing a brick factory. Militia wages were disbursed through work-point distributions, and surplus grain was employed to procure equipment. This self-sacrificial approach enabled the primitive accumulation of capital, effectively embodying the collective spirit of "placing the greater good above personal interests." Subsequently, the profits generated by the brick factory were loaned to newly emerging village-level enterprises, providing a financial foundation for the subsequent stage of industrial competition. The 1980s and 1990s marked the initial phase of industrial competition, wherein Zhanqi Village's main focus centered on establishing new enterprises and expanding existing ones. These new enterprises sprouted like mushrooms, a direct outcome of the cumulative competitive spirit. By the mid-1980s, competition had reached its pinnacle, prompting enterprises to seek expansion through indebtedness. This commendable performance of Zhanqi's enterprises owed much to the preceding phase of accumulation. The second phase of industrial competition, spanning the 1990s to the twenty-first century, witnessed the decline of several enterprises due to the path dependence of capital expansion and the tumultuous macroeconomic environment. Evidently, the spirit of collectivism first, formed in the preceding stage, may have weakened to some extent during this phase but nevertheless laid the groundwork for the subsequent phase of industrial development.

During the ecological competition stage, Zhanqi Village's triumphant achievements were attributed to its ability to effectively integrate the highly fragmented rural space through grassroots collective economic organizations. This, in turn, relied on the spirit of collectivism first, forged during the initial stage. In 2002, Secretary Li Shili, who assumed office in Zhanqi Village, drew inspiration from Huaxi Village and Xiaogang Village, recognizing that although the household responsibility system could stimulate enthusiasm, it hindered overall village development. Consequently, upon returning, he initiated land consolidation, transferring a portion of natural risks, market risks, and transaction costs to the village collective. In doing so, the village rediscovered the value of its land, aligning its efforts with the development plan of Pixian County, and reaping additional institutional benefits. The process of land consolidation unfolded in distinct phases. Firstly, party members and cadres assumed a leadership role, followed by group leaders who were entrusted with mobilizing members within their respective groups. Secondly, the village collective reinforced the notion that "achieving a better life necessitates implementing large-scale operations," reigniting the collective memory of Zhanqi's villagers, who yearned for an improved existence. Lastly, it was the historical camaraderie forged between the party and the people that engendered complete trust and anticipation in the party organization and village collective, prompting the villagers to willingly surrender their land in exchange for subsequent benefits. This accomplishment embodied a level of organization and collectivization rarely witnessed in other villages. In essence, Zhanqi Village's ability to maintain a leading position nationwide during the third phase of ecological competition and to establish a long-lasting mechanism for resource rights was contingent upon this crucial step of land consolidation. Absent the spirit of collectivism first, the land consolidation of Zhanqi Village would likely have remained an insurmountable challenge.

Undoubtedly, the realization of the spirit of collectivism first and unity and mutual assistance owes much to the guidance of the Party and the government. The interplay between collective prioritization, unity, and mutual assistance under the auspices of the Party and the government played a paramount role in Zhanqi Village's development, ensuring the perpetuation and magnification of the collective spirit.

3 Unwavering Diligence, Fearless Pursuit of Innovation

Zhanqi Brigade, once destitute, now proudly witnesses its Zhanqi fluttering in the wind. The hardworking people of Zhanqi illuminate the canvas of time. In the 1960s, amidst limited technology and capital, the infusion of labor instead of capital became a crucial catalyst for increased grain production. Guided by the rallying cry of "Raise the flag high, never forget the line; toil arduously for 3–5 years, effecting a triple transformation in mindset, land, and productivity," and inspired by the indomitable spirit of self-reliance and tenacious struggle, the leaders and masses of Zhanqi Village nurtured an enduring spirit of mutual upliftment and unwavering resilience.

Above all, Zhanqi's cadre exemplified the essence of hardship and perseverance in their lives and work. Hailing mostly from impoverished farming families, these dedicated individuals embraced frugality, actively engaged in labor, and shunned wastefulness. Their professional conduct remained unblemished, for not a single member of the 13-strong cadre had ever harbored a selfish interest in public funds. By personally embodying the arduous struggle, the cadre not only curtailed production and management costs within the brigade but also set an exemplary standard, bolstering the people's trust in their leaders and fortifying the cadre's influence over the masses. Thus, a virtuous cycle of mutual oversight and encouragement flourished.

Moreover, the masses of Zhanqi willingly embraced the spirit of tenacious struggle. Tales of hardship played out time and again, passing down the torch of unwavering determination from one generation to the next. The Zhanqi Brigade's Party branch maximized the substitution of labor for capital, unifying the deployment of skilled craftsmen and internalizing the costs associated with constructing village facilities and repairing tools. These measures rallied an extensive workforce for the betterment of agricultural and water management projects.

Especially notable was the mobilization of women and militia members, showcasing their unyielding spirit in the face of adversity. Empowered by newfound status, female laborers surged forth with unwavering vigor, offering invaluable support to agricultural endeavors. Among them, figures like Li Shifang, a female militia member doubling as a skilled tractor operator, not only kindled motivation within their male counterparts but also exemplified the unflagging determination of women. With the growing ranks of female militia members, the status of women soared, further fueling their spirit of indomitable struggle.

If the spirit of tenacious struggle laid the bedrock for Zhanqi's development, then the dauntless spirit of innovation unfurled its banner for all to behold.

A glimpse into Zhanqi's developmental journey reveals an unwavering thread of innovative spirit. In the late 1960s, through relentless trial and error, the Zhanqi Brigade pioneered an innovative framework that harmoniously united agriculture and sideline occupations. By incentivizing workers with grain allocations and fertilizer distribution based on their respective contributions, a harmonious balance between animal husbandry and crop cultivation emerged, heralding an era where both spheres flourished in tandem, yielding abundant harvests. Furthermore, Zhanqi Brigade steadfastly upheld the collective rearing of sows for sideline endeavors, ensuring a stable supply while simultaneously empowering impoverished households, thereby narrowing the wealth gap within the village. During the restructuring of collective enterprises, Zhanqi Village boldly devised a novel approach: leasing and selling the enterprises' fixed and liquid assets to new proprietors at fair market value. The unpaid dues were transformed into loans, attracting a nominal 10% interest rate imposed by the collective. This ingenious strategy not only preserved the fruits of Zhanqi's generations-long struggle but also ignited the "first seed capital" for further economic prosperity. In the realm of land consolidation, Zhanqi Village adroitly employed a distribution model comprising "guaranteed rent + 50% profit sharing," thereby safeguarding the well-being of its inhabitants.

To conclude, the spirit of unwavering struggle bestowed upon Zhanqi Village the first seed capital for agricultural and industrial development, while relentless innovation ensured its growth in leaps and bounds.

4 Adapting to the Times, Mastering Policy Artistry

Success in development is a lesson to be learned, but not a mere copy-and-paste affair. The reason why Zhanqi Village soared high was its firm grip on the winds of change blowing through the era. Embracing the present, Zhanqi Village astutely employed policies like the militia system and land finance, seizing the opportunity to become a "pilot village" and letting the momentum of the times elevate their fortunes.

Back in the 1960s and 1970s, Zhanqi Village, with its exceptional strides in militia construction, became a shining model of military-civilian collaboration in Pixian County. This achievement garnered a trove of political and economic resources, laying a rock-solid foundation for the village to seize future development opportunities. During the era of militia construction, the Armed Forces Department joined forces with the leadership of Zhanqi Village, dedicating themselves to militia affairs and military training. The disciplined militia, prompt in their response, owed their success to the village's skillful utilization of policies and the establishment of a robust organizational framework. In 1970, in their pursuit of better execution of the "three tasks" of the militia, Zhanqi Village undertook a series of measures to revitalize their militia work. These actions transformed Zhanqi's militia into a critical force, maintaining order within the village and becoming an indomitable power in agricultural production and irrigation projects. In response to the call for agricultural development exemplified by the "Learning from Dazhai in Agriculture" movement, Zhanqi Village rallied the labor force of women, actively fostering the growth of women's militias and harnessing their unwavering dedication. These women's militias played a vital role in supporting agricultural production, while the increased participation of female militiamen and cadre members further invigorated the labor force of women.

The efficacy of their militia efforts forged a deep bond between Zhanqi Village and the county's Armed Forces Department. During the nascent stages of industrialization, Zhanqi Village, bolstered by their militia construction, enjoyed access to coveted resources, effectively reducing the costs associated with industrialization.

In the competitive period of industrialization spanning the 1980s and 1990s, Zhanqi Village took proactive steps in conducting urban–rural interaction experiments, attracting a substantial influx of talented students from esteemed institutions. By seizing the opportunities for development, Zhanqi Village not only became a prominent symbol of Pixian County but also stood as an unwavering force, transcending the barriers between urban and rural domains.

From 2011 to 2015, Zhanqi Village accomplished the defining of collective membership, the assessment of collective assets, and the quantification of shares. Thus, the establishment of Zhanqi Asset Management Co., Ltd. in Tangchang Town, Pixian County, became a reality. Capitalizing on Pixian County's selection as one of the 33 pilot counties for nationwide rural land system reforms, Zhanqi Village capitalized on this opportunity by listing their unused construction land on the land resource trading center, successfully becoming the province's trailblazer in bringing collective-operated construction land to the market. This strategic move awakened the dormant resources within the village, gradually unleashing the dividends of reform.

In the era of ecological competition, with an escalating focus on sustainable growth and issues surrounding agriculture, rural areas, and farmers, Zhanqi Village actively sought transformation towards industrial ecology and ecological industrialization. By upholding regional distinctiveness, cultivating picturesque ecological landscapes, fostering diverse industries, and nurturing a rich local culture, Zhanqi Village became the epitome of a model village for rural revitalization.

Presently, Zhanqi Village proudly houses the Zhanqi Rural Revitalization Training Institute, exemplifying their ability to keep pace with the times and astutely harness available resources. On February 12, 2018, during a visit to Zhanqi Village, General Secretary Xi Jinping lauded the village's efforts in party building activities, industrial development, and cultural integration. Remarkably, Zhanqi Village was the inaugural destination chosen by General Secretary Xi Jinping after the inception of the rural revitalization strategy, signifying his acknowledgment of the village's commendable adaptability in embarking on the transformative path of ecological development in sync with the changing times.

5 Prioritizing the Common Good, Fearlessly Engaging in Struggles

Struggle, a defining element of the collective era, unfolds as a relentless contest between national rationale, collective rationale, and individual rationale, propelling the spiraling ascension of Zhanqi Village. It embodies the indomitable spirit of Chinese farmers, who epitomize this formidable battle not only against nature but also in the arena where public confronts private, and collective confronts individual.

Indeed, before Zhanqi Brigade's inception, a tumultuous struggle raged between the state, the collective, and individuals. During the infancy of the People's Republic of China, Pidu County and Chongning County witnessed the eruption of the "May 25th Uprising," with Chongning County spearheading the crusade against banditry and feudal domination. Through a multitude of means like mass gatherings and clashing with grain-hoarding landlords, they ensured the smooth execution of grain requisitioning, laying a firm groundwork for the monumental land reform of 1951. This transformative process ushered in a society where arable land was evenly distributed among the masses, igniting the fervor for individual production and restructuring the social fabric and power dynamics at the grassroots level. As the march towards industrial advancement gained momentum in 1953, the cooperative movement took center stage. Intensive socialist education reshaped the mindset of countless cadres and masses, rectifying their misguided economic, political, ideological, and managerial perspectives. It was within this crucible of struggle that Zhanqi Brigade emerged, drawing strength from its turbulent milieu. Alongside societal battles, Zhanqi Brigade confronted a relentless natural struggle. In 1966, an unanticipated inferno devoured the nascent collective thatched houses, yet the conflagration failed to incinerate the aspirations of the resilient people of Zhanqi. On the contrary, it kindled an unwavering determination. Echoing the rallying cry, "Fear knows no flames; Zhanqi forges a brighter path," the brigade embarked on the arduous task of rebuilding their cherished abode. This tale of resilience repeated itself throughout the annals of Zhanqi Village, a testament to the unwavering spirit shared by its humble inhabitants, who, akin to countless Chinese compatriots, never relinquished their struggle against the forces of nature.

Through the crucible of criticism and self-reflection, Zhanqi Brigade instilled in its cadre and masses an innate recognition of their fallibility, impelling them towards redemption. Consequently, in the realm of agricultural and subsidiary industry development, collective rationale triumphed over individual rationale, harmoniously maximizing their collective gains, paving the path for primitive capital accumulation within the village community.

In retrospect, the magnetic allure of Zhanqi Brigade's developmental trajectory stemmed from the party's visionary leadership, undergirded by its resilience to external forces. It fearlessly embraced responsibility, cherishing the collective above all, fostering unity and reciprocal support. Unyielding in the face of adversity, they ceaselessly pioneered novel approaches, adapting to the evolving times, and adroitly harnessing policies to their advantage. Embedded within this noble struggle was an unwavering commitment to the "common good" cause, weaving together a tapestry of spirits that amalgamated into the ethos of Zhanqi. Guided by this resolute spirit, Zhanqi Brigade crafted an intricate web of collective actions, harnessing a low-cost capital accumulation blueprint that expedited its transformation into an industrious agricultural village by seizing the opportunities that materialized in the mid-to-late 1970s.

CHAPTER 17

Rationality in Rural Community: The Essence of "Three Livelihoods" and "Three Governance" in Rural China

Like creatures in nature's tapestry, humans adapt their survival strategies to the natural environment. Therefore, it is inevitable that agriculture, as an ancient form of civilization, shares an inseparable bond with its surroundings. Understanding the profound influence of the natural environment on humanity is a fundamental prerequisite for a robust existence and progress. Since ancient times, the impact of geographical surroundings on human civilization has captivated scholars, as demonstrated by Herodotus' portrayal of Egypt as a blessing from the Nile.[1]

This understanding has evolved through three stages. The first phase witnessed early proponents of geographical determinism, who viewed the geographical environment as the decisive force behind cultural development and historical evolution. Despite evident flaws, this theory sheds light on the significant influence of the natural environment on personal, societal, and political transformations.

The twentieth century ushered in the second phase, marked by a reevaluation and disavowal of geographical determinism. It emphasized human agency in relation to the natural environment, introducing theories that explored the "probabilistic" influence of humans on the environment, the power to "adapt" and shape it, and the "cultural-historical

[1] Fang Xiuqi, Ge Quansheng, Zheng Jingyun. Progress and prospects in the study of the impact of environmental changes on Chinese civilization. Journal of Historical Geography, 2004(1): 85–94.

© Peking University Press 2024

X. Dong, *Zhanqi Village Over Fifty Years*,
https://doi.org/10.1007/978-981-97-5426-7_17

layer theory" underscoring the reciprocal impact of culture and the environment. Consequently, the sway of the natural environment diminished, yielding to a greater emphasis on human subjectivity. Sadly, this era witnessed a prolonged period during which human prowess was unduly extolled, as the environment's carrying capacity was callously disregarded during exploitative endeavors.

Following the 1960s, a shift in perspective emerged as the deteriorating state of the natural environment compelled introspection on humanity's detrimental impact. Rather than viewing humans as adversaries of nature, a vision took shape—human development within the bounds of ecological sustainability, the concept of endurance.

Simultaneously, the development of geographic science and technology burgeoned, further illuminating the profound repercussions of environmental changes on human society. A plethora of evidence revealed the backdrop against which many momentous events in human history unfolded—environmental transformations. Ancient Egypt, ancient India, and the civilizations along the Indus Valley succumbed to the ravages of climatic desiccation, while the ebb and flow of Chinese dynasties danced in tandem with climatic oscillations. These discoveries have cemented the understanding that the geographical environment exerts a profound influence on the trajectory and evolution of civilizations.

As a result, the Eastern and Western civilizations, sprouting from disparate geographical realms, exhibit inherent dissimilarities, each forging a distinct path in response to the constraints imposed by their respective environments.

1 Eastern Agriculture and the Rationality of Governance

Government rationality, a concept steeped in profound political philosophy, finds its interpretations primarily within the realm of political science. It posits that the government, as a collective entity serving societal interests, stands upon theoretical, temporal, guiding, and self-aware foundations. The research team delved into this notion to dissect the triumphs of China's industrialization during the nascent years of People's Republic of China. Contrary to the emphasis on individualistic rational economic actors propagated by the doctrine of free markets, they observed an emergence of government rationality fueling China's economic growth. As an integral participant in the national economic system, the government exemplified characteristics akin to what Douglas C. North referred to as "governmental corporatism." Here, we explore the genesis and implications of government rationality in the context of China's historical progression, particularly focusing on the predominant agricultural civilization.

1.1 The Genesis of Government Rationality

The inception and evolution of civilization share an inseparable bond with water. Along the banks of mighty rivers, numerous illustrious ancient civilizations flourished. China, a country plagued by the caprices of drought and flood, engaged prominently in flood control, a quintessential pursuit of the Chinese nation, vital for sustaining civilization. This agricultural civilization bore the arduous responsibility of grappling with the ever-changing forces of nature. Through a tumultuous history marked by recurrent river diversions and the ravages of floods, the ancestors dwelling in these regions were compelled to unite. Thus, tribes were born, and each encounter with a significant calamity necessitated the mobilization of more manpower and resources to undertake water management endeavors. Consequently, tribes congregated, birthing settlements that gradually evolved into city-states, laying the foundations for nascent nationhood. Through geological investigations in Qinghai, Chinese geological and archaeological teams unearthed evidence of a cataclysmic flood in the Yellow River basin around 1920 BCE. Scholars participating in this research speculate that this deluge catalyzed a transformation in China's societal structure, transitioning from tribal chiefdoms to a system founded upon political governance. Qin, the first unified empire in Chinese history, thrived and solidified its dominion by constructing the Dujiangyan irrigation system, a benevolent hydraulic engineering marvel that laid the groundwork for the subsequent unification of six states. These narratives eloquently illustrate the seminal role of water management throughout the annals of Chinese civilization. The specific circumstances and resources upon which these undertakings hinged exerted profound ramifications, engendering what scholars would label as path dependence.

Subsequently, let us delve into the formation of government rationality in the East. China, initially a realm replete with remarkable diversity and conspicuous disparities, underwent a metamorphosis into a unified nation. The revelation of the Liangzhu culture (良渚文化) in Zhejiang, courtesy of archaeological endeavors, elucidates this transformation. Meticulous excavations within the Liangzhu ancient city unveiled a plethora of sophisticated hydraulic systems. Given the scale of these engineering feats, constructing the Liangzhu ancient city and its encompassing water systems necessitated the labor of hundreds of thousands, if not more. Yet, without a political entity, how could such a mobilization of human capital transpire? Considering the population distribution of the time, it becomes conceivable that provinces such as Anhui and Jiangxi fell under the purview of this nascent political entity, facilitating effective labor coordination to embark upon the grand construction endeavors associated with the ancient city and its hydraulic infrastructure. Bold conjectures thus arise, positing that the exigencies of harnessing water resources, safeguarding against water-related perils, and effectively harmonizing the labor force propelled the formation of a national political framework. Moreover, the inherent tensions between human settlements and the finite land resources, coupled with the invasions of northern nomadic tribes, engendered an imperative for a compelling centralized authority.[2]

To exemplify, the archaeological discoveries at the Shuanghe Tree Site (双槐树遗址), which reverberated across the globe, substantiated that flood prevention and control constituted a central tenet in the urban layout even during the reign of the Yellow Emperor. Situated within the riverine junction of the Yellow River and Luo River, the ancient state of Luohe, harbored within the Shuanghe Tree Site (refer to Fig. 1), epitomized the heartland of Chinese civilization.

Delving into the functional layout of the Shuanghe Tree Site (refer to Fig. 2), one readily discerns the encompassing three-tiered moats encircling the ancient city. In antiquity, these moats served the primary purpose of flood defense, ingeniously harnessed by the ancients who exploited the propensity of water to gravitate towards lower regions by constructing circular or elliptical ditches. Over time, as human conflicts escalated, the moats evolved into formidable defensive bastions warding off encroaching hostile forces. Evidently, flood control has persistently occupied a position of paramount importance within ancient civilizations. The characteristic traits of early civilization permeated through the annals of time, forming an unbroken thread of China's agrarian heritage spanning millennia.

[2] Excerpt from Professor Wen Tiejun's 2019 address, titled "The Disparity between East Asian Agricultural Civilization and Western Civilization," presented at Sansheng Valley Academy.

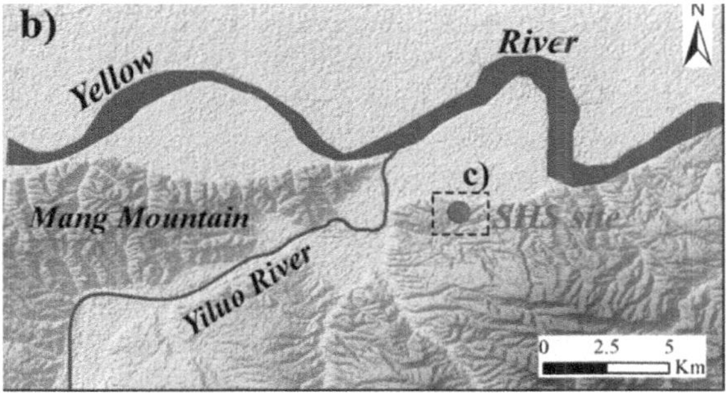

Fig. 1 Geographical location of the ancient state of Luohe

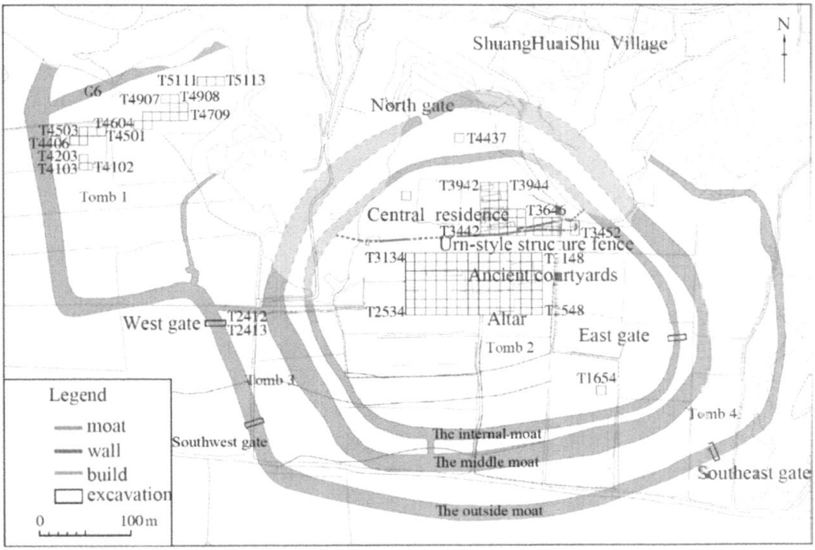

Fig. 2 Functional layout of the Shuanghe Tree Site

Western scholars, too, acknowledge the impact of geographical landscapes on the formation of political systems. Rousseau, in his magnum opus "The Social Contract," poignantly postulates, "I envision a time when the impediments in nature surpass the individual's ability to overcome them for self-preservation... and the only way for humanity to survive lies in the consolidation of collective strength, wherein each individual, while merging with the whole, remains free." Rousseau's concept of the "social contract" serves as a bedrock to comprehend the formation of political systems. Nevertheless, owing to stark disparities in geographical environs, the West failed to engender a government rationality reminiscent of its Eastern counterpart. Across the expansive and sparsely populated Western domains, where maritime trade thrived, the rapid accumulation of capital in private hands heralded the ascendancy of individual rationality, paving the way for a culture that extolled liberty and the maximization of individual interests.

1.2 The Impact of Government Rationality

In the fierce competition of national political forms, the preservation of a civilized and stable continuity relies on a distinctive government rationality that also shapes subsequent historical progress. During the era of warring states, the State of Qin constructed three major water conservancy projects, with the renowned Dujiangyan Irrigation System standing out among them. Upon completion, this water management marvel swiftly transformed the Chengdu Plain into a crucial granary for Qin, turning Ba-Shu (巴蜀) into a vast and prosperous strategic rear, altering the longstanding equilibrium among the mighty forces of Qin, Chu, and Qi. Qin rose above its rivals, leading the way. And so it came to pass that, with an audacious and resolute king at its helm, the wealthy and formidable Qin swept through six kingdoms, achieving ultimate unification. Thus, the era of feudalism was left behind, paving the way for a unified county system—a political form where central authority could effectively mobilize the nation's resources and power, expanding its reach beyond the homeland. This prowess proved instrumental in countering the northern nomadic tribes' southward pressure amidst the chilling climate change. Though the Qin Dynasty's reign in Chinese imperial history resembled a meteor's transient flash, its radiant glow laid the bedrock for China's centralized political structure. Consequently, when humanity entered the competitive arena of national political forms, China's millennia-old agrarian civilization persisted, unwavering.

In the early days of People's Republic of China, the government rapidly attained primitive accumulation through rationality. Post-1949, as a means to sustain the state's industrialization, which was internally driven by a mechanism of "capital accumulation excluding labor," the government had no choice but to embark on rural collectivization. It was the only way to extract surplus from a highly dispersed small-scale agricultural economy, thus forging an inward-oriented "primitive capital accumulation" fueling industrialization. Nevertheless, operating within the macro environment of engaging billions of minimally surplus small farmers imposed unavoidably exorbitant transaction costs. Thus, the government aimed to address this quandary, establishing necessary institutional arrangements. By drawing lessons from the ruling party and the people through protracted wars, as well as harnessing the militarized centralization system stemming from those conflicts, indispensable mechanisms and organizations for national industrialization were constructed.

It was with the aid of a dual system arrangement rooted in rural collectivization and urban unit structures—demonstrating the state's highly concentrated and monopolistic control over resources (refer to Table 1)—that the central government ensured a consistently high accumulation rate of up to 30% during the industrialization process lasting less than 30 years. This transformation propelled China, once a quintessential traditional agricultural nation in the early 1950s, struggling amidst an inhospitable global environment bereft of external markets and foreign investments, into a preliminary industrialized state boasting over 70% industrial output, a comprehensive spectrum of industries, and meticulous specialization.

In the contemporary era, government rationality plays a pivotal role in resolving both internal and external crises. With the advent of economic globalization, crises have reverberated and spread under its pervasive influence. Presently, humanity confronts two momentous crises—a global financial crisis born from financial surplus and an ecological crisis confronting the collective human race. Examining the global financial crisis first, since embarking on an era of comprehensive financial surplus, these crises have followed predictable cycles. Our research team's "Crisis Theory" probes China's remarkable resilience in extricating itself from the quagmire of financial crises, repeatedly rising from the ashes. For instance, barely a decade after People's Republic of China's establishment, confronted by a tense international landscape, the government invested 205.26 billion yuan into the Third Front construction. This bold initiative relocated key defense and basic industries from vulnerable coastal regions to secure the Third Front territories, effectively safeguarding China's industrial infrastructure. Yet, from an economic rationality standpoint,

Table 1 China's urban and rural dual economic system arrangement. *Source* He Huili, Qiu Jiansheng, Gao Jun, Wen Tiejun. "Government Rationality and Village Rationality: China's Two 'Comparative Advantages'." Journal of the National Academy of Governance, 2014(6):39–44

Institutional category	*Function*
Rural collective system	In order to implement the "price scissors," a policy involving the centralized collection of low-priced agricultural products determined by the government and the mandatory acquisition of high-priced urban industrial products, there was a significant mobilization of labor resources on a large scale and in a militarized manner for the purpose of national infrastructure development. This was done with the condition of maintaining basic stability in rural areas to serve as a soft landing for urban crises
Urban unit system	Comprehensive support for the young, elderly, sick, and deceased was provided to maintain a relatively closed and low-level basic standard of living for laborers and their family members. This was done in coordination with the national capital's pursuit of surplus maximization and minimal welfare payments to achieve the short-term goal of industrialization and initial accumulation of capital

the accomplishments of the Third Front construction were modest, incurring substantial human and material costs. Consequently, Western scholars criticized it as an endeavor undertaken "at the wrong time and place." However, the Third Front construction movement decisively propelled China's military and heavy industries, fortifying the defense industry, with its true value defying simple cost–benefit calculations. Subsequently, the nation harnessed its collective strength to invigorate rural areas, channeling abundant resources into the countryside, not solely motivated by maximizing returns but also to avert social upheaval through expanded investments in risk-free assets. Moreover, in 2020, the eruption of the COVID-19 pandemic accentuated China's government rationality with resounding clarity. Unifying the nation's efforts, the swift containment of the virus showcased the government's execution and response capabilities, standing in stark contrast to Western nations.

In sum, China's political and cultural civilization, founded upon the governance of water, has perpetually maintained stability throughout millennia of civilization's evolution. While ancient civilizations from the same era have faded into oblivion, this venerable nation east of the

Himalayas continues to forge ahead amid cyclic climatic changes, intermingling and assimilating diverse cultures, and the intertwined fate of disasters and transformations.

2 The Rationality of Rural Community: A Crucial Element in Rural Development

Earlier, we explored the contrasting Eastern and Western civilizations from a grand perspective, considering geographical and cultural disparities. The agrarian societies of the East favored stability, while the adventurous maritime civilizations of the West thrived. They showcased collectivism's altruistic ideals and individualism's pursuit of self-interest. Additionally, Eastern civilizations exhibited centralized government rationality, while Western societies embraced the individual rationality of liberal democracy. These broad strokes hint at the underlying dynamics, urging us to delve into the extension of Eastern civilization within the fundamental building block of society—the village.

Why, you may ask, is China's rural landscape referred to as the "Three Lives in One (三生合一)"? This concept encapsulates the inseparable fusion of ecology, production, and living in the rural domain. Let's first examine the ecological aspect. China's geographical features consist of "seven mountains, two waters, and one-third farmland." Astonishingly, Chinese arable land accounts for a mere 7% of global resources, while its water resources comprise a modest 6.4%. Moreover, less than 10% of the nation's territory possesses suitable conditions for agriculture in terms of water, soil, light, and heat. Compounding matters, China predominantly experiences a subtropical monsoon climate, exacerbating the uneven distribution of water resources and restricting agricultural production. Curiously, China harbors a staggering 20% of the world's population. How does East Asia, beset by resource scarcities and land pressures, manage to feed such a substantial populace? Contrastingly, the sparsely inhabited expanse of the Americas, blessed with fertile soil, finds itself grappling with insurmountable challenges within a century of development. Professor Franklin H. King surmises that China's resolve lies in its traditional agricultural practices—intensive cultivation, resource recycling, and conservation.[3] Eastern Asia's production system, rooted in sustainable agriculture, stands in stark contrast to the industrialized and modernized models fixated on immediate gains and resource depletion. The geographical resource characteristics enable community members to meet their daily needs within the confines of their locale, promoting flourishing industries alongside agricultural pursuits. Formed through kinship and geographical boundaries, the rural society envisioned by Fei Xiaotong—the realm of familiar faces—ultimately gives rise to a cultural tapestry and governance order defined by the village's distinct attributes.

The intertwined fabric of this rural society, encapsulating the "convergence of three lives," engenders a superstructure of "three governance" principles—people, water, and the village. This triad adheres to a logical progression, where water governance assumes precedence for effective village management. In agrarian societies devoid of substantial industrialization, food production reigns supreme as the fundamental "capital." Elevating grain production necessitates the construction of water infrastructure. This arduous undertaking demands extensive human engagement, a torrent of manpower, resources, and financial investment. Crucially, water management hinges on upstream–downstream cohesion, necessitating unwavering cooperation and coordination among community members. Huang Zongzhi's comparative study of the Yangtze River Delta and the North China Plain reveals the pivotal role played by water-related projects in shaping kinship organizations.[4] Thus, village governance and the innate characteristics of the "integration of three lives" in rural society become inseparable companions. Our research team christens this collective rationality, which stems from an economic framework grounded in the bifurcation of collective ownership and individual usage rights within a defined territorial scope, while fostering bonds forged through blood relations and geographic proximity, as "village community rationality." We shall illustrate the village's transformative growth fueled by this inherent rationality derived from the "integration

[3] Franklin H. King. Farmers of Forty Centuries: Permanent Agriculture in China, Korea, and Japan [M]. Translated by Cheng Cunwang and Shi Yan. Beijing: Dongfang Publishing House, 2011.

[4] Philip C. Huang. The Small Peasant Economy and Social Change in North China [M]. Beijing: Zhonghua Book Company, 2000.

of three lives" and channeled into the realms of the "three governance" through the prism of Zhanqi Village.

2.1 Hydrologic Prosperity: The Genesis of the Zhanqi

In the aftermath of the rational government-led social mobilization movement within the People's Commune, while other regions faced the looming demise of their collective economies, why did Zhanqi Village emerge as a paradigm of collective economic development in the new era? In their quest to answer this question, the villagers have ventured into three distinct camps: the elite theory, the opportunity theory, and the cultural theory. The elite theory emphasizes the influential role of the village's elites in governance and contributions, culminating in the triumph of Zhanqi today. Advocates of the opportunity theory contend that Zhanqi Village astutely aligned its pivotal choices with the prevailing social trends at a crucial turning point, thereby securing substantial institutional advantages. Conversely, the cultural theory places paramount importance on the resolute spirit of unity and trailblazing exhibited by the people of Zhanqi, which has enabled their Zhanqi to soar across generations. Each perspective possesses its own validity, offering partial insight into the reasons behind Zhanqi Village's remarkable success.

Historian Xu Zhuoyun (许倬云) regards individuals as the feeblest presence in the annals of history, followed by society, culture, and ultimately nature. This hierarchy aptly reflects the three-tiered historical viewpoints encapsulated by these three perspectives. The elite theory delves into the individual's impact, the opportunity theory encompasses societal considerations, and the cultural theory, grander than its counterparts, encompasses the transformative journey of both individuals and society. Yet, conspicuously absent is a broader vantage point—nature—through which to decipher the developmental experiences of Zhanqi Village. Hence, from this pivotal standpoint, we shall endeavor to address the fundamental question of "why Zhanqi prospered."

Firstly, let us acquaint ourselves with the fundamental natural setting of Zhanqi Village nestled within the Western expanse of the Sichuan Plain. The origins of this plain trace back approximately 5000 years to the Himalayan mountain-forming epoch. As the Qinghai-Tibet Plateau rapidly ascended, the Western region of Sichuan gradually descended, paving the way for the sedimentary deposition of sand and gravel borne by the Minjiang and Tuojiang rivers. Over time, this process sculpted the present-day plains, while the obstruction of the Hengduan Mountains resulted in the stagnation of moist air currents from the Pacific and Indian Oceans, engendering abundant precipitation. The dry, frigid air currents from the northwestern hinterlands, however, struggled to penetrate the plains' interior, thus engendering a bountiful subtropical monsoon climate replete with rainfall. This combination of alluvial plains and copious precipitation proved highly conducive to agricultural endeavors, making the western Sichuan region one of the earliest cradles of ancient Chinese agrarian civilization. It was within this realm that the ancient civilization epitomized by the Sanxingdui (三星堆, Three Star Mound) culture flourished. Naturally, this geographical milieu bore its limitations. The distinct seasonal distribution of rainfall associated with the subtropical monsoon climate, coupled with the vulnerability of the plains' topography to ravaging floods, engendered recurrent droughts and deluges. The Dujiangyan Irrigation System (refer to Fig. 3) revolutionized the hydraulic landscape, satiating the irrigation needs of the fertile lands in the western Sichuan Plain while mitigating the perils of inundation. This monumental feat earned the region the appellation of the "Land of Abundance." Subsequently, successive dynasties diligently maintained and fortified the Dujiangyan Irrigation System. Following the establishment of the People's Republic of China, the nation embarked on comprehensive reforms of the Dujiangyan hydraulic system, ensuring perpetual benefits for its populace. Thus, this perspective ostensibly underscores the commanding role of rational government intervention in water conservancy infrastructure. Nevertheless, scholars have posited that the intricacy of the Dujiangyan irrigation area's hydraulic facilities surpasses the river governance of North China. As a result, distinct from the autocratic "gentry society" prevalent in the Orient and the autonomous agrarian communities of North China, the Dujiangyan irrigation area engendered a collectivist society distinguished by its communal attributes.[5] This collectivization is predominantly manifested in two aspects.

Firstly, the water conservancy management system forged within the Dujiangyan irrigation area bears collective traits. In general, large-scale water conservancy infrastructure projects guided by rational government initiatives tend to be transient, incapable of ingraining themselves within the daily fabric of grassroots governance. By contrast, the western Sichuan

[5] Lv Dewen. The Nature of Water Conservancy Society. Development Research, 2007(6):11–13.

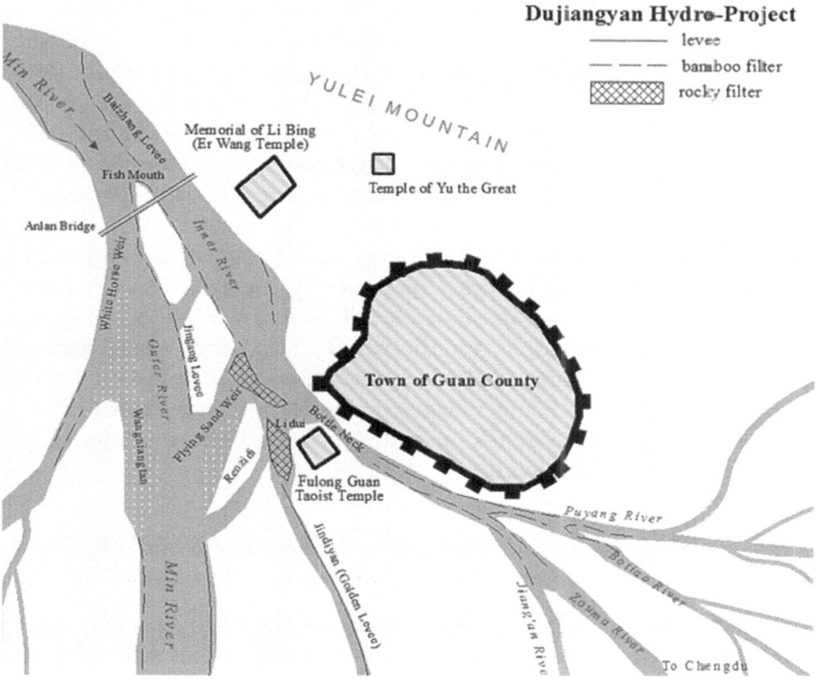

Fig. 3 Functional Diagram of the Dujiangyan Irrigation System

Plain's "gentry" lacks conspicuous prominence, instead directing their water conservancy endeavors towards institutional design. Measures such as planned water volume control and segmented, scheduled channel irrigation have fostered a collective management structure centered around water rights concentration. Secondly, the operational framework of the Dujiangyan irrigation area epitomizes collectivism. Although the farmers of the western Sichuan Plain reap the bounteous benefits of the Dujiangyan Irrigation System, these advantages hinge upon collective investments of labor, resources, and finances. Consequently, the region witnessed the emergence of "water releasers," who functioned outside the purview of the state's grassroots political power system, alongside water conservancy funds imbued with a philanthropic nature facilitating internal irrigation operations.

Thus, viewed through this lens, the western Sichuan Plain has forged a water conservancy society embodying collective characteristics rooted in its distinctive hydraulic infrastructure. Consequently, while water conservancy systems in other regions faltered due to the government's rational retreat—a consequence of the People's Commune disintegration and the malfunctioning of grassroots governance following fiscal and taxation reforms—the Dujiangyan irrigation area persevered, sustained by its collectivist operational model. In essence, the extraordinary Dujiangyan water conservancy project itself engendered an intrinsic necessity for collective endeavors. Consequently, the fiscal system's collective attributes, underpinning rural overall planning founded upon the principles of "by the people, for the people," and the management of public affairs in accordance with the conventions of a close-knit society, persevered. Naturally, Zhanqi Village, a mere twenty kilometers from the Dujiangyan Irrigation System's epicenter, became integrally intertwined within this societal framework.

2.2 *The Mechanism of "Internalizing External Risks" During Rural Industrialization's Primitive Accumulation*

Every industrial development is a process of densifying capital, where capital accumulation takes precedence as capital becomes scarce. In the early stages of rural industrialization's primitive accumulation, the entire nation faces an acute scarcity of capital. Zhanqi Village's journey appears fraught with obstacles, burdened not only by extreme capital scarcity but also carrying a debt of nearly 700 yuan from its inception. The puzzle of how to develop collective economy and emerge as a standout during the primitive accumulation stage of rural industrialization perplexed the first-generation leaders of Zhanqi Brigade. Approaching this challenge within the framework of capital accumulation, it breaks down into two further inquiries: firstly, addressing the issue of capital scarcity encountered during primitive accumulation, and secondly, resolving the negative externalities resulting from capital's original accumulation. By relying on the rationality of village communities that emanate from the collectivized nature of the Dujiangyan water conservancy system, lies the crux of overcoming these two significant issues. In an era where agricultural industrialization becomes the sole path for agriculture, only villages with high social connectivity possess the potential to develop industrialized agriculture.[6]

1. "Self-Capitalization" for Primitive Accumulation

The initial step involves "self-capitalization," wherein the scarcity of capital is substituted by the infusion of labor within the village community, rapidly completing the primitive accumulation. Zhanqi's primitive accumulation can be divided into two stages: the inception of industrial accumulation, propelled by an ample agricultural accumulation to bolster industrialization, and the phase of industrial development, achieved through a distribution system that concentrates and recirculates capital. Zhanqi's trajectory of industrial development closely mirrors China's path towards industrialization. During the early stages, both sides harnessed the collective system to extract agricultural surplus, fostering the development of industrialization. Water management and field transformations played pivotal roles within the agricultural accumulation process. Zhanqi Brigade was endowed with a surplus of "rotten fields" and "wet fields" at the time. These results stemmed from Zhanqi Village's location within the Minjiang alluvial fan area, characterized by ice-water ice-cobble terraces, ice-water alluvial fan plains, and floodplains. The contact points between these landforms exhibited varying permeability due to dissimilar rock compositions, ultimately leading to the formation of wet fields.[7] Compromised air circulation, compacted soil, disrupted soil granular structure, and low soil temperatures in the wet fields hindered root development, resulting in not only diminished agricultural output but also root decay and death. In addition to soil challenges, Zhanqi's irregular land shapes proved highly disadvantageous for cultivation. Consequently, rectifying the low productivity of agriculture necessitated the transformation and regulation of the "wet fields" and "rotten fields."

The critical determinant for converting wet fields into fruitful farmland rests with efficient drainage, contingent upon the quality

[6] He Xuefeng, Tong Zhihui. On the Social Connections of Villages—A Discussion on the Social Foundation of Village Order. China Social Sciences, 2002(3): 124–134, 207.

[7] Sichuan Province Pixian County Compilation Committee. Pixian County Annals. Chengdu: Sichuan People's Publishing House, 1989.

of the ditches. The existing channels within the Dujiangyan irrigation area proved inadequate to fulfill the water conservancy needs of farmland, compelling Zhanqi Brigade to renovate their existing farmland water conservancy projects. However, such a renovation endeavor demands the contribution of numerous factors, including manpower and material resources. "In the early 1970s, Zhanqi Brigade consisted of nine production teams, 283 households, and a total population of a mere 1194 individuals. Subtracting half-laborers and children, the available labor force barely exceeded 560 individuals. Apart from regular production activities, the mobilization of robust labor could only be accomplished through the formation of a militia company." Leveraging the mobilizing power of the militia construction, Zhanqi Brigade successfully organized a contingent of vigorous laborers, facilitating the construction of farmland water conservancy. Consequently, they transformed the "rotten fields" and "wet fields" into level plots, substantially augmenting agricultural yields. By 1972, rice yields per mu reached 813 catties (including 710 catties for early rice and 103 catties for late rice). In 1973, the yield further escalated to 983 catties (including 683 catties for early rice and 300 catties for late rice). By 1975, Zhanqi Brigade's grain reserve amounted to 400,000 catties.[8] This formidable stockpile laid a solid material foundation, accomplishing the arduous task of early-stage primitive capital accumulation.

Established with the aid of the grain reserve, the brick factory became the iconic enterprise that marked the commencement of Zhanqi's industrialization. During this stage, Zhanqi Brigade maximized the value of labor factors through militia construction while employing a work-point system to maximize surplus capital for industrial investment.

2. Internalizing to Resolve Negative Externalities of Primitive Capital Accumulation

As a general rule, primitive capital accumulation inherently carries a nature of deprivation. Zhanqi Village's ability to extract copious amounts of agricultural surplus from within the collective, specifically for industrial construction, within a remarkably short span

[8] Source: Zhao Renchun. Zhanqi Village Chronicles (Unpublished).

> without triggering significant collective resistance can be attributed to a foundation based on "values rationality rooted in blood ties and village communal identity, characterized by intergenerational division of labor and external collaborative behavior."[9] In essence, the surplus generated throughout the entire process of agricultural village industrialization belongs collectively to the village residents. This accumulation method, perceived as a form of "self-deprivation," permits the "internalization" necessary to mitigate the negative externalities arising from primitive capital accumulation. This is manifested in Zhanqi's collective enterprises, where maximizing profits does not reign supreme as the primary business objective. While pursuing profitability, these enterprises concurrently shoulder the responsibility of financing the village's public affairs, ensuring equitable employment opportunities and fair distribution systems for the village's residents.

For instance, during the 1980s, the collective allocated a portion of the brick factory's surplus to construct the "Yinglong Mountain Villa" with an investment exceeding 200,000 yuan. Subsequently, in 2006, the village further invested over 1.2 million yuan, transforming it into the largest cultural venue at the village level in the Western region—the Zhanqi Village Cultural Courtyard—fulfilling the spiritual and cultural needs of the villagers. Moreover, during Zhanqi's collective enterprise restructuring process, the village collective retained a share of the enterprise's profit rights, thus transitioning from managing enterprises to operating assets and collecting rent income (land rent, factory rent, and equipment rent).

In conclusion, the two mechanisms of "self-capitalization" for accomplishing primitive capital accumulation and "internalization" to resolve the negative externalities of primitive capital accumulation enable Zhanqi Village, renowned as the "Village Standing on Water," to smoothly and expeditiously transition from agriculture to industry during the era of rural industrialization. Furthermore, Zhanqi perpetuates the "Three Lives" (ecological, productive, and living) culture born from water

[9] He Huili, Qiu Jiansheng, Gao Jun, Wen Tiejun. Government Rationality and Village Rationality: China's Two "Comparative Advantages." Journal of the National School of Administration, 2014(6): 39–44.

management, while achieving a highly integrated "Three Governance" (governing people, governing water, and governing the village).

2.3 Cooperative-Based Land Transfer: Unveiling Rural Development

As urban industries, capital surpluses, and financial abundance continue to escalate, rural regions, once experiencing a net exodus of the three production factors, now stand at the threshold of newfound opportunities. Capital is retracing its steps, resolute on awakening dormant rural assets and reaping profits by facilitating the elevation of agricultural industries and realizing the value of resources. Yet, the desiccated villages, longing for rejuvenation, find themselves grappling with the enigmatic nature of capital. Whether driven by idealism or sheer greed, capital perpetually grapples with the invisible forces and informal systems unique to the countryside. In turn, villagers perceive a semblance of hope in these external investments, albeit disconnected from any substantial benefits. From the very onset of capital influx, a clandestine dance of vested interests ensues, veiled in ambiguity and entanglement.

The symbiotic relationship between capital and villages assumes two possible outcomes—a harmonious alliance or a binary opposition, giving rise to adverse externalities, as depicted in Fig. 4. Capital, under rational village governance, fuels rural development. A well-established governance system mobilizes dispersed small-scale farming organizations, reducing the burdensome transaction costs incurred from individual dealings. Moreover, through the consolidation of robust collective organizations, the negotiating power of the village collective is fortified, enabling the majority to partake in the fruits of communal progress. Conversely, when capital and rural communities stand in opposition, impediments to capital inflow emerge, accompanied by amplified operational risks and the unfortunate transference of negative externalities onto the village. This strains the village enterprise relationship and leaves villagers feeling detached from the burgeoning development.

Zhanqi Village, post collective restructuring, witnessed the dawn of a new era—the "first pot of gold" in the twenty-first century. The culmination of labor-driven progress paved the way for a transformative phase, wherein land reform took center stage as the linchpin of village development. Drawing from a rich developmental history, Zhanqi Village adeptly seized the opportune moment. In 2003, the village spearheaded land

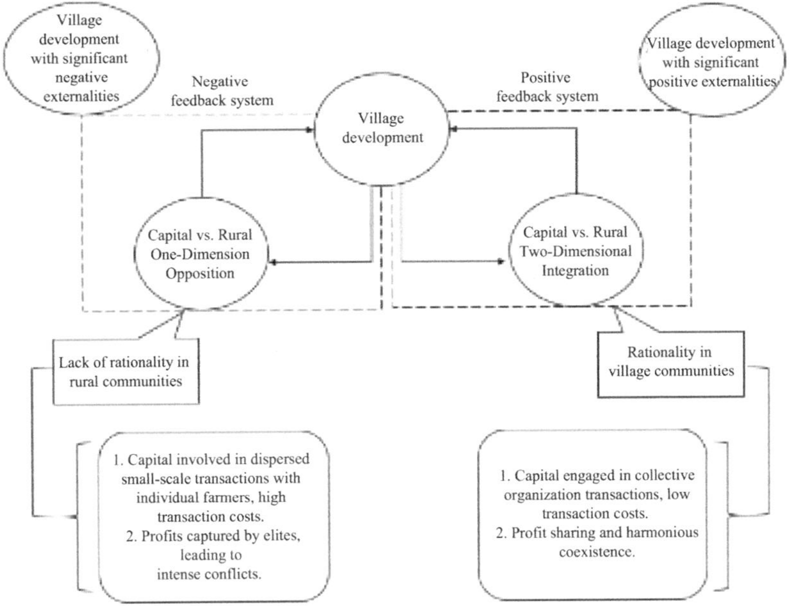

Fig. 4 Two possible outcomes of capital entering rural areas. 村庄发展总体负外部性大|村庄发展总体正外部性大 Village development with significant negative externalities | Village development with significant positive externalities, 负反馈系统|村庄发展|正反馈系统 Negative feedback system | Village development | Positive feedback system, 资本与乡村一元对立|资本与乡村二元融合 Capital vs. Rural One-Dimension Opposition | Capital vs. Rural Two-Dimensional Integration, 村社理性缺失|1.资本同分散的小农交易，交易成本高昂。2.收益被精英俘获，冲突激烈。Lack of rationality in rural communities | 1. Capital involved in dispersed small-scale transactions with individual farmers, high transaction costs. 2. Profits captured by elites, leading to intense conflicts, 村社理性在位|1.资本同集体组织交易，交易成本低。2.收益共享，和谐共处。Rationality in village communities | 1. Capital engaged in collective organization transactions, low transaction costs. 2. Profit sharing and harmonious coexistence

concentration, ultimately amassing 100 mu of land. Subsequently, in 2006, Zhanqi Village established a specialized cooperative for vegetable production, concentrating 500 mu of land. Pioneering market-oriented operations, the village became the inaugural test bed for the linkage between land and developmental initiatives in the city by 2007. The resounding echo of progress reverberated throughout the province in September 2015 when Zhanqi Village became the first to integrate collective construction land into the market. Maigao Tourism Resources Development Co., Ltd. secured a 40-year land use right for 13.447 mu of collective construction land, at a price of 525,000 yuan per mu, amounting to a total auction price of 7.06 million yuan. By that time, the per capita disposable income of Zhanqi Village had surpassed 20,000 yuan.

Throughout the land concentration process, the village community played a pivotal role, its rationality guiding the way. To ensure a seamless land transfer, safeguarding the villagers' interests, Zhanqi Village's approach neither relied on project-driven initiatives nor succumbed to commercial capital development. Instead, it primarily relied on voluntary internal transfers within the village during the initial phase and purposeful guidance from village-level organizations during subsequent stages. Table 2 outlines the measures undertaken concerning land in Zhanqi Village from 2003 to 2015.

The intrinsic mechanisms driving land concentration in Zhanqi Village become evident through several facets. Firstly, harnessing the industrialization accrued during prior stages, the village capitalized on collective enterprises, successfully reallocating a substantial portion of the agricultural labor force to the industrial realm. Unlike other rural areas plagued by hollowing-out crises, Zhanqi Village defied the odds, with 80% of its labor force gainfully employed within the village. However, the allure of higher wages in non-agricultural sectors significantly increased the opportunity cost associated with agricultural pursuits, exacerbating the issue of abandoned lands. One villager aptly explained, "Let me be frank, with young folks working in companies like Rongzhen Mushroom Industry, women earn over 3000 yuan, men over 5000 yuan, and a young couple can rake in 8000 yuan per month. Do you think they'd still choose to till the land? They handed over their fields to the village collective for unified management—it's more convenient. You may hear whispers of paltry monthly land rental fees of 100 yuan, but truth be told, cultivating

Table 2 Measures related to land in Zhanqi Village from 2003 to 2015. *Data Source* Zhanqi Database, interview records of the research team

Year	*Measures*	*Results*
2003	Field study	The idea of "In order for a village to develop, land must be concentrated" was determined. In that year, 100 mu of land were concentrated
2006	Established the Zhanqi Vegetable Professional Cooperative, carrying out land concentration progress	The total area of concentrated land reached 1100 mu, with a guaranteed minimum dividend of 800 yuan
2007	Implemented the "Demolish and Rebuilding Courtyard" project and applied for the pilot reform of 'Innovative Rural Grassroots Governance Mechanism.'	The scattered farming households occupying 400 mu of land were reorganized, using 200 mu of land to build new houses, and the remaining 200-plus mu of homesteads (collectively owned land parcels) were linked to urban land auctions, generating revenue of 130 million yuan. In addition to repaying 115 million yuan in financing principal and interest, the remaining 15 million yuan was earmarked for the construction of infrastructure for the Zhanqi Village Modern Agricultural Industrial Park, and a new Zhanqi community with an area of 91,000 square meters was built (data excerpted from a research report by Tsinghua University)
2008	The Chengdu Municipal Committee and Municipal Government issued the "Opinions on Strengthening Farmland Protection and Further Reforming and Improving the Rural Land and Housing Property Rights System (Trial Implementation)."	Taking this policy as an opportunity, Zhanqi Village began to promote the qualification certification of collective economic organization members
2009	Renamed as the Zhanqi Vegetable Professional Cooperative in Tangchang Town, Pixian County	More than 2300 mu of farmland were concentrated, of which more than 500 mu were not leased out and were independently operated by cooperatives for vegetable cultivation. The remaining 1800-plus mu were all leased out, with a uniform land rent of 1200 yuan per mu

(continued)

Table 2 (continued)

Year	*Measures*	*Results*
2010	Zhanqi Village introduced the "Method for Recognizing Members of Collective Economic Organizations."	Collective membership was based on households, with no increase in births and no reduction in deaths. As of April 20, 2011, a total of 1704 people were determined as members of the collective economic organization
2015	Applied for the pilot reform of rural collective profit-oriented land entering the market exchange and established the Pixian Tangchang Collective Assets Management Co., Ltd	The approved village collective assets amounted to over 40 million yuan, all of which were injected into Zhanqi Asset Management Co., Ltd. The company was initiated by members of the village council (35 people) with a registered capital of 17.04 million yuan. Each member of the collective economic organization held 10,000 yuan in shares, and the remaining collective assets were valued as share premium. 40% of the net income of the collective asset management company was allocated to surplus funds for company development; 30% of the net income was allocated to public welfare funds for collective public welfare and charity projects; 10% of the net income was allocated to a risk fund to cover losses, and the remaining 20% was distributed as dividends to all members

the land would impact income far more."[10] Around 1991, the first signs of land transfer emerged as villagers within specific groups collectively leased approximately 10 mu of land to local vegetable growers.

Secondly, the dominant role of the collective economy in mobilization was fortified, promoting land concentration through cooperative measures. Initially, Zhanqi Village's village committee refrained from directly coercing villagers into land transfers. Instead, they sought to shape their perceptions, evident in the village's transformative moments.

[10] Data source: Interview record with the head of Group 7, Zhanqi Village, October 4, 2019.

Delegations comprising village committee members, production group leaders, and representatives of village-run enterprises—approximately 30 to 40 individuals—journeyed to coastal regions, such as Jiangsu, Shandong, and Tianjin. These expeditions aimed to enlighten villagers on the pivotal role land concentration played in propelling villages like Huaxi towards robust collective economies and overall progress. Such endeavors laid the groundwork for subsequent land concentration initiatives. Furthermore, guided by the village community's rationality, villagers were encouraged to act collectively, avoiding radical extremes. When asked why villagers agreed to land transfers, one villager responded, "Back in 2003, when land concentration first took root, only two households in Group 7 initially entertained the idea. However, through the village committee's persuasive efforts and witnessing the widespread adoption of land concentration, they eventually succumbed to the herd mentality and agreed." Fueled by kinship and geographical networks, villagers sought to uphold their "relationships" while simultaneously fostering village development, driving them towards shared goals. Moreover, the distribution system, allowing the collective benefits to be enjoyed by all villagers, further solidified the collective economic structure. During the period of collective membership determination, the village committee formulated a charter for village autonomy, resolving conflicts among villagers. This charter addressed matters ranging from the distribution of benefits within the village to regulating the conduct of villagers. Through these initiatives, the village's governance order was enhanced, significantly bolstering the village committee's efficacy.

Post land concentration, both the village and its residents reaped the rewards of resource integration. Firstly, the consolidation and reorganization of land liberated approximately 200 mu of collective construction land. This not only afforded villagers a quality of life akin to urban neighborhoods but also raised their living standards, while simultaneously augmenting the collective assets through the entry of construction land into the market. From the perspective of urban capital, the scale and organization of land minimized entry barriers, obviating the exorbitant costs associated with fragmented village transactions. Furthermore, cooperative endeavors facilitated by cooperatives and asset management companies mitigated aversions typically exhibited towards external entities in a closely-knit community, endowing Zhanqi Village with exceptional appeal to investors. Records from Tianyancha reveal substantial investments in the village: Rongzhen Mushroom Industry Co., Ltd. in 2007

(90 million yuan), Chengdu Fifth Season Investment Co., Ltd. in 2010 (130 million yuan), and Sichuan Maigao Tourism Resources Development Co., Ltd. (70 million yuan). These three enterprises alone injected a staggering 290 million yuan into the village, dramatically improving living conditions, enhancing infrastructure, and generating numerous employment opportunities. Crucially, resource allocation, driven by the village community's rationality, mitigated the confrontational nature of capital and the village, strengthening the collective's bargaining power and safeguarding their substantial stake in resources. By fortifying the village's position, the risk of being at a disadvantage against capital was averted. This ensured that the benefits of village development were not excessively siphoned away and forestalled the unwarranted transference of negative externalities from capital to the village.

2.4 *Driving the Shift Towards Ecological Transformation*

For decades, Zhanqi Village endured the arduous journey of agricultural industrialization, with labor and land taking turns in the spotlight. Through extracting surplus labor and capitalizing on land value, coupled with absorbing urban surplus capital, Zhanqi Village shed its shackles of a meager 700 yuan debt and embraced capital as a vital force propelling its development in this new era. The question of harnessing the power of capital emerged as the next challenge for Zhanqi Village. Simultaneously, the macro environment, experiencing rapid advancement, reached a pivotal fork in the road as the collective eruption of negative externalities from radical industrialization and urbanization, such as environmental pollution and resource constraints, rendered the ride on this express train unpleasant and faltering. Consequently, achieving the structural transformation and upgrade of industries emerged as a macro strategy for the nation.

In 2015, the Central Committee of the Communist Party of China introduced the structural reform of the industrial supply side, emphasizing the need to reduce capacity, destock, deleverage, cut costs, and address weaknesses. Among these priorities, capacity reduction took center stage. In December 2015, during the executive meeting of the State Council, Premier Li Keqiang made it clear that enterprises in industries with excessive capacity failing to meet national standards for energy consumption, environmental protection, quality, safety, and exhibiting prolonged losses should be shut down, transformed, or divested through restructuring.

Enterprises consistently running losses for over 3 years and deviating from the direction of structural adjustment should be "cleared out" through asset restructuring, equity transfer, or bankruptcy to eliminate "zombie enterprises." In the same year, Chengdu enacted the "Chengdu Drinking Water Source Protection Regulations," encompassing Zhanqi Village within the protected water source area. Thus, Zhanqi Village, bearing its iconic Zhanqi, once again altered its developmental course due to the flowing Baitiao River, marking the commencement of a new chapter in ecological transformation.

Adhering to the requirements of the "Chengdu Drinking Water Source Protection Regulations," Zhanqi Village shuttered eight heavily polluting enterprises. Every transformation entails costs and anguish. In this "cleaning up" process, Zhanqi Village suffered the loss of millions of yuan in revenue solely from closing down its steel foundries, delivering a heavy blow to the collective economy. Yet, it is crucial to note that while this transformation was primarily driven by external influences, internal rationality also played a role within the village. Among the eight closed enterprises in Zhanqi Village, not all were polluters jeopardizing the water source. Nonetheless, considering the overall ecological environment, Zhanqi Village, with a broader perspective in mind, decisively abandoned outdated production capacities, advancing boldly towards a stage of green development.

If eliminating obsolete capacities represents the first stride towards ecological transformation, the subsequent critical juncture lies in how to reintegrate, utilize, and develop resources. How does one traverse the path of ecological transformation? Zhanqi Village implemented two primary measures.

Firstly, establishing an external screening mechanism and macro-level control over industrial structure. In contrast to villages merely driven by a scarcity of assets, indiscriminately welcoming capital, Zhanqi Village, leveraging accumulated experience and adeptness in macro policies, selectively invited enterprises into its embrace. To achieve this, Zhanqi Village initially introduced the "Fifth Season · Mama Farm" project, subsequently earning the distinction of being the first 4A-level scenic spot in Pixian District. Revered as Chengdu's "Provence," it blossomed into a new brand for rural ecotourism in the region. With the surge in sightseeing tourism, Zhanqi Village, aiming to enhance visitors' experiences, thoughtfully introduced agricultural activities like blueberry and strawberry picking, optimizing industrial complementarity and maximizing benefits. Furthermore, within the self-established "Zhanqi's 18 Rural Workshops" project, Zhanqi Village rigorously adhered to an approval system, subjecting all enterprise and product applications to the collective scrutiny. Adhering to the operational system of "highlighting intangible cultural heritage in the first phase, emphasizing cultural and creative industries in the second phase, and prioritizing gastronomy in the third phase," Zhanqi Village meticulously selected distinctive products or brands capable of showcasing the production process on-site, thus forestalling the detrimental impact of homogeneous competition within the scenic area.

Secondly, propelling organizational innovation and multidimensional collaboration to exploit spatial resources. Ecological spatial resources bear multifaceted functionality, encompassing economic, social, cultural, and ecological security, and boasting highly positive externalities for the nation and society at large. The pursuit of rural ecological spatial resources has become a coveted aspiration among urban middle-class communities. Consequently, effectively tapping into rural ecological spatial resources and elevating the level and value of rural industries have emerged as transformational objectives. However, the cohesive nature of "mountains, waters, fields, forests, lakes, and grass" as integrated resources makes it challenging for them to independently manifest their natural ecological and socio-cultural functions. Moreover, with regards to property rights structure, these resources fall under rural collective ownership, forming an interconnected system with the "integration of production, living, and ecological functions" within the village. It proves arduous to enforce physical or legal means to forcibly segregate them. Thus, the intrinsic structural cohesion of spatial elements necessitates a development approach that hinges on collective organization and comprehensive planning. Initially, in 2006, Zhanqi Village established the Zhanqi Agricultural Cooperative, allowing villagers to participate by investing their land contracts. By quantifying income rights as shares for cooperative members, usage rights were consolidated within the collective, creating a favorable condition for negotiations with external investors. Subsequently, in 2008, a vegetable cooperative was established, assuming the responsibility of attracting investment. Prior to attracting investment, the village collective secured a 1.3 million yuan loan, earmarked for interest subsidies, in the cooperative's name. A portion of the funds was allocated to land improvement and related infrastructure construction, thereby augmenting land rent value and facilitating the introduction of organic agriculture ventures with tertiary industry functions, such as strawberry and blueberry gardens. Broadly speaking, the vegetable cooperative chiefly undertakes five functions: agricultural product cultivation, land management (to avoid duplication by managing introduced plant varieties), rural urbanization (enhancing the villagers' quality of life), alignment with policies pertaining to rural revitalization, and providing financing services to enterprises, as illustrated in Fig. 5.

Consequently, it becomes apparent that Zhanqi Village, embedded within its specific geographical environment, organically devised effective governance measures. Through geographic, economic, cultural, and structural interconnections, a harmonious village governance structure

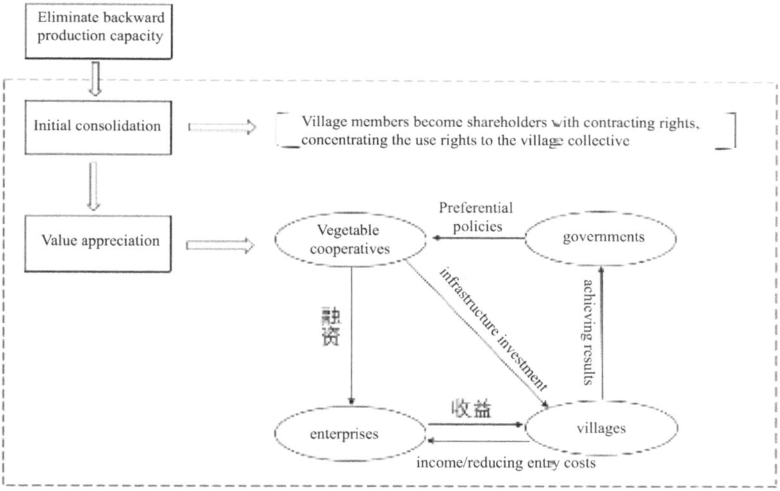

Fig. 5 Mechanism for Advancing Ecological Transformation in Zhanqi. 淘汰落后产能Eliminate backward production capacity, 初始整合|村民以承包权入股，将使用权集中到村集体Initial consolidation|Village members become shareholders with contracting rights, concentrating the use rights to the village collective, 提升价值|蔬菜合作社、政府、村庄、企业|优惠政策、取得成果、收益/降低进入成本、调控产业结构/融资、基础设施投资Value appreciation|Vegetable cooperatives, governments, villages, enterprises|Preferential policies, achieving results, income/reducing entry costs, regulating industrial structure/financing, infrastructure investment

took shape, optimizing the village's developmental trajectory. Unlike the internalized and chaotic outcomes resulting from atomized villages, Zhanqi Village epitomizes rationality at the governance level, demonstrating constructive and protective functions in the construction of the village.

* * *

Property rights theory, in all honesty, is often depicted as culturally unrestricted, universally applicable. The role of ownership is to grant owners residual control rights over assets in the absence of contractual provisions, thereby resolving potential conflicts. In simpler terms, clear-cut property delineations and a rational compensation framework are of paramount importance to prevent efficiency-impairing speculations and evasive behaviors.

Should the aforementioned approach to problem scrutiny hold true, then the ability of ownership to effectively tackle internal organizational issues sans formal regulations is contingent upon cultural interplay. This ability can be deemed culturally predisposed in many instances. Hence, orthodox property rights theory is not universally applicable; it solely finds relevance in low-λ cultural environments. When λ assumes a low value (indicating a lack of mutual trust), the presence of comprehensive legal provisions regarding ownership, compensation, and other regulations becomes crucial. Absent the binding force of such rules, low-λ organizations fall prey to inefficiency. Conversely, for a high-λ society, where inter-organizational competition and other concerns take precedence, formalized property rights, and legally enforceable regulations are less significant.

To illustrate further, let us delve into the commonplace phenomenon in business practices known as lock-in relationships or lock-in effects. The lock-in effect refers to the scenario wherein parties invest in relationship-specific ventures. The worth of this investment within the relationship surpasses its value outside. For instance, workers' human capital investments made today specialize in the enterprise, and the future remuneration for their human capital depends on specific enterprise attributes. Thus, a lock-in effect arises between the enterprise and the workers.

When lock-in effects exist, and λ takes on a low value, the establishment of long-term contracts becomes imperative to curtail opportunistic behavior or formally induce people to "cooperate" and establish effective lock-in relationships. However, in cases where parties find it arduous or unfeasible to enter into comprehensive long-term contracts due to unobservable outcomes or exorbitant contract enforcement costs, ownership emerges as a prerequisite for maintaining efficiency. Owners of tangible assets possess residual control rights and the authority to instruct employees on their usage.

For any sprawling economic organization, the key to triumph lies in eliciting obedience from certain individuals towards others' directives. From the vantage point of property rights scholars, the sole means of ensuring compliance among certain individuals (employees) to the directives of others (owners) during the pursuit of economic interests, while avoiding potential conflicts within the team, is by instituting a well-defined ownership framework. Low λ or distrustful behavior stands as a fundamental assumption among game participants in conventional property rights theory. Its fundamental nature is such that economists do not explicitly reference it as an assumption.

Conventional property rights theory might fundamentally hold true in a low-λ society. However, if a society can be characterized as high-λ, where mutual trust prevails, individuals can still invest in their relationships and maintain connections even without formal ownership rights. In such instances, the necessity for a well-defined owner vested with explicit rights to exclude others from their assets might be obviated. In a high-λ society, where cooperative abilities and desires abound, it becomes unnecessary, or even preferable, to induce good behavior through the threat of termination. Stated differently, in a high-λ society, the decisive nature of well-defined property rights might be diminished. Nonetheless, the significance of well-defined property rights fluctuates across diverse societies due to disparities in individuals' cooperative capacities.

It is worth noting that in a high-λ society, implicit contracts may prove more efficient than explicit ones. In such a society, individuals may opt for implicit contracts over explicit ones for myriad reasons. It could save time and effort expended in negotiations, contract observance, verification, and enforcement. It might also be attributable to the "incentive effect" intrinsic to implicit contracts. When individuals are cooperative and mutually trusting, employees approach their tasks with the same seriousness and responsibility as if they were residual claimants or owners, adeptly handling unforeseen incidents unaccounted for or impossible to detail in formal contracts. By contrast, explicit contracts might confine employees to performing solely the tasks stipulated in the employment agreement. Thus, implicit contracts potentially carry stronger motivational impetus than explicit contracts.

In general, the costs of explicit contracts, encompassing negotiation, observation, outcome verification, and contract enforcement, present a continuum. Correspondingly, λ values in different societies exhibit a similar continuum, reflecting disparities in cooperative abilities and desires among individuals in diverse societal contexts. Consequently, the costs and benefits associated with employing explicit versus implicit contracts differ across societies, engendering a spectrum of trade-offs between the two. Real-world scenarios might arise where cooperative individuals opt for "gentlemen's agreements," denoting implicit contracts founded on custom, goodwill, reputation, and other self-imposed constraints, while individuals with low λ values might require explicit contracts to forestall opportunistic behavior.

CHAPTER 18

Resource Rights and Interests: Realizing and Preserving Rural Resource Value—A Case Study of Township and Village Enterprise Restructuring and Mama Farm

Development is the essence of resource capitalization. Thus, resource rights and interests represent the ultimate capitalization returns for resource owners—a matter of distributing the benefits of resource capitalization.

The outbreak of the COVID-19 pandemic reaffirmed the pivotal role of rural areas as the cornerstone of national comprehensive security and a soft landing. Utilizing grassroots methods like village and road closures, rural communities constructed a formidable prevention and control system, rooted in their unique autonomy and governance. Their low-cost community-wide defense contributed significantly to stemming the spread of the virus. Simultaneously, the crisis unveiled the profound inclusiveness and diversity of the "convergence of the Three Lives," a traditional cultural concept that had undergone rapid industrialization and urbanization. Presently, as we reflect on the flaws of extensive and quantity-oriented development, a window of opportunity for ecological transformation opens, with rural resources poised to benefit from the momentum of rural revitalization and structural reforms in agricultural supply. Any village able to seize the moment possesses the prerequisites to capitalize on institutional opportunities.

© Peking University Press 2024
X. Dong, *Zhanqi Village Over Fifty Years*,
https://doi.org/10.1007/978-981-97-5426-7_18

However, rural resource development encounters structural contradictions. Within the urban–rural duality, numerous rural resources either suffer from organizational deficiencies and a dearth of capital or fall captive to various elites capitalizing on rural assets, ultimately resulting in hollow returns. Over a century of industrialization, rural areas have remained passive in service of national industrialization and urban modernization, exacerbating the deepening "three rural issues." On one hand, due to adjustments in the fundamental operating systems, rural production and operations have reverted to a highly fragmented landscape of part-time smallholder farmers, accentuating the trend of "de-organization" within rural domains. Moreover, the dominant capital element responsible for rural resource allocation flows towards urban areas alongside the commercialization and restructuring of banking institutions. This dynamic triggers a comprehensive net outflow of land, capital, and labor from rural regions, rendering rural areas a hollow composite.[1] In such a backdrop, any external party faces the dilemma of transaction costs, inhibiting the formation of a credit-based market economy within rural domains. Consequently, the extensive "dormant" resources remain incapable of independent development and external market valuation. On the other hand, profit-driven urban industrial and commercial capital fails to assume the role of the primary driving force for rural resource development. Capital's encroachment into rural territories contradicts the logical fabric of familiar rural social networks, thereby triggering various forms of resistance. Stable alignment of interests with the elderly, weak, and disabled rural population left behind becomes increasingly challenging, fueling social conflicts and contradictions within rural areas. Attempts to collude with rural elite farmers to minimize transaction costs further obstruct sharing the benefits of resource capitalization with ordinary farmers, inevitably reducing their well-being.

Presently, constrained by the scarce endowment of human and natural resources within our country, space within a certain range has been fully utilized through the integration of primary, secondary, and tertiary sectors, as well as the implementation of three-dimensional circular agriculture. However, the separation of land ownership and usage rights introduces a new quandary regarding the allocation of "space use rights." Furthermore, due to the prolonged agricultural utilization of land,

[1] Jiang Shaojing, Luo Pan. Research Progress and Achievements of Hollow Villages [J]. China Population, Resources and Environment. 2014 (6): 51–58.

primarily classified within the primary sector, the added value and revenue generated from tertiary sector development gravitate towards operators, leading to the dissipation of spatial rent. This unjust distribution of resource development and utilization benefits manifests as a new form of "hidden deprivation." It erodes not only the distribution rights of rural collectives as resource owners but also exacerbates the degradation of rural environments and the accumulation of social conflicts.

In light of these circumstances, this chapter endeavors to retrospectively examine the historical facts surrounding the restructuring of Zhanqi Village's township and village enterprises. By analyzing the divergent approaches employed in the transaction process concerning surface rights and underground rights, it sheds light on the multifaceted nature of rural resources. Moreover, within the framework of ecological competition in the contemporary era, this chapter integrates the negotiation process between villages and external capital, represented by Mama Farm, elucidating the pivotal mechanisms for realizing resource rights and interests in the development and utilization of ecological spatial resources.

1 Dissecting the Complexity of Resources

The multifaceted attributes of goods and services have captivated the minds of Western economists delving into the realm of property rights theory. Yoram Barzel, commencing his analysis with the attributes of goods, artfully elucidates the notion that "goods possess numerous distinct attributes, varying in levels from one commodity to another, and it is the unique attributes that form the foundation of transactions."[2] Furthermore, as the definition of multiple attributes carries inherent transaction costs, resources left undefined fall within the public domain,

[2] In his book "Economic Analysis of Property Rights," Yoram Barzel illustrates the attributes of goods through examples such as cherry trading, the use of photocopiers, and the gasoline supply during the era of U.S. price controls. In the process of buying and selling cherries, characteristics like color, shape, size, and freshness determine the quality of the product. The observable attributes dictate only a partial value of the goods, while intangible attributes, such as sweetness and nutritional content, reside in the public domain, justifying customers' direct tasting behavior. When a business leases a photocopier, the attributes include the manufacturer's repair rights, the operator's business rights, and even the residual claim rights resulting from employees' personal use. Similarly, the U.S. gasoline price control in 1971 led to oil shortages and the phenomenon of queuing, adding the additional service attribute of "waiting time" to gasoline transactions.

becoming "rented" and discovered by opportunistic seekers of various skill levels. Barzel advocates for the "decomposition of ownership of identical goods among different individuals" to prevent losses stemming from attributes being consigned to the public sphere.[3] Similarly, in his examination of transaction costs in the market exchange process, North unveils the necessity of incurring measurement costs due to the multiple attributes of goods and services. He asserts that "determining the hierarchy of individual attributes for each unit of exchanged goods or services requires the payment of information costs, forming the costly foundation of transactions in this regard."[4] These insights prompt reflection: first, a comprehensive understanding of the multiple attributes of goods or services is imperative as transactional entities; second, the presence of transaction costs in economic activities is an irrefutable reality.

Glancing through history, the grassroots land system practice that emerged during the Song Dynasty echoes these perspectives to a certain extent. Following the Song Dynasty, the system of granting land use rights gained official recognition as the means of land disposition. Landlords would bestow land use rights while reserving the right of redemption, granting the lessee operating and disposal rights while paying land taxes to the state. Thus emerged the division between the landlord's "land bone" and the grantee's "granted industry." In fact, through outright sales, the grantor could even relinquish both the right to use the land and the first redemption right of the granted land. During the Southern Song Dynasty, tenant farmers obtained steadfast tenancy rights, leading to the subsequent emergence of permanent tenancy rights for both official and private lands. This evolution eventually birthed a management model in which the operating rights and land ownership rights were dissociated, resulting in a scenario where the same plot of land housed undisturbed surface owners and underlying owners, aptly dubbed "one field, two owners." While surface owners paid land rent, underlying owners paid land taxes. Evidently, within the framework of the granting system, land bore dual prices: the value of its intrinsic natural resource, represented by absolute rent or annual rent, and the appreciation in

[3] Li Zhongqiu. "The Connotation and Nature of Goods Attributes in Barzel's Theory of Property Rights." Journal of Hebei University of Economics and Business, 2019, 40(1): 26–31.

[4] Douglas C. North. "Institutions, Institutional Change and Economic Performance." Translated by Liu Shouying. Shanghai: Shanghai Sanlian Bookstore, 1994.

land value due to socioeconomic development and capital investments, manifested through differential rent or land price. Consequently, the determination of land lease prices found its foundation in the complete rent theory. Conversely, many developing nations find themselves coerced into striking low-priced resource deals with multinational corporations, unable to partake in the premiums offered by external markets. Consequently, the gains obtained through relinquishing ownership pale in comparison to the post-redevelopment profits. These nations, devoid of long-term impetus, become ensnared within market systems controlled by developed countries, hopelessly trapped in a cycle of political dependency and economic destitution. Hence, reevaluating the multiple attributes of resources and wielding resource rights and interests as a guiding principle within transactional processes emerge as new imperatives for rural resource development.[5]

2 Zhanqi Village's Success at "One Fell Swoop"

In 2013, General Secretary Xi Jinping, during the Jiangsu delegation meeting at the 12th National People's Congress, unveiled the significance of rural reform as the vanguard of China's path to progress. He emphasized that the initial breakthrough in the reform and opening up process was the all-encompassing responsibility of rural communities. While the establishment of a unified and individualized family contract system was proposed, the practical outcome revealed an inherent challenge in achieving effective collective management. To fortify the rural collective economy, various avenues such as share cooperative economies, specialized farmer economic organizations, and township enterprises were advocated. Reiterating this sentiment in 2016 at the rural reform symposium in Xiaogang Village, Anhui Province, Xi Jinping underlined the

[5] Translator's note: After Shakespeare, in Macbeth, act iv, scene 3, where Macduff learns his wife and entire family are murdered:

Ro. Wife, Children, Servants, all that could be found. [...].
Macd. [...] All my pretty ones?
Did you say All? Oh Hell-Kite! All?
What, All my pretty Chickens, and their Damme.
At one fell swoope?

The imagery is of a bird of prey ("hell-kite") ransacking a whole nest at one blow, fell meaning "terrible, cruel, savage." In later uses of the expression, the force of the metaphor is reduced or lost.

necessity of preserving the collective ownership of rural land, ensuring an ample cultivated land base, safeguarding food production capacity, and protecting the interests of farmers.[6] Xi's statements constituted the bedrock for advancing rural reform. Undeniably, the development and empowerment of a novel collective economy hold universal value in alleviating rural impoverishment and harnessing the advantages of collective operational systems. However, Zhanqi Village's distinctive approach of institutional innovation through collective asset restructuring, elevating the prominence of resources, self-development, and maximizing returns on resource appreciation, truly stands out.

2.1 Transcending the Zero-Sum Game: How to Fill Two Needs with One Deed

In Zhanqi Village's entrepreneurial revival of the collective economy, the 2003 transformation of township enterprises emerges as a beacon of progress. By delineating the rights to subterranean and surface realms during the transactional process, the village firmly grasped the reins of its development.

Systemic transformation derives from the convergence of supply and demand, wherein the erosion of collective resource rights and interests became a fundamental impetus for adapting operational structures. Viewing land as a multifaceted commodity, distinct layers of prices manifest in myriad forms of "rent." During the collective era, the collective enterprise's total rent value was internalized and equitably distributed among all members. However, the subsequent era of shareholding saw a silent partitioning and appropriation of rent value, propelled by deteriorating market conditions and the institutional allure of privatization. Alas, this spawned opportunistic tendencies among enterprise operators, gradually dwindling the annual dividends received by the collective. In the late 1990s, enterprise employees were offered a discounted opportunity to acquire 40% ownership, leading to instances where some operators disavowed the collective land ownership, absolving themselves from land rent obligations, asserting statements such as, "The enterprise is my personal asset. If I manage it well, your (the collective's) investment of

[6] "Jinghua Times. Xi Jinping: Cannot Undermine Collective Ownership of Rural Land" [EB/OL]. (2016-04-29) [2021-01-21]. http://m.cnr.cn/news/20160429/t20160429_522018106.html.

50,000 yuan will be duly returned." Moreover, despite the theoretical efficacy of the shareholding model as a resource allocation mechanism, its implementation costs remain exorbitant within the unique socioeconomic fabric of rural communities. The incongruity between the superstructure and economic foundation fostered a milieu of blurred ownership, semi-private and semi-public realms, and inadequate oversight. These predicaments reflect the objective consequences of institutional disharmony, as confirmed by subsequent interviews: "The emergence of such behavior among operators is quite ordinary. In our village, the collapse of enterprises was deemed a normal occurrence. Given the operators' advanced age and limited education, it is unrealistic to expect them to adopt modern management ideologies. If we do not address this issue promptly, the enterprises will inevitably perish." Consequently, the impetus to transcend the zero state stems from both subjective desires and objective laws.

Transactional endeavors commence at the genesis of resource demarcation, and the collective's retention of partial ownership over the enterprises becomes a vital prerequisite for savoring the "dual delights." First and foremost, the five enterprises participating in the restructuring were established during the collective era, rooted in agricultural accumulation or village-operated enterprise funds. They were inherently borne from collective origins and embodied the essence of collective enterprises. Since 1994, the village enterprise's operating model transitioned into a share cooperative system under the unified leadership of Chengdu Jifeng Industrial Corporation. Each factory functioned autonomously, and the collective received a 50% share dividend. Despite characterizing this period as a nadir amidst macroeconomic crises and the "phoenix's downfall" amid industrial competition, the collective retained certain prerogatives such as collecting rent for fixed assets like factories and land, irrespective of the business's profitability. This norm endured (refer to Table 1), preserving the collective's traditional strengths, resource endowments, and institutional bedrock. It endured, undeterred, albeit diminishing in scope. In the ensuing game with enterprise operators, this foundation laid the groundwork for the collective to reclaim a dominant position and attain a "phoenix-like rebirth." In contrast to numerous contemporaneous collective enterprises, burdened by regional disparities and the onus of urban–rural dichotomies, leading to debt-laden operations and eventual embezzlement of collective assets through related-party transactions, these enterprises ceased to exist entirely. Thus,

Table 1 Shareholding reform period—collective dividends and management fees, Unit: 10,000 yuan. *Data source* Zhanqi Village Archives, Chengdu Jifeng Industrial Corporation Profit Distribution Plan (1995–2003)

	19954E	*19964E*	*19974E*	*19984E*	*19994E*	*20004E*	*20014E*	*20024E*	*20034E*
Share dividends	19.21	22.49	17.57	15.59	21.77	16.18	8.43	5.89	14.75
Pay management fees	9.95	12.80	9.74	6.35	8.95	9.34	6.90	7.52	6.12

the collective economy was reduced to an ephemeral concept, bereft of substance. How then could it propel village development?

The process of trade unfolds amidst the contrasting forces of negotiation power and fluctuating prices, replete with the dynamics of game theory, conflict, interaction, and choice. Embedded within this tapestry are the objective realities of transaction costs, which invariably influence the manner in which exchanges are conducted.

Back in late 2002, the village collective astutely engaged the services of esteemed professors from Southwest University of Finance and Economics. Together, they rallied factory managers, accountants, sales personnel, village officials, and town leaders for comprehensive deliberations on matters pertaining to property rights and economic development within the realm of the share cooperative system. These discussions sought to disseminate vital knowledge surrounding the intricacies of operating rights and ownership. Throughout this process, the inherent tensions became evident. Operators and the collective organization alike had recognized the various deficiencies present within the share cooperative system. Discrepancies in matters of enterprise rights attribution and share allocation remained unresolved. The collective assets belonged to all villagers, with the village collective acting as their custodian and leasing the assets to operators. In theory, the separation of ownership, contracting, and operational rights was imperative. However, the accumulation of collective assets differed from the collective land, which was based on natural member rights. The growth of assets necessitated continuous injections of capital and the expertise of skilled human capital to ensure successful operations and management. This cumulative effort became the crux of the debate surrounding the necessity of rewarding operators with shares. Furthermore, the composition of the board of directors for Jifeng Industrial Corporation, entrusted with safeguarding collective interests, faced the challenge of securing favorable reforms, as only two out of five members represented the collective. Faced with this predicament, circumventing the board of directors and acquiring individual employee shares to secure a substantial collective stake appeared as a more viable option. According to the provisions stipulated in the Company Law of the People's Republic of China, internal transfer of corporate equity was permissible. Acquiring shares dispersed among employees provided an advantageous position for the collective in terms of stock ownership. The competitive bidding for collective shares aligned seamlessly with shareholders' innate pursuit of potential returns. By March 2003, Zhanqi had successfully reclaimed shares from Xianfeng Machine Brick Factory employees at a rate of 1.5 yuan per share. Similarly, in May 2004, shares from Xaifeng Brewing Factory employees were reclaimed at a rate of 1 yuan per share. The commitment to maintain a connection with the village employees, regardless of contracting parties, solidified bonds while providing a measure of reward to the original operators.

Having laid the groundwork and made preparations, the true expression of resource rights and interests lay within the transaction process itself, with its diverse treatment of resources based on their unique attributes. Zhanqi Village's pivotal mechanism rested upon two pillars: First, leveraging time as a strategic move, capitalizing on negotiation timing to solidify its sovereign position. Second, employing multiple games to mitigate risks and prevent dissipation of rent-seeking opportunities.

Leveraging time operated as a strategic asymmetrical information game. After conducting a thorough inventory and disclosing the accounts of various factory assets, liquid assets such as raw materials, semi-finished products, and finished goods were auctioned off. The lessees were required to make a lump-sum payment equal to the purchasing capital. These liquid assets could sustain normal operations for a period ranging from 2 to 3 years at minimum and around 11 years at maximum.[7] This direct conversion into cash yielded a sum of 4.2 million yuan, thus earning its moniker as "leveraging time." The approach to handling liquid assets

[7] Source: Interviews with Gao Demin and Luo Zunrong, June 9, 2019.

involved internal negotiations on pricing within the village, followed by an open bidding process. The collective wielded the power to establish rules governing the auction of liquid assets. With incomplete information at their disposal, the collective could preemptively capture the attendant value of surface rights.

Allow me to briefly recount the auction process for Xianfeng Machine Brick Factory and Huifu Douban Factory, exemplifying the astute and highly strategic nature of these negotiations. After due deliberation, the pricing for red bricks at Xianfeng Machine Brick Factory settled at 0.1 yuan per piece, while water clay garnered a valuation of 0.08 yuan. The bidding procedure unfolded as follows: Each bidder deposited 5000 yuan, non-refundable for the triumphant bidder yet returned to unsuccessful ones. The opening bid stood at 40,000 yuan, with increments of 1000 yuan for subsequent bids.[8] The auction proceeded publicly, culminating in a final transaction of 61,000 yuan. Prior to the auction of raw materials at Huifu Douban Factory, the collective convened to determine a pricing framework. Minutes from the April 27 meeting reveal that the factory's inventory stood at 644,900 yuan. It was unanimously decided to prioritize the needs of Wang Jianhui (王建辉), offering a preferential price of 600,000 yuan. However, Wang Jianhui expressed reluctance to participate if prices exceeded this threshold. Subsequently, the members engaged in fruitful discussions concerning the starting price and potential reductions. The resulting proposal unfolded as follows: First, set the bidding price at 645,000 yuan. If there are bids, the highest bidder prevails. Should no bids materialize, reduce the price by 100,000 yuan to 545,000 yuan, giving priority once again to Wang Jianhui. Should Wang Jianhui decline, proceed with a fresh round of bidding. If bids emerge, the highest bidder prevails. If not, reassess the situation. Second, establish a minimum bid price of 601,000 yuan. The final decision crystalized as follows: "Set the base price at 645,000 yuan. If no one desires it, reduce the price by increments of 10,000 yuan until satisfied. Each reduction shall prioritize Wang Jianhui. If still unclaimed, the company shall reclaim it." A day later, the auction plan was publicly announced, and the bidding conference for Huifu Douban Factory convened on April 30. Each bidder deposited 10,000 yuan, with 645,000 yuan serving as the starting price. Yang Kui

[8] Source: Meeting minutes of Zhanqi Village, April 9, 2003.

emerged as the triumphant bidder. Contracts were signed on the spot, with the remaining balance to be settled within three days.

Through this intricate dance, the collective devised a profit structure characterized by "rent and rewards." Firstly, fixed assets were monetized through rentals. Xianfeng Machine Brick Factory adhered to the original agreement regarding land fees, while Huifu Douban Factory paid an annual rental fee of 50,000 yuan, in addition to land fees. The Compound Fertilizer Factory contributed an annual rent of 80,000 yuan (inclusive of land rent). Secondly, the utilization of liquid assets proved advantageous. The collective procured a one-time influx of cash amounting to 4.2 million yuan through the auctioning of liquid assets, while contractual agreements safeguarded the preservation of collective assets. By extending these newfound financial resources through loans, the collective generated additional income in the form of interest.

"Multiple games" entailed charging rent for fixed assets such as land, buildings, and machinery, thereby reflecting the owner's benefits. Conversely, the pricing of mobile assets such as raw materials and brand assets was conducted separately. This one-time transaction disentangled them from fixed assets, achieving equilibrium between returns and risks while maximizing the value of surface and underground rights. This comprehensive approach truly embodied resource rights and interests. It is worth noting that prior to this endeavor, the village had garnered an annual fixed rental income of 285,000 yuan. By engaging in multiple transactions, they were able to secure 320,000 yuan solely through leasing factory buildings and land, akin to obtaining an "empty shell." Under the leasing system, village-run enterprises became risk-free assets, relieving the collective of the burdens associated with entrepreneurial risks. For instance, in June 2004, when the brick factory operator proposed constructing a glazed tile kiln at the factory entrance, the collective responded with a resolute stance: "We have no involvement in terms of investment or the project itself. You may lease it for as long as you wish, but upon expiry, demolition is mandatory." This starkly contrasted with previous concerns raised by certain operators regarding the collective's financial contributions. The dichotomy was striking: "Does the collective possess the necessary funds? If we need 500,000 yuan to purchase machinery for reforms, will the village contribute 250,000 yuan?" Such inquiries now paled in comparison, for the collective had emerged as the rightful beneficiary of its status as the resource owner. As one village resident eloquently stated, "Although our village does not boast substantial wealth, with fixed assets amounting to merely a few million yuan, it signifies the shared ownership of 1704 individuals from Zhanqi Village. It is not the possession of any individual contractor!" Additionally, lease contracts with each factory carried a duration of 3, 5, or 10 years, affording the collective the opportunity to adjust rental rates in response to fluctuating land values. This iterative game strategy ensured the preservation of long-term benefits. Following the initial foray into the market with construction land, the value of land for construction acquired the chance to mirror the rights and benefits enjoyed by urban land. The recent inspection by General Secretary Xi further bolstered the appreciation of land value. The floating rent system presented landowners with the opportunity to savor the benefits derived from the appreciation of land value due to socio-cultural factors. In this manner, they derived value from underground and surface income, forging a solid financial foundation that transitioned them from a dormant state to one of development. This duality of benefits is akin to partaking in a sumptuous multiple gains, as rent becomes concentrated.

Yet, Zhanqi Village's endeavors are not an isolated tale of rarity. An equally fascinating narrative unfolded in 2001, as the Chongqing model emerged to tackle the issue of non-performing loans in banks. Under the guidance of Chongqing Yufu Holdings Group Co., Ltd., a subsidiary of the Chongqing State-Owned Assets Supervision and Administration Commission, banks underwent restructuring and subsequent listing. Through this process, a single asset underwent three successful sales, resulting in multiple increments of value appreciation. Huang Qifan (黄奇帆) dubbed this triumphant phenomenon the "triple gains from one act."

2.2 *Resonating Echoes of Shared Gains*

The essence of sharing incremental gains derived from resource valorization lies in the embodiment of resource rights and interests. Li Shili, the former secretary, succinctly described this approach: "With 4.2 million yuan, we had two options: immediate distribution or employing it as the seed capital for Zhanqi Village's renewed development. We gathered the masses to discuss both avenues, and if I had proceeded as such, 90% of the people would have readily accepted distribution—a plausible scenario.

However, lacking a clear solution, we found ourselves compelled to seek knowledge and guidance from external sources."[9]

While the benefits of enterprise restructuring may not have translated into an immediate surge of personal wealth for the villagers, they did contribute to the overall welfare of the village, ensuring sustainable development and establishing an institutional framework for ecological transformation. Collective assets belonged to the entire village community, exemplifying the social distribution of gains. This arrangement not only served the imperative of safeguarding owners' rights to self-development but also harnessed the organizational potential of capital, facilitating public governance and fostering reorganization. By transcending the confines of time and space, the impact of institutional benefits became more remarkable and enduring.

Primarily, the cash obtained from raw material auctions bolstered the collective assets, offering much-needed relief to the financial strains of collective enterprises and fostering a symbiotic ecosystem between the village and its businesses. Notably, perusing post-restructuring meeting materials reveals the collective's provision of loan support to numerous enterprise operators. By lending the cash at an annual interest rate of 10%, the village secured risk-free returns. A summary of some loans is outlined in Table 2.

Furthermore, a portion of the accrued gains was allocated to village accumulation, funding public services, and supporting social-cultural

Table 2 Village loan status after 2003

Date	*Reason for borrowing*
2004.02.21	Yang Kaifu borrowed 100,000 yuan a year with a monthly interest of 6%
2004.03.12	Yang Kui borrowed 100,000 yuan, and the interest was paid as usual
2004.03.26	The steel casting factory borrowed money, and the 300,000 yuan acceptance bill was collateral
2005.01.06	Yang Kaiff borrowed 100,000 yuan to purchase raw materials for production
	Xianfeng Brewing Factory borrowed 200,000 yuan to pay employees (short-term loan, if there is money to pay wages, it will not borrow money)

[9] Source: Interview record of Li Shili on June 7, 2019.

endeavors. This infusion enriched the spiritual and cultural lives of the villagers while propelling the integration of organizations, serving as the bedrock for spatial reconstruction and social harmony. Concurrent with the near-completion of enterprise restructuring, the collective embarked on land consolidation experiments, road construction, ditch maintenance, and land reclamation. Gradually progressing from small-scale trials to the establishment of professional cooperatives, the collective played a pivotal role in addressing local farmers' employment concerns and mitigating conflicts. In 2004, the Village Committee adopted resolutions such as "the village assumes all agricultural taxes, water fees, and medical insurance costs" and "each child in our village receives a subsidy of 30 yuan per semester, while kindergarten fees for our village children are 20 yuan lower than those for children from other villages."[10] In 2006, Zhanqi Village proactively embraced the "University + Party Branch + Farmers" initiative spearheaded by the County Party Committee Propaganda Department. Subsequently, the village initiated reforms in public services and social management, establishing a cultural hub, installing fitness equipment, and cultivating a diverse range of cultural activity groups. Selected expenditures are itemized in Table 3. Consequently, Zhanqi Village's prominence soared, affording it tangible benefits stemming from various pioneering endeavors and exceptional achievements. Undeniably, small-scale peasant opportunism poses a common obstacle to mobilizing villagers in present times. However, Zhanqi Village artfully neutralized this menace by proffering an expectation of shared benefits, deftly deploying social integration. Throughout this journey, the villagers' well-being flourished while the village organization's mobilization capabilities continually strengthened.

Sustaining the infusion of support into collective enterprises and facilitating socialized services necessitates a substantial capital threshold. Hence, Zhanqi Village's manifold accomplishments in ecological competition trace back to the foundation laid by enterprise restructuring. Just as a shallow source runs dry prematurely, achieving lofty heights proves elusive without a solid groundwork to build upon.

[10] Excerpted from the meeting records of Zhanqi Village Committee on April 7, 2004, and July 9, 2004.

Table 3 Detailed breakdown of social and cultural expenditures in Zhanqi Village in 2006. *Source* Financial records for 2006, released in March 2007 by Zhanqi Village Committee

Items	*Amount (yuan)*
Subsidies for brewery retirees	1630
Subsidized kindergarten	960
Expenditures on "Cultural Yard" and village infrastructure construction	677,456.70
Costumes and equipment for the art team	6022
New Year's greetings to the veterans and the 80-year-old man	4979.40
Pay "holiday allowance" to members, 40 yuan per person	65,840
Medical insurance (two years)	32,190
Expenses for the "College Students Entering Farmhouses" activity	38,717.14
Compulsory blood donation subsidy	640
Order newspapers and magazines	1034

3 Mechanisms for Embodying Spatial Resource Rights and Interests in the New Era

3.1 Rural "Peril" and "Opportunity" from a Macro Perspective

> Though rural areas may yield slender profits, their returns remain steady in the long run, as the era of exorbitant real estate gains has waned. Hence, rural resources are boundless.
> As players in the real estate game, we hold an unyielding fondness for land. Alas, urban resources dwindle by the day, leaving rural regions to hold the future of land resources.
> Source: Field research records, October 3–5, 2019.

Following the East Asian financial storm, China embarked on nationwide investment-driven initiatives, laying the foundation for comprehensive infrastructure development. Amid a global excess of capital, an influx of Western industrial investments poured in, catapulting China to the forefront as an industrial capital powerhouse in the first decade of the twenty-first century. The surge of trade, currency circulation, and industrial, commercial, and financial capital reached a tipping point of saturation and overflow, culminating in three formidable "surpluses." Scholars' calculations reveal a persistent decline in the growth rate of national fixed asset investments since 2009, accompanied by a dwindling return on capital, indicating an overabundance of urban investment.[11] As the aforementioned interviews elucidate, the lure of real estate bubbles and financial saturation compels business capital to search for novel investment domains, ultimately presenting rural landscapes as a "blue ocean" ripe for capitalizing on surplus crisis. After accomplishing their historical duty of distorting prices to alleviate the costs of industrialization and urbanization, rural elements have seized the opportunity for market-driven exploration and value augmentation by external capital. Simultaneously, the burgeoning middle class, with their appetite for green, secure consumption, aligns seamlessly with the multifarious agriculture and diverse civilization inherent in rural settings.[12] Consequently, rural spaces, imbued with natural and cultural panoramas, assume the mantle of scarce resources that possess economic worth and developmental viability—an embodiment of rural "opportunity."

However, rural spatial resources predominantly reside within the realms of land, serving as long-standing pillars of agricultural production. Given their characteristics as non-excludable and non-competitive public goods, these resources defy singular valuation and computation. Consequently, the development of rural resources frequently engenders a facade of developer-driven prosperity, wherein commercial capital tends to reimburse the cost of transforming agricultural land for commercial purposes at agricultural price levels. This often results in the resource owners' aggregate absolute rent not displaying a conspicuous increase. Moreover, the consequences may entail an exacerbation of wealth disparities and an abrupt escalation in prices. A multitude of villages, lured by the allure of immediate income, fall into the quagmire of underdeveloped realms, relinquishing the rights to their net land through auctions or market sales, thereby exchanging the potential for reserve resource development with a one-time windfall. Pricing resources and equitably

[11] Tang Li, Liu Yahui, Dong Xiaodan. Analysis of Innovative Mechanisms in Land Ownership and Urban Dwellers' Return to the Countryside[J]. Journal of Fujian Agriculture and Forestry University (Philosophy and Social Sciences Edition), 2018, 21(2): 1–5.

[12] Wen Tiejun, Liu Yahui, Zhang Zhen. Transformation of Agriculture, Village, and Farmers under the Ecological Civilization Strategy[J]. Journal of National School of Administration, 2018(1): 40–46,149.

distributing benefits emerge as novel trials in the realm of rural spatial resource development.

How does the trend of real estate developers venturing into rural domains harmonize with the mechanism for realizing rural resource rights and interests? With consideration for the holistic and indivisible nature of spatial resources, coupled with the prevailing collective land ownership system in rural regions, it becomes paramount to acknowledge rural collective economic organizations as the custodians of property rights. By consolidating and pricing comprehensive spatial resources, and subsequently introducing external investors through methods like land equity participation, diverse development can be stimulated, ensuring that village members partake in the augmented returns of multifaceted transformation.[13] Only then can an all-encompassing growth environment be fostered. Subsequent exploration will delve into the partnership between Zhanqi Village and the pioneering external investor, Mama Farm.

3.2 *Strategic Partnerships Unleash a Ripple Effect*

Mama Farm, backed by Chengdu Fifth Season Investment Co., embarked on its construction journey in 2011 and swiftly bloomed in 2012. Its essence lies in the cultivation of imaginative agriculture and the allure of agritourism, catering to diverse consumer demands like weddings, training, vacation getaways, and recreational pursuits. With a workforce exceeding 100 individuals, this agricultural haven sprawls across a sprawling expanse of 389.82 acres. Within this domain, 371.52 acres are devoted to agricultural and construction purposes, while the remaining 18.3 acres encompass channels, roads, and riverbanks. The particulars of rental arrangements can be found in Table 4.

In harmony with the cooperative, the farm adopted a "minimum payment + profit sharing" paradigm for agricultural land. This translated into a guaranteed annual income of 1200 yuan per acre, affording villagers a monthly subsidy of 100 yuan specifically designated for grain. This entitlement shields them from operational risks while reaping the rewards. When the year concludes, a surplus dividend, assessed by a neutral third-party evaluation agency based on the company's profitability,

[13] Tang Li, Liu Yahui, Dong Xiaodan, Wen Tiejun. Establishing and Perfecting the Pricing System for Rural Spatial Resources to Avert "Latent Deprivation" in Rural Areas[J]. Economic Guide, 2019(3): 76–78.

Table 4 Rental payments at mama farm[14]

Items	*Rent*
Agricultural land	The annual rent is 1600 yuan/mu, rising by 5% every five years. Regardless of profit or loss, a guaranteed income of 1200 yuan/mu per year is guaranteed. The remaining part (400 yuan/mu per year) is invested in shares, accounting for 5% of the shares, and enjoys premium dividends
Construction land	The annual rent is 2800 yuan/mu, rising by 5% every five years; the transfer fee for collective profit-oriented construction land use rights is 500,000 yuan/mu per year

is amassed. After an appropriate portion is reserved by the vegetable professional cooperative, the remaining sum is distributed equally among its members. This symbiotic risk-reward scenario affords all villagers an opportunity to partake in the benefits derived from the development of the tertiary industry. Notably, the initial agreement stipulated that construction could commence only upon completion of rental payments, ensuring the avoidance of future payment disputes.

As for the construction land, a lease arrangement was instituted, wherein the enterprise assumes responsibility for rental remittance and operational usage of the land surface, while underground ownership rights remain with the village collective. To obtain usage rights for the 40-year term, the enterprise procures land use rights registration and a collective construction land use permit, involving a payment of 500,000 yuan per acre as a construction land transfer fee. This grants the enterprise economic privileges such as transfer, rental, and mortgage of usage rights. At the expiration of the contractual period, the collective retains the right to reclaim the land's usage without remuneration. This duality allows the collective to harness rental income from surface rights while preserving its position as the rightful owner of the subterranean domain. Akin to a delectable feast for the village, this arrangement bears semblance to the proverbial "having one's cake and eating it too" following the transformation of the leasing system by the enterprise. Testimony from a village

[14] Based on transcripts compiled from interviews with the project leader conducted on October 3, 2019. During these conversations, it was noted that both agricultural and construction land rents were set according to the grain market prices announced each September 30th, constituting the obligatory minimum rental payments. Moreover, a proportion of the profits was allocated to villager dividends.

resident provides explicit insight into the village collective's rationale in managing resource rights.

> Having sold all the land, what lies ahead for us? Where do we find our sustenance? Where is the soil that defines our existence? Our identity as farmers, be it modern or the venerable old guard, necessitates a connection to the land. This immutable truth permeates our thoughts. Therefore, the land within our village shall remain unsold, though the rights to its usage are entrusted to the enterprise, while ownership belongs to the village itself. We shall not relinquish complete control of the village's assets, nor the assets of our 1700-strong populace, to the enterprise's management. Such a perilous venture bears excessive risk.[15]

Following the settlement of Mama Farm, its vibrant lavender fields kindled an exponential rise in popularity. The enterprise further endeavored to establish an exhibition area for space vegetables, an agricultural flagship store, and more. As agricultural investments typically yield meager returns with prolonged recovery periods, the company initially incurred substantial learning costs. Nevertheless, as the village's pioneering integrated tertiary industry venture, Mama Farm elicited positive external effects by transforming the village's spatial landscape. Emphasizing tourism, this industry naturally necessitates the preservation of the overall environment. Many visitors expressed discontent with the lingering odor emanating from nearby foundries, tarnishing their tourism experience. Coupled with the implementation of water source protection policies, the village collective's valorous decision to halt foundry and fertilizer plant operations materialized—a symbolic farewell to an era of unsophisticated industrial development. Simultaneously, Mama Farm emerged as an irresistible magnet, drawing blueberry farms, strawberry farms, and ecological agriculture projects. These enterprises mutually partake in the village's tourism resources, fostering a complementary and diversified range of industries. Consequently, this rich tapestry enhances the scenic allure and elevates the experiential worth, enabling Zhanqi Village to seamlessly transition into a bastion of "industrial village with agricultural characteristics." Mama Farm thus bore the ecological transformation costs for the village, reaping manifold benefits. By transferring the risks

[15] Based on transcripts compiled from interviews with villagers conducted on October 5, 2019.

to external investors, the collective steadily shares the remaining profits, thus cementing Mama Farm's status as a strategic partner.

3.3 *Aggregation of Elements as Prerequisite and Organizational Integration as the Key*

> "Once the cooperative was established and residents were resettled, he used the surplus land that had been sorted out for investment promotion."
> The prerequisite for land valuation and stock participation in the company is that we are a cooperative. The village's land has already been included, so it's not about negotiating land with each household. When the investor is making an investment, they are least willing to deal with villagers.
> I (referring to the company) asked him (Secretary Gao Demin) about some policies, and he said he could fulfill all of them. Firstly, I said I don't want to deal with villagers because it's too laborious... He said, 'We have a cooperative there, it has already been established.' So he brought me here. 'Our land is simple, just sign an agreement with the village, and we can give it to you tomorrow.'
> Source: Field research records of the project team from October 3 to 5, 2019.

As mentioned in the above interview records, the advantage of Zhanqi Village in dialogue with external capital lies in its organization and scale. The cooperative, with the endorsement of the village collective, has become an important platform for absorbing agricultural land within the village for circulation and operation. External capital can directly connect with the cooperative, obtaining a sizable land area and greatly reducing transaction costs in negotiations.

This leads to an important foundational mechanism in the ecological competition of the new era, which is often overlooked but crucial for the realization of resource rights and interests: the structural stickiness of the overall ecological spatial resources and the contradiction between fragmented land operated by small-scale farmers and the spatial range of land. This situation poses high transaction costs for any organization entering rural areas. To break through the institutional barriers of comprehensive ecological spatial resource integration, it is necessary to make organizational integration a prerequisite for element aggregation and spatial reconstruction on a large scale. Looking back at the process of village reorganization, it also fills the time and space gap between enterprise restructuring and capital entering rural areas as discussed in this topic.

1. Aggregation and Integration of Spatial Resource Elements

Aggregation of elements is necessary to promote structural restructuring and functional optimization. The previous section briefly reviewed three stages: the initial concentration of Group 5 and Group 7, the establishment of cooperatives for unified circulation after "dismantling and rebuilding courtyards," and the overall integration. The "three-step approach" represents the practical realization of the village collective's concentration of land. The first step is the experiential starting point of breaking the scattered state of land. The traditional factors of personal relationships, trust, and acquaintances played an important role, and collective consciousness began to recover after undergoing "de-organization." The second step is the government's policy of scale operation, carrying funds to rural areas and promoting infrastructure improvement and cooperative establishment. The third step is the integration of residential land, which helped achieve a "risky leap" towards comprehensive land concentration. Through asset exchanges such as land-for-employment and land-for-social welfare, the various social functions attached to the land were untied. The collective has successfully transformed farmers into community residents and achieved the goal of concentrating 94% of agricultural land, gaining control over a sizable land area and thus dominating the development of comprehensive spatial resources.

After achieving the scale, organization, and centralization of elements and meeting the conditions for government-scale operation, various hardware facilities are built to support the entry of any enterprise without relocation costs. The required road facilities for daily operations are also basically met. The value of agricultural land in Zhanqi Village has become apparent. For example, the land rent was at least 800 yuan per mu in 2008, already double that of neighboring villages at the time[16]

[16] According to records of interviews conducted by project team members with the project leader on October 3, 2019: "Other villages haven't sorted out their land. Before the 2008 earthquake, the land rent in other villages was 400 yuan per mu, but in our Zhanqi Village, the minimum was already 800 yuan per mu. Why? We fixed all the roads

2. The Organization of Large Trading Entities

   The train raced with fervor, propelled solely by its determined engine. To unleash the potential of factor aggregation, a collective economic organization must serve as the conduit. This brings us to the crucial aspect of grassroots organizational development in Zhanqi Village. By fortifying these foundations, nurturing trust and esteem within the villagers, we foster a mechanism of "strong credibility, strong expectations, and strong mobilization." This, in turn, reduces transaction uncertainties, empowering the novel collective economic organization, guided by Party principles, to act as the pivotal force in harmonizing village resources.

In early 2018, during his visit to Zhanqi Village, General Secretary Xi Jinping spoke heartfelt words, proclaiming himself as a diligent steward of the people, dedicated to their service. This sincere sentiment epitomizes the historical backdrop of Zhanqi Village, where party members and cadres relentlessly advance, each carrying a banner. The role of the new collective economic organization, steered by Party principles, in the attainment of rural resource rights and interests is primarily characterized by its close connection to the masses, fostering an environment of constructive criticism and self-reflection, and setting a leading example. These noble virtues foster a new structure, mitigating transaction costs incurred during land concentration and overcoming the pervasive predicament of elite exploitation in resource distribution.

Foremost, Zhanqi Village imposes stringent demands on its leadership, ensuring they exemplify virtue while adamantly avoiding misconduct. They adhere to the principle of “no trivial matter escaping the community’s attention, no significant issue escaping the village’s purview.” Land concentration stands as a paramount concern in the village’s development. From the inception of small-scale pilot projects, village cadres, party members, and village representatives convene numerous meetings to address conflicts arising during the concentration process. Each parcel of land is assigned to responsible individuals with clearly defined deadlines, regular progress reports, and a mandate for timely rectification. In 2003, during the land allocation conference, concerns arose among

around the entire village, so big vehicles can enter, and they loaded vegetables on the side of the road.”

the masses regarding corrupt officials. In response, the village enacted a financial management protocol, clarifying the work objectives of party members and cadres: "Certain party members and representatives shirk their responsibilities, while others contribute significantly. As representatives of the Party, it is our duty to lead, ensuring all tasks are accomplished through the joint efforts of party members and village cadres. The 5th, 7th, and 9th communities shall take the initial steps in land allocation, while the other communities continue their work." To rectify misconduct observed among a few party member team leaders who engaged in unauthorized land leasing, which hindered the realization of the village's land concentration plan, the branch leadership embarked on an educational campaign, emphasizing the paramount importance of "subordination to the organization, majority rule, adherence to the hierarchical structure, and the Party's unwavering allegiance to the central leadership." Consequently, party members and cadres experienced a paradigm shift, enhancing their ideological stance.[17] In 2007, when the new community construction demanded a 40% prepayment, they called for the village's "two committees" to lead by example, followed by production team leaders and party group leaders, and finally, the party members themselves. In 2008, Zhanqi Village was designated as a pilot village for "innovative rural grassroots governance mechanisms," with party members and the masses contributing a special party fee of 16,800 yuan to support post-disaster reconstruction efforts.[18] During the Lavender Festival organized by Mama Farm, despite the influx of tourists, drawn by Chengdu's "Provence" moniker, the basic infrastructure remained incomplete, straining its limited capacity. Nonetheless, all staff and party members ardently engaged in upholding order, hosting over 400,000 visitors throughout the Lavender Festival.

Moreover, Zhanqi Village skillfully unites diverse forces, rallying university students and veterans to partake in community initiatives while fostering an environment of constructive criticism and self-reflection within the Party. In early 2004, as the leadership team conducted their annual work assessment, they acknowledged their inadequate grasp of policies and the lingering impact of unresolved land allocation issues.

[17] Source: Interview record of Gao Demin on December 26, 2019.

[18] (Source: "Zhanqi Village 2008 Target Task Completion and Year-end Summary" archived in the Zhanqi Village Archives.

Subsequently, they established clear targets for the upcoming year. In May 2006, following the successful "University + Party Branch + Farmers" collaboration, the village initiated an extensive discussion, "What should the village's 'two committees' do? How should party members and villagers contribute?" Group leaders pinpointed deficiencies in the organizational prowess of village cadres, emphasizing the need to sustain the fervor for work. They stressed punctuality, particularly during meetings, warning against empty rhetoric and self-serving agendas. They demanded unity and coordination, emphasizing the human-centric approach that should permeate all endeavors. They seized the opportunity to fortify the ideological fabric of party members and the masses, drawing inspiration from the leadership of the propaganda department and the town party committee and government. They emphasized the necessity of engaging intimately with each household, delving deep into the lives of the masses. They concluded by affirming the profound bond forged between students and farmers during this endeavor, urging the village to continue hosting university student activities, enriching their lives with diverse experiences. During the symposium on Army Day in 2008, several veterans voiced their opinions, highlighting existing issues in village affairs and offering personal suggestions. Mr. Yu Changfu passionately expressed how veterans brought the military's ethos back to the countryside, dutifully executing party policies. However, he acknowledged economic shortcomings, particularly concerning concentrated living, where diverse construction units caused delays in worker wages, undermining policy effectiveness. Mr. Yang, drawing upon their military training and education, emphasized the imperative of making substantial contributions to local economic development, supporting village initiatives, and serving as exemplars for their fellow villagers.[19] This vibrant interaction among diverse groups fortifies the sense of belonging and responsibility among village members, ensuring that party members consistently engage in self-reflection and vigorous action. In 2003, a group member posted a notice at the village committee office, exposing the leader's tardiness in disclosing financial accounts. The village promptly organized party members, cadres, and representatives to conduct an investigation, demanding that the results be made public. The village established a regulation mandating timely financial transparency, safeguarding every

[19] Source: Minutes of Zhanqi Village Committee Meetings, 2003–2013, archived in the Zhanqi Village Archives.

villager's right to information and oversight. Following the centralized living arrangement in 2009, to ensure uninterrupted signal connectivity, the village planned to erect additional mobile signal towers. Despite several obstacles encountered during site selection, including concerns from some villagers regarding potential health risks from radiation, a few party members were also influenced. The village invited experts to dispel doubts, urging party members to lead the charge in persuading the masses. Through diligent efforts, a party member liaised with several households, ultimately resolving the impasse surrounding the tower's construction. The time-honored tradition of party members actively engaging with the masses endures to this day. As the secretary aptly remarked, "The Party branch assumes an all-encompassing, absolute leadership role. Party members silently work behind the scenes, while the village committee exudes a heartfelt human touch, eschewing the mere dissemination of hollow propaganda. It's all about substance." Thus, a united force composed of the party, government, military, civilians, and academics collaboratively orchestrates grassroots governance, ensuring congruity between space, resources, and landscapes, while establishing an elevated platform for discourse with external capital.

In light of the aforementioned, factors serve as the guiding principle, while organization represents the ultimate objective. By placing due emphasis on organizational construction and facilitating factor integration, the guiding principles and ultimate objectives converge harmoniously. Thus, Zhanqi Village triumphs over the inherent challenges faced by ordinary villages, such as fragmented distribution of land and spatial resources, effectively realizing resource rights and benefits throughout the process of capital infusion into rural realms.

4 Conclusion

The realization and preservation of resource rights and interests embody the crucial essence of a village's self-development. It encompasses the pricing of resources and the equitable distribution of accrued benefits. This study centered around the restructuring of the township enterprises and the integration of real estate in the rural landscape, endeavors to unearth a viable path by immersing itself in the village's prevailing circumstances. Whether through the reformation of township enterprises or the resultant distribution pattern of capital influx, both endeavors invariably unfold within the overarching framework of the collective village economy, underscoring the imperative need to cultivate a burgeoning novel collective economic model. Every village aspiring to negotiate from a position of strength during the process of capital infusion must perforce undertake a comprehensive restructuring, a forging of alliances aimed at capitalizing on the increasingly scarce spatial resources. Zhanqi Village's shining exemplar lies in the astute monetization of collective assets, realized through the ingenious approach to fill two needs with one deed. Guided by the core socialist value of "equality," Zhanqi Village accomplishes the socially conscious redistribution of gains, a key prelude to the consolidation of spatial resources. Simultaneously, leveraging social leverage, it harnesses social capital and capitalizes on collective economic organizations, thus enticing fresh resources, and in turn, nurturing an organic transition towards ecological transformation, with the dividends of tertiary industry development shared equitably among village members. Zhanqi Village, with its trailblazing institutional innovations synchronized with macro policies, successfully assumes the vanguard, an inspiration to emulate.

CHAPTER 19

Spatial Equity—China's Distinctive Approach to Resource Allocation and Income Distribution at the Grassroots Level

1 Background

Ever since the 18th National Congress of the Communist Party of China, our nation has embarked upon a strategic transformation towards an era of ecological civilization. The 19th National Congress of the CPC introduced the "Rural Revitalization" strategy, emphasizing the need to establish a grassroots governance system that combines autonomy, rule of law, and moral governance. The Fourth Plenary Session of the 19th CPC Central Committee further stressed the importance of "adhering to and improving the system of ecological civilization." In the midst of the profound integration of urban and rural areas, it becomes imperative to lead the way while also exploring innovative approaches. This necessitates breaking away from the traditional reliance on village's "two committees" and the limited mindset of local villagers, and instead embracing green ecological industries alongside urban dwellers venturing into the countryside. By incorporating a broader spectrum of social forces, we can drive innovation in grassroots governance, ensuring that the benefits of resource capital are not monopolized by large corporations but rather shared among various stakeholders. In doing so, we simultaneously achieve the economic objectives of rural industrial development and the social goals of promoting the well-being of farmers, fostering the harmonious and comprehensive development of rural communities.

In this context, "social enterprises" emerge as a unique organizational model that strives to maximize overall social benefits. These enterprises

© Peking University Press 2024
X. Dong, *Zhanqi Village Over Fifty Years*,
https://doi.org/10.1007/978-981-97-5426-7_19

highlight the application of market mechanisms and business strategies to integrate social resources, develop ecological economies, and tackle societal challenges. Within China's strategic transformation towards ecological civilization in the modern era, this organizational framework holds significant value. Employing social enterprises within rural communities as a means to engage diverse external investment entities, promote socialized agriculture, and enhance village governance represents a promising avenue for effective organizational innovation in rural industrial development. This approach not only bridges the gap between urban and rural integration but also facilitates the participation of diverse social entities, thereby propelling the collective and prosperous development of various economic components. By embracing social enterprises as a conduit for inclusive production methods, we surpass the limitations of traditional rural societies and unlock their potential for agricultural strength, scenic rural landscapes, and flourishing farmers. Consequently, social enterprises emerge as a vital component of "effective governance" and a pivotal innovative direction within the rural revitalization strategy, facilitating the construction of new collective economic frameworks and private enterprises.

In contrast to other nations worldwide, China's urban and rural landscapes boast staggering scales and proportions. This realization underscores the necessity for our nation to address social governance challenges through indigenous experiences, as opposed to emulating foreign solutions. Thus, the exploration of social enterprises in China's rural regions demands our unwavering attention. Drawing inspiration from the exemplary case of Zhanqi Village, we can examine the development model anchored in collective economy and rural collective ownership, unveiling an important trajectory for rural social enterprises to fulfill the dual objectives of economic progress and social advancement.

2 Social Enterprises: Embracing Local Roots

Discussions surrounding "social enterprises" initially emerged in the West, and since the 1990s, this organizational form has swiftly gained ground, wielding its dual nature of social responsibility and economic viability to break the shackles of the Western capitalist welfare conundrum and address societal issues constructively. As the twenty-first century unfolded, theories and practical experiences of social enterprises gradually infiltrated China from foreign shores. However, due to disparate political and economic landscapes, the precise definition of social enterprises varies across nations. Presently, the prevailing notion of "social enterprise" hails from Western countries, with many certification standards also originating from the West. In contrast to their Western counterparts, Chinese scholars have engaged in relatively limited discussions regarding social enterprises, struggling to establish clear-cut characteristics for these ventures. The integration of China's national circumstances with the definition and categorization of social enterprises remains a matter of contention within academic circles, further compounded by the dearth of comprehensive research and organization regarding China's unique experiences with social enterprises, particularly in rural areas. Nonetheless, upon delving into history, it becomes evident that social enterprises are anything but "imported goods."

2.1 An Idyllic Tapestry in Rural China: Favors are More Important than Property

As the Fei Xiaotong elucidated, the fundamental unit of Chinese rural society is the village, wherein each village exists in isolation, separated by invisible barriers. Consequently, rural life embodies an intimate regional essence, encapsulating a society where people are born, live, and ultimately perish. Examining the blood and geographical ties in rural society, Fei posited, "In an intimate society governed by blood relations, commerce cannot thrive. This does not imply that transactions are absent in such a society, but rather that they are sustained through the exchange of personal affections—a reciprocal bestowal."[1] In these communities of familiarity, economic activities intertwine seamlessly with social endeavors due to the omnipresence of blood connections. Likewise, the esteemed Liang Shuming contended that traditional Chinese society, with its bedrock in the countryside, witnessed the emergence of all cultural and social organizations upon this rural foundation. Liang further maintained that the defining characteristic of this social structure lies in its ethical nucleus—ethics commencing within the family and extending into society at large. Thus, family relationships serve as the bedrock, subsequently expanding into extended familial connections and ultimately permeating the entirety of society. Consequently,

[1] Fei Xiaotong, From the Soil, Beijing: People's Publishing House, 2008.

in ancient times, families and clans were a microcosm of the broader social fabric. Within an ethical society, the union of husband and wife and the bond between parents and children becomes indivisible, transcending the division of property—a concept known as "shared wealth (共财之义)." However, acknowledging the inherent hierarchy within ethical emotions, practical considerations necessitate living separately, resulting in the inevitable limitation of communal wealth. Consequently, among siblings or close relatives, the notion of "dividing wealth (分财之义)" comes into play. For acquaintances, friends, and neighbors, sharing wealth becomes an act of camaraderie, a principle aptly known as "communal sharing (通财之义)." In principle, communal sharing entails an obligation for repayment, yet extending assistance without seeking reimbursement remains a prevailing norm, representing the broadest form of ethical relationships. To summarize, economic interdependence intertwines with mutual responsibility, where failure to adhere to these principles renders one a pariah in the community's discerning eyes. Moreover, the existence of communal resources such as ritual fields, benevolent institutions, and educational endeavors serve as shared assets within clans. Similarly, social granaries, benevolent storehouses, and communal fields become communal properties within rural communities, employed primarily for the upliftment of the destitute, bridging wealth disparities within the extended family, and bolstering education.[2]

It can be seen that traditional village communities have strong geographical limitations, with isolation between villages, each maintaining its isolated social circle, while within the village, it is considered a large family, governed by social ethics. Members within the village community need to support each other economically, or they may be accused of being unjust. This support is provided through communal property such as the "Yi Cang" (Justice Granary), "Zu Chan" (Clan Property), "Cun Xue" (Village School), and other shared resources to assist the impoverished, widowed, and poor, and to alleviate wealth disparities within the "extended family," as well as to provide educational assistance, among other things.

In his work "The Great Transformation: The Political and Economic Origins of Our Time," Karl Polányi argues that before the nineteenth century, human economic activities were embedded in society. At that

[2] Liang Shuming. Essentials of Chinese Culture[M]. Shanghai: Shanghai People's Publishing House, 2005.

time, economic activities were subservient to politics, religion, and social relationships, and were referred to as "ethical economies."[3] He uses Western Europe as an example, pointing out that until the late Middle Ages, various economic systems were organized based on principles of reciprocity, redistribution, and household economy, or a mixture of the three, with clear ethical implications. In contrast, in rural China, economic activities based on the foundation of small village communities can also be considered an ethical economy: in conditions of high resource scarcity, rural communities operate on a village level, where members must prioritize "human relationships over material wealth," help each other, integrate economic and social relationships, and pursue both economic and social goals to achieve sustainable development

2.2 Localized Social Enterprises in Modern China

In rural China, amidst limited resources, the humble farming families tread the path of ethical economics, achieving sustainable growth. This cherished social and cultural tradition serves as fertile ground for the sprouting of Chinese-style social enterprises. Unlike their Western counterparts, China's nascent enterprises do not draw a clear line between society and business, but rather fuse them together, employing the enterprise as a vessel for societal progress—a harmonious integration of economics and social values.

Following the Qing government's defeat in the cataclysmic Sino-Japanese War, a league of local luminaries, spurred by the urgency to repel imperialist forces, embarked on a quest for national salvation, birthing enterprises that sought to "industrialize the nation." The likes of Zhang Jian (张謇), founder of Nantong's Dah Sheng Cotton Mill, and Lu Zuofu (卢作孚), the visionary behind Beibei's Minsheng Company, launched their ventures with a profound mission—beyond mere profitability—to resuscitate the nation through industrious pursuits and nurture a new generation of citizens. These were tumultuous times, with internal turmoil and external perils casting a pall over the land. Native enterprises struggled to procure external resources to fuel their operations amidst the tempest of war and the tempestuous Western economic crisis. Meanwhile, within the local realm, the governance structure of rural regions

[3] Polanyi, K. (1944). The Great Transformation. Foreword by Robert M. MacIver. New York: Farrar & Rinehart.

teetered on the precipice of transformation, succumbing to an unsettling state of disarray. Recognizing the imperative of relying on internal resources to forge China's industrial destiny, these intrepid entrepreneurs endeavored to establish social order and embark on community development at the grassroots level. Thus, the Minsheng Company, led by Lu Zuofu, undertook the remarkable task of transforming Beibei's Jialing River Three Gorges into a testament of economic and social fusion, where both facets coexisted symbiotically, yielding resounding success. Weathering the storm of inner and outer strife, Minsheng Company, through its engagement in localized rural development, bolstered the organization and skills of local farmers, fortified infrastructural foundations, and deftly marshaled the local labor force and resources, all at a modest cost. Consequently, operational expenses dwindled, while the comprehensive tapestry of progress unfurled in Beibei—from social security to education, culture, and infrastructure—providing vital security for Minsheng Company's maritime exploits. Concurrently, Minsheng Company, at the zenith of its operational triumph, orchestrated a remarkably fruitful experiment in Jialing River Three Gorges, spearheading the formation of student volunteer brigades, molding them through military-style training, and enlisting their participation in upholding public security and propelling communal initiatives within the Beibei community. A bevy of public cultural facilities sprung forth, expanding the collective consciousness of its citizens.[4]

In the crucible of adversity, these intrepid entrepreneurs harmoniously melded with China's indigenous rural society, harnessing its human capital, natural resources, and vibrant social tapestry, thereby obviating the exorbitant costs of material acquisition and labor procurement, while simultaneously breathing life into a frugal operational ecosystem. Emboldened by China's cultural fabric, enterprises seamlessly interweaved economic endeavors with social engagement, for they recognized that the nourishment of enterprises stemmed from the very soil of rural society. Thus, reaping bountiful rewards demanded reciprocation towards the local community. This virtuous cycle heralded an unprecedented amelioration in the production and living conditions of the locale, constituting an enduring testament to the potency of social objectives. In turn, the locale's unwavering stability furnished an environment conducive to

[4] "Localization of Social Enterprises and Social Governance: A Case Study of Lu Zuofu's Minsheng Company and Beibei Construction" by Du Jie, Zhang Lanying, and Wen Tiejun. Exploration, 2017(3):141–142.

the enterprises' burgeoning expansion, nourishing their economic aspirations. Therefore, during the Republican era, these trailblazing social entrepreneurs resolutely opted for localized growth, anchoring their factories in rustic hinterlands and channeling the returns on local resource capitalization back into the very heart of the community—a sublime interplay between economic and societal realms. Scholars have christened this breed of enterprise, steadfast in their pursuit of dual economic and social objectives, as "localized social enterprises."[5]

2.3 Township and Village Enterprises in the 1980s

After the establishment of the People's Republic of China, the intertwined pattern of economic activities and social ethics remained unchanged. In the early stages of reform and opening up, township and village enterprises developed rapidly, embodying the essence of the "social enterprise" with dual economic and social objectives. Following the call by the Central Committee of the Communist Party of China in 1958 for "large-scale development of local industries by people's communes," large-scale commune enterprises were established nationwide to support the country's industrialization. In 1978, the Third Plenary Session of the Eleventh Central Committee of the Party was held, and the "reform and opening up" policy swept across the country like a spring breeze. The Decision on Several Issues Concerning the Acceleration of Agricultural Development (Draft) (《中共中央关于加快农业发展若干问题的决定（草案)》) passed at the meeting stated that "commune enterprises should achieve significant development." Subsequently, the Party Central Committee issued continuous documents emphasizing the support policy for commune enterprises, aiming to gradually increase their share of income in the commune's three-tiered economy.[6]

[5] Du Jie et al., "Exploration and Innovation of Local Social Enterprises in Modern China: A Case Study of Zhang Jian's 'Dah Sheng Group' and Modern Nantong Construction," Journal of Shanghai University: Social Sciences Edition, 2018, 35(1):11–22.

[6] On July 3, 1979, the State Council issued the "Provisional Regulations on Several Issues Concerning the Development of Commune Enterprises《国务院关于发展社队企业若干问题的规定（试行草案）》," which called for active support of commune enterprises by various departments, including planning departments and various industrial departments, specifying how they should support the development of commune enterprises. On September 28, 1979, the Fourth Plenary Session of the Eleventh Central Committee of

In March 1984, along with the rural "household responsibility system" reform, the Central Document No. 4 renamed "commune enterprises" as "township and village enterprises." If we talk about the rural areas of the 1980s, township and village enterprises played a prominent role. Taking the industrialization development in southern Jiangsu Province in the 1980s as an example, the region relied on village and community organizations to develop the economy by substituting labor inputs for scarce capital elements in the absence of sufficient capital or even burdened with debts. It transformed agricultural land, a resource form, into industrial land, an asset form, at extremely low costs. Through the mobilization of internal resources, it achieved initial capital accumulation. Additionally, the southern Jiangsu region made full use of the social and cultural traditions of village and community organizations. By forming fair income distribution within the villages and communities, it mitigated potential external problems such as "capital excluding labor" and social differentiation that could occur during the initial accumulation phase. The fair income distribution within the villages and communities highly valued the rights of community members, ensuring that all members received basic guarantees for production needs and prioritized collective interests in collective actions. This is an important manifestation of the social objectives of township and village enterprises.

Scholars define this phenomenon, which relies on village and community organizations to form stable internal cooperative relationships and internally address the external issues brought about by the market-oriented operation of enterprises through fair income distribution within the villages and communities, as "village community rationality." Although rural areas have undergone various changes, and the current institutional arrangements have undergone significant differences from the past, compared to villages where the disappearance of "collective economic organizations" after rural reforms led to the loss of social functional subjects, the villages where the former township and village enterprises were located retained the "collective economy," avoiding the disappearance of social functional subjects and forming relatively effective social governance. Based on the premise of the communal property

the Party passed the Decision on Several Issues Concerning the Acceleration of Agricultural Development《中共中央关于加快农业发展若干问题的决定》, reaffirming the support policy for commune enterprises outlined in the 1978 draft. The support from the central level played a significant role in promoting the development of commune enterprises.

relationship of land and other assets, "rural community rationality" can alleviate negative externalities such as social differentiation and labor-capital conflicts brought about by industrial development within the villages and communities through internalization thus forming effective social governance.

3 The Social Enterprises in Zhanqi Village

3.1 The Genesis: Fusion of Economy and Society in the Collective Era

In the infancy of People's Republic of China, an agrarian nation with feeble industrial foundations, the pursuit of industrial development served as the bedrock for modernization and a pivotal point in international relations. The nation, mindful of the adage "lag behind, get thrashed (落后就要挨打)," envisioned prioritizing heavy industry for swift advancement. To achieve national industrialization, the entire populace toiled tenaciously, embracing self-reliance, tightening their belts, and funneling resources towards heavy industry. Urban cadres and workers endured meager wages and frugal lifestyles, while rural regions embraced collectivization to curtail transaction costs with myriad small-scale farmers, augmenting agricultural surplus and accentuating the divergence between labor-intensive industry and agrarian production

In 1965, the Zhanqi Brigade emerged as an independent entity, splitting from the Jinxing Brigade. This newfound autonomy spurred a fervent pursuit of land improvement and diversification of subsidiary occupations. With collective support, even struggling households devoid of labor found solace in venturing into pig farming through credit-based initiatives, bolstering their income streams. The collective's provision of productive capital for impoverished households to engage in pig farming not only assuaged internal wealth disparities but also yielded a symbiotic relationship between social and economic gains. Intriguingly, this emphasis on member rights within the village community and the allocation of collective resources in a community-centric, egalitarian manner was not exclusive to Zhanqi Village alone. It echoed what the venerable Liang Shuming dubbed as the "principle of common wealth" in traditional China. Village communities, driven by a focus on collective interests, factored in the sustainable development of economically and socially disadvantaged groups while considering their inherent conditions. In traditional rural China, this was referred to as "ethics-based primacy" by Liang Shuming, while modern scholars termed it "rationality of rural community."

It becomes evident that the era of collectivization, under the aegis of a planned economy, pursued not only dual economic and social goals but also wielded political objectives. Viewed through an organizational lens, the village collective structure assumed roles as a political, economic, and social entity. Guided by political and economic tenets, these organizations shouldered the responsibility of agricultural and subsidiary industry development, while their political and social attributes compelled them to address the living conditions of their members. As a composite organization tasked with "triple objectives," their economic and social aspects functioned separately when serving the country's political goals. The economic aspect ceased to revolve around the internal allocation of economic resources within the village collective, instead catering to the nation's macro perspective of accumulating the raw materials for industrialization. This entailed not only labor-intensive and low-wage work in agricultural and subsidiary industries but also the relentless dedication of Zhanqi Village's inhabitants, who, unfettered by labor costs, invested their energies tirelessly. "Work points may not have soared, for our work was plentiful, and excessive toil deflated their value."[7] The social aspect, in turn, manifested in providing the collective's members with production and livelihood guarantees. In the realm of subsidiary occupations, the Zhanqi Brigade, through their control over allocation rights, not only curbed market price fluctuations and shielded pig farmers from market risks but also bolstered the underprivileged and middle-to-low-income farmers engaged in pig farming through credit-based assistance, thus narrowing the wealth gap within the community. In terms of agricultural production, the collectivization era's unified collective operations ensured that village members received work points that bore minimal discrepancies. The distribution mechanism within the brigade, guided by egalitarian principles, sustained the villagers' basic survival needs while contributing to the nation's macro-industrialization. It embodied an ethical, value-driven approach to collective decision-making. Stripping away the ideological debates surrounding the efficiency of the collectivization era, when viewed from a national perspective, the village collective

[7] Source: Interview record with Li Shibing on June 12, 2019.

organizations prioritized member survival and accomplished accumulation under the constraints of limited resources. Such an approach had its merits. What sets Zhanqi Village apart is its remarkable ability to maintain efficiency amidst collective egalitarianism, with its members brimming with enthusiasm, leading to Zhanqi Village's remarkable progress during the collectivization era, transforming it into a radiant role model.

In conclusion, the village collective organizations, despite their differing outward manifestations, converged upon the same destination when compared to the pre-1949 traditional rural community system hinged on kinship and geography. While serving the country's industrialization, these village collective organizations shouldered the responsibility of their members' production and livelihoods. Regarding production, their emphasis on equality and fundamental security prioritized the establishment of an egalitarian distribution system within the collective through work points. Under conditions of high accumulation and low consumption, these village collective organizations made tremendous contributions to the nation's primitive accumulation for industrialization. Stripping away the political nature of the collective organization, the village collective organizations during the collectivization era resembled localized social enterprises. Operating within the confines of stringent conditions, unable to extract resources externally and compelled to provide agricultural accumulation for the nation's industrialization, these organizations thrived by harnessing the essence of the local rural society. They mobilized their members to partake in cost-effective internal development within Zhanqi Village, ensuring the survival needs of their members while providing the prerequisites for the nation's industrialization.

3.2 *From Reality to Obscurity: Market's Unyielding Expansion and the Village's Internalization of Market Relations (Late 1970s to the Early Twenty-First Century)*

Since the 1970s, bolstered by the social capital accrued through politicized competition and agricultural surplus, the Zhanqi Brigade took the initiative to steer its members towards industrial transformation. Their brainchild, the Zigzag kiln, propelled Zhanqi Village into the nascent stages of industrialization. Despite the pervasive influence of the surging market economy from the '70 s to the '90 s, Zhanqi Village's collective enterprises remained deeply ingrained in its societal fabric.

1. The Village's Internal Accumulation Nurtured Zhanqi Village's Industrial Endeavors

   Having tasted success in agricultural and sideline productions, the industrious folk of Zhanqi Village cast their aspirations towards industry. It was the village secretary, Li Shibing, who, after visiting Dazhai, resolved to transform the living conditions of the villagers by constructing new dwellings. Recognizing the need for bricks, the fiercely self-reliant residents decided to forsake their humble adobe kiln, built in 1969, in favor of a superior curved kiln boasting greater productivity and quality. The completion of this curved kiln addressed the brick requirement for the new settlement, simultaneously providing a significant source of revenue through the sale of vibrant bricks. Thus, this pivotal moment can be viewed as Zhanqi's inaugural step towards industrialization. In 1979, the curved kiln was succeeded by an upgraded round kiln, marking the establishment of Zhanqi Village's maiden collective enterprise—the Xianfeng Brick Factory. Flourishing brick sales catapulted the factory into a nurturing ground for subsequent collective enterprise ventures within Zhanqi Village. The surplus generated acted as seed money for these enterprises, perpetuating a cycle of accumulation. For instance, the establishment of Zhanqi Village's second collective enterprise, the Xianfeng Brewing Factory, owed its existence to the surplus generated by the brick factory. The profits gleaned from the honeycomb coal factory fueled the birth of the Xianfeng Broad Bean Paste (Douban) Factory, while the construction of the flour mill and machinery replacement were financially facilitated by the existing brick and brewing factories of Zhanqi Village. By 1987, Zhanqi Village boasted a total of 10 enterprises, including the brick factory, bean paste factory, prefabricated components factory, trading company, Fengguan Liquor Factory, resin factory, orchard, foundry, agricultural machinery factory, and joint foundry. The brick factory, with its extensive workforce, outshone the rest and employed 62 resilient militiamen. By 1992, Zhanqi Village housed over a dozen collective enterprises, encompassing the Xianfeng Brewing Factory, Huifu Bouban Factory, compound fertilizer factory, resin factory, and flour mill.

   This transition from agriculture to industry precipitated a momentous surge in collective earnings for Zhanqi Village, endowing its members with enhanced production and living standards.

First and foremost, this transformation eased the strain on surplus labor within Zhanqi Village, alleviating the perils of labor over-concentration prevalent in agricultural and sideline industries. Concurrently with the construction of the zigzag kiln, Zhanqi Village tenaciously established eight enterprises, ranging from agricultural machinery to agricultural and sideline product processing, brick production to construction, fireworks to hairdressing, slaughterhouse to sewing. In 1979, 110 diligent members straddled the realms of industry and agriculture, constituting 24% of the total labor force. Moreover, the brick factory's income swiftly burgeoned into the primary industrial revenue for the Zhanqi Brigade, in tandem with the economic profits amassed by other enterprises. This surge bolstered Zhanqi Village's mechanization endeavors, with the enterprise's output value reaching a staggering 175,000 yuan in 1979, of which the brick factory contributed 92,000 yuan. The enterprise's output value accounted for 29% of the total output value of agricultural and sideline industries, totaling 605,000 yuan, equating to a per capita output value of 121 yuan.

Ultimately, this industrial progress fostered a notable improvement in the material well-being of the people of Zhanqi Village. In an interview, Li Shibing declared, "The cultural livelihood of the masses was encapsulated by the kindergarten. When it was absent in the village, we took it upon ourselves to establish one. Our kindergarten thrived during those times. We also initiated the establishment of a primary school, and a medical station was set up to cater to the villagers' healthcare needs. Thanks to the support of higher authorities, doctors were dispatched to offer medical services. Slaughterhouses, supply points, and free everyday commodities, including haircuts, were readily available to the villagers. We made it clear that they needn't pay; instead, we kept a record of their contributions." The economic returns derived from industrial development were judiciously reinvested into the social and cultural growth of the brigade, thereby substantially augmenting the quality of life for its members. By the late 1970s, the Zhanqi Brigade boasted a complete infrastructure, including schools, auditoriums, offices, medical stations, and retail stores. Notably, a select group of farmers even found solace in newly constructed residences, generously provided by the collective.

2. The Triumph and Fall of Collective Enterprises in the Arena of Industrial Competition

Zhanqi Village's former secretary, Li Shili, revealed in an interview that back in 1980, the average disposable income for rural residents in China stood at 468 yuan, while their urban counterparts earned around 439 yuan. Notably, Zhanqi Brigade soared well above the national average.[8] As the winds of reform and openness swept through the land, rural areas experienced an undeniable transformation in the 1980s. In 1981, Zhanqi Brigade sought the opinions of farmers regarding family contracting. Only three households embraced the idea of working independently, while the remaining 500 households dissented. The crux of the matter lay in the fact that the three agreeing households boasted a larger labor force, envisioning greater benefits from self-reliance. Consequently, in 1981, Zhanqi Brigade petitioned the county party secretary, Yang Xizong (杨析综), to postpone family contracting for a year. However, with reform as the irresistible tide, Zhanqi Brigade commenced the implementation of a dual management system called "unified distribution and individual incentives" in 1982. Although the land still maintained a collective nominal status, after being distributed among households, the system of labor points, hinging on land as its foundation, was abolished. This left the enterprise unable to holistically evaluate agricultural and industrial gains through labor points, thus hampering the mobilization of collective members' enthusiasm. Consequently, they resorted to wage incentives to motivate the factory workers. However, the interdependence between Zhanqi's farmers, collective, and collective enterprises remained unscathed. The industrial output value of the village-operated factories became the bedrock of Zhanqi's economic structure. While attaining their own economic goals, the village-operated factories, under the guidance of the village collective, further fostered comprehensive development throughout the village, ultimately realizing social objectives.

[8] Source: Interview record with Li Shili, January 11, 2020.

During the 1980s, Zhanqi Village, through its vanguard brick factory, continued to nurture collective enterprises, providing assistance to enterprises during the contracting period. This reciprocal relationship between the village community and collective enterprises saw the profits returned to the community. In 1989, for instance, "60% of the village's labor force evolved into a novel breed of farmers, adept in both industry and agriculture. Members of the village committee, selected through the trust of the masses, transformed into leaders of village factories, well-versed in production technology and modern management."[9] The village collective gained command over the collective enterprises, which, in turn, generated abundant employment opportunities for villagers. Moreover, "the fees paid by the village party branch, primarily allocated for loan repayment and further development, were mostly dedicated to the village's endeavors and the welfare of its members."[10] In terms of progress, the village allocated nearly ten thousand yuan from the fees paid by enterprises to water conservancy projects, hybrid rice seed procurement, grain storage incentives, and support for pig farming, stimulating agricultural production development through the paradigm of "industry supporting agriculture." Concerning member welfare, festivities like the Double Ninth Festival embraced elderly citizens, and support was extended to disadvantaged households. At year-end, each member received a dividend of 20 yuan. All the communal expenses, including the wages of village and community cadres, as well as three kindergarten teachers, were covered by the fees paid by enterprises. By returning enterprise profits to the village community, the improvement of production and living conditions for the villagers ensued. The stability of their lives and the vibrancy of cultural activities maintained social order within the village, successfully eradicating feudal superstitions and gambling.

As the 1990s unfurled, the relentless expansion of the market economy gravitated towards coastal regions and export-oriented endeavors. The state virtually disengaged from rural society, resulting in village-operated collective enterprises losing their prior preferential treatment in terms

[9] Source: "Zhanqi Village Persists in the Development of Collective Enterprises" (December 26, 1989), Archives of Pidu District, Sichuan Province, File No. 152-001-0272-007, p. 1.

[10] Source: "Zhanqi Village Persists in the Development of Collective Enterprises" (December 26, 1989), Archives of Pidu District, Sichuan Province, File No. 152-001-0272-007, p. 3.

of loan amounts and fiscal policies. Consequently, during the industrial competition phase, Zhanqi Village, beset by the realities of the market economy and internal structural issues, witnessed the collapse of five collective enterprises. In 1994, Zhanqi Village became a test ground for the reform of township and village enterprises in Pixian County. However, unlike the forceful measures applied to revamp underperforming state-owned enterprises in the 1990s, the reform process in Zhanqi Village adopted a more lenient approach. Notably, the village merged and reformed major entities such as the brick factory, bean paste factory, brewing factory, flour mill, and compound fertilizer factory. The shareholding structure comprised 50% village collective, 20% operators and workers, and 30% corporate legal entity. Thus, Zhanqi Village acknowledged the contributions of all villagers by assigning a 50% stake to the village collective and a 20% stake to operators and workers, effectively securing the collective's voice in decision-making. The existence of the collective economy laid the groundwork for the village collective's authority, facilitating the smooth execution of various village collective endeavors.

Tables 1 and 2 depict the ranking of village-level economic strength in Pixian County for the years 1996 and 1997.

In the records of remarkable achievements provided by the Tangchang Town Party Committee Office in 1997, Zhanqi Village stood out among three advanced villages for its notable collective economic strength. Serving as the economic backbone for effective social governance in the rural setting, Zhanqi Village's Party branch embarked on a robust journey

Table 1 Top five ranked village-level economic strength in Pixian County in 1996. Rank | Unit | Net Income Per Capita (yuan) | Disposable Income of the Village (10,000 yuan) | Total Output Value (10,000 yuan) | Industrial Output Value (10,000 yuan) | Agricultural Output Value (10,000 yuan) | Comprehensive Score | 1995 Ranking | Change in Ranking (Absolute Value)

Strength ranking	Unit	Net income per capita (yuan)	Village disposable income (ten thousand yuan)	Total output value (ten thousand yuan)	Industrial output value (ten thousand yuan)	Agricultural output value (ten thousand yuan)	Overall score	Ranking in 1995	Ranking rise and fall (absolute value)

Table 2 Ranking of Village-level Economic Strength in Pixian County in 1997. Rank | Unit | Net Income Per Capita (yuan) | Disposable Income of the Village (10,000 yuan) | Total Output Value (10,000 yuan) | Industrial Output Value (10,000 yuan) | Agricultural Output Value (10,000 yuan) | Comprehensive Score | 1997 Ranking | Change in Ranking (Absolute Value). *Source* "Ranking of Village-level Economic Strength in Pixian County for the Year 1996" and "Ranking of Village-level Economic Strength in Pixian County for the Year 1997," Archives of Pidu District, Sichuan Province, File No. 149-001-0538-0086

Strength ranking	Unit	Net income per capita (yuan)	Village disposable income (ten thousand yuan)	Total output value (ten thousand yuan)	Industrial output value (ten thousand yuan)	Agricultural output value (ten thousand yuan)	Overall score	Ranking in 1995	Ranking rise and fall (absolute value)

of developing collective enterprises. With the establishment of a brick factory, they witnessed a remarkable snowball effect in their business growth, ultimately giving rise to over a dozen enterprises. As a result, the collective economy flourished, paving the way for the smooth execution of various village-wide endeavors.

1. On the production front, Zhanqi Village extended support to agricultural activities through a two-pronged approach known as "work to subsidize farming (以工补农)" and "work to promote agriculture (以工促农)." In the former, the village allocated funds to aid agricultural pursuits. They annually set aside a substantial sum of 20,000 yuan for canal repairs, hybrid rice cultivation, and inviting agricultural experts and professors to disseminate knowledge and techniques, as well as promote new agricultural varieties and technologies. Moreover, the village purchased several thousand Zhangzhou pomelo saplings for the farmers, creating a sprawling fruit and flower base covering nearly 100 mu. In addition, subsidies totaling 21,000 yuan were provided to facilitate the purchase of combine harvesters, revolutionizing the harvesting conditions for the farmers. The village further invested 53,000 yuan in 1996 to construct a nearly 1-kilometer-long, three-sided open ditch in

the central area. In 1999, an additional 2000 yuan was invested to acquire seedling germination machines and transplanting trays, promoting the adoption of transplanting techniques. The latter approach, "work to promote agriculture," aimed to explore avenues for agricultural products and drive the restructuring of the agricultural industry. Notably, one of the collective enterprises, Pioneer Brewery, introduced pickled vegetable seeds to farmers for cultivation. With a guaranteed purchase price, farmers reaped tangible benefits, and the enthusiasm for cultivating pickled vegetables soared. By 1999, Pioneer Brewery had signed contracts with 420 households, offering a protected price of 0.3 yuan per kilogram for pickled vegetables. Consequently, the village witnessed a significant expansion in pickled vegetable cultivation, covering an area of 1200 mu, equivalent to two-thirds of the village's arable land. With a favorable market price of around 1 yuan per kilogram, an average yield of 2000–2500 kilograms per mu, and an income exceeding 1000 yuan per mu, farmers in the village were able to collectively augment their income by approximately 800,000 yuan.

2. In terms of improving livelihoods, Zhanqi Village made substantial collective investments in 1996. Amounting to 450,000 yuan, these funds were allocated to construct a state-of-the-art village office building and dedicated activity rooms for the party and youth organizations. These developments enhanced the organization of village-level activities. Furthermore, in 1997, the village collectively invested an additional 60,000 yuan to collaborate with the government in widening and paving Tangbao Road, significantly enhancing transportation convenience within Zhanqi Village.

Despite the impact of a market-driven economy and the reform of shareholding systems, collective enterprises in Zhanqi Village, although witnessing a decline in their owned operating income, remained under the control of the village collective. By bolstering the collective economy, the village successfully established an economic foundation for effective village-level autonomy, ensuring the continued benefits from collective enterprise revenues, which have been instrumental in supporting the village community since the 1980s.

However, as the twenty-first century unfolded, the challenging financing and market environments posed considerable hurdles to the development of township and village enterprises. Consequently, privatization and restructuring became inevitable. In 2002, following a change in leadership, Li Shili assumed the role of Secretary of the Village Party Branch, with Gao Demin being elected as the Village Director. To mitigate potential issues like collective asset erosion resulting from enterprise privatization, the new leadership launched a fresh round of restructuring of township and village enterprises within the village in 2003. Diverging from the "privatization without joint-stock holding (能私不股)" approach, the village collective, driven by a strong collective consciousness, sought to regain ownership of enterprise fixed assets through restructuring. By leasing collective enterprises via auctioning movable assets, the village collective secured annual rental income from the lessees, safeguarding collective benefits. This distinct choice made by Zhanqi Village in response to the deteriorating external business environment not only showcased their unwavering collective consciousness but also reflected their unwavering commitment to prioritizing collective interests. Although the enterprises continued to contribute to the collective economy by generating income, the proportion of income transferred to the collective was significantly curtailed compared to the post-shareholding reform era. Consequently, the grandeur of collective enterprises gradually waned. While the collective retained ownership, they had largely withdrawn from active involvement in enterprise operations. Furthermore, the change in enterprise operators diluted the social attributes of these entities. A telling example was observed in the Chongqing entrepreneur who leased the village's compound fertilizer plant, shifting their hiring preferences from "villagers" to "young labor." In the pre-twenty-first-century era, township and village enterprises prioritized employing local labor, fortifying the nexus between collective enterprises and the villagers' interests, thereby embodying a strong social attribute. However, post-restructuring in the twenty-first century, operators were freed from the constraints imposed by village communities and their members. Guided by the principle of maximizing enterprise interests, the focus shifted towards recruiting young labor to enhance profitability. Consequently, within the context of an expanding market, the product of the collective enterprise era gradually faded away, losing its erstwhile significance.

3. The Social Enterprise Essence of Collective Enterprises

> Collective enterprises, born from the embrace of rural communities, harness the combined efforts and frugal utilization of internal village resources by their members. Through this, they achieve primal accumulation and adeptly internalize externalities through the village's rational framework. This unique Chinese path to industrialization mitigates the inherent contradictions that surface during the enterprise's growth. It is apparent that even amidst financial scarcity, the Xianfeng Brick Factory achieved primal accumulation, ensuring its steady operation until 2003. Notably, it provided substantial contributions, serving as a bedrock for subsequent collective enterprises. The industrial ventures in Zhanqi Village owe their prosperity to the nurturing of the Xianfeng Brick Factory, its progenitor.

The Xianfeng Brick Factory, driven by the concerted efforts of the entire village, utilizes the three vital production elements—land, capital, and labor—cost-effectively within the village's bounds. Bolstered by the village's rational mechanisms, the Factory weakens the conflicts that arise during this process, facilitating Zhanqi Village's industrial takeoff and economic aspirations. Consequently, the enterprise's profits reverberate within the village community itself.

Throughout the 1970s to the 1990s, although township and village enterprises faced the transformative winds of restructuring, their profits remained a crucial force propelling and empowering the collective economy of Zhanqi Village. They played a pivotal role in elevating the village's standards of living and production, ultimately fulfilling the enterprise's social development ambitions within the community's embrace. In summation, Zhanqi Village's township and village enterprises embody the essence of a social enterprise. As the market economy expands, the erstwhile brilliance of township and village enterprises wanes, but the tenacious people of Zhanqi Village set their sights on fresh horizons.

3.3 *Substance in Harmony: Resurrecting the Village Collective Economy*

In 2002, as the tides shifted around Zhanqi Village's leadership, the daunting task of restoring its former glory weighed heavily on the new regime. On one hand, the collective enterprises had lost their luster, while on the other, the widening chasm between agricultural and industrial incomes diminished the villagers' reliance on the land. Recalling those times, Zhanqi Village's secretary, Li Shili, shared, "Around 2000, the village witnessed an influx of migrant workers. With over 1600 residents, more than 400 toiled outside the village, with most gainfully employed within local enterprises."[11] Consequently, farming seemed less lucrative to the villagers, prompting a common practice of outsourcing land cultivation. Furthermore, the collection of agricultural taxes from scattered households consumed copious amounts of time and energy for village officials. Faced with the transformations of the twenty-first century, the new leadership pondered on a path for Zhanqi Village's revival.

1. The Significance of Village Collective Economy for Rural Governance

   Following the rural reform of the 1980s, the dissolution of the administrative system of people's communes left a void that was filled by grassroots organizations like villagers' committees to manage internal village affairs. Diverging significantly from their urban counterparts, these village committees, by virtue of the law, oversaw the collective ownership of land and other assets, thus holding the reins of collective property. Besides fulfilling their duty of public service provision, they were obliged to "support and organize villagers in legally developing various forms of cooperative and other economic activities" and "respect and back the independent economic ventures of collective economic organizations, exercising their lawful autonomy." This fusion of political, economic, and social functions made the village committees unique. In rural communities, a typical economic structure consisted of four levels: individual households engaged in contracted farming, cooperative economic organizations, collective economic organizations within production teams, and village-level economic organizations. Those supervised by the village committees, the collective economic organizations, and cooperative economic organizations, erected a social system rooted in collective land ownership and the intimate fabric of rural society. While navigating commercial operations, they remained mindful of the communal responsibilities ingrained in the village.

[11] Source: Interview transcript with Li Shili, January 10, 2020.

Since the introduction of the "household responsibility system" in 1982, China's rural landscape witnessed the implementation of a dual-track management structure: "unified distribution and individual operation." This system, propelling farmers into action, unleashed their productive fervor, resulting in noteworthy achievements. Over time, the struggle of fragmented small-scale farming became apparent in the face of market-driven mechanisms, rendering agriculture an unprofitable and undignified occupation. As a consequence, a wave of laborers migrated to urban centers, seeking employment opportunities and entrepreneurial ventures, leaving rural areas engulfed in desolation. Within village communities, the lack of emphasis on the layer of unified operation by the collective in the dual-track system resulted in the gradual erosion of the collective organizational function. Consequently, the village autonomous committees lost the impetus to rally the villagers, causing a disconnect between the village collective and individual households. As a grim consequence, the significant policy funds delegated to village communities bypassed the collective, only trickling into the hands of millions of scattered small-scale farmers. This predicament failed to reinvigorate rural society or adequately meet the growing demands for public services from farmers.

Acknowledging the realities of rural China, the reform and opening-up era ushered in an era where individual-scale production and operation ceased to cater to the demands of agricultural modernization. It was then that the village collective economy assumed the responsibility of unified operation by the collective, giving rise to village-level autonomous organizations capable of serving their constituents and fostering effective democratic self-governance. Simultaneously, the central role and fortification of the village collective economy strengthened the bond between the collective and individual farmers, bolstering their organizational cohesion. Consequently, policy support gained traction, while the costs associated with engaging external market entities diminished, enabling farmers to augment their income and satisfy their increasing public service needs. The rural collective economy, an integral component of the socialist public ownership framework, embodied the essence of socialist public ownership within rural domains. Only through the cultivation of the village collective economy could the cherished vision of rural renaissance become a tangible reality.

2. Rise of the Zhanqi Vegetable Cooperative: A Snapshot of Progress

   In the Chinese countryside, farmer cooperatives have emerged as vital catalysts, bolstering the collective economy of villages and pioneering innovative rural governance models. Expanding their scope of services, these cooperatives have evolved into various forms, including shareholding, credit-based, and Specialized Cooperatives, as well as cooperative unions. Notably, community-based shareholding cooperatives, blending stock ownership and cooperative principles, have played a significant role in enhancing village community governance, leveraging collective economic foundations and the institution of "collective ownership in rural areas." This article delves into the social enterprise attributes of a community-based shareholding cooperative, exemplified by the Zhanqi Vegetable Specialized Cooperative in Chengdu's Pidu District.

   Under the impetus of Chengdu's comprehensive urban-rural policies, Zhanqi Village, situated in Tangchang Town, Pidu District, embarked on land transfer explorations around 2006. Seeking to combat land abandonment and address management issues associated with concentrated land, the villagers ingeniously converted their land contracts into shares. In 2006, the Zhanqi Agricultural Cooperative came into being with an injection of 500,000 yuan from the village collective enterprise—Chengdu Jifeng Industrial Corporation. It's worth noting that due to the absence of registration procedures for specialized cooperatives in the "People's Republic of China Farmers' Specialized Cooperative Law" enacted in 2006, the cooperative was formally registered in 2008 under the moniker of Pixian Zhanqi Mushroom Specialized Cooperative. Subsequently, in 2009, it was renamed the "Pixian Tangchang Town Zhanqi Vegetable Specialized Cooperative," and in 2017, it further evolved into the "Chengdu City Pidu District Zhanqi Vegetable Specialized Cooperative." The cooperative earned recognition as a "Good Social Enterprise" after obtaining certification from the China Charity Fair in 2018. Concurrently, it found a place on Chengdu's roster of observed social enterprises.

   Around 2007, in addition to the land under cooperative management, several large-scale farmers entered into land lease agreements with local farmers. Nevertheless, a pivotal shift occurred in 2009 when over 90% of the village's agricultural land gradually concentrated within the cooperative. Formerly signed agreements between individual farmers and landholders transitioned to contracts inked with the village committee, owing to the cooperative's nascent stage and the committee's established credibility.[12] This distinction sets apart the Zhanqi Vegetable Specialized Cooperative as it garnered the endorsement of the village committee during its formative years, diverging from Specialized Cooperatives spearheaded by prominent local farmers. In essence, the cooperative, representing the entire village populace, utilized the mantle of a specialized cooperative to assume the comprehensive cooperative functions of all villagers. By 2011, the cooperative had achieved stable land consolidation, with all agricultural land in the village under its operational and managerial purview, excluding a few households engrossed in vegetable and fruit cultivation on a smaller scale.

Capitalizing on the centralized agricultural land resources, the cooperative pursued superior infrastructure development through incentives provided by higher-level policies. Enhancing the differential land rent, it could lease the land at higher prices to specialized farmers, reaping economic benefits. In addition to engaging in agricultural cultivation, the cooperative selected partners involved in high-value-added ventures such as vegetable and nursery plant cultivation, as well as the cultivation of lucrative cash crops. Consequently, this strategy further heightened the differential land rent, granting Zhanqi Village an increased share of land rent income. An illustrative case involves the establishment of Chengdu Rongzhen Mushroom Industry Co., Ltd. in Zhanqi Village's modern agricultural park in March 2007. This venture not only bolstered the village's land rent income but also provided employment opportunities for surplus labor within and surrounding the village. Consequently, it augmented off-farm income for villagers, curbed the phenomenon of left-behind elderly and children, retained

[12] Source: Interview record with Fang Lei, the cooperative's accountant, on October 2, 2019.

young individuals, and stimulated land transfer dynamics, effectively promoting large-scale land management.[13]

In a statistical report from 2009 encompassing village (community) collective economic income in Tangchang Town, Zhanqi Village soared to first place among the 23 villages with an "accumulated collective economic income" of 12.8 million yuan and an "annual disposable collective income" of 560,000 yuan. Comparatively, other villages reported the highest "accumulated collective economic income" at 1 million yuan and the lowest at 0 yuan, while the range for "annual disposable collective income" stood between 10,000 yuan and 0 yuan.[14] This indisputably showcased Zhanqi Village's remarkable collective economic prowess. In their 2010 work summary, Zhanqi Village articulated, "By December 2010, the cooperative encompassed 495 farming households and 1551 members, managing 1820 mu of land. Among these, 1420 mu of land were leased to large-scale farmers for cultivation, while the cooperative directly operated 320 mu of land. Over the course of the year, the village's total collective income reached 2.9537 million yuan, with the cooperative accounting for 2.3537 million yuan in revenue and the collective enterprise accruing 600,000 yuan through leasing" [Source: "Zhanqi Village 2010 Work Summary and Next Year's Work Plan" (December 2010), Archive No. 149-2010-175].

Post-2011, the cooperative embarked on a journey of growth, attracting investment and collaborating with Dahang Hongye to initiate the Mama Farm project. This endeavor materialized into a 200 mu facility dedicated to agricultural sightseeing, encompassing a 30,000-square-meter leisure club, rural hotels, and other interactive industries. Notably, the "Zhanqi Fifth Season" lavender field became a renowned attraction, successfully securing a national 3A-level scenic spot designation in 2013. In its inaugural year, this idyllic locale enticed almost 400,000 visitors, propelling the influx of people and subsequently attracting enterprises such as Blue Rainbow Ecological Agriculture Co., Ltd. and Chengdu Yuxiang Agricultural

[13] Source: Interview record with Yang Yong, current village director of Zhanqi Village, on October 5, 2019.

[14] Source: "Village (Community) Collective Economic Income Statistics Table" (June 2009), Archive No. 149-2009-99.

Technology Co., Ltd. to establish a presence in Zhanqi Village. This played an instrumental role in fortifying the village's collective economy and augmenting employment opportunities and income for its residents (Table 3).

3. The Status of Zhanqi Vegetable Cooperative

The cooperative thrives with village locals, each household represented by an individual. On one hand, by consolidating land and engaging in independent operations and external contracts, the

Table 3 Statistics of collective economic income of villages (communities) in Tangchang Town in 2009, Unit: 10,000 yuan. *Source* "Village (Community) Collective Economic Income Statistics Table" (June 2009), Archive No. 149-2009-99

Name of village (community)	*Accumulative income of collective economy*	*Disposable collective income*	*Name of village (community)*	*Accumulative income of collective economy*	*Disposable collective income*
Jinxing Village	45	6.1	Henshan Village	60	3.2
Xianfeng Village	40	1.8	Zhulin Village	60	1.8
Jianfeng Village	80	3	Mingfeng Village	100	10
Pingle Village	40	4.2	Qingchun Village	2	1.08
Xingluo Village	15	3.5	Liujia Village	40	1.5
Bailu Village	10	2.5	Jinsha Village	50	2
Xibei Village	80	5	Pingkang Village	50	0.8
Huohua Village	20	1.2	Dongjie Village	10	0.35
Zhanqi Village	20	1.8	Xijie Village	0	0
Vegetable Community	1280	56	Nanjie Village	0	0
Xinsheng Street Community	20	0.5	Beijie Village	0	0
Xinsheng Street Community	1	0			

cooperative achieves agricultural industrialization, empowering the village collective economy and fostering the development of public services and communal initiatives. Since 2009, the village collective has annually distributed "elderly benefits" to villagers, granting a monthly allowance of 50 yuan to those aged 60–70, 100 yuan to those aged 70–80, 150 yuan to those aged 80–100, and 300 yuan to those surpassing 100 years.[15] Additionally, the collective procures basic medical insurance, significantly bolstering its credibility and communal cohesion in decision-making. The financially substantial Zhanqi Village successfully facilitates cultural hygiene, community governance, and essential amenities like Zhanqi Kindergarten, Elderly Association, Health Station, Convenience Service Center, and Rural Supermarket, effectively catering to the daily needs of its residents.

On the other hand, farmers relish stable and diverse income sources, thus elevating their financial standing. Firstly, there's the land lease rent, with participating farmers receiving an assured rent of 1200 yuan per mu annually. Secondly, adhering to the principle of "accumulate more, distribute less," 50% of the surplus land value above the guaranteed rent is shared among shareholder farmers as secondary profits, while the remaining 50% bolsters the cooperative's expansion endeavors. Thirdly, when leasing land, the cooperative prioritizes collaboration with enterprises that address greater employment needs, providing villagers opportunities to work as agricultural laborers within the industrial park, securing steady wages, and mitigating the exodus of labor from the village.

During our visit, Luo Xiaojun, the leader of Group 2 in Zhanqi Village, generously acquainted us with various village benefits.[16] At 65 years old in 2019, Luo Xiaojun resided with his family of five, while his son, daughter-in-law, and grandson resided in Pidu District. He assumed responsibility for the horticultural greening work at Mama Farm, earning a monthly salary of 2000 yuan. He and his spouse received a monthly "elderly benefit" of 50 yuan each from the village. Moreover, the village collectively procured basic medical insurance for all residents (should farmers desire more advanced

[15] Source: interview records with Yang Hongqing on October 4, 2019.

[16] Source: interview records with Luo Xiaojun on October 4, 2019.

medical coverage, the village collective would convert the annual basic medical insurance expenses into cash payments to villagers; in 2019, basic medical insurance amounted to 220 yuan). Furthermore, as a cooperative shareholder, Group 2 leader Luo not only received the guaranteed annual rent of 1200 yuan per mu but also enjoyed a year-end bonus. In 2018, each villager received a dividend of 350 yuan.

According to Fang Lei (方磊), the current cooperative's accountant, agricultural production encounters substantial influences from natural factors, exhibiting seasonal and long-term characteristics. Coupled with significant market fluctuations in agricultural product prices, the cooperative's annual revenue remains unsteady, unlike the predictability of industrial production. Besides the guaranteed annual rent bestowed upon farmers, the cooperative occasionally subsidizes dividends to villagers by balancing interests across various areas. Funds are reallocated from "collective enterprise rental income," ensuring that villagers receive dividends higher than previous years rather than lesser—a similar approach to how Zhanqi Brigade provided price-stable piglets to pig farmers during the collectivization era.

4. The Social Enterprise Essence of Zhanqi Vegetable Specialized Cooperative.

   In the realm of China's charitable exhibition in 2018, the Zhanqi Vegetable Specialized Cooperative from Tangchang Town, Pidu District, Chengdu City, emerged as an agricultural Specialized Cooperative society. It proudly secured a spot on the esteemed roster of China's Charity Fair, earning the title of a "Good Social Enterprise." Additionally, it found a place in Chengdu's 2018 roster of observed social enterprises.

The cooperative society's pronounced social essence resonates deeply within the confines of Zhanqi Village. With the village committee's endorsement, this cooperative society, inclusive of all members, spearheads its development. By fortifying the village's collective economy, it establishes an economic foundation that caters to the material and cultural needs of the villagers. It uplifts the standard of public services within the village and propels the advancement of public initiatives. Despite the agricultural nature of its endeavors, which renders fixed revenue uncertain, the cooperative society pledges that the villagers' annual dividends shall not dwindle compared to the previous year. It assumes the responsibility of shielding farmers from market risks, offering them a much-needed peace of mind. In selecting collaboration partners, the cooperative society prioritizes enterprises capable of generating more employment opportunities, thereby ensuring local employment for numerous villagers and diminishing the count of abandoned children and elderly. With the collective economy of the village thriving, the village collectively purchases basic medical insurance for each villager, extends support to the elderly through pension disbursements, and augments various public amenities. It brings forth the construction of convenience service centers, cultural courtyards, and the like.

In the wider scope, the cooperative society remains a profit-driven organization. Since its inception, it has diligently pursued support from higher authorities, capitalizing on favorable policies and enhancing ancillary infrastructure. This concerted effort leads to the elevation of land rent differentials. Principally, the cooperative society operates land autonomously, leasing it to agricultural tourism companies, both within and outside the village, and engaging in the development of primary, secondary, and tertiary industries, encompassing vegetable and seedling cultivation. Through this approach, it soars to new heights, transcending the confines of differential land rent. In 2011, following the concentrated resettlement of Zhanqi Village, a comprehensive assessment of collective membership qualifications and land rights redistribution took place. Member farmers, having ostensibly acquired an equal portion of land, discovered the dissolution of land boundaries. The village collective now commands full control over all land, eliminating the challenge of linking dispersed rural resources with external entities and larger markets. Compared to fragmented, small-scale land transfers, the cooperative society boasts exceptional negotiation prowess, considerable land rental income, and an enhanced ability to navigate market risks.

All things considered, the Zhanqi Vegetable Specialized Cooperative intrinsically embodies a social essence. Primarily, as a safeguarding production factor, land assets operate under comprehensive management, naturally yielding dual social and economic benefits. Especially when the majority of rural regions teeter on the edge of decline, social benefits take precedence. Moreover, underpinning community-based shareholder cooperatives, the cooperative society assumes centralized management of the village collective's agricultural land assets under the auspices of the village committee. Empowered to handle and adjust these assets, it assumes a public role, shouldering the responsibility of harmonizing the village's agricultural land resources and mobilizing farmers. By centralizing and consolidating the village's resource-based assets, it generates income, obliging it to channel the returns back to the village collective. In doing so, it effectively addresses the production and livelihood needs of farmers that neither the government nor the market can resolve, forging a stronger connection between the collective and the villagers. Lastly, the unwavering collective consciousness of Zhanqi Village, fostered by the bonds of familiarity and geography, facilitates the implementation of social enterprise-like market activities at a lower cost. It adeptly tackles challenges pertaining to farmers' employment, elderly care, cultural pursuits, and other predicaments, cultivating a low-cost social governance system fortified by an unyielding social essence, at times even superseding its economic counterpart. Furthermore, by capitalizing on the rural collective land ownership framework, the village collective economy avoids the restrictions encountered by urban community-based social enterprises, imbuing rural social governance with heightened vigor. This indigenous experience rooted in China's soil manifests as a distinctive rural economic organizational model that warrants meticulous exploration and research.

Given the absence of legal regulations governing the development of community-based shareholder cooperatives in China, their legal status remains ambiguous. In earlier years, community-based shareholder cooperatives registered as specialized cooperatives. Presently, registration and regulation are entrusted to agricultural and rural committees across different regions, resulting in varying standards and regulatory frameworks. Community-based shareholder cooperatives are unable to register as conventional businesses, unlike their counterparts, owing to their identity as community-based economic organizations operating under the supervision of the village committee and relying on the village collective economic organization for support. This naturally amplifies their administrative disposition relative to regular enterprises. The legal representative of the cooperative society generally assumes the role of village branch secretary, with board members concurrently serving as members of the village's "two committees." Furthermore, when engaged in weak industries such as agriculture and serving marginalized groups like farmers, the cooperative society necessitates policy resources to sustain operations. While enjoying specific policy benefits, it may also encounter certain limitations. Nevertheless, it is precisely these circumstances that render the community-based shareholder cooperative's service-oriented welfare attributes overt and fundamentally aligned with the essence of a social enterprise.

In essence, the community-based shareholder cooperative possesses distinct and prominent social and economic attributes, profoundly impacting rural community governance. However, the present development of community-based shareholder cooperatives faces certain challenges. Their range of business activities and community welfare services remain relatively limited, their legal status remains nebulous, and administrative inclinations tend to prevail. Overall, community-based shareholder cooperatives are in an exploratory phase, where both strengths and limitations become evident. Nonetheless, as rural social enterprises deeply ingrained in China's soil, they merit comprehensive research and exploration, unraveling a unique path for rural community governance bearing the hallmark of Chinese characteristics.

4 A Glimpse Ahead: The Novel Phase of Rural Community Development

In 2015, seizing the opportunity presented by the public listing and trading of collectively constructed land, Zhanqi Village embarked on a comprehensive evaluation of all non-agricultural assets, fixed assets, collective resources, and other resource assets. This endeavor birthed the Zhanqi Asset Management Company. Beyond managing the non-agricultural assets within the village collective, this company took charge of overseeing the operations of "18 Rural Workshops," Chengdu Jifeng Business Services Co., Ltd., and Chengdu Jifeng Investment Management Co., Ltd. Collaboratively, the cooperative and asset management company ventured into the realm of operating and managing village assets, igniting the flame of collective economic growth within the village.

Presently, Zhanqi Village's cooperative and asset management company find themselves still in the throes of development. They stand at the threshold of transforming scattered assets such as land and houses owned by villagers into a cohesive and organized asset platform, primarily focused on elevating the quality of rural households' lives through the enhancement of public infrastructure and services. However, the cooperative and asset management company's future prospects extend far beyond this realm. As they venture into monetizing the village community's resource-based assets, they can daringly explore diversifying their business scope to tackle issues concerning farmers' production and livelihood, mutual assistance for the elderly, education, healthcare, financial cooperation, and funding support for rural entrepreneurship. This audacious stride will undeniably propel the development of rural communities, elevating the material and cultural fabric of rural life.

As the 19th National Congress report aptly underscored, agriculture, rural areas, and farmers constitute the bedrock of national well-being. In China's march towards modernization, resolving social governance challenges encountered by rural areas necessitates drawing from indigenous experiences to effectively surmount developmental hurdles. The quintessential cornerstone of rural China lies within its collective land system, and under the vigilant guardianship of the village committee, the village collective economy, rooted in the land system, emerges as a formidable gateway to rural community governance.

Epilogue

At the behest of the Zhanqi Training Institute for Rural Revitalization, our team, under the guidance of Professor Wen Tiejun, embarked on several research expeditions to Zhanqi Village in Chengdu's Pidu District. Armed with archives, literature, statistics, and publicly available government documents and news reports, graciously provided by Zhanqi Village and the Pidu District Archives, we adopted a comprehensive analysis approach, fusing macro and micro perspectives, as well as the dimensions of time and space, to meticulously trace and synthesize Zhanqi Village's journey and the wisdom it has garnered. Thus, this book came to fruition.

As we present this work, our foremost gratitude goes to Professor Wen Tiejun, who has devoted years to scholarly pursuits and arduous international and domestic investigations, culminating in a remarkable ideological framework. We owe this research endeavor to the financial support garnered from numerous vertical and horizontal projects that Professor Wen Tiejun has presided over or served as an academic advisor to. We express our sincerest appreciation for this invaluable assistance.

Associate Professor Dong Xiaodan from Renmin University's School of Agriculture and Rural Development took the helm of this project, contributing to the formulation of key insights, guiding the writing process across various chapters, and ultimately overseeing the manuscript's completion. Dr. Zhang Yiying, a lecturer at Southwest University's College of Rural Construction, along with Du Jie, the office director, Associate Professor Pan Jia'en from Chongqing University's Institute of Higher Research in Humanities and Social Sciences, master's

© Peking University Press 2024

X. Dong, *Zhanqi Village Over Fifty Years*,
https://doi.org/10.1007/978-981-97-5426-7

student Pei Diao, and doctoral student Ma Li from the Law School, as well as Liu Yahui, Tang Li, Cui Fanglin, Xu Wenjing, Chen Chunwen, Chen Lu, Zhou Yaxi, Zheng Lu, Chen Yuyi, and undergraduate student Mi Yang, conducted meticulous and comprehensive field research while taking charge of the respective written segments.

The specific allocation of writing responsibilities is as follows:

Overview: Zhou Yaxi, Zheng Lu, Cui Fanglin. Chapter 1, Sects. 1 and 2: Zhang Yiying. Chapter 2, Sects. 3–6: Ma Li. Chapter 3, Sects. 7 and 8: Cui Fanglin, Xu Wenjing. Chapter 3, Sect. 9: Chen Yuyi. Chapter 4, Sect. 10: Xu Wenjing. Chapter 4, Sect. 11: Zheng Lu. Chapter 4, Sect. 12: Zhou Yaxi. Chapter 4, Sect. 13: Cui Fanglin. Chapter 5, Sect. 14: Zhang Yiying, Bai Tianyi, Zhang Yixin, Cui Leqi. Chapter 5, Sect. 15: Zhou Yaxi. Chapter 5, Sect. 16: Zheng Lu. Chapter 5, Sect. 17: Pei Diao, Du Jie.

Gao Xiang, Qi Jia'en, and Cui Leqi, master's students from Renmin University's School of Agriculture and Rural Development, contributed to discussions and writing in certain sections of this book.

Throughout the course of our research and writing, Dr. Yan Xiaohui, Mr. Jia Linzhou, Ms. Li Cuihuan, and Mr. Chen Jingjing from the Guoren Rural Construction Enterprise Alliance, as well as Lecturer Zhang Junna from Fujian Agriculture and Forestry University's School of Economics and Management, and doctoral students Tang Zhenghua and Yang He, provided significant support, for which we express our heartfelt gratitude.

We extend our thanks to the staff at the Pidu District Archives for preserving a wealth of archival materials, enabling the smooth progress of historical research on this subject.

Our immense gratitude goes to the Zhanqi Training Institute for Rural Revitalization, the Wen Tiejun Workshop, and the Gao Demin Workshop, as joint contributors to this book, for their unwavering support in its creation and successful publication. We offer a special acknowledgment to the institute for coordinating research efforts, assisting in data collection, and proofreading the manuscript during the writing process.

We would like to express our appreciation to Gao Demin, Secretary of Zhanqi Village Party Committee and a National Model Worker, Yang Yong, Director of the Village Committee, former Party Branch Secretaries Li Shibing, Gao Yuchun, and Li Shili, as well as Luo Huifu, the founding director of Zhanqi Village's Brick Factory, and Feng Zhonghui, Zhao Renchun, and others for their invaluable assistance.

We also extend our thanks to the various departments, institutions, and individuals who provided support and assistance in various forms to the research team during the field investigations and manuscript writing.

Our gratitude goes to Director Wei Xueping and Editor Yang Shuang from Peking University Press for their unwavering dedication in bringing this book to life.

Lastly, the research team wishes to express profound gratitude to all the villagers of Zhanqi Village. "The people, and only the people, are the motive force in the making of world history." It is a great honor for our team to record the illustrious and momentous struggle of Zhanqi Village. When faced with the vastness and profundity of history, words often seem inadequate. May this book convey a compelling Zhanqi tale that embodies both depth and detail, vitality, and inspiration.

The entire research team.

The manufacturer's authorised representative in the EU is Springer Nature Customer Service Centre GmbH, Europaplatz 3, 69115 Heidelberg, Germany. If you have any concerns regarding our products, please contact ProductSafety@springernature.com

Printed and bound by CPI Group (UK) Ltd, Croydon, CR0 4YY
01/10/2026
02225854-0018